A New Buddhist Movement II

THE COMPLETE WORKS OF SANGHARAKSHITA include all his previously published work, as well as talks, seminars, and writings published here for the first time. The collection represents the definitive edition of his life's work as Buddhist writer and teacher. For further details, including the contents of each volume, please turn to the 'Guide' on pp. 801–809.

FOUNDATION

1 A Survey of Buddhism / The Buddha's Noble Eightfold Path
2 The Three Jewels I
3 The Three Jewels II
4 The Bodhisattva Ideal
5 The Purpose and Practice of Buddhist Meditation
6 The Essential Sangharakshita

INDIA

7 Crossing the Stream: India Writings I
8 Beating the Dharma Drum: India Writings II
9 Dr Ambedkar and the Revival of Buddhism I
10 Dr Ambedkar and the Revival of Buddhism II

THE WEST

11 A New Buddhist Movement I
12 A New Buddhist Movement II
13 Eastern and Western Traditions

COMMENTARY

14 The Eternal Legacy / Wisdom Beyond Words
15 Pāli Canon Teachings and Translations
16 Mahayana Myths and Stories
17 Wisdom Teachings of the Mahayana
18 Milarepa and the Art of Discipleship I
19 Milarepa and the Art of Discipleship II

MEMOIRS

20 The Rainbow Road from Tooting Broadway to Kalimpong
21 Facing Mount Kanchenjunga
22 In the Sign of the Golden Wheel
23 Moving Against the Stream
24 Through Buddhist Eyes

POETRY AND THE ARTS

25 Poems and Short Stories
26 Aphorisms, the Arts, and Late Writings

27 Concordance and Appendices

COMPLETE WORKS 12 **THE WEST**

Sangharakshita

A New Buddhist Movement II

EDITED BY VIDYADEVI

Windhorse Publications
38 Newmarket Road
Cambridge CB5 8DT

info@windhorsepublications.com
www.windhorsepublications.com

First published in 2022.

Cover design by Dhammarati
Cover images: Front: Sangharakshita being interviewed for BBC
Radio in London in the late 1960s, Urgyen Sangharakshita Trust.
Back flap: Sangharakshita at Yale University, USA, 1970,
Urgyen Sangharakshita Trust.

Typesetting and layout Tarajyoti
Printed by Bell & Bain Ltd, Glasgow

**British Library Cataloguing
in Publication Data:**
A catalogue record for this book is
available from the British Library.

ISBN 978-1-911407-79-9 (paperback)
ISBN 978-1-911407-78-2 (hardback)

CONTENTS

Foreword xi

THE 1960S

Buddhism and the Bishop of Woolwich 2
The Lamas of Tibet 12
The Heights and Depths of the Spiritual Life 21
The Buddha's Philosophy of Right Speech 31
Introducing Buddhism 1: Is Religion Necessary? 39
Introducing Buddhism 2: Why Buddhism? 49
Introducing Buddhism 3: The Approach to Buddhism 58
Introducing Buddhism 4: Buddhism in England 67
Evolution – Lower and Higher 82
Buddhism and Psychoanalysis 91
Buddhism and the Language of Myth 102
Buddhism and the New Reformation 112
A Visit to a Buddhist Vihara 129
Aspects of Buddhist Psychology 1:
The Analytical Psychology of the Abhidharma 138
Aspects of Buddhist Psychology 2:
The Psychology of Spiritual Development 150
Aspects of Buddhist Psychology 3:
The Depth Psychology of the Yogācāra 166

Aspects of Buddhist Psychology 4:
Archetypal Symbolism in the Biography of the Buddha 179
Aspects of Buddhist Psychology 5:
Psycho-Spiritual Symbolism in the *Tibetan Book of the Dead* 194
Aspects of Buddhist Psychology 6:
The Mandala: Tantric Symbol of Integration 209
Aspects of Buddhist Psychology 7:
Zen and the Psychotherapeutic Process 224
Religion: Ethnic and Universal 235

THE 1970S

From Alienated Awareness to Integrated Awareness 258
The Question of Psychological Types 270
Padmasambhava, Tantric Guru of Tibet 285
Levels of Going for Refuge 301
The Manu, the Buddha, the Guru, and the Tertön 317

THE 1980S

Buddhism, World Peace, and Nuclear War 338
A Buddhist Dawn In the West 363
Twenty Years on the Middle Way 385
The Next Twenty Years 396
Fifteen Points for New – and Old – Order Members 411

THE 1990S

My Eight Main Teachers 426
Dilgo Khyentse 446
The Message of Dhardo Rimpoche 452
The Five Pillars of the FWBO 461
Fifteen Points for Old – and New – Order Members 473
The Rain of the Dharma 492
The Disappearing Buddha 518
Intellect, Emotion, and Will 533
Reflections on Going Forth 545

A Life for the Dharma 561
Communicating the Dharma 580
Looking Ahead a Little Way 591
Living and Working Together 602
Seeing Things As They Really Are 610
The True Miracle 618

THE 2000S

The Celebration of Sangharakshita's Seventy-Fifth Birthday 630
Fields of Creativity 634
Looking Back – and Forward 649
On Tārā 659
Forty Years On: The Six Distinctive Emphases of the FWBO 663
The Growth and Prosperity of the Sangha 674
Recollections of my Early Life, and Some Reflections on Rebirth 681
Mingling Souls 691

Sources 700
Notes and References 701
Index 761

A Guide to *The Complete Works of Sangharakshita* 801

FOREWORD

Many of Sangharakshita's talks – the Noble Eightfold Path series, 'Mind Reactive and Creative', the various series on Mahāyāna *sūtras*, 'The Taste of Freedom' – were quickly transcribed and published, to become an important aspect of the Buddhist movement he founded, and eventually to find their way into these *Complete Works*. But what about the talks which for whatever reason were never published? When I began to edit this book, I was curious, as perhaps you are too, to know what this collection would be like. One surprise was how many unpublished talks there were, with more coming to light up to and beyond the last minute before publication. But would the collection be a treasury of hidden gems, a heap of words from the cutting-room floor, or a glorious ragbag, as Sangharakshita once described another collection of Dharma teachings?

It has elements of all of these, but it's something else too – something I wasn't expecting. The book covers such a diverse range of themes that it didn't make sense to try to organize it thematically, so I decided instead to try putting the talks in chronological order, and the experiment seemed to be a success. Looked at in this way, the collection spans the period from 1965 to 2011, tracing the course of Sangharakshita's Dharma teaching career in the West from his early days at the Hampstead Buddhist Vihara, before the FWBO began, to his visits to Triratna centres and festivals near the end of his life. To my surprise, this simple organizational scheme seemed to give the collection coherence, and to tell a story in a way that no other volume of the *Complete Works* quite does.

After I'd compiled *The Essential Sangharakshita* (*Complete Works*, vol. 6, first published in 2005), a friend noticed something I hadn't: that the whole substantial collection of teachings barely mentions the FWBO (now Triratna) at all. We concluded that all those teachings were *for* the Buddhist movement Sangharakshita founded rather than *about* it. By contrast, as this volume proceeds through time, we get a sense of how the FWBO formed and grew, through a tangible process of co-creation. The words are Sangharakshita's, but the subjects he addresses and the ways he expresses himself are clearly in response to the needs of the people to whom he was speaking. The talks are a collaboration. In a talk given in 1966 (his first ever talk on evolution), he told those listening that when a talk is being given:

> We must not think of speaker and audience as two different things. There is a distinction, obviously, but at the same time the two are inseparable. The relationship between the speaker and the audience is like that between the conductor and the orchestra. At a concert the music you hear is the product jointly of the members of the orchestra and the person conducting them, and similarly, I often feel that a lecture is a joint product. Everybody is playing as well as listening. This is what we should try to feel. One person may be speaking, but that person speaks for everyone present.

In those early days at the Hampstead Buddhist Vihara, whether he knew it or not, he was moving towards the founding of a Buddhist movement which would be neither monastic or lay, although at that time such a thing did not exist. Still thinking in terms of monks and lay people, in a talk (on the New Reformation) also given in 1966, he said:

> When a monk turns up, sometimes people wonder, 'Why is he wearing a yellow robe? How does he come to be living in a monastery?' But if they find that the Buddhist is someone who looks like them, if he is wearing an ordinary suit or she is wearing an ordinary dress, people are sometimes a little more receptive, and at first this counts for a lot.

He went on to say, and one can sense behind the words his experience of the challenges he faced and the determination to overcome them:

> We have to confess that it isn't easy to be a Buddhist in this country. The odds are against it. To be a Buddhist, you need a certain amount of backbone, intelligence, sheer obstinacy, and indifference to what other people think. It isn't easy to preach any religion nowadays, and to preach an exotic religion coming from the East isn't easy for anybody, though we have to carry on somehow. A vihara like this should be thought of as a kind of spiritual research station, not the Buddhist equivalent of the local parish church with a congregation of the faithful flocking there every Sunday to receive their weekly dose of uplift. In fact, the vihara should be the centre of the new Buddhist reformation.

In a talk given nearly thirty years later – an example of how this volume offers different perspectives on the same events as time passes – Sangharakshita reflected on this period:

> I was happy in robes in India, where they were quite convenient, especially in hot weather. But in Britain I decided after a few years not to wear robes except on ceremonial occasions when a little colour was called for. I also allowed my hair to grow. In fact, I must confess I allowed it to grow somewhat longer than it is now, and this upset some people very much indeed. It was an eye-opener to me how much it shocked them. I was just the same, I was still myself, I'd only changed the externals, but externals mean a lot to people. I realized in the end that some people at least had become upset because I'd disturbed their projections onto me. But on the whole I found that I was able to communicate better, heart to heart and mind to mind, and I was therefore able to communicate more effectively. And at that point I founded the FWBO, but that's another story.

It is that other story that this volume tells. One can feel it taking shape in the talks that precede the FWBO's founding – the exhortations to his listeners to come to Buddhism freshly, not thinking that they already know all about it, and to do whatever they could to help Buddhism grow. In 'Buddhism in England' he said:

> It is incumbent upon each and every person coming here to do their utmost to improve themselves, to try to raise their intellectual and cultural level, to learn more about Buddhism and also more about their own culture, otherwise it will be impossible to attract intelligent people to the movement.

Clearly with the creation of sangha in mind, he went on to say:

> When we get together, it shouldn't be just a social gathering. The Buddhist spiritual community shouldn't be a symbiotic community substitute. It should have a spiritual purpose. When you get together with other Buddhists, discuss Buddhism, discuss the Buddhist movement and what can be done to help it progress, to make it more active, more alive. Leave aside purely personal things or questions of politics, or what you read in the newspaper. If in the present British Buddhism, which means all of us, can do as I have suggested, then its future will be assured.

The story of his efforts to bring Buddhism alive in the modern West is told elsewhere in the *Complete Works* in various ways, but this volume gives a unique perspective on how he went about it. It features only one of many (evidently unrecorded) talks given at the 'College of Psychic Science' in Kensington among the pre-FWBO talks, but it does include the first talks ever given in FWBO days. He recalled in a talk given many years later:

> The very first course of lectures I gave under the auspices of the FWBO took place at Kingsway Hall in Holborn, and it was on aspects of Buddhist psychology. Psychology was very popular in those days, and those who thought of themselves as Buddhists used to read mainly psychological literature – Freud, Jung, Stengel, Sullivan, Erich Fromm – so we decided to lure them in with the magic word 'psychology'. But under this heading we had the analytical psychology of the Abhidharma – good tough material to begin with – and the depth psychology of the Yogācāra, which brought in lots of Buddhist metaphysics, and even the archetypal symbolism of the life of the Buddha, because archetypal was another word that really attracted people. We also had a talk about the *Tibetan Book of the Dead*, and to my surprise people came

> flocking to that lecture, which was the most successful one of the whole series. So under the banner of psychology I was able to put across a lot about Buddhism.

By the 1970s, he was talking to an audience of committed Dharma practitioners, most of whom would have been meditating for a number of years. At the FWBO's early centre, Pundarika, and then at the new London Buddhist Centre, sharing some thoughts about Padmasambhava, he took the theme of psychological integration to a new, more challenging level:

> We have to think of ourselves as living in a world of scattered energies which we have to claim and collect and bring together and incorporate into the spiritual life, so that our individual spiritual lives and the collective spiritual life of the spiritual community can be reinforced.

By now the true significance of the act of Going for Refuge to the Three Jewels had occupied his mind for two decades, more or less since his *bhikkhu* ordination in Benares. Over time his thoughts had multiplied and deepened, until they emerged as the very heart of his project. Confiding in a gathering of Order members, he articulated some key elements in his thinking for the first time, very much still work in progress:

> I'm going to speak tonight about an aspect of Going for Refuge about which I've recently been thinking quite a lot, but about which I've so far not communicated anything to anybody, so far as I recollect.

He began with a sequence of stories about his relationship with the Three Refuges:

> It strikes me now as rather odd that it didn't occur to me to wonder why so little was explained about what we were doing when we chanted those Pāli words and took, as I suppose one can say, the Refuges and Precepts.

and then tried out various terms for the 'levels' he wanted to identify. 'Provisional' Going for Refuge seemed 'not at all satisfactory' as a way of putting it (though no better term was ever found), but 'effective' Going for Refuge was coined 'perhaps more happily'.

His introduction to 'The next twenty years', given in 1987, on the twentieth anniversary of the founding of the Order, shows the contrast between his formal expressions of his thinking and his more informal and spontaneous style when addressing Order members:

> The day after tomorrow I shall be reading a paper on the history of my Going for Refuge. This is something to which I've given a great deal of thought, something I've composed very carefully. But I haven't prepared a lecture for this evening. It's going to be more of a semi-impromptu talk on the basis of some rough notes. I'm not going to try to predict what's going to happen, because there are so many unknowns. What I'm going to do is simply share with you some of my hopes and fears with regard to the next twenty years.

In the 1986 talk 'A Buddhist Dawn in the West', he teased his audience that although he now preferred to write and present a paper, 'having rather gone off giving talks, to be frank' (as he was to continue to protest for many years to come), he had noticed people stifling their yawns during the paper he read the previous year, and thought when preparing this year's presentation,

> Oh dear. I'm starting to write a paper, and I really mustn't. People are coming along to celebrate the anniversary of the FWBO. They want to have fun, they don't want to listen quietly, carefully, and attentively to a paper that needs a lot of concentrated thought.

He relished the chance to reminisce about the early days that such occasions gave him, but also used them to reflect on and guide the new movement as it took shape. In this pivotal talk he sketched out the outlines of what he later called the six distinctive emphases of the FWBO. (That talk appears later in this volume.) He also talked about how the conception of ordination had developed, the emergence of a new retreat centre for women, Taraloka, and the supportive conditions which had been developed in the FWBO, which should enable those involved to do much better than he had done himself. For the first time he expressed his wish to hand on his responsibilities – 'The FWBO is less and less "my" movement every day, and I'm very happy to see that. It's *your* movement' – and he suggested ways of strengthening one's motivation to work for the Dharma.

Strong motivation would be needed. The talks of this period show how much he expected of Order members. One year he urged them to take up the study of the classics, and on another occasion, mindful of the need to support the spread of the Dharma to as many countries as possible, he prompted everyone to learn a second language. In 1988 he put it to them that 'in a gentle and kindly and non-violent way' they should do everything in their power to counteract the menace of racial prejudice, and also to take a stronger stand on the destruction of the environment:

> In the next twenty years I would like to see the Order developing an ecological dimension, and I would like to see some Order members working in this field on the basis of their Buddhist commitment, perhaps in some cases working alongside non-Buddhists who share this concern.

By the 1990s Triratna was an increasingly international community. In talks given in America and Germany we see Sangharakshita as a kind of ambassador, explaining the Buddhist movement he had founded to people who had not come across it before, and offering his own perspective on it. Also in this period, in talks on the five pillars of the FWBO, the place of will in the spiritual life, the dimensions of going forth, and the mystery of the 'disappearing Buddha' we see his mind reaching out to add a dash of colour here, some guidance or extra clarity there. In a meta moment, he even offered a series of practical tips on giving Dharma talks ('don't conceal your ignorance', 'don't be apologetic', 'dress appropriately', and so on).

Having spoken on the occasions that marked the long-anticipated handing on of his responsibilities, his work now done, in his last talks he tended to speak personally and spontaneously on topics on which he happened to have been reflecting – on old age, on the experience of losing his sight, on dreams ('I wasn't expecting to talk about dreams, but I think I will'), and death and rebirth. In a talk on 'fields of creativity', he indulged in some self-assessment:

> It occurs to me that, to be quite honest, I'm not a religious-minded person in the conventional sense. I don't think I've ever been pious, and I wouldn't like to be described as religious. It seems to have all the wrong connotations. So how would I describe myself? I think I'd like to describe myself as a creative person, someone whose life has been an expression of creativity, even if only in a small way.

And at an international retreat held at Taraloka, he explored the Buddha's advice on the growth and prosperity of the sangha. It was 2008, and at the age of 82 he was speaking in a large marquee against the sound of pouring rain on the forty-first anniversary of the founding of the FWBO. The talk brings this volume full circle, from the early days when he shared his imaginings about what a sangha could be to that tent where he stood surrounded by a crowd of men and women from many countries, gathered together in an atmosphere of collaboration and friendship, their very presence bearing out the truth of the Buddha's words – and the progress, so far, of Sangharakshita's work.

Vidyadevi
Herefordshire
November 2021

THE 1960S

BUDDHISM AND THE BISHOP OF WOOLWICH

Burgh House, Hampstead, 12 May 1965

This might seem a rather strange topic. What could an Eastern religion and an Anglican bishop possibly have in common? To answer this question, I must take you back with me to India. I spent twenty years there, and for most of that time I was based in a little town called Kalimpong, in the Himalayan foothills not far from Darjeeling and in full view of the snow ranges that interpose themselves between India and Tibet. Kalimpong is a quiet place, or at least it was until recently, and not many sounds from the outside world reach it, but about three years ago, even in that remote spot, we heard echoes of a debate – one might even say a controversy – which was going on here in England. At my vihara in Kalimpong I received various English magazines and journals, mostly religious, and they started referring to a recently published book called *Honest to God*. The Unitarian weekly *The Enquirer* featured articles and letters about it, and other journals and even the daily papers devoted a lot of space to the book and its ideas, as well as to the discussion that arose from its publication. Having heard that this book had created such a stir in England, and knowing that I would in all likelihood find myself back here before long, I made a mental note to read it as soon as I had settled down here. Not long after my arrival at the Hampstead Buddhist Vihara, I was browsing through our library when I found a dog-eared copy of this very book, which had obviously been read by quite a large number of people in our community. Being something of a bookworm, for me to see a book that I want to read is to start reading it, so that very night I sat up late and finished it at one sitting, and I must say that I found it of very great interest indeed – not merely of academic, theoretical, or intellectual interest, but something much more than that.[1]

In the course of the last century there has been in the West a great development in the study of comparative religion. It was at first confined to scholars, especially professional orientalists, but gradually people who had no technical interest in philology, sociology, or anthropology, but were interested in religion, began to pay attention to the religions of the world, not just as anthropological or exotic curiosities, but as faiths in which people believe and by which they live, and in which, therefore, Westerners began to think that there must be something of value, even though they might not choose to regard it as being quite so valuable as what they find in their own religion.

On my return to England after twenty years, I was pleasantly surprised by the degree of interest in non-Christian religions, including Buddhism, to be found among sincere Christians, especially as my encounters in India with the official representatives of the various churches in the form of missionaries had not been very happy. Having had a certain amount of contact with Christian bodies in England, as well as with individual Christians, I have come to see that the attitude of the missionaries towards other religions is not representative of the more advanced religious thinking in England today. Not many years ago I went from Kalimpong to Pedong, on the Bhutan border, where there was an annual fair to which the people of the area brought their produce. There were competitions with prizes, and exhibitions, and various Christian missionaries had pitched their tents and were busy proclaiming the gospel. They buttonholed me, and one of them told me that my fate after death would be far worse than that of other people. When I asked why, he said, 'Not only have you gone astray yourself in becoming a Buddhist, but you are leading others astray too.' I certainly haven't encountered this sort of attitude in this country, and I've come to the conclusion that it is out of date. Those who go as missionaries to places like India are apparently anachronisms, unable to fit into the religious life of this country today.

Since my return to England, my contacts with Christians of various denominations have been extremely cordial. I might especially mention the Anglicans, the Methodists, the Quakers, and the Unitarians. In all these four bodies there are quite a number of people who are interested in Buddhism. Not long ago I spent a pleasant weekend at an old farmhouse in Kent with a group of young Methodists. Every evening we sat up late discussing Christianity, Buddhism, Methodism, Wesley, the Buddha, Zen, and so on, and I was surprised to find that one of them, a lay preacher in the Methodist church, had not only acquired a sound understanding of Zen but was extremely appreciative of it. When I suggested to him that there is in John Wesley's teaching and example something faintly redolent of Zen, and pointed out one or two parallels, he admitted that although it hadn't occurred to him before there was a very interesting resemblance. It's very pleasing to find that many religious people in this country are not only interested in Buddhism theoretically but willing to learn from it, though without actually becoming Buddhists.

It is therefore only right that there should be Buddhists who are interested in understanding modern developments in the field of Christianity. Not long ago in Rome the first and second sessions of the Second Vatican Council were held, and it was interesting to note the widespread interest they aroused, the proceedings of the Council being followed with sympathy all over the world by religious-minded people.[2] Personally I was rather disappointed at the outcome of the Council, which reminded me of the saying about the mountain being in labour and producing a mouse, but what I want to emphasize is that in our current situation it is only natural that at least some Buddhists should be interested in the Bishop of Woolwich and his remarkable book, *Honest to God*. In this book the bishop is trying to come to grips with a problem which all religious people have to face today, though perhaps not to the same degree: the problem of how to restate traditionally received spiritual truths in a language that is meaningful to contemporary humanity. In the case of Christianity, the problem is perhaps more acute than it is in some of the other religions. The example that the Bishop of Woolwich has given in writing this book is therefore of interest to us all.

Before addressing the contents of the book, I must say something in appreciation of the spirit in which it has been written. Almost my first impression on reading it, even though I went through it very rapidly the first time, was that the writer is an intensely sincere and honest person. He cares very deeply about the religious and spiritual life, but he does not shut his eyes to the contemporary world, and he is concerned that religion should be relevant to life here and now. He has the courage to reject, or at least to be willing to reconsider, formulations that have become a trifle outworn or even out of date. With this sort of spirit, although he may not always command the agreement of Buddhists he can certainly command their sympathy and respect.

I can't hope to deal with all the issues raised in the book, which, though small, is rich in ideas. I therefore propose to deal with two or three major issues that may be of particular interest to Buddhists. The first of these, and the most important, is the issue of God. Historically speaking, Christianity is a form of theism, affirming the existence of a personal God, the Supreme Being, endowed with all perfections, the creator and governor of the universe. In modern times, belief in God is coming increasingly under attack. There are many people today, even in the churches, who are deeply and sincerely religious, but feel that the traditional idea of God is not only unacceptable, but even meaningless. Even many of those who are most profoundly religious, whose attitude towards life is most truly spiritual, find the traditional theism of Christianity unacceptable. One of the greatest merits of the Bishop of Woolwich is that he has had the courage to face up to this and try to take it into consideration, even try to do something about it. For a Christian it must be a terrible thing to have to face up to the fact that what was for centuries a cherished conception has suddenly become meaningless, even to some extent ridiculous. But the bishop does face up to it.

He does so in the first and second chapters of *Honest to God*, which are entitled 'Reluctant Revolution' and 'The End of Theism?'. Though the title of the second chapter is cast in the interrogative, the bishop does not leave us in much doubt that in his opinion traditional theism is finished. He goes into this in considerable detail, and I won't repeat all the steps of his argument. He says that at the beginning of the scientific period in modern thought, the conception of a God literally or physically 'up there' in heaven, above the earth, became unacceptable, and was replaced, gradually and insensibly, by the conception of a God who is spiritually or metaphorically 'out there'. But now even this more refined formulation has become obsolete. The whole conception of a transcendent being is unacceptable. These ideas are not new. As the bishop himself admits, he is indebted to Paul Tillich and Dietrich Bonhoeffer.[3] His originality consists, it seems to me, not in what he has said, but in the fact that whereas before it was said in the pages of obscure learned journals, in the exchange of confidences between theologians and scholars, the bishop has had the courage to bring the issue into the open, almost into the market place. Despite the many changes which have taken place in the West and in the church, the office of bishop still commands great respect, even authority, so it is significant that the Bishop of Woolwich has chosen publicly to espouse these views, knowing that they are highly controversial. He espoused them because he honestly believed in them and felt that they should be brought more emphatically to people's notice. He felt that *someone had to speak*.

In this, it seems to me, the bishop is not unlike the little boy in the well-known fairy story of the emperor's new clothes. As you may remember from your childhood, the emperor engaged two rogues to weave for him a new set of robes. These rogues told him that the robes were so marvellous that only the pure and virtuous could see them. Not liking to admit that they were not pure and virtuous, the emperor and his ministers pretended that they could see the robes, and the emperor walked naked in a procession. No one in the crowd said anything because nobody wanted it to be thought lacking in purity and virtue, but at last the voice of a small boy piped up and said, 'But Daddy, the emperor isn't wearing any clothes!' To my mind, without any disrespect, that is exactly what the Bishop of Woolwich has done. People were thinking that they believed in God, that they accepted him as part of their creed, but he has had the courage and honesty, the childlike quality, to get up and say, 'But we don't really believe in God, do we?' The repercussions are continuing even now, as the bishop himself has made clear from time to time. As far as I can see, his originality consists in his being a lonely voice of truth within the Church.

In the bishop's later book, *The New Reformation?*, he has included an appendix headed 'Can a truly contemporary person not be an atheist?' This seems a startling question for a bishop to ask, but he not only asks it but gives a definite answer, in the course of which he concedes that God is intellectually superfluous, emotionally dispensable, and morally intolerable. For a bishop to concede so much – well, what are we coming to? A hundred years ago, when poor Bishop Colenso of Natal dared to state publicly that he didn't think the first five books of the Old Testament were really written by Moses, he was practically declared a heretic, and excommunicated for a while.[4] Some people might like to excommunicate the Bishop of Woolwich, and some people certainly think him a heretic, but whether or not one agrees with him, one can certainly admire his courage.

So where does all this lead? I don't know whether this was in the bishop's mind when he wrote his book, but as far as I can see, it leads in the direction of non-theistic religion, and even, paradoxical as it may sound, to non-theistic Christianity, that is to say, Christianity without God, the possibility of which the bishop seems to envisage. This is a startling, indeed revolutionary, idea, and apparently a contradiction in terms. But although the bishop seems to be quite aware of the direction in which he is moving, he does not seem to be aware – on the evidence of these two books at least – that the idea that religion can be non-theistic, that there can be spiritual life in its fullness without the idea of a personal God, is very ancient. In the West, and in the Middle East too, at least since classical times, religion has been theistic. If you were religious, you believed in God, and if you believed in God, you were religious. But this has certainly not been the case in the East. In ancient China, Daoism and Confucianism were both very great moral and spiritual teachings, but neither said a word about God. In India, Jainism, a little older than Buddhism, didn't mention God either, and later on in India the non-dualist Advaita Vedānta got along perfectly well without God. If God comes into the Vedānta at all, it is just as a relative truth, by way of a concession to the ignorance of people. 'If there is a God,' Śaṅkara says, 'it is the absolute seen through the veil of nescience.'[5] But the most prominent example of non-theistic religion is that of Buddhism. We might even go so far as to say that Buddhism is the perfect example of a spiritual way of life which has been worked out fully, in all its details and in all its ramifications – ethical, psychological, philosophical, metaphysical, artistic – without a single reference to the idea of God.

This being so, we can begin to appreciate the significance to a Buddhist of the Bishop of Woolwich. He represents a movement within the bosom of the Church, at least on the level of ideas, towards a non-theistic form of religion, and therefore a movement of approximation to Buddhism. I don't know whether the bishop himself realizes this. He might be horrified to think of himself as a crypto-Buddhist. In *Honest to God* there is no reference to the Buddha whatsoever. There is a rather unfortunate quotation from Bonhoeffer, who speaks of the followers of other religions worshipping monstrous animal forms and so on, but I don't think the bishop takes that very seriously. In *The New Reformation?* there is one passing reference to the Buddha, as well as one to Mohammed, but one has no means of understanding from this what the bishop feels about Buddhism, which is rather a pity.[6] I can't help thinking that a knowledge of Buddhism – not just an acquaintance with the facts, but a real understanding – and especially of that very special form of Buddhism that we call Zen, would help the bishop quite a lot in his spiritual life. Perhaps one day he will get around to studying Buddhism seriously. I shouldn't be at all surprised, because it seems to me that he is heading in this direction, whether he knows it or not.

Chapter 4 of *Honest to God* has the striking title 'The Man for Others', and in this chapter the bishop deals with Christ. Obviously if he rejects traditional theism the bishop is faced with a problem, as traditionally Christ is regarded as God incarnate. One of the reasons, if not the main reason, why the Quakers and the Unitarians are excluded from the World Council of Churches is that they are unable to regard Christ quite in this way. But if the traditional conception of God is not valid, what happens to Christ? If he is not God incarnate, if he is not the second person of the Trinity, who or what is he? The bishop's approach to this problem, I was very happy to note, is rather Buddhistic: he keeps firmly to the middle way. He is well aware that the traditional conception of Christ as the incarnate second person of the Trinity must go, but he doesn't go to the other extreme, as some liberal Christians do, of regarding Christ just as a very good man. He doesn't go to the humanistic extreme. This is very interesting to Buddhists, because we look at the Buddha in rather the same way. What I mean by that I have tried to explain elsewhere, but let me briefly recapitulate. The Buddha obviously isn't God incarnate, because in Buddhism there is no God, but at the same time he is not just an ordinary man. According to Buddhist tradition, the Buddha was an Enlightened human being, a human being who had become fully, perfectly assimilated to the transcendental spiritual reality. To put it in popular, rather imprecise language, the Buddha is a human being who has become one with reality. We don't say that the Buddha is God, nor that he is merely man. He is an Enlightened man, a man become one with reality. The two have become interfused, so that one cannot say which is the human being and which is reality. For this reason, neither a purely supernaturalistic nor a purely humanistic assessment of the Buddha is possible. It seems to me that the Bishop of Woolwich is struggling towards a similar conception of Christ. He cannot regard him as God incarnate, but he is reluctant to regard him just as a very good man, a great ethical teacher. He therefore takes over, as the title of the chapter indicates, Bonhoeffer's idea of Christ as 'the man for others'. Moreover, the bishop makes the same point that Bonhoeffer made: that transcendence, or a sort of metaphysical dimension of reality, is experienced in concern for others. In concern for others you transcend yourself, and in that self-transcending, there is a participation in absolute reality.

The conception of living for others is a very noble one, but even if one regards Christ as 'the man for others', that does not make him unique, although the bishop would still like to think that he is. After all, there have lived in the world many people who lived for others. The bishop doesn't say, though he might have said, that Christ died for others, no doubt because the very conception of dying for others, or the atoning death of Christ, is part of the dogmatic structure that the bishop is trying to abandon. But we can say that Socrates died for others, the Vietnamese monks who set themselves on fire several months ago died for others, and even secular heroes and heroines like Edith Cavell died for others.[7] So this idea of living for others is not sufficient to establish the uniqueness of Christ. It seems to me that here the bishop perhaps wants to have his cake and eat it too. To me, the Buddhist idea of the compassionate bodhisattva, the great being who in the popular version of the teaching renounces his own salvation, his own Nirvāṇa, in order to dedicate himself to the salvation and well-being of others, expresses clearly and adequately the truth that the bishop is trying to work his way towards. In Buddhism compassion is not merely an emotion, not just a feeling of pity. It is the way in which one acts, or what one manifests, when one has a deep and true realization of non-selfhood. In Buddhism compassion is regarded as the flower of wisdom, wisdom being understood as an experience of the truth of non-self and non-duality, or what we call *śūnyatā*, the voidness which is not just emptiness, but reality itself. Only when one has had this sort of experience can one really live for others in the deepest and truest sense. But to this metaphysical, deeply spiritual level the bishop doesn't penetrate. He seems to think of living for others more in terms of social service and so on, which to the Buddhist is comparatively superficial.

One who throws traditional theism overboard, as the Bishop of Woolwich has done, has difficulties not only in restating his Christology but in many other ways. If there is no personal God, no supreme being, what becomes of prayer? What becomes of worship? If there is no God, what function do the churches serve? What do you go to church to do every Sunday? The bishop is aware of all these difficulties, but he doesn't go into them very deeply. He certainly doesn't seriously consider the possibility of meditation. If there is any real defect in his book I think it is that he doesn't quite see the connection between non-theistic religion and meditation. Prayer, worship, and theism all go naturally together, and in the same way, with non-theistic religion comes concentration, meditation, mind development, or whatever term one might like to use. When he comes to the practical side of the other-regarding life, the bishop becomes a bit vague and tends to reduce it to various forms of social service.

But I don't want to give the impression that I'm criticizing the Bishop of Woolwich. I think that he has introduced a very important and necessary catalyst into the Church of England, and into the whole Christian religion, at least in this country. As a Buddhist, I can only hope that that catalyst will do its work, and that Christianity will gradually become non-theistic, not only in principle but also in practice. It is my own view that if that happens, what is produced will cease to be Christianity in any recognizable sense. Historically, Christianity is a theistic religion, and if we get a non-theistic Christianity emerging, it will be much more like Buddhism than like Christianity as we have known it so far.

We are all in certain respects very conservative, if not politically, at least psychologically. We don't like change where deep-rooted assumptions about our religious life are concerned, and it seems to me that even though he is almost a revolutionary thinker, or popularizer, the Bishop of Woolwich quite naturally, and even quite rightly, has an emotional attachment to the tradition to which he belongs. Sometimes it seems as though he is going all the way forward, but then he pulls himself back a bit and hesitates. This is the sort of thing that happens to all of us when we are reaching out towards something new, towards a fresh interpretation of our spiritual life and experience. But it seems to me that if he pushes on and follows his present line of thought to its logical conclusion, it will be very difficult for him not to come to a position closely approximating to that of Buddhism, or even to Buddhism itself. However, human beings are not rational, and it would be irrational to expect anyone to behave rationally. In religious and spiritual matters perhaps they *shouldn't* behave rationally. So I don't have any great expectations of getting a knock on my door from the Bishop of Woolwich and a request to admit him into the fold of Buddhism. But I think it is inevitable that the bishop will come closer to Buddhism in the course of years, whether he knows it or not. I am quite sure that if he comes to know something about Buddhism, and if he comes into contact with Buddhists, he will be delighted to recognize some resemblance between his present views and those which have been the views of Buddhists for thousands of years.

This is all to the good. Buddhists are not anxious to make converts. They are always happy, naturally, when someone joins them in their quest for truth and reality, but they also see that people have to tread their own individual paths, and that ultimately the choice is one's own. I am sure that whether the bishop carries on in the Church of England or whether he takes any other step, whether he comes to know about Buddhism or not – or whether he even retracts all that he has said, as he might possibly do – Buddhists will always have towards him great good will for his courageous attempt to break through convention and tradition and come nearer to a position which they feel is Buddhistic. In these days, when religion is generally rather on the defensive, it is not a bad thing that members of different religions should find themselves coming closer together. Buddhists, of course, are very loyal to their own principles, one of the most important of which is that Buddhism is a non-theistic religion. No concession can be made on that front. But we are happy if we find people in other religions, even in Christianity, coming to hold that view within the limits of their own faith, because we feel that they have thereby come nearer to the truth, to Enlightenment. Perhaps it will now be felt that there is not so great a disparity between Buddhism and the Bishop of Woolwich as might at first sight have appeared.

THE LAMAS OF TIBET

College of Psychic Science, Kensington, 9 June 1965

In the ten or fifteen years since the unhappy invasion of Tibet by the Communist Chinese, we have heard quite a lot about the lamas of Tibet, especially about the Dalai Lama, the Panchen Lama, and various other incarnate lamas of that great Buddhist country. This evening we're going to try to understand who the lamas of Tibet really are. There is quite a lot of misunderstanding about the meaning of the word lama, so let's deal with that topic first. The word literally means superior, and it is said to translate the Sanskrit word *uttara*, which also means that which is higher or superior. 'Lama' means superior in the sense of being spiritually superior, and this introduces an extremely important idea which underlies not only practically the whole of Tibetan Buddhism but practically the whole of Buddhism itself and in fact any system of spiritual life and thought: the idea of spiritual hierarchy.

To understand this, we have to understand the concept of degrees of reality, the idea that the level of experience we usually occupy – waking experience, the experience that comes through the five senses and the lower mind – is just one level of the experience of reality. Above this there are other, higher levels of consciousness. The whole of existence is like a great ladder on which we occupy the lowest rung, speaking in terms of human understanding and experience and consciousness. In all spiritual systems, whether Buddhism or Hinduism, Platonism, Neoplatonism, Sufism, and so on, one gets this conception that there are degrees of reality in the structure of existence. This has an important corollary in terms of experience. If there are degrees of reality, there are degrees of spiritual experience, even degrees of Enlightenment in accordance with the degree of reality that is being experienced. On our present level there is objectively a certain level of reality, a comparatively low one. Corresponding to that on the subjective side is our experience of that lower level of reality, which is itself an experience of a lower kind in the hierarchy of experiences. So objectively one has a hierarchy of degrees of reality and subjectively one has the hierarchy of degrees of experience or even levels of Enlightenment. This being the case, we have also a hierarchy of being: there are beings occupying the lower reaches of the hierarchy and others who are on the higher levels and thus occupy a higher place in the hierarchy of beings.

When we enter upon the spiritual life, we automatically take our place in a hierarchy of spiritual beings, some of them above us and some, perhaps, below us. Usually we will find that most of the beings who are already members of that spiritual hierarchy are our spiritual superiors, belonging on a higher level of reality by virtue of their higher degree of spiritual experience. In relation to us they are what the Tibetans call lamas. This way of thinking is of course distasteful to the modern mind. We don't like to think in terms of anybody being spiritually superior, preferring to think that everybody is on the same level. It may be that in terms of an ultimate spiritual essence nobody is superior or inferior to anybody else, but in terms of the manifestation of that inner essence, some are higher and some are lower, and in the Buddhist tradition considerable importance attaches to the recognition of this hierarchical principle. For instance, when one is ordained as a *bhikṣu*, a Buddhist monk, the time of the ordination is noted, so that if you meet another monk and discover that you were ordained fifteen minutes before he was, that makes you senior to him. The idea is that in the sangha there can't ever be complete equality in respect of the position you occupy in the hierarchy, in this case not the spiritual hierarchy, but merely the ecclesiastical hierarchy.

In English the words superior and inferior have unpleasant connotations because of how we look at things, but in the East no one minds being inferior and no one objects to anyone being spiritually superior. According to Buddhist tradition, reluctance to recognize others as spiritually superior and therefore as deserving of respect and even reverence is a sign of egotism, and it is emphasized that until this is overcome, until one is able to look up to those who are spiritually superior and adopt a more receptive attitude, very little spiritual progress is possible. There is a living chain of spiritual beings from the heights right down into the depths, and according to Tibetan Buddhism (and general Buddhist teaching) up and down that living chain of spiritual beings there run all sorts of spiritual influences. From below there rises a current of reverence, devotion, even worship, and descending from above is a current of what the Tibetans call *chin lap*, which is very difficult to translate, but means something like a blessing or even grace, a transmuting force or power (Sanskrit *adhiṣṭhāna*). According to the Tibetan tradition, the blessing or grace takes a certain form and it is essentially this that is known as the teaching, the guidance upon the path. Usually we think of teaching in more intellectual, conceptual terms: the four noble truths, the twelve links of conditioned co-production, and so on, but according to Tibetan Buddhism the teaching is a current of spiritual energy descending from higher to lower planes, from those who are spiritually superior to those who are spiritually inferior, in such a way as to help and guide them, and the doctrinal teaching is only one manifestation of this. So a lama is not only a spiritual superior, but also a spiritual teacher, and this is the real meaning of the word. When we refer to the lamas of Tibet, we really mean the spiritual teachers of Tibet.

The word 'lama' is used rather loosely by Western writers and travellers as though it means 'monk', but this is not accurate, though a lama may be a monk and a monk may be a lama. There are other terms in Tibetan for monk, the most general being *drapa*, which means simply 'student'. For the fully ordained monk, the *bhikkhu* as he is called in Pāli or *bhikṣu* in Sanskrit, the Tibetans use the term *gelong*; the Tibetan equivalent of the *śrāmaṇera* or novice monk is *getsul*; and the Tibetan term for the *upāsaka* or *upāsikā*, the lay brother or lay sister, is *genyen*. Some Western writers have created confusion by speaking of all monks as lamas, and by speaking of married monks. If by monk you mean *bhikṣu*, a married monk is a contradiction in terms. What they're really referring to is a married lama. Usually, especially in the Gelug tradition, a lama is a monk, but among the Nyingmapas and Kagyupas it often happens that the lama is a layman, who may in some cases be married. So a married lama is not a monk but a spiritually advanced layman who is functioning as a spiritual teacher.

The general Indian word for a spiritual teacher is guru, so when we speak of the lamas of Tibet we mean the gurus of Tibet, those who are spiritual teachers within the framework of Tibetan Buddhism, and Tibetan Buddhism, broadly speaking, is a direct continuation of Indian Buddhism. Indian Buddhism lasted for about 1,500 years, from about 500 BCE to about 1000 CE and during that time it passed through three great phases of development, each of which lasted for about 500 years. First of all it passed through the phase of Hīnayāna or basic Buddhism, then through the phase of the Mahāyāna or developed Buddhism, and then through the phase of the Vajrayāna, or esoteric Buddhism, as it is sometimes called. During the phase of basic Buddhism, the Dharma went from India to Ceylon, so the Buddhism of Ceylon (now Sri Lanka) represents Indian Buddhism of that first phase of development. Buddhism went to China during the second phase, the Mahāyāna phase, so Chinese Buddhism is Indian Buddhism in that stage of its development, Hīnayāna plus Mahāyāna. But Buddhism went to Tibet during the third great phase, so what went to Tibet from India was basic Buddhism plus developed Buddhism plus esoteric Buddhism. Tibetan Buddhism is often referred to as Mahāyāna Buddhism but it isn't just that – it's all three *yānas* integrated into a single system. Tibetan Buddhists themselves often refer to *triyāna* Buddhism, and according to Tibetan tradition these three *yānas* are not mutually exclusive but represent three successive stages of spiritual progress.

The lamas of Tibet are thus gurus in a threefold sense, functioning on three different levels. When a lama is functioning on the Hīnayāna level he has the function of the *upādhyāya* (Sanskrit) or preceptor, one who has completed at least ten years as a fully ordained monk. It is the *upādhyāya* who gives to others the Refuges and Precepts and presides at the time of conferring monastic ordination. If you want to be ordained, you have to gather together at least five fully ordained monks in the same place, and among them there has to be one who is able to function as *upādhyāya* within that context. Within the context of the Hīnayāna the lama also teaches basic Buddhism and gives instruction in elementary concentration and meditation.

Within the context of the Mahāyāna, the lama functions as what is known as the bodhisattva, one who occupies a high place in the spiritual hierarchy, who is nearing Nirvāṇa, but renounces Nirvāṇa for himself. The idea is that as one progresses in the spiritual life, as one dissociates oneself more and more from the things of this world, the *saṃsāra*, it becomes possible to complete the dissociation, to cut oneself off from the world and remain in a state of spiritual peace and calm, quite apart from the other beings of the universe. This individual or private Nirvāṇa is a possibility when you reach a certain level of your spiritual development, but if you are a bodhisattva, you don't take up that possibility. You decide to remain in contact with beings within *saṃsāra* and devote the spiritual knowledge and experience you have acquired to helping others to make spiritual progress and become free. This is what is meant by the lama as bodhisattva within the context of the Mahāyāna. According to Tibetan tradition, not only does he renounce his own Nirvāṇa, but he voluntarily allows himself to be reborn on this earth to continue his work of guiding and teaching other living beings. The bodhisattva ideal is common to all the Mahāyāna countries, but in Tibet it has been given a very special development. The Tibetans are a practical people. They are not satisfied with generalities and abstractions. They want to come down to details. So they weren't satisfied with just being told in a general way that bodhisattvas renounce their individual Nirvāṇa and allow themselves to be reborn on earth to help others. They wanted to know where they were and who they were. They wanted to locate them, almost to hunt them down. In this way there developed the institution of what became known as *tulkus*, incarnate lamas, though they're not so much incarnate lamas as incarnate bodhisattvas. The most famous ones are the Dalai Lama and the Panchen Lama, but there are many others, and there are books describing how they are discovered and identified and trained.

In my observation, over the generations in Tibet there has arisen some confusion in the popular mind on the subject of incarnate lamas. Nowadays, Tibetan Buddhists usually think that if a child can be identified as the reincarnation of a certain deceased abbot or teacher, he is automatically a *tulku*, an incarnate lama or bodhisattva, but strictly speaking you'd have to prove that the original abbot or teacher was himself a bodhisattva before you could speak of his reincarnation as an incarnate bodhisattva. In the whole of Tibet in the old days there were about 2,000 people who were popularly regarded as incarnate lamas. I regret to say that out of all of them there is only one woman.[8] Christmas Humphreys once put the matter rather well in a lecture, saying that most incarnate lamas are really the equivalent of the local vicar reborn. Very few out of the 2,000 can be regarded as incarnate bodhisattvas – maybe the Dalai Lama and the Panchen Lama and a few others, some of whom I've known, but not many more than that.

On the Mahāyāna level, as a bodhisattva, the lama is a teacher in two ways. First of all, he is a teacher by virtue of his mere presence in the world. Tibetans attach great importance to the simple fact that there is such a spiritually superior being in the world. He doesn't necessarily have to do anything, say anything, or teach anything. The mere fact that he is here, that in the midst of ordinary people there is someone who is spiritually more highly attained than they are, carries its own influence and its own blessing. But secondly, the lama functions as a teacher of the Mahāyāna, and especially of the *śūnyatāvāda*, the philosophy of the Mahāyāna, and of the six perfections that lead to Buddhahood: *dāna* or giving, *śīla* or ethics, *kṣānti* or patience, *vīrya* or vigour, *samādhi* or meditation, and *prajñā* or wisdom. In the context of the Mahāyāna the lama gives to others the bodhisattva vow and ordination, and the bodhisattva precepts. This is on the comparatively ecclesiastical level but it does have its own function and importance.

On the level of the Vajrayāna, the lama functions as the Vajrācārya, or Tantric guru. The lama as preceptor and even as bodhisattva is provisional, but the lama as Tantric guru is the real, ultimate meaning of the word 'lama'. If a Tibetan Buddhist says, 'So-and-so is my lama', he doesn't mean that he has taken the precepts from him or that he is studying Buddhist philosophy with him, but that he has received from him Tantric initiation, or *wong* (also called *wang*). The guru or lama is of supreme importance in all stages of the Buddhist life, but in the Vajrayāna or Tantra the lama appears as a fourth refuge. In all other forms of Buddhism we go for Refuge to the Buddha, the Dharma, and the Sangha, but in the Vajrayāna there is also refuge in the guru, and this fourth refuge comes first. Tibetan Buddhists say that the lama refuge is the esoteric form of the Buddha Refuge; that is, what is Buddha in relation to the whole Buddhist tradition is lama in relation to you individually. They consider this so important that they separate this esoteric aspect of the Buddha Refuge and make it into the first refuge, preceding refuge in the Buddha, the Dharma, and the Sangha. Vajrayāna Buddhism encourages the attitude that one should regard one's Tantric guru as the Buddha himself, and revere him accordingly. You never find fault with or criticize your own Tantric guru, or anybody else's, or indeed any spiritual teacher. Tibetans require the absolute obedience of the pupil to the teacher.

The classic example is that of Milarepa. His early days were passed in sinful fashion – he practised black magic and killed a number of people – and then he had a change of heart and came within the influence, or even into the clutches, of a famous guru called Marpa, who was extremely strict. Marpa didn't set Milarepa studying the scriptures or practising meditation; he set him building towers on the tops of hills. He made Milarepa carry the stones on his shoulders and great sores developed, but when he showed these to his guru, all Marpa did was show him how to fold a piece of sacking to protect his back. Milarepa built a tower and the guru said it was all wrong and made him pull it down again. In this way he built several towers and they all had to be pulled down, except the last one. In this way he was subjected to trials and austerities until the guru said that all his sins had been thoroughly purified, and only after that did he get initiation.[9] The life of Milarepa is often cited as an example of how the disciple should behave towards the guru.

There's another well-known example from the *Life of Milarepa*. In Tantric Buddhism the tradition is that when you receive an initiation, you have to make an offering, and if it's a very important initiation, you have to offer everything that you have in order to get it: your money, your household furniture, your pots and pans, your rice and barley, even your beer. The attitude you're trying to express is that what you are going to receive is so precious that it requires everything you've got in return. One day Marpa was due to give an initiation of this sort and all his disciples came. One of them was a very old man who came a long way and brought his family and all his possessions with him, his wives and his children, his flocks and his herds, sacks of rice and barley and barrels of beer, even gold and jewellery. He offered them all to the guru, but Marpa said, 'This isn't good enough. You haven't brought everything.' The disciple said, 'I think I have,' but Marpa said, 'Think again.' The disciple thought and thought, and then he remembered that he had a she-goat who was so old she couldn't walk. Thinking that she wasn't a suitable gift for the guru, he'd left her behind. The guru said, 'Back you go and get that goat,' and he had to go back about five hundred miles to get her, and everybody had to wait until he came back carrying her on his shoulders. Then the guru said, 'Now you've offered everything, you can have the initiation.' This is the sort of person Marpa was, and the story illustrates the importance of devotion and obedience to the Tantric guru.[10]

In the Tibetan Tantric tradition there is a practice called the *guru yoga* whose purpose is to help you to attune yourself to the mind and heart of the guru and make you receptive to his spiritual influence. The Tibetans believe that it isn't enough to learn teachings from the guru, or even to do as he tells you. Your heart must be tuned into the guru's heart so that you know spontaneously what he wants you to do and behave accordingly. It's sometimes said that there are three kinds of disciple. When the guru tells the first kind to do something, they don't do it. When the guru tells the second kind to do something, they do it. But the third kind do it without having to be told, and it's the third kind of disciple whom the *guru yoga* is meant to form, the kind of disciple who knows instinctively what the guru wants him to do because he's tuned into the mind and the heart of the guru, and is receptive to his spiritual influence. The *guru yoga* attunes the disciple not just to their personal guru, but the guru's guru, and so on, all the way up the hierarchy.[11]

The *guru yoga* follows immediately after the four preliminary practices, also called foundation yogas or *mūla yogas*. The first of these is Going for Refuge, with various prostrations and visualizations. In early Buddhism and in the Mahāyāna you simply recite 'To the Buddha for Refuge I go, to the Dharma for Refuge I go, to the Sangha for Refuge I go' three times. But in Tantric Buddhism, you visualize a Refuge Tree, a great tree rooted in the earth with its branches spreading to the heavens, and sitting in the branches of the tree you visualize the lamas or gurus of your hierarchy: your own guru in the middle and his guru above him, and his guru above him, then other great gurus like Padmasambhava and Milarepa and Marpa all sitting in the branches of the tree. You visualize all this, you clearly see it all in meditation, and then you make full prostrations, reciting at the same time formulas that mean 'I take refuge in all the gurus, all the lamas, the Buddha, the Dharma, the Sangha, the sacred scriptures.' This you do up to 100,000 times. It's rather a strenuous practice. The second of the *mūla yogas* is development of the *bodhicitta*, the will to Enlightenment. This consists in reciting up to 100,000 times the bodhisattva vow: the fourfold great vow or any other formulation of the aspiration to gain Enlightenment for the benefit of all living beings. You recite it over and over again until it becomes part of your mind and consciousness. The third *mūla yoga* is the recitation of the mantra of Vajrasattva, and this is practised for the purpose of purification – not only to purify you from all sins and faults, but to reveal to yourself the fact that your essential, intrinsic nature remains pure all the time, was pure from the very beginning and is never stained, whatever you do or say or think. The mantra of Vajrasattva has a hundred syllables, and you go on reciting it, together with visualizing the white figure of Vajrasattva. And the fourth of the *mūla yogas* is the offering of the mandala, a symbolical representation of the entire universe which you offer to the Buddhas and bodhisattvas and lamas and teachers, reciting a verse while you do so. There are several ways of doing this: the great offering, the middle offering, and the little offering. The little offering of the mandala simply involves making a *mudrā* with your fingers, to represent the whole universe, with Mount Sumeru in the middle (the centre of the earth, according to traditional Buddhist cosmology) and the four seas all round. What the Tibetans usually do is put a little rice in each palm, lift their hands up in this *mudrā*, and recite a verse which means, 'I offer the whole universe to the Buddhas and bodhisattvas and the gurus.'[12]

Inasmuch as the lama functions in all these ways, he is clearly of great importance in the context of Tibetan Buddhism, but it's the Vajrayāna or Tantric guru who is the most highly regarded. In the Hīnayāna the lama is a spiritual teacher, in the Mahāyāna a spiritual presence, but in the Vajrayāna, in Tantric Buddhism, the lama as the Tantric guru functions as the bestower of spiritual power at the time of Tantric initiation or *abhiṣeka* (as it is called in Sanskrit) or *wongkur* (as the Tibetans call it). This initiation is fourfold, for the body, the speech, the mind, and the unity of all three. The idea is that the spiritual power which you receive from the Tantric guru at the time of initiation enables you eventually to transmute your body, speech, and mind, and their unity, into the body, speech, mind, and their unity of a Buddha. This is why in Tantric Buddhism the lama is regarded as being of the utmost significance.

THE HEIGHTS AND DEPTHS OF THE SPIRITUAL LIFE

Hampstead Buddhist Vihara, 19 September 1965

This topic is connected with one of the most important aspects, if not *the* most important aspect, the most important principle, even, of Buddhist thought: the law of conditionality, the law that whatever arises, arises in dependence upon conditions and ceases when those conditions cease to exist. Whether in the material world, the mental world, the emotional world, or even the spiritual world, whatever arises, arises in dependence upon conditions. There is no chance, no accident, no fate, no destiny, but a process of universal conditionality on all levels of existence from the very bottom to the very top of mundane phenomenal existence.

Broadly speaking, there are two ways in which the principle of conditionality can operate: the cyclical and the spiral. The cyclical mode of conditionality is a process of action and reaction between opposites, as when you go from pleasure to pain, or from life to death, birth to rebirth, and so on. The other, the spiral order or mode of conditionality, is a process of action and reaction between factors which progressively augment one another. For instance, you go from pleasure to happiness, from happiness to joy, from joy to rapture, and from rapture to bliss, in an ascending progressive spiral.

The process of action and reaction between opposites – happiness and unhappiness, pleasure and pain, birth and death, loss and gain – is in Buddhist language the *saṃsāra* or the wheel of conditioned existence, within which we revolve round and round within the two great opposites, birth and death. Within this process there are many pairs of opposites, and this evening we will be considering one of them, the heights and the depths – not in the abstract, but within the context of the spiritual life. Broadly speaking, there are two kinds of pairs of opposites: the horizontal, when the pair are both on the same level, and the vertical, when the pair are arranged hierarchically. As an example of the first we could take the pair of opposites represented by the two sexes, man and woman, whereas teacher and disciple are a pair of opposites on the vertical in a hierarchical order. When we speak of the heights and the depths, obviously we are concerned with a vertically arranged pair of opposites, and the words themselves suggest that the heights are up there and the depths are down there. But what exactly is meant by these expressions in the context of the spiritual life? Very broadly speaking, the heights represent consciousness, and the depths represent what is usually called the unconscious, or we could say that the heights represent mind or thought or intellect and the depths represent instinct, emotion, will, volition.

Perhaps it's best to explain the relationship between the heights and the depths not by way of an abstract definition, but using an illustration. As I prepared this talk, there came floating into my mind's eye a picture of an iceberg. An iceberg is an enormous mass of ice, and the strange thing about it is that by far the greater portion of it is beneath the waves. The relationship between the conscious and the unconscious, the thought and the emotion, intellect and volition, is like that. The submerged portion is very much greater. Alternatively, we can compare the relationship to a mountain. The peak of the mountain is very narrow, culminating in a point, while the base of the mountain is very broad. The relationship between the conscious and unconscious, between thought and emotion or instinct, is just like this. There is a tremendous disparity, the heights almost infinitesimal and the depths almost infinite.

This brings us directly to the central problem of the spiritual life. If we think we know something about the Buddha's teachings, that knowledge has probably come from what we've read and heard. We may have come to be well acquainted with the life of the Buddha, the *Jātaka* stories, the history of Buddhism, how the Order was founded, the various doctrines, the schools, the principles of meditation, and so on. But although we could give a fairly coherent account of the Buddha's teaching and explain the different paths leading to Nirvāṇa, although we might even be able to give an account of what Nirvāṇa is, we have to admit that we're not Enlightened. We know it all, but in another, profounder sense, we don't know anything at all. So why is this? The reason, very obviously, is that we know only superficially, only with the unsubmerged portion of ourselves. We know intellectually, but that is all. We don't know profoundly, we don't know emotionally, instinctually. We might say that we know in the heights of our being, but we don't know in the depths, and we might even go so far as to say that we therefore don't know at all.

It is not even a question of half and half. If it was, a real spiritual tension would be set up, and out of that something might come. But the conscious part of us is like the tip of the iceberg, so we know only with a seventh or eighth part of ourselves, and even then not very thoroughly or seriously, and we don't know at all with the rest of our being. We come to lectures, read books, and just for a minute we are mentally lifted up to the heights. But we put the book aside, leave the vihara, go home, turn on the television, listen to the radio, go to the cinema, whatever it happens to be, and with that we're back down in the unregenerate and incoherent depths. There is a mild oscillation going on like this all the time, not even a real tension, much less an actual conflict. Some people are quite happy to go on like this in a Christian context. They go to church on Sundays, half sleep through the sermon, sing a hymn or two, say 'amen' at the end, and then go home and carry on living their lives. They feel a little uplifted – you can't say it hasn't done them any good – but it doesn't last long. There's a danger that Buddhists may do the same thing. You might come along to a meeting or a lecture, even go to the summer school for ten whole days, and you're uplifted while you're there, but you can't keep it up, and you slip back down into the depths. Most people are quite happy to go on like this, with an occasional bit of uplift to keep them feeling good, to prevent too much tension from developing. They burn a little incense at the shrine of religion, and that's that. The problem that faces us is how to know not just in the heights, mentally, but emotionally, in the profoundest places of our being, so that we know from the top to the bottom of ourselves wholly and totally. We can't ignore the depths. Out of the depths come our energies of instinct, emotion, and will, and somehow they have to be harnessed to the chariot of the spiritual life; otherwise they will drag us in some other direction. They've got to be harnessed, they've got to be integrated, and it's here that the devotional side of Buddhism comes in.

Devotion is one of the most important ways in which the energies of instinct and emotion can be refined, sublimated, and gradually integrated with our mental understanding, contributing their energies to that understanding and helping us in the direction of the actual realization of what we've so far merely understood, refining and sublimating those emotions which otherwise would be dissipated and perhaps even pull us in the opposite direction to the one that we're trying to take. In the Buddhist countries, the worship of the Buddha, paying homage to his memory and to the spiritual ideal he represents by offering flowers and incense, chanting the scriptures and so on, occupies a very important place indeed. At the summer school recently I was very interested to find how warm a response there was to the devotional meetings that were held on the last three evenings. I had imagined that perhaps ten or twelve pious people would come along, but practically everybody turned up. They even left their coffee to attend these meetings, and some people said afterwards that the meditation that followed went much better for them on account of the devotional meeting, usually called a puja. Evidently the puja had not merely aroused but harnessed those emotions that are usually dissipated, so that the energy of those emotions was there behind the meditation. All the devotional exercises in Buddhism have, among other purposes, this reason for their existence: they refine and sublimate the emotional nature and place this energy at the disposal of the spiritual life.

There are various other ways of refining and sublimating the emotional side of our nature. Some people do it through the arts in their more refined forms. In the Buddhist art of ancient India, China, Japan, and Tibet, the traditional arts are impregnated with spiritual values, even if not explicitly expressed in religious terms, and many people looking at a Chinese landscape painting or a sculpted image of the Buddha develop the state of refined emotion that others get from devotional practices. There is also the practice of the four *brahma vihāras*, the systematic cultivation in meditation of the sublime sentiments of love or *maitrī*, friendliness, loving-kindness; *karuṇā* or compassion; sympathetic joy, *muditā*; and tranquillity and equanimity, or *upekṣā*. I was interested to find when I started teaching meditation on my return to England a year ago that many people had great difficulty with the practice of the development of loving-kindness. It seemed to point to a certain difficulty of refining and sublimating their emotional nature. Those who find the *maitrī bhāvanā* difficult usually find the mindfulness of breathing much easier, and they may be tempted to follow the line of least resistance and concentrate on the practice they find easiest, but that temptation should be resisted. We need to cultivate that which is weakest in us; otherwise our development will be lopsided, so whichever side you find more difficult, whether it's the emotional side or the intellectual side, that's the side you should cultivate.

This is the significance of that famous teaching, the five spiritual faculties: faith and wisdom, energy and concentration, and mindfulness.[13] These constitute two pairs and a balancing faculty. Faith is the emotional and devotional side of the spiritual life, wisdom is the intellectual and cognitive side, and these two must be balanced; otherwise, the following of the higher spiritual life is very difficult, for one must be emotionally and intellectually in harmony. The extrovert and the introvert, the active and the meditative, have to be balanced as well. And both pairs have to be balanced with the fifth faculty, mindfulness, which is described in the Pāli canon as being always useful.[14] Here we're especially concerned with keeping faith and wisdom in balance, for otherwise spiritual progress will be hindered, or even delayed.

So far we have considered the heights and the depths in a comparatively mundane manner, but we can go further and deeper, even much deeper. As we lead our spiritual lives, as we get more and more – I don't like to say 'advanced', because it isn't a very pleasant expression – but as we become a little more accustomed to it, as we get more into the way of it, as we make a certain amount of progress, especially in meditation, there come to us various experiences. To begin with, they are comparatively superficial. Some people see lights or hear sounds when they meditate, but these are not to be taken seriously, just to be noted and passed over as you progress. As you go further than that, higher than that, other experiences come of a loftier, rarer kind, experiences we may call transcendental, glimpses – even if only from a great distance – of ultimate reality, truth, Enlightenment. There are various terms used to describe these glimpses. The Theravādins talk in terms of flashes of insight, of *vipassanā*; the Mahāyānists talk in terms of perfect wisdom, or transcendental wisdom, which dawns upon the meditating disciple; and the Zen people talk in terms of *satori*. In plain English we might call it Enlightenment experience, not the full or total experience of Enlightenment, but glimpses, flashes seen from afar. These experiences constitute the peaks of our spiritual life. They're very rare, but when they come, and later when we think back on them, they're very encouraging. Sometimes it's hard work sweltering along the plains of the spiritual life, but if we look up and see the peaks in the distance, and know that one day we will get there, that gives us a great deal of encouragement and hope. These transcendental experiences represent the heights of the spiritual life.

If you have a flash or a glimpse of this sort, you might think, 'This is it. I've got there at last.' But although you've attained something, and it might be a very profound experience, it might move you very deeply, it might even shake you to the foundations of your being, it isn't the end. We might even go so far as to say that Buddhism doesn't end with Enlightenment, or even that it's once you're Enlightened that your spiritual life really starts. By Enlightenment in this context I don't mean the full, ultimate, complete and perfect Enlightenment, but the initial glimpse or vision which many people mistake for the ultimate goal or the whole experience. It's after that initial glimpse has been attained that the real work begins. Before that we're just trying to make a start. The start is really made once that transcendental experience has occurred, or a whole series of transcendental experiences have occurred, and the work we have to do consists in the transformation of the whole being at all levels, in all aspects, in accordance with that experience. It's not enough to leave the experience hanging up there. It has to descend into the depths and illumine and transform them, sublimate and refine them, and integrate them with that experience so that there is one illumination from top to bottom, not just a little sunlight on the peaks and the rest below in total darkness.

So it comes about that in Buddhism there are taught two paths: the *darśana-mārga*, the path of vision, and the *bhāvanā-mārga*, the path of becoming or path of transformation. The path of vision represents the initial transcendental experience and the path of transformation represents the working over of one's entire nature in accordance with that experience. The Noble Eightfold Path is one of the best-known aspects of the Buddha's teaching, but people very often don't realize that there are really two eightfold paths: the mundane eightfold path and the transcendental eightfold path. Considered as a transcendental eightfold path, the first step, right understanding, which can also be translated as right vision, *samyag-dṛṣṭi*, represents the path of vision. It represents actual spiritual experience. It's not just an intellectual understanding, not just the ability to name the four noble truths, but at least the initial experience of the underlying reality of that teaching. This is the first step, and the other seven steps – right thought or intention, right speech, right action, right livelihood, right effort, right mindfulness, and right meditation – represent the path of transformation, the bringing into harmony of all our different aspects with that initial transcendental experience so that it pervades our whole being instead of remaining isolated at the peaks of our existence. For example, in the transcendental path the last stage, right *samādhi*, right concentration and meditation, isn't just using the right technique or even getting the right results, but the absolute pellucidity and clarity of one's entire emotional nature, the complete illumination of our depths, so that the depths become one with the heights, with that initial transcendental experience. Thus the great teaching of the path of vision and the path of transformation illustrates this relationship between the depths and the heights in our spiritual life.

Another illustration is that of the four *ārya-mārgas*, the four noble paths. There's the path of the Stream Entrant, the one who has entered the stream leading to Nirvāṇa, who will be reborn not more than seven times and after the end of those seven lives will gain Nirvāṇa finally and completely. Then there's the once-returner, the one who has got so far with their spiritual life that they have to return and be reborn only once; then the *anāgāmin*, the non-returner, the one who won't return at all, who after death will go direct to Nirvāṇa from some higher level of existence; and finally the *arhant*, the one who in this life itself has broken the web of birth and death, become emancipated, gained supreme knowledge, wisdom, and illumination. According to Buddhist tradition there are ten fetters binding us to the wheel of life. The Stream Entrant has broken three. First, there's *satkāya-dṛṣṭi*, the wrong belief in a separate, unchanging self. Secondly, there's *śīlavrata-parāmarśa*, attachment to moral rules and religious observances – not that moral rules and religious observances are wrong or unhelpful or unnecessary, but one should not become attached to them as ends in themselves. One should follow a middle path, neither dispensing with them nor becoming stuck in them, but practising them as a means to an end. Thirdly, there's *vicikitsā*, the inability to settle down or to take a firm decision, just shilly-shallying, wobbling, unable to commit oneself to the spiritual life and its consequences. This is usually translated as doubt, but that is a very inadequate translation. These three fetters have one thing in common: they are all intellectual. Breaking the fetter of *satkāya-dṛṣṭi* means giving up the wrong belief in a separate, unchanging self; breaking the fetter of *śīlavrata-parāmarśa* means understanding that moral rules and religious observances are not ends in themselves; and breaking the fetter of *vicikitsā* obviously represents the need to commit oneself, which includes coming to a clear understanding of things.[15]

Coming to the next of the paths, the once-returner weakens the next two fetters: *rāga* or desire and greed and *lobha* or anger. The third, the *anāgāmin*, the non-returner, finally breaks these two fetters. This tells us that the intellectual fetters may be comparatively easy to break, but the emotional fetters are very, very difficult to break. One can break the intellectual fetters even at the first of these stages, but at the second stage one can only weaken the emotional fetters, and only at the third stage, when one is very near Nirvāṇa, can one finally break them even in their subtle forms. This teaching thus shows the extreme difficulty of refining one's emotional nature as compared with correcting one's intellectual attitude. It's relatively easy to get the right ideas, to understand and accept the truth intellectually, but to bring the emotional side of one's nature into harmony with that, to transform the depths, is very difficult indeed.

Just one more illustration, this one of a more symbolical nature. In the Mahāyāna Buddhism of medieval India there are two great philosophical schools known as the Yogācāra and the Madhyamaka. The followers of the Yogācāra are the practitioners of yoga and meditation, while the followers of the Madhyamaka follow the middle way. The Yogācāra is called the sublime Yogācāra and the Madhyamaka is called the profound Madhyamaka, and these characteristics are illustrated by the stories about their respective origins. The Yogācāra school was founded by the great teacher Asaṅga, who, we are told, ascended in meditation to the Tuṣita *devaloka*, the heaven or state of continued happiness, and there encountered the future Buddha, Maitreya, from whom he received five books of teachings, five sets of insights or illuminations, and these form the basis of the Yogācāra school.[16] So the Yogācāra descended from the heights, from sublime spiritual experiences. Whether one accepts the mythological presentation of it or not, something comes down from an infinitely sublime range of transcendental experiences. But in the case of the perfection of wisdom, which is the basis of the

Madhyamaka school, it's exactly the opposite. We are told that the Buddha preached these teachings during his lifetime, but they were so difficult that they were kept hidden in the depths of the ocean, among many other treasures, and they were retrieved from the depths by the great teacher Nāgārjuna, the founder of the Madhyamaka school. This scene is very often depicted in Tibetan Buddhist art. We see a great ocean and a raft on which Nāgārjuna is sitting, and coming up from the depths is a serpent maiden with the books in her hands. This represents the arising of these profound realizations out of the very depths of our being. In Tibetan Buddhism these two schools have been united, the Yogācāra being considered the relative truth and the Madhyamaka being considered the absolute truth, the first the foundation of the second and the second the completion of the first. This also represents the necessity of uniting the heights and the depths in one's spiritual life, of bringing the heights down to the depths and the depths up to the heights so that one is fully, perfectly integrated, whole, and harmonious. To put it into more Western terminology, we might say that the spiritual life means above all else what William Blake calls the marriage of heaven and hell, heaven representing the pure abstract understanding and hell representing not the hell of conventional Christian thought, but the vortex of undeveloped inchoate energy that needs to be harnessed and integrated.[17] What is necessary above all else in the spiritual life is the bringing together, the integration, of these great pairs of opposites, the heights and the depths.

But how does this affect us here and now? How does it affect you? How does it affect me? As you come here from time to time for these lectures, as you sit here calm and receptive, you should gain intellectual understanding, but there should be something a little more than that, something a little clearer, more refined, purer – not quite insight, but not just intellectual understanding, something that represents the possibility of insight, even if not actually insight itself. So then what do you do? Do you go away and forget about it, do you put it aside as you walk out of the door? What you *should* do during the week is try to embody that insight in your day to day life. Here at the talk you get the path of vision, and during the week you should get the path of becoming, the path of transformation, and this process must go on all the time, week by week, year by year, until the heights and the depths in your spiritual experience become one. The whole business of the spiritual life lies in the attainment of this unity or, to put it more Buddhistically, this non-duality, this overcoming in the fullest possible way of the dichotomy that usually exists between conscious and unconscious, thought and will, understanding and emotion. We overcome it at higher and higher, or deeper and deeper, levels of our being until we can truly say that the heights and the depths, the inner and the outer, have become one. When we succeed in this great task, then we shall be Enlightened, because there will be in us the fullness of wisdom and also the plenitude of compassion. So this is the goal: a state of full, complete and final integration at the very highest, or very deepest, level, making one the heights and the depths of our spiritual experience.

THE BUDDHA'S PHILOSOPHY OF RIGHT SPEECH

A talk with this title was given at the Hampstead Buddhist Vihara on 21 November 1965, but the content of this version makes it clear that it was given on a retreat. We haven't been able to find out when the retreat was given, but it was possibly one of the early ones held under the auspices of the FWBO.

If you have been acquainted with Buddhism for any length of time, you will know that it has a prodigious quantity of sacred writings. There's an enormous collection in Pāli, some forty thick volumes. In Tibetan there are no less than a hundred (in some editions 108) massive xylograph volumes of scriptures, and in Chinese there are some fifty volumes, comprising some 1,660 independent works. There are also lots of odd or loose or scattered Sanskrit *sūtras*. Sometimes a newcomer is rather bewildered by all this richness of Buddhist sacred literature, but fortunately there are a few texts embedded here and there in this vast mass of literature which give us the essence of the whole thing in just a few pages. Among the Perfection of Wisdom *sūtras* we have the famous *Heart Sūtra*, which gives us the heart of the Perfection of Wisdom in just one page of writing, and in the same way, among the Pāli scriptures there's a little work called the *Dhammapada* which gives us the gist of all the Buddha's teachings in the Pāli canon in a very short compass indeed. It consists of 423 verses arranged subject-wise in twenty-six chapters. There's a chapter on the mind, a chapter on the wise man, a chapter on the Enlightened man, a chapter on flowers, a chapter on the pairs, a chapter on the monk, on the Brahmin, on sin, on anger, and so on. It is one of the most famous and popular of all the Buddhist scriptures and has the distinction of having been the first Pāli text to be published in Europe. (Pāli is one of the ancient Indian languages and it is canonical for the Theravāda school of Buddhism.) In 1855 the *Dhammapada* was translated not into any modern language, but into Latin, by the great Danish scholar Viggo Fausbøll, who published it in Copenhagen, and there are now translations in many languages. The *Dhammapada*, being so short and handy, enables us to get at the content of the Buddha's teaching very easily and simply.

This evening I'm going to talk about a verse from chapter eight of the *Dhammapada*, the *Sahassavagga* or Chapter of Thousands. (*Sahassa* is 'thousand', and *vagga* is simply 'chapter'.) This chapter is so called because most of the verses make mention of a thousand things. In each chapter of the *Dhammapada* the verses are strung together to illuminate different facets of the subject, and in each of the verses of this chapter, a thousand, or sometimes a hundred, things of lesser value are contrasted with one thing of greater value. The whole chapter may thus be viewed as one long exhortation to discriminate between one thing of greater value and many things of lesser value, and to prefer the former to the latter, an exhortation which is very necessary, especially nowadays. Most people are unconsciously very much impressed by sheer size or sheer number. There's a book by René Guénon called *The Reign of Quantity and the Signs of the Times*[18] – rather an imposing title, but one could very well speak of the reign of quantity in contemporary life, because we tend to attach importance to quantity, not quality, and this shows itself in many ways, both big and small. If in a few days' time someone came up to you and said, 'In the ten days of the retreat I've read twenty books', you'd be quite impressed by that, more impressed than if they said they'd read one book. You might not stop to ask about the comparative value of those books. The twenty books might have been anything – novels, murder mysteries, science fiction – and the one work might have been a dialogue by Plato or a Buddhist *sūtra*, but the tendency is for us to be more impressed by quantity than by quality. Likewise, we tend to assume that it's a good thing to live to be 80 and a tragedy to die at 20, but we don't ask about the quality of the life lived. Your eighty years may have been useless, wicked, and harmful, and your twenty years may have been full of creativity and promise. John Keats died at the age of 25 and practically all his major creative work was produced in a single year.

The Buddha applies the principle of valuing quality over quantity to the question of speech – hence the verse that we're going to consider this evening:

> Better than a thousand meaningless words is ... a single meaningful word on hearing which one becomes tranquil.[19]

In contrasting a thousand meaningless words with one word full of meaning, the Buddha uses a little humour; he was fond of a touch of irony. He suggests that our speech is usually meaningless, and he delicately hints that the ratio of meaningless words to meaningful words is about a thousand to one. That ratio is perhaps a bit on the generous side. The Buddhist scriptures list thirty-two kinds of idle and useless talk,[20] and surely in the present day they would count many more. We have to admit that our conversation generally consists of a selection of these kinds of idle and useless speech, and that very rarely among our friends and acquaintances do we ever hear anything which sinks deep into our consciousness and which we remember for a long time afterwards, any meaningful word that gives us peace.

The Buddha clearly attached great importance to speech: right speech, or Perfect Speech, is the third step of the Noble Eightfold Path, and abstention from false speech is the fourth of the list of five precepts which it is incumbent upon every professing follower of the Buddha to observe. In the West we are familiar with a twofold classification of the human being into body and mind – or sometimes a threefold classification into body, soul, and spirit, St Paul's classification[21] – but in Buddhism the human being is classified into body, speech, and mind, which is surely very significant, because it means that in Buddhism speech is given the same importance as body and mind. It is speech, perhaps above all else, that distinguishes human beings from the animals. Without language, there would be no civilization, no culture, no thought, no literature, no philosophy, no real communication between one human being and another. Speech, the principle of communication, is thus of the utmost significance and should be given as much consideration in the moral and spiritual life as action and thought.

What exactly is right speech? Usually it is described as speech that is truthful, affectionate, helpful, and promoting of concord, and wrong speech is the opposite of these things: untruthful, harsh, harmful, and promoting of discord. I'm afraid that most contemporary expositions of Buddhism present this in a superficial, moralistic manner, and no attempt is made to penetrate the psychological and spiritual depths of the subject. This is true of our approach to the Buddha's teaching as a whole. Sometimes, misled by the apparent simplicity of the Buddha's teaching, people are content to remain on the surface, thinking that they have mastered it, and never going into the depths. Those who write about right speech usually think that truthfulness, kindliness, helpfulness, and the promotion of concord are four separate attributes sort of 'stuck onto' right speech, but these four qualities really represent four successive levels of speech, each deeper than the one before, or even four progressive stages of communication. So let us look at each of them in this light. We shall then be in a position to appreciate what the Buddha meant by that rare and precious thing, a meaningful word.

First of all, right speech is truthful. We may think we know what is meant by that, but do we really? We surely don't mean just factual accuracy, though it's very important to be precise when we speak. There's that famous remark of Dr Johnson, speaking on the subject of training children, that if a child mentions seeing something through this window when in fact he or she saw it through that window, the child should at once be corrected, because once the habit of untruthfulness begins, there is no knowing where it may end.[22] We should accustom ourselves to accuracy of narration; this is the first thing required if we are to speak truthfully. Very few people are content to describe something exactly as it happened. They usually tend to exaggerate or minimize a little, to make it look a little better, or a little worse, as the case may be. We all know that we have this tendency and that it is extremely difficult to be truly honest. Some years ago in Kalimpong I attended a Wesak celebration, the anniversary of the Buddha's Enlightenment.[23] There was a nice little meeting – about a hundred people attended – but I was rather surprised when a month later I saw a report in a Buddhist magazine describing it as a mammoth meeting. You can hardly describe a hundred people as a mammoth meeting, but no doubt whoever wrote the report thought, 'It will increase people's faith and devotion when they hear that in Kalimpong there was a mammoth meeting on the occasion of the anniversary of the Buddha's Enlightenment,' so they didn't hesitate to deviate from strict factual accuracy. Apparently it's very difficult for human beings to present a thing exactly as it is. So factual accuracy is the first thing that we must train ourselves in.

But speaking the truth involves not only factual accuracy, but psychological and spiritual accuracy, and to speak in this way we have to be honest and sincere, saying what we really think and what we really know. But do we really know what we think? Most people live in a state of chronic mental confusion, so they cannot speak the truth. Most of the time, even when we think we're speaking truthfully, we're only repeating something we've heard or read. We haven't made it our own. We don't really know that it is so. To speak the truth in this fuller sense, we must know what we think, and this means that we must clarify our ideas, think more clearly, and be much more intensely aware of ourselves, and much more honest with ourselves, than we usually are.

So speaking the truth is by no means easy, and most people rarely do it. We may not exactly tell lies, but we don't quite tell the truth either, and some people go through the whole of their life without ever once speaking the truth. If you think about your relationships with other people you will realize that there are very few people to whom you can really speak your mind. Very often we can't say what we really think even to those who are supposedly nearest and dearest to us. There's always something we feel is not proper to say, or we dare not say, or we can't say because we think it might hurt the other person. We can't speak the truth until we know it, but even when we know it, we don't speak it in its fullness. When you go into the witness box in a court of law you swear to speak the truth, the whole truth, and nothing but the truth, but very few people find it possible to speak that truth to anyone. If it ever happens that we can for once say what we really think, it's a great relief. Perhaps we're worried about something, maybe something to do with our health, or our finances, or somebody with whom we're involved, and for some time we can't talk about it to anybody, so it becomes a heavier and heavier burden. If we're able one day to tell someone – a friend, or even a doctor or psychoanalyst – it's as though a great weight has been lifted and we feel free. We may go so far as to say that it's only when we're speaking the truth in the fullest sense that we are truly being ourselves, giving expression not to what we would like to appear to be, but what we are and what we know we are. This is speaking the truth, the first level of communication, and this in itself is difficult enough to achieve.

But the truth is never spoken in a vacuum. You don't go out into the garden and speak it to the trees and the flowers. That isn't psychologically possible, apparently. The truth is always spoken to another person, and this brings us to the second stage of communication. Right speech is affectionate and loving, not in a gushing or sentimental way, but spoken in full awareness of the person to whom one is speaking. If we reflect, we may recollect, perhaps to our horror, that usually when we speak to people, or when they speak to us, we don't really look at them. If you don't even look at the person you're talking with, you can't be really aware of them. One definition of love is that it is the awareness of the being of another person. We can't speak truthfully or affectionately to another person if we don't see them as they are, and we won't see them as they are if we don't take the trouble to look. But usually if we are conscious of another person to any extent, we tend to see them in terms of our emotional reaction to them. It's like our response to the weather. If we want to go out and the sun is shining, we say it's a lovely day. But if the farmer wanted rain for his crops, he would say it was a lovely day if it was raining heavily. Our judgements tend to be subjective, and it's like that with regard to people. If they do and say what we like, we say how good and kind they are. Usually we never get to the core of the person because we're never aware of them, never know them, and we tend to communicate with our own mental projections onto them. This is why there are so many misunderstandings and why so often we're disappointed by the people we meet, and even people we've known for a long time.

If we really, truly know the person to whom we are speaking, we will know what they need, and this brings us to the third stage of communication. We should say that which is useful – not just in the ordinary sense, but that which promotes the spiritual growth of the person to whom we are speaking, that which helps them, in the words of the *Dhammapada*, to become tranquil. Useful speech doesn't necessarily consist in spiritual instruction – it doesn't mean that you've got to be talking about Nirvāṇa, or right livelihood, or anything like that. It means that through your awareness of the other person and your appreciation of their needs, you speak in such a way that they are stimulated and their growth is promoted. The subject can be anything you like. What matters is that we should speak to people in such a way that they are raised in the scale of being and consciousness, and become more alive.

We all know that some people we meet have a very depressing effect on us. Whatever we want to do, they've got a reason for not doing it. They dampen our enthusiasm like a wet day. We should watch ourselves and try to be positive, appreciative, and constructive. Lama Govinda is a good exemplar of this. I've known him for practically twenty years, and I think I can say that there has never been any occasion on which he was negative, or disapproved of anything, or even criticized anything. Whatever I suggested, or whatever he commented on, he always spoke in a positive and constructive and appreciative way. Even if confronted by a rather unpromising situation, he would still manage to be positive about it.[24] This is a rare faculty, and one that we should do our utmost to cultivate. Even if we can't speak usefully to someone in the full sense of stimulating and promoting their spiritual growth, at least we can be positive, constructive, appreciative, and creative. If in addition to this we can give some spiritual guidance, the gift of the Dharma, so much the better. But even here, there's no question of giving in the abstract, just as a form of cold words, but only in the context of truthfulness and love, because it's only then that the instruction becomes effective.

If we are aware of another person's needs and concerned to provide for them, which means thinking about them, we shall tend to forget about ourselves, just as a mother does when she is caring for her baby. In this way we come to the fourth and deepest level of right speech, the promotion of harmony. This is not just intellectual agreement. It's not just sharing the same ideas, following the same religion, accepting the same philosophy, belonging to the same political party. It means mutual helpfulness, leading to mutual self-transcendence. You think about somebody else's needs so much so that you tend to forget about yourself, and the other person is so preoccupied with your needs that they tend to forget about their own self. Thus you get a situation of mutual helpfulness leading to mutual self-transcendence, a reciprocity of helpfulness within a context of increasing selflessness. In this way we come to the very perfection of communication: when understanding is so perfect that nothing needs to be said. When you meet someone for the first time there's a lot to talk about, but the better you know them, the less there is to talk about, and in this way right speech culminates in silence.

So right speech is by no means the simple matter that it might at first appear. We can perhaps begin to understand why in the *Dhammapada* the Buddha said that better than a thousand meaningless words is one word full of meaning, upon hearing which one is at peace. As we have seen, most people find it very difficult to communicate. Sometimes they go on talking and talking, in the hope, almost by accident, of being able to communicate something, but only too often it doesn't happen, and they get more frustrated than ever. Obviously something is seriously wrong – so much so that one may have to have recourse to exercises to help restore one's lost faculty of communication. This is where the communication exercises we are going to do on this retreat come in. The exercises are quite simple, and they start by helping us to become more aware of other people. We're out of communication with other people in the first place because we're simply not aware of them, and we're not aware of them because we don't take the trouble to look at them. So the first thing we do in these communication exercises is to learn to look at another person. It's simple, but people find it helpful and enjoyable, and it paves the way to real communication.[25]

INTRODUCING BUDDHISM 1: IS RELIGION NECESSARY?

Hampstead Buddhist Vihara, 2 January 1966

If you've seen the advertisement on the noticeboard, you will know that this series is entitled 'Introducing Buddhism'. That may come as a surprise, even a shock, to regular members. You may be thinking, 'We've been studying Buddhism for months or even years. Surely by this time we know at least the elements of the teaching quite well. What is the need for an introduction?' It's rather like going to a party and being introduced to someone who turns out to be an old friend. This idea of a series introducing Buddhism is excellent for newcomers, but is it really necessary for those who come faithfully week after week to go over the same ground again?

But it isn't a question of going over the same ground. In fact, it is just the opposite. What I am asking you to do is to see the Buddha's teaching afresh, with new eyes, not just as you've always seen it, but as though you've never seen it before in your life. Try to put your old understanding of Buddhism behind you, and see it objectively, afresh. If we can even think of the elementary teachings of Buddhism as old ground, that means that we're approaching them not with the mind and the experience that we have now, at this very moment, but with the mind and experience that we had last week or the week before, or last year, or ten years ago. We have to keep our insight into Buddhism up to date, not living on our past capital, but renewing it, making it ever more living, day by day, even minute by minute. Familiarity with Buddhism won't breed contempt, but it may breed staleness. We may settle down in our understanding of Buddhism, think that we know it, and not try to exert ourselves and penetrate into it afresh. Instead of confronting ourselves with the principles and truths the Buddha taught, we may be confronting ourselves with our previous understanding of those principles and truths, and thereby limiting ourselves. We must constantly be on our guard against this, and to guard against it we have to go back again and again to the principal teachings and turn them over afresh in our minds. Don't think, 'Well, five years ago, I made a thorough study of the five aggregates (*skandhas*), and I remember what I understood then.' This week, today, ask yourself, 'What did the Buddha mean by the five aggregates? What does this teaching signify?' After five years of practising Buddhism, you should have evolved a bit more, your understanding should be a little clearer and brighter, so that when you direct your mind to the five aggregates, your understanding of them should be a little more advanced than it was five years ago, however good that might have been. Instead of resting on your laurels, instead of carrying over the understanding of the past, recreate an even better understanding in the present. This is what we must do again and again with all aspects of the teaching, both theoretical and practical.

It's like reciting the Refuges. Very often one ceremonially repeats 'To the Buddha for Refuge I go, to the Dharma for Refuge I go, to the Sangha for Refuge I go.' In the East they sometimes recite the Refuges weekly or daily, and some pious people recite them morning and evening, so it's as though you're doing the same thing over and over again. But you're not, because in the interval between these repetitions, your understanding of the Buddha, Dharma, and Sangha, through your study and your practice, should have deepened. You understand them better, and the better you understand them, the more effectively, the more deeply, you can go for Refuge. Your going for Refuge to the Buddha, Dharma, and Sangha this week shouldn't be the same as it was last week or last month or last year, or ten years ago. If it means exactly the same to you, that means you haven't made any progress in experience or understanding. We can never really go for Refuge 'again'. We just go for Refuge here and now. One should always recite the Refuges as though for the first time, with a certain freshness, directness, newness. It's the same with studying the teachings. Always approach the truths and the principles as though you had never approached them before. In as much as your past study and practice will have helped you to grow and develop a little more, your attempts to understand the principles and apply them here and now will go a little deeper, carry you a little further, and in this way your study and practice of Buddhism will never become stale. It will always be a fresh, self-recreating thing, with the wonder and impressiveness of what is new.

In our new series, 'Introducing Buddhism', so far as newcomers are concerned, the material covered will be in the ordinary sense quite new, but to the oldcomers it should be doubly new, because you can approach it with a fresh mind, fortified by the study and practice of previous years, but approaching the material directly and seeing it anew. If there is anyone present who thinks they know anything about Buddhism, forget it. You may have been studying for years, but whatever you remember about the four noble truths, the Noble Eightfold Path, *pratītya-samutpāda*, karma, Nirvāṇa, bodhisattvas, meditation, ethics, put it all out of your mind. You won't be able to put it out of your being, but that is not wanted. Just put it out of your conscious mind. Make your mind a complete blank as far as Buddhism is concerned. Go back to the time before you'd heard of Buddhism, if you can remember that, and imagine yourself in a state of complete – I won't say ignorance, but innocence. And then go back in imagination even further than that. Imagine yourself without any religion at all. Imagine getting up in the morning, going to work, coming home in the evening, reading a novel or a newspaper, listening to the radio or looking at the television, but being quite devoid of religion. And then imagine, one day in the midst of this irreligious existence, asking yourself the question with which we're concerned this evening: 'Is religion necessary?' In the course of conversation, you might be asked this question quite casually. It's a question that we have all faced, and which we have still to face on other people's behalf. We can't ignore it, living in this modern world, just after the middle of the twentieth century. We have to ask it, and we have to try to answer it.

The question breaks itself down into three interconnected questions. Firstly, what do we mean by religion? Secondly, what do we mean by necessary? And thirdly, necessary to what, or to whom? So first, what do we mean by religion? There are many definitions of this protean word. At one end of the scale there's that rather sarcastic description of Voltaire's: 'Religion originated when the first rogue met the first fool.'[26] At the other end of the scale is Whitehead, who said that 'religion is what the individual does with his own solitariness'.[27] This certainly gives us something to think about, but we're not really concerned at this stage of the proceedings with abstract definitions. For the present, we'll take the word religion to mean a collective designation for all the individual religions. There are so many religions in the world, even if sometimes we're blind to all of them except the one in which we happen to be brought up. There's Christianity, Islam, and Judaism. In the East there's Buddhism, Hinduism, Daoism, Confucianism, Shinto, Zoroastrianism. There are modern cults like the Mormons, the Bahá'ís, and the theosophists. There are all sorts of tribal beliefs and primitive cults, even all sorts of dead religions – those of the Egyptians and Babylonians, the Syrians, the Hittites, and the Aztecs. Let's take this word religion for the present as covering all these teachings.

When we look at religions even casually, we notice that there are many differences among them. They can be distributed into various classes. Some are ethnic religions – that is, they're the religion of a single group, united by ties of blood, or by loyalty to a single piece of territory. Hinduism or Judaism are more or less ethnic religions. Others are universal religions, not based upon distinctions of blood or soil or culture. Christianity, Buddhism, and Islam are the three great universal world religions. Then, adopting other classifications, there's a theistic group of religions, including Judaism, Christianity, and Islam, which believe in a supreme being, a personal God, and there's a non-theistic group, consisting of Buddhism, some forms of Hinduism, Daoism, and Confucianism. There's another distinction between those religions that are humanistic, positing human values, and those that are authoritarian, imposing upon human beings values that come from outside humanity, usually considered to be given by God by way of revelation.

But religions also have a number of features in common. They all address three main issues: who we are as human beings in relation to ourselves, who we are in relation to other human beings, or other living beings of all kinds, and who we are in relation to ultimate reality. Take Christianity. According to the Christian teaching, who we are in relation to ourselves is that we know we were created by God, who created us as good, but that we sinned, on account of which we are no longer good, even completely evil. Christianity further teaches that all men and women, being children of the same father – that is, created by the same God – are brothers and sisters, and that therefore the appropriate relation among us is one of mutual love. In Christianity the ultimate reality is God, the Supreme Being, the Creator himself, and he is considered to be known not directly but indirectly, through Christ, who is regarded by the orthodox as the son of God. Christianity teaches that Christ died on the cross for us all, and that if one believes this, one's sins will be wiped out and one will attain salvation. So the basic pattern is quite clear.

Buddhism says that we are conditioned beings, undergoing again and again the process of suffering on account of birth, old age, disease, and death, and that our rebirth, whether into the human world or into any other world, higher or lower than this, is due to our ignorance of the spiritual truth, and our craving and selfish desires, which are based upon and grow out of this ignorance. But although we are conditioned, there is in us an element that is unconditioned, that has some kinship, some affinity, with ultimate reality, and because of this, we are capable of attaining Enlightenment, capable of realizing the truth. Buddhism inculcates compassion for all beings without exception, whether human or animal, because all beings are subject to the universal rule of suffering. According to Buddhism we should also have respect for other beings because all, though conditioned in this way or that, have some aspect that is unconditioned, that is capable of Enlightenment. Whatever anyone may appear to be right now, however wicked or misguided they may appear to be, we should respect them, because fundamentally the potentiality for Enlightenment is there. In Buddhism, ultimate reality is not thought of as a personal God, a supreme being. Buddhism says that you can't think of ultimate reality at all, it's beyond thought, beyond speech. We might say, conventionally, that it constitutes the 'objective' content of Enlightenment. It's what we experience when all mental conditions, from the highest to the lowest, have been removed or transcended. So like Christianity, though in a rather different way, Buddhism revolves around these three great issues: the relation of human beings to themselves, to other living beings, and to ultimate reality.

To generalize, we could say that religion consists in the achievement of a state of complete psychological and spiritual wholeness and relating to other beings, and also to reality, in that wholeness. To put it even more simply, we can say that religion consists in total concern with what is of ultimate value.

But, to come to the second of our three questions, when we ask whether religion is necessary, what do we mean by 'necessary'? In ordinary parlance, when we say that something is necessary to us, we mean that it's indispensable to our existence. Food and sleep are necessary because without them, human life just breaks down. Is religion indispensable in the same way? Well, apparently not. There are millions of people who apparently get on perfectly well without religion. The vast majority of people in this country seem to have no real contact with any of the churches. Our ancestors throughout history have had a close contact with religion in some form or other, so it's something quite new to have no contact with conventional organized religion, but it would seem that the traditional language of Christianity is meaningless to most modern people. Terms like God, soul, sin, redemption, and sanctification, which represented burning issues in the past, just leave people cold. It's not that people are anti-Christian; nowadays we are post-Christian. We are no more anti-God than we are anti-Jupiter; they don't mean enough for us to be against them. If we consider them at all, we dismiss them with a shrug. God is dead? Well, sorry to hear it. Everyone has to die some day, even God. Just put another nail in the coffin, shovel some earth on it, let it go out of sight. Traditional, conventional religion means very little to us, especially in its churchified form.

But I would say that modern man (that's a rather grand expression – I just mean you and me, all of us) is irreligious more in appearance than in reality. Conventional religion, quite frankly, has become quite flat and stale. Not long ago, I had a conversation with a young Anglican, and we were talking shop. (Even Anglican curates and Buddhist *bhikkhus* can talk religious shop.) He was asking me how long I speak for when I give a lecture, and I told him I usually speak for an hour or an hour and a quarter. Once at the Buddhist Society I got interested in the subject and spoke for an hour and three-quarters. He said, 'Good heavens! I never speak for more than ten minutes. People aren't interested enough.' In church these days, people listen to the sermon because that's the traditional routine, like passing round a plate for the collection. It's all flat, all stale, and modern people are quite right to lose interest in it. There is no life in it, no vitality, no deeper significance. What is the point of continuing this meaningless routine week after week, month after month? Of course some well-meaning people still think in terms of a revival of religion, hoping to get tens of thousands of people back into church, sitting on those hard wooden seats or getting down on their knees and confessing their sins, beating their breasts if necessary. But it's impossible. One would perhaps like to put the clock back in many parts of the world. I would certainly like to put it back ten or fifteen years in Tibet. But one can't. There are a few people even in the Church of England, like the Bishop of Woolwich, who realize this and try quite sincerely to cope with the situation. When you are going to be shipwrecked, you throw everything heavy overboard because your life is in danger. You might have a box of diamonds, but if it's making the boat sink, you'll throw it overboard without hesitation, because life is more precious.

If conventional religion has become non-religion, there are some non-religious areas of life and culture that have come to have spiritual significance. As we have seen, religion means that which contributes to our wholeness, that which gives us some sense of ultimate values at least in the plural if not in the singular. There are lots of people nowadays who can't find this in conventional religion but find it to some extent elsewhere. Some people find that if they listen to a fine piece of classical music they feel uplifted, as if they have a certain insight into things, and they feel more whole, integrated, and refined. Others find it in poetry, whether ancient or modern. Others again find in philosophy, reading Schopenhauer, Kant, or Plato, or even spiritual philosophers such as Plotinus. So it would seem that religion in the true sense is necessary at least to some people, so they'll find it somehow, perhaps in classical music or poetry. But there are lots of people who get along not only without religion in the conventional sense, but without classical music, poetry, philosophy, or any cultural interest at all. They are quite satisfied with their home and family, their job, their television, their washing machine, the car in their garage and all the rest of it. Apparently they manage to live – or at least exist – in a perfectly respectable, decent, philistine way. It reminds me of a line of T. S. Eliot: 'And the wind shall say: "Here were decent godless people."'[28]

This brings us to the third question: 'To what or to whom is religion necessary?' This is perhaps the most important of the three questions, because it provides us with a clue to the answer to our main question: 'Is religion necessary?' I am going to say something which may come as a surprise: religion is not for everyone. We're brought up to think that everyone must be saved, that Jesus died for all. For hundreds of years missionaries have been sent forth to convert the heathen, because they must all be saved. But if religion is not for everyone, who is it for? Let's recall our definition. In the first place, religion consists in the attainment of complete psychological and spiritual wholeness. This implies a conscious effort. You don't become psychologically and spiritually whole if you just allow yourself to drift along, even if you drift along to the vihara on Sundays, however regularly. It will take conscious, deliberate, willed, determined, regular, systematic effort, and that is impossible without the attainment of self-awareness. This is what really distinguishes human beings, or at least some human beings, from the animals. Most people are more animal than truly human.

If one surveys the vast world of living things, one sees that one can sort existences into various classes. First of all, there's the great division between the non-living and the living. (I am not going now into the metaphysical question of whether everything, even a stone, is in the ultimate sense living.) Living things can be divided into two classes: those that are merely sensitive, the vegetable world, and those that are not only sensitive but conscious, the animal kingdom. And conscious living beings can be further divided into those beings that are simply conscious and those that are not only conscious but also self-conscious. Evolution proceeds from the non-living to the living, from the sensitive to the conscious, and from the conscious to the self-conscious. So a human being – cutting the whole thing short – is a conscious being in the process of becoming self-conscious or self-aware. One who has become even intermittently self-aware can strive to become psychologically and spiritually whole, and one who has not become self-aware cannot.

Up to the level of self-consciousness, the process of evolution is collective and automatic; it just goes on irrespective of the individual effort made by individual beings, so it's very slow. For the vegetable kingdom to evolve into the animal kingdom took millions upon millions of years, for the animal kingdom to evolve into human beings took millions of years, and for human beings to develop from consciousness to self-consciousness or self-awareness has taken several thousand years and only a few have been able to do it. This attainment, this higher evolution from the conscious to the self-conscious or self-aware, unlike the whole process of evolution in nature, is not collective or automatic but individual, and proceeds only through individual, deliberate, aware, self-conscious effort. It is therefore much quicker. It has been said that there is a greater difference between an Enlightened one and an unenlightened human being than between an unenlightened human being and an animal. To go from the state of animal to unenlightened human being has taken millions of years, but to go from the state of unenlightenment to Enlightenment – representing an even greater difference – can take just a few years if the right effort is put in.

Religion is the sum total of all those teachings and practices that makes this achievement possible. So religion is obviously only for those who have developed some degree of self-awareness and who, as the next stage of their evolution, feel the need of achieving psychological and spiritual wholeness. Religion is for those who know that they don't yet know, and who desperately want to know it. So religion is for the minority, at least until such time as all human beings become more or less self-aware, which they certainly are not at present.

But what about all those millions of devout Christians, faithful Buddhists, pious Hindus, strict Confucianists, and so on, in all the temples and churches all through the centuries? Can't one say that they were religious? Strictly speaking, one can't, because they weren't self-conscious. They weren't deliberately and consciously using the teachings and practices and observances of the religion to which they belonged as a means of achieving wholeness. Theirs was a mere passive, semi-conscious participation. Sometimes the masses of nominal followers were using religion in a fundamentally irreligious way. We're familiar with this in all religions. Even those who go to church aren't participating in a self-aware way for the sake of their higher evolution. They just conform; they're getting some emotional satisfaction, blindly, half-consciously, which is quite a different thing. Go to a Buddhist country like Ceylon or Burma or Thailand or Japan, and it's much the same. The vast majority are not conscious participants, but passive beneficiaries. Religion, even when nominally professed by everybody, is definitely for the minority, because the masses tend to use religion in a fundamentally irreligious, semi-magical way to help them get what they want. This is one of the reasons for the failure of the church; it has become conventionalized in accordance with the non-religious, or pseudo-religious, needs of the masses.

A while ago I was reading a book about the non-belief in Christianity in modern England in which the writer said, 'It's not the non-belief of the non-Christians that shocks me, it's the belief of the Christians.' For example, she met a woman who for thirty years had been a pious Christian, going to church every Sunday, putting sixpence in the collection plate, attending prayer meeting on Wednesdays and Mothers' Union on Fridays – all the rigmarole. The writer met this woman after an interval and said, 'How are you feeling? I know you've been ill.' And she said, 'I've lost all my faith. I feel so bitter to think I've been a good woman all these years, I've believed in God, I've gone to church, and God let me down, because all the same I fell ill and suffered.' In another case, she met a woman coming from the funeral of her best friend, a young woman who had died in childbirth. She said, 'I've been a good Christian all these years but I am losing my faith. My friend died in childbirth, a respectable married woman. That so-and-so girl in the next street had an illegitimate baby and she didn't die. What kind of God is this, to allows such things to happen?' Conventionally religious people are trying all the time to twist religious teachings to satisfy their needs and desires, and because fundamentally irreligious people have got control of the machinery of religion at all levels – there they are, sitting on the bench of bishops and in the prebendary stalls and all the rest of it – the church has failed. To be quite honest, in the East, Buddhist organizations also fail so far as sincerely spiritual people are concerned. The churches and sects often become clubs for the non-religious and even the irreligious, and the main thing is to belong to the club.

So our main question has been answered. Religion is a total concern with what is of ultimate value, and the means to achieve complete wholeness. It isn't necessary to everybody, but it's indispensable to the existence of those who are self-aware, those to whom the achievement of psychological and spiritual wholeness, and in that wholeness relating to others and to ultimate reality, are matters not of just passing intellectual interest but of life and death.

INTRODUCING BUDDHISM 2: WHY BUDDHISM?

Hampstead Buddhist Vihara, 9 January 1966

So religion is essentially the achievement of a condition of psychological and spiritual wholeness, and in that state of wholeness relating to other people, and to ultimate reality. Contrary to what people usually take for granted, religion isn't necessary for everybody, but only for those who have begun to be self-aware, and who ardently desire to embark on a higher evolution to psychological and spiritual wholeness. Now let's suppose that we're not just motivated by instinct or custom. Suppose we really are self-aware; suppose we really are considering our place in the universe, the whole scheme of things. Suppose we're trying to understand the purpose of life itself. And suppose, being self-aware in this way, we make up our minds that we wish to pursue the higher evolution. Suppose we want to achieve psychological and spiritual wholeness in the full sense, at the highest level, and suppose we want to have recourse to religion for this purpose. Then we're confronted by a serious problem. Though I have been speaking of the necessity of religion, religion doesn't exist in the singular, but only, bewilderingly, in the plural. Even within this one great city of London we can encounter not only Christian churches and Buddhist organizations, but representatives of Islam, Hinduism, Judaism, the Bahá'í, the theosophists, so many groups, sects, schools, and religions. So even if we come to the conclusion that religion is necessary for us, which one are we going to choose? Most of us sitting here have more or less definitely chosen Buddhism, but why?

Before we go into this, we'll briefly consider one or two preliminary questions. First of all, there's the whole question of choice. Should we be free to choose our religion? Some people think that the choice should be made by some other authority, and some even say that we shouldn't think in terms of choice at all, but simply follow the religion into which we happen to have been born. I used to be asked by Hindus in India why, having been born into a Christian family, I abandoned Christianity and took to Buddhism, and when I tried to explain, they said, 'That doesn't matter. You should have stuck to Christianity. After all, you were born into that,' as though that was the last word on the subject. This idea is strong among Hindus because it is linked with the caste system.

Both Buddhism and Hinduism are referred to in the original Indian language as *dharma*, but in each the word has different connotations. What it means for Buddhism you know, at least to some extent, but in Hinduism it has a rather different connotation, relating to a socio-religious tradition called the caste system. In modern India there are about two thousand separate castes, but they can all be classified under four main ones. There's the caste of the Brahmins, the priests and teachers, although nowadays you often find them doing very different kinds of work; secondly, there's the Kshatriyas, the land-owners and rulers, warriors; thirdly, the Vaishyas, the shopkeepers, traders and merchants, sometimes peasants; and fourthly, the Shudras or labourers – the menials, the servants, the coolies. The outcastes, including the so-called untouchables, are outside this system altogether; they're lower than the low. The Hindus take the view that there is a particular religious duty appropriate to the caste to which you belong, and what they mean by *dharma* is the set of customs, practices, and duties appropriate to the caste into which you happen to have been born. The *dharma* of the Brahmin is to teach, the *dharma* of the Kshatriya is to fight, the *dharma* of the Vaishya is to make money, and the *dharma* of the Shudra is to serve the other three castes. Hindus hold that it is a sin to depart from the *dharma* of the caste into which you were born. Orthodox Hindus even hold that the Buddha committed a great sin because, having been born into a Kshatriya family, instead of devoting himself to fighting, he took up the *dharma* of the Brahmin and had the temerity to teach religion.

Sometimes it happens, I need hardly tell you, that the religion into which you are born doesn't suit you. But what are you to do? Obviously you should be free to choose some other teaching. In ancient times this was hardly possible, but nowadays horizons have widened and a global culture is beginning to develop. In the years since the last war, people in this country have been learning to appreciate previously unknown things like Indian music, Chinese poetry, and Japanese prints. This is as it should be. Every human being should have some appreciation of the cultural traditions of countries other than their own, and in the West we should have some appreciation of the great cultures of the East. Likewise, in the sphere of religion and philosophy we should acquaint ourselves with the highest achievements in these fields, regardless of their place of origin. It is incumbent upon us to know the philosophy of Śaṅkara, the great Vedāntic Hindu philosopher, just as we know the philosophy of Plato, and to be as familiar with the sayings of the Buddha as we are with the sayings of Christ. Cultural and religious parochialism has no place in the modern world. We should have a look around and see what else there is in the world. Any other attitude is unworthy of a thinking and reflecting human being. Having surveyed the religions and philosophies of the world, we may decide that we will continue to follow the religion into which we've been born, but then we will be following it not out of ignorance, but out of positive choice.

This brings me to the important question of the teaching of religion in schools. Nowadays religious instruction usually means the teaching of the Bible, and generally it is done in a dull and unimaginative way by someone who doesn't believe in those teachings. When I was at school, we were taught the Bible by a teacher who was an atheist, and the way he taught it was certainly not conducive to any kind of faith in Christianity. He simply ridiculed what he was supposed to be teaching. The teaching of a religion by someone who doesn't believe in it can have a dreadful moral effect upon the mind of the child. Children are very quick to understand whether or not you believe what you tell them. You might think you've palmed them off with an explanation with which you're not really satisfied yourself, but the child will detect the lack of conviction in your voice and your slight uneasiness, and know intuitively that you don't believe what you're saying, and that will undermine your authority. Any lack of conviction will communicate itself to the child, who may be left with the impression that the whole business of religion is fundamentally dishonest. Many people feel that sectarian religious instruction should be replaced by the study of comparative religion.

Sometimes at the Vihara we get invitations from schools to give lectures on Buddhism, and this is an extremely healthy development. Instead of trying to ram the tenets of a particular teaching down the children's throats, teachers should try to arouse their interest in and sympathy with the spiritual quest of humanity. They should try to show that the questions dealt with by religion are important, and that the children themselves will have to face them one day. The acceptance of a religion is a matter about which everybody has to make up their own mind. One can't take one's religion ready-made from someone else. Even if one accepts the religion into which one has been born, one must remould it in the fire of one's own personal conviction and experience.

But why should we choose between the different religions? Some people recommend browsing through them all and taking what appeals to you from each one, an attitude known as eclecticism. It may seem a good idea to garner whatever is best in all the great religions, but in practice adopting this attitude won't get you far in the spiritual life. Usually people take what appeals to their prejudices or flatters their preconceptions, not what they need from a spiritual point of view. In fact, usually they don't know what they need. Eclecticism usually involves an evasion of the real issues of the spiritual life. If you want to practise religion seriously, you have to practise according to a particular discipline. If you want to practise meditation, for example, you can't just sit down and do it – you have to follow a particular system of practice.

If we have decided to choose a religion, why choose Buddhism? First of all, let's rapidly survey the whole field. We'll leave aside the so-called dead religions (though it's the people who followed them that are dead, not the religions themselves). No one is likely to want to worship Isis and Osiris, or Apollo or Mars, at least not consciously, though in fact people are doing just that all the time. But in terms of living religions, some eleven independent religions at present exist in the world.

In more or less chronological order, first comes Hinduism, the ancient indigenous religion of India, based on a set of scriptures called the Vedas. In modern times, Hinduism has been represented to the West by three prominent thinkers, Swami Vivekananda, Sri Aurobindo, and Sri Ramakrishna, whose writings have made the complex teachings of Hinduism familiar to most educated people.

Secondly, we have Zoroastrianism, one of the religions of ancient Persia, founded by the sage Zoroaster. It's a dualist system which posits two fundamental principles in the universe – good and evil – and says that it's our moral and spiritual duty to side with the forces of good and thereby help ensure their eventual victory. Zoroastrianism was displaced in Persia by Islam many centuries ago, though there are still some Zoroastrians in Iran, and Zoroastrianism also survives among the 30,000 or so Parsees of Bombay. I have a number of Parsee friends, and have had the opportunity of coming quite close to their religion. They are rather exclusive, though. They don't allow non-Parsees into their fire temples, and if a Parsee marries a non-Parsee, he or she is at once excommunicated.

Then we come to Judaism, the religion of the Jewish people, the Hebrew race, which for 2,000 years had no homeland until very recently. The Jews regard themselves as being the people chosen by God.

Next we have Jainism, which was founded by and named after Mahāvīra, an elder contemporary of the Buddha who received the title of Jina or 'conqueror', the one who conquered mundane existence. Most of its sacred books have been lost, unfortunately, so we don't know much about its early teachings, but we do know that it advocates strict nonviolence and a rigorous asceticism as the path to emancipation. It's confined to various parts of India – there are Jains in Rajasthan, in Mysore, and also in central India.

Then there is Daoism, one of the indigenous religions of ancient China. Originally Daoism was a sublime mystical philosophy, but over time it became corrupt and degenerate, and in modern times the name has become attached to a system of crude popular magic and superstition. Complementary to Daoism is Confucianism, a teaching systematized by Confucius, who lived in about the sixth century BCE, and consisting mainly of a comprehensive code of social morality.

Then we have Buddhism and Christianity, about which I don't propose to say anything special. Next on the list is Shinto, the indigenous national cult of Japan, which consists in various practices of purification, both physical and mental, and of nature worship.

Next we have Islam. The word Islam literally means submission – submission in this case to God. It's sometimes referred to as 'Mohammedanism', because it was proclaimed by Mohammed in the seventh century CE, but Muslims strongly object to this name, because they say that the religion didn't originate with Mohammed, but with God himself. Mohammed was only its prophet or revealer. Islam is an uncompromising monotheism of a particularly rigorous and even intolerant kind. Its sacred book is the Koran, which is regarded as being quite literally the word of God, dictated by God to Gabriel, and handed on by Gabriel to Mohammed.

After Islam, chronologically, we have Sikhism, which was founded by Guru Nanak in India in the thirteenth century. It is more or less monotheistic and highly devotional, and was refounded by the tenth Guru in the seventh century as a semi-military brotherhood, which is what it is today.

Apart from these religions, there are a number of modern fringe religions or cults, representing various degrees of eccentricity and eclecticism. We're going to leave those aside – they're far too numerous and perhaps not particularly rewarding to consider. So for practical purposes our choice is limited to the eleven major religions mentioned. Why follow Buddhism in preference to any of the other great religions?

The list of religions falls into two great groups: ethnic religions and universal religions. Ethnic means 'pertaining to a group of people united by ties of blood and ties of soil', sometimes but not invariably also by ties of language. An ethnic religion is the religion professed or practised by a particular ethnic group, and it is inseparable from the culture of the country and the people amongst whom it arises. The most prominent example is Hinduism, which is the religion of the majority of the people of India. Apart from Indians living overseas, it's limited to the soil of India. It's not a proselytizing religion, and it is inseparably bound up with Indian culture, geography, social life, institutions, and customs. Zoroastrianism, Judaism, Daoism, Confucianism, and Shinto are all ethnic religions. Zoroastrianism was bound up with the soil of Persia, then transplanted to Bombay. Judaism was bound up originally with the soil of the Holy Land, but after that with the Jewish people wherever they live. Daoism and Confucianism were confined to China, and Shinto to Japan. Jainism and Sikhism were not originally ethnic religions, but have become such. Jainism is the religion nowadays of a particular caste of people contained within Hinduism, and Sikhism is similar. It is characteristic of ethnic religions that by their very nature one can't be converted to them. Generally speaking, one can only belong to an ethnic religion by being born into it. One does occasionally hear of conversions to Judaism, usually through marriage, but these are limited to the liberal or reformed branches. So your choice is already rather restricted. You can't choose an ethnic religion; it has to choose you in that you have to be born into it. If you want to make a choice, you are in effect confined to the universal religions, which are explicitly meant for people all over the world, potentially. Sometimes they are called founded religions, because they go back to individual founders, or missionary religions, because they try to convert other people, or at least explain themselves.

The universal religions to which our choice in practice is narrowed down are only three in number: Buddhism, Christianity, and Islam, and they in turn can be divided into two groups: theistic and non-theistic. *Theos* means 'God' – that is, a personal God, a supreme being, creator of the universe – so theistic means 'pertaining to the belief in such a God'. Christianity and Islam are both theistic religions, and that affects their whole character. Buddhism is the sole representative of non-theistic universal religions. In Buddhism there is no place for a personal God, a supreme being or a creator, and this affects its whole character, nature, and structure. I don't want to labour this point, but this is the basic issue. So far as this talk is concerned, I'm not trying to determine whether theism or non-theism represents the truth. I am being merely descriptive.

It is a striking fact that today in the West, an increasing number of religious-minded people find it difficult to accept the theistic form of religion. This question 'Why Buddhism?' can't be answered without reference to this. I'm sure that most of those who think of themselves as Buddhists have chosen Buddhism rather than Christianity or Islam because Buddhism is a religion which talks the language of the spiritual life, the language of Enlightenment, without any reference to a supreme being. Not long ago I was reading a book by Julian Huxley called *Religion Without Revelation*. In the chapter called 'Personalia' he relates how when as a young man he came to the realization that there could be religious life without a personal God, it came as a tremendous relief. One is not forced to make an almost impossible choice between religion and God on one hand, and no God and no religion on the other.[29]

One of the major attractions of Buddhism for the modern mind is that it's a complete system of spiritual life without the personal God which previously in the West people have considered indispensable to religion, and we shouldn't attempt to water down this fact. Sometimes people come along to a Buddhist class and ask rather timidly, 'What does Buddhism have to say about God?' One might think 'Well, perhaps this person believes in God so if I say that in Buddhism there is no God, it might be a rather nasty shock.' One might thus be tempted to compromise and say, 'Well, er, Buddhism doesn't use the word God, but it talks about Nirvāṇa and Enlightenment, and that's the same sort of thing. It's all right, don't worry.' This is the approach that some people, in the goodness of their hearts, are tempted to employ. It's true that one should take people step by step in easing them from the known to the unknown, but one shouldn't betray the cause of Buddhism itself. People have a perfect right to choose theism if it appeals to them, but we should make it perfectly clear that Buddhism is a non-theistic religion; otherwise, we're guilty of slipshod thinking, even intellectual dishonesty. If one puts it as crudely and bluntly as saying, 'It doesn't matter what it's called. You call it God, we call it Nirvāṇa,' that shows that one hasn't really understood what Buddhists mean by Nirvāṇa, or even what Christians mean by God.

I would go so far as to prophesy that the whole future of religion in the West is bound up with this issue of theism and non-theism. Lots of thinking people realize this already. The title of Julian Huxley's book, *Religion Without Revelation*, really means religion without God, because revelation is bound up with the idea that God reveals himself to humanity, and that revelation, either through his son, or the messenger or prophet that he sends, is at the heart of religious life. In Buddhism there is no revelation of truth from God to man, but the discovery and realization of the truth by a human being through his own efforts.

I'm not one of those people who likes to recommend Buddhism to non-Buddhists by describing it as a scientific religion. I think this is a misnomer, and based on great confusion of thought. At the same time, there's a certain analogy between Buddhism and science, even though their fields and methods are rather different. Both Buddhism and science represent an effort to ascertain the truth. Science is concerned with the truth about material phenomena, while Buddhism is concerned with spiritual truth, but inasmuch that this spiritual truth is to be discovered and realized by human effort, there is an analogy with science, because when speaking in terms of discovering and realizing spiritual truth, Buddhism places a great emphasis on the personal, direct experience of that truth. In our series of talks on Zen Buddhism we saw the emphasis of Zen on direct experience, but that's really the emphasis of the whole Buddhist tradition.[30] This is why meditation is so important.

It represents the practical corollary of the nature of Buddhism itself, because meditation is regarded as a royal road leading to the direct experience of truth or reality for oneself. Buddhism is rich in systems of meditation, as we will see in a later talk in this series. One could go on pursuing the ramifications of the fact that Buddhism is a non-theistic religion, but this isn't necessary. Once one grasps the fact that Buddhism is non-theistic, and that it emphasizes the value of direct, personal experience of reality, the importance of meditation follows automatically. As the proverb says, if one grasps the bull by the horns, the tail comes along of its own accord.

So if we wish to have recourse to religion as a means to psychological and spiritual wholeness, we're confronted by a choice among eleven major religions. If we go into the matter more deeply, eight are excluded because they're ethnic religions into which one has to be born, and that leaves us with the three universal religions, Buddhism, Christianity, and Islam. These fall into two categories, the theistic and the non-theistic. This means that if it's impossible for you to think of religion in theistic terms, your only option is Buddhism. So this is the basic answer to the question 'Why Buddhism?' We choose it essentially because it is a non-theistic universal religion. Because it's non-theistic, there's no question of revelation. It stresses discovery, the realization of spiritual truth by our own efforts, the value of personal experience, and the importance of the practice of meditation. We also choose it, many of us, because it's a non-dogmatic, tolerant teaching, because of its rich cultural traditions and associations, and because of its comprehensiveness, the fact that it embraces not only metaphysics and psychology, but art, ritual, yoga, and many other things. But all these considerations are secondary or even tertiary. The essential reason why we choose Buddhism is because it is a non-theistic system of spiritual self-development. Having made that choice, having committed oneself in this way, having decided the matter once and for all, another question arises: how are we to get to know this teaching properly, if possible perfectly? How are we to approach it? This is what we shall be dealing with next week.

INTRODUCING BUDDHISM 3: THE APPROACH TO BUDDHISM

Hampstead Buddhist Vihara, 16 January 1966

As we discovered, the primary answer to the question 'Why Buddhism?' is that most people take it up because it is a non-theistic universal system of spiritual self-development. But having settled this question, another question arises. We've discussed religion as the instrument by means of which the self-aware person pursues the higher evolution, and Buddhism answers to this description. Buddhism is also a teaching which functions as an instrument by means of which the self-aware person, the person who is spiritually alive, conscious of their spiritual destiny, pursues the higher evolution from unenlightened humanity right up to Enlightened humanity or Buddhahood. We may even go so far as to say that Buddhism is better adapted to such an end than any other spiritual teaching known to us. But how do we make contact with it? How do we get a grip on it? How do we actually make use of it, as distinct from knowing about it or contemplating it or seeing pictures of it?

For those who live in a Buddhist country, this isn't a problem. In those countries, whether or not people actually practise it, Buddhism is always available. If you want to learn to meditate, within a few miles of your home you'll find a vihara or monastery where you can do that. If you want to study the Buddhist scriptures, you'll find some learned monk who is capable of instructing you. If you're troubled by the deeper questions of the spiritual life, the chances are that in your district there are at least a few monks, or even a few lay people, who have fathomed these questions for themselves and can answer your questions. But in the West it's a very different story. We may know Buddhism from books, but we may have no contact with the Buddha's teaching as an actual way of life or culture. Sometimes we have no real contact with other Buddhists at all.

I have become very much aware of this in my work here at the vihara. Every now and then I meet someone or receive a letter from someone who says that they've considered themselves Buddhist for years, but they've never met another Buddhist. I met two or three people like this last year at the summer school. They said that was the first time they'd had contact with other Buddhists, and it was quite impossible to convey what that meant to them. Many years ago this was my own case. I considered myself a Buddhist at the age of about 16, so I got started pretty early. I came to this realization after reading two important Buddhist texts, the *Diamond Sūtra* or *Vajracchedikā Sūtra* and the *Sūtra of Wei Lang* as in our ignorance we used to call it. (Now it's called the *Sūtra of Huineng* or the *Platform Sūtra*.) When I got hold of these two works, I read them very quickly (they're very short, though very profound and concentrated in content), and I had an intuitive apprehension that this was the truth. I had never before come into contact with anything that surpassed this or even approached it. The truth was here, not in the sense of a particular set of words, teachings, or doctrines, but in the sense of some metaphysical, transcendental dimension suggested by the words, hinted at by the thoughts and ideas and teachings, which was essentially beyond them all but nevertheless in some way communicated or mediated by them. I felt that this was the truth, the absolute truth. Not only that. There was also the intuitive understanding that this was nothing new. It wasn't that I didn't know it yesterday and I've come to it today. I not only knew it, but knew that I had always known it, that I had always been a Buddhist without knowing it.

This happened in London, but I didn't learn of the existence of a Buddhist movement in London until considerably later. I happened to be reading a translation of the *Dao De Jing*, a Chinese Taoist work, and at the back there was an advertisement for a magazine called *Buddhism in England* (now known as *The Middle Way*), the organ of the Buddhist Society at Eccleston Square. I wrote off for the magazine, became a subscriber, and entered into correspondence with the editor, who was then Clare Cameron; she is still alive, still in this country, and still in touch with me.[31] In time I started writing articles for *Buddhism in England*, the first of them being on the unity of Buddhism, a subject which I've pursued with some enthusiasm ever since.[32] And eventually I plucked up my courage, joined the society (it was then based in Great Russell Street, and now there's a bookshop on the premises), and started attending meetings. But during the two years from the time I read the *Diamond Sūtra* and the *Sūtra of Wei Lang* up to the time I went to the society at Great Russell Street, I hadn't met a single other Buddhist.

There have been many changes since then, but there are still quite a number of people in this position, especially people living outside London, and for them this question of the approach to Buddhism constitutes a very real problem. How to make contact? For us who are in a society it seems obvious that you come along and join, but for someone who has never heard of the existence of a society and doesn't know how to begin looking, it is a real problem. Only the other week, a young man from the provinces came along to this vihara and told me that he had been interested in Buddhism for about a year. He had written me one or two letters, but he'd had no contact with any other Buddhist, or ever met or even seen one. It was a great relief to him to be able to speak the word Buddhism, to discuss Buddhism with other people who were also Buddhists. It seems to me that I was saying very ordinary things, answering very elementary questions, but so far as he was concerned, my comparatively commonplace remarks were pearls of wisdom. When he first arrived at the vihara, he said to the young man who opened the door to him, 'Do you know, you're the first Buddhist that I've ever seen in my life?' It was a historic occasion. This shows us how careful we must be. We may be at any time the first Buddhist that somebody else has ever seen. There may come a knock on the door of the vihara, and it might be someone who has plucked up courage to come and knock. It may be that the whole of the rest of their life will be determined by the response of the person who opens the door, and that might be you. If you open it with a smile that at least makes an initial good impression, but if you open it with a frown because whatever you were doing has been interrupted, that person might not come again. When the subject of religion comes up and you say, perhaps with a certain amount of bashfulness, 'Well, I am interested in Buddhism', or even 'I am a Buddhist' (you might as well be hung for a sheep as for a lamb), it may be that the person to whom you are speaking has never seen a real live Buddhist before. That is, assuming that you are a real live Buddhist and not a dead and stuffed one! This is something that deserves some serious thought, that someone's whole spiritual life can be affected for better or worse by their impression of you, your knowledge, your sincerity, at that moment.

Anyway, getting back to the main question of the approach to Buddhism, it's possible to approach it in many ways, some more adequate than others, and a few positively wrong. What we have to do in the first place is to approach Buddhism as Buddhism. That might sound obvious, but we don't always do it. In the first talk religion was defined as the achievement of a state of spiritual and psychological wholeness, and in that state relating to other people and to ultimate reality. Religion is also the sum total of all the doctrines, teachings, and methods conducive to this achievement, and Buddhism reflects this definition perhaps in a purer and less distorted form than any other teaching. In its own language Buddhism is the way to Enlightenment, the raft to carry us to the other shore of Nirvāṇa, perfect peace of mind, freedom, insight, wisdom, compassion, and so on. In more modern terms, the Dharma is the instrument of the higher evolution of humanity, each individual human being evolving from an unenlightened to an Enlightened state. Unless one understands this, one may think that one is approaching something, but it will not be Buddhism; at best it will be a rather serious distortion of Buddhism.

Let me give you one or two examples. From time to time at the vihara we have the pleasure and privilege of receiving visitors from Buddhist countries, from Thailand, Burma, Japan, Tibet, and so on, and some months ago we had a charming visitor from Japan. He was a priest of the Shin sect, quite a prominent figure in the Buddhist life of his country, and he was on a world tour. He naturally called on us, and in conversation he said, 'I must tell you about something which pleases me very much. On my way from Japan I called in at Rome, where I had the honour of an audience with the Pope. Not only that, but the Pope gave me a letter in which he expressed very high appreciation of Buddhism.' When I heard this, to be frank I became a bit suspicious. It didn't sound quite Pope-like to me. So I said, 'Have you any objection to my seeing this letter?' Delighted to show it to me, he produced it out of his briefcase. It was on a beautiful piece of parchment-like paper embossed with an enormous coat of arms, and it was indeed from the Pope, though it didn't carry his signature, and he did indeed write about Buddhism, saying, 'Buddhism is to be commended because it is an excellent human teaching.' To anyone who knows a little of Catholicism, it's very clear what this means. There are two kinds of religion, revealed religion and natural religion; transcendental, one may say, and merely humanistic. So the Pope neatly classified Buddhism as a human teaching, a teaching of just a man, not of any really religious figure, not of a saviour, not of a son of God, but just an ordinary human being. It's quite good on that level, but it's just a system of ethics, not capable of leading one to salvation. The Japanese priest didn't quite get this because he wasn't familiar with Western culture. He thought that Buddhism was being praised; he didn't realize that it was being undermined and depreciated. This is the general line taken in books by orthodox Roman Catholics. Yes, Buddhism is very fine, very noble, but it's a human creation, not a revelation, and therefore it can't conduce to salvation. One of these writers, after a scholarly survey of Buddhist teachings, ends by saying, 'What a pity, all these millions of people embark on the raft of the Dharma, and the raft simply founders and all go down with it.' This is the official attitude among Roman Catholics. They don't regard Buddhism as a way to Enlightenment, they don't approach it on its own terms, so there can be no real understanding of Buddhism, but only a distortion. The only genuine approach to Buddhism is as a way to Enlightenment; otherwise there's just a very learned missing of the mark.

The Roman Catholics aren't the only offenders. Orthodox Hindus, particularly Brahmins, also have great difficulty in approaching Buddhism as Buddhism. As soon as you mention Buddhism, they say at once, without waiting for another word on the subject, 'Oh yes, it's only a branch of Hinduism.' That little word 'only' at once gives you a clue that the whole idea is of depreciation or limitation. Even good Hindu scholars, finding that certain Buddhist doctrines are not found in Hinduism, say, 'These can't be part of Buddhism at all. Buddhism is a branch of Hinduism, so any doctrines that are not found in Hinduism must be corruptions introduced by devious Buddhist monks.' Some Hindu scholars, even Dr Radhakrishnan, try to argue quite seriously that the Buddha did not teach the *anātman* doctrine, but that it was the invention of later monks.[33] It's the same with the non-theistic attitude of Buddhism. Some go so far as to try to argue that the Buddha did believe in God but he didn't like to tell his followers because it might upset them. But if we really want to approach it, Buddhism has to be approached as Buddhism. You have to understand that it's a means to psychological and spiritual wholeness, a way to Enlightenment, the instrument of the higher evolution. Otherwise, you may approach something, but it won't be Buddhism, just your own distorted version of it, your own subjective interpretation.

The culmination of approaching Buddhism as Buddhism is Going for Refuge to the Three Jewels, the Buddha, the Enlightened teacher, the Dharma or the way to Enlightenment, and the Sangha, the community of those who are walking that way leading to Enlightenment. But even if you don't take that step, you should at least seriously ask yourself whether you regard Buddhism as the means to Enlightenment, the instrument of the higher evolution, or whether you have any other ideas or lack of ideas about it. Are you coming to this vihara with the understanding that you're trying to approach something which is a way to Enlightenment, trying to lay hold of the instrument of your own individual higher evolution from an unenlightened to an Enlightened state? This is the question you should ask yourself.

Now we come to another crucial point. It isn't even enough to approach Buddhism as Buddhism. We have to approach Buddhism as a whole. Buddhism is a very ancient religion, with 2,500 years of history behind it. It spread through practically the whole of Asia, and through the centuries underwent a process of continual transformation and development, its fundamental doctrines being adapted to the conditions and needs of the people amongst whom it found itself. In this way many different schools and traditions came to be established. Historically speaking, Buddhism is all of these.

Broadly speaking, there are in the world three major forms of Buddhism. There's South-east Asian Buddhism, current in Ceylon, Burma, Thailand, Cambodia, Laos, and a few other places. It is based on the Pāli canon, the version of the Buddhist scriptures handed down by the Theravāda, the School of the Elders, one of the most ancient of all the schools of Buddhism. There is Chinese Buddhism, and its offshoots Japanese, Korean, and Vietnamese Buddhism. Chinese Buddhism is based on the Tripiṭaka or 'three treasuries', the collection translated into Chinese of the Indian Buddhist scriptures of all schools, Mahāyāna, Sarvāstivāda, Sautrāntika, and so on. And thirdly, there's Tibetan

Buddhism, including the Buddhism of Mongolia, Bhutan, and Sikkim. This is based on two great collections of canonical and semi-canonical works: the Kangyur, the translated word of the Buddha, and the Tengyur, the translated commentaries by the great *ācāryas*, the great Buddhist philosophers and spiritual teachers. All three are branches of the original trunk of Indian Buddhism. South-east Asian Buddhism represents the first phase of development of Indian Buddhism, lasting from about the *parinirvāṇa* or death of the Buddha to about the beginning of the Christian era, a period of 500 years; this is the Hīnayāna phase of development, where Buddhism is stated predominantly in ethical and psychological terms. Chinese Buddhism represents Indian Buddhism in its second phase of development, an amalgamation of Hīnayāna plus Mahāyāna, which added the more devotional and metaphysical expressions of the Buddha's teachings. This phase lasted from about the time of the origin of Christianity to about 500 CE. And Tibetan Buddhism represents the third phase of development of Buddhism in India, the phase lasting from about 500 to around 1000 CE. This is Hīnayāna plus Mahāyāna plus Vajrayāna or yogic and symbolically ritualistic Buddhism. All three major forms of Buddhism include numerous schools and sub-schools. In South-east Asia the differences are largely national – Sinhalese Buddhism differs from Burmese Buddhism, Burmese Buddhism from Thai Buddhism, and so on – but there are individual sects or schools within each country. In Thailand they've got two major sects, the Mahā Nikāya and the Dhammayuttika Nikāya, and in Chinese Buddhism there are about a dozen important schools, including the Tiantai, the Huayan, and the Chan school, usually known as Zen. Japan has schools of its own which it developed independently of Chinese influence, especially the Shin school and the Nichiren school, and in Tibet there are the Gelugpas, the Nyingmapas, the Kagyupas, and the Sakyapas.

When we approach Buddhism, we don't approach just this school or that school; we approach the total Buddhist tradition. We certainly don't treat one school of Buddhism as though it was the whole Buddhist tradition. Unfortunately this is sometimes what happens. In the introduction to one book on Buddhism I found the incorrect statement, 'The Buddhist scriptures are to be found in the Pāli Tipiṭaka.' It's correct to say that the Theravāda Buddhist scriptures are to be found in the Pāli Tipiṭaka, but if one says 'Buddhist scriptures', one is leaving out of consideration the Chinese canon, the Tibetan canon, and several other minor canons, and regarding the Pāli canon as the Buddhist scriptures as a whole. In another pamphlet I found the statement 'Buddhism teaches salvation by faith in Amitābha.' It's quite true that the Shin school of Japanese Buddhism teaches this, but it isn't at all correct to say that 'Buddhism' teaches it. Another booklet states, 'The Dalai Lama is the head of the Buddhist religion.' The Dalai Lama is certainly the head of the Tibetan branch of the Buddhist religion, but he isn't the head of the whole Buddhist religion. Here again the part is being confused with the whole. So one's approach to Buddhism should be not sectarian, but synoptic. One should approach the whole of Buddhism, whole in time and whole in space, and try to fathom the essence of it all, not just one aspect.

One's approach to Buddhism should also be balanced. Human nature has many aspects. We have emotional aspects and intellectual aspects. Some people are more introvert, others more extrovert. There are so many differences, all of which are represented, incidentally, in the formula of the five spiritual faculties, faith and wisdom representing the emotional and intellectual, meditation and energy representing the introvert and extrovert, and all of them balanced by mindfulness or awareness.[34] Buddhism should be approached in all these ways. One shouldn't have just an emotional approach or just an intellectual approach, or just a meditative approach or just an active approach. Our nature comprehends all these aspects; we feel, we think, we act, and we sometimes just sit still. We should approach Buddhism through all these aspects, with our total being, not just part of it. We shouldn't just feel and not try to think or understand, and nor should we just try to understand without feeling. Don't look within all the time; but don't look outwards so much that you never pause to look within. There's a time and place for all these things, and if possible we should try to do all of them all of the time. As we ascend higher and higher in our spiritual development, we will find that we can think and feel, act and be still, simultaneously. It sounds impossible but that's only because of the limitations of our present way of thinking. Eventually, as our spiritual life develops, all these four apparently contradictory aspects will be fused and harmonized into one spiritual faculty, one being which is forging ahead. Unless we have this balanced approach of head and heart, there's no real commitment, no real dedication to Buddhism as a way of Enlightenment, as an instrument of the higher evolution.

So we should approach Buddhism as Buddhism, as the way to Enlightenment, the instrument of higher evolution. We should approach it as a whole, not just the Theravāda or just Zen, or just Shin, or just Tibetan Buddhism; we should try to assimilate the best elements of all these traditions. And we should approach it in a balanced manner with the whole of our being. I had intended to say something about the approach to Buddhism with regard to conditions here in England, but this is a big subject, and as it happens I have a rather important engagement on the other side of London for which I don't wish to be late, so I will postpone the consideration of this aspect of the subject to next week, when we shall in any case be considering Buddhism in England.

INTRODUCING BUDDHISM 4: BUDDHISM IN ENGLAND

Hampstead Buddhist Vihara, 23 January 1966

We saw in last week's talk that we should approach Buddhism as Buddhism, approach it as a whole, and approach it with our whole being. But there's a more specific, more concrete approach to Buddhism, in terms of conditions here and now in this country, in the midst of the twentieth century. But why as part of a series introducing Buddhism do we have to consider Buddhism in England at all? Why not get straight on with the exposition of Buddhism, the philosophical first principles, the spiritual and ethical path? Why pause to consider something so apparently irrelevant, even though of interest, as Buddhism in England? Well, the position isn't as straightforward as that. As I'm sure you've gathered by this time, in this vihara we're concerned with Buddhism not just theoretically, not just as a subject of study, not just as a matter of intellectual research and investigation, but practically, as a matter above all else of the actual spiritual life. And if you've tried, you know that it's very difficult indeed to lead a spiritual life, whichever religion you follow, in complete isolation from other people who are following that path. It's a struggle to lead a spiritual life by oneself, just with the help of books, with no one to talk to, no one whose advice one can ask, no one on whom one can rely, no one to whom one can turn in difficulties, or at least for a little encouragement, inspiration, or guidance. As I mentioned, there are quite a number of Buddhists scattered up and down this country who have no contact with any other Buddhists, and it seems that they have quite a difficult time, which is why they look forward so much to occasional trips to London, where they can meet other Buddhists, or to Biddulph for meditation, or to a sojourn at the Buddhist Society summer school.

Aristotle says that if a man can endure to live alone, he's either a beast or a god.[35] Most people, as he goes on to say, are neither beasts nor gods, but somewhere in between, and they need society, companions, friends. This is the case in the spiritual life perhaps even more than in ordinary social life. Most people find that they can lead the spiritual life most easily as a member of a spiritual group. One may not be in contact with anyone who is highly advanced spiritually, but if one spends time with other people following the same spiritual path as oneself, that gives mutual encouragement and stimulation. When I myself took up the monastic life, I found it very helpful indeed that there were two of us together. I was ordained as a *śrāmaṇera*, a novice, at the same time as my friend Buddharakshita, who is now in charge of a vihara in Bangalore, but even before that we travelled together, and stayed together in ashrams and hermitages, sometimes in mountain caves. If one of us flagged a little, it was encouraging that the other was there. If one wanted to get up late, the other was there to say, 'No, we must get up early and meditate.' Or if one of us was studying and didn't quite understand what he was reading, there was the other one to discuss it with.[36] This sort of thing is very helpful, not only in the monastic life, but in our spiritual life as lay Buddhists. We can get a great deal of encouragement and stimulation from those who are following the same path and aspiring to the realization of the same spiritual ideals. As Buddhists, our spiritual lives are not lived in isolation. As John Donne wrote, 'No man is an island, entire of itself.'[37] We're all linked, underground or undersea, to the continent, to the larger life of the group. Our spiritual lives as Buddhists are part of the larger spiritual life of the group to which we belong, whether it's the Hampstead Buddhist Vihara, the Buddhist Society, or a little group in Birmingham or Oxford. Ultimately, the whole English Buddhist movement is the larger spiritual group to which we all belong, and we can't separate ourselves from it if we want to lead a spiritual life as Buddhists in the fullest possible sense. The majority of English Buddhists in any case don't want to separate themselves from the larger spiritual life of the group, because they find it so helpful.

But a word of caution. We shouldn't use the Buddhist group as a community substitute. Suppose someone's rather lonely. They live on their own, don't go to church, don't belong to a club (perhaps it's too expensive), don't like sports or games, not even chess. And then they learn that there's a nice little organization near at hand. Nice people meet there every Sunday afternoon and sometimes during the week. It's pleasant to go along and have a little chat, and if you have to listen to the lecture too, that's a price which no one minds paying for the sake of the social amenities. In this way, the Buddhist group comes to be used as a community substitute. Up to a point this is legitimate, but it's not really what it's there for. I'll come back to this topic later.

If the Buddhist group is properly used, it provides us with the immediate context of our spiritual life. As has already been made clear in this series, although you can lead a conventional religious life without self-awareness, you can't have any meaningful, constantly progressing spiritual life without it. One might even say that the whole spiritual life is a process of the progressive intensification of self-awareness. I've said that our spiritual life is bound up with that of the spiritual group or spiritual community to which we belong. Putting it in Buddhist terminology, Going for Refuge, *śaraṇa*, is an intrinsic part of being a Buddhist, and you can't be a Buddhist and go for Refuge to the Buddha and the Dharma, but not to the Sangha. Going for Refuge to the Sangha is part of the very definition of being a Buddhist. Self-awareness should therefore include awareness of ourselves as members of the spiritual group to which we belong. Otherwise, we're not fully aware of ourselves, because our membership of the group is part of the very definition of ourselves. We can't be truly spiritually self-aware unless we're also aware of the movement of which we are a part. If we understand the Buddhist movement in England, its history, its significance, and its possible or probable destination, we shall understand all the better what we as individual Buddhists are, and what we're trying to do.

Many people don't know this, but Buddhism has been known in this country for well over a hundred years. Before that, in all Western countries there was complete, fantastic ignorance of Buddhism. According to one early writer at the beginning of the nineteenth century, the Buddha was none other than the Egyptian god Apis, the white sacred bull. During the second half of the nineteenth century, however, this dense ignorance began to be dispelled through the work of a number of distinguished orientalists. The earliest of these was Robert Spence Hardy, who made a special study of monastic life in Ceylon.[38] Then there was Robert Caesar Childers, who went to Ceylon to work for the Civil Service, learned Pāli, translated Buddhist scriptures into English, and compiled the first Pāli–English dictionary.[39] And then there was the great T. W. Rhys Davids, who inaugurated the systematic translation and publication of all the Pāli Theravāda texts, and launched the Pali Text's Society's *Pāli–English Dictionary*, besides founding the Pali Text Society itself.[40] These three great orientalists were all workers in the field of Pāli Buddhist studies. At the same time, in the field of Sanskrit Buddhist studies we had Max Müller. His life's work was the study and translation of the *Rig Veda* and various other Hindu works, but he devoted a considerable amount of time and attention to Buddhist Sanskrit texts – the Mahāyāna *sūtras* and so forth – and translated a number of them himself.[41] For Chinese Buddhist studies, there is the well-known figure of Samuel Beal, who published his *Catena of Buddhist Scriptures*, which includes material that is still very valuable indeed.[42] There were also translations into English of works on Buddhism by various continental scholars, and a number of Buddhist texts and scriptures were translated into English in this period by scholars in other oriental languages, for example Bishop Bigandet, an Anglican bishop in Burma who compiled an enormous work from Burmese and Pāli sources on the life and teachings of the Buddha.[43] It's a little out of date now, but it is still a valuable work and a very worthy effort for its time.

In this way, a great deal of the Pāli canon and at least some Mahāyāna *sūtras* came to be translated into English, and knowledge of Buddhism began to be introduced in this country. But there were considerable limitations. This knowledge was on the whole confined to scholarly circles, both those of people who were working or living in the East and had an administrative interest in the religions of the people over whom they were ruling and those of students of comparative religion and ancient thought. An important part was played by the Theosophical Society, which was founded in the United States in 1873 by Madame Blavatsky and Colonel Olcott and quickly spread to this country. The Society has three main objects: the formation of a nucleus of universal brotherhood, the comparative study of religions, and the investigation of occult powers. With this broad platform, it helped to spread a number of Buddhistic ideas in this country and elsewhere in the West, sometimes in a slightly garbled form. One great merit of the Theosophical Society's work was that it familiarized people with the idea of Buddhism as a living religion. The oriental scholars tended to present it as something dead, or that's the impression one often gets from reading their works, but the Theosophical Society made it quite clear that Buddhism was a living religion which people could follow, not just an exotic oriental curiosity. At about the same time, Edwin Arnold's famous poem on the life of the Buddha, *The Light of Asia*, published in the 1870s, did a great deal of good work in spreading knowledge about the Buddha and his teaching. This work is still a bestseller; I believe it has run into practically a hundred editions.

With the beginning of the twentieth century, a new phase began. People born and educated in Britain began adopting Buddhism as their way of life, so that Buddhism was no longer just an object of intellectual interest, but became a living religion. The first Buddhist organization was started exactly sixty years ago in 1906 by two stalwarts, R. J. Jackson and J. R. Pain.[44] And in 1908 Ananda Metteyya, who was born as Allan Bennett, of Scottish origin, returned to this country after six years in the East as a monk, having gone out to Burma in 1902 with the object of studying Buddhism, so as to be able to return and preach it in this country. After his return, the first Buddhist periodical, *The Buddhist Review*, was started. These three – the organization, the monk, and the magazine – carried on until 1923, when Ananda Metteyya died.

It's rather remarkable that we can claim that the British converted themselves to Buddhism. It's perhaps unique in the history of Buddhism. One usually finds that some missionary monk goes from India to China, or India to Tibet, or China to Korea, or Korea to Japan, and introduces the teaching of the Buddha to the indigenous inhabitants, but in our case, British people themselves took interest in Buddhism, studied it, and decided to go to the East (in the case of Ananda Metteyya), gain a deeper knowledge, and then return to this country and disseminate it. This is characteristic of the whole development of British Buddhism. It has always been independent, relying on its own effort, its own study, and its own thought. This isn't surprising, because over the last few hundred years Buddhism has not been in a very active condition in the East. The most creative phases were a thing of the past, and very little life and energy, at least organizationally, were left.

After Ananda Metteyya's death in 1923, the gap was filled by an important series of thirty-six lectures by a disciple of R. J. Jackson called Francis Payne,[45] and then in 1924, Christmas Humphreys founded the Buddhist branch of the Theosophical Society, which the next year became the Buddhist Society as an independent organization. The Buddhist Society is the oldest surviving Buddhist organization not only in this country, but in the whole of the West.[46]

During this period, important additions were made to the literature about Buddhism available in English. At this time Dr D. T. Suzuki started publishing his writings and articles about Zen, and these have assumed a tremendous importance in the development of Buddhism, not only in this country, but in the United States.[47] At the same time, Dr Evans-Wentz who had studied in Sikkim, launched the Oxford Tibetan series with translations of some very important Tibetan texts, *The Life of Milarepa*, *The Tibetan Book of the Dead*, *Tibetan Yoga*, *Secret Doctrines*, and so on. These contributions enormously enriched our knowledge of Buddhism, which had hitherto been confined mainly to the Theravāda Pāli canon and certain selected Mahāyāna *sūtras*. Dr Suzuki's writings in particular marked a turning point because they succeeded in penetrating into circles where Buddhism had been hitherto unknown. Philosophers, psychologists, and students of comparative religion, including famous people like C. G. Jung and Erich Fromm, devoted themselves to Dr Suzuki's writing and were apparently deeply influenced, or at least impressed, by him.

During the war there was a lull in Buddhist activities in this country, but immediately after it there was a considerable expansion. The Buddhist Society became much better known, and scores of new books on Buddhism were published. In particular, one can refer to Christmas Humphreys' *Buddhism*, published by Pelican, 300,000 copies of which have so far been sold. That is quite an achievement. It's quite reasonable to assume that many of these copies will have been read by two or three people, and that would bring the total readership above the half million mark. Buddhism is beginning to make an impression, it seems. On a much profounder level, there are Dr Conze's translations from the Perfection of Wisdom *sūtras*, which belong to the same period. These are perhaps the most important group of *sūtras* in the whole of Mahāyāna Buddhist canonical literature. There are about thirty-six of them, some several volumes long, some just a page in length. Dr Conze has completed the enormous task of single-handedly translating all of them; many have been published, and others are available in typescript.

In my opinion this is one of the great pioneering works of Buddhist history. It's remarkable that one man should have been able to achieve so much despite very little encouragement. In 1955, just ten years ago, the English Sangha Trust and the English Sangha Association were founded.[48] The idea behind these two bodies was mainly to send trainees to the East to study and be ordained as monks, and to arrange for their support and provide them with facilities for teaching after they returned to this country. And with this, we come down to the present day.

So where does the Buddhist movement stand now, in 1966? Well, to begin with, the name of Buddhism is quite widely known. When I left these shores twenty-one years ago, hardly anybody had even heard of it, but now thousands or perhaps even millions of people have at least heard the word. That's a small thing, but it's a beginning. We can't say that there's much understanding of Buddhism. Those who know a little about it are to be numbered in thousands, or perhaps not even that. But lots of people, especially younger people, are eager to learn something about Buddhism. Here at the Vihara we get lots of invitations to give talks in schools, comparative religion classes, and even religious knowledge classes; that's a very encouraging sign for the future. Unfortunately, however, apart from Suzuki, no Buddhist has yet succeeded in penetrating or even touching the religious and intellectual life of this country.

At present, organizationally speaking, the Buddhist movement in this country comprises the Buddhist Society, the oldest and largest Buddhist organization in the West, and ourselves, the English Sangha Trust and Sangha Association, which run this Hampstead Buddhist Vihara. These two between them are the two poles supporting the axis upon which the British Buddhist movement revolves. There's also the Chiswick Vihara run by the Maha Bodhi Society of Ceylon and the Richmond Vihara run by the Thai government, which has the advantage of vast resources upon which to draw. And there are about twenty provincial groups scattered up and down the country, from Brighton in the south to Newcastle in the north. Some have only a dozen or so members, some have thirty or thirty-five, and I've visited practically all of them. Buddhists are linked by two magazines, *The Middle Way*, published by the Buddhist Society, and *The Buddhist*, published by ourselves, and by the Buddhist Society's annual summer school, to which people come not only from all over Britain, but from the Continent too.

But the Buddhist movement here is still very small. I'm often asked by journalists how many Buddhists there are in this country. The other day I heard the figure of 30,000, but my own estimate is that there are about 3,000, and that would be generous, not insisting that every one of them has fully gone for Refuge to the Three Jewels or strictly observes the five precepts, but including those who are pretty interested and fairly committed, and who pay their subscriptions to the Association after only one or two reminders. Out of those 3,000 I would say that about a hundred are really involved in the Buddhist movement. The other 2,900 just read about Buddhism or subscribe to Buddhist magazines, and if they're in London they attend a few lectures. So this is our movement so far. It's one of the smallest religious movements in this country, if not the smallest. However, it's quite clear that we are expanding, even though very slowly. Another encouraging fact is that our average age is steadily going down. In some of the provincial groups one doesn't see this yet. In one or two of them the average age must be about 74! But here I've noticed since my arrival nearly a year and a half ago that from about 55, it has crept down and now it's about 40, perhaps, which is pretty good.

This brings us to the future of Buddhism in this country. The future will obviously grow out of the present, just as the present has grown out of the past, so let's begin our little excursion into the future by taking a broader and perhaps deeper view of the present. I've observed already that Buddhism is very much a minority religion, and hasn't yet made any real impact. Life and thought go on just as though such a thing as Buddhism had never existed. Whether in the future Buddhism will ever be able to make an impact depends, I feel, upon whether Buddhism has anything which is consonant in some way with the character and culture of the English people. So here I want to pause and take a look at the nature of the English.

I think I perhaps have a right to generalize about the English character because I've been out of this country for twenty years, so I've seen it from a distance, and can perhaps be more objective. I've also had an opportunity of hearing what the Indians, the Burmese, the Chinese, the Tibetans, and various other nationalities have to say about the English. It's sometimes quite revealing. I would say that the most distinctive trait of the English character is that it is empirical. That is, the English mind, at its most representative, proceeds from facts to theories, rather than from theories to facts, and sometimes it doesn't bother about the theories at all. If something works well enough, people don't bother about why it works, or what would happen if they did it in some other way. This pragmatism is especially observable in the political life of this country. We haven't produced any great political philosophies, at least none which have been operative in daily life, but nevertheless we have had a very active political life and a great history of constitutional development. Now Buddhism is a sort of spiritual empiricism. It asks us to take nothing on trust. The Buddha himself asks us not to believe something simply because he says it. We are to test it, verify it, experience it even, ourselves. The Zen form of Buddhism is perhaps particularly attractive from this point of view. It stresses something immediate and direct, to be experienced by ourselves here and now, in the same way that we experience the coldness of water when we drink it, not taking it on trust, not just believing it. So Buddhism and the English have empiricism in common.

Also, the English character is very tolerant. In England there's a long tradition of freedom of thought and belief and religious practice, coming down from Anglo-Saxon times, certainly from the days of John Wycliffe, who was sometimes referred to as the morning star of the Reformation.[49] Even during the Middle Ages, when many bloody persecutions took place in different European countries, religious persecution in England, though it certainly happened, was at least much rarer than anywhere else in Europe. And Buddhism is probably the most tolerant of all religions. It's never persecuted anyone, or launched a religious war. So this is another point of affinity between the English character and Buddhism, though in Buddhism the basis is ultimately transcendental rather than secular.

England has been a Christian nation for many centuries, ever since St Augustine of Canterbury came here and converted us from paganism, but my personal feeling is that Christianity has never really suited the English. It's never really fitted us, like a suit we inherited which was made for somebody else and hangs a bit loose. If we study the history of England, the greatest achievements have hardly any connection with Christianity. In the whole field of law, whether it's the common law of England or any other form of law, there's no direct connection with Christianity, but this is the field in which some of the greatest achievements of the English have taken place. Often, in fact, political, legal, and penal reforms have been made in the teeth of church opposition. For example, in 1810 a bill which had already passed the Commons was introduced into the House of Lords for the assent of the peers temporal and spiritual. The bill related to capital punishment, and one of its provisions was that the penalty of death for stealing something worth five shillings should be abolished. Of course it was voted out – it didn't stand a chance – but it's interesting to see that at the head of the list of those voting against it were all the bishops who were in the House of Lords at that time.[50]

Now suppose we take a look at the arts. If there's anything or anyone in English literature that we can be proud of, it's Shakespeare, so let's look at his plays. You can go through Shakespeare with a fine-tooth comb and cut out every line where Christianity is mentioned, even every line where God is mentioned, except so far as swearing is concerned, and it will make hardly any difference. Shakespeare will still be Shakespeare. Of course, scholars like Tillyard tell us that Shakespeare's world picture was derived from medieval thought – the three-storey universe, the idea of degree and so on,[51] and that's true, but specifically Christian content and feeling are not there in Shakespeare at all. By contrast, if you take away the Christianity from Dante's *Divine Comedy*, there's nothing left; almost every line is permeated with it. So there is a very significant contrast here. The greatest of the Italian poets is Christian through and through, but the greatest of the English poets couldn't care less, apparently. Some people even say that Shakespeare wasn't a Christian, but an initiate who knew things that Christians of his day didn't and deliberately disseminated them through his plays, and if one goes through the plays carefully, one wonders whether it might perhaps be true. Some people might object that Dante is medieval, whereas Shakespeare is post-Renaissance, so you can't really compare the two, but if you want a medieval English poet to compare with Dante, take Chaucer, a thoroughly secular poet, though you can find bits of Christianity here and there in his *Canterbury Tales*. He describes the monk and the friar, the priest and the canon, but none of them very flatteringly. He doesn't seem to have much sympathy with the church. These great poets are thoroughly secular.

The same is true of the paintings of the three greatest English painters, William Hogarth, Thomas Gainsborough, and J. M. W. Turner. Hogarth painted street scenes and people getting drunk in Gin Lane and various stages of debauchery; Gainsborough painted elegant portraits of the aristocracy; and Turner painted sunrises and sunsets and trains rushing through the mist. If you put all their paintings together, there's hardly a Holy Family between them, whereas if you turn to Italian or Spanish painting, or even German or French painting in its early stages, it teems with Holy Families, and Madonnas, and Crucifixions. Where in English art do you find this? You have to go right back to the early medieval period to find a few wooden painted panels.

Likewise, British philosophy has virtually no connection with Christianity at all. Sir Francis Bacon paid it lip service, but he was busy laying the foundations of induction and the scientific method.[52] George Berkeley had a nominal connection with the Church – after all, he was a bishop – but you can't detect Christianity in his work.[53] And the British have never shone in the field of theology. There's Bishop Butler, but very few people read him nowadays, and perhaps he isn't worth mentioning.[54] It is significant, though, that if we go through English literature, there are a number of important moralists, especially in the seventeenth and eighteenth centuries, and sometimes the psychological analysis of these moralists – for instance Samuel Johnson – is very acute and perceptive indeed.

What about saints, those experts in Christianity? How many saints has this country produced? You have to go back to Edward the Confessor and Martyr in the seventh century, or Thomas More, canonized in this century by the Roman Catholic Church, apparently to annoy the Protestants. We haven't produced any saints to compare with St Francis or any of the other great founders of religious orders on the Continent, like St Bernard, St Benedict, and St Dominic. We've produced very few mystics and hardly any religious thinkers. There were the Cambridge Platonists of the seventeenth and early eighteenth century, but they were really only half Christian, as their name suggests. Their main inspiration came from Plato.[55]

So it seems that Christianity in this country has had a certain social and political importance, but the spiritual and cultural life of the country has proceeded quite independently of Christianity, especially since the Reformation and the spoliation of the monasteries. It's almost as though the English couldn't really thrive, couldn't really do their best, on Christianity. My own conviction is that we shall do very much better with Buddhism, but for this to be possible, two things at least are necessary. First of all, there's image. Nowadays, people are very concerned with image. When I first came back to this country, I thought people were talking about idol worship, and it *is* idol worship, but in a rather different sense. But the image of Buddhism as something oriental, mysterious, exotic, Lobsang Rampa-ish, must go.[56] Otherwise, there's very little chance for Buddhism in this country. Historically speaking Buddhism originated in the East, as Christianity also did, but in its essence, intrinsically, substantially, Buddhism is no more Eastern than Western, any more than Christianity is. So British Buddhism, if it's to spread and have a real influence, must gradually shed its oriental trappings. There aren't many of them, and British Buddhism has done this to some extent already, but it will have to be able to get along, at least so far as the average British Buddhist is concerned, without Pāli or Sanskrit, Chinese or Tibetan, without Eastern-style rituals, though we may devise some of our own, and without Eastern dress, even for monks. Otherwise our appeal will be very limited. The test for British Buddhists will be whether we can extract the non-geographical, supra-cultural essence of Buddhism and distil it and create out of it our own cultural form, whether we can distinguish the essential in Buddhism from the nonessential, the kernel from the husk. The husk is historically important, but we mustn't hesitate to discard it if we want to eat the kernel.

Secondly, it's very important that British Buddhism should link up with those elements in British thought and culture which are Buddhistic – not Buddhist, but Buddhistic. There's a very important book by R. H. Blyth called *Zen in English Literature and Oriental Classics*, in which he discusses Zen concepts, quoting from the Zen or Chan masters, and shows by quoting extensively from English poetry that the same ideas, the same sorts of experience, are adumbrated in poets like Wordsworth, Keats, Shelley, and Shakespeare. Blyth was well-versed in English literature, having been a professor of it in a Japanese university for many years. This linking up is the kind of thing that needs to be done.[57] In the same way we need research into English philosophy, mysticism, ethical thought, and so on. For instance, in Buddhism there's the important Vijñānavādin philosophy, one of whose principal exponents is Vasubandhu, and in English thought there's something very similar in the philosophy of Berkeley, so someone should compare Berkeley and Vasubandhu and see what comes of it. There's a vast field of work, but unfortunately no workers – very few people seem interested in pursuing things in this way.

The Renaissance was the rebirth of European culture in the fifteenth and sixteenth centuries due to the rediscovery of Graeco-Roman literature and art. Arthur Schopenhauer, who was very much influenced both by the Upanishads and by Buddhism, predicted that 'the Renaissance which will be brought about in the West as a result of the discovery of Eastern thought, Eastern spirituality, Eastern religion, will exceed in importance the Renaissance brought about in the fifteenth to sixteenth centuries through the rediscovery of the literature of Greece and Rome.'[58] Buddhism is the flower, the consummation, of Eastern spirituality, especially in its Chan or Zen form, and Britain has a very highly developed secular culture which it seems is now in need of fresh inspiration, a fresh impetus, so when these two come together, there is no knowing what could be produced.

The British Buddhist movement is the spearhead of this convergence between Buddhism and British secular, largely non-Christian culture, and the spearhead of the British Buddhist movement is here among all of us, so this should make us think. We should try to realize our historic responsibility. We're all interested in Buddhism, and we have all inherited, in one way or another, some measure of British culture, so in each one of us, not only collectively but individually, these two streams, these two tendencies, these two historical traditions, spiritual and secular, Buddhist and British, are coming together. We should all make some effort to contribute to and enrich this.

The other day I attended the memorial meeting for the late Indian Prime Minister, Mr Shastri, at the Albert Hall.[59] As you can imagine, it was quite a grand occasion with many important people present, and among the speakers were the Prime Minister and Lord Mountbatten. Both of them, and all the other speakers, made a number of references to Indo-British friendship. They said that the Indian people and the British people must work together, and all the sorts of things that are usually said on such occasions. But contact on the political level is comparatively superficial, and doesn't go far enough or deep enough. It's on the spiritual level that contacts have to be made and exchanges have to take place, so perhaps what is happening here is even more important than what happened the other evening in the Albert Hall. Here, though the numbers involved are fewer and the people involved are much less prominent, the level on which the contact and exchange are taking place is immeasurably higher, and therefore of immeasurably greater significance.

At present, we have in this country only two English Buddhist monks – Bhikkhu Mangalo at Biddulph and myself – and the number isn't likely to increase much in the near future.[60] Perhaps very shortly we shall be losing Bhikkhu Mangalo, who will be going into retreat for an indefinite period. It must be admitted that the life of the Buddhist monk in the West is not easy. Even after spending a number of years in the East, one finds that the pressures and claims of life in the West are all pulling one in a quite different direction from Buddhism, and one has to stand very firm indeed so as not to be carried away. With the prospect of only a very small number of monks in this country, because even among those who are deeply interested in Buddhism the number of people who wish to become monks is microscopic, the laity will have to take an increasingly responsible role. This doesn't mean that unqualified people should start acting as though they were qualified, but the laity should make a much greater effort to qualify themselves to undertake some of the duties and responsibilities which traditionally in Buddhism are the prerogative of the monk. They must study Buddhism harder, meditate harder, and give up more and more all those activities that are inconsistent with Buddhism, apart from those necessary for maintaining themselves and their families. In the case of some, especially those who are single and without responsibilities, they should try to reorganize their lives as much as possible. If they can't become monks, at least they could take a job that doesn't demand too much of them and devote as much as possible of their time to the study, practice, and dissemination of Buddhism.

As I've emphasized, our Buddhist movement in this country is very small, and we can't comfort ourselves with the old saying that it's quality that counts, not quantity, because I'm afraid we must admit that at present our intellectual and cultural calibre is rather low. It is incumbent upon each and every person coming here to do their utmost to improve themselves, to try to raise their intellectual and cultural level, to learn more about Buddhism and also more about their own culture, otherwise it will be impossible to attract intelligent people to the movement. Those who are more advanced in their study of Buddhism should take up particular topics for research and study, pursue them, and try to exhaust them. Someone might take up Buddhism and psychoanalysis. Someone else might make a special study of Buddhist art, or decide to read as much as they can about Chinese Buddhism. In this way, each seriously interested person should try to become an expert, at least in a small way, in some branch of Buddhist studies, or Buddhism in relation to some aspect of Western culture, and periodically they should give a lecture or write an article, so that everyone can share the fruits of what they have discovered.

The mention of the responsibility of the laity introduces the question of the whole social side of Buddhism. I feel strongly that all Buddhists should get to know one another as well as they possibly can, especially those who are based at a vihara or any such institution. A serious effort should be made to develop amongst ourselves a spirit of brotherhood. The Theosophical Society have 'the creation of a nucleus of universal brotherhood' as their first objective, and I can say from my own experience of the society that they try very sincerely to put that into practice. Buddhists should try to cultivate this spirit too. But when we get together, it shouldn't be just a social gathering. The Buddhist spiritual community shouldn't be a symbiotic community substitute. It should have a spiritual purpose. When you get together with other Buddhists, discuss Buddhism, discuss the Buddhist movement and what can be done to help it progress, to make it more active, more alive. Leave aside purely personal things or questions of politics, or what you read in the newspaper. If in the present British Buddhism, which means all of us, can do as I have suggested, then its future will be assured.

EVOLUTION – LOWER AND HIGHER

A combination of a talk given on 6 February 1966 at the Hampstead Buddhist Vihara (material from which also appears in Who is the Buddha?, Complete Works, *vol. 3) and another talk of the same name given in 1969.*

In this lecture we shall be concerned with what is possibly the most important subject that we could ever concern ourselves with, under practically its most significant aspect: humanity – that is to say, ourselves. We shall not be concerned with any merely general or abstract idea of the human being, but with human beings as we actually and potentially live and evolve and aspire – not as something static, fixed, final, finished once and for all, but as developing, progressing from lower to higher and ever higher levels of being and consciousness. We shall be concerned with the vitally important subject of human evolution.

Most of the time we are preoccupied with external things. I am sure that today most of you have been busy with household chores, other people, your job, all sorts of everyday things. I know that in some cases it has not been easy for you to get here. One gentleman almost staggered up the stairs and collapsed on the top landing, he had had so much difficulty with the traffic. Preoccupation with external things seems to be an inevitable part of modern living, and we do not often get time just to be still and take a look at ourselves, feel our own existence. I wonder how long it is since you had the opportunity to sit down in a room by yourself, with nothing in particular to do, no job, no duty, nothing to rush out for, and be still for as long as you wanted, time just to think and be yourself? Someone once defined religion as what we do with our solitude, but nowadays, unfortunately, only too often we do not have any solitude and therefore, perhaps, we do not have any religion.[61]

But in this lecture we shall be trying to stop and consider ourselves. We shall be trying to see how far we have come in the evolutionary process and how far we have yet to go. We will need to be very careful not to think of human beings as distinct from ourselves. Quite a lot of people who attend lectures have a sort of genius for insulating themselves from the subject being talked about. If the speaker mentions negative emotions, they think, 'Yes, lots of people have negative emotions,' but they never think, '*I* have negative emotions. The lecturer is talking about *me*.' They insulate themselves from what is being said, as though it was purely objective and didn't concern them. Even with regard to a subject like human evolution, it is only too easy to sit back as though it were about a being living on some other planet in some other galactic system millions of miles away, and never think, 'This concerns me, this is about me, this *is* me.' We manage to put up such an effective screen between ourselves and what is being said. We just look at it as it were drifting by 'out there', and never make the application to ourselves. But in the course of this talk we must avoid doing this at all costs. Our study is self-study, and we will be studying ourselves all the time.

We should also be careful not to divide ourselves into speaker and audience, as though these are quite different. Lecture halls are often designed so that the speaker is up on a platform, which has the practical advantage that everybody can see him or her, but the effect can be to create a feeling of separation between lecturer up here and audience down there. The lecture supposedly creates a sort of bridge, but often instead it tends to emphasize the separateness of the speaker and the audience. But we must not think of speaker and audience as two different things. There is a distinction, obviously, but at the same time the two are inseparable. The relationship between the speaker and the audience is like that between the conductor and the orchestra. At a concert the music you hear is the product jointly of the members of the orchestra and the person conducting them, and similarly, I often feel that a lecture is a joint product. Everybody is playing as well as listening. This is what we should try to feel. One person may be speaking, but that person speaks for everyone present.

It is no exaggeration to say that evolution is probably the most important general concept of modern thought. I say 'modern thought' advisedly because although the idea of organic development was known in earlier times, it was known only in a vague, almost dreamy, poetic way, and if there was any understanding of evolution, it was more a matter of inspired guesswork than any scientific, objective, grounded knowledge. As a scientifically demonstrable principle, the concept of evolution will be forever associated with the name of Charles Darwin, who first traced the operation of the principle in detail within one particular field of human knowledge: biology. He showed decisively, in the face of a great deal of dogmatic Christian opposition, how one form of organic life develops into another, the simpler forms developing into the more complex, and the more complex developing into the more complex still. Since those days, only a hundred years ago, the principle of evolution has been discovered to be at work in every field of knowledge and every department of life. Wherever you find life, there you find evolution, there you find development; the ramifications of this great principle extend throughout the universe at all possible levels. Julian Huxley wrote:

> The different branches of science combine to demonstrate that the universe in its entirety must be regarded as one gigantic process, a process of becoming, of attaining new levels of existence and organisation, which can properly be called a genesis or an evolution.[62]

This is the inspiring vision held up for our contemplation by science, a vista of an evolving universe on a gigantic scale which contrasts very much with the cramped and static picture of the universe presented by traditional religions. But wonderful as this vision of cosmic evolution is, there is something still more wonderful about it, and that is the fact that we ourselves are included in this process. We ourselves are part of the universe, part of nature. We tend to think of ourselves, feel ourselves, as separate from nature, but we must never forget that we are part of the universe, and intimately connected with nature. We may look out at nature, but our looking at nature is also nature looking at herself, contemplating herself through our eyes. Shakespeare wrote, 'This is an art / Which does mend nature, change it rather, but / The art itself is nature.'[63] So we too, being a part of nature, part of the evolving universe, are in a process of becoming. We too are all the time attaining new levels of existence and organization, and with this realization we come to the threshold of the distinction between the lower evolution and the higher evolution.

But before crossing that threshold, I want to go a little more deeply into the nature of evolution. Evolution is a word that we know very well, but we don't usually stop to think what is meant by it. What is evolution really? Or, to put it differently, when a lower organism develops into a higher one, what happens? Principally there are two answers to this question: a mechanist one and a vitalist one. The mechanist account of evolution would say that all that happens when a simpler organism evolves into a more complex one is that previously existing elements arrange themselves into a more complicated pattern. It would maintain that nothing new has come into existence, and would add that elements arrange themselves in more and more complicated patterns quite fortuitously. This explanation is sometimes called derisively by its opponents the monkey and typewriter theory of evolution. It is said that if you gave a monkey a typewriter and enough time, say a few hundred million years, he would eventually produce, quite by accident, the collected works of Shakespeare, and in the same way, if you have enough atoms banging around in infinite space and infinite time, they will eventually produce, entirely by chance, all the phenomena of existence as we know them. The vitalist answer, however, speaks in terms of life force, saying that the evolutionary process is not the product of chance, but is guided by an immanent life principle or life force which is trying to attain through the evolutionary process a definite goal.

Neither of these answers is very satisfactory. The mechanist one entirely overlooks the fact that at least on the human level qualities can come into existence that the universe did not contain before. With the higher cultural and spiritual life of humanity, something new comes into existence that cannot be explained in terms of any rearrangement, however complicated, of previously existing elements. The vitalist explanation, on the other hand, is really a description of what happens rather than an explanation of how it happens; even if one accepts the vitalist view, the nature of the goal of the evolutionary process is not very clear. But despite its drawbacks, the vitalism explanation is capable of some enlargement, and this is what I now propose to do, to enlarge the vitalist conception until it comes a little nearer to the truth.

We have to begin to do this rather dramatically by taking what Shin Buddhists sometimes call the Great Sideways Leap.[64] We have to begin by positing an absolute reality above and beyond the evolutionary process, which is neither matter nor mind as we usually think of mind. We can call this reality absolute or universal mind, and it is a mind in which there is no distinction of subject and object, just one pure, non-dual, universal, cosmic awareness which is all-comprehending, transcendental, and blissful, which in Buddhist language is devoid of separate individuality, and which is above and beyond the evolutionary process, transcending it even at its highest level, existing in a different dimension. I propose to posit this absolute reality, not prove it, because no proof is possible. The evidence we have to go on, and this is very important, is the unanimous, unassailable testimony of the mystics, inspired seers, and visionaries of all ages, all sects, and all religions who down the ages have testified to the existence, above and beyond the senses and the ordinary mind, of this absolute reality, this universal mind, which transcends and transfigures all that we ordinarily know.

This absolute reality is that which manifests through the whole evolutionary process. It cannot manifest all at once. If it did, it wouldn't be a manifestation, but absolute reality itself. Absolute reality manifests through the evolutionary process by degrees. The greater the complexity of the organism through which it manifests, the more reality is able to manifest through it. At the same time, it is the presence of this absolute reality behind the evolutionary process which makes it possible for the organism to attain ever higher levels of complexity. Looking at the matter more broadly, we may say that life in the process of evolution is able to manifest new qualities which were not there before, which were unprecedented, because all the time life is able to draw on the inexhaustible reservoir of absolute reality. Evolution is essentially a self-transcending process. What was not there before comes into existence. When circumstances are favourable, the succeeding stage of development is able to transcend the preceding one. This perpetual self-transcendence is possible because life, the evolutionary process, is itself eternally transcended by the absolute reality upon which it perpetually and everlastingly draws. And the goal of this process is to manifest this absolute reality, this universal mind, more and more fully. Whether a complete manifestation is possible at all within time is a question into which we cannot enter now. Indeed, it is time that we crossed the threshold to the second part of this evening's lecture.

EVOLUTION: LOWER AND HIGHER

I have said that we are going to explore the higher evolution of humanity, but if there is a higher evolution, there must be or have been a lower evolution. How are we to distinguish between the two? Any evolving phenomenon, from an egg to an empire, can be studied in two ways: in terms of its past and in terms of its future, in terms of its origins and in terms of its destination, or, in more technical language, either genetically or teleologically. We ourselves are part and parcel of the evolutionary process, as we have already seen, so let's consider ourselves at our best. Sometimes, unfortunately, we human beings are very far from being at our best, but let's let ourselves off lightly and consider a self-conscious, aware human being, intelligent, sensitive, balanced, harmoniously developed, and responsible. We can try to understand this being in two ways: in terms of what they have developed out of, and in terms of what they can potentially develop into, and in fact what they are already developing into. The first of these constitutes the lower evolution and the second constitutes the higher evolution. The lower evolution is dealt with by science, especially the biological sciences, whereas the higher evolution is covered by psychology, the arts, and religion in the more spiritual sense of the term, and by what John Middleton Murry calls the metabiological sciences, those sciences that go beyond the ordinary biological framework.[65] This may sound a little complicated, so let us start thinking diagrammatically. I was going to ask you to close your eyes and imagine a right-angled triangle, but this might be rather difficult for some people to do, so I decided that instead I would get someone to draw a simple diagram on the blackboard. I hope this will make clear the nature of the difference between lower and higher evolution.

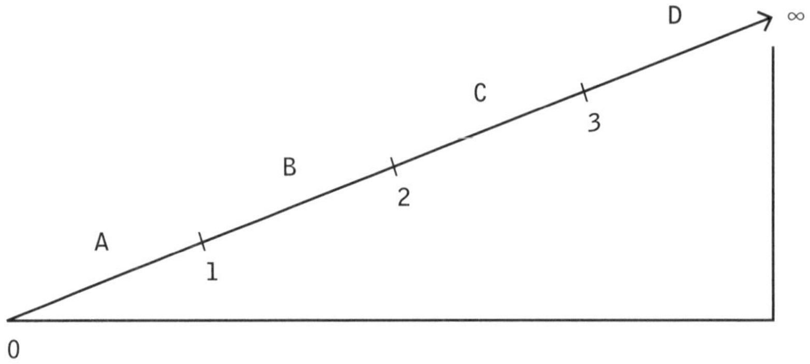

If we look at this triangle, we shall see that along the hypotenuse there are various numbers and letters. Point 2, right in the middle, represents our aware human being. The section of the hypotenuse from 0 to 2 represents the process of the lower evolution, the distance that we have come, and the section from 2 onwards represents the higher evolution, the distance that we have yet to traverse. Each of these two sections is in turn divided. Point 1 represents the point at which consciousness emerges, the point at which the animal becomes human. Animals, especially some of the higher animals, possess a rudimentary consciousness, but I am thinking here of consciousness in its distinctively human form. Point 3, at the middle of the section representing the higher evolution, is the point at which transcendental awareness, or awareness of absolute reality, emerges in a decisive manner, when it starts to be a permanent faculty or a directive principle of one's life. In traditional Buddhism this is called the point of no return because it is the point beyond which it is impossible for the individual to fall back.

With the points zero and infinity, we now have five distinct points. Zero obviously represents the starting point of the whole evolutionary process. In terms of physics this is the subatomic unit, and in terms of biology it is the amoeba. Point 1 is the point at which human consciousness emerges, and self-consciousness or awareness emerges at point 2. The majority of us are a bit below this point. In fact, some people are not much above point 1. One can't help feeling sometimes that a lot of people are not much more than animals. Not long ago I read an article about someone's claim (on the basis of scientific investigation) that all human beings facially resemble either pigs or birds. Apparently it is possible to look around at one's friends and immediately classify them as either pigs or birds. It's quite a thought, that we have so much of the animal nature still clinging about us. For the majority of people, humanity is something that is yet to be achieved. We usually refer to the human race as if every statistical individual were a fully-fledged human being, but this can't be taken for granted. The vast majority of people are still living very much at the animal level, preoccupied with purely animal needs and interests, and comparatively few succeed in rising to any extent above that. It is all very well to talk about leading a religious or a spiritual life as though we could all go straight off and do that, but the first thing most people need to do is to make sure they are leading a truly human life. We have to apply this to ourselves too. Are we yet really and truly and fully human? Have we really established ourselves on the human level? Do we really behave like human beings, or are we just animals whose marvellous brains have placed a bit of technology at their disposal? This is something we should ponder very seriously. Point 3 is the point at which transcendental awareness emerges, the awareness of reality that begins to carry us above the human, and infinity is of course the point of the arising of what in Buddhism we call Nirvāṇa or Enlightenment or Buddhahood, the state of a fully perfected or Enlightened human being.

These five points divide the hypotenuse representing the evolutionary process into four distinct stages. Stage A is the infra-human, the sub-human, i.e. the mineral, vegetable, and animal kingdoms, stage B is the human, both primitive and civilized, stage C we may describe as the ultra-human, and stage D is the supra-human or even the trans-human. In this way we cover the whole process of evolution, beginning with the amoeba, continuing through the unenlightened human being, and culminating in the Buddha, the one who is fully awake to and identifies with absolute reality. With the help of the conception of evolution in this extended sense, science and religion, the lower and the higher evolution, biology and metabiology are combined in a single vast sweep which comprehends the whole of life in all its manifestations, at every conceivable level. This is surely a most inspiring and even consoling prospect, because it enables us to understand ourselves better than ever before. It makes sense of human existence. We can begin to see where we stand. We can see that the human being occupies the middle point in the whole evolutionary process. We have come a long way and we have a long way still to go, but we can advance joyfully because the path is clear before our feet.

As illustrated by this diagram, the lower and the higher evolution are in a sense continuous, the higher growing out of the lower. At the same time there are radical differences between the two, the biggest difference being that the lower evolution proceeds collectively whereas the higher evolution is an individual matter, occurring one organism at a time, separately, by itself, alone. This is why the development of self-consciousness, awareness, mindfulness, upon which Buddhism places so much emphasis, is so supremely important. It is this consciousness of oneself as an individual in the true sense which constitutes the growing point of the higher evolution. Among vegetables, and among animals of the same species, members of the same species cannot outstrip one another in the evolutionary process. One individual may be bigger or stronger, but it is not essentially different from any other member of the same species. But a human being can become different in kind, can become a Buddha, an Enlightened or awakened one – not just the old human being reissued in a slightly improved edition, but an altogether new species. One could even speak in terms of a fresh biological or even metabiological mutation. What we call religion or spiritual life is, or should be, concerned with the production of this new kind of being, but unfortunately it often isn't. Only too often religions are concerned with other things – enlisting converts, or putting up great big buildings, or proving or demonstrating something. Any truly spiritual movement should not be wasting time and energy on inessentials, but should be concerned with producing what Buddhism calls the Enlightened being, the Buddha, and thus contributing to the process of the higher evolution.

BUDDHISM AND PSYCHOANALYSIS

A talk with this title was given at Caxton Hall, Westminster, under the auspices of the Buddhist Society (chaired by Christmas Humphreys) on 9 March 1966, but the content of this version makes it clear that it was given on a retreat. We haven't been able to find out when the retreat was given, but it was possibly one of the early ones held under the auspices of the FWBO.

Those of us who are students of language know that very often it is the simplest words that are the most ambiguous. Take, for instance, the title of our talk this morning. What is meant by Buddhism should have become clear in the last few days, at least in a general way, even for those who have had no previous connection with Buddhism, and psychoanalysis is almost a household word, so we will have a general idea of what is meant by it. But the title of the talk is 'Buddhism *and* Psychoanalysis'. What is the significance of this little but highly ambiguous word 'and'? Obviously some kind of comparison between Buddhism and psychoanalysis is intended, but why should one want to compare these two fields of knowledge? One might say that we make the effort to compare things only when their existence constitutes for us a problem. It is the desire to solve the problem that is the motive for the comparison.

From 1944 to 1964 I was in the East, mainly in India, and for the last fourteen years of my sojourn there I lived in the Indo-Tibetan borderlands, in Kalimpong. During my stay in the East I was occupied with the study of Eastern religions and philosophies, especially Buddhism, both in theory and in practice, and as my studies progressed and I became a little more experienced, I did a certain amount of teaching. I used to go down into the Indian plains at least once a year and engage in marathon preaching tours all over the length and breadth of that vast subcontinent. And as I travelled around, people would come to me with their problems. These problems were usually quite ordinary. Perhaps an irate father would say, 'My boy has stopped going to school. I'm sending him to you tomorrow morning. Please make him realize he must study.' He would want me to put the full force of my authority behind his demand that his son should study because that is the high road to a government job, which is the 'nirvana' of modern Indian life. Sometimes a husband would complain about his wife, or a wife would complain about her husband, or perhaps someone had got mixed up with two or three wives, and quite a lot of sorting out was required. Less often there were psychological problems, and rarest of all were spiritual problems. It was my custom to help as best I could, whatever the nature of the problem, and in this way I developed quite an insight into aspects of worldly life with which I had no direct personal connection. But during the whole period that I was in the East, I had very little contact with modern psychology. In the East one gets along without psychology quite well. Buddhism has its own system of psychology, and in the Buddhist countries they usually manage quite well with this, without any help from the various systems of modern psychology.

When I paid my first return visit to England at the beginning of August 1964, almost from the day of my arrival, just as in India, people came to me with problems of various kinds, but I started noticing a difference. Here, hardly anyone came to consult me about domestic problems, and neither did they ask questions about Buddhist philosophy. I would say that nine out of ten people came to ask my advice about their psychological problems. Usually they started off by telling the story of their life. Sometimes it was long and interesting, and sometimes it was long and not so interesting. Some people would go into great detail and others would just mention a few salient facts. I used to listen patiently, take it all in, and make a few mental notes. Gradually, as I listened to more and more people, two facts emerged. Well, they didn't just emerge; they clamoured for attention. The first thing that struck me was the large number of people who were mentally and emotionally disturbed, many more than in the East, where people seem much more relaxed, and much more emotionally and mentally balanced. And the second thing was how many of the people coming to me had been psychoanalysed. Whether it was Freudian analysis, Jungian analysis, or existentialist analysis, an extraordinarily large number of people seemed to have had analysis, or were still having it. One woman claimed the record, having been in analysis for seventeen years, two or three times a week;

she didn't seem noticeably better for it, but I'm sure that's not the fault of psychoanalysis. In India, psychoanalysis is available only in two or three of the big cities, so it plays an insignificant part in people's lives, but in the West it's clear that it plays a very important part indeed, and nobody who is concerned with the teaching of Buddhism or any other religious system can ignore its influence. So within months of my return to this country I started turning over in my mind the relation between Buddhism and psychoanalysis, and this morning I want to share with you some of my thoughts about it.

Obviously, it's a vast and complex subject which one can't fully explore, or even properly introduce, in an hour or so. In the first place, Buddhism comprises hundreds of different schools of thought, and they don't all speak with one voice. There's Theravāda Buddhism, the Mahāyāna, Zen, and Tibetan Buddhism, and there are many subdivisions representing different aspects of the total Buddhist tradition: metaphysical, psychological, ethical, and so on, a vast plethora of schools, teaching the same basic things but with many important differences of emphasis. Whereas Buddhism is 2,500 years old, psychoanalysis was started by Freud at the beginning of the twentieth century, so it's not even a hundred years old yet, but already there are quite a number of different versions. Within a century of the Buddha's passing away eighteen schools of Buddhism came into existence, and almost as many schools of psychoanalysis developed in Freud's own lifetime. There's Jung and his analytical psychology, and Adler and his individual psychology. There are orthodox Freudians and various kinds of neo-Freudians and revisionist Freudians. We've also got the humanistic type of psychoanalysis and the existentialist type of psychoanalysis, and there are the schools of Harry Stack Sullivan, Erich Fromm, and Karen Horney. Obviously, with so many schools of Buddhism and so many types of psychoanalysis, I can't make a detailed comparison between the two systems, so I propose to attempt to compare basic Buddhism with basic psychoanalysis. By basic Buddhism I mean the body of teachings common to all the different schools, and by basic psychoanalysis I mean principles common to the orthodox Freudians, Jungians, neo-Freudians, and so on. I hope that those who are more interested in Buddhism may be stimulated to study a little psychoanalysis and those who are more interested in psychoanalysis may be stimulated to go a little more deeply into Buddhism.

Buddhism and psychoanalysis are both human-centred, not God-centred. Neither is concerned with any form of supreme being, except empirically as a psychic image. For this reason it is sometimes doubted whether Buddhism is a religion at all. Books about comparative religion written by Christian ministers or missionaries sometimes say that Buddhism is a very decent, ethical system, but it isn't really a religion, and that's true, if you define religion as belief in and worship of a supreme being. But if you define religion as a way of life that takes into account the existence of something transcending the senses and the mind, some ultimate spiritual reality behind the universe, filling the universe, Buddhism is a religion in this broader sense. Nowadays, people are beginning to recognize that there are two major kinds of religion in the world: the theistic and the non-theistic. All those systems that posit the existence of a personal God, a supreme being, a creator, are theistic – the Semitic religions, plus some popular forms of Hinduism. But there are a number of important religions that get along quite well without the concept of a personal God, including the more philosophical forms of Hinduism, like the Vedānta, as well as the religions of China (Daoism and Confucianism), Shinto, the indigenous religion of Japan, and Buddhism.

In this country we've been brought up to think that religion is necessarily theistic, and that the practice of religion means going to church on Sundays, but in modern times, even within Christianity, some extraordinary developments have been taking place. People have been talking about a non-theistic Christianity centred upon Christ rather than God. This outlook is associated with the name of the Bishop of Woolwich, who seems to believe that the traditional Christian concept of God is finished and must be got rid of, to be replaced with the idea of the 'ground of being', which has an oriental, even Buddhistic ring.[66] In fact, I can't help thinking that the Bishop of Woolwich, whether he knows it or not, is moving in the direction of Buddhism.

No doubt, being a modern man, he has been influenced to some extent by psychoanalysis. Freud has tried to show that the traditional conception of God is as a father figure. When we're born, we're completely helpless. We don't remember this stage, so we tend to overlook it, but for several years the human infant is in a condition of complete dependency. The only thing it can do to help itself is cry at the top of its lungs. If it's cold, or hungry, or afraid, it cries. If it feels angry, it cries very loudly indeed.

When it gets into difficulties, or when it wants something, it cries. The infant becomes a child, and then a man or woman, and as they grow up, they begin to encounter all sorts of difficulties in living and dealing with other people. Sometimes they cope, but only too often something goes wrong and they don't know what to do. Very often what happens then, according to Freud, is that the adult, in desperation, unconsciously regresses to an infantile attitude. Just as when you are a child, you have an omnipotent mother or father who will come running and do anything you want if only you let out a loud enough yell, when an adult gets into difficulty, they imagine an all-powerful figure, someone who can do for them what they can't do themselves. Just as the infant lets out its wail, the adult imagines a personal God, an omnipotent being, and cries out in distress. This is often what prayer is – a cry for help.

If we live in the city, it doesn't really matter to us whether it rains or not, though rain may be a nuisance if we want to go for a walk, but for some, life utterly depends upon that rainfall. You may have ploughed your land, planted your seeds, and everything may be coming up nicely, but if there is no rain – only the sun mercilessly shining all day, and the crop gradually drying up and withering away – all is lost. Before irrigation and water storage were thought of, primitive humans could do nothing except pray for rain. It's the same in some places today. About twenty years ago I was staying in a village in Nepal, and one day I saw a procession going around the bazaar, led by the governor of the locality. The magistrates, the police, a few soldiers, the merchants, and all the local population, carrying images of gods and goddesses, were shouting, '*Mahādeva pani dot, Mahādeva pani dot*,' which means 'Oh great God, give me rain.' And I suspect that if you went into the depths of the English countryside in summer, in some village churches you might hear the parson praying for rain.

You may smile at this, thinking that it's rather a caricature and that people don't regress in this way any longer, but has modern civilization entirely wiped out this attitude? If we reflect, we realize that it is still a very human tendency to pray for the removal of one's difficulties. During the war, whenever things were a bit sticky, a day of national prayer would be ordered and everyone would pray to God for victory. This was an official policy, proclaimed by government edict, but it was a pure and simple regression to an infantile attitude. Some of the Germans were praying too, which exposes the absurdity of the whole procedure.

According to psychoanalysis, this is an example of mass regression to an infantile attitude and to be discouraged, but such regressions are not uncommon, not only in time of war but at any time. If we think about our own lives, sometimes we are up against a problem we can't resolve. We feel completely helpless, but we want to do something. In fact, something must be done. What do we do? Most people, regardless of their religious beliefs, pray. Sometimes they don't even know to whom they are praying or what they are asking for, but their instinct is to regress to this infantile attitude. Even the atheist does it, though this isn't a proof of the existence of God, however much well-meaning theists want it to be. It only shows that our tendency to regress to an infantile attitude of dependence is so strong that even the convinced atheist can't help himself sometimes.

It reminds me of a little story told by the great modern Indian teacher Ramakrishna about a parrot that had been taught to recite the name of God. In India people are fond of teaching birds to talk. Dhardo Rimpoche, my old friend in Kalimpong, had a collection of birds and cats and dogs, and he had taught one of his birds, a mynah, to recite *oṃ maṇi padme hūṃ*. It lived in a cage on the veranda and as you went up the stairs to see the Rimpoche it would sing out *oṃ maṇi padme hūṃ* and you would look around thinking you had heard a human voice. If the Rimpoche wanted to show a visitor the bird's tricks he would give it a piece of fruit and say, 'Mynah, *oṃ maṇi padme hūṃ*' and at once the mynah would say it. In England I'm afraid people often teach parrots to say swear words, but in the East they teach talking birds to say holy words. Ramakrishna said that if you teach a bird to recite the name of God, he will do it all day long, but if the cat suddenly springs up and catches the bird by the neck, he will forget all about the name of God and let out his natural squawk. In the same way, when you are not in difficulties, you may be a secularist, an atheist, or even a Buddhist, but when you get into difficulties, when you are really seized by the throat, the tendency is to put all your philosophy aside, regress to the infantile attitude and say, 'Oh God, please help me.' This doesn't prove that there is a God; it only goes to show how easily we revert to our original nature, not in the Zen sense but in the evolutionary sense.

According to psychoanalysis the idea of God is a father figure, and we see the same thing in early Buddhist teaching. The Buddha made it clear that belief in a personal God (a belief which was held by some of his contemporaries) tends to make us dependent and stultify our ethical and spiritual life, because if you think that God will save you or help you, this prevents you from getting on with your spiritual evolution by your own efforts.[67] The Buddha said, 'Don't rely on anyone outside yourself.'[68] Be independent, be responsible, realize that your spiritual and ethical development depends upon your own efforts. However great the difficulties that arise, don't think that any Father in heaven is going to sort it out for you. This applies not only to the individual but on a national, even on a global, scale. We have got ourselves into a mess, with our hydrogen bomb and all the rest of it, but it is no use thinking that if we all go to church and pray, we will be saved from the consequences of our own folly. Buddhism and psychoanalysis both say, 'You've got yourself into this mess, and you've got to get yourself out of it.' If you think that God will intervene, you're only postponing the day of the solution of the problems by which you are confronted.

The figure of God, or Brahmā as he is called, appears from time to time in the Buddhist scriptures but I am sorry to say that he often appears as a comic and childish figure, because according to the Buddha's teaching belief in God is a childish attitude. The *Dīgha Nikāya* tells the story of a monk called Kevaddha who had a problem – a spiritual problem, rather than a psychological one. I won't go into what it was, but he naturally wanted to find an answer. He couldn't find it on earth, he couldn't get the answer from his teachers, so he ascended into the various heavens and asked the gods and goddesses, and the angels and archangels, but he still couldn't get an answer. They kept referring him to a higher authority, and eventually he found himself in the highest heaven of all and in the presence of Brahmā. Thinking, 'Now I've come to the right person at last,' he put the question, and Brahmā replied, 'I am the great God. I have made everything, I am omnipotent, I know everything, I can do everything.' The monk said, 'Excuse me, I haven't asked about that. I want the answer to this problem.' Again God said in a loud voice, 'I am the great God, I am all-powerful, I know everything, I can do everything.' And again the monk patiently and politely said, 'I am not interested in all that. I just want the answer to my problem.' So eventually God said, 'Come here,' and he pulled him by the sleeve and took him aside. He said, 'I didn't want to say anything in front of all these minor gods, but I don't know the answer to your problem. But I think I know someone who might know. There is a man called Gautama the Buddha who is said to be Enlightened. You had better go back to earth and ask him.' So Kevaddha descended through all the heavens, found the Buddha, put his question, and the Buddha was able to resolve it.[69] The fact that Brahmā referred Kevaddha back to the Buddha really means that our questions as human beings must be answered by ourselves. The Buddha was an Enlightened man, not a god or an incarnation or a prophet. It is significant, incidentally, that Kevaddha's question was a metaphysical question about the nature of consciousness.

So Buddhism and psychoanalysis are both humanistic, and they are both concerned with human beings not just theoretically but also practically. Buddhism is not just a system of metaphysics, however wonderful, but a way of life, and in the same way psychoanalysis is not just a system of descriptive psychology giving a catalogue of mental states and functions, but also a therapy. I think we may correctly describe Buddhism as a therapy too. It is significant that in the scriptures the Buddha is called the great physician, whereas in the Bible Christ is often called the good shepherd.[70] To compare the founder of a religion with a physician is implicitly to compare his followers to the sick, and to compare him with a shepherd is to compare the followers with sheep. If you go to an analysis, the analyst doesn't do it all for you; you've got to cooperate intelligently. But sheep simply allow themselves to be led.

Not only is the Buddha called the great physician, but traditionally a connection is made between medicine and one of his best-known teachings. The four noble truths are often regarded as summarizing the whole of Buddhism. The first noble truth is that there is suffering in this world, both mental and physical. The second noble truth is the cause of suffering, which is basically our wrong mental attitude, especially our thirst or craving. The third noble truth is the cessation of suffering, which comes about through the cessation of craving, and is ultimately identical with a state of supreme bliss or Nirvāṇa. And the fourth noble truth is the way leading to the cessation of suffering – that is, the Noble Eightfold Path. According to scholars these four noble truths are based on an ancient pre-Buddhist medical formula: the disease, the cause of the disease, the cure, and the treatment leading to the cure.[71] This resemblance is no accident, because to discover the causes of suffering or of disease one has to go very deep. Both Buddhism and psychoanalysis are concerned with the human being at a very deep level because the sources of suffering, the sources of disease, are found not on the surface but in the depths.

So both Buddhism and psychoanalysis are concerned not only with the conscious mind, the surface mind, but with the unconscious. These conceptions are found in traditional Buddhism; in Theravāda Buddhism, for instance, you get the *viññāṇa-sota*, the stream of unconscious mental activity, and the Yogācāra school has the concept of the *ālaya-vijñāna* or store consciousness, in which impressions are stored up and of whose contents we are usually unconscious.[72] Both Buddhism and psychoanalysis are aware that the mind has depths, that beneath the conscious there is the subconscious, even the unconscious, and both regard the mind as a process, not a thing. They don't see it as a *tabula rasa*, a blank slate, as Locke thought, but conceive of it dynamically as a force, an energy.[73] Psychoanalysis speaks in terms of libido, which means vital impulse or energy, especially sexual energy, and Buddhism speaks of human beings as being dominated and controlled, driven even, by *taṇhā* or *tṛṣṇā*, which literally means thirst and refers to craving. In Buddhism there are three kinds of thirst or craving: that for sensuous experiences through the five physical senses, that for continued individual existence, and that for annihilation.[74] Buddhism has always recognized that there is in some people a craving for death, corresponding to Freud's death wish, and in the Buddhist conception of craving for continued existence and also craving for annihilation, we can see a correspondence with what Fromm calls biophilia or love of life and necrophilia or love of death.[75] It is also significant that the Buddha seems to have regarded many of the religious teachings of his time as rationalizations of craving, either for continued personal existence or for annihilation.[76] Traditionally in Buddhism, any form of belief in a supreme being with its corollary of personal immortality after death is regarded as a rationalization of our craving for continued existence.

Psychoanalysis also speaks in terms of the id, a term coined by Freud to refer to the impersonal mass of interacting energies or forces constituting the unconscious. With this we come to the heart of the therapeutic process. Freud says, 'Where there was id there shall be Ego' – ego with a capital E, not in the ordinary undesirable sense. Ego represents the conscious personality, the conscious individuality, and psychoanalysis is essentially concerned with the bringing of the unconscious into consciousness, with the transformation of the incoherent mass of the id into the comparatively organized patterned harmony of the Ego. Psychoanalysis effects this transformation by means of various techniques of free association. Buddhism has the same preoccupation. It wants to replace thirst or craving by Nirvāṇa. In the language of the Mahāyāna, it wants to transform the passions into Enlightenment, to transmute the five poisons into the five wisdoms. It effects this transformation by means of mindfulness, concentration, and meditation, and under these three headings there are various practices. We see therefore that both Buddhism and psychoanalysis emphasize the importance of self-knowledge in the sense of self-understanding: not objective rational knowledge, not knowledge of oneself as an object, because this would be merely descriptive psychology and would have no therapeutic value, but a living experience in awareness of one's own being.

So are Buddhism and psychoanalysis practically the same thing? This brings us back to people coming to me with their problems. Some people have come to me after analysis and said that according to their analyst they are now cured, but they still feel terrible: 'I feel that life is completely empty. I feel I've got nothing to live for. I've got no meaning and no purpose.' Here we come to the crux of the matter, and begin to become aware of the limitations of psychoanalysis. We can see these more clearly if we try to reverse the situation. Just imagine a Buddhist going to an analyst and saying, 'I've got a problem. According to Buddhism, I'm Enlightened. I've gained Nirvāṇa, I've got full wisdom and compassion, I'm a real-life bodhisattva. But life is so empty. I've nothing to live for.' The mere idea is absurd.

The analyst might not let us get away with this so easily. They might say that if anyone says after analysis that they're not happy, they're not really cured. Maybe they don't want to adjust. Maybe further analysis is required. To my mind, this indicates a weakness in psychoanalysis in many of its forms – the tendency to think of the return to normality in terms of adjustment to existing conditions. If you're disturbed or neurotic or unbalanced, many psychoanalysts will give you a few sessions and regard you as being cured if you can go back to your job happily, return to normality, carry on within the existing set-up. Such psychoanalysis tends to perpetuate the status quo. It helps you to adjust to the existing order of things, regardless of whether that order is good, bad, or indifferent. It may be that you can't carry on with your work, settle down, get married, have children, all the rest of it, because you are neurotic, but although in many cases when the neurosis is removed the person readjusts quite happily, sometimes they refuse to adjust, as if they are rebelling, and this kind of neurosis can be quite healthy. If you are in this situation, the fault may lie not with you, but with the conditions in which you live, including yourself as you are at present. It is beginning to be recognized by some psychoanalysts that many examples of so-called neurosis are healthy symptoms of rebellion against a social order that is itself fundamentally unhealthy. This goes to show that psychoanalysis will have to deepen its understanding of human beings and realize that we have many potentialities that can't be satisfied by the existing set-up. The existing set-up needs to be changed so that a healthy person can live in a healthy environment, and to see this, psychoanalysis could use the help of a non-theistic religion like Buddhism. There are many similarities between the two, and there is no reason why they should not cooperate where they can, each benefiting the other and both contributing to the advancement of the human race and the greater happiness of humanity in all respects.

BUDDHISM AND THE LANGUAGE OF MYTH

A talk with this title was given at the Buddhist Society in Eccleston Square, Pimlico, on 13 March 1966, but the content of this version makes it clear that it was given on a retreat. We haven't been able to find out when the retreat was given, but it was possibly one of the early ones held under the auspices of the FWBO.

This morning I spoke about Buddhism and psychoanalysis, and this evening our subject is Buddhism and the language of myth. I have a definite reason for selecting this topic, and I'll illustrate it by telling you the parable of the blind men and the elephant. Apparently in ancient India in the days of the Buddha there was a certain king who, to create a little amusement for himself, had an elephant brought into the palace courtyard. Then he sent his minister out into the streets of the city to collect about a dozen blind men, and they were led to the elephant and asked to feel it and describe it. One caught hold of the ear and said the elephant was like a great winnowing basket. Another caught hold of the trunk and said the elephant was like a snake. Another caught hold of the tail and said the elephant was like a broom. Another caught hold of a tusk and said the elephant was like a ploughshare. Another stood underneath the elephant and caught hold of the belly, and said the elephant was like a great pot. Another caught hold of a leg and said the elephant was like a pillar supporting a house. In this way they gave various contradictory descriptions of the elephant. None of them believed any of the others, and they started fighting and quarrelling. The king was highly amused by this incident, which apparently created a pleasant diversion for him.[77]

This little story illustrates the dangers of a one-sided approach to the truth. The truth is total, multidimensional, multifaceted, but we tend to take one dimension, one facet, and call it the truth, not realizing that there are many other aspects, dimensions, and facets. One could also use the story to illustrate the history of the study of Buddhism in the West. Like the elephant, Buddhism has many aspects, dimensions, and facets, and like the blind men examining the elephant, scholars have different impressions of Buddhism. One says that it is humanitarianism, another that it is mysticism, another that it is atheism, another that it is a form of oriental philosophy. One scholar says that one form of Buddhism is rationalism tinged with mysticism, and another is mysticism tinged with rationalism.[78] In this way they all give their different accounts of Buddhism, all one-sided, all containing some element of the truth, but none true as a generalization.

But there's a difference between the blind men in the story and the scholars who describe Buddhism. In the parable the blind men start quarrelling, but with regard to the study of Buddhism, each scholar, having examined one aspect of it, goes away and writes a book about it. In this way you get very many one-sided presentations of Buddhism. If we look at some of the books written even forty or fifty years ago by Western scholars, we can only be astonished, because within this short period our knowledge of Buddhism has grown so much, meagre though it still is, that those earlier presentations are very outdated. If you read Waddell, you can't help laughing at some of his descriptions of Buddhism, as when he says that its philosophy is sophistic nihilism, that the Tibetans worship fiendesses, and so on.[79]

Many of these one-sided presentations of Buddhism are still widely current, and this is perhaps not surprising in view of the fact that Buddhism is such a vast and complex system, or perhaps we should say organism. It has so many different aspects, levels, dimensions, applications, and ramifications that it's like one of those old gothic cathedrals. It's not surprising that we can't grasp it in its totality all at once, or immediately. But we don't have to acquiesce in any of these one-sided presentations. As the years go by, more and more reliable, authentic material on Buddhism is becoming available in Western languages. For example, Dr Conze, in a monumental labour of love, has recently translated the whole of the Perfection of Wisdom corpus of scriptures. Nearly every morning we've been reciting the *Heart Sūtra*, the heart of the Perfection of Wisdom, and although this *sūtra* occupies only one page, it gives the essence of the Perfection of Wisdom. But there are more than thirty *sūtras* or discourses of the Buddha dealing with the Perfection of Wisdom, some of them several volumes long. At the other extreme, there's the Perfection of Wisdom in a single letter. It's all said to be concentrated in one letter, the letter A; how that comes to be, we are not going to examine just at present. But thanks to the labours of Dr Conze, now there's no excuse for not having a good idea of what is meant in Mahāyāna Buddhism by the Perfection of Wisdom. Even more recently, Dr David Snellgrove has edited and translated the *Hevajra Tantra*, the first Buddhist tantra to be translated in its entirety into any European language, so far as I know.[80] Of course, if you go through it by yourself you won't make head or tail of it. Even Dr Conze, when he came to review the work, confessed that he wasn't able to make much sense of it.[81] It is not sufficient just to read a text like the *Hevajra Tantra*; one has to study it with a teacher and practise according to the teacher's instructions. But my point is that we now have more and more opportunities of correcting and enlarging our picture of Buddhism. It's now possible to begin to see it as a whole, and there's less excuse than ever for relying upon one-sided and thus misleading interpretations of the Buddha's teaching.

One of the one-sided presentations that is still widely current is that Buddhism is rationalistic (not rational, but rationalistic). This presentation says that Buddhism appeals only, or at least primarily, to reason. It says that Buddhism is a philosophy rather than a religion. About forty years ago Dr George Grimm, a great German Buddhist scholar, wrote a thick book entitled *The Doctrine of the Buddha, the Religion of Reason*, but in the recent new edition the title has been changed to *The Doctrine of the Buddha, the Religion of Reason and Meditation* – rather a significant change, even though meditation comes as an afterthought.[82] Forty years ago one could publish a book called *Buddhism, the Religion of Reason*, but nowadays one has at least to genuflect in the direction of meditation.

This rationalistic presentation of Buddhism is also beginning to be found in the East. During my time in India, I was often told by Eastern Buddhists that Buddhism is based on pure reason, or sometimes that it is scientific. It is a popular ploy nowadays to say that Buddhism anticipates modern science. Some Eastern Buddhists have written books to demonstrate that all modern scientific inventions, including things like nuclear weapons, are anticipated by the Buddha, and can be found in the Abhidharma. Sometimes I have even been told that modern science proves Buddhism, or that Buddhism is pure science. But I'm afraid that all this is very naive. It's not that there are no non-rational elements in Buddhism in the Theravādin countries. There are plenty, fortunately, otherwise Buddhism would have died in those countries long ago. To put the matter a little paradoxically, it's better to have a bit of superstition than too much rationalism. We could perhaps compare rationalism to a garden made entirely of rock and gravel. It may look neat and clean, it may be beautiful, or at least hygienic, but it will be sterile; nothing will grow. But superstition is like a garden full of weeds. Even though the weeds are undesirable, they at least show that the soil is fertile. The rationalistic type of presentation is beautiful but sterile, a stone garden, whereas a more superstitious presentation, though much needs to be weeded out, proves the fertility of the soil.

I sometimes found that monks in the East were rather ashamed of the non-rational elements in popular Buddhism. When I first went to Ceylon at the end of 1944, I visited a temple not far from Colombo, and immediately to the left of the courtyard was a temple with images of all sorts of Hindu gods and goddesses: Shiva, Ganesh, Lakshmi, and all the rest.[83] I thought, 'That's strange. Perhaps I've made a mistake. Maybe I haven't come to a Buddhist temple at all.' A Buddhist monk came up, so I asked him, 'What are all these gods and goddesses doing here?' He said, 'Oh, they're just for the local people to worship.' This attitude I felt at the time, and still feel, was potentially dangerous. If you've got a rationalistic monastic order and a superstitious laity, a schizophrenia of the Buddhist community develops. It's not unlike the situation in Britain in the eighteenth century. Many of the clergy, even though they continued to administer the sacraments and preach, were at heart sceptics and rationalists, but their congregations continued to believe firmly in Christianity, so the two were alienated from each other, and a split in the religious community occurred. In Ceylon, when official Buddhism didn't allow the non-rational elements to find expression within the field of Buddhism, but was kept all clean and bleak and rational, those non-rational elements found expression outside Buddhism. A lengthy correspondence in one of the Sinhalese Buddhist magazines on the subject of the *kōvil*, as the Hindu temples in Ceylon are called, suggested that more Hindu temples were being built in Ceylon than Buddhist temples, even though the population of Ceylon is predominately Buddhist. The reason was that lay Buddhists were building temples to the Hindu gods, because they corresponded to those aspects of the Sinhalese psyche that official, rational Sinhalese Buddhism was unable to cope with and did not recognize. I think this is a very significant and interesting situation, which if the Sinhalese Buddhists are not careful may mark the beginning of the end of Buddhism in Ceylon.

We mustn't go to the other extreme and deny that there is a rational element in Buddhism. Its rational element is very strong; we may go so far as to say that Buddhism is the most rational of all the great religions. But it is by no means *purely* rational. After all, Buddhism is essentially trying to communicate a mystery, the mystery of the Buddha's Enlightenment, to unenlightened human beings, in such a way we can participate in it to the measure of our capacity. When Buddhism tries to communicate this mystery, it's trying to communicate it not just to a part of us, but to us in our totality, in all our aspects, all our dimensions, and as we know, a human being is not a simple being, but a composite. To put it simply, we consist of three things: head, heart, and hand. Or, to put it another way, we consist of conscious surface and unconscious depths. To communicate fully the mystery of the Buddha's Enlightenment, Buddhism has to speak to all of these as best it can, otherwise there's no real contact, no full communication. It communicates with the head, with the conscious mind, by speaking the language of reason and knowledge, making use of concepts, reasoning, metaphysics, philosophy, epistemology, and psychology. But it communicates with the heart, with the unconscious mind, by speaking another, equally valid, powerful, and important language, the language of myth, and it speaks this language with the help of symbol, legend, ritual, music, and poetry.

All religions speak this language, and they sometimes speak it very powerfully indeed. Christianity has some very impressive myths and symbols: the fall of man, the virgin birth, the crucifixion, the resurrection. These myths and symbols strongly appeal to the emotions, the unconscious mind, the heart, but unfortunately in official Christianity they are usually interpreted literally. Take the myth of the virgin birth. According to official Christianity this means that the mother of Christ was a virgin at the time of conception, and remained a virgin. It is regarded as historical fact that if you could have been present at that time, and if you could have subjected the Virgin Mary to a medical examination, you would have found that she was a virgin. This is crudely literal. If one looks a little deeper, one finds that virgin motherhood is a universal symbol found not only in Christianity, but in other religions, including the pagan religions of Greece and Rome and Egypt. So what does this myth of the virgin birth really mean? Virgin means that which is pure or one who is pure, and virginity represents not just the state of sexual purity, but purity in the complete sense. So the virgin birth means that the Christ consciousness, the higher consciousness, can come into existence only in the mind that is pure, that is virgin. This is the real meaning of the myth, but official Christianity interprets it in this literal, historical way and therefore misses its significance. Myth is hardened into dogma, and belief in this dogma is regarded as essential to salvation. The spiritual meaning is not entirely lost, but it is usually very much obscured.

In Buddhism the position is rather different. Christianity spoke the language of myth from the beginning. From the beginning its appeal was more to the heart, more to the unconscious mind. Only later did it learn to speak the language of reason and logic, and even then only rather imperfectly. But the initial appeal of Buddhism was to reason, to the intelligence, and only afterwards, especially when it spread among the masses, did it start speaking to the emotions and the unconscious mind. This development is fully in accordance with the spiritual path in Buddhism. As I explained in the eight lectures we had on the Buddha's Noble Eightfold Path, the path of the higher evolution, the spiritual path, is divided into two great stages: the *darśana-mārga* or the path of vision, and the *bhāvanā-mārga* or the path of transformation.[84] The path of vision represents the initial spiritual experience or insight, and the heights of one's being, and the path of transformation, represents the gradual transformation of one's whole being in all its aspects in accordance with that original vision. The first, the path of vision, is also the path of the Stream Entrant, and the second is the path of the once-returner, the non-returner, and the *arhant*. The path of vision represents the realization of truth by the conscious mind, and the path of transformation represents the penetration of that truth into the depths of the unconscious. The path of transformation is much more difficult, because the unconscious mind is much more difficult to transform than the conscious mind. It takes much longer, and that's why the path of transformation is subdivided into three stages, of once-returner, the non-returner, and *arhant*, whereas the path of vision consists of only one stage, the stage of the Stream Entrant.

We get the same sequence in the canonical literature of Buddhism. The earlier texts, especially those in the Pāli canon, appeal more to the conscious mind, speaking the language of abstract thought, concepts, and reason, but the later scriptures, those which are later literary records, appeal to the unconscious mind, speak the language of image, myth, and legend, although there are exceptions – the Pāli scriptures certainly have what we would regard as mythical elements, and many of the Perfection of Wisdom *sūtras* are quite late but continue to address the reason. The history of Western Buddhism has followed a similar course. In the West Buddhism was first of all grasped intellectually, and that's more or less our current position, but now we have to start assimilating it emotionally. We've listened to the language of logic long enough; now we have to start listening to the language of myth.

Symbol, myth, legend, and ritual are all parts of the same language. One could also add poetry and parable. I may speak about the psychology of ritual later on in the retreat, so I'm not going to say anything about that for the moment.[85] I'm going to concentrate on myth and legend. These two terms are often used synonymously and loosely. Most people think that they are both stories of ancient gods and heroes, like you find in Homer. Strictly speaking, however, a myth usually explains the origin of a certain object or custom. For example, in Greek mythology Prometheus is supposed to have stolen fire from heaven. This is a myth to explain the origin of fire. Primitive man didn't have fire, except by accident, so how did he learn how to make it? Well, this myth explains that a kind god, a titan called Prometheus, stole it from heaven, because fire is in the sky in the form of the sun and the stars, and brought it down to earth. A legend, by contrast, is a pseudo-history; it speaks about kings and battles and so on, though it doesn't correspond to anything we can call historical fact. Until only a few hundred years ago there was a legend in this country that Brutus had founded a kingdom here, and that Britain was named after him, but that is a legend, a pseudo-history, like King Arthur and his knights. I hope I am not disillusioning anybody.

But a myth is not history at all. Myth represents psychological experiences and spiritual truths, which may be couched in terms of historical events, but are not to be taken literally. If we look at the fall of man as a myth, we are not to think that so many thousand years ago there was a man called Adam who lived in a garden called Eden which you could find on the map if you looked hard enough, and that this Adam ate an apple which he had been commanded not to eat, and because he was disobedient he fell. It's very difficult for us to grasp this because there has been such a revolution in our ideas, but as recently as a hundred years ago, Adam eating the apple was considered in Christian countries to be a historical fact which no one seriously questioned. Not many years ago I met a farmer in Devonshire who was astounded when I told him that Adam was not a historical person, and refused to believe it, saying, 'It's all there in the good book.' It says in the margin of some Bibles that the fall of Adam happened in 4004 BC, and theologians used to work out the exact day of the week and the hour of day on which he ate the apple, so that it was plain it was all historical fact. But the myth of the fall of Adam has nothing to do with anything that happened in time. It refers to something that takes place every time we follow the dictates of our lower nature. It might have happened five minutes ago, or five seconds ago, or it might be happening at this very minute. The myth of the fall of man doesn't convey a mere historical fact, but embodies an eternally valid spiritual and psychological truth about human nature, a truth about every man and every woman.

This evening I'm going to take some examples from the life of the Buddha to show Buddhism's non-conceptual, mythical approach to the heart, to the unconscious depths. The Buddha lived some 2,500 years ago, but we know quite a lot about him. There are a number of biographies in existence, both canonical (that is, part of the Buddhist scriptures) and semi-canonical, apocryphal. For instance, in the Pāli canon there are long sections of the Vinaya Piṭaka, *The Book of the Discipline*, which are biographical, recreating various important episodes in the career of the Buddha.[86] Then, in what is called Buddhist Hybrid Sanskrit, or Mixed Sanskrit, there is the *Mahāvastu*, the 'great story'. Other works include the *Lalitavistara*, literally the 'extended sports', the *Abhiniṣkramaṇa Sūtra*, the discourse on the Going Forth of the Buddha, the *Mahāparinirvāṇa Sūtra*, a detailed account of the last weeks of the Buddha's life, and the *Buddhacarita*, a beautiful epic poem in classical Sanskrit written by Aśvaghoṣa in the Indian Middle Ages.[87] All these accounts of the life of the Buddha contain not only indubitably historical facts but also a lot of legendary material and mythical elements.

Leaving aside the legends, let's take up the myths, which are of two kinds. The first are those that represent the Buddha exercising supernormal powers. Some episodes in the scriptures show that the Buddha is telepathic – that is, he knows what is going on in somebody's mind.[88] It used to be fashionable to dismiss telepathy as an old wives' tale, but it is now being demonstrated to be empirically verifiable. I would say that the passages in the Buddhist scriptures that represent the Buddha exercising supernormal powers such as telepathy are not myths proper, but historical facts which are now regarded as myths owing to the limitations of the modern scientific approach. But in the biographies there are elements that are myths in the true sense, representations of psychological experiences and spiritual truths. These elements are a source of some embarrassment to modern Western scholars, some of whom just cut them out when they write about the Buddha, saying, 'Oh, it's all a lot of nonsense.' They are even a source of embarrassment to some rationalizing Eastern Buddhists, who would apparently be happier without them.

[*At this point in the lecture, four mythical incidents from the life of the Buddha were described: the victory over Māra, calling the earth goddess to witness, Brahmā's request, and the appearance of the serpent king Mucalinda. This part of the lecture was repeated in 'Archetypal Symbolism in the Life of the Buddha', which is where it will be found in this volume.* *See pp. 186ff.*]

These four mythical incidents are just a few examples chosen almost at random, and it's obvious from the way some of them seem to have gripped your attention that the language of myth still speaks very effectively to the human heart and to the unconscious. It is by speaking the language of myth that Buddhism gets through to the unconscious depths. You surely know from your own experience that when something is expounded logically and rationally you experience it in a certain way, but when you listen to a myth or a story you feel it in quite a different way. There's a different atmosphere, and the reason is that the logical exposition reaches the head, but the myth and the story, the parable and the poem, reach the heart, and even the unconscious depths of the psyche. This is not only how but why Buddhism speaks the language of myth, and it does so on a grand scale in Mahāyāna *sūtras* like the *Saddharma Puṇḍarīka Sūtra*, the *Sukhāvatī-vyūha Sūtra*, the *Gaṇḍavyūha*, and the *Avataṃsaka*.

It is the language of myth that we must now learn to understand, so that we can not only grasp Buddhism intellectually but also assimilate it emotionally. So far in the West our approach to Buddhism has been one-sidedly intellectual, and it's time we tried to redress the balance. The Buddha gained Enlightenment sitting beneath the bodhi tree, and the tree is one of the most important Buddhist symbols. I've not got time to go into its significance, but one thing we can note about it is that the roots of a tree go down very, very deep. As high and wide as the branches spread, so deep and wide do the roots have to go. If the tree has a massive trunk and enormous branches and thousands of twigs but only tiny roots, it is very easily blown over. The roots must be deep and strong, just as the branches are lofty and large. And it's just the same with us. The great tree which is Buddhism must spread wide and high within our conscious mind, but its roots must go deep down into our unconscious. Only then will the tree of the Dharma be firmly established in our lives, and in this way perhaps we also may speak on behalf of Buddhism the language of myth.

BUDDHISM AND THE NEW REFORMATION

Hampstead Buddhist Vihara, 12 June 1966

More than a year ago, I gave a talk on 'Buddhism and the Bishop of Woolwich', not here in the vihara, but not far away, at Burgh House in Hampstead. On that occasion, for some reason – perhaps the weather wasn't propitious – we had fewer people than we usually get for talks of this sort, but that didn't matter much because the talk was tape-recorded, and it has been played many times not only here at the vihara but elsewhere and has become quite well known. In fact, it got as far as the episcopal ears of the Bishop of Woolwich himself, and out of this there have come some interesting developments, not the least of which is that some months ago the bishop and I had a personal meeting. I believe that isn't the end of the story. He is just back from holiday and I am on the point of going away for a little rest, but it seems we shall be meeting again. But meanwhile I thought it might be a good idea to have a follow-up to that talk, which is why today we have for our subject 'Buddhism and the New Reformation'.

The religion which we in the West know as Buddhism, usually referred to in the East as Dharma or Dhamma or *chös*, and the religion known as Christianity are radically different in many ways, and I would be the last person to equate them. At the same time, we must recognize that both these great systems are what we popularly call 'religions' – not a word which is much in favour at present but we don't have any other. Some time ago in India, I started saying 'normative', rather than 'religious', which I thought rather good, but it didn't catch on. Today, both Buddhism and Christianity find themselves surrounded by, almost overwhelmed by, problems of various kinds. Christianity, which is if anything the more overwhelmed of the two, is trying to face up to some of those problems, and so is Buddhism, so we can learn from each other. In the talk on Buddhism and the Bishop of Woolwich, I was more concerned with what the bishop could perhaps learn from us. I know from my meeting with him that he is an open-minded man and he expressed a wish to make a proper study of Buddhism. I pointed out that it couldn't be done by reading just two or three books, but that he would have to embark on a serious course of study, and possibly he is thinking of doing that.

One of the things I feel that Christianity could learn from the Buddhist tradition is the non-theistic approach. For modern Christians, one might say, God has become a considerable embarrassment. Many of them feel, as the Bishop of Woolwich seems to feel, that Christianity would get along much better without God altogether. That's a radical conclusion but it seems that they have been almost forced to it. Buddhism supplies an example of a religion, a faith, a way of life, which has got on without recourse to belief in or prayer to God very well. This is perhaps the principal point that Christianity in general and the Bishop of Woolwich in particular – inasmuch as he represents a sort of advanced guard of contemporary Christian thought, at least in this country – can learn from Buddhism. But in this talk I am concerned with what we can learn from him. Some Buddhists in the East like to sit back complacently and think that there are no problems for Buddhism. Just as in the old days people used to quote the Bible as the solution to every difficulty, in some Eastern Buddhist countries people say, 'Well, the Buddha said ...' and that is often considered to represent the last word on the subject. But it isn't as easy as all that, and in this country those of us who are Buddhists recognize that.

We feel that with regard to some problems we have a bit of an edge over Christianity. We are not embarrassed by the idea of God, having got on very well without him all these centuries, so we don't have to face up to the problem that today people aren't interested, broadly speaking, in a theistic, anthropomorphic approach to religion. But we do live in the modern world, with all its remarkable developments and problems. The world in the midst of which we find ourselves, willingly or unwillingly, is a very complex, difficult one – one, in short, in which it isn't always comfortable to live. Some people dream of the past, thinking that they would like to have lived in the heroic age of ancient Greece or in the Middle Ages, the Age of Faith, when intellectual problems arising within a religious context were just matters of exposition or presentation within a wider generally agreed doctrinal framework. Such nostalgic dreaming is all right for an occasional afternoon, but it doesn't help us in the long run. We live in this modern, complex, difficult world, and as religious people we need to try to become more and more deeply aware of its problems and needs. We can't stand aloof, or even be really objective. Whether we like it or not, inasmuch as we live at this time and in this place, we are involved in those problems and share those needs.

The New Reformation? is the bishop's new book, following on from *Honest to God*. It is just over a hundred pages long. Perhaps the bishop realized that even though what he had to say was very valuable, if he enshrined it – or entombed it – in a weighty tome, no one would read it except the reviewers and the professional theologians, a short book being all that the average layman these days can take of religion in one dose. The book consists of four chapters: 'Troubling of the waters', 'Starting from the other end', 'Towards a genuinely lay theology' and 'Living in the overlap' – all quite arresting titles. Each of these chapters is concerned with a particular problem or, to speak in less negative and defensive terms, a particular area of opportunity or challenge.

The title *The New Reformation?* suggests that there has already been an old Reformation, and indeed there has, that inaugurated by Martin Luther when he rather bellicosely nailed his ninety-five theses on the church door at Wittenberg.[89] It was out of that old Reformation that there eventually emerged a welter of Reformed and Protestant churches, including our own dear old Church of England. The Reformation split Christianity in two, the Roman Catholic church on one side and all the Reformed and Protestant churches on the other. But what about the new Reformation? The bishop is convinced that it has already begun, thinking it essentially means the adaptation of Christianity to the needs of our times. He's deeply aware, as we saw in *Honest to God*, that there's a great deal of theological and ecclesiastical lumber to be cleared away. A lot of it is kept up in the attic out of sight, but he is of the opinion that the attic ought to be cleared, and the essentials of the Christian message restated in a way that people can understand, though without any loss of integrity.

The bishop is well aware that the new Reformation about which he speaks, in which in fact he is involved, cannot be confined to the West. In *The New Reformation?* he refers to Parrinder's book *The Christian Debate: Light from the East*,[90] and he makes it clear that he is well aware that whatever is said on this sort of subject within the limits of Christendom is, as he puts it, overheard by the followers of other religions, especially by Hindus and Buddhists. But we can go even further than this. It's not so much that Hindus and Buddhists and followers of other Eastern religions overhear what is going on in the new reformation within Christianity. We Buddhists are having a new reformation of our own. That may not be obvious to Western Buddhists, but that's simply because they have comparatively little contact with traditional forms of Buddhism. This new reformation is certainly in evidence here and there in the Eastern Buddhist countries, although the 'new' is a little out of place if it suggests that Buddhism has had just one reformation, for Buddhism has had several.

But what might a reformation be within the context of Buddhism? Basically a reformation is a restatement of the essentials of a religion in terms that are meaningful to contemporary culture. It's not just locking away the bad and preserving what is good. Reformation means getting down to the essentials of what you think, what you believe, and what you are trying to practise, and finding a new way of expressing that intangible essence which is more relevant to the needs of the people around you than any of the old ways of putting it. That essence may be the same as what previous generations were trying to communicate, but your way of communicating it must be uniquely your own, uniquely suited to the needs of your generation. It's this communication, whether doctrinal or institutional or of any other kind, that we call a reformation.

Buddhism has had a very long history, and in the course of its 2,500 years it has certainly needed to put its message into fresh terms. If you assume otherwise, you're really assuming that during that time the people among whom Buddhism was preached and practised didn't change. In India alone, Buddhism had a history of 1,500 years, and obviously over such a long period there's going to be a tremendous amount of change. Just as our own country changed over that time, the India of 1000 CE wasn't anything like the India of 500 BCE, the India of the Buddha's own day. It is thus inevitable that in the course of its history Buddhism should have changed, and indeed its fundamental message was restated again and again in accordance with the needs of the times. We know as a matter of fact that the message of Buddhism has been restated at least four times in the course of its history; in other words, in the course of Buddhist history there have been four major reformations.

This may come as a surprise. You may have heard of the Reformation in Europe in the fifteenth century, but perhaps you've never heard of even one Buddhist reformation, let alone four. This is perhaps due to a misunderstanding. You may have heard of the three *yānas* of Indian Buddhism, Hīnayāna, Mahāyāna, and Vajrayāna, and these are often wrongly described as schools or even sects of Buddhism, but in fact they are three successive stages in the development of Buddhism in India. Or, to rephrase it, they are three restatements of the essentials of the Buddha's teachings. It's isn't stretching the terminology too far to describe each of them as a reformation. Of course, there is a difference. When we speak of the Reformation in Europe, we think of violence and burning at the stake, forcible conversion, the bloody wars of religion that so disfigured the face of Europe before a final religious settlement. But in the history of Buddhism there is nothing forced, no bloodshed, but complete tolerance, in accordance with the much more pacific nature of Buddhism.

It is significant that each of these three *yānas* was dominant in India for a period of about five hundred years, in the course of which one might expect considerable changes to have taken place. The Hīnayāna, the first of these reformations, as we may now say, is Buddhism stated in predominantly ethical and psychological terms, especially in the form of the Abhidhamma. In modern times the Theravāda, one of the eighteen schools of the Hīnayāna, is the most prominent representative of this approach. The Mahāyāna, the next reformation, expresses the essence of Buddhism in predominantly devotional and metaphysical terms, attaching great importance to the worship of the Buddhas and bodhisattvas and also discoursing at length on the nature of reality, the nature of Mind, and so on. And the Vajrayāna, the third reformation, is very much concerned with all that pertains to meditation, especially that of a more esoteric type, and as coordinated, at least at the lower levels, with various kinds of symbolic ritual. Each of these three stages of development represents a restatement of the preceding one.

The fourth major reformation wasn't an Indian development. When Buddhism went from India to China, there developed an attempt to restate Buddhism in terms of Chinese life, thought, and culture, and this, at least from one point of view, is what we call Chan or Zen: not a school or sect but a complete reworking of the whole message of Buddhism. It's as though the great Indian teachers who went to China went with completely open minds; well, their minds were Enlightened, so naturally they were open. It's as though they put aside their own Indian psychology and tried to communicate directly with the hearts and minds of the Chinese people. They spoke to them in terms of Confucianism, and especially in terms of Taoist conceptions like acting through non-action, although that was a little foreign to the Indian mind. The result of this effort to put across the truth of Buddhism in terms that could be assimilated by the Chinese mind was the fourth reformation.

I feel that a fifth reformation is inevitable as people in the West get to know about Buddhism, and also as Western culture and scientific knowledge, and even unpleasant things like industrialism, gradually move into Buddhist cultures. This modern world of ours is a very secular one, and nowadays religious approaches and terminology aren't at all popular. If you want to discuss the profounder questions of life, so far as the average person is concerned you can discuss them more satisfactorily in secular language. So this is what Buddhism has got to do. In addition to using the traditional means, it has to state its essence in terms which are acceptable to and understandable by people who consider themselves to be secular. This means that Buddhism has to put itself across in terms of secular philosophy and psychology, in the language of Freud and Jung, and the language of secular ethics. We shouldn't be saying, 'You can't do this, there's a commandment against that.' No discussion of ethics on that sort of basis will get you anywhere nowadays. We have to discuss ethics in secular terms, even in terms of secular spirituality. Works of literature and art produced by people who are quite oblivious to any sort of spiritual or religious motivation very often have something that gives life to them, some touch of the spiritual. We have to be able to use that.

This doesn't mean identifying Buddhism with philosophy or psychology. Unhappily, some people get a little knowledge of Buddhism and a little knowledge of Jungian psychology (for example) and assume that the two are the same. Instead of talking about Buddhism in terms of Jungian psychology, they get it all mixed up. They talk sometimes about Buddhism, sometimes about Jung, and in the end they don't know which they're talking about. Instead, knowing the terms of Jung's system of psychology, and also knowing, which means experiencing, or being, the essence of Buddhism, you should put across to people who are familiar with Jungian terms your feeling, understanding, and experience of Buddhism in those terms. As you do this, a new dimension, a new range of meaning, will be added to the terms you are employing. Language is a very subtle, elastic thing. You can give words almost any meaning you like. You can begin by using a term like 'archetype' in a strictly Jungian sense, but as you go on talking to someone who knows about archetypes, whether you are aware of it or not, you'll start injecting meanings derived from Buddhist sources into your usage of the word 'archetype'. Since you've established common ground, the person you're talking to won't notice this at first, or even if they notice it, the meaning will have got across, and the range and connotations of the word archetype will have been expanded.

Let's get back to the bishop's book, *The New Reformation?* Its first chapter, 'Troubling waters', is mainly concerned with what we have been talking about so far. The bishop is concerned to assure us, or to convince us if necessary, that the new reformation has already begun. There's no question, apparently, of deciding to have a reformation. Whether we like it or not, the new reformation is already in our midst. Most Christians don't realize this, and many no doubt write off the Bishop of Woolwich and people like him as eccentrics, the sort of person the Church of England can afford to accommodate, a sort of safety valve for the young person. They don't want to face up to the fact that there's a new reformation within Christianity, but continue grimly hanging on to the old ways. If they talk at all of reformation, they tend to think of getting everybody who has drifted away from the Church back into the pews. After all, the buildings are there, with hundreds of empty seats waiting, and they think reformation means getting people into those empty seats, perhaps with a little gentle pressure. They're not thinking in terms of changing the Church.

I'm sorry to say that we sometimes find the same sort of thing in Buddhism. Having smiled a little at Christianity, it's time to smile at ourselves. Well, not exactly, because we find this sort of thing not so much in the West, but in the Buddhist East. There, monks and elderly ladies often complain that the young people, especially Western-educated ones, have very little time for Buddhism. They're not against it, they just don't bother with it. To them it seems irrelevant. I remember some young men in one of the Buddhist countries telling me, 'We don't go to the temple because the custom is that you must kneel on the floor, which is all right when you're wearing a lunghi, but when you're wearing a nicely pressed pair of Western trousers, you don't want to spoil the creases in your trousers.' That's a trivial example, but it illustrates the sort of thing that happens. Western-educated young people, especially those who have some scientific knowledge, tend to drift away from Buddhism, and one must say in fairness to them that in some parts of the Buddhist East very little effort is made to make Buddhism intelligible to people who have received a Western education.

It's often the same when monks come to preach Buddhism in the West. There are lots of innocent Buddhists in the East who think it would be glorious to come and preach Buddhism in the West. It's a laudable ambition, but the vast majority have no idea what they're up against. They just don't know how difficult it is to preach religion of any sort here. It's difficult even for Dr Billy Graham, I believe, so how much more difficult is it going to be for a Buddhist coming from the East?[91] They tend to think of repeating the old familiar formulas over here, which is natural when they haven't had any experience of conditions here, but it won't get Buddhism in the West very far.

This is one of the reasons why in the West there are so many types of national Buddhism. When Christian missionaries went to the East, they could usually be distinguished according to sects: the Catholics, the Protestants, the Methodists, the Baptists, and so on. But those coming from the East to preach Buddhism in the West are usually distinguished on a national basis – the Sinhalese Buddhists, the Tibetan Buddhists, the Thai Buddhists – because they all tend to try to reproduce their own national religious and cultural patterns rather than producing something suitable for the indigenous patterns of this country. In an article published last week in the *Observer* newspaper about the Buddhist movement in this country, they pointed out that the full-moon day was celebrated by different Buddhist groups on different days. According to the calendar the full moon was on Friday, but the Sinhalese Buddhists in London celebrated their full-moon day on Thursday, because that was the correct day according to the Sinhalese calendar, whereas the Thai Buddhists observed it on Friday, presumably because their calendar agreed with the English one. The *Observer* went on to point out that the English

Buddhists (referring to ourselves) weren't going to have their full-moon celebrations on the full-moon day at all, but on Sunday immediately after their lecture, theirs being the pragmatic approach – pragmatic apparently being laudable according to that particular reporter. This is a simple example of how difficult it is for Eastern Buddhism coming to the West to drop their national religious and cultural patterns.

When I speak of the need to adapt to local conditions, I don't mean a compromise. What is needed is an attempt to speak about Buddhism in terms with which people are familiar. For the Eastern Buddhist this seems to be very difficult, perhaps partly because in many parts of the Eastern Buddhist world Buddhism is having to adopt an increasingly defensive posture, so they tend to withdraw within themselves. But if Buddhism is to spread in this country, whoever spreads it, whether they are from the East or from the West, they will have to learn to speak not only the English language but the cultural language of this country at this time. These are the points to which the Bishop of Woolwich has drawn attention in a Christian context and which I'm now trying to transpose into the Buddhistic context.

Chapter 2 of *The New Reformation?* is 'Starting from the other end' – a rather intriguing title, by which the bishop means that we need to start from human beings and their problems instead of from God. Orthodox traditional Christian theology begins with God, who has made the universe, this world, you and me, and thus imposed certain duties on us. He not only made us but sent his son to save us, and we have to accept that salvation. So you start with God and eventually come down to humanity. This is the deductive rather than the inductive approach to religion. The bishop says that this has to be reversed. He says that Christians have to start from the other end, not with God coming down to humanity, but with human beings working their way up to God. For traditional Christianity this inductive approach would be not reformation but revolution, because once you introduce this way of thinking there's no knowing where it might end. As I suggested in my previous talk, you may end up, even if you're a bishop, outside the church and in the bosom of Buddhism.

This sort of approach is commonplace for Buddhism. Buddhism has always started from human beings. We don't work our way up to God, of course – we leave God out of it altogether – but we work our way up to whatever we do work our way up to from the experience of human life. This is illustrated very well by the four noble truths. You start with suffering. Suffering is a fact. Birth is suffering, sickness is suffering, old age is suffering, death is suffering. This is what we start with in Buddhism as classically stated – not with abstractions or transcendental first principles, but down here on earth, with the undeniable fact of human suffering. The second noble truth goes on to reveal the cause of suffering, the third the cessation of suffering, and the fourth the way to its cessation, and right at the end of that path, when you've gone very far indeed, you come to what we call Nirvāṇa, about which it seems the Buddha preferred to say very little, though he said a great deal about the four noble truths, especially suffering.

So it would seem that Buddhists don't have much to learn about 'starting from the other end'. But I need to introduce a word of warning. Sometimes one is asked the question, 'What is the goal of Buddhism? What as a Buddhist are you aiming at?' The usual answer given is that the goal of Buddhism is Nirvāṇa or Enlightenment, but this seems a little too easy, even a little too slick. We know that in a sense Enlightenment is the ultimate goal of Buddhism, but we shouldn't trot out 'Nirvāṇa' as the answer too quickly, we shouldn't just pop up like a jack-in-the-box with an automatic, inevitable, irrefutable reply, as if that settles it. Sometimes you do get that in traditional circles in the East, among both monks and lay people. They produce Nirvāṇa very much as the Christians produce God. But it isn't as easy as that. Nirvāṇa should emerge, very much as it emerged for the Buddha. First be aware of suffering – the fact of it. Then go deeply into the cause of suffering, then the cessation of suffering, then the way to the cessation of suffering, and finally, at the end of that, Nirvāṇa. Nirvāṇa should emerge, if it emerges at all, as a possible solution from a deep analysis of a given problem, not just be produced like a rabbit out of a conjuror's hat.

In Tibetan Buddhist circles, when one meets a teacher for the first time, there's a little procedure which one goes through. Rather crudely, Western people usually come straight to the point. They meet a lama or Buddhist teacher, and after they've shaken hands, they sit down and say, 'Well, what's Nirvāṇa? I've heard the word a lot, but what is it?' Of course, it's impossible to give a reply on the spot. The Tibetan procedure is different, as I've experienced myself many times. In the East they still have a lot more time than we do, so they can afford to be leisurely. What usually happens when you meet someone is that first of all there are mutual enquiries after health, and sometimes they go into quite a lot of detail in a way which an English person might consider embarrassing. Then they ask where you come from and why you've come, and your experiences along the way, and then somehow Buddhism slips into the discussion. You get talking about manners and customs and rules, a bit about discipline, a bit about monasteries or festivals. Then they'll come on to something about the life of the Buddha, and a bit about doctrine, and very cautiously edge their way to something about meditation. By this stage the discussion, which might have been going on for two hours, has brought about a certain rapport between the people engaged in it. They've got to know one another a little. Almost insensibly, profounder questions slip in, and sometimes even questions like Nirvāṇa come up. But they come up naturally. It's very different from some Western globetrotter trotting along and saying, 'Well, what's it all about?' and expecting a reply on the spot.

And this is how it should emerge for us too. We shouldn't trot out the profounder aspects of Buddhism too glibly or slickly or readily. They should emerge as the end result, by way of a deep analysis of a given problem, and they certainly shouldn't be prescribed in advance. So perhaps there is something for Buddhists to learn from this chapter, 'Starting from the other end'. We know the end to which we are going, Nirvāṇa, but we shouldn't take it for granted that it's evident to other people. We should start with their problems and difficulties, go into them deeply, try to throw light on them, and if eventually that light seems to be the light of Nirvāṇa, or a faint glimmer of it, so much the better. We shouldn't be in too much of a hurry to bring in ultimate things. Let them come in naturally, let them emerge.

Chapter 3, 'Towards a genuine lay theology', is for me the most interesting of the four chapters, full of thought-provoking reflections. The bishop refers to four different types of theology, borrowing the classification from another writer, as he acknowledges, but making very full use of it. The first of these types is the episcopal theology created by bishops in accordance with the needs of their teaching and pastoral function. The second is monastic theology, created in the monasteries in accordance with the spiritual needs of monks. Third, is scholastic theology, created in the interests of professional thinkers, theologians, and philosophers during the Middle Ages. And fourthly, there's seminary theology, taught to equip a person to be a priest. But beyond these four kinds of theology, the bishop says, we need a lay theology. Lay people are after all the majority of the church. He says that what is wanted is a statement of Christianity (by which he means a fully-fledged expression) not for episcopal administration, monastic life, scholastic preoccupations, or seminary requirements, but designed for the life of lay people.

This applies to Buddhism too. We need a statement of Buddhist principles for lay life. Traditionally, Buddhism is a strongly monastic movement. Throughout the centuries, the sangha, the monastic order, has been the backbone of the Buddhist community. Dr Conze goes so far as to say that without the monastic sangha, Buddhism wouldn't have survived at all.[92] We've no time to go into the historical reasons for this, but one practical result has been that the presentation of Buddhism has traditionally been cast in a form adapted more to the requirements of monks than to those of lay people. There are a few discourses in all the collections of scriptures addressed especially to lay people, but for every one of them there must be ninety-nine addressed to monks, and this sometimes gives the wrong impression that Buddhism is a purely monastic religion, and has no place for a laity.[93] In India one finds this view widespread among Hindu scholars, who want to discourage people from taking an interest in Buddhism and thus present it as being purely for the monks, and are able to produce quite a lot of historical evidence to support their contention. It is true that in some Buddhist countries, the laity play a very minor, subordinate role. If you ask the average lay Buddhist in Ceylon or Burma or even Tibet what the main function of the lay Buddhist is, he would say that it is to support the monks. But alongside that duty one finds in practice that lay people have a crude popular religion of their own. In Ceylon, for instance, the lay people are very devout, they look after the monks and support the monasteries, but their own religious life often tends to be centred around Hindu shrines. Some people in Ceylon are quite worried about this.

So we very much need to reformulate the principles of Buddhism in terms of lay life, especially now that Buddhism has come to the West. We can claim that this has already been done to some extent in the Mahāyāna. It was part of the Mahāyāna's reform to translate the teachings of Buddhism out of the monastic language in which they had been handed down into lay terms. Taking its stand upon the beautiful idea which we call the bodhisattva ideal, it stressed that the lay person just as much as the monk could be a bodhisattva, could take Enlightenment as his or her goal. When we make this restatement, when we try to put Buddhism across in the West, the bodhisattva ideal must be our ultimate foundation. But although the Mahāyāna has made this fruitful start, there is still a great deal of work to be done to translate monastic expressions into lay ones. I'll give you just a few examples.

One of the precepts for the monks is what is called 'abstention from untimely eating'. The popular interpretation of this in most Buddhist countries is that the monk should not eat after midday, and they follow this quite strictly. But how does it work out in terms of lay life? What is the principle involved? It isn't just a matter of the lay person occasionally doing what the monk does. The principle involved is simply that of moderation. Translating this monastic precept of not eating after midday in terms of lay life, it means observing a consistent moderation in diet. In the Buddhist East it's very often thought the monk has to observe the rule of not eating after midday, but the lay people can stuff themselves as much as they like. It's almost as though the whole practice of the religion is left to the monks and the laity satisfy themselves with supporting the monks and being Buddhist by proxy.

Dāna, giving, is definitely a Buddhist virtue, but that doesn't mean you can forget about the others. Some years ago I was told the story of King Thibaw, the last king of Burma, by his son-in-law, Prince Ata, who would have been king of Burma had the country still been a monarchy. Apparently at King Thibaw's court all the Buddhist formalities were kept up. The king was so pious that he insisted that food should be ceremonially served in the palace to at least a hundred monks every day. The last days of the Burmese monarchy were overshrouded by all sorts of palace intrigues, and the king became very suspicious and starting having a number of his close relations killed, afraid that they were trying to usurp the throne. It's a matter of history that he arranged for the killing of about three hundred of his relations, so that only one or two were left, among them Prince Ata, who told me that every day there would be executions in the palace grounds. The executions were carried out in a very painful way, apparently according to traditional Burmese custom. King Thibaw sent to Antwerp, of all places, for beautiful red velvet bags. The person who was to be executed was put alive in one of these bags, the bag was tied up, and the person was trampled to death by elephants. This was the traditional mode of execution for members of the royal family. A Burmese orchestra would be playing music at the same time, and while this was going on, the king continued to offer *dāna* to the monks, because he was a very pious Buddhist. This is an extreme example, but it shows the sort of thing that can happen when there's an assumption that the layman's only duty is to offer *dāna* to the monks. We must safeguard against this by translating the teachings of Buddhism into the terms of lay life. With regard to food, the monk may observe the precept of not eating after midday, but the sincere lay Buddhist will observe an unwritten precept of consistent moderation and simplicity.

Another example is the rule that every year the monk goes into retreat for four months. Nobody bothers him, and he can meditate, or study, or do whatever he likes, as long as he stays in one place, completely secluded. If this four-month retreat is of some spiritual value, there must be a principle involved which would be useful to the lay person. Obviously they're not going to be able to make a four-month retreat every year, however much they might like to, but what about a one-week retreat? Some people here have already done this, going on a week's meditation course up at Biddulph, doing in principle what a monk does when he observes the rainy season retreat.[94] They've gone into retreat for a period, isolated themselves from all worldly concerns, and tried to lead a purely spiritual life, at least for that week. Of course they eat and drink (in moderation), but apart from that they're occupied exclusively with the things of the Dharma, the things of the spirit. One could go even further than that. What about an occasional retreat from social activities? There are some people who would welcome that, letting go of all meaningless, frivolous social engagements. If you're naturally introverted, you might instead be encouraged to go out and meet people a bit more, but if you're a natural extrovert, which more people seem to be even in the Buddhist movement, you could cut down a bit on your social life, go on retreat a bit more, try to give more time and energy and thought to spiritual things.

The two simple examples I've given are on the ethical plane, but one can go much further. All of Buddhist thought and practice needs to be translated into the terms of lay life. If we have what the bishop calls a lay theology, the lay person will be much more closely integrated into Buddhism. I've noticed in South-east Asia that lay Buddhists are very loosely connected with Buddhism. The monks get on with religion, and the lay people get on with secular life – it's a sort of division of labour. But that isn't good enough. If the fundamental concepts and practices of Buddhism are restated in terms of lay life so that the lay person can practise at home, and in the office or factory, just as the monks practise in the monastery, the lay Buddhist will be brought much closer to Buddhism, and closer to the monastic community too. We'll find, I'm sure, that the lay person will become more active and play a more responsible role. This is in fact starting to happen in the East. For the last thirty or forty years, some individual Buddhist laymen have come to play a much more active part than they used to do. In the past, by which I mean any time before the beginning of the twentieth century, you hardly heard of a prominent Buddhist layman, unless he was a king and making magnificent endowments. But in a small way it has been quite a feature of Buddhist life and work in the Asian countries in this century that lay people have taken an increasingly active part. One very active Eastern lay Buddhist whom we know quite well is Dr Malalasekera, the High Commissioner for Sri Lanka in this country.[95] He is probably better known than any monk, which simply would not have been possible one or two hundred years ago, but it is a sign of the times. There aren't many like him, but there are a few.

If lay Buddhists are more closely integrated in the Buddhist movement, more active and more responsible, secular, non-Buddhist society will tend to be infiltrated more and more by Buddhist values. The monk can't infiltrate society without people knowing about it because his robe gives him away at once and puts people on their guard. But a lay Buddhist who has a definite role in the Buddhist movement may be sitting quietly at his desk in the office in his blue or grey suit, and no one will know that he is a Buddhist. He just sits there awaiting his opportunity. In the course of conversation he may drop in little hints, little ideas, not deliberately but because he can't help it, which point in the direction of Buddhism. One day someone will say to him, 'Your way of looking at things is quite interesting. What makes you think like that?' He'll think, 'Now the moment has come, this is it', and he'll say, wiping the sweat from his brow, 'Well, to tell the truth, I'm a Buddhist.' But by that time his colleagues will have got used to his ideas and they won't be too shocked. He looks quite normal, after all, so his ideas are acceptable. Many people quite frankly fight shy of people who appear ostentatiously religious, especially when they wear robes, and one doesn't get the chance of getting near to them, but the committed lay Buddhist can infiltrate much better.

This topic came up last week when we had our question-and-answer meeting and I made the point that we need a sort of third order, an order of committed lay people intermediate between the vast mass of what Christians would call 'the unchurched' and the little inner circle of the sangha, a third order of people who have one foot firmly in the secular world and the other firmly within Buddhism, within the vihara. It's not unreasonable to predict that for quite a few years, if not generations to come, the Buddhist monastic order will be very small. That isn't altogether a disadvantage, provided the calibre is sufficiently high, but it's important that those monks shouldn't have to spend their time doing things that the committed lay person can do just as well. For instance, here at the vihara we get a lot of invitations to give talks to schools, socialist groups, Conservative associations, and the like. This is the sort of engagement with which the dedicated lay Buddhist can cope very well, sometimes better than a monk. When a monk turns up, sometimes people wonder, 'Why is he wearing a yellow robe? How does he come to be living in a monastery?' But if they find that the Buddhist is someone who looks like them, if he is wearing an ordinary suit or she is wearing an ordinary dress, people are sometimes a little more receptive, and at first this counts for a lot. There's a great deal of work of this sort which lay Buddhists can do, freeing the monks for other work – either their own meditation or study, or teaching those who are going out and mixing with people.

The fourth and last chapter of the bishop's book also has an interesting title: 'Living in the overlap'. By overlap, we gather, the bishop means a period of transition between a traditional religious approach and a modern secular approach. We Buddhists are also living in this overlap. There's an overlap in all our lives between the traditional and the modern, the religious and the secular. English Buddhists live in a double overlap, not only the overlap between what we may call the Christian and the post-Christian period, but also the overlap between Christian and post-Christian on the one hand and Buddhist on the other. I for one don't regret that. In fact, living in a double overlap is doubly exciting because it's double the challenge. No doubt we'll have a double reformation, and also double the responsibility.

We have to confess that it isn't easy to be a Buddhist in this country. The odds are against it. To be a Buddhist, you need a certain amount of backbone, intelligence, sheer obstinacy, and indifference to what other people think. It isn't easy to preach any religion nowadays, and to preach an exotic religion coming from the East isn't easy for anybody, though we have to carry on somehow. A vihara like this should be thought of as a kind of spiritual research station, not the Buddhist equivalent of the local parish church with a congregation of the faithful flocking there every Sunday to receive their weekly dose of uplift. In fact, the vihara should be the centre of the new Buddhist reformation.

The Bishop of Woolwich's ideas and suggestions in *The New Reformation?* are of considerable interest and value, even of help to us in our life and work here. As I said at the beginning, my talk on Buddhism and the Bishop of Woolwich was tape-recorded and eventually sent to the bishop himself. On this occasion I rather hope that the tape won't be sent to the bishop, because I feel that his book has been covered rather inadequately. However, I'm quite sure that if Mr Revill gets it into his head to send it to the bishop, nothing will stop him. I once thought of giving a talk on Buddhism and Roman Catholicism but I didn't dare to do it because I knew that Mr Revill would send it to the Pope! In any case, I shall be away for a few weeks having a rest from lectures, and even from the Bishop of Woolwich, and while the cat is away, the mice tend to play, so perhaps this tape will be sent after all.[96] While I'm away – this is just by way of conclusion – the Sunday meetings will continue, and I hope that all of you will continue to come.

A VISIT TO A BUDDHIST VIHARA

A talk delivered to teacher training students, 1966

Perhaps I should begin with a few words about myself. I went out to India more than twenty years ago, and when I came back to England after being away all that time, I noticed a number of changes. I got quite a few surprises and even a few shocks, but there was one change which it gave me great pleasure to observe. When I was a boy, we hardly ever heard any mention of any religion other than Christianity. We had Bible class, but so far as I recollect not one of our teachers at any time pronounced the name of any other religion. We were not even given to understand that there were any other religions in the world. But now it would seem that people's minds are becoming more and more open. Though they may be ardent Christians, or convinced of the truth of humanism or some other system, they have a great interest in learning about other religions. In ancient times, people were almost completely ignorant of how people in other countries lived, but today, through books and films, you know much more about the customs and traditions of other countries than your forefathers did, you have a much broader, more cosmopolitan outlook, and it's only natural that this great change should extend to the sphere of religion. Despite devastating setbacks from time to time, I think we can state with some confidence that as the years go by the human race is tending to become more and more one great family, more and more interconnected, even more and more united. Perhaps the day will come when we see the development not only of a global government but of a global culture, even of global religious and spiritual aspirations. I welcome the development of this tendency within the field of religious studies.

When I was a boy, I was fond of poetry, and there was one line of Rudyard Kipling which has always struck me very forcibly: 'What should they know of England who only England know?'[97] I can verify the truth of this. When you know only your own country, your own customs, your own culture, you don't really know them, because you've no standard of comparison. Knowledge is essentially comparison. You come to understand a thing by comparing it with another thing, so if you know only one thing, you don't really know even that thing. After spending twenty years in the East, I feel that I understand England much better than if I had remained here. Things I would have taken for granted I now see in comparison with things I've seen in other countries, so I see them in a new light, and I can appreciate and understand them more deeply.

Likewise, you can't understand your own religion except in relation to other religions, and this is one of the values of the study of other religions. You may not abandon your own religion as a result; in fact you may be more securely anchored in it, because you come to know it better. It is a very healthy sign that you, who are if anything Christians, should have taken up the study of other religions. Buddhists are usually willing to learn about and from other religions, and if that tendency is spreading among Christians too, that's surely to the benefit of both faiths. Recently I had the opportunity of meeting the Bishop of Woolwich, who is well known, even notorious, for his book *Honest to God*, in which he makes the point that the traditional image of God must go. We had a discussion lasting about two and a half hours, and we felt by the end of it that we had quite a lot in common. He's gone to the United States to give some lectures, but just before we parted he said, 'I look forward very much to visiting you at the Hampstead Buddhist Vihara after my return.' Even twenty years ago the idea of a Christian bishop calling on a Buddhist monk would have been quite shocking, but as the world grows smaller, people are drawn ever closer together.

So this afternoon you've come to try to understand something about Buddhism. Buddhism has a vast and complicated teaching, with a history of 2,500 years, and many schools, systems, and traditions, but in this short time I won't be able to say much about it. I can only give a brief, simple, and inadequate summary, in the hope that that will spark off some interest in you and that you will pursue that interest later on by yourselves. The word Buddhism comes from the word Buddha. The Buddha is the founder of Buddhism in the same way that Christ is the founder of Christianity. The word 'Buddha' isn't a proper name, but a title, just as 'Christ' is also a title. 'Christ' means 'the anointed one', and 'Buddha' means 'the one who knows' or 'the one who is Enlightened'. It's sometimes translated as 'the one who is awake', the idea being that most people are asleep, or dreaming at best, subject to all sorts of illusions and delusions. The Buddha is one who has awoken from all those.

Let us examine briefly the main facts of his life. You probably know that he was Indian, or not quite Indian, having been born at a place called Lumbinī, in what is now Nepalese territory, about five hundred years before Christ. He was born into a rather aristocratic family. According to the traditions his father was a raja. 'Raja' has two meanings, a hereditary monarch, or a sort of elected president of the clan or tribe, and when the future Buddha was born, his father was the latter, serving a twelve-year term as the elected raja of the Śākya tribe, one of the many little republics in north-eastern India in those days. The Buddha-to-be – his name was Siddhārtha – received a very good education. He was initiated into the customs of the clan to which he belonged, which was a tribe of the warrior (Kshatriya) caste, and became skilled in martial arts, as well as learning genealogy and history. When he was about 16, he was married to one of his cousins, and not long afterwards a son was born to them.

It is obvious that from a worldly point of view there wasn't anything that Siddhārtha lacked. He had social position, health, youth, and a happy and contented family life. He was educated and cultured. He seemed to have everything. But despite that, it seems that from a very early period he was dissatisfied. He developed the habit of spending time by himself, thinking about things. 'Well, here I am, but what's the meaning of it all? Why is one born into this world at all? After death, what happens? What's the purpose of life?' Such questions started troubling him, even tormenting him. Some of the early scriptures put it in the form of what some people regard as a legend, which may for all that have actually taken place. We are told that on one occasion he decided to go out from his palace on an excursion. He called the palace charioteer, who whipped up the horses, and off they went. As they were spinning along, Siddhārtha saw by the roadside, tottering along, a very old man. In India, an old man often looks very old indeed, and this old man was white-haired, thin and bony. Siddhārtha was very much struck by this, because according to the legend he had been secluded from all unpleasant sights, his father wanting that he should see only beautiful things and beautiful people. Never having seen an old man before, he asked the charioteer, 'What is this?' The charioteer thought, 'Well, now the moment has come,' and he said, 'This is an old man.' 'But how did he get like this?' 'Well, it's natural, I'm afraid. It happens to everybody.' Then Siddhārtha asked, 'Even me?' And the charioteer said, 'Yes, although now you are young, strong, and healthy, one day even you will be cast down by old age.' This made Siddhārtha very thoughtful. He started thinking, 'If youth ends in this state of emaciation and suffering and weakness, what is the use of it?' Very slowly and thoughtfully he turned back to the palace. And this is what is called the first sight.

On a subsequent occasion, he went out and saw another sight: a sick man lying at the side of the road with an attack of fever, tossing this way and that. He asked the charioteer, 'What is this?' and the charioteer said, 'It's a sick man.' Siddhārtha asked, 'Am I likely to suffer in this way?' and the charioteer said, 'Yes, sickness is something we can't prevent. It might come at any time. At any moment you or I or anybody else may be struck down.' This also made Siddhārtha very thoughtful, and again he went back to his palace, thinking it all over.

On the third occasion when he went forth, he saw a corpse being carried along by a group of mourners. In India, people don't put a corpse into a coffin. They just put a white sheet over it, and with the face exposed they carry it on an open bier through the streets. So Siddhārtha said to the charioteer, 'Why are they carrying that man? Why is he so stiff? Why is he so quiet? What's happened?' The charioteer said, 'He is dead.' And the young man asked, 'Shall I come to this state? Must I also die?' And the charioteer said, 'Yes. You must die. I must die. Your father must die. Everybody who is born must one day die. Life ends in death. This is an inexorable law. No one can escape it. Death is the king of all.' This made Siddhārtha more thoughtful than ever, and he went back to the palace, plunged deep in thought.

But there was a fourth occasion, we are told, when Siddhārtha went forth, and this time he saw not an old man, or a sick man, or a corpse, but a living man walking along in the saffron-coloured robe worn in India by those who give up domestic ties and social obligations and wander about devoting themselves to the search for truth. They are supported by alms: people give them food and invite them to their houses, this kind of generosity being considered very meritorious. This is the system in India even now. Such people are called *sadhus*, which simply means 'good people'. So on the fourth excursion Siddhārtha saw one of these *sadhus*, just walking along with a begging-bowl and a shaven head. He looked quite different from anyone Siddhārtha had ever seen. He was calm, quiet, contented, peaceful, serene. Siddhārtha asked the charioteer, 'Who is this?' and the charioteer said, 'He is one who has given up all worldly ties. He has no wife, no family, no domestic responsibilities, social or political obligations. He is solely concerned with the truth.' This also made Siddhārtha very thoughtful, and again he went back to his palace.[98]

In this poetic way the story is told, and whether or not we take it literally, the meaning is clearly that during his youth Siddhārtha was deeply impressed by the facts of old age, disease, and death, by the fact that this human life of ours is lived under these limitations. We may ignore them, we may try to escape them, but they are there all the time. He came to realize this, and he also saw that there might be a way of coming to understand the meaning of it all. So we're told that after thinking it over for a long time, he came to a decision. He decided that he would become a *sadhu*. He felt he couldn't rest until an answer was found. He couldn't stay at home, he just had to get out, be free to search, to think, to meditate. So one night, we are told, he left home without anybody knowing, went out into the dark, into the jungle, took off his princely robes, donned the saffron robe of a wandering *sadhu*, and set out in search of truth.

We are told that he searched for six whole years. He went from one teacher to another and learned what they had to teach, which included quite advanced meditation, but he wasn't satisfied, finding that each teaching took him a certain distance but not to the ultimate goal. He practised self-mortification, asceticism, and found that that didn't work either. And about six years after he left his palace, at a place now called Bodh Gaya, he found a tree, afterwards known as the bodhi tree, sat down beneath it, and made a resolution that whatever might happen, he would not leave that spot until he'd gained the knowledge that he was seeking.[99] Day after day, night after night, he remained deep in thought, and eventually, on the full-moon night of Wesak, the month of April/May, when he was deep in meditation, he suddenly saw the answer to the problem that had tormented him – not only saw it, but understood it, became one with it, realized it, and in this way became the Buddha, the Enlightened or the Awakened One.

After this great realization, which took place when he was 35, he spent forty-five years wandering the plains of north-eastern India, teaching whoever would listen to him: princes, kings, peasants, housewives, merchants, monks, all sorts of people. And eventually, having collected a following, having founded a sangha or an order, he passed away at the age of 80 with his teaching, which we call the Dharma or Buddhism, firmly established. So this in very brief outline is the story of his life.

One fact to which I want to draw your attention is that the Buddha, according to his own declaration, is simply an Enlightened human being. He comes into the world just as we do. He's perplexed by the mystery of life just as we sometimes are, and he struggles and strives to find the solution just as we sometimes do, to find some light in the darkness. He found it, whereas we are still looking, but the point to remember is that the Buddha, even after the consummation of his search, was an Enlightened *human* being. He did not claim to be God, or an incarnation of God, or the son of God, or a prophet or messenger of God. He claimed to be no more than a simple human being who, by his own efforts, had realized the truth and then, after realizing it, proclaimed it to other human beings so that they might realize it for themselves by their own efforts. This is the most important thing that we have to realize about the Buddha.

In Hinduism, Krishna and Rama claim to be incarnations of God, or it is claimed on their behalf by their followers. Christ is believed to be the son of God. Mohammed is believed to be the messenger of God. The Jewish prophets are believed to be prophets sent or inspired by God. But the Buddha, alone among the founders of the great religions, doesn't make any such claim. He simply says, 'I am a human being and by my own human efforts I have realized the truth.' That doesn't mean, though, that the Buddha is just an ordinary ethical teacher, like Socrates or Marcus Aurelius. In the eyes of Buddhists, one who has realized the truth, one who is Enlightened, is the highest of all beings in the universe. This is something else we have to understand.

So if the Buddha is not God, or an incarnation or messenger of God, what is his relationship to God? What is the place of God in Buddhism? The answer may surprise or even shock you. In Buddhism there is no place for God at all. Buddhism is a non-theistic religion. You may have made the assumption that religion is by definition theistic. The dictionary tells us that religion means 'a system of belief in worship of God, the supreme Being'. But the dictionary definition overlooks a very important fact. If we examine all the major religions of the world, we see that broadly speaking they fall into two groups: theistic and non-theistic. The theistic religions include Christianity, Islam, Judaism, and some forms of popular Hinduism. They all believe in one God who created and rules the universe, who is the father of all human beings. The non-theistic religions are Daoism and Confucianism in China, philosophical Hinduism, Jainism (another religion originating in India around 500 BCE), and Buddhism. Adherents of these faiths don't believe in God at all. This realization alone should open your eyes a little, should make your outlook broader. You may have thought that if someone believes in God they are religious, and if they don't believe in God they're not, but for thousands of years there have been hundreds of millions of people who have led meaningful spiritual lives, made spiritual progress, even gained Enlightenment, without resort to the conception of a personal God. This is why the Bishop of Woolwich's book, *Honest to God*, has made such an impact. This is why it has pleased some people and outraged and shocked others: because he says, simply, 'God must go.'

Every Buddhist is supposed to follow the Noble Eightfold Path, developing right understanding and the right emotional attitude, practising right speech, right action, right livelihood, right effort, right mindfulness, and finally right concentration and meditation leading to Enlightenment. This is the path, and the Buddha says emphatically, 'You must walk the path yourself. I can't walk it for you. No man can purify another.'[100] Purity and impurity depend upon one's own efforts, or lack of effort. Self-help is one of the fundamental principles of Buddhism. That's why it is sometimes said that Buddhism is a do-it-yourself religion. Nobody can do it for you. You have to tread the path with your own two feet. The Buddhas only show the way. But Buddhism also says that anyone who makes the effort can attain the goal. It is not that there are a chosen few who can do it and others who can't. Everybody who makes the effort can obtain the same results. If you put your mind to it, if you resolve that you are going to practise right understanding, right emotional attitude, right speech, and so on, as time goes on you can make progress, you can grow gradually towards Enlightenment. You don't even need to call yourself a Buddhist. The main thing is to accept the principles and follow the practices. If you do that, you'll get the right results.

In Buddhism there is no compulsion. In Pāli, the Dhamma, the Buddha's teaching, is called *ehipassiko dhamma*, the teaching which says *ehi* (come), *passiko* (see). Come and see for yourself. Don't believe things just because the Buddha tells you. Don't believe things because I tell you. Believe only what you can understand, experience, and verify for yourself. In one of the most remarkable passages in the scriptures, the Buddha says to his followers, 'Don't accept anything out of respect for me. Just as gold is tested in the fire, test my words in the fire of your own spiritual experience.'[101] In Buddhism there is complete tolerance. Buddhism says that we must all find out the truth for ourselves. We must all find our own path. We can't force anybody else to follow our path. We must allow others the same freedom that we claim for ourselves: freedom to grow, freedom to develop spiritually, each in our own way.

When I lived in Kalimpong, in north-eastern India, I came to know a lot of Tibetan Buddhists, mostly newly arrived refugees. They used to say to me, 'I went to the market place and what do you think I heard? I couldn't believe my ears. There was a Christian missionary abusing Buddhists. He's supposed to be a priest, but he was abusing another religion.' For them this is unthinkable. One of my Tibetan students came to me one afternoon, and said, 'I've made a great discovery. Christianity and Communism are the same thing!' I said, 'How do you make *that* out?' He said, 'Well, I've just been along to the bazaar and I heard one of the Christian missionaries attacking Buddhism. He was asking, "What is this bowing down to wood and stone? Do Buddhists think that an image can help them? And the monks are all parasites, living on the fat of the land. They should be made to work." In Lhasa, I used to go to Communist meetings, and they said exactly the same thing. So it's quite clear that Christianity and Communism are the same.' When I came back to this country I was happy to discover that that attitude is becoming very rare, and some clergy to whom I related these incidents were sorry to think that there could be, in the middle of the twentieth century, Christian missionaries who recommend their faith by running down the faith of other people, but unfortunately here and there you get missionaries still adopting this attitude. One can't imagine, unless one has had contact with Tibetan Buddhists, how much it shocks them to hear the follower of one religion running down another. It isn't that they are Buddhists and they don't like to be criticized by a Christian missionary. If they heard a Buddhist speaking like that about another religion, they would feel it equally deeply. You may disagree with someone, you may think they're completely wrong, but you should treat their ideas with respect. If you argue, argue courteously, without heat, politely, coolly. Try to convince them of your point of view, but don't abuse or criticize in a bad spirit. In Buddhism we have had no religious wars, no persecution, no Spanish Inquisition, but perfect freedom of religion, perfect tolerance, and an effort to understand the points of view of the followers of other religions.

That brings us back to the point we started from. As I've made clear, Buddhism originated in India. It died out there, for various reasons I won't go into now, after fifteen hundred years, but it's now extant all over the East and is very quickly spreading to the West. There are Buddhist movements in most of the European countries, and perhaps the biggest movement so far is in this country. Here, the movement is centred upon London, where we have not only this place, the Hampstead Buddhist Vihara and its Sangha Trust and Sangha Association, but also the Buddhist Society at Eccleston Square, which is the oldest and best-known Buddhist organization in the West. Since my return to this country, I have been very impressed by the interest shown in Buddhism. I get invitations from all over the place. One week I may be lecturing up in Glasgow, another week across in Bristol, and a few days later in Oxford or Cambridge; and then regularly here in London. It is very encouraging to see this awakening of interest. We don't expect everybody to become Buddhists but at least we hope that as this world gets smaller and smaller, Christians will take interest in Buddhism, just as we hope that Buddhists will take interest in Christianity and in other faiths. In this way, we come to appreciate different points of view, to educate ourselves in the true sense, to become people with broad and liberal, truly catholic outlooks and attitudes. This is, I believe, the spirit in which you've all come along this afternoon, and I hope that this visit to a Buddhist vihara, and this experience of listening to a talk on Buddhism, has been of some value.

ASPECTS OF BUDDHIST PSYCHOLOGY 1: THE ANALYTICAL PSYCHOLOGY OF THE ABHIDHARMA

The first in a series of seven lectures on 'Aspects of Buddhist Psychology', 1967

Nowadays, both in the East and in the West, we find a widespread interest in psychology, and it is easy to understand why. Psychology, as the term suggests, is concerned with the psyche, with mind, and one may say emphatically that the mind is the most interesting thing about us, and we are beginning to wake up to this. It has been suggested that the word 'mind' and the word 'man' are etymologically connected, which is perhaps of some significance. Psychology is both theoretical and practical. We all know, some of us only too well, that the pressure of modern life produces all sorts of mental tensions, even breakdown, and we have various systems of psychotherapy to relieve us from states of that kind. When I returned to this country some three years ago, after twenty years in the East, and started getting to know people, I was extremely surprised to find how many people suffer from mental strain in some form or another, and indeed how many have to have analysis. Not only is there this interest in psychology; there is also a growing interest in Buddhism. Recently I have been up and down the country visiting Buddhist groups, giving lectures, and holding meditation classes, and I have noticed a quickening of interest everywhere, so much so that some of us feel that a new stage in the development of Buddhism in this country has been reached. With this great interest in psychology and this growing interest in Buddhism, albeit on a considerably smaller scale, it is inevitable that sooner or later Buddhism and psychology should come together, that there should be some dialogue (to use the fashionable term) between them, and this is why I have decided to organize these lectures. Over the next seven weeks we will be studying aspects of Buddhist psychology, and this evening we will start with the analytical psychology of the Abhidharma.

But before we embark on any consideration of Buddhist psychology, we have to understand what Buddhism is. There are many answers to this question, but to be brief, historically, Buddhism is the spiritual tradition inaugurated by Gautama the Buddha in India some 2,500 years ago, around 500 BCE. The tradition he founded continues down to the present day in the countries of South-east Asia as a living, vital tradition. Essentially, Buddhism is the systematic development of awareness at the highest possible level. This awareness has several dimensions, and for Buddhism the two most important of these are wisdom and compassion. In this context, by wisdom I mean complete and utter freedom from subjectivity, both affective and intellectual, and by compassion I mean the spontaneous activity that springs up in accordance with the needs of living beings within the framework determined by wisdom.

So much will suffice for a general description of Buddhism. What about Buddhist psychology? Strictly speaking, there is no such thing, which might seem a rather odd thing to say at the beginning of a series of lectures about Buddhist psychology. But if we look at Buddhism, we see that it is a fully integrated teaching. It all hangs together: take up any one aspect of it and all the others follow. This fully integrated teaching has a number of different aspects, and when we study Buddhism, which Buddhists themselves call the Dharma or the *sāsana*, from a Western point of view, we isolate these different aspects from the whole and apply to them various Western terms. In this way we come to speak of Buddhist philosophy, Buddhist ethics, Buddhist logic, Buddhist epistemology, Buddhist ontology, Buddhist art, Buddhist culture, and even Buddhist sociology and Buddhist anthropology. But these terms really belong to a totally different universe of discourse, and in trying to make them fit Buddhism, we can seriously distort the whole picture. So in a sense there's no such thing as Buddhist psychology. There's no independent field of study that Buddhists know or label as psychology. At the same time, the term psychology isn't entirely inappropriate. So far as the present series of lectures is concerned, by Buddhist psychology I mean simply all of Buddhism's teachings about the nature and functioning of the mind, especially as this has to do with the spiritual life in general and the practice of meditation in particular.

We will not be dealing with the subject in a strictly systematic manner. This, in fact, would be impossible. The history of Buddhist psychology has yet to be written. We don't yet have any systematic study, though a few aspects have been touched upon remotely and in passing. I have selected for this course certain important aspects which I hope will enable us to approach the subject from a number of different angles and to penetrate deeply into them. At the same time, we should be able, through Buddhist psychology, to penetrate into the nature of Buddhism itself.

So, let us come to this evening's subject, the analytical psychology of the Abhidharma. Despite the expression analytical psychology, I'm afraid there's no connection here with Jung, but I shall have something to say about him later on in the series. Unless you've made a serious study of Buddhism, you will not have come across the term Abhidharma, but historically it represents one of the most important developments in the whole field of Buddhism, and it is widely and intensively studied in many parts of the East today, though I'm afraid that in some Eastern Buddhist circles a great mystery is made out of it. When you say the word 'Abhidharma', people hold their breath, as though it's something mysterious and profound, something that only monks know anything about. The impression is heightened by the fact that the texts of the Abhidharma are sometimes written in gold on beautiful palm leaf manuscripts, bound in golden covers studded with jewels. People get the impression, heightened by their devotional feelings, that the Abhidharma is something aloof and mysterious which ordinary people can't touch or even think about. But this impression of mystery is quite unnecessary. In principle the Abhidharma is, I won't say simple, but certainly straightforward.

As to the meaning of the word Abhidharma, *dharma* here means the doctrine or teaching of the Buddha, and *abhi* is a prefix meaning higher, superior, or further, so the Abhidharma is the higher doctrine or the further teaching. To understand precisely what this means, we have to go back to the life and teaching of the Buddha himself. The Buddha taught very extensively but, like Christ and Mohammed, he wrote nothing. He walked from place to place meeting all kinds of people – monks, princes, wealthy Brahmins, peasants, beggars, scavengers, courtesans – and he talked to them and taught them the Dharma. His ministry went on for forty-five years, in the course of which he gave thousands of discourses as well as participating in dialogues and conversations, answering questions, and so on. Around him was a circle of disciples, and they treasured up the words that fell from his lips, reflected upon them, repeated them to one another, and in this way committed to memory whatever he had taught them, or as much of it as they could. When they were old, they transmitted what they had learned to their disciples, and they to their disciples, and in this way the teaching was preserved for several hundred years, until it was eventually written down.

So after the Buddha's death, there was an enormous amount of Dharma teaching in existence. He had tens of thousands of monk disciples and they used to gather together regularly to recite what they remembered of his teaching, trying to reduce it to certain standard forms, but it was not systematically arranged. They remembered that on a certain occasion the Buddha had spoken in such and such a way to a certain Brahmin who asked a question, or that another time he'd called the monks together and given a discourse on a certain topic, but it was all mixed up. Long discourses were mixed up with short ones, poetry was mixed up with prose, teachings about the mind were mixed up with teachings about the elements, teachings about cosmology were mixed up with history and legend and marvels and biography. But within a few decades after the Buddha's death, or perhaps a century or so, the monks gradually started sorting it all out. Some of the more brilliant, more retentive minds started studying the whole mass of the tradition and organizing it systematically, and in this way it was worked over by hundreds of monks over a period of several hundred years. The result of this sorting out process was the Abhidharma, the higher teaching or the further doctrine.

Broadly speaking, the Abhidharma does three things. In the first place, it establishes the meaning of technical terms. Many terms hadn't been precisely defined; in one context they were used in one sense and in another context they were used in another. The Abhidharma does away with all that, delimiting the meaning of terms, establishing a technical meaning for them and developing a strict and almost scientific terminology. Secondly, the Abhidharma collates different discussions of the same topic. The Buddha might have spoken about Nirvāṇa twenty times, but one reference to it was here, another reference was there;

in one context he spoke from this point of view, in another context from that point of view. The Abhidharma collated references of this sort, compared them, and tried to extract from them a single teaching and a definitive meaning. Thirdly, the Abhidharma expounds the whole range of the Dharma systematically. Instead of presenting it bit by bit, according to circumstances, according to what question was asked, the Abhidharma organizes it into a totality and expounds it systematically. This is the achievement of the Abhidharma, and it is certainly a very great achievement indeed.

The Abhidharma dominated Buddhism in India for about a thousand years. It is a very important tradition, and if we do not know at least something about its basic viewpoint, its recurrent themes, and its distinctive emphasis, we can't really understand the development of Buddhist thought in India. At the same time, it must be confessed that the Abhidharma had its negative side. It banished from Buddhism the human element. It took out of the teachings everything biographical, everything historical. It banished myth, legend, and above all poetry. In the Abhidharma, the impersonal, the scientific, and the rational reign supreme. Eventually, inevitably, the banished elements reasserted themselves in the Mahāyāna, the great way, and the Vajrayāna, the adamantine way, but that's another story.

The two great schools of early Buddhism, the Theravāda and the Sarvāstivāda, each had its own independent Abhidharma tradition which they eventually committed to writing. The Theravāda version was written down in Pāli and forms part of the Pāli canon found in Ceylon, Burma, Thailand, and Cambodia, whereas the Sarvāstivāda version of the Abhidharma was written down in Sanskrit and in translation forms part of the Chinese canon, the original Sanskrit texts having been lost. The teachings coming down from the Buddha through disciples and disciples of disciples were written down in their unsystematized, earlier form to constitute what we know as the Sutta Piṭaka, and the systematized version, the Abhidharma, constitutes the Abhidhamma Piṭaka, and these two, together with the Vinaya Piṭaka, or Collection of Discipline, make up the Tripiṭaka, or threefold collection, of the schools of early Buddhism.

Both the Theravāda and the Sarvāstivāda Abhidharma Piṭakas contain seven voluminous books, but they are quite different sets. The Theravādins regard the Abhidharma Piṭaka as being the word of the Buddha. According to the commentarial tradition, it was preached by the Buddha in the Tāvatiṃsa *devaloka*, a higher heavenly realm, and thousands of beings came to listen, including the Buddha's mother, who came from where she was living in the Tuṣita heaven to listen to her son's teaching.[102] Then the Buddha descended from that higher realm and repeated what he'd taught his mother to Śāriputra, the wisest of his disciples, who taught it to his disciples, and in that way, the Abhidharma tradition was handed down. But the Sarvāstivādins frankly admit that the contents of the Abhidharma Piṭaka are the work of disciples, which would seem to be the case.

The Abhidharma literature is by no means confined to the two Abhidharma Piṭakas. These constituted only a beginning, and over the centuries hundreds of other works were produced. From a literary point of view the Abhidharma is a very rich, vast field indeed. But among all the writers of Abhidharma texts, two names tower above all the others, both of them belonging to the fifth century CE. On the Theravāda side there is the great scholastic commentator Buddhaghosa, author of the *Visuddhimagga*, the *Path of Purification*. He was a native of India, but lived and worked in Ceylon. And on the Sarvāstivāda side there is the great figure of Vasubandhu, the author of the *Abhidharmakośa*, or *Treasury of Abhidharma*, which is the major Abhidharma work in existence. He lived and worked in north-western India and in his old age became a follower of the Mahāyāna and one of the founders of the Yogācāra school of Mahāyāna philosophy.

Long before the days of Buddhaghosa and Vasubandhu, the Abhidharma had gone far beyond its original objectives. From analysing and classifying the Buddha's teachings, it started analysing and classifying the whole universe, indeed the whole of existence. Philosophically speaking, the position of the Abhidharma is what has been very well called by Dr Radhakrishnan pluralistic realism.[103] The Abhidharma believed that the whole of existence, mental and physical and spiritual, conscious and non-conscious, can be broken down into a limited number of ultimately real, discrete, elements. It's a psychophysical atomism. These elements it calls *dharmas*.

We must distinguish several meanings of this word *dharma*. It usually means doctrine or teaching, but in the technical sense of the Abhidharma it means the ultimate, irreducible, discrete elements into which the whole of existence is analysed, and beyond which analysis can't go. According to the Abhidharma, it is these *dharmas*, these ultimate irreducible elements, which in various combinations and permutations make up the whole phenomena of life. The Abhidharma maintains that these *dharmas* can be classified in various ways. In fact, this process of classifying *dharmas* is the chief work of the developed Abhidharma. It goes into it in enormous detail, though this evening we can be concerned only with the main outlines.

The Sarvāstivādins enumerate seventy-five *dharmas*, and the Theravādins count many more, but there is no difference of principle between the two traditions. Taking the entire mass of *dharmas*, both the Theravādins and the Sarvāstivādins divide them first of all into two groups: *saṃskṛta* and *asaṃskṛta*, literally compounded *dharmas* and uncompounded *dharmas*, usually translated conditioned *dharmas* and unconditioned *dharmas*. According to the Theravāda there is only one unconditioned *dharma*: Nirvāṇa, but according to the Sarvāstivāda there are three: space and two kinds of Nirvāṇa. All the *dharmas* other than these three, or in the case of the Theravāda this one, are conditioned. So you've got a very small group of unconditioned *dharmas* and a much larger group of conditioned *dharmas*. Rather importantly, for the Abhidharma this is not a distinction between real and unreal. For the Abhidharma, all the ultimate elements, whether conditioned or unconditioned, are equally real, equally ultimate, in the sense that none of them can be reduced to any of the others.

The conditioned *dharmas* are divided into four great groups, and it is here that the Abhidharma departs from the *sutta* tradition, the tradition of unsystematized Buddhism. In his original discourses, the Buddha divides conditioned existence into the famous five *skandhas*. If you have even a nodding acquaintance with Buddhism, you will have come across the five *skandhas*, the five heaps, or the five aggregates, as they're sometimes called, which are said to comprise the whole of phenomenal existence. They are *rūpa*, or material form; *vedanā*, or feeling; *samjñā*, or perception; *saṃskāra*, or acts of volition; and *vijñāna*, or consciousness. In the unsystematized teaching, the whole of phenomenal existence, especially the empirical personality or individuality, is reduced to just these five heaps, but the Abhidharma adopts a different classification, dividing the conditioned *dharmas* into four groups. First, and here there's an agreement with the five *skandha* classification, there's *rūpa*, or material form. Secondly, there's *citta*, which means mind or mental states. Thirdly, there's *caitta*, functions associated with mind or consciousness. And fourthly, there's *cittaviprayukta saṃskāras*, elements existing independently of mind. The whole of the Abhidharma turns on this grouping, which, as you can probably see, is much more systematic than the *sutta* classification into the five *skandhas*.

Each of these four groups is subdivided again. The Sarvāstivādins include under the group of material form fifteen *dharmas* or ultimate elements. Under the second heading, under mind or *citta*, they include only one *dharma* – mind itself. Under the third heading, functions associated with mind or consciousness, they include forty-seven *dharmas*, and under the heading of *dharmas* not associated with mind they include fourteen *dharmas*. The Theravādins, however, recognize only three subdivisions, but they divide the second group, the group of *citta* or mind, which the Sarvāstivādins leaves as just one single *dharma*, into eighty-nine *dharmas*. The Sarvāstivādins argue that mind is essentially one, that there are many mental states but they are all phenomena of consciousness, not independent, but the Theravādins do not agree with this.

Perhaps you can begin to see why I speak of the *analytical psychology* of the Abhidharma. I am obviously not using the term quite in the Jungian sense. The Abhidharma's analysis of mind is one application of its analysis of the whole of life, and for Buddhism, this analysis as applied to mind is the most important of all. Why and how this is, we shall see in a minute. Meanwhile, let us go back to our four groups of conditioned *dharmas* and go into them a little further.

The first group is that of the *dharmas* that make up material form, *rūpa*. The Sarvāstivādins enumerate fifteen *dharmas* under this heading and the Theravādins enumerate twenty-eight. Broadly speaking, here the Abhidharma investigates the nature of what we would call matter, and this investigation belongs more to philosophy than to psychology, so we need not pursue it here. And the fourth group is that of the *dharmas* dissociated from mind. These are fourteen in number, and in Western terms they comprise a mixture of philosophy, psychology, and epistemology. We have no need to pursue this group further, and in any case its existence is not recognized by the Theravāda. So that leaves us with the second and third groups, with *citta*, mind and mental states, and *caitasika*, the functions associated with mind. The interest of the Abhidharma as an analytical psychology centres here, so let us devote a little time to these two groups. Let us see what the Theravāda has to say about *citta*, and what the Sarvāstivāda has to say about *caitasika*. In that way, I hope we shall get a balanced picture of the Abhidharma.

As we've already seen, the Theravāda enumerates eighty-nine *cittas* or mental states. This is one of the most celebrated and difficult of those famous Buddhist lists, but this evening I'm not going to give you the complete list, though if you are interested I can refer you to books that do.[104] We are going to concern ourselves with certain general principles of classification, certain groupings of mental states. The first and most fundamental grouping within the eighty-nine *cittas* is an ethical one, or more correctly a karmic one. In the first place, the Theravāda Abhidharma distinguishes three kinds of *citta*, three kinds of mind or mental state. First, there's what it calls *kuśala*, which means skilful or wholesome or good mental states, those states of mind that make for ethical and spiritual progress and are productive of good karmic consequences. There are twenty-one of these, all dissociated from craving, hatred, and delusion. The second great classification of *cittas* identifies those that are *akuśala*, unskilful or unwholesome, which bind us to the world and eventually result, under the law of karma, in suffering. These are twelve in number. It is interesting to note that out of these twelve unskilful or unwholesome mental states, eight are rooted in craving, according to the Abhidharma, while only two are rooted in hatred and two in delusion, which suggests that we have to be most on our guard against craving. And the third group consists of what are described as *avyākata*, or karmically neutral mental states. These are neither skilful nor unskilful, and they are forty-seven in number. They can be further broken down, according to the Theravāda, into two subgroups, the first consisting of forty-four mental states that are the results of good and bad karmas committed in the past, and the second being three that are automatic mental functions. This second group is particularly interesting. It consists of automatic mental functions connected with the five senses, automatic mental functions connected with the mind, and, rather beautifully, the smile of the *arhant*, the smile of the Enlightened one.[105] This too is considered to be spontaneous. It has no real cause – it just comes. When you wander in the arid wastes of the Abhidharma, it's a relief to come across the smile of the *arhant* – it cheers you up on your journey.

So much for the Theravāda's ethical classification of the *cittas*, or mental states. The Theravāda also classified them according to the plane on which they occur. According to Buddhism there are three planes in the phenomenal universe: the *kāmaloka*, or world of sensuous desire, the *rūpaloka*, or world of form, and the *arūpaloka*, or formless world. Or, to paraphrase, we may speak of the material world, the archetypal world, and the spiritual world. The first plane is that experienced through the five senses, while the second and third plane are experienced only in higher states of meditation. There is also a fourth plane, the transcendental plane, though it's not a plane in the sense of being a fourth above the third, but more like a fourth dimension, in a quite different direction altogether. On this plane which is a non-plane there occur the thoughts – not just ideas, but thoughts, experiences – which have as their object the unconditioned *dharma*, Nirvāṇa. The Theravāda proceeds to distribute its eighty-nine *cittas* among these four planes. Karmically wholesome and karmically neutral *cittas* occur on all four planes, but unwholesome *cittas* occur only in the world of sensuous desire, the material world.

Broadly speaking, the Abhidharma analysis reveals that the higher the plane, the fewer the mental states involved. This is illustrated by its treatment of the five *citta*s belonging to the world of form, or the archetypal world, which are identical with the four *dhyānas*, or four superconscious states, experienced in meditation. In the first *dhyāna* there are five mental factors present, in the second *dhyāna* only four, in the third only three, and in the fourth only two. In other words, in meditation there is a process of the progressive unification of consciousness. In one of his works on the Abhidharma Lama Govinda speaks in terms of a pyramid of consciousness.[106] There's a broad base: in the lower realms of consciousness many mental factors operate. But as you go higher, to the world of form and the formless world, more and more factors are eliminated, and consciousness – mind – is progressively unified and integrated. With the help of the Abhidharma classification and distribution of *dharmas*, we see this process very clearly and beautifully. Modern psychology is familiar only with normal mental states and with what it calls abnormal mental states, but the analytical psychology of the Abhidharma extends to supernormal states, occurring in states of meditation, of superconsciousness, so the Abhidharma analytical psychology includes a psychology of mystical states or experiences. This it does not in any vague or woolly way, but in a cool, almost scientific manner.

These two groupings of the eighty-nine *cittas*, according to ethical value and according to plane, are among the most important classifications in the Abhidharma, but there are many more, and you can lose yourself in the maze if you're not careful. In any case, we've no time to go further into this matter this evening. We have to proceed to the Sarvāstivādin treatment of mental functions. According to the Sarvāstivāda, there are forty-six of these, and it divides them into six subgroups. Firstly, there are ten mental functions which are common to all mental states or *cittas* whatsoever, whether ethically good, bad, or neutral. One of these mental functions is of special interest: *samādhi*, or concentration. It is interesting to see that according to the Sarvāstivādin Abhidharma, in every mental state, in every experience, an element of concentration is present. This suggests that the capacity for developing *samādhi*, the capacity for meditation, is there all the time. People often say that they find it difficult to concentrate, but you are concentrated, at least in an embryonic sense, all the time. You are always concentrating on something. All you need to do is develop your concentration and switch it onto the right object, and that is what meditation is. Potentially, meditation is present in every mental state. This is one of the very striking insights of the Abhidharma.

Secondly, there's the subgrouping of mental functions that are common to all skilful mental states, and these also are ten in number: faith, energy, equanimity, modesty, shame, freedom from craving, freedom from hatred, harmlessness, peacefulness, and mindfulness. Whenever one entertains a skilful thought or mental state, all these ten mental functions are present. Thirdly and fourthly, we have mental functions arising in connection with unskilful and defiled states of mind, and these are altogether eight in number. Fifthly, there are mental functions arising in connection with certain defiled states of mind but not others – there are ten of these. And sixthly and lastly, we have eight mental functions which are not included in any of the previous five groups.[107] One could say much more on this subject, for the classification, analysis, study, explanation, and exposition of mental functions occupy a central position in the Sarvāstivāda Abhidharma and volumes upon volumes have been devoted by the great Abhidharma writers to this topic, but we haven't time for any more this evening.

Before concluding, just a few words on the bearing of the Abhidharma on the spiritual life. The Abhidharma has such a bearing because it is an aspect of Buddhism, which is concerned with the development of awareness at the highest possible level. First of all, the analytical psychology of the Abhidharma helps us to sort out our mental states. It helps us to distinguish skilful states from unskilful states, and when we can do that, we know what we have to cultivate and what we have to eliminate. This knowledge is extremely useful, especially to the meditator, making clear the whole rationale of the spiritual life. Secondly, the analytical psychology of the Abhidharma helps us to understand, even to realize, that what we usually think of as the self, or 'I', is nothing but an ever-changing combination of mental states and functions, and this realization is of supreme importance. For Buddhism, this constitutes wisdom: thinking not in terms of 'I', 'me', and 'mine', but contemplating the flow, the flux, the impersonal procession of the *dharmas* in their various groupings and combinations.

I hope that this evening I have been able to give you at least a glimpse of the analytical psychology of the Abhidharma, so that you can see in what sense the Abhidharma is analytical, in what sense it is a psychology, and also the general nature of its connection with its great parent, Buddhism.

ASPECTS OF BUDDHIST PSYCHOLOGY 2: THE PSYCHOLOGY OF SPIRITUAL DEVELOPMENT

The second in a series of seven lectures on 'Aspects of Buddhist Psychology', 1967

All of us were young once – in some cases rather a long time ago – and when we were young, most of us heard fairy tales. Some of you may remember from that far distant period hearing the story of Sleeping Beauty, who slept for a hundred years in a beautiful garden surrounded by an enormous hedge bristling with thorns, and how the prince who was to wake her with the proverbial kiss had to struggle through that thick thorn hedge to get to her. You may have been thinking that we are in a similar predicament as we try to approach the sleeping princess of Buddhist psychology. Last week we had to struggle through the thick thorn hedge of the Abhidharma, and I understand that some of us got a little scratched. I'm happy to inform you that this week we will be on easier, more negotiable ground, and we shall emerge, I hope, comparatively unscathed. Even if we are unable actually to get through to the princess, we may be able to pick a few flowers here and there. We come this evening to an aspect of Buddhist psychology which is difficult to apply and difficult to practise but perhaps not so difficult to understand, at least theoretically: the psychology of spiritual development.

I must admit to begin with that I don't much like this word 'spiritual'. If I had been able to do so, I would have chosen a better word, but ransack the dictionary as I might, I'm afraid I couldn't find one. Many years ago, when I was in India and writing books and articles on Buddhism, I coined the word 'normative', which I hoped might gain currency as a substitute for 'spiritual', but no one liked it, it never caught on, and eventually I had to drop it. So I'll carry on using the word spiritual, but when it occurs in this lecture, it is to be understood as connoting whatever conduces, either directly or indirectly, to the attainment of what Buddhists call Enlightenment.

In considering the psychology of spiritual development, it will be obvious straightaway that I am using the word psychology in a wider sense than usual. Last week we saw that the Abhidharma classifies mental states – *cittas* – according to their ethical value: whether they are skilful states dissociated from craving, anger, and delusion, or unskilful states associated with craving, anger, and delusion. We also saw that *cittas* are classifiable according to plane, whether they are associated with the sensual plane, the archetypal plane, the higher spiritual or noumenal plane, or even the transcendental plane. In this way, the Abhidharma developed a psychology not only of 'normal' mental states, the states we usually experience in our ordinary waking and dream consciousness, but supernormal states, those states that are experienced only in comparatively lofty states of concentration and meditation. The Abhidharma thus developed its own scientific psychology of what are loosely known as mystical experiences.

This evening we will be covering much the same ground, but much more practically. Let us start off with the whole idea of spiritual development. The dictionary defines development as 'gradual advance or growth through progressive stages'. In more Buddhistic terms, it consists in the arising of a higher stage in dependence upon, conditioned by, a lower stage. To use the traditional phraseology, development in Buddhism is a type of dependent origination or conditionality. To speak in these terms is to go right to the very heart of Buddhist thought, so perhaps we'd better start at the beginning. Perhaps we'd better go back to the Buddha.

After six years of strenuous spiritual struggle in the jungles and caves of north-eastern India, the Buddha gained supreme Enlightenment, *samyak sambodhi*, a profound spiritual experience which was a turning point not only in his own life, but in the life and history of Asia, indeed of the world. The scriptures tell us that after gaining Enlightenment, he remained immersed in the bliss of it for seven whole weeks. One can just imagine with what tremendous relief he plunged into that experience. Six years before, he had left his palace, his parents, his wife, his child, and for all these years he had struggled, sometimes despairing of success, sometimes wondering whether the light was ever going to dawn, sometimes fasting, sometimes fainting, sometimes with friends and followers, sometimes quite alone. But he'd struggled on, despite everything, and at last he had reached the goal and there was nothing for him to do but remain immersed in that transcendental experience. For seven weeks, he didn't so much as stir from that place.

But towards the end of this period, a train of reflection started arising in his mind. He started wondering whether he could ever reveal to other human beings the truth he had discovered, the secret of his spiritual experience. We are told that after a supreme spiritual crisis he decided, out of compassion for humanity, to reveal what he had discovered, to make the truth known, to teach the Dharma.[108] But no sooner had he made that decision than a problem, or at least a difficulty, arose. This is what we call nowadays the problem of communication, a problem which has been faced not only by the Buddha, but by all those throughout the history of humanity whose insight and experience has gone beyond the average. How is one going to put across to other people what one has found, or experienced, or discovered? Those whom we regard as exceptional people, geniuses, are often lonely, often feel that they are voices crying in the wilderness, because the problem of communication is so great. They have some knowledge or vision to impart, but there is no one to hear it, receive it, understand it. In some cases the rest of humanity starts catching up only centuries later.

This was the problem that confronted the Buddha. He had experienced the greatest of all experiences, Enlightenment, something absolutely beyond the ken of the ordinary person. How was he to communicate that? Here was someone ploughing a field, there was someone sowing, there was someone trading, someone else philosophizing, someone else just passing the time of day. How was he to communicate his experience of Enlightenment to them? What formulation could bridge the tremendous gap between the Enlightened mind and the unenlightened mind?

The Buddha's solution to this problem was simple, or at least apparently simple. He flung a slender bridge across the gulf between the Enlightened mind and the unenlightened mind in the form of the law, or the principle, or the truth, of conditionality. This was the link. It is stated in the Buddhist scriptures with deceptive brevity and simplicity – but genius often is very simple: 'Whatever arises on any plane of existence arises in dependence on conditions, and in the absence of those conditions, ceases.'[109] According to the Buddha's teaching, this law governs the whole of the universe on all planes: on the sensuous plane, the archetypal plane, and the spiritual plane, in all their aspects, not only physical, but psychological, and not only psychological, but spiritual. This statement of the truth, this principle of universal conditionality, *pratītya-samutpāda*, is the basis of the whole teaching of the Buddha.

To us nowadays this has a familiar ring; it sounds almost ordinary. But in the Buddha's day, when most people believed in divine, miraculous intervention, irruptions of the supernatural into ordinary life, this concept of universal conditionality was absolutely revolutionary, and it literally created a revolution in Indian thought, psychology, and spiritual life. Indeed, the concept of conditionality governing every level and aspect of human life was revolutionary even in this country a hundred years ago. When Charles Darwin applied this idea to the origin of species, when he propounded his theory of evolution, many people found it very difficult to accept. It was revolutionary even sixty years ago, when Freud applied an application of this principle to the workings of the subconscious mind. People used to think that things just popped into the mind, and they weren't interested in the why and the wherefore of it until Freud formulated certain laws and found conditionality working at that level. We may even go so far as to say that this concept of universal conditionality is revolutionary even today, as applied to the spiritual life. We tend to think that spiritual experiences happen by chance: we have a mystical experience and that's that. We don't know how it comes or how it goes: we think we have no control over it. But Buddhism says, 'The law of conditionality is at work here. The experience arises in dependence on certain conditions, and it ceases when those conditions are no longer there.' This great principle – translated variously as the law of conditionality, or dependent origination, or conditioned co-production – was explained by the Buddha.

He also expounded two trends in this law of conditionality: the reactive trend and the progressive trend, the cyclical mode and the spiral mode. The first type of conditionality consists in a process of action and reaction between pairs of opposites. For instance, there's loss and gain. You lose something, you get it back, you lose it again – there's an action and reaction between these two opposite poles. In the same way, you react from pleasure to pain, from pain back to pleasure. Or there's sleeping and waking; you sleep in order to wake and you wake in order to sleep, and in this way your life goes on. A Buddhist would say that you also oscillate between birth and death. You are born only to die; you die only to be reborn. In this reactive or cyclical mode of conditionality, the mind oscillates or vibrates between opposite states, never at rest, but never truly going forward. This is the state of most of us most of the time, as a little honest reflection will quickly reveal. We know no rest, but we move not an inch forward. The second type of conditionality, the progressive or the spiral, is different. It consists in a process of cumulative reactions – we have to use that word because we've got no better one – between factors which are not opposites but augment each other, each succeeding factor augmenting the effect of the preceding one. If you experience pleasure, from pleasure you move not to pain but to happiness; from happiness you move not to unhappiness but to rapture; from rapture you move not to despair but to bliss; and so on. There is a progressive, cumulative spiral.

In the material world, only the cyclical type of conditionality is at work. Everything, sooner or later, passes over into its opposite and back again. But in the mental and spiritual world, both cyclical and spiral conditionality are active. The cyclical type of conditionality is symbolized by the Tibetan wheel of life, which is not just a pretty picture on a monastery wall, but shows us accurately and minutely the way our minds work when they revolve between the pairs of opposites. And the spiral type of conditionality is symbolized by the sequence of the stages of the path to Enlightenment, which shows how the mind grows in a cumulative fashion from lower to higher states of being and consciousness.

At the hub of the Tibetan wheel of life there are three animals: a cock, a snake, and a pig. These symbolize the three principal aspects of the reactive mind: the cock representing craving, the snake representing aversion or anger or hatred, and the pig representing mental and spiritual blindness and ignorance. Each animal is biting the tail of the one in front, and this means that craving, aversion, and delusion are interconnected – you can't have one without the other two. These are the three principal aspects of the reactive mind, the mind that reacts to pleasant experiences with craving, to unpleasant ones with aversion, and to those which are neither pleasant nor painful with indifference based upon mental and spiritual blindness and ignorance.

Around the hub of the wheel is a circle divided into two segments, a white one in which people are moving upwards with happy peaceful expressions, and a black one in which people are plunging downwards with expressions of horror and despair. These two segments represent the ethical life and the unethical life. But all this is within the wheel. The truly spiritual person can never become unspiritual, but the person who is merely good in the conventional sense can become bad, so the conventionally religious life is included within the wheel of life, part of the reactive mind. The next circle out is divided into the six planes of rebirth according to traditional Buddhist cosmology: human beings, hungry spirits, animals, divine beings, titans, and beings in states of torment. And the third and outermost circle is divided into twelve segments representing the twelve *nidānas* or links, each of which is illustrated with a little picture, explaining in detail the workings of the cyclical type of conditionality on the level of the individual mind.

The first *nidāna*, the first link, is *avidyā*, which means spiritual blindness, unawareness, ignorance – the ignorance of the previous life. In dependence upon this ignorance there arise various *saṃskāras*, activities productive of karma, the results of which you have to reap at some time in the future. These two *nidānas* are the cause process of the past life. Very often the first is compared to the state of being drunk and the second to performing actions in that state of drunkenness. Overpowered by spiritual blindness and ignorance, we perform actions of body, speech, and mind that are productive of karma which we call the *saṃskāras*, sometimes translated as karma formations or mental formations.

In dependence upon the ignorance and ignorance-inspired activities of the previous life, there arises at the beginning of this life, in the womb of the mother, the initial seed or pulse of consciousness, *vijñāna*. Then in dependence upon that, there arises *nāma-rūpa*, the entire psychophysical organism. In dependence on *nāma-rūpa*, there arise the *ṣaḍāyatanas*, the six sense organs. In Buddhist psychology, the ordinary mind is considered to be in a rather humble position. We don't regard it as in any way superior to the eye or the ear or the nose. It's merely a sixth sense. Then, when the six senses come into contact with their respective sense objects, arises *sparśa*, which means contact. In dependence upon contact there arises feeling or *vedanā*, which may be pleasant, painful, or neutral. Then in dependence upon that feeling, especially pleasant feeling, there arises *tṛṣṇā*, craving. We start hankering after pleasant experience. In dependence upon craving there arises *upādāna*, clinging or attachment. We start getting attached to the pleasant side of life, clinging to our pleasant experiences. In dependence on that clinging there arises *bhāva*, becoming or coming to be, the process of being conditioned by your limitations, your clinging, your attachment. This is the last *nidāna* of the present life. In dependence upon that there arises, as the first *nidāna* of the next life, the future life, *jāti*, or birth. And in dependence upon that arises *jarā-maraṇa*, or old age, disease, and death. These twelve links are distributed over three lives: *avidyā* and the *saṃskāras* in the previous life; *vijñāna*, *nāma-rūpa*, the *ṣaḍāyatanas*, *sparśa*, *vedanā*, *tṛṣṇā*, *upādāna*, and *bhāva* in the present life; and *jāti* and *jarā-maraṇa* in the future life. But though the twelve links are distributed over three lives, all twelve are also operative in our ordinary, cyclical mode of consciousness all the time, every minute of the day.

*Nidāna*s are of two kinds, those that are the causes of future results, and those that are the results of previous causes. You get groups alternating in this way: a karma or action group and then a result group; then an action group and again a result group. We can say that *nidānas* one and two, ignorance and the activities based on ignorance, constitute the karma or action process of the past. It's because of entertaining this ignorance and performing these *saṃskāras* that we experience the result process that follows, which consists of *vijñāna*, consciousness; *nāma-rūpa*, the psychophysical organism; the *ṣaḍāyatanas* or six sense organs; *sparśa* or contact; and *vedanā* or feeling. Following upon *vedanā*, we get *tṛṣṇā*, or craving, *upādāna*, or clinging or attachment, and *bhava*, or coming to be. These three make up the cause process of the present life, because they set into motion effects that we will experience in the future. And in the future life, we have *jāti*, or birth, and *jarā-maraṇa*, or old age, disease, and death. These represent the result or effect process of the future life.

There are three junctures occurring where one process passes over into another. There is a juncture between *saṃskāras* and *vijñāna*, between the previous life and the present life. Then there's a juncture between feeling and craving, feeling being the last *nidāna* of the effect process of the present life and craving being the first *nidāna* of the cause process of the present life. And thirdly, there is a juncture between *bhāva*, or coming to be, and *jāti* or birth, in other words, between the last *nidāna* of the present life and the first *nidāna* of the future life. It is the middle one of these three junctures which is of the greatest importance, the juncture between feeling and craving. It's here, according to the Buddha's teaching, that all the trouble begins, and because it begins here, it can also be made to end here. *Vedanā*, feeling, stands for all the experiences of the external world by which we are confronted. All the time sense impressions and mental impressions are pouring in, and we react to them all. For the most part, if not entirely, we react automatically with craving, aversion, fear, jealousy, or craving, and in this way the wheel of life continues to revolve. This, according to the Buddha's teaching, is the psychology of the reactive mind, the psychology of bondage.[110]

So how is this process of the reactive mind to be stopped? How is one to check the revolutions of the wheel? There are two methods, the sudden method and the gradual method, both representing the psychology of spiritual development, the psychology of liberation. The sudden method is illustrated by a significant incident in the life of the Buddha. It is said that in those days there was a man called Bāhiya who lived on the west coast of India. He'd practised meditation, but doubt arose in his mind as to whether he was on the right path. He came to hear of the Buddha, so he set off on foot, hundreds of miles, until he came to Śrāvastī, where the Buddha was staying. On the morning he arrived, he was told that the Buddha had already gone to the nearby village to beg his supply of food for the day. Bāhiya was so keen to meet the Buddha that he hastened into the village, and sure enough, he saw a slow and stately figure moving gently ahead, going from one door to the next, standing for a few minutes with his begging-bowl in his hand, and waiting for a few morsels of rice and curry to be put into it. So great was Bāhiya's eagerness to receive a teaching that he went straight up to the Buddha and without a word of introduction said, 'Lord, give me a teaching!' The Buddha's practice was to maintain silence when he was on his almsround, so he said nothing, but just moved on. But Bāhiya wasn't to be put off. He walked along behind the Buddha and again he said, 'Lord, give me a teaching!' The Buddha still took no notice. But Bāhiya, desperately now, put his request a third time. The Buddha's custom was that if you asked him a question for the third time, whatever it was and however disastrous the answer might be for you, he would reply. So he turned round and gave Bāhiya what the scriptures call an 'elephant look' – that is, turning his whole body to face Bāhiya – and said, 'In the seen, only the seen; in the heard, only the heard; in the tasted, only the tasted; in the touched, only the touched; in the thought, only the thought.' With that he turned and went on his way, and Bāhiya, we are told, became Enlightened on the spot.[111]

I don't know how many of you became Enlightened when I said that just now, but if you didn't, you may be wondering what the Buddha meant by 'In the seen, only the seen; in the heard, only the heard.' He meant: cultivate towards all experiences an attitude of pure awareness. Don't react. When you see something, just see it. Don't start thinking, 'Oh, look at that tree – that needs cutting down,' or 'Yes, those apples are getting ripe, I'd like to eat those.' Usually the reactive mind starts working at once. But the Buddha advises us just to look, just to see. Just experience the pure sense impression, with nothing added from your side, no subjective reaction. Be like a mirror, reflecting everything without distortion. Be purely aware, purely objective. Stop reacting. And Bāhiya, fortunate man, was able to do this. He saw what the Buddha meant, immediately cut off all his reactions, and was Enlightened on the spot. Anyone who adopts this attitude, who, as though with a sword, can cut off all reaction, not react to anything, just mirror all sensations with perfect objectivity, can gain Enlightenment. As you can imagine, this is very difficult to do. It's for spiritual heroes, not for ordinary people. But there's a gradual method too, and this is represented by the twelve positive *nidānas*. They wind up and out of the wheel of life from the point between *vedanā* or feeling and *tṛṣṇā*, thirst or craving. They are a sequence of progressive states of being and consciousness, representing the whole process of the transition from *saṃsāra* to Nirvāṇa. They are not exactly the stages of a path, though we can refer to them like that. They are more like stages of growth or development, the succeeding stage arising in dependence on the preceding one, growing out of its fullness, so that no stage of growth can be bypassed.

The series of twelve positive *nidānas* begins with suffering, which in this sequence of positive *nidānas* corresponds to *vedanā*, feeling, among the twelve reactive or cyclical *nidānas*. We can say that it is through the experience of suffering, through the pain and stress of human existence, that we become aware. Unfortunately, we are often most aware when we are suffering. When we have it easy, very often we lapse into spiritual forgetfulness and unawareness, but pain stings and startles us out of this somnolent state and we begin to become aware.

And without awareness, there is no spiritual life, indeed, no truly human life. Without awareness, we are just a mass of blind animal reactions, cyclical reactions, humanoid rather than human.

Suffering (Sanskrit *duḥkha*) covers not just painful experience – a cut finger or a toothache – but the unsatisfactoriness of ordinary life. Even pleasant experiences are ultimately unsatisfying. This was certainly the Buddha's experience in the days when he lived at home with his parents and his wife. He had everything that the world could offer, but there was a corner in his heart that those things could not fill. It was to fill that corner that he left home and struggled for six years, and eventually he found something that did fill it: his experience of supreme Enlightenment. It is the experience of many people that even when we are doing what we most enjoy, when we are with the people we like best, there's a grain of dissatisfaction, some little corner of the heart which is not filled, which hankers after something more, something greater, something beyond. Most of us pretend it's not there, or say, 'Well, I should be satisfied, so I suppose I am really.' But we should cherish our dissatisfaction, allow that little empty corner to remain unfilled until we find that which alone can fill it. It's because of this underlying dissatisfaction that we feel restless, and because we feel restless, we go in search of something more, something higher. At first we don't know what we're searching for; we're groping in the dark. But eventually, if we search for long enough, we come up against something higher, or something that is a symbol of something higher. We may read a book or see a picture or meet a person or have an experience which convinces us that there is something that can fill that empty corner in our heart. And when we encounter it, we feel a response. We know at once, in those familiar words, 'This is it.'[112]

This heartfelt response is what in Buddhism we call *śraddhā*, or faith, which is the second of the positive *nidānas*. In this way, in dependence upon *duḥkha*, suffering, there arises *śraddhā*. This is not just believing something to be true, or even an emotional state. *Śraddhā* is the response of what is ultimate in us to what is ultimate in the universe. For Buddhists, faith is specifically faith in the Three Jewels: the Buddha, the Dharma, and the Sangha, which represent the ultimate values for the sake of which all other things exist. The Buddha represents the ultimate spiritual ideal of Enlightenment. The Dharma represents the path of the higher evolution, the whole spiral mode of progression. And the Sangha is the spiritual community within which the path is followed and spiritual development takes place. Faith is our total response to these values, and that response manifests in a positive commitment which we call Going for Refuge to the Three Jewels. Going for Refuge to the Buddha means accepting him as teacher. Going for Refuge to the Dharma means accepting that as one's way of life. And Going for Refuge to the Sangha means finding oneself in the midst of a spiritual community of people following the same path to the same goal, with the opportunity to learn from those with more spiritual experience.

Next, in dependence on faith there arises joy or delight (Sanskrit *prāmodya*). We've found what we were looking for, or at least we've begun to find it, so we feel pleased and contented. At this stage, we may want to express our happiness and gratitude through practising devotional exercises like offering flowers to the Buddha image, lighting sticks of incense, chanting, and so on. We may also feel great love and devotion for our spiritual teachers. More even than that, the delight we experience begins to transform our lives. We become less and less self-centred. We start to be weaned away from ourselves – we become more generous, more open-hearted and open-handed, and our lower nature starts coming under control, especially in matters such as food, sex, and sleep. We start leading a comparatively harmless, simple, and sane life, and this too makes us feel happy, contented, and carefree, at peace with ourselves. We enjoy a good conscience. This doesn't mean that we are complacent, but we know within ourselves that we are on the right path. Buddhism attaches great importance to this experience, teaching that not being on good terms with yourself, or not approving of yourself, or have an unconscious or half-conscious awareness that you've done something you shouldn't have done or have left undone something you should have done, blocks further progress. In some Buddhist traditions, we therefore have confession rituals, as for instance in our Sevenfold Puja, when we confess our faults in front of all the Buddhas. In this way our feeling of guilt is purged, our feeling of joy and delight is restored, and we can go on with our spiritual progress.

Then, in dependence upon that joy arises rapture (Sanskrit *prīti*), an emotion of intense joy. In fact, we could even translate *prīti* as ecstasy. *Prīti* is experienced not only mentally, but also in the physical body, with several degrees of intensity. In the first, there is a slight thrill of ecstasy, and the hairs of the body stand on end. The second type of *prīti* is a momentary but electrifying stimulation, a sudden flash of ecstasy, like a flash of lightning: but before you can absorb it, or even recover from it, it's gone. Thirdly, there is what is described as a flooding emotion of ecstasy which descends on the body again and again, like the breaking of waves on the seashore. In the fourth kind of ecstasy, the whole body is surcharged, like a mountain cave being swept by a mighty flood of water – this is the traditional comparison. And the fifth kind of *prīti* is what is called the transporting, in which the body may even be physically lifted from the ground, and levitation occurs.[113] Most people have had some experience of *prīti*. You may not have been literally lifted from the ground, but you may experience something like *prīti* when you see a beautiful sunset, or hear a beautiful piece of music and you're so deeply moved that a lump comes into your throat and tears come into your eyes. *Prīti* is like this, but much more intense, especially when heightened by the practice of meditation.

In dependence on rapture arises *praśrabdhi* (Pāli *passaddhi*), which means calming down or pacification. At this stage, the physical side effects of rapture calm down. The hair no longer stands on end, the body no longer feels flooded, not because the rapture has become less, but because it has become more. Because your spiritual experience has expanded and become more profound, you can contain and assimilate it better, and it doesn't overflow onto the physical plane. The comparison given is with an elephant taking a bath. An elephant is so big that if it steps into a small pond to take its bath, the water splashes out at the sides, but if it lowers itself into a great river, there's hardly a ripple. The elephant descending into the pond is like the experience of *prīti* – there's a great physical disturbance because of one's limited experience and practice. But the elephant submerging itself into the great river with hardly a ripple is like the experience of *praśrabdhi*.[114] One's spiritual experience has expanded, so that even though the ecstasy is there, it is contained within, and doesn't show itself in physical manifestations.

In dependence upon pacification arises bliss (*sukha*), a state of intense happiness, purely internal, without any physical manifestation, which represents the complete unification of all the emotional energies, which have been made positive, transmuted, and made to flow together into one great harmonious stream. In this stage there is the experience not only of bliss, but of peace, love, and joy. There are no negative emotions

– no hatred, no fear, no craving – certainly not in the conscious mind, though perhaps just very slightly in the unconscious mind.

In dependence on bliss arises *samādhi*. *Samādhi* has a number of meanings, but here it means concentration, and this experience is based on an important psychological principle, which is that when one is completely happy, when all one's emotional energies are unified, when no energy overflows or leaks away, then one is concentrated. A concentrated person is a happy person. If you're unhappy, you're restless. If you're happy, you're concentrated, you're absorbed. And the happier you are, the longer you can stay concentrated, because the less need there is to change to something else. This can be illustrated by another story from the scriptures. One day a certain king went to call upon the Buddha, and discussion arose between them as to who was the happier. The king thought to himself, 'Well, it's obvious. I've got all those palaces, I've got this army and all this treasure, and all these women. Surely I'm happier than the Buddha.' But the Buddha said, 'No, I'm happier than you.' The king said, 'Prove it.' So the Buddha said, 'All right. Just sit here, cross-legged, eyes closed. Do you feel happy?' The king said, 'Yes, quite happy.' So the Buddha said, 'Suppose you were to sit like this for an hour. Would you still be happy?' And the king said, 'Yes.' And then the Buddha said, 'If you were to sit here for the whole day, would you still be happy?' The king said, 'Er, well, I might be.' So the Buddha said, 'What about a week? Could you sit here for a week?' The king had no answer to that. But the Buddha said, 'I could sit here without moving not only for an hour, not only for a day, but for seven days and seven nights, enjoying uninterrupted perfect happiness.'[115]

All this relates to our own practice of meditation. Meditation begins with concentration, and it's well known that most people find concentration rather difficult. If that's your experience, it's probably because you're not very happy. You don't enjoy it because your emotional energies are not unified. Some of your emotional energy is leaking away here, some is leaking away there, and there's very little left for the meditation practice, so you have to make a tremendous effort to forcibly fix your mind on the concentration object. But that is not the way to do it. If your emotional energies are not unified and you try with a conscious effort of will to fix your mind on a point and hold it there, there's a danger that there will be a reaction from the unconscious mind. If you go on a meditation retreat without proper preparation, if you dash there from the office or a hectic weekend away without having meditated for two or three weeks, and then think, 'Right, now I'll get down to it,' and forcibly put your mind on the object, there will be a reaction because your emotional energies have not been unified, and they will give you a lot of trouble. This is why preparation for meditation is so important. In preparing, we disengage our psychological energies from other things and direct them all in one channel. When we are fully prepared, concentration exercises just put the finishing touch. If all our emotional energies are flowing together, when we sit to become aware of the breath going in and out, we're automatically concentrated, with no struggle and hardly any effort.

In dependence on concentration arises knowledge and vision of things as they really are (*yathābhūta-jñānadarśana*), in other words insight into reality. This stage is of crucial importance, because it marks the transition from meditation to wisdom, from the psychological to the truly spiritual, or better, to the transcendental. In this stage we start escaping from the gravitational pull of *saṃsāra* and start feeling the gravitational pull of Nirvāṇa in the opposite direction. From this stage, the eighth positive *nidāna*, there is no falling back. The attainment of Enlightenment is assured. Knowledge and vision of things as they really are is twofold, corresponding to the first two kinds of *śūnyatā*. In the last talk we saw the Abhidharma distinction between unconditioned and conditioned *dharmas*. The first kind of *śūnyatā* consists of the emptiness of conditioned *dharmas* in respect of the Unconditioned. The conditioned *dharmas* are impermanent, unsatisfactory, and unreal, so Nirvāṇa, the unconditioned *dharma*, which has the opposite characteristics, is not to be found in *saṃsāra*. The second kind of *śūnyatā* is the emptiness of the Unconditioned in respect of the conditioned. Unconditioned existence is permanent (it's above time), supremely blissful, and ultimately real, characteristics that one does not find among the conditioned *dharmas*. Just as the conditioned is empty with regard to the Unconditioned, the Unconditioned is empty with regard to the conditioned. These are the first two kinds of *śūnyatā*. Knowledge and vision of things as they really are consists in seeing this clearly, not just as an intellectual understanding, but as a direct perception and experience which changes one's whole outlook. From this point on, one's whole being, one's whole life, is oriented towards the Unconditioned rather than the conditioned.

Then, in dependence upon knowledge and vision of things as they really are there arises withdrawal (*nirveda*). This is sometimes translated as revulsion or disgust, but that is much too psychological – one has gone beyond reactions of that sort. It's just a smooth movement of withdrawal from involvement in things that you have seen through, by which you are no longer deluded. It's like seeing a mirage in a desert. When you realize it's a mirage, though it may look very beautiful, and the fruit on the trees may look very tempting, you're no longer deceived. Withdrawal represents an attitude of sitting loose to life, not taking it too seriously, doing what is objectively necessary but not getting subjectively caught up.

In dependence on withdrawal arises dispassion (*vairāgya*). Withdrawal is the movement of detachment from conditioned existence. Dispassion is the state of being detached. In this state, we can't be moved by any worldly happening or experience. It's a state of complete imperturbability, like that of the Buddha sitting under the bodhi tree and repulsing the armies of Māra, the evil one.

In dependence on dispassion arises freedom (*vimukti*). Nowadays there's a lot of talk about freedom of various kinds, and only too often we're tempted to think that it means freedom to do as we like. But the Buddhist conception of freedom is quite different. In Buddhism, freedom is twofold: *ceto-vimukti*, or freedom of mind, consisting in complete freedom from all subjective emotional bias, and *prajñā-vimukti*, or freedom of wisdom, freedom from all wrong views – ignorance, unawareness, and so on. This freedom is the ultimate goal of Buddhism, synonymous with Enlightenment. As the Buddha says, 'Just as the great ocean has but one taste, the taste of salt, so my teaching has one taste, the taste of freedom.'[116]

In dependence on freedom arises knowledge of the destruction of the *āsravas* (*āsravakṣayajñāna*). One isn't only free; one knows that one is free. *Āsrava* is one of the most untranslatable words in the whole of Buddhism, but it means something like a mental poison that floods the mind. There are three *āsravas*: *kāmāsrava*, or the poison of the desire for sensuous experience; *bhavāsrava*, the poison of the desire for any form of conditioned existence, even existence on a higher plane as a heavenly being; and *avidyāsrava*, the poison of spiritual ignorance or unawareness.[117] When these are extinct, and when one knows that they are extinct, then one is free, one is truly Enlightened, one has gained Buddhahood.

We've come a very long way, and traversed a lot of ground rather rapidly, but these are the twelve positive *nidānas*, the twelve stages of the spiral path, winding from the point between feeling and craving all the way up to Enlightenment, to Nirvāṇa. This great sequence of states and experiences constitutes the psychology of spiritual development, a development of which each and every one of us present here this evening is capable, if only we make the effort.

ASPECTS OF BUDDHIST PSYCHOLOGY 3: THE DEPTH PSYCHOLOGY OF THE YOGĀCĀRA

The third in a series of seven lectures on 'Aspects of Buddhist Psychology', 1967

This evening we are going to be concerned to some extent with psychological themes and technicalities, as we were in the first lecture, but also, as in the second lecture, with the spiritual life itself, and we will be concerned with the first as subordinate to the second. Broadly speaking, this evening's lecture follows a middle way between the subject matter of the first lecture and the subject matter of the second. Of course, the first question that arises is 'What is the Yogācāra?' I'm sorry we keep having to have all these Sanskrit and Pāli words, but until they become naturalized in English there's no other way. Yogācāra literally means the practice of yoga: *ācāra* (Pāli) means practice, or application, or even conduct. We shall be going a little more deeply into this later on. For the present, all we need to know is that the Yogācāra is one of the schools of ancient Indian Buddhism. Buddhism was extinct in India for many centuries until its revival in the twentieth century and the Yogācāra school is no longer known there, except as a subject of academic study.

So the Yogācāra is a school of ancient Indian Buddhism. More specifically, it is a school of the Mahāyāna form of Buddhism. In the first lecture I remarked that poetry and myth – the whole non-rational approach – had been practically banished from Buddhism by the Abhidharma, and that those more mythical, poetic, intuitive elements reasserted themselves in the Mahāyāna and the Vajrayāna. So let us look into this a little bit more. We all know that Buddhism originated in India, but it's not always appreciated that it lasted in India for 1,500 years, longer than Christianity has been known in Britain. The history of Buddhism in India lasted from about 500 BCE to about 1000 CE or a little after, when it was finally destroyed. (See pp. 237ff.) During that history, Buddhism passed through three great phases of development, known in Buddhism as the three *yānas*. *Yāna* literally means a vehicle, but in this context it means a path or a way. Each of the three *yānas* was dominant for 500 years in the history of Buddhism in India.

So what were these three *yānas*? As this is only introductory to our main subject matter, I am going to be very brief and schematic. The first *yāna* is the Hīnayāna, which literally means the 'little way', so called because (in the view of those who later called it that) it taught the goal of individual emancipation, individual realization and attainment of Nirvāṇa, without thinking so much about other people. The Hīnayāna stressed ethics, especially in the form of disciplinary rules, and, as we saw in the case of the Abhidharma, analytical psychology. It attached great importance to the monastic life; indeed, it tended in practice to identify the spiritual life with the monastic life. The Theravāda and the Sarvāstivāda are the two most prominent representatives of the Hīnayāna phase. The second great phase in the history of Buddhism is the Mahāyāna, which likewise was dominant in India for about 500 years. Mahāyāna literally means 'great way' or 'great vehicle', and it is so called because it teaches the goal of universal emancipation. It says, as the bodhisattva vow it taught makes clear, that one should be concerned not only with one's own spiritual development, but also with that of other people, and one should help them to the utmost of one's ability, according to one's spiritual qualifications and experience. The Mahāyāna stressed metaphysics in the sense of ontology; it was preoccupied with the nature of the Absolute; and it gave an important place to the emotional and devotional side of the spiritual life, including ceremonies, rituals, and devotions to Buddhas and bodhisattvas. The Mahāyāna attached great importance to living in the world but not of it, and maintained that the dedicated household life, devoted to the realization of spiritual objectives, was just as good as the monastic life. And the third phase was that of the Vajrayāna, the adamantine way, perhaps better known as Tantric Buddhism. This also accepted the Mahāyānistic goal of universal salvation, but taught its realization by means of a 'short cut'. It stressed symbolic ritual and the practice of esoteric meditation.

On the philosophical side, there are two great schools of the Indian Mahāyāna: the Madhyamaka and the Yogācāra. Madhyamaka means 'middle way', and this school is so called because it followed a middle way between the extreme metaphysical positions of affirmation and negation. It tried to see reality not in terms of existence or non-existence, but in terms of a third factor above and beyond those two extremes. And the Yogācāra, as we've already seen, means the practice of yoga. These two schools have certain fundamental things in common, but each has its distinctive emphasis. The Madhyamaka emphasizes the primacy of wisdom, and its approach to reality is dialectical, logical, philosophical, even intellectual, while the Yogācāra places greater emphasis on meditation, approaching reality not through the intellect, but through meditation, through one's own spiritual experience.

Each of these schools is associated with a particular group of Mahāyāna *sūtras*. *Sūtras* are discourses given by the Buddha, and they are the most important scriptures of the Buddhist tradition. The Madhyamaka is associated with the Prajñāpāramitā or Perfection of Wisdom *sūtras*. There are more than thirty of these texts in Sanskrit and Chinese and Tibetan. Most of them survive in the original Sanskrit, and they have all been translated into English by Dr Edward Conze. The Yogācāra is associated with a *sūtra* called the *Saṃdhinirmocana*, which means 'Explication of Knots', and especially with the *Saddharma Laṅkāvatāra Sūtra*, 'the entry of the Good Law into the island of Lanka', the *Laṅka* for short.

The Madhyamaka school was initiated by the great Indian thinker and sage Nāgārjuna, and the Yogācāra was founded by Maitreya, or Maitreyanātha. Scholars disagree as to whether Maitreya is a historical or a non-historical figure, just as they dispute whether Bodhidharma, and even the Buddha, was a historical figure. Scholars tend to be fond of disputes of this sort. But according to tradition, Maitreya or Maitreyanātha, the founder of the Yogācāra tradition, is identical with the bodhisattva Maitreya, the coming Buddha. Among Buddhists there is a belief that another great Enlightened teacher will arise when the teaching has been forgotten and once again proclaim it to humanity. Buddhists of practically all schools believe that the next Buddha is now the bodhisattva Maitreya, and lives on a higher plane of existence imperceptible to human beings except when in advanced states of meditation. According to the Yogācāra tradition, the great teacher

Asaṅga, who lived in the fifth century, is supposed to have visited the Tuṣita heaven, where Maitreya lives, and to have received instruction from him, which he wrote down in the Five Books of Maitreya, as well as in various independent works of his own, and these works constitute the literary foundation of the Yogācāra school. Some scholars dismiss this legend, saying that Maitreya, or Maitreyanātha, was a human, historical teacher of the fourth century and Asaṅga simply received instruction from him. Perhaps it doesn't matter very much which is true. But there's at least one point of interest in the traditional account, according to which Asaṅga visited Maitreya in the Tuṣita heaven. In Buddhism a heaven, a *devaloka*, is a higher plane of consciousness. In the first lecture we saw that the Abhidharma classifies mind according to planes, including planes of consciousness that rise above the level of so-called normal consciousness. The Tuṣita *devaloka* represents one of the higher planes or states of consciousness, and the story of the origin of the Yogācāra school may be taken to mean that Asaṅga received the inspiration, even the guidance, for his work from a higher level of consciousness in the course of his own practice of meditation. This is in keeping with the whole emphasis of the Yogācāra school, and the name of the school, which means simply the practice of yoga. In this context yoga means not physical exercises but meditation, so the Yogācāra is the school of the practice of meditation. This brings us to a very important principle, which is that one who meditates, whether a follower of the Yogācāra school or any other, sees things in a way that is very different from how one who does not meditate sees them. This is the first thing we have to realize, otherwise we shan't understand very well what follows.

The ancient Indian Yogācārins meditated; that is, they experienced states of consciousness above and beyond the functions of the ordinary conscious mind, states much nearer to reality than those we normally experience. They not only attained them; they dwelt in them, lived and moved and had their being on those higher levels. It's only natural that these experiencers of higher states of consciousness should have seen things very differently from how other people saw them. They saw them truly, saw them as they were in reality, and they formulated their vision in terms of the Yogācāra philosophy. This isn't philosophy in the modern academic Western sense of the term. A couple of years ago, not long after my return from India, I paid a visit to Oxford to give a lecture, and before the lecture I had a talk with Dr Conze, who was living there and giving lectures. Knowing his great knowledge of Indian thought and Buddhist philosophy, I said, 'Surely there must be a tremendous interest in oriental philosophy in Oxford, especially since you are here?' But he smiled a bitter smile and said, 'Interested in oriental philosophy? In Oxford? Good heavens, no. They're not even interested in Western philosophy here.' And then he said, with his usual scathing expression, 'All they're interested in is linguistic analysis.' The Yogācāra philosophy isn't philosophy in that sense. Like any other form of Buddhist philosophy, even the Abhidharma, it attempts to describe what is essentially a spiritual experience.

But what was the nature of this experience? What did the Yogācārins see in their meditation? We can put this very simply, because the Yogācārins themselves did so. What they saw in these higher states of consciousness was that nothing exists but mind: that all things are in reality mind, and that mind is all things. This wasn't something they thought about – the thinking came later. It was something they saw and realized and directly experienced. This is the famous Yogācārin doctrine of *citta-mātra*, usually translated as 'mind only', only mind, nothing but mind. The *Laṅkāvatāra Sūtra* expresses this experience in a number of ways. In one place the Buddha says, revealing his own inner experience, 'The world is nothing but mind.' And again, in another place, 'Nothing is seen outside the mind.' In yet another place, 'The triple world (the three levels of existence, sensuous, archetypal, and pure form) is mind itself.' And again, 'The triple existence is nothing but mind.' And even more briefly and simply, 'All is mind.'[118]

Similar statements are found throughout Mahāyāna literature, especially in Zen texts. For instance, the great Chinese Chan or Zen master Huángbò, who lived in the ninth century, says in his teaching, as recorded by one of his disciples from his verbal instructions:

> All the Buddhas and all sentient beings are nothing but the One Mind, beside which nothing exists. This Mind, which is without beginning, is unborn and indestructible. It is not green nor yellow, and has neither form nor appearance. It does not belong to the categories of things which exist or do not exist, nor can it be thought of in terms of new or old. It is neither long nor short, big nor small, for it transcends all limits, measures, names, traces and

> comparisons. It is that which you see before you – begin to reason about it and you at once fall into error. It is like the boundless void which cannot be fathomed or measured. The One Mind alone is the Buddha, and there is no distinction between the Buddha and sentient things, but that sentient beings are attached to forms and so seek externally for Buddhahood. By their very seeking they lose it, for that is using the Buddha to seek for the Buddha, and using mind to grasp Mind. Even though they do their utmost for a full aeon, they will not be able to attain to it. They do not know that if they put a stop to conceptual thought and forget their anxiety, the Buddha will appear before them, for this Mind is the Buddha, and the Buddha is all living beings. It is not the less for being manifested in ordinary beings, nor is it greater for being manifested in the Buddhas.[119]

The Mind Only doctrine of the Yogācāra can be understood on two different but related levels: the epistemological level, and the metaphysical level. Understood epistemologically, it is a form of what we would call in the West subjective idealism, and understood metaphysically, it is a form of what we would call absolute idealism, though in both cases one is speaking in terms not of an academic philosophical construction, but of inner spiritual experience. Western philosophy tends to distinguish between subjective idealism and absolute idealism, but in Buddhism the two are different poles of the same experience. I need hardly remind you that for Buddhism, epistemology, metaphysics, and psychology are all interconnected, and related ultimately to the concerns of the spiritual life.

Epistemologically speaking, the Yogācāra denies the existence of any object external to the mind. It maintains that all that we perceive are ideas, ideas in this context meaning mental presentations. What we think of as an external object, the Yogācāra says, is simply the sum total of a number of impressions or perceptions. For instance, we say that we see a tree, but what do we really see? We have a visual impression of green, brown, a certain shape, a certain size, and that assemblage of impressions we call a tree. According to the Yogācāra, there exists behind those impressions no object independent of them which possesses the qualities of colour, shape, size, and so on. Such an object behind the impressions, the Yogācāra would say, is an erroneous mental construction. All this is more or less familiar ground. It is very similar to the subjective idealism of Bishop Berkeley in the eighteenth century,[120] and also to the position adopted by Jung when he points out that all reality is psychical, in the sense that we can't perceive a thing apart from our perception of it, so that – so far as we are concerned at least, and Jung certainly goes as far as this – nothing exists except ideas, impressions, perceptions.

Both the Yogācāra and Bishop Berkeley appeal to the testimony of dreams. They say that, as we all know, one can experience certain things, even a whole life, in the dream state, but there's no corresponding external object. Here we have a clear and generally admitted case of something perceived without any objective material substratum. Both Bishop Berkeley and the Yogācāra say if this can happen during the dream state, why not also during the waking state? In both cases there is a stream of impressions and perceptions, and in neither case is it necessary to refer them to an external objectively existing object. In principle there's no difference between the waking state and the dream state. The Yogācāra goes a step further than Bishop Berkeley, being able to appeal to meditation experience. In the course of one's meditation, even in not very advanced stages, one sees all sorts of eidetic images. Your eyes can be closed, there can be no influx from the senses at all, you may not be conscious of the physical body, but you see images. They may be abstract or they may take form: discs of colour, light, flowers, mountains, a figure of the Buddha, a mandala. But it's all subjective: there's no external object corresponding to that perception. Images are vividly perceived, even more vividly than things we see on this earth here and now, but there is no external object which is being perceived. From this source, the Yogācāra argues that everything that we perceive is like this. If you can perceive an image in a dream or in a state of meditation without any independently existing object of that perception, there's no reason why you shouldn't experience the same thing during waking life. In this way the Yogācāra abolishes the object altogether. There's a stream of impressions, perceptions, forms, images, and so on, but no external object standing behind them. The Yogācāra concludes that there's no such thing as matter in the ordinary sense of the term. There's no real external object. All that exists is the mind, perceiving ideas. And one can go even further than this. If there is no object, if there are only ideas, presentations to the mind, there's no subject either, no ego, no empirical self, because the object and the subject are correlative. If the object is there, the subject is there too. If the subject is there, the object is there. But when you reduce the object to a set of impressions and thus abolish it, you abolish the subject at the same time. In this way, the whole subject–object duality breaks down.

So what is left? According to the Yogācāra, when one breaks down subject and object in this way, what is left is the One Mind – Mind Only, in the absolute, metaphysical sense of the term, mind free from the division into subject and object, mind that is pure, radiant, illuminating, blissful, calm – and mind that is also *śūnyatā*. According to the Yogācāra, this One Mind isn't just something to be discussed and speculated about, as we're doing at present. It's something to be experienced. The Yogācāra emphasizes very strongly indeed the importance of inner experience, of realization. We find this emphasis resounding throughout the *Laṅkāvatāra Sūtra*, which doesn't make much use of the term *bodhi*, usually translated as Enlightenment, because *bodhi* is a bit too intellectual, and in the *Laṅkāvatāra* the Buddha wants to avoid the intellectual emphasis, so he usually speaks of *pratyātmagocara*, a Sanskrit word meaning inner perception, inner realization.[121] It may be partly for this reason that the *Laṅkāvatāra Sūtra* was so popular with Bodhidharma, who took Buddhism from India to China and founded Zen. According to legend, he went wafting over the ocean on a reed, and the only things he took with him were his robe, his bowl, and a copy – it must have been a palm-leaf manuscript – of the *Laṅkāvatāra Sūtra*. With its emphasis on personal experience, inner realization, the *sūtra* had a tremendous affinity with and influence upon the development of Chan or Zen in China and Japan.

The Yogācāra sees clearly that this experience of Mind Only is quite opposed to our ordinary experience, which is firmly and securely based on subject–object dualism. All our experience, all our knowledge, all our thinking, takes place within the framework of this dualism – subject and object interrelated, interdependent, and inseparable. But the One Mind – *citta-mātra*, Mind Only – is free from this dualism. So far as one sees in all directions, up, down, on all sides, there's just One Mind, without any trace of subject or object. It's like a great expanse of water, absolutely pure, absolutely transparent, with nothing in it, not one single speck, other than the water itself. Between the experience of the One Mind and the experience of the empirical self, the subject–object relationship, there is a great gulf, and to go from the one to the other, to go altogether beyond subject–object dualism, requires a tremendous change, a complete reversal of all our usual attitudes. The Yogācāra insists most firmly upon this. It says that the spiritual life doesn't consist in a little chipping away here or there, a small improvement here or there. It means a complete reversal, a great death, as the Zen people say, and then a great rebirth. The Yogācāra emphasizes very strongly indeed that there must be a complete turning about, or a turning upside down, a turning topsy-turvy, of all our established values and attitudes and ways of looking at things. This great change, this great death and rebirth, the Yogācāra terms *parāvṛtti*, which literally means turning about, turning round, turning upside down.[122] This is the central theme of the *Laṅkāvatāra Sūtra*, and indeed the central concern of the spiritual life. If the spiritual life doesn't turn you upside down, if you don't feel as though you're hanging head downwards in a void, then it isn't the spiritual life. If you feel all safe and secure and firm and nicely going ahead step by step, you haven't really got onto the spiritual path. *Parāvṛtti* – turning about – is synonymous with conversion, as we usually call it, in a very deep and radical sense.

The Yogācāra explains the mechanism of this incredible transformation with the help of its teaching of the eight *vijñāna*s. *Vijñāna* is usually translated as consciousness, but a more literal translation would be 'discriminating awareness'. (*Jñāna* is awareness, *vi* is to discriminate, to divide.) These eight types of discriminating awareness operate at several different levels, at different depths, hence the *depth* psychology of the Yogācāra, which sounds even greater depths than modern depth psychology. The eight *vijñāna*s are, firstly, the five sense *vijñāna*s; secondly, going a little deeper, the *mano-vijñāna*, or mind consciousness; thirdly, the *manas*, or *kliṣṭa-mano-vijñāna*, the afflicted or soiled mind consciousness; and fourthly, the *ālaya-vijñāna*, the repository or store consciousness.

The five sense *vijñāna*s, or the five sense-discriminating awarenesses, include discriminating awareness of form and colour through the eye; sounds through the ear; smells through the nose; taste through the tongue; and heat and cold, hardness and softness and so on through touch, through the skin. This is quite clear and straightforward.

Secondly, the *mano-vijñāna*, or mind consciousness, is discriminating awareness through the mind of ideas, mental objects. Mind, by the way, the *mano-vijñāna*, is usually classified in Buddhism as a sixth sense alongside the five sense consciousnesses, not given a special eminent position. According to the Yogācāra psychology, there are two aspects of the *mano-vijñāna*, the first consisting in the mind's awareness of impressions presented to it by the five senses, and the second in its awareness of ideas that arise independently of sense perception, out of the mind itself. The latter are of three kinds: first, ideas and impressions arising in meditation, as when one sees a light that doesn't have its origin in any sense impression but comes from the mind; second, functions such as those of imagination, comparison, and recollection; and third, images perceived in dreams that come not from sense impressions, but directly from the mind.

Thirdly, there's the *kliṣṭa-mano-vijñāna*, the seventh consciousness. *Kliṣṭa* literally means afflicted or suffering and it also means defiled, and the *kliṣṭa-mano-vijñāna* is so called because it is afflicted or defiled by the dualistic outlook, because it sees everything in terms of subject and object. Very often the *kliṣṭa-mano-vijñāna* is referred to simply as *manas*, often translated as mind, as *citta* also is, which tends to produce a certain amount of confusion. The *kliṣṭa-mano-vijñāna* or *manas*, the afflicted or defiled consciousness, is what we usually regard as the empirical self. It may also be described as the middle consciousness, because it is situated between the sense *vijñāna*s and the *mano-vijñāna* on one hand, and the *ālaya-vijñāna* on the other. The *manas* faces two ways: it looks outwards or downwards towards the five senses and the mind consciousness, and it looks inwards or upwards towards the *ālaya*. From below, the *manas* receives sense impressions and ideas, and these it interprets in terms of an external world existing objectively behind the impressions. All sorts of perceptions flow in upon the *manas*, and it isn't content just to perceive these perceptions and ideas – red and blue and green, big and small, hot and cold – but constructs behind them a mental world of objects in which it regards them as inhering. In the same way, from above it receives, reflected in itself, the *ālaya*, and this reflection the *manas* interprets in terms of a separate, real self. In this way the dualistic pattern of experience is set up: the *manas* misinterprets the impressions from the senses and the mind, and also misinterprets the reflection of the *ālaya* in itself, and sets up out of these elements, these impressions and reflections, a dualistic world revolving around the experience of subject and object.

Fourthly, comes the eighth *vijñāna*, which is the *ālaya-vijñāna*, the eighth consciousness. Strictly speaking, this is not a *vijñāna* at all, because here there's no discrimination. The word *ālaya* literally means a repository or store, or an abode or treasury, as for instance in the word Himalaya: *hima* is snow, *ālaya* is abode or store, so Himalaya means the store or treasury or abode of snow. The *ālaya*, the eighth consciousness, has a relative aspect and an absolute aspect. The relative *ālaya* consists of all the impressions deposited by our previous experiences, in this life and previous lives, not unlike Jung's collective unconscious. The impressions deposited in the relative *ālaya* are not passive, like the impression made in wax by a seal; they're active, conceived by the Yogācāra as being like seeds which will sprout and produce fruits whenever conditions are favourable. The *ālaya* in its absolute aspect is reality itself, pure awareness free from any trace of objectivity and subjectivity. The *ālaya* in its absolute aspect is the One Mind – not numerically one, but metaphysically one.

So these are the eight *vijñāna*s of the Yogācāra. The *parāvṛtti*, the turning about, takes place not at the level of the *manas*, the ordinary mind, the empirical self, but at a much deeper level, the level of the *ālaya*, which is why it is also called revulsion at the base, or revulsion in the depths. The *Laṅkāvatāra Sūtra* is not explicit about this, but it seems that the *parāvṛtti* takes place on the borderline between the relative and the absolute *ālaya*. So what exactly happens? It isn't easy to describe, but we may say that as the result of our thoughts, words, and deeds, there accumulate in the relative *ālaya* more and more impressions, known as impure seeds. Ultimately, according not only to the Yogācāra, but to the Buddhist tradition in general, these are the causes of our future rebirth. But it's also possible to accumulate pure seeds, active impressions produced or deposited by skilful thoughts, words, and deeds. The more skilful actions we perform, the more pure seeds accumulate in the relative *ālaya*, and when there are enough of them, the absolute *ālaya*, which is just verging on them, presses upon the pure seeds, and pushes the impure seeds right out.

It's this pushing out of the impure seeds that constitutes the turning about which brings about a transformation in the entire *vijñāna* system. The eight *vijñāna*s are transformed into the five *jñānas*, transformed from modes of discriminating awareness to modes of pure awareness or wisdom. The five sense *vijñāna*s are collectively transformed into what is called the all-performing wisdom. The mind consciousness is transformed into what is called distinguishing wisdom. The mind perceives the differences of things, the infinite variety of existence, and there's nothing wrong in this, but one must not construct behind that variety an unreal world, an objective world quite separate from it. Thirdly, the defiled or afflicted mind consciousness is transformed into the wisdom of equality. Formerly, the *manas* saw everything in terms of subject–object. Now it perceives everything in terms of the One Mind; it sees only the One Mind everywhere, so it becomes the wisdom of equality – all things are equally Mind, equally *śūnyatā*, equally real. Fourthly, the relative *ālaya* is transformed into the mirror-like wisdom, so called because it reflects everything impartially like a mirror. It just reflects – there's just pure awareness. But the absolute *ālaya* is not transformed at all, because there is no need for it to be transformed. It is the wisdom of the *dharmadhātu*, the absolute wisdom. These five wisdoms are personified as five Buddhas, of whom we shall be hearing in a later lecture in this series.

When the eight consciousnesses have been transformed into the five wisdoms, the One Mind has been thoroughly realized in all its aspects. Enlightenment, to use the more well-known Buddhist terminology, has been attained. But how is this turning about to be induced? Obviously it doesn't come about by accident. Normally we function at the level of the seven consciousnesses: five sense consciousnesses, mind consciousness, and defiled or afflicted mind consciousness. We're not aware of the relative *ālaya*, the abode of the seeds of purity and impurity, and much less still are we aware of the absolute *ālaya*, perhaps not even conceptually. The highest level we experience is the *manas*. So we have to start from there. We have to start within the dualistic pattern and, to begin with at least, take up religious practices and exercises which are based upon it. We have to take up especially the practice of meditation. In this way, as we practise, day by day, week by week, year by year, more and more pure seeds will be deposited in the relative *ālaya*, until it becomes full of them, and in this way, eventually, the turning about will take place.

This is not something that can be accomplished in a day, but though it takes time and much effort, one should not be discouraged. Many years ago, in South India, I spent some time in the ashram of a famous Hindu teacher now deceased.[123] Someone apparently once asked him, 'How is it that we practise week after week, month after month, year after year, but there is no result? We do all this meditation, we read all these scriptures, we give all this *dāna*, but we're the same, apparently, as we were before. What is happening? Why is there no improvement?' In reply, the teacher said, 'Once upon a time, there was a man who wanted to split in two an enormous rock. He went up to the rock with a sledge hammer, and swinging it with all his might, he delivered a terrific blow right in the centre. But nothing happened. He drew a deep breath, flexed his muscles, and gave another great blow on the same spot. Nothing happened. The rock was just as it was before, perfectly intact. Sweating more and more, panting for breath, he delivered nineteen tremendous blows. But the rock was just as before – not a mark, not a dent. So he thought, "All right, now or never," collected all his strength, and gave one last blow. And with that twentieth blow, the rock split, cleanly and quietly, into two.' So the teacher said, 'Were the first nineteen blows completely useless? Was it just that last blow that did the trick? No, all twenty were needed. Every time he gave a blow, though no result could be seen, the rock was being weakened along the line where the hammer struck, and the twentieth blow gave the last touch which split the rock.'

It's the same with our practice of the precepts, meditation, and study. We're hammering the rock of the empirical self with tremendous blows again and again, or in the language of the Yogācāra, we're depositing more and more seeds, but they fall down into the depths and accumulate there, where we can't see them. For a long time it's all happening in the dark. But all we have to do is carry on, and one day the rock will split, the *parāvṛtti*, the turning about, will take place, and our whole eight consciousness system will be reoriented. The five wisdoms will spring forth, and the aim and object not only of the Yogācāra but of the whole of Buddhism – the realization of the One Mind, or Enlightenment – will at last have taken place.

ASPECTS OF BUDDHIST PSYCHOLOGY 4: ARCHETYPAL SYMBOLISM IN THE BIOGRAPHY OF THE BUDDHA

The fourth in a series of seven lectures on 'Aspects of Buddhist Psychology', 1967

Tonight we come to a turning point, not just the middle lecture in the series, but another kind of turning point too. In the first three lectures, we became increasingly preoccupied with the spiritual life. Even though we were ostensibly concerned with aspects of Buddhist psychology, we saw that for the Buddhist tradition, psychology is not an autonomous subject cut off from the rest of Buddhism. It is not studied for its own sake; it's a by-product of the quest for metaphysical self-knowledge, even the quest for Enlightenment. At the same time, our approach to the subject was intellectual, conceptual. Both the Abhidharma and the Yogācāra address themselves to the conscious mind, to reason, to the intellect, and thus they use the language of ideas, concepts, abstract thought. But as we know, we are much more than our conscious mind. Consciousness is like a light froth playing and sparkling on the surface, but the unconscious is like the vast ocean depths, dark and unplumbed, lying far beneath. The unconscious, non-rational part is by far the larger part of our nature, and its importance is far greater than we generally care to recognize. If we want to appeal to the whole human being, it isn't enough to appeal to the conscious, rational mind, the intelligence; that only touches the surface. We have to appeal also to something else, and speak an entirely different language: the language of images, poetry, myth, and legend, a language that many modern people have forgotten how to speak fluently. But Buddhism speaks it no less powerfully than it speaks the language of concepts and abstract thought, and it is to the language of images and myth that we must now begin to listen. This is the real turning point in this series: from the conceptual, abstract, mental approach to the non-conceptual, from the conscious mind to the unconscious mind. Up till now we have been talking about the depths, but from today we will begin to descend into them.

Today we are going to encounter in those depths some of what I have called the archetypal symbols in the biography of the Buddha. I say 'encounter' advisedly. We are not just going to think about them, not just going to understand them intellectually. We have to do something more than that: we have to be receptive. We have to take in these archetypal symbols, open ourselves to them, listen to them, and allow them to speak to us in their own way, especially to our unconscious depths. We have not just to think about them, but to experience them, assimilate them if we can, and eventually allow them to transform our whole lives.

But before we embark upon our encounter with these archetypal symbols, there is a serious misunderstanding to be cleared up. I've said that Buddhism speaks the language of images, to use a rather contradictory expression, but I know that some people are under the impression that Buddhism is a strictly rational system which speaks only the language of concepts, reason, and abstract thought. When you mention the word Buddhism to them, you can see from their reaction that they think, 'Now we're going to hear something very dry and abstract.' It's almost as though they hear the skeleton rattle. That there should be such a misunderstanding here in the West is quite natural. After all, the greater part of our knowledge of Buddhism is derived from books, magazines, and lectures, and all these things appeal to our capacity for abstract thought, so our approach is automatically conceptual, and we tend to get the impression that Buddhism speaks only this language. But in the Eastern Buddhist countries, Buddhism certainly isn't just a matter of rational understanding. In fact, they tend to go to the other extreme, being influenced by the images all around them and not very able to give an intellectual account of what they believe, even though it may move and influence them a lot. When I first went to live in Kalimpong, I was surprised to find that many of my Tibetan and Sikkimese and Bhutanese friends, who were ardently practising Buddhists, had never heard of the Buddha. If they mentioned his name at all, it was as an unreal and distant historical figure. To them, it was the archetypal forms – Padmasambhava, the mandala of the five Buddhas, Maitreya – that were real, not the historical facts and figures. But we have to try to unite the conceptual and the non-conceptual, appeal both to the rational mind and also the unconscious depths that lie beneath. We need a balanced spiritual life in which both the conscious and the unconscious play their part. In the West, a lot of attention has been given to the conceptual, analytical, intellectual approach to Buddhism. We now have to give much more attention to images, poetry, myth, and legend, letting Buddhism begin to sink into the unconscious mind, which is, after all, the greater part of ourselves.

Next, we need to define one or two key terms. What do we mean by archetypal symbolism? What is an archetype? Broadly speaking, following the dictionary, an archetype is the original pattern of a work, or a model from which a thing is made or formed, but Jung used the term in a much more specialized sense which is hard to elucidate precisely. His usage of it is fluid and shifting, and the meaning is not always conceptually clear. He tends to rely on examples of archetypes to show the meaning of the term, and in doing this he no doubt proceeds deliberately. So perhaps it's best for us to follow his example, and make the meaning of this term clear by citing examples. But what about symbolism? A symbol is generally defined as a visible sign of something invisible, but philosophically, religiously, it is more than that. A symbol is something existing on a lower plane that corresponds with something existing on a higher plane. To cite a common example, in the theistic traditions the sun is a symbol of God, because the sun performs in the physical universe the same function that God, according to these systems, performs in the spiritual universe. The sun sheds light and heat, and in the same way God sheds the light of knowledge, the warmth of love and so on, in the spiritual universe. So the sun is not just a sign of God, but a symbol, in the sense that the sun is on a lower level that which God is on a higher level. You get the same reality existing on different levels and manifesting in different ways. It's the old Hermetic idea of 'as above, so below'.[124]

Today we are concerned with archetypal symbolism in the biography of the Buddha. Various Western scholars have written detailed biographies of the Buddha, and there's a lot of traditional material available, because a number of biographies were written in ancient India. There is, for instance, the *Mahāvastu*, the 'Great Relation', a bulky work in three volumes in the English translation which contains some very ancient and interesting material, including a biography of the Buddha, but also a great deal of other matter, especially *Jātakas* and *Avadānas*. Then there's the *Lalitavistara* and the *Abhiniṣkramaṇa Sūtra*, both Mahāyāna *sūtras*. The *Lalitavistara* is a poetic work, with a lot of devotional and literary appeal, on which *The Light of Asia*, Sir Edwin Arnold's famous poem, is primarily based. Then we have the *Nidānakathā*, which is Buddhaghosa's commentary in Pāli on the *Jākata* stories, and there's Aśvaghoṣa's *Buddhacarita*, the 'Acts of the Buddha', a beautiful epic poem in classical Sanskrit.[125] Western scholars have explored all these sources pretty thoroughly, but their method is usually to go through them and divide the material into two heaps. On one side they put whatever they consider to be a matter of historic fact – that the Buddha was born in a certain family, that he spoke a certain language, that he left home at a certain age, and so on – and on the other side they put the myths and the legends. This is all right so far as it goes, but they don't just make this division; they start indulging in value judgements, and most of them say that only what they consider to be the historical facts are useful and relevant. The myths and legends, all the poetry of the accounts, they usually say are mere fiction – by which they mean untrue, false, and to be discarded as worthless. This in my view is a great mistake. There are two kinds of truth. There is scientific truth – the truth of concepts, the truth of reasoning – but in addition to this, and some would say above it, there is poetic truth, the truth of the imagination, of images, of the intuition. Both are important, and the second kind of truth is revealed in myths and legends, as well as in works of art, in symbolic ritual, and in dreams.

The archetypal symbolism of the biography of the Buddha belongs to this second category. It's meant to be poetic, imaginative, even spiritual truth, not scientific factual information. It is not concerned with the external events of his career, but is meant to suggest something about his inner spiritual experience, and thus shed light on the spiritual life for all of us. We find archetypal symbolism not just in the life of the Buddha, but in the biographies of Nāgārjuna, Padmasambhava, Milarepa, and many others. In all of them there are incidents which are not based – and are not supposed to be based – on historical fact, but have a symbolic significance which points to inner experiences and realizations. Sometimes it's difficult to decide whether something belongs to the historical order or to the symbolic, intuitive, imaginative order. The Buddhist tradition usually seems to take the myths and legends just as literally as the historical facts. It's as though in early times people didn't possess the capacity, or perhaps the willingness, to distinguish between them. Everything was truth of its own kind. There's no harm in trying to make up our minds what constitutes the factual, historical content of the Buddha's biography and what represents its archetypal and symbolic content, but we must be careful not to undervalue the mythical and legendary elements.

This evening I propose to give a few examples of archetypal symbolism from the biography of the Buddha, drawing on some of the texts I have mentioned. I won't do this in chronological order because with the exception of one sequence the chronological order doesn't seem to be of any importance. I'm going to start off with a simple example: the twin miracle, the *yamaka pāṭihāriya* (Pāli), which according to the scriptures was first performed by the Buddha at Śrāvastī, and subsequently on a number of other occasions. For example, it's described in the *Mahāvastu* as being performed at Kapilavastu. Here's the canonical account:

> Then the Exalted One standing in the air at the height of a palm tree performed various and divers miracles of double appearance. The lower part of his body would be in flames, while from the upper part there streamed five hundred jets of cold water. While the upper part of his body was in flames, five hundred jets of cold water streamed from the lower part. Next, by his magic power, the Exalted One transformed himself into a bull with a quivering hump. The bull vanished in the east and appeared in the west. It vanished in the west and appeared in the east. It vanished in the north and appeared in the south. It vanished in the south and appeared in the north. And in this way the great miracle is to be described in detail. Several thousand *koṭis* of beings, seeing this great miracle of magic, became glad, joyful and pleased and uttered thousands of bravos! at witnessing the marvel.[126]

I'm not going to say anything about the Buddha's transformation of himself into a bull. The bull is a universal symbol in mythology and folklore, and it deserves a study of its own. I'm going to concentrate on the twin miracle proper. First of all, the Buddha stands in the air. In some other versions, he is represented as walking up and down in the air.[127] So what does this signify? It signifies a change of plane, showing that this incident does not happen on the earth, on the historial plane, but on a higher, spiritual, metaphysical plane of existence. The twin miracle is not a miracle in the ordinary sense, something magical or supernormal happening here on this earth. It's something archetypal, spiritual, symbolic, something happening on a higher plane of existence. The presence in Buddhist art of a lotus flower has the same significance. If any figure is depicted sitting on a lotus, it shows that they are on a trans-human, transcendental plane, because the lotus symbolizes severance of contact with the world. In sculptures of the twin miracle, since the sculptors are not able to represent the Buddha up in the air, they represent him sitting on a lotus flower. There's an example in one of the cave temples at Kanheri.[128]

Standing in the air, in this metaphysical dimension, the Buddha emits fire and water simultaneously, fire from the upper half of the body and water from the lower and then vice versa. If we were to take this literally, it would be a mere conjuring trick, but the Buddha certainly didn't indulge in conjuring tricks, so what does it signify on this higher plane of existence where he now stands? Fire and water are very ancient symbols indeed. They are found all over the world, in all cultures and all religions. Fire always represents spirit, or the spiritual, and water always represents matter, the material. Fire represents the heavenly, the positive, and the masculine principle; water represents the earthly, the negative, and the feminine principle. Fire represents the intellect and consciousness; water represents the emotions and the unconscious. Thus, fire and water between them represent all the cosmic opposites. They stand for what are known in the Chinese tradition as yang and yin, terms you may know from your consultations of the *I Ching*. The fact that the Buddha emitted fire and water simultaneously represents the conjunction of these great pairs of opposites, and at the highest level of all this is synonymous with Enlightenment. Enlightenment is a state of what the tantras call *yuganaddha*, 'two-in-oneness', and it is this union or integration of opposites that is represented by the Buddha's simultaneously emitting fire and water. There's an interesting parallel in the Western alchemical tradition as explored by Jung, where the union of fire and water is said to be the secret of alchemy – alchemy not in the sense of producing gold, but in the sense of a process of spiritual transmutation.[129] Sometimes in alchemical texts this union of fire and water is spoken of as the marriage of the red king and the white queen. In this episode of the twin miracle, the general significance is the same. The incident says to us that Enlightenment is not a one-sided affair, not a partial experience. Enlightenment is the union of opposites at the highest possible level.

Let's turn now to another episode. In the first lecture we saw that the Buddha, according to the Theravāda tradition, preached the Abhidharma to his deceased mother in the Heaven of the Thirty-Three. According to the same tradition, the Buddha thereafter descended to the earth by means of a magnificent staircase, attended by gods and divinities, angels, and so on. In the Buddhist texts, the archetypal significance of the Buddha's descent from the Heaven of the Thirty-Three is enhanced by glowing descriptions of gold and silver and crystal, coloured light, panoplies of coloured umbrellas and flowers falling and music sounding. This is all to enhance the archetypal significance and make a strong appeal not to the conscious mind but to the unconscious depths.[130] The staircase or ladder between heaven and earth, or a silver or golden cord linking the two, is a universal symbol. In the Bible there's Jacob's Ladder,[131] and on a more popular level there's the Indian rope trick, where the magician throws a rope up into the air, climbs up it with his disciple, cuts his disciple into pieces and the pieces come falling down, and then the disciple is reconstituted. In Shamanism the conception of the link between heaven and earth is found in all the Arctic regions.

An important variant on the theme of the union of opposites is what is generally known as the world tree, or cosmic tree. According to the traditional account, the Buddha gained Enlightenment at the foot of a peepul tree. From a historical point of view we don't know whether he sat under a tree or not. He was in the jungle, and he gained Enlightenment in the month of May, which is the hottest time of the year, so it's more than likely that he was sitting under a tree for the shade, but we don't know. The oldest accounts make no mention of a tree. But as the legendary and mythical element in the biographies grew, the Buddha came to be more and more associated with sitting at the foot of a tree at the time of his Enlightenment. A tree's roots go deep down into the earth, and its branches tower high into the sky, so like the ladder or stairway, the tree links heaven and earth, and it too is a symbol of the union or harmony of opposites. The world tree is found in most mythologies in the world. There's the Norse Yggdrasil, the world ash – roots deep down, branches up in the heavens, and all the worlds suspended on the branches. The Christian cross has the same significance, and it is often represented as a tree. Like the world tree, the cross links heaven and earth cosmically in the same way that Christ, according to the Christian tradition, unites the human and the divine natures psychologically.

Closely associated with the idea of a staircase, ladder, or tree is the idea of the central point. In the legendary accounts of the Buddha's Enlightenment, he is represented as gaining Enlightenment sitting on the *vajrāsana*, the diamond seat or diamond throne. The diamond, the *vajra*, the *dorje*, always represents the transcendental element, the metaphysical base, and according to tradition this *vajrāsana*, the spot where the Buddha sat when he gained Enlightenment, was the centre of the universe.[132] One can compare this with the corresponding Christian tradition that the cross stood on the same spot as the tree of the knowledge of good and evil from which Adam and Eve took the apple, said to be the exact centre of the world. The centrality in the cosmos of the diamond throne suggests that Enlightenment consists in adopting a position of metaphysical or transcendental centrality, which amounts to the same thing as the union of opposites. We can go on in this way almost indefinitely. The traditional biographies are full of material of this sort, which has not so far been explored in the West. In a forthcoming book, *The Three Jewels*, an introduction to the study of Buddhism, I have dealt slightly with this aspect of the Buddha's biography, but not in great detail.[133]

At this stage I want to take up a sequence of archetypal symbols connected with the most important event in the Buddha's life, his attainment of Enlightenment. These symbols are represented by incidents that are usually regarded as historical or partly historical, but their significance is much deeper. The first one is the victory over Māra, Māra being the Evil One, the 'Satan' of Buddhism. According to some of the later legendary accounts, the Buddha-to-be, Siddhārtha, was sitting meditating at the foot of the tree when he was attacked by terrible demon hosts, all sorts of foul and unsightly and misshapen figures, led by Māra Pāpīyān, the evil one. This scene is vividly evoked in Buddhist art and poetry. There's the calm figure of the Buddha-to-be, seated under the bodhi tree with his eyes half-closed, peacefully meditating, and on all sides there are monstrous figures like something from the canvasses of Hieronymus Bosch.[134] You get demons with the heads of crocodiles or wolves, demons with ten arms, demons with eyes in the middle of their chests, all trying to attack the calm figure under the tree. Some are throwing stones, some are spitting flames, some are discharging bows and arrows; all very menacing and frightful. But Siddhārtha is unmoved. His eyes remain closed and he remains in meditation with a smile on his lips. There is a great radiance about him, a five-coloured radiance of white and blue, yellow and red and orange, and when the demons' weapons reach the edge of this halo, they're transformed into flowers which fall at his feet. The significance of this doesn't need to be explained, only to be felt.

The myth goes on to relate that Māra wasn't finished. Having failed to frighten Siddhārtha with his demon hosts, he tried a subtler approach, if one can call it that, sending his three daughters, whose names were Lust, Passion, and Delight, to dance in front of Siddhārtha and exhibit their charms. But Siddhārtha didn't take any notice at all. In some versions of the story the three beautiful daughters of Māra turn into withered old hags and creep away.[135]

What does all this represent? All these figures, the demon hosts, Māra the evil one and his daughters, all surging around the Buddha-to-be and attacking him, represent the unregenerate forces of the unconscious mind, the passions and cravings that swirl about in the pit of the unconscious, in conflict not only with the conscious mind and its aspirations, but even among themselves. The demons represent negative emotions like fear, anger, hatred, jealousy, wrath, and fury, the daughters represent different aspects of craving, clinging, lust, and desire, and Māra himself, the father of the three daughters, the leader of the demon hosts, represents primordial ignorance, spiritual ignorance, darkness, blindness, and confusion. The name Māra literally means death, the principle of impermanence in its negative form, so this great myth of the Buddha's victory over Māra represents the victory of his Enlightened consciousness over all the negative forces, and even the positive forces, within his own unconscious mind.[136]

The second incident is known as 'calling the earth goddess to witness'. According to the myth, the spot where Siddhārtha was sitting beneath the bodhi tree was the centre of the universe, the diamond throne, the *vajrāsana*. In order to gain Enlightenment, the Buddha-to-be takes up his position on the central point, and this symbolizes the middle way. You must be perfectly centred and balanced before you can hope to gain Enlightenment. Māra's attempts are by no means finished, and now he challenges Siddhārtha's right to occupy the seat on which all previous Buddhas sat before gaining Enlightenment. Māra says, 'What makes you worthy to sit there? How do you know that you are going to gain Enlightenment, that you are not deluding yourself?' So Siddhārtha says, 'I have observed the perfections, the *pāramitās* (generosity and ethics, patience and vigour, meditation and wisdom), for hundreds of lives. I have prepared myself. I am worthy to sit on this seat.' Māra sneers, 'That's your story. I don't know anything about these previous lives, and all this practice of the *pāramitās*. I never saw you. Who is your witness?' Māra, it is sometimes said, was the first lawyer; he wants evidence.

In reply, Siddhārtha touches the earth with his fingertips – this is the famous *bhūmisparśa mudrā*, the earth-touching gesture, depicted in many images – and says, 'I call the earth to witness, because all these lives were lived on the earth.' In response to the summons arises the earth goddess, bearing a vase of riches in her hand, for the earth is the source of all riches, and she says, 'I have been here all the time. Men may come and men may go, but the earth always remains. I have seen all the thousands of lives in which he practised the perfections. I bear witness that he is worthy to sit on the seat of the Buddhas of old.'[137] This scene is often depicted in Buddhist art. Sometimes the earth goddess is shown dark green in colour, sometimes a beautiful golden brown, and she is always depicted emerging from the earth, like the figure of Mother Erda, in Wagner's *Ring* (Erda means the earth) and Hertha in Swinburne's famous poem of that name.[138] The significance of the earth goddess is a whole subject by itself, but essentially she represents the same forces as those represented by Māra's daughters, now tamed and subdued, ready to help instead of to hinder.

The third incident is known as 'Brahmā's request'. We are told that after his Enlightenment, the Buddha was inclined to remain silent. He reflects, 'This Truth which I have discovered is so difficult to see, so sublime, so transcendental, that ordinary people, their eyes covered with the dust of ignorance and passion, are not going to be able to see it or appreciate it. Better not to preach, better to remain silent, better to stay under the bodhi tree.' But then a great light shone forth, and in the midst of the light was the ancient figure of Brahmā Sahāmpati, lord of a thousand worlds. He appeared before the Buddha with folded hands and said, 'Please preach the truth. There are a few with little dust on their eyes. They will hear, they will appreciate, they will follow.' So the Buddha opened his divine eye, looked forth over the world, and saw all beings just like lotuses in a pond, some submerged, some just starting to open their petals, and some standing clear of the water. And he said, 'All right. For the benefit of those with just a little dust on their eyes, I will preach the Dharma.'[139] We shouldn't take this literally. We are not to think that a god literally appeared and reminded the Buddha of his duty. He knew that anyway; he was Enlightened. The figure of Brahmā represents the forces of compassion and love springing up within the Buddha's mind as part of the Enlightenment experience, which compelled him to make known the truth he had discovered.

The fourth and last episode, which is rather more complex and interesting, is the Mucalinda episode. For seven weeks, we are told, the Buddha sat at the foot of the bodhi tree and other trees in the vicinity, and in the middle of the seventh week there arose a great storm. By now it was the middle of July, the beginning of the rainy season, and in India, when it rains, it really rains. In moments, the whole sky goes black and rain descends in torrents. The Buddha was sitting under a tree, wearing just a thin robe, when out of the undergrowth came Mucalinda, the serpent king, and he wrapped his coils round the Buddha and stood with his hood spread over the Buddha's head like an umbrella, and protected him from the downpour. This incident also is often depicted in Buddhist art, sometimes almost comically; you see the snake like a coil of rope with the Buddha's head poking out and the hood like an umbrella over him. Then the rain stopped, the storm clouds cleared away, and Mucalinda assumed the form of a beautiful youth of about 16 years of age, and bowed before the Buddha.[140] I'm afraid that some scholars try to force some factual meaning from this and say, 'Oh yes, it's well known that in the East snakes are sometimes quite friendly with holy men,' but we can't accept this pseudo-historical interpretation. We are on a different level of meaning altogether. Mucalinda the serpent king represents the forces of the unconscious in their most positive and beneficent aspect. All over the world, water represents the unconscious, and the *nāgas*, the serpents or dragons, represent the forces of the unconscious. In Indian mythology, the *nāgas* live in the depths of the ocean and represent powerful, beneficent forces dwelling in the depths of the unconscious mind. Mucalinda is the king of the *nāgas*, and we can see now what he stands for. The falling of the rain represents a baptism, and all over the world baptism – sprinkling water on someone or something – represents the investment of that person, or that object, with all the powers of the unconscious mind. The rain fell at the end of the seventh week, and Mucalinda wrapped his coils seven times round the seated figure of the Buddha. This repetition of the figure seven is no coincidence. Mucalinda also represents what the tantras call the *caṇḍālī*, the fiery path or the fiery one, which Hindus call the *kuṇḍalinī*, the coiled-up one, or the serpent path, which represents the powerful psychic energy surging up inside a person, especially in meditation, through the central channel. The coils winding seven times round the figure of the Buddha represent the seven psychic centres through which the *kuṇḍalinī* passes in its ascent, and Mucalinda's assumption of the form of a beautiful 16-year-old youth represents the new personality born as a result of this upward movement. Mucalinda in that new form salutes the Buddha, and this represents the perfect submission of all those powers and forces of the unconscious to the Enlightened mind.

It's obvious that these four incidents have a deep psychological and spiritual significance. They are not pseudo-history, nor just a fairy tale, though fairy tales have a significance. They are invested with a powerful symbolic, archetypal meaning. The four main figures – Māra the Evil One, Vasuṃdharā the Earth Goddess, Brahmā, and Mucalinda – form a definite set, and the order in which they appear is rather interesting. I'm going to draw what some people may feel is a bold analogy, but I think it has great significance. It seems to me that these four figures correspond to some extent to the four principal archetypes according to Jung, and their appearance in this order represents an integration of these contents into the conscious mind, what Jung calls the individuation process. Māra corresponds to what Jung calls the shadow, that darker side of ourselves of which we are ashamed, which we usually try to keep under. If any spiritual progress is to be made, this has to be dealt with. We have to see our own darker side and integrate it into our conscious attitude. We have to recognize it as our shadow, not project it outwards onto other people, but recognize it as part of ourselves, behaving in that way, and integrate it into the conscious attitude by resolving it. The earth goddess represents the anima, the repressed feminine part of the masculine psyche. Every psyche is both masculine and feminine, but in the case of a man the feminine side is repressed, unconscious. In the case of a woman the repressed side is called the animus. So the earth goddess represents the repressed feminine side of the masculine unconscious which also must be brought up, just as the earth goddess appears in the myth, and integrated into the conscious mind. The Buddha, being a man, has an anima; in the case of a woman, it would be an animus. Brahmā represents the wise old man archetype, the teacher. In Buddhist art he's represented with white hair and beard, a God-the-father figure. He represents the voice of the higher consciousness which has to be heard not just as a voice coming from outside of oneself but integrated into one's conscious attitude. And Mucalinda represents the archetype of the young hero. The world's religions have many myths of the birth of the young hero, who represents the higher consciousness which is born out of the stress and conflict of the spiritual life. Mucalinda represents this emergence of this higher self or higher personality at the end of the individuation process.

There's also a correspondence with the principal figures of Christian mythology. Māra corresponds to Satan, the earth goddess to the Virgin Mary, Brahmā to God, and Mucalinda to Christ. I don't think this is too far-fetched. If we study these things carefully, and go into them deeply, the analogy is clear. In Tantric Buddhism there's a similar set: the guardian or protector, the *ḍākinī*, the guru, and the *yidam*. But although I've drawn these comparisons, there's a great difference of principle between the Buddhist and the Christian attitudes towards the archetypes of their respective traditions. In Buddhism these archetypal figures are regarded as aspects, projections, of one's own mind, but in Christianity they're regarded as objectively existing beings. It's thought that there is a being called Satan, a Virgin Mary up there in heaven, God the Father also in heaven, firmly seated upon his throne, or nowadays perhaps not so firmly, and a Christ figure objectively present out there, Christ the saviour. In Buddhism, it's always categorically stated that all these archetypal forms are phenomena ultimately of one's own mind, all projections from one's own unconscious, and all of them are to be integrated, but in Christianity, the archetypes are regarded as objectively existing beings, so it isn't possible fully to resolve them. You can't resolve an archetype in the sense of incorporating it, as representing unconscious contents, into your conscious mind, your new personality, your new self, unless you realize that in the last analysis it is not something objectively existing, but something you have projected from some hidden source within yourself. On account of this limitation in the Christian tradition, with the exception perhaps of the experience of a few heretical mystics, there's no full resolution of the archetypal figures, but in Buddhism, all the archetypes can be dissolved, resolved, or drawn back into one's own conscious mind, and integrated there to enrich and perfect and beautify it. The individuation process can be carried to its conclusion. Enlightenment, to use the traditional language, can be attained.

Today I've touched on only a few of the archetypal symbols occurring in the biography of the Buddha. I would like to have mentioned many more. I would have liked, for instance, to have said something about the Buddha's begging-bowl, about which there are many interesting legends. One could say that the Buddha's begging-bowl occupies in Buddhist legend a position analogous to that of the Holy Grail in Christianity, with much the same significance. There's no time to talk about that now. But before we close, I would remind you, even warn you, that these archetypes are not just of historic or literary interest. They are not foreign to us. Each and every one of them is present within us all. We can even say that we are all present in them. We share them; we've got them in common. They share us; they have us in common. And in our spiritual life, especially as we practise meditation, these archetypes tend to emerge into consciousness. Sometimes they show themselves, at least by way of glimpses, in dreams, in meditation, or in waking fantasies. We all have to encounter the shadow, the dark, unpleasant side of ourselves that we'd rather forget, the side that appears in dreams as a black dog snapping at our heels. We have to face, come to terms with, even assimilate this darker side of ourselves, just as the Buddha faced and overcame Māra and his hosts. Repression is no solution. The shadow must be saturated with awareness and resolved. The Buddha didn't start emitting flames to counteract the flames of Māra's hosts, or start throwing stones. When their missiles touched his aura, they turned into flowers. So that's what we have to do with our shadow: look at it, recognize it, accept it, and transmute it into what the Tantric tradition calls a guardian, a protector.

In the same way, we have to summon the earth goddess, though not necessarily to bear witness. In psychoanalytical language, we have to face and free ourselves from the anima or animus. Men have to bring up and integrate into their conscious attitudes their unconscious femininity, and women have to bring up and integrate into their conscious attitudes their unconscious masculinity. When this is done, there will no longer be any question of the projection of these unconscious, unrealized contents onto members of the opposite sex, and the problem, as it's sometimes called, of sex, will have been solved. This is a very important aspect of spiritual life.

Next, we have to learn from the wise old man. Sometimes we may quite literally have to sit at the feet of a teacher, or at least have some ideal image to which we owe allegiance, and then, perhaps after many years, we have to incorporate all the qualities which that figure represents – wisdom, knowledge, and so on – into ourselves.

And lastly, each one of us has to give birth to the young hero, create the nucleus of a new self, a new being. In traditional Buddhist language, we have to give birth within ourselves to the Buddha-nature itself. If we do this, if we face our own shadow, call up our own anima or animus, learn from our own wise old man, give birth within ourselves to our own young hero – give birth to ourselves – then we shall recapitulate in our own lives, at all levels, in all aspects, the archetypal symbols that appear in the Buddha's biography.

ASPECTS OF BUDDHIST PSYCHOLOGY 5: PSYCHO-SPIRITUAL SYMBOLISM IN THE *TIBETAN BOOK OF THE DEAD*

The fifth in a series of seven lectures on 'Aspects of Buddhist Psychology', 1967

Last week we reached a turning point in our course on aspects of Buddhist psychology. Until then, we had been addressing the conscious mind, but last week we started trying to speak to the unconscious mind, using the language of images, myth, legend, and poetry. Today we will continue that exploration within a rather different context: the context of death. Now, death is not a popular subject – or so one might think. I was going to say that people don't exactly come flocking to a lecture on death, but to my surprise, it seems that that is just what they do. A couple of years ago, when I gave a series of fortnightly lectures in Kensington over a whole year on various aspects of Buddhism, the biggest attendance was when we had a lecture on Buddhism and the problem of death. It was perhaps because in the neighbourhood there were rather a lot of spiritualists, but it may also have been because quite a lot of people think of death as a problem – a problem which we will all have to face sooner or later. You may not be interested in meditation or Buddhist philosophy or psychology, but a human being can hardly help being interested in death – at least, so one would have thought. But here in the West, people are often reluctant to face up to the fact of death. In some circles it seems to be considered rather indecent to refer to it too openly or bluntly. It is perhaps significant that we have a large number of euphemisms for the plain and simple fact of death. Instead of saying that someone has died, we tend to say 'passed away', or 'passed on', or 'passed over', or 'he is no more'. This reluctance to face up to the fact of death is due basically to fear. We don't want to die, so we try to pretend that we won't. We shut it out of our minds, force it into the background of our consciousness, where it lurks, ever ready to spring out but always kept in the shadows, not recognized, much less still accepted.

Having lived in the East for some twenty years, I would say that death is accepted much more readily there. Often, quite ordinary people – not saints or sages or yogis or mahatmas – look forward to death. They look forward to old age too, because they think their children and grandchildren will be grown up and they won't have much to do, so they can grow old gracefully, accumulate merit, and look forward to dying. In Chinese Buddhist circles, they order their coffin well in advance, beautifully carved and lacquered, and keep it in state in the sitting room. The great Indian poet Rabindranath Tagore writes, 'Because I love this life, I know I shall love death as well.'[141] This is typical of the Eastern attitude. You accept that life and death are two sides of the same coin, and if you love one, you can hardly help loving the other too.

In Buddhism, historically an Eastern spiritual tradition, great attention is paid to the question of death. Buddhists of all schools are exhorted to be mindful all the time of the inevitability of death, to remember in the midst of life, youth, health, and pleasure that one day we will be no more. One day we will come face to face with death, which appears to us almost as a terrible reality. Recollection of death – being constantly mindful of one's inevitable end, or at least the end of the physical body – is one of the methods of meditation designed to cure us of the disease of craving, and there are many teachings on the subject of death, in various languages, canonical and non-canonical. But there is one literary source that stands out above all others, and synthesizes the whole of the Buddhist teaching on the subject of death, as well as adding unique esoteric elements of the highest value. This is the text with which we are concerned today: the *Tibetan Book of the Dead*.

This is not its real title, though it's a very good, expressive one. Its title in Tibetan is *Bardo Thödol*, and what that means we shall see a little later on. If not in its present literary form, at least insofar as its contents and teachings are concerned, the *Tibetan Book of the Dead* goes back to one of the greatest and most fascinating and colourful figures in the history of Buddhism: Padmasambhava, the lotus-born guru. He was a great Indian teacher of the eighth century CE, a scholar, a sage, a philosopher, a mystic, a yogi, and a perfect master of the occult sciences and the esoteric traditions. Many students of Buddhism believe that he was the greatest master in this field who has ever lived, next to the Buddha himself. It was Padmasambhava who above all others was responsible for the establishment of Buddhism in Tibet, and he afterwards became the founder of the Nyingma school, the oldest school of Tibetan Buddhism, going right back to Indian traditions. Sometimes it's referred to as the Red Hat school because when performing certain ceremonies the initiates of this sect wear red conical hats, whereas the Gelugpas wear yellow ones. Padmasambhava, the lotus-born guru, or Guru Rimpoche, as the Tibetans call him, is regarded by his followers as the second Buddha, which gives some measure of his greatness. I would like to say much more about him, but there is no time at present. Perhaps one day it may be possible for me to give a complete lecture on his life, career, and teachings.[142]

According to tradition, when Padmasambhava established what later became the Nyingma tradition, he saw that there were many subtle, esoteric Dharma teachings for which the Tibetans were not then prepared, so he wrote them down and hid them away in caves and other places in the Himalayan area. We are told that over the centuries some of these texts were found, but many have not yet been discovered. They are known in Tibetan as *termas*. *Terma* literally means 'that which is taken out', or 'a treasure', and in Tibetan literature there is a substantial collection of them, supposedly written centuries ago by Padmasambhava and subsequently taken out in different parts of Tibet at different times by different teachers. At present the collected edition comprises some sixty-four volumes. Sets of these are very rare, and I have only seen two, one owned by the Maharaja of Sikkim in Gangtok and one belonging to one of my own teachers in Kalimpong.[143] So far as I know, the only set in the West is in Rome, with Professor Tucci.

The Nyingmapas, the followers of Padmasambhava, regard the *Rinchen Terdzö*, as they call this collection, as canonical, equal in authority to the scriptures which purport to be the word of the Buddha himself. Tibetan tradition attributes a large number of prophecies to Padmasambhava. One of my friends in Kalimpong once told me that one of his teachers in Tibet had told him a prophecy attributed to Padmasambhava which said, 'When the iron birds fly in the sky, my teaching will go to the West.'[144] We all know what the iron birds are, and it certainly seems as though the prophecy has been fulfilled in the case of the present work, the *Tibetan Book of the Dead* or the *Bardo Thödol*.

The *Tibetan Book of the Dead* is one of these *termas*, discovered or taken out by a great teacher called Rinchen Karmalingpa in the thirteenth or fourteenth century. (The tradition is a bit vague about timing.) It was given that title by Dr Evans-Wentz, who was the editor of Kazi Dawa-Samdup's English translation of the *Bardo Thödol*, by way of analogy with the *Egyptian Book of the Dead*, which had been translated from Egyptian hieroglyphics some years earlier by Sir Wallace Budge. The English translation of the *Tibetan Book of the Dead* was first published in 1927 and attracted a great deal of attention, including that of the great psychologist Jung, who wrote about it in his commentary on the work, published in the third edition of the translation: 'For years, ever since it was first published, the *Bardo Thödol* has been my constant companion, and to it I owe not only many stimulating ideas and discoveries, but also many fundamental insights.'[145]

Thödol means liberation by hearing, and *bardo* means 'between two' (*bar* meaning between and *do* meaning two) or, more colloquially, in between, so *bardo* is usually translated as 'the intermediate state', the state in between two other states. In this sense, *bardo* corresponds to the Sanskrit term *antarā-bhava*, *antarā* meaning in between or inner and *bhava* meaning state. The *bardo* teaching is one of the most profound aspects of Buddhism, and to the best of my knowledge it has never been publicly expounded in the West before. To understand it, we must go back to something I have referred to before in this series: the two types of conditionality, the cyclical type and the spiral type. The cyclical type is where you have an action and reaction between opposite factors, and the spiral type is action and reaction between factors which progressively augment one another. The cyclical type of conditionality is illustrated by the Tibetan wheel of life, and the spiral type is illustrated by the stages of the path, whether in terms of the twelve positive links or *nidānas*, or the seven *bodhyaṅgas* (Pāli *bojjhaṅgas*) or limbs of Enlightenment, or any other formulation.

This evening we are concerned with cyclical conditionality. We have many examples of this process, for instance the natural process of breathing in and breathing out, the reaction between hunger and satiety, sleeping and waking, and above all between life and death, or between birth and rebirth. So far as the individual human life is concerned, the process of cyclical conditionality is set forth in detail in the twelve *nidānas* or links, from ignorance right down to old age and death. The twelve *nidānas* are distributed over three lives, the past life, the present life, and the future life, and between the cause process and the effect process. In this way, we have the cause process of the past, consisting of two *nidānas*, then the effect process of the present, consisting of five *nidānas*; then the cause process of the present, consisting of three *nidānas*; and finally the effect process of the future, consisting of two *nidānas*. There are three junctures at which one process changes into or is succeeded by another: firstly, the moment of birth, when the cause process of the past changes over into the effect process of the present. This is the moment of birth or, strictly speaking, the moment of conception; secondly, the point where the effect process of the present passes over into the cause process of the present; and thirdly, the moment of death and rebirth, when the cause process of the present passes into the effect process of the future. The second of these three junctures is the most important from the point of view of Buddhist teaching – the point where feeling, the last link of the effect process of the present life, is succeeded by craving, the first link of the cause process of the present life. If one can prevent craving arising in dependence on feeling, then one can stop the whole cause process of the present, and enter upon the path to liberation on the spot. The spiral path winds out from this point.

I have sketched this rather rapidly because here we are really concerned with the underlying principle that there is a cyclic process, a movement of action and reaction between opposites, like the swinging of a pendulum. But in between there is a middle point, where the effect process ceases and the cause process has not yet begun. Just for an instant the pendulum is at rest. It is at this knife-edge point that we can make our escape, the point where one process has ended and the other has not yet begun. Here we can break through and find our way up the spiral into another dimension, and this in principle is the intermediate state, the *antarā bhava*, the *bardo*. If one considers it from this point of view, spiritual life consists in being on the lookout for such moments and taking advantage of them. There are many such points, but the Indo-Tibetan Buddhist tradition distinguishes six of them as being of particular significance: the *bardo* of life, the *bardo* of dreams, the *bardo* of meditation, the *bardo* of the moment of death, the *bardo* of reality, and the *bardo* of rebirth. This evening we are particularly concerned with the last three, but I shall say a few words about each of the others.

THE *BARDO* OF LIFE

According to this teaching, life itself is an intermediate state between birth and death. It's also intermediate between the cyclic process and the spiral process, between the wheel of life and the stages of the path. It's in this life that we can choose whether to continue to go round and round the wheel of life or up and up the spiral, whether to be reactive or creative. In all schools of Buddhism, very great importance is attached to human life. Human life represents a marvellous opportunity, because in this life there is the possibility that one could attain the state of ultimate, transcendental centrality which we call Buddhahood. This *bardo*, this intermediate stage of human existence, is therefore seen as rare and valuable, and not to be wasted.

THE *BARDO* OF DREAM

The dream state is intermediate between the waking state and the deep sleep state, or between two waking states. In the dream state, it is possible to come in contact with deeper levels of reality, with the help of archetypal images. The images which come in these archetypal dreams differ from ordinary dreams in being brilliantly coloured in jewel-like rainbow hues, and they're endowed with a great significance. Very often, after one of these archetypal dreams, one wakes up feeling that something profound has happened; one feels changed, and one does not easily forget. Those who have studied Jung's psychology will know that dreams of this sort play a very important part in the individuation process.

In Buddhism, there are many methods of meditation based upon the dream state, in which great progress can be made, for some people more easily and more quickly than in the waking state. One can receive teachings which one never forgets, and initiations of various kinds. According to tradition, some people have even gone so far as to attain Enlightenment in the dream state. We shouldn't think that Enlightenment can be attained only in the waking state: that's just our prejudice. Most methods of meditation to be practised in the dream state involve prolonging mindfulness into the dream state so that when you're having an archetypal dream, you know that you are dreaming and that it is you dreaming. You are fully aware of the reality of these states and experiences, but your mindfulness is not lost. There are various psychophysical methods of inducing mindfulness in the dream state, so that you can control your dreams and even have the dreams that you want.

THE *BARDO* OF MEDITATION

You might be surprised to find that meditation is included here. In what sense is meditation an intermediate state? It's intermediate between two states of so-called 'normal' consciousness. More precisely, from a certain point of view it's intermediate between two thoughts. But what does this mean? As we begin to realize when we learn to meditate, we are usually dominated by a constant succession of thoughts. If you have practised meditation you will know that as soon as you sit down and close your eyes, you become aware of a great torrent of thoughts rushing through your mind, and you have to struggle with this. You watch it, you're aware of it, and gradually the torrent starts to slow down. A stage comes when you see the whole process becoming more spaced out. You start becoming aware of each thought individually, and the intervals between them. There's a thought, you are aware of it coming, staying, going, and then there's a gap. You're aware of this, you experience it, and then another thought comes. With practice, these intervals lengthen. There's an interval of 'thoughtlessness', at least for a little while, maybe five minutes, eventually half an hour. There is no real meditation without this experience. It's only in this state of no thought, in this empty space between thoughts, that one can contact reality.

Now we come to the last three *bardo*s: the *bardo* of the moment of death, the *bardo* of reality and the *bardo* of rebirth. It is with these that the *Tibetan Book of the Dead* is mainly concerned. They are really all part of one single *bardo*, in the sense that they are all intermediate between death and rebirth, or re-conception. This brings us to a rather important difference between different schools of Buddhism. According to the Theravāda tradition, death is followed immediately by rebirth, or re-conception, but all the other schools, the Sarvāstivāda and the Mahāyāna schools (the Chinese, Tibetan, and Japanese schools) hold that there is an interval between them. According to the *Tibetan Book of the Dead*, this interval lasts for forty-nine days. The number – seven times seven – is obviously symbolical, indicating that we're concerned here with a quite different time scale.

This is what the Tibetans call the *chikhai bardo*. At the moment of death, consciousness is withdrawn from the senses. One no longer hears anything – sounds fade away. One no longer sees anything – everything is a blur, and eventually no blur. There are no tactile sensations, no olfactory sensations, no taste. Consciousness is withdrawn from the five senses, from the physical body, and breathing itself ceases. One draws in one long, last breath, and then sighingly exhales (the famous rattling in the throat); then there is a long silence, and no further breath is drawn in. To those nearby it seems as though the person is unconscious, in a coma. At this point, consciousness is dissociated completely from all mundane things: from the senses, from the lower mind, from all the things one was interested in during life, from all one's passions and attachments, likes and dislikes. And at that moment, according to the *Tibetan Book of the Dead*, one experiences, just for an instant, what the text calls the clear light of reality – just a blinding flash which dawns, and then disappears. It's what Buddhists call the *dharmakāya*. For most people it lasts only an instant, but for others it lasts longer. There's a basis for this, especially in the case of those who practise meditation. So far as most people are concerned, when at the time of death reality is experienced in this way, it's not only instantaneous, but terrifying. Most feel intensely afraid of this glimpse, this revelation, and they shrink back from it, because the last thing that they want is reality. As T. S. Eliot wrote, 'Humankind cannot bear very much reality.'[146] It has been suggested, I believe by Aldous Huxley, that our whole psychophysical organism is designed to shield us from the impact of reality, so that we get it just in dribbles and can assimilate it.

But according to the *Tibetan Book of the Dead*, for those who do not shrink back, this experience represents a great opportunity. If one is not afraid, if one accepts it, at that moment one can unite with that reality. But in order to be able to do this in this split second, one must recognize the clear light not as coming from outside, not as anything terrible bursting in, but as the radiance of one's own true mind at its deepest or loftiest level, the light of the One Mind, which is one's own mind, even as it is everybody else's mind. According to *The Tibetan Book of the Dead*, if one has recognized the clear light of reality in the course of one's life, perhaps in meditation or in some spontaneous mystical experience, then recognition and even union at the moment of death is easier, because one recognizes an old friend, something that one has experienced before. But it's still difficult, because death is an experience that, so far as we remember, has not befallen us before. We may be confused, so a little external help is necessary. It is recommended that a spiritual teacher or a *kalyāṇa mitra* (spiritual friend) should be sitting by your side at the time of death quietly whispering in your ear, reminding you that what you are now experiencing is the clear light of reality, your own mind. 'Don't be afraid; allow yourself to be drawn to the light, and absorbed by it.' This is why the full title of the work is the 'Liberation by Hearing in the Intermediate State'. You hear the reminder, and you think, 'Oh, yes, no need to be afraid. This experience is the clear light of my own mind. Let me unite with that.'

If you have had any previous meditative or mystical experience it is easier to unite at that time, and if you unite, you are liberated and all is well. You have attained reality, you are emancipated from birth and death and rebirth. But if you are unable to grasp the experience, you experience reality a second time, but rather more obscurely. This is the secondary clear light, and according to the *Tibetan Book of the Dead* it dawns about half an hour after breathing has ceased. From this stage also, liberation can be attained, but once again a teacher or friend must remind you of your spiritual practice during your lifetime, saying, 'Don't forget your experiences in meditation. What you are experiencing now is the same kind of thing, so don't be afraid, allow yourself to be drawn to it, to unite with it.' In some cases, liberation occurs at this stage, but in many, it doesn't. Those who are not liberated fall into a deep swoon, an unconscious state which lasts some three or four days, and then they go on to the next *bardo* state, the *bardo* of reality or the *chönyi bardo*.

THE *BARDO* OF REALITY

When the *bardo* of reality dawns, the deceased person wakes up not in a gross physical body, but in a subtle body. We are told that they can see their own corpse and hear their relations weeping. At this stage you do not know that you are dead. You have to be told by the lama or friend who is still sitting by your corpse, 'Now you are dead. You've left your physical body, you've left this life, you've left your relations, left your home. Don't be attached, forget all about it. You've left all these people and things for good, so put it all behind you. Just think about what is to come.' And the dead person should be assured that liberation is still attainable.

You now experience a series of visions, archetypal dreamlike experiences. You see, in Tibetan Buddhist terms, a hundred and ten peaceful and wrathful deities, various Buddhas and bodhisattvas. These are the psycho-spiritual symbols of the *Tibetan Book of the Dead*: psycho-spiritual because experienced mentally, psychically, and because their significance goes far beyond that of the ordinary conscious mind, or even the personal unconscious. These archetypes of which you now have visions represent descending degrees of reality: as you progress, you get further and further away from reality. The visions, which last for fourteen days, are rich, colourful, and complex, and there's no time to describe them in detail, or even enumerate them, but I will touch on what are known as the peaceful deities, who appear one by one with their entourages in the first seven days. On the first day, the whole of space in all directions appears a deep rich brilliant blue colour. You experience nothing but a deep blue luminosity on all sides, above and below. From the central region of this blueness appears the Buddha Vairocana the Illuminator. He is a brilliant dazzling white, like snow shining in the sun, and he is seated on a throne supported by lions, holding a golden wheel, the *dharmacakra*, or wheel of the law, embraced by his consort, and symbolizing the wisdom of the *dharmadhātu*, the wisdom of ultimate reality.

From the heart of Vairocana, there issues a dazzling blue light, and at this point the teacher, still sitting by your corpse, tells you not to be afraid, saying, 'This is the light of the wisdom of the *dharmadhātu*, the wisdom of ultimate reality. Don't be afraid – this is ultimately innate in your own mind.' But at the same time there comes from the world of the gods a dull, dirty white light. The world of the gods is one of the six realms of sentient existence in the wheel of life according to Buddhist cosmology. At this stage, one can either follow the brilliant blue light back into the heart of Vairocana and in this way be liberated, or one can follow the dull white light and be reborn in the world of the gods. The teacher urges you to choose the former. Thus passes the first day.

On the second day, all around is an incredibly brilliant clear white radiance, and from the east there appears a deep dark blue Buddha, Akṣobhya the Imperturbable, on a throne supported by elephants, embraced by his consort, attended by bodhisattvas, to make up a mandala of symbolic forms. From the heart of Akṣobhya there issues a pure brilliant white light, the mirror-like wisdom. But at the same time from the lower realms, the realms of suffering, there shines forth a dull, smoky-coloured light. And once again you must choose: either you are liberated in the realm of Akṣobhya or reborn in a state of suffering. On the third day, a yellow Buddha, Ratnasambhava, appears from the south, and a bright yellow light shines from his heart, the light of the wisdom of equality, while at the same time from the human world a dull, bluish-yellow light shines. And once again you have to choose. The same pattern repeats itself in different aspects and levels and dimensions – always this question of choice. On the fourth day, a deep red Buddha dawns. This is Amitābha, the Infinite Light, and from his heart a brilliant red light shines forth, the light of the distinguishing wisdom, while from the *pretaloka*, the world of hungry ghosts, comes forth a dull red light, and once again you have to choose. Here we can see the connection between the tradition of the *Tibetan Book of the Dead* and the Pure Land school of Buddhism. On the fifth day appears the green Buddha, Amoghasiddhi, and from his heart a bright green light shoots forth, the light of the all-performing wisdom, while from the *asuraloka*, the world of the titans who are warring with the gods, there streams forth a dull green light, and again there's a choice to be made.

On the sixth day, all the five Buddhas with their consorts and their families appear simultaneously, and all five wisdoms shine forth with all their different-coloured radiances. These are the five Buddhas of the mandala; we will be studying them in more detail next week. Rays also shine forth from the six worlds of conditioned existence. There's still a chance of liberation, still the possibility of choice, if only – and this is the supreme condition – one recognizes that all these forms, figures, archetypes, psycho-spiritual symbols, are in their ultimate essence phenomena of one's own mind.

On the seventh day appear the knowledge-holding deities, and from the eighth to the fourteenth days the wrathful deities appear. The appearance of these deities indicates an increasing alienation from reality on the part of the deceased person. At this stage, if your consciousness can't sustain itself at the higher levels, your consciousness bounces down to its natural level, like a ball bouncing down a flight of steps. The wrathful deities are reflexive appearances of the peaceful deities;

as you become alienated from the peaceful aspects of reality, it assumes a wrathful aspect corresponding to the degree of your alienation. It's increasingly difficult to recognize these wrathful forms as phenomena of your own mind, because you become too terrified to be able to do so.

Towards the end of these days, there is a swirl of monstrous semi-animal forms, and here contact with reality is practically lost. Even at this point, if by any chance you are still hearing the voice of the teacher, and you recognize that all these archetypal experiences are phenomena of your own mind, you can be liberated, but if you can't sustain even that level, there follows the sixth *bardo*, which is the *bardo* of rebirth, the *sidpa bardo*.

THE *BARDO* OF REBIRTH

There's much material about this *bardo* in the *Tibetan Book of the Dead*, but this evening I've time only for a few brief remarks. The dead person is still in their subtle body and still sees their relatives. They're in a grey, twilit state as though under water, and they have various experiences in this state: pleasant, painful, or neutral according to their past karma. Those who have been cruel in their previous life may hear voices threatening: 'Kill, burn, slay, pierce, cut!' Later on, they may feel as though they are fleeing, pursued by terrible winds, or falling over precipices, but there are still possibilities of escape. I won't go into all the methods mentioned, but most people cannot avail themselves of them and are eventually reborn. They are roaming about in this grey twilight state, pursued by all sorts of terrifying visions and experiences, and looking for some refuge, some place to hide themselves, and then they see in the distance their future parents at the moment of sexual intercourse. The text says that if you are about to be reborn as a male, you feel an intense jealousy of the father, but if you are about to be reborn as a female, you feel an intense jealousy of the mother. This is obviously of great interest to the Freudians. You try to get in between your copulating parents and at that instant conception – reconception – takes place, and you lose consciousness, fall into a swoon, and you're back in this world.

Such are the psycho-spiritual symbols of the *Tibetan Book of the Dead*. I wanted to say much more on the subject, but there isn't time. I wanted to say, for instance, something about the correlation of the last three *bardo*s with the three bodies of the Buddha – there's a very important, intimate connection – and also with the three Tantric initiations. We must leave all this material to another occasion. But I'd like to emphasize one thing: that there is a close correspondence between the intermediate state of meditation and the intermediate states during and after death. Meditation is a death, death is a meditation, and in both these states liberation is possible. The texts tell us that the nearer we get to reality in meditation during life, the more clearly we see it, the better our chance of experiencing reality and gaining liberation after death.

The *Bardo Thödol* is not only a book of the dead. As Lama Govinda has emphatically insisted, it is also a book of life.[147] The key to death is the key to life. Ultimately both life and death are illusions, and we must go beyond them both. I should like to conclude this lecture by reading you the Root Verses of the Six Bardos, which form part of the nucleus of the *Tibetan Book of the Dead*. In the light of what has been said, their meaning may be a little clearer.

THE ROOT VERSES OF THE SIX *BARDOS*

O now, when the Birthplace *Bardo* upon me is dawning!
Abandoning idleness – there being no idleness in (a devotee's)
  life –
Entering into the Reality undistractedly, listening, reflecting, and
  meditating,
Carrying on to the Path (knowledge of the true nature of)
  appearances and of mind, may the *Tri-Kāya* be realized:
Once that the human form hath been attained,
May there be no time (or opportunity) in which to idle it (or
  human life) away.

O now, when the Dream *Bardo* upon me is dawning!
Abandoning the inordinate corpse-like sleeping of the sleep of
  stupidity,
May the consciousness undistractedly be kept in its natural state;
  Grasping the (true nature of) dreams, (may I) train (myself) in
  the Clear Light of Miraculous Transformation:
Acting not like the brutes in slothfulness,
May the blending of the practising of the sleep (state) and actual
  (or waking) experience be highly valued (by me).

O now, when the *Dhyāna Bardo* upon me is dawning!
Abandoning the whole mass of distractions and illusions,
May (the mind) be kept in the mood of endless, undistracted *Samādhi*,
May firmness both in the visualizing and in the perfected (stages) be obtained:
At this time, when meditating one-pointedly, with (all other) actions put aside,
May I not fall under the power of misleading, stupefying passions.

O now, when the *Bardo* of the Moment of Death upon me is dawning!
Abandoning attraction and craving, and weakness for all (worldly things),
May I be undistracted in the space of the bright (enlightening) teachings,
May I (be able to) transfuse myself into the heavenly space of the Unborn:
The hour hath come to part with this body composed of flesh and blood;
May I know the body to be impermanent and illusory.

O now, when the *Bardo* of the Reality upon me is dawning,
Abandoning all awe, fear, and terror of all (phenomena),
May I recognize whatever appeareth as being mine own thought-forms,
May I know them to be apparitions in the Intermediate State;
(It hath been said), 'There arriveth a time when the chief turning-point is reached;
Fear not the bands of the Peaceful and Wrathful, Who are thine own thought-forms.'

O now, when the *Bardo* of (taking) Rebirth upon me is dawning!
One-pointedly holding fast to a single wish,
(May I be able to) continue the course of good deeds through repeated efforts;
May the womb-door be closed and the revulsion recollected:

The hour hath come when energy and pure love are needed;
(May I) cast off jealousy and meditate upon the *Guru*, the Father-Mother.

'(O) procrastinating one, who thinketh not of the coming of death,
Devoting thyself to the useless doings of this life,
Improvident art thou in dissipating thy great opportunity;
Mistaken, indeed, will thy purpose be now if thou returnest empty-handed (from this life):
Since the Holy Dharma is known to be thy true need,
Wilt thou not devote (thyself) to the Holy Dharma even now?'

Thus say the Great Adepts in devotion.
If the chosen teaching of the *guru* be not borne in mind,
Wilt thou not (O *shiṣḥya*) be acting even as a traitor to thyself?
It is of great importance that these Root Words be known.[148]

ASPECTS OF BUDDHIST PSYCHOLOGY 6: THE MANDALA: TANTRIC SYMBOL OF INTEGRATION

The sixth in a series of seven lectures on 'Aspects of Buddhist Psychology', 1967

Nowadays a lot of people are much exercised by what they call the problem of communication, and it seems significant that communication should have become a problem. Broadly speaking, there are two principal modes of communication between human beings: communication in terms of concepts, thoughts, and ideas, and communication in the form of images. The first type is addressed to the rational intelligence, and is employed by science and philosophy, while the second type aims at the unconscious depths that lie beneath the rational intelligence, and is employed by all forms of imaginative literature. Spiritual traditions employ both, but in their more popular forms they tend to rely more on images, thus trying to stir the unconscious depths. In this series of lectures we've passed from one mode of communication to the other, starting with a more conceptual approach, but soon finding ourselves in the midst of images, symbols, and archetypes, and today we come to the mandala, which the subtitle of the talk describes as the Tantric symbol of integration. Three questions naturally suggest themselves. What is a mandala? What do we mean by integration? And in what way is the mandala a symbol of integration? I am going to deal with these, but not in a strictly logical fashion. We can't deal with material of this sort in a logical sequence, and even if we could, it would give a false impression about the nature of the material.

First, though, we need to address another question. If the mandala is the Tantric symbol of integration, what do we mean by Tantric? What are the tantras? To understand this, we have to refer back to the three *yānas*, those three great stages or phases of the development of Buddhism in India, the land of its birth. Each flourished for a period of about 500 years, and each produced its own canonical literature or sacred scriptures. The Hīnayāna produced the Tripiṭaka, the three baskets or collections of scriptures: the Vinaya or monastic code, the *sūtras*, and the Abhidharma, the higher or further doctrine. The Mahāyāna produced the *vaipulya sūtras*. *Vaipulya* means extended or amplified, and some of these *sūtras* are very lengthy indeed, a single discourse sometimes being the length of a whole volume. They include great texts like the *Saddharma Puṇḍarīka Sūtra*, the *Laṅkāvatāra*, and the Prajñāpāramitā *sūtras*. And the Vajrayāna produced the tantras.

The word 'tantra' is from a verbal root meaning to weave, so a tantra is that which is woven or put together, compiled – in other words, a book. In Sanskrit literary usage the term can be applied to any type of work – in Indian literature a number of works on mathematics are called tantras – but within the field of Buddhism, the term is usually applied specifically to the Vajrayāna scriptures, and there are a great many of them in existence. All the tantras were originally written in Buddhist Hybrid Sanskrit or Mixed Sanskrit, but many of them have been lost over the centuries. Those that have survived, apart from a few that are available in Nepali and Sanskrit, are found in the Tibetan canon. No one knows exactly how many there are, but I have been told that there are at least three hundred tantras in Tibet, preserved by the Nyingma school of Tibetan Buddhism and not recognized by the Gelugpas. And I have heard (one of my friends has been doing research in this field) that the Sanskrit originals of a number of Nyingma tantras which some scholars had thought to be original Tibetan compositions have recently been located in Nepal in out-of-the-way Buddhist monasteries and temples. It's a staggering thought that out of all these hundreds of important works, so far only one, the *Hevajra Tantra*, has been translated in its entirety into English, and I'm afraid the translation doesn't help us much. The distinguished scholar Dr Conze read the English translation of the *Hevajra Tantra* with great interest (not knowing Tibetan to that extent, this was his first access to this material) and wrote a review in which he remarked that he was no wiser than before.[149] Why this should have been may become clear in a minute.

The tantras are very different from other types of canonical literature. The Tripiṭaka texts are mainly conceptual in their approach, which is one of the reasons for the great appeal of many parts of the Pāli canon. The approach is rational, understandable; one can get at it with the rational intelligence. The Mahāyāna *sūtras* are of both kinds, some of them being couched in conceptual terms, others more in terms of images and myth. For instance, the Perfection of Wisdom texts, the Prajñāpāramitā *sūtras*, use the language of concepts almost exclusively, but the approach of the *Saddharma Puṇḍarīka Sūtra* is more dramatic, poetic, mythical, and archetypal, and it is therefore only just beginning to become popular among Western Buddhists. But the tantras are entirely non-conceptual. The *Saddharma Puṇḍarīka Sūtra* has at least some organization from a literary point of view, but the tantras are absolute chaos, just a jumble of images, archetypes, and cryptic practical instructions. There's no logical arrangement at all. This is what Dr Conze found so baffling about the English translation of the *Hevajra Tantra*. There's apparently no organization: just a flow of images, concepts, practices, descriptions, and advice, all mixed up, so it's very difficult to sort out.

Among the topics dealt with in Tantric literature is the mandala, so we come back to the question 'What is a mandala?' Literally, a mandala is a circle. Some writers on Buddhism call it a magic circle, but this could be rather misleading – it depends what you mean by magic. Perhaps the best short definition of the mandala is 'a circle of symbolic forms'. In a complete Buddhist mandala there are at least five symbolic forms, one in the middle, and one at each of the four cardinal points. They are the forms of Buddhas and bodhisattvas, personifications of various attributes of Enlightenment, archetypal images. In all these mandalas, the central symbolic form is reality itself, and the forms at the four cardinal points represent the four principal aspects into which that reality can be split up. So this is the basic scheme of the mandala: five archetypal Buddhas arranged in this pattern. The mandala has many other features: for instance, the symbolic forms, whatever their number, are placed within a square enclosure with four gates, and this is placed within a series of three concentric circles. What all this means we shall see a little later on. But first, let us take a closer look at the symbolic forms.

There are hundreds of different sets of these figures in different mandalas, but they all follow the same basic scheme: the central point radiating in the four main directions. The Chinese have a saying that a picture is worth a thousand words, so I shall try to paint in words a picture of a mandala. I'm going to take the simplest of all the mandalas, but also the most important: the mandala of the five Buddhas. We briefly encountered them last week when considering the *Tibetan Book of the Dead*, but today we are going to look at them in greater detail and try to get a vivid picture of them. These five Buddhas represent the five principal aspects of Buddhahood. In conceptual terms, they represent the five wisdoms. To add to the confusion, in different traditions, different Buddhas are associated with different wisdoms, depending on the context, the spiritual tradition, and so on. There are two or three more or less standard patterns and we're going to follow one of those, but it's not an invariable one. Each of the five Buddhas is also associated with a particular direction, point of the compass, colour, emblem, and *mudrā* or gesture of the hands.

VAIROCANA, THE WHITE BUDDHA

The name Vairocana means Illuminator. In Vedic times and later, Vairocana was one of the names of the sun, or even of the sun god, and it's as though Buddhahood or Reality is conceived of as a spiritual sun. Just as the material sun illumines the material world, so Vairocana, the Illuminator, the sun of Enlightenment, illumines the whole of the spiritual world. In the Shingon sect of Japan, Vairocana, who is their principal Buddha, is known as the 'Great Sun Buddha'. Appropriately, Vairocana holds in his hands a golden *dharmacakra*, a Wheel of the Law, with eight spokes, often beautifully decorated. His *mudrā*, the gesture of his hands, is what is called the wheel-turning, the *dharmacakrapravartana mudrā*, which is associated with the Buddha's first sermon at Sarnath, whose title is the *Dhammacakkappavattana Sutta*, the 'turning of the wheel of the doctrine', this being an idiom for propagating the Buddha's teaching.[150] So Vairocana's gesture is this wheel-turning *mudrā*, turning the Wheel of the Doctrine, shedding the light of the doctrine on all living beings.

Vairocana embodies the wisdom of the *dharmadhātu*, which is the basic, central wisdom – in a sense, Enlightenment itself. *Dharmadhātu* is one of the most difficult terms to translate in the whole of Buddhism. *Dhātu* means a sphere, a field, a realm, or even a kingdom, while *dharma*, which sometimes means the teaching and sometimes a mental state, here means reality, so *dharmadhātu* means the whole universe, the whole of the cosmos, conceived of as the sphere of the manifestation of reality, pervaded by reality, and the wisdom of the *dharmadhātu* is the wisdom that sees directly that the whole universe, in all its heights and all its depths, on all sides, in all directions, to infinity, is pervaded by one sole reality which penetrates everywhere, just as the whole of space is penetrated by the light of the sun. This is the central experience of Enlightenment.

The other four wisdoms are aspects of this wisdom, just as the other four Buddhas are aspects of Vairocana. This is why Vairocana occupies the centre of the mandala, and why his colour is white. White is the union of all the colours of the rainbow, the colours being a refraction of the purity of the white light, so Vairocana, representing reality in its absolute, central aspect, undifferentiated, is white. If any Buddha or bodhisattva is represented as white (you sometimes get a white Tārā or white Avalokiteśvara), this means that they are being represented in their absolute aspect. Regardless of their usual place in the pantheon, when they become white they are invested with all the attributes of absoluteness and become a symbol of Buddhahood itself in its perfection, its supreme state.

AKṢOBHYA, THE DARK BLUE BUDDHA

It is said that Akṣobhya is dark blue like the midnight sky without any stars, an almost impenetrable blue, verging on black. The name Akṣobhya means the Imperturbable, the Unshakeable, the one who can't be moved or disturbed in any way, and Akṣobhya represents the firmness and stability and indestructibility of the Enlightenment experience. Akṣobhya occupies the eastern direction and his emblem is the *vajra*. The Sanskrit word *vajra* means both thunderbolt and diamond, and it is the hardest of all things. The *vajra* can cut everything but nothing cuts the *vajra*. The wisdom of Enlightenment is like that. It cuts everything, but nothing cuts it.

The *mudrā* of Akṣobhya is the earth-touching gesture. We heard something about this a couple of weeks ago, because it's associated with the Buddha's victory over Māra. Remember how the Buddha sat unperturbed under the bodhi tree, even as he was attacked by the hosts of Māra, all those terrible misshapen forms, and how all their weapons turned to flowers and fell harmless at his feet, and then how he touched the earth to call the earth goddess to witness his practice of the perfections. Akṣobhya, with his earth-touching *mudrā*, is associated with this episode in the life of the historical Buddha.

Akṣobhya is associated with the mirror-like wisdom, that aspect of the Enlightened mind that sees everything, understands the true nature of everything. If a mirror is free from dust, if it's perfectly polished, it reflects whatever is in front of it. It reflects everything but is affected by nothing. It can reflect a thousand things, but nothing leaves a trace on its surface. Nothing sticks to it, there's no subjective reaction. The mirror-like wisdom represents the pure, perfect objectivity of the Enlightened mind, which reflects everything, sees everything, knows everything, understands everything, penetrates through everything, but is not touched or affected by anything, does not stick anywhere or settle down anywhere, but moves freely on.

RATNASAMBHAVA, THE GOLDEN BUDDHA

Ratnasambhava means the Jewel-Producing One, and he represents the beauty and richness and abundance of the Enlightened mind. He occupies the southern quarter of the mandala and his emblem is the *cintāmaṇi*, or wish-fulfilling gem. In Hindu and Buddhist mythology, the *cintāmaṇi* is rather like Aladdin's lamp. If you hold it in your hand and wish, you get whatever you wish for. In Hindu mythology, the gods and powerful kings are constantly trying to get hold of this *cintāmaṇi* so they can get their wish. But what is the true, the real, *cintāmaṇi*? It is the Enlightened mind itself, because that gives you in the ultimate sense whatever you can wish for. All beauty, all riches, all abundance, it's all there in the depths of your own mind. Ratnasambhava, the jewel-producing Buddha, has as his emblem this *cintāmaṇi*, this wish-fulfilling gem, suggesting that the true wish-fulfilling gem is Enlightenment itself.

Ratnasambhava's golden colour links him with the earth, which is sometimes golden, and whose depths are the source from which all treasures come. Likewise, all spiritual treasures are dug up from the depths of the Enlightened mind, and especially the jewel of the *bodhicitta*, the will to Enlightenment, the aspiration to gain Enlightenment not just for oneself, but for all living beings.

The *mudrā* of Ratnasambhava is that of *varada*, supreme giving, because he represents that aspect of Enlightenment which bestows spiritual gifts on all people without discrimination. Ratnasambhava is associated with the wisdom of equality or sameness, because the Enlightened mind sees things with no preferences, no likes or dislikes, no reactions, whether positive or negative. The Enlightened mind sees all equally, and has the same love, the same compassion, towards all.

AMITĀBHA, THE RED BUDDHA

The word Amitābha literally means 'infinite light' – not just light, but also warmth – and Amitābha, the red Buddha, represents the love aspect of Enlightenment. Red is the colour of love, and Amitābha's emblem is a lotus of a deep rich red colour. Amitābha represents the maturing power of love. We all know that love is necessary to both psychological and spiritual growth. Some time ago I read about an orphanage where some of the infants were treated in a very objective, hospital-routine way, without any personal attention or handling, and another group of children were carried about in people's arms and given a great deal of attention. It was found that those children who were deprived of human contact almost withered, while those who were given human contact, sympathy, and love did much better. For all human beings, and even all animals, some element of love is necessary for growth and development. Amitābha symbolizes the love aspect of Enlightenment, the light and warmth of the Enlightened mind which matures all living beings in a spiritual sense.

Amitābha sits with his hands in the *dhyāna mudrā*, the *mudrā* of meditation, and he occupies the western quarter, where the sun sets. To some Buddhists, especially those in Japan, the setting sun, with its rich red colour, is reminiscent of Amitābha. When the sun goes down, light is gradually withdrawn from the earth, and this symbolizes the withdrawal of our consciousness from the senses. When the light fades away, darkness comes, and when we withdraw our attention from the senses and focus the mind within, it's as though the external world, even our own body, is a darkness to us.

Amitābha is associated with the discriminating or distinguishing wisdom. The Enlightened mind sees things in their unity, their sameness, but it also sees them in their diversity. The one doesn't obstruct the other. The Enlightened mind sees things at the same time as one and as different. In metaphysical terms, Buddhism is neither a monism nor a pluralism. It neither reduces difference to unity, nor unity to difference. It sees both – in a sense it goes beyond both. Unity doesn't obliterate difference, and difference doesn't obscure unity. Both are seen together by the Enlightened mind. In the *Gaṇḍavyūha Sūtra*, this state is compared to the mutual intersection of innumerable beams of coloured light. They all intersect, they all penetrate one another from all directions, but they all retain their own individuality.[151]

AMOGHASIDDHI, THE GREEN BUDDHA

Siddhi means success or ripeness or perfection, and *amogha* is unobstructed or unimpeded, so Amoghasiddhi is the unobstructed success, or the unimpeded perfection, and he represents the practical aspect of Enlightenment, the mysterious, almost occult activity of the Enlightened mind. It's not necessarily external – it may be an activity of non-activity, action in non-action, as the Taoists and Zen people say – but it is very mysterious, and very efficacious. Amoghasiddhi occupies the northern quarter of the mandala and his emblem is the double *vajra* – two vajras placed one across the other – which represents the union of the positive and negative forces of the cosmos and of the human psyche. Just as the colour green is a union of blue and yellow, the double *vajra* represents the conjunction of all the positive and negative forces in the universe.

Amoghasiddhi has the *abhaya mudrā*, the *mudrā* of fearlessness. The experience of Enlightenment bestows fearlessness or confidence. One can't imagine an Enlightened person being afraid. There are many episodes in the Buddha's life that reveal his characteristic confidence and fearlessness. When he was going through a dark jungle infested with bandits when people threatened to beat him up, or even murder him, he didn't turn a hair. Once a band of murderers had been hired by his enemies to do away with him. Alarmed, his disciples gathered together and made a great ring around him. The Buddha said, 'What is this?' They said, 'Lord, we've heard that your enemies have sent murderers to kill you. We need to protect you.' But the Buddha said, 'You can all go away. A Tathāgata (a Buddha) needs no protection from anyone.' So he sent them all away and sat there by himself all night. And nothing happened. The murderers apparently just melted away.[152] Amoghasiddhi's *abhaya mudrā* represents this aspect of Enlightenment. In the Mahāyāna especially, great importance is attached to this quality. If you're not fearless, if you're not confident, if you're not even bold, you can make no approach to Enlightenment. You need not be aggressive or over-confident, but there's no need to be timid or hesitant or humble in the Uriah Heep sense – these are not Buddhist virtues.[153]

Amoghasiddhi is associated with the all-performing wisdom, the aspect of the Enlightened mind which actively devotes itself to the welfare of all living beings, and devises many skilful means, *upāya-kauśalyas*, as they're called, to help them. It does this naturally and spontaneously – there's no question of thinking about how to help, what to do.

So this is the mandala of the five Buddhas. They are correlated with various other sets of five, for example the five aggregates (*skandhas*) into which all of conditioned existence can be analysed (form, feeling, perception, impulses, and consciousness), the five poisons or passions, the five elements, five animal emblems, and so on. We will see more about this later on. But now let's go on to the second of our three questions. What do we mean by integration? Or, to put it another way, what do we mean by disintegration? Disintegration is the state of being split up, broken, fragmented, and modern human beings are very much in this condition psychically. There's a great chasm between our rational intelligence, our conscious mind, and the deeper, more unconscious or even totally unconscious levels of our psyche. This split is reflected in our increasing alienation from nature. We're getting further and further away from a natural way of life, especially those of us who live in cities, who have become industrialized, urbanized, commercialized, computerized, and all the rest of it. That part of ourselves which is responsible for all this, the rational intelligence, has got almost completely out of hand. It has almost entirely broken loose from the rest of the psyche and cut itself off, except for a thread, from the deeper sources of life and vitality. It is functioning almost in a void. Sometimes the unconscious rebels and erupts into consciousness in a violent, disruptive manner, in various forms of what we usually call insanity, which is a forcible attempt on the part of the unconscious contents of the mind to secure some recognition. The majority of us don't go as far as insanity – or at least it's nice to think that we don't – but there's still considerable tension. The chasm still yawns. There's a conflict between the conscious and the unconscious. It's not just a question of repressed desires that are incompatible with conscious attitudes; it goes much deeper than that. It's a conflict between the ego-centred intellect and the deeper, transpersonal psychic and spiritual life deep down within ourselves, from which we have become divorced. In Buddhist terms, there's a tension between the *manas* and the relative *ālaya*.

In this situation, we need some third, reconciling factor, something that will combine the clarity, sharpness, and crystalline purity of the conscious mind with the richness and colour of the unconscious. This third, higher factor is the mandala. Jung found that his patients produced mandalas, these symbols of integration, quite spontaneously in their individuation process.[154] The mandala, though the word is Sanskrit, is a universal symbol. We find mandalas everywhere. Coleridge said about Sir Thomas Browne, referring to his work *The Garden of Cyrus*, that Browne saw quincunxes everywhere, in the heavens and on earth, a quincunx being an arrangement of five points just like a mandala.[155] In all spiritual traditions, and in great art and literature, mandalas can be seen. One has only to think of our great European cathedrals, with their enormous rose windows filled with stained glass of beautiful colours and filaments raying out from a centre. Patterns of stars with rays streaming from a central point, all sorts of jewel-like structures, flowers, especially lotuses, chrysanthemums, and so on, and wheels – these are very often mandalas. And wherever we encounter mandalas, whether in the East or in the West, whether in art or literature or religion or philosophy or dreams, they all have the same significance. They represent a resolution, or at least the beginnings of a resolution, of the conflict between the conscious and the unconscious, a reintegration of the psyche on higher and higher levels in which nothing is left out, no element is excluded or repressed, everything finds its place in a complete, harmonious, organized, and unified pattern.

Buddhist mandalas are symbols of this integration on the highest possible level, the level of complete or supreme Enlightenment, and the fact that Enlightenment can be pictured in this way shows that it isn't just a blank, featureless, inert state. When we speak about Nirvāṇa or Enlightenment, people sometimes think, 'How dreary! – just a void, some great empty hole in which you tumble headlong, a great blank nothing.' After all, we're told that there's nobody there, no mind, no thought, no speech – so what is there? It could seem a dreary place, rather like the Christian heaven in a sublimated way. But Enlightenment isn't like that, and the tantras and the symbol of the mandala make this clear. It's much better to think that Enlightenment is red or blue or green than that it is just a state of nothing. It's much better to conceive of it pictorially than to picture it just negatively. The mandala symbolizes the fact that Enlightenment is a state of beauty, harmony, colour, spiritual life, and spiritual activity.

Historically speaking, the mandala emerged at a critical stage in the history of Indian Buddhism, at the very end of the Mahāyāna period and the beginning of the Vajrayāna period. In the last days of the dominance of the Mahāyāna, Buddhism had retreated into the big monastic universities. In places like Nālandā, you got thousands of monks going through the academic routine, studying texts, writing commentaries, debating, refining the principles of logic, and so on. The tradition had become over-intellectualized and over-conceptualized. And at this point, when Buddhism in India seemed to have lost contact with its own sources, when it had become too intellectual, too much an affair of the conscious mind, the mandala emerged, and became a means of reintegration for Buddhism itself. The emergence of the tantras represented a rebirth of Buddhism – not a corruption or degeneration, as many people think without even studying these traditions – by re-establishing contact with the primordial depths which had been lost. The mandala in one or another of its forms can do the same for us today. It isn't just an exotic symbol, something that floats in from the East with all the colours of the East upon it. It reflects processes that are going on within each of us all the time – certainly within all those of us who are attempting in any way to lead a spiritual life, to achieve an understanding of ourselves and the universe in which we live. Like the Tibetan wheel of life, the mandala is a picture of the contents of our own mind.

Now we come to our third and last question, which is perhaps the most important of all. In what way is the mandala a symbol of integration? The question has already been answered in very general terms, but let's be more specific. First of all, let's take a closer look at some of the details of the typical mandala. Let's consider first of all the centre and the circumference. At the centre of the mandala is a symbol or image, and this represents the nucleus of the new self, born out of the conflicts of the old, the nucleus around which the entire contents of the psyche at all levels must be grouped and organized. In the mandala of the five Buddhas, at the centre is Vairocana, Enlightenment itself, and at the circumference of the mandala, there are three concentric circles that enclose the whole mandala. The outermost circle is a circle of flames, within that is a circle of *vajras*, and within that is a circle of lotuses. What do these signify?

Fire is a symbol of transformation. One must imagine the mandala as a disc of light with fiery edges, standing out against the darkness of the unconscious. The light of consciousness, not just the consciousness of the intellect, but the higher consciousness, is burning the surrounding darkness, the surrounding chaotic forces of the unconscious – not only burning them, but transforming them into beautiful shapes which can then be admitted within the confines of the mandala. This is the significance of the circle of flames.

Within that is the circle of *vajras*, placed end to end like a chain. The *vajra* is the thunderbolt or diamond, it is indestructible, and it represents the transcendental, so it signifies the fact that the mandala is a higher state of consciousness, a higher self (a psychological rather than a theological higher self), a sacred area which can't be destroyed by the forces of the unconscious. The symbolism is linked with that of the diamond throne, the *vajrāsana*, that point of absolute immutable stability, that transcendental spot on which the Buddha sat to gain Enlightenment.

Within the circle of *vajras* is the circle of lotuses. The mandala itself is a lotus and it's surrounded by lotuses. The lotus is always a symbol of spiritual rebirth, spiritual awakening, initiation. In both Buddhist and Hindu mythology a cosmic lotus, often golden, floats on the waters of existence.[156] The waters are the primordial unconscious, and the lotus is consciousness, which is born there. In the mandala we've got the same symbolism transposed to the highest level – rebirth, awakening, initiation, Enlightenment.

In between the circle of *vajras* and the circle of lotuses one often finds a circle containing eight cremation grounds. The burning ground is another symbol of transmutation, the gateway between the lower world, this earth, and the higher world, the world of the heavens. I've seen this gateway quite clearly a number of times. I'm thinking in particular of the cremation of an old lady who was a friend of mine. At about four o'clock one afternoon we took her body on a lorry down from Kalimpong to the river Teesta and cremated it on the banks of the river. We set fire to the pyre just as the sun was setting. All the four elements were there: earth, the riverbank; water, the river flowing by; fire, the burning corpse; and air, the sky. As the sun set, the stars came out. I have rarely, if ever, seen a more beautiful scene: the water and the earth below, the sky above, and in between, the pyre, burning. One could see very clearly how fire is a symbol of transmutation, the gateway from a lower to a higher world. One could literally see the physical body being transmuted by the fire into something subtler – into smoke, into ash, which was eventually just blown away. The remaining ashes are usually thrown into the river and then nothing is left. The transformation is complete. The cremation ground symbolizes something of this sort, the transmutation of the individual human mind into the higher mind, the universal consciousness. But why are there eight cremation grounds in the mandala? All these numbers have a significance. They represent the eight *vijñāna*s, the eight discriminative consciousnesses, which, as we saw in the third lecture, must be transmuted into the five wisdoms.

I could mention many more details of the mandala, but there's no time. I'll just make one more point. Within the three circles of the mandala is a palace, and this palace is the mandala proper. The five divisions of the mandala of the five Buddhas are all located here. The symbolism of the palace is a whole subject in itself, but at present I'll make just one point: the palace has four gates opening in each of the four directions, and each gate has a guardian, a terrible figure, usually black or blue, wrathful in appearance, with a red tongue hanging out, glaring eyes, and a thick body, surrounded by flames. This is the guardian of the gate of the mandala, of the integrity of the higher self. But it's not just a guardian. It's not just a question of keeping out the surging forces of the unconscious. The guardian is ready to take the offensive, to sally forth from the gate. In other words, the higher consciousness must not only defend itself against the inroads of unconsciousness. It must actively appropriate the contents of the unconscious and transform them, and include them within the mandala. In a sense the mandala gets bigger and bigger, including more and more, until eventually in a sense the whole earth, the whole of existence – or at least the whole psyche – becomes one great mandala, with everything integrated, everything harmonized. That state is the state of Enlightenment.

Now let us move on to the sexual symbolism of the mandala. I've described the five Buddhas singly, but they're usually represented with their consorts. These consorts are described as the five wisdoms, but they are not to be confused with the five wisdoms already mentioned, the five *jñānas*. The Buddha's consorts are the five *prajñās*, also translated as wisdoms. They are also known as the five female Buddhas. You might be surprised to learn that there are female Buddhas – you perhaps thought that only masculine Buddhas exist – but in the tantras you get female Buddhas too. These five are also known as the five great *ḍākinīs*.

Vairocana, the illuminator, has as his consort Ākāśadhāteśvarī, the lady of the sphere of infinite space. Vairocana represents the light of the sun, and his consort represents the infinity of space through which the light shines. Akṣobhya, the imperturbable, has for his consort Locanā, her name meaning the seeing one, the one with an eye, awareness, knowingness. Ratnasambhava, the jewel-producing, has for his consort Māmakī. Māmakī means mine-maker, because the Enlightened mind regards all things, all beings, as its own, as 'mine' – not in a sense of belonging to me, but in the sense of my own, dear to me. Māmakī is that aspect of the Buddha mind that regards all things as beloved. Amitābha, the Buddha of infinite light, has for his consort Pāṇḍaravāsinī, the white-robed one, also known as White Tārā, who is a form in her own right also. And Amoghasiddhi, infallible success, has as his consort Green Tārā, the savioures, who represents the redeeming power of Enlightenment.

The five Buddhas are represented as being in sexual union with their five consorts. Some people naturally find it surprising, even shocking, that religious representations should be of this sort, but the Tibetans and the Nepalese regard these images as being particularly sacred. They are not shocked, and there is no reaction of an erotic nature, no little giggle. I've seen on many occasions Tibetans going into a temple with these paintings on the wall and at once their attitude is one of devotion and respect. We have to try to understand the meaning of these things. The masculine Buddha represents the active, compassion aspect of Enlightenment, his consort, the female Buddha, represents the passive, wisdom aspect of Enlightenment, and their sexual union represents the inseparable unity of these two elements. Iconographically they are two persons, but spiritually, truly, they are just one Enlightened mind fully integrated at the highest possible level – wisdom and compassion fully integrated.

Integration is necessary at all levels of the spiritual life, and there is much sexual symbolism in Tantric literature. To give one extraordinary example, the Tantric practitioner is sometimes advised to have intercourse with an untouchable or low caste maiden. (One can see this in the *Hevajra Tantra*, which twice mentions taking an untouchable – called by the outcast group name Dombi – as a sexual consort.) What on earth does this mean? The tantras are supposed to be leading you to Enlightenment, but apparently they are encouraging immorality. Isn't this a degradation, a betrayal of the Buddha's teaching?

The clue is in 'untouchable' or 'low caste'. In India, the caste system is very rigid, and divided into about two thousand subdivisions, many of whose members do not intermarry or interdine. The untouchables are at the very bottom of this system, and they are looked down upon by the other castes: 'They're uncultured, they're immoral, they've got all sorts of dirty habits' and so on. In other words, psychologically the higher castes project their shadow onto lower caste people, just as some white people do onto black people. In this way, the untouchables, especially untouchable women, become identified with the unconscious in the widest sense. The higher castes are the more conscious, cultured, and intellectual, they would say – and actually it is the case that the higher castes in India, especially the Brahmins, are intellectual. People at the other end of the scale tend to be not so intellectual, but much more emotional.

So the higher castes represent the standpoint of the conscious mind, but the tantras are saying to such people that no spiritual progress is possible unless you recognize the unconscious, unless you overcome that gulf, unless you 'marry the untouchable girl' who represents your own unconscious, not just the repressed part, but the whole deeper unrealized side of your psychic life. This is a dramatic illustration of the way the mandala functions as a means of integration. You can imagine what a shock it would give some holy monk to be told that he had to have intercourse with an untouchable girl, but the shock itself should have got him thinking, 'Why should I be shocked?'

Before we close, a reminder. The mandala is not just an exotic symbol. It's not just of artistic interest. We all suffer from psychic disintegration. We must find that higher point, that nucleus, which reconciles conscious and unconscious. Around that we have to reintegrate our own psychic contents, give birth to our own mandala, and then we shall truly understand for ourselves the mandala, the Tantric symbol of integration.

ASPECTS OF BUDDHIST PSYCHOLOGY 7: ZEN AND THE PSYCHOTHERAPEUTIC PROCESS

The seventh in a series of seven lectures on 'Aspects of Buddhist Psychology', 1967

Today we come to the last lecture in the series. As the course has progressed from the conceptual to the non-conceptual approach, we have begun to appreciate, I hope, the importance of myths and symbols and legends and the poetic imagist element generally in the spiritual life. I hope that having come so far, you will have been able to appreciate something of the richness and profundity of the psychological side of Buddhism. Today our subject is Zen and psychotherapy, and here I have a confession to make. The lectures were decided upon some time ago, and I had a fairly clear idea of what the contents of each of the first six lectures would be, but when I put down the title 'Zen and Psychotherapy', I had no idea at all what I was going to say on this subject. Perhaps that is appropriate. One shouldn't perhaps know in advance what one is going to say about Zen; perhaps if one does, it isn't Zen.

But why include Zen at all? There are two reasons. First of all, I included it simply for the sake of completeness. I can't leave Zen out, and someone would object if I tried. In one of the lectures I referred to the three major forms of Buddhism representing the three principal phases of its development in India, the three *yānas*. But Zen, as I'm sure most of you will agree, is too important to be included under any of these headings, so I decided that there should be a separate lecture on Zen, even though I didn't know what I would be saying about it. In this way we would cover the whole field of Buddhism, all the principal forms. Secondly, I decided to include a talk on Zen because so many people nowadays are interested in it. If you talk to them about Buddhism, there's a bit of a response, but if you talk about Zen, even if you say exactly the same thing, at once people start perking up. The name has a magic about it. Sometimes people are interested in Zen, or what they think is Zen, for entirely the wrong reasons. There are misunderstandings about Buddhism, but they're nothing compared with the misunderstandings about Zen. I hope that this evening I shall be able to clear up at least a few of them. To begin with, Zen is a form of Mahāyāna Buddhism, although many Zen devotees don't realize this, and try to treat it as something standing quite independently, with no roots in Buddhism, with its roots in the sky. And Buddhism, of which Zen is one form, is a religion, though many people don't realize this either, very often thinking that it's cold, abstract, scientific, and purely rational – the North Pole among the thought systems of the world. But although Buddhism isn't a religion in the theistic sense – there's no supreme being, no personal God – it is a religion all the same.

I propose to deal with the subject of Zen and psychotherapy in three progressive stages: psychotherapy and religion, Buddhism and psychotherapy, and Zen and psychotherapy. So first of all, what is psychotherapy? For a brief but compendious definition, let us turn to Karl Jaspers. In *The Nature of Psychotherapy* he says,

> Psychotherapy is the name given to all those methods of treatment that affect both psyche and body by measures which proceed via the psyche. The cooperation of the patient is always required. Psychotherapy has application to those who suffer from many types of personality disorder, psychopathies, to the mildly psychotic patient, to all people who feel ill and suffer from their psychic state and almost without exception to physical illnesses which so often are overlaid with neurotic symptoms and with which the personality must inwardly come to terms.[157]

He goes on to describe the various means of influencing the psyche which psychotherapy has at its disposal, classifying them under various headings. He enumerates, for instance, methods of suggestion such as hypnosis, cathartic methods (in which he includes all forms of psychoanalysis), methods involving practice and training (including various kinds of breathing exercises), methods of re-education, and methods that address themselves to personality.

Taking Jaspers' basic definition of psychotherapy, 'all those methods of treatment that affect both psyche and body by methods which proceed via the psyche', here religion and psychotherapy stand on common ground. They both address themselves not to the superficial layers of human nature, but to the deepest part, which we call the psyche, the mind, the heart, or even the soul. Secondly, Jaspers says that psychotherapy is applicable to 'all people who feel ill and suffer from their psychic state'. This is extremely important. But what is meant by feeling ill and suffering from one's psychic state? Jaspers, it seems to me, is deliberately being very general here, even vague. Your conception of health will depend on your conception of illness, and your conception of therapy or cure will depend on your conception of health. If your conception of illness is superficial, your conception of cure will be superficial too, but if your conception of illness is profound and far-reaching, your conception of cure will also be profound and far-reaching. So there are two kinds of psychotherapy corresponding to two different conceptions of illness, adjustment therapy and character therapy, though the latter isn't a very satisfactory term.

As its name suggests, adjustment therapy is therapy that enables you to adjust. Adjust to what? To society, to the business of living in the world, earning a living and so on. Let's take a simple example. A young man is getting on quite well and everything seems all right, but one day he is attacked by feelings of intense nausea, and that keeps happening, until eventually it becomes almost continuous, and so bad that he has to stop working. He goes to see a psychotherapist, and he is treated for a few weeks or months. The cause of the trouble is located (maybe some childhood experience), it's resolved, the nausea disappears, and the young man goes back to work. So the therapy has enabled him to adjust to society, but the question is never raised as to whether the society to which he has adjusted is good or bad. It may be thoroughly immoral. He may have been enabled to resume work as a stockbroker, or an income tax consultant, or a tobacconist. But according to this way of thinking, that doesn't matter. You have got to adjust to the existing state of affairs, the world as it is, and psychotherapy helps you to adjust, just as in the old days some forms of religion helped you to accept the status quo. Some psychotherapists are becoming increasingly dissatisfied with this method. Many of them feel that they are in effect prostituting themselves to an immoral social order, but there's very little that they can do about it, because after all they too have to earn a living.

But character therapy goes far beyond the concept of adjustment. Let's take another example. Imagine a man of 45, with a moderately successful career and a comfortable domestic life. The children are doing quite well at school and he plays golf every Sunday. He has no symptoms. But deep down in himself, he feels ill. In Jaspers' language, he suffers from his psychic state. This is not an illness in the ordinary sense, but a spiritual malaise. He may be overwhelmed by a feeling of intense boredom or a sense of complete futility. He may feel that nothing he is doing has any value. And he may therefore ask himself, 'What is the use of it all? Why am I here?' In the old days he would have turned to religion and consulted his priest, but for many Western people this is now impossible, so he goes to the psychotherapist. But what is the psychotherapist to do? There's no question of helping this patient to adjust to society, because he's perfectly well adjusted already. The psychotherapist has to go deeper than that, and point out to the patient that he's ill because he is not being fully himself. He's got all sorts of deeper potentialities which have been overlaid by the business of so-called living. The patient has related successfully to society, but now he has to relate to life itself, to reality, and this requires a great change of character, attitude, outlook, vision. This psychotherapy is therefore called character therapy. It isn't just a matter of change, however radical. Before this patient can be brought to terms with himself and with reality, before he can be cured, there has to be a conversion, a spiritual rebirth. Adjustment therapy has very little in common with any religion, except superficial, popular forms of consolatory religion. It may even be profoundly anti-religious. But character therapy, in its concept of illness, health, and therapy, seems to come quite close to religion. If psychotherapy has a religious aspect, or at least a religious bearing, religion in the true sense is therapeutic, and this is certainly the case with Buddhism. This brings us to Buddhism and psychotherapy.

Both Buddhism and psychotherapy are humanistic, concerned with human beings in their totality, their heights and their depths, in all aspects of their being and character. Both are concerned just with human beings, not with God. Erich Fromm distinguishes between what he calls humanistic religion and what he calls authoritarian religion.

He claims that psychoanalysis and humanistic religion have much in common, which is no doubt true, but when he goes on to say that the distinction between humanistic religion and authoritarian religion cuts across the distinction between theistic and non-theistic religious systems, because both theistic and non-theistic religions can be either humanistic or authoritarian, I can't quite agree with him.[158] It seems to me that the theistic systems almost inevitably tend to be authoritarian, especially in their strict monotheistic forms. St Augustine said, 'God's thundering commands are to be obeyed,' and in more modern times, Cardinal Manning said, 'I don't think. The Pope does my thinking for me.'[159] This is authoritarianism with a vengeance. But Buddhism, Daoism, and Confucianism, which are all non-theistic, are definitely humanistic – Buddhism above all, perhaps, because it's the most fully articulated. An authoritarian Buddhism is a contradiction in terms. A Buddhism that says 'you must do this' or 'you must do that' doesn't sound like Buddhism at all.

Psychotherapy (or at least character therapy) has more in common with Buddhism than with any other religion because both are concerned with human beings as being psychically and spiritually sick. It is often said that the essentials of Buddhism are contained in the four noble truths: the truth of suffering; the truth of the cause of suffering (which is blind craving); the truth of the cessation of suffering, or the supremely blissful state of Nirvāṇa; and the way leading to the cessation of suffering, the Noble Eightfold Path. According to some scholars, this doctrinal formula is based on an ancient pre-Buddhistic Indian medical formula consisting of disease, the cause of the disease, the cessation of the disease, or state of perfect health, and the therapy.[160] The Buddha himself is known as the great physician. In Mahāyāna Buddhism there is a Buddha called Bhaiṣajyarāja, which means King of Healing, and there's a *sūtra* devoted to him in the Mahāyāna canon.[161] Tibetan Buddhism also has a set of seven Medicine Buddhas who are very popular indeed.

Even more interesting is a passage from one of the most famous and beautiful of the Mahāyāna *sūtras*, the *Vimalakīrti-nirdeśa*, the *sūtra* of the instruction of Vimalakīrti. According to the text, Vimalakīrti was not a monk, but a great householder bodhisattva of Vaiśālī (in present-day Bihar) in the days of the Buddha, and he was famous for his profound, far-reaching wisdom. One day he fell ill, and when the Buddha heard about his sickness, he wanted to send someone to enquire how he was getting on, but among all the disciples, all the great bodhisattvas and *arhant*s, no one was willing to go, because they were so afraid of Vimalakīrti's wisdom. He'd caught them out, every one of them, on more than one occasion in the past. But eventually no less a person than Mañjuśrī, the Bodhisattva of Wisdom, volunteered to go. He went to visit Vimalakīrti with a great train of disciples and followers, and a famous dialogue ensued. This evening we are concerned only with the beginning of this dialogue. When Mañjuśrī entered Vimalakīrti's room, he sat down by his bed and asked, on behalf of the Buddha, 'What is the cause of your sickness?' In ancient Indian medicine they had a theory somewhat like the Western medieval idea of the four humours – bile, blood, and so on. If these get out of balance, you fall sick. Mañjuśrī perhaps had something of that sort in mind. But Vimalakīrti replied, 'I am sick because beings are sick.'[162] This is one of the most profound and significant statements in the whole of Buddhist literature, and its significance is twofold. First of all it reveals Vimalakīrti's great compassion. Wisdom and compassion are basically the same thing: no wisdom without compassion; no compassion without wisdom. Vimalakīrti had both, so he identified himself with all living beings, and therefore he said, 'I am sick because beings are sick,' – not just physically sick, but spiritually sick. This is a thought for us to ponder. All beings, without exception, are sick.

There's an even more remarkable statement often attributed to the Buddha: 'All *pṛthagjanas* are mad.' According to Buddhism, there are two kinds of people: *āryas* and *pṛthagjanas*. The *āryas* are the holy ones: the Buddhas, the bodhisattvas, the *arhant*s, the non-returners, once-returners, and Stream Entrants, all those who have reached the higher stages of the spiritual path. Everybody else, even beings in higher heavenly realms, is a *pṛthagjana* or worldling. And we are being told that anyone who's not a Buddha, an *arhant*, or at least a Stream Entrant, is quite literally mad.[163] It isn't an exaggeration. If we look around, we see that we are living in the midst of a vast hospital, because everybody is sick. We are living in the midst of a vast lunatic asylum, because everybody is mad. Everything that everybody does in this world is the action of a madman or a madwoman, and we see glimpses of sanity only here and there. Of course, people like to think that they're sane, normal, and healthy, but it isn't really so. Their so-called health is sickness and their so-called sanity is insanity.

Not long ago I was looking into the writings of Vladimir Solovyov, that great Russian mystic and poet, and he gives a good example of how we think that we are sane when really we are insane. Discussing the question of sexual perversion, he takes the example of fetishism, the fixation of erotic interest on a particular part of the body or an article of clothing. Solovyov says that the perversion consists not in the sexual feeling itself, but in the fixation of the sexual feeling on a part instead of on the whole, but then he raises an interesting question. Is the whole body really the whole, or is it part of a whole? And he concludes that it's only part of a person. The person is body, soul, and spirit – he is using the Christian terms – so that to love or to be erotically interested in the body only is a perversion, and sexual perversions are forms of insanity. But the world doesn't see it like that. If your sexual interest is confined to someone's hand, or foot, or shoe, then you're a fetishist, but if it's directed only to someone's body, ignoring their mind and soul, that's perfectly normal. This is the example Solovyov gives of the way we think we're sane, when it would be much truer to say that we are mad.[164]

Anyway, it is time we got onto Zen and psychotherapy. Of course, as Zen is a branch of Buddhism, what I have said about Buddhism and psychotherapy holds good for Zen. Zen means meditation, and the word is used in three different, though related, senses. First of all, Zen is deep mental concentration, perfect one-pointedness of mind, as well as all those exercises, methods, and techniques that induce that state. Secondly, Zen is the realization of the One Mind, about which I spoke in the lecture on the depth psychology of the Yogācāra. Zen is awakening to the One Mind, above and beyond and behind and identical with all phenomena. Zen in this sense is practically synonymous with Enlightenment. And thirdly, Zen is certain special techniques and unconventional methods used by Zen masters to awaken disciples to the truth, methods such as shouts or even blows, the koan, the *mondō*, and so on. There's also a fourth kind of Zen, 'mouth Zen' – the Zen of people who talk about Zen and never do any practice. This form of Zen is extremely popular in the West; it's a very well-organized sect here, with several eminent masters.

According to tradition, Zen began with the Buddha in India. Some people think that Zen started in Japan, but that's a great mistake. We may even go so far as to say that Zen has nothing to do with Japan, or with India either – nothing to do even with the East or with the West.

Zen is like the lotus blossom. The lotus grows out of the mud but we must be careful not to define it in terms of the mud it's growing out of. Lotuses grow all over the world, and wherever they grow, they are the same lotuses.

In speaking about Zen, there are two mistakes to be avoided: saying too little and saying too much. By saying too little, I mean remaining completely silent. We hear of masters going up onto their platforms to give a lecture on Zen and just sitting there in silence. This is certainly very profound and meaningful, and it might help the advanced disciple, but the average person would become bored and restless and even resentful. By saying too much, I mean saying so much about Zen that people start thinking they've understood it, which is fatal. If they think they've understood Zen, they go away and forget all about it – or write a book about it. So this evening I'll try to follow a middle path. I'll speak on four fundamental principles of Zen, embodied in a well-known verse from the Tang dynasty, I'll point out some analogies with psychotherapy, and then we're going to leave psychotherapy far behind us.

> A special transmission outside the scriptures;
> No dependence upon words and letters;
> Direct pointing to the mind;
> Seeing into one's own nature and realizing Buddhahood.[165]

The first line of this verse takes us right back to the birth of Zen, in India in the days of the Buddha. Zen tradition tells us that one day the Buddha was sitting in a jungle clearing in the midst of a great crowd of his disciples. Great bodhisattvas were there, great *arhants*, Stream Entrants, monks, nuns, lay people, princes, ministers, and pandits. They were all sitting round the Buddha, all completely silent. This was apparently one of the features of the Buddha's ministry. Lots of discourses are attributed to the Buddha, but often he sat with his disciples in silence far into the night, no one saying a single word. This is the customary setting for a Mahāyāna *sūtra*, the atmosphere in the midst of which the Buddha begins to speak. On this occasion, the Buddha said nothing, but eventually, in the midst of the silence, he lifted up a golden flower. All the disciples saw it, but only one of them understood what it meant, and that was Mahākāśyapa, one of the oldest, wisest, and most experienced of all the disciples. He understood and he just smiled. So the Buddha said, 'Mahākāśyapa, I now transmit my Dharma to you.' And this, we are told, is the origin of Zen. This is how the special transmission started. It was a transmission from the Buddha to Mahākāśyapa, from the heart of the master to the heart of the disciple, in silence. And this is how the transmission continues, even down to the present day.

The question that people inevitably ask is 'What was transmitted?' What was this Dharma, this truth, that was handed over by the Buddha to Mahākāśyapa? After all, the Buddha didn't just give him a flower. One could say that Zen itself was symbolized by the golden flower, but this doesn't help us much. Going deeper, we can say that what was transmitted was the realization that there is nothing to transmit, nothing to hand over, and when the Buddha held up the golden flower, it was this that Mahākāśyapa understood. Those who were expecting something from the Buddha were mistaken, because there was nothing to transmit. So there's nothing for the Buddha to transmit to us. We usually think we go to the Buddha to receive Enlightenment, receive instruction, but there's nothing to receive. The Buddha simply points. He says, 'There's no need to go to Buddhism for what you are seeking, no need to go to Zen. There's nothing to be transmitted: you have it already. If you look for it, you'll lose it.' On a lower level, it's the same in psychotherapy. The patient has nothing to gain from the therapist. The therapist doesn't hand you health and sanity on a plate. He or she simply helps you to mobilize your own dormant curative and creative powers. That's all – and it's a great deal. Returning to the verse, this process, so far as Zen is concerned, takes place outside the scriptures. Not that the scriptures are useless – they're very useful – but they represent a crystallization of somebody else's experience, and this is no substitute for our own experience of the truth that there is nothing to transmit. It is all with us, every bit of it, already.

Secondly, 'No dependence on words and letters.' There's no dependence on second-hand experiences, on what somebody else says – in a word, no dependence on authority. Most people are afraid to stand on their own feet. They want to believe in someone, place their faith in someone, cling to someone. They don't want to carry the burden, as they feel it, of responsibility. They're afraid of freedom. They want someone to tell them to do what they want to do. Sometimes when people come and talk to me, it soon becomes quite clear what they really want to do. Why don't they go and do it? Well, they want me to tell them to go and do it. In this way people set up authorities, create father figures. The most familiar father figure is that of God, but there are many others: the state, the leader, the party. There are also mother figures – Mother Church, for example. People don't want to be independent. They want to go back to the womb, because it's so nice and cosy. They don't want freedom, they don't want the open air, they don't want responsibility.

One of the most dangerous authorities of all is the authority of the Book with a capital 'B', and especially the Sacred Book: the Bible, the Koran, *Das Kapital*, the 'Little Red Book', *Hansard*, the newspaper.[166] Some people swear by *The Times*, or the *Financial Times*; lots of you, I know, swear by the *New Statesman*. Whichever of these you swear by, the attitude is the same: slavish dependence. But the attitude of Zen is quite different. Japanese Zen paintings show the Sixth Patriarch, Huineng, tearing up the scriptures, especially the *Diamond Sūtra*. And it's just the same (on its own level, in its own context) with psychotherapy, which tries to resolve this attitude of infantile dependence and help people to stand on their own feet, or at least to realize that they have a backbone.

The third line speaks of direct pointing to the mind. The mind being pointed to is one's own. Most of us find it easy to look at other people's minds but very difficult to look at our own, but Zen says, 'Look within.' Maybe you've never looked there before. You may know the whole cosmos, with all its planets and stars and galactic systems, you may be able to weigh the stars, but if you don't know your own mind, it's all useless. And it isn't a question of knowing the mind as an object, knowing it as something 'out there', as the subject matter of psychology. What is meant here is something quite different. It is knowing the mind beyond the mind: not the lower mind knowing the higher mind, not even the higher mind knowing the lower mind, but mind, or the knowingness of mind, where there's no subject and no object, where they're merged. But there's no question of knowing this mind, which is neither subject nor object, as an object. If one wanted to be paradoxical, one could only say one can only know it by a not knowing, or an un-knowing.

Psychotherapy doesn't go so far as this, but it is well aware of the importance, and the difficulty, of knowing ourselves, even on the psychological level. Psychoanalysis, especially, knows how much we repress, how much in ourselves we allow to remain undeveloped, unrealized, unrecognized – not only lower things, but so much that is higher, rich and meaningful and spiritual. Psychoanalysis also knows how much we project from our unconscious depths onto people and places and things around us. All these repressions must be resolved, all these projections withdrawn. Both Zen and psychotherapy in their own ways point to the mind and say, 'Look there.'

In the fourth and last line of our verse, 'Seeing into one's own nature and realizing Buddhahood', a much more metaphysical, transcendental dimension begins to be disclosed. Here one penetrates into the ultimate depths of one's own true nature, and one emerges into Buddhahood, because Buddhism would say, and Zen would say most emphatically, in the depths of one's being, far beyond the mind, far beyond even the higher mind, is another dimension altogether, one of which most of the time we're not aware. There, you are Buddha, were Buddha, and always will be Buddha, not in time, but out of time altogether, and therefore you have nothing to gain. There's no Buddhahood to gain, it's there all the time. You have never really lost anything. When you wake up to the fact that in the depths of your being, in your ultimate nature, you are Buddha, a tremendous creativity and spontaneity is released, because you are in touch with the source of reality. Reality therefore flows through you, and you are reality. You have gone far beyond psychotherapy, far beyond Zen, and far beyond all the aspects of Buddhist psychology.

RELIGION: ETHNIC AND UNIVERSAL

From the series 'The Higher Evolution of Man', 1969

I lived in the East for some twenty years, and spent fourteen of them in Kalimpong, a small township in the foothills of the Himalayas some 4,000 feet above sea level. It is situated in a strategic spot. To the south is the great Indian subcontinent, to the north you have Sikkim and Tibet, away to the west there is Nepal, and to the east is Bhutan. Being at the juncture of all these territories, Kalimpong is a cosmopolitan place where one can meet not only Indians, Nepalese, and Sikkimese but Bhutanese, Tibetans, Chinese, Europeans, and even sometimes the odd American. Here, about two miles out of town, I established a small vihara, a hermitage, which commanded a magnificent view of the Himalayas. When I sat up in bed in the morning, I could see shining in the distance the snow peaks of the great Kanchenjunga range. At dawn this was a beautiful sight. First of all you would see them glimmering a ghostly white, and as the sun rose they turned a brilliant crimson and then a glowing gold; and then the gold would die away and they would be left a dazzling white. I saw this sight almost every morning of the year, especially in the autumn, when the skies are blue and cloudless and the peaks shine forth even more brilliantly than usual. It was here, with this view before me, that I established my hermitage, and in this spot I studied and meditated and wrote books and received friends for many years. Every now and then, once or twice a year, I would go out on tour down to the heat and perspiration of India, and wander among the new Buddhists of central and western India, but I always made a point of being back in Kalimpong for the rainy season, which in Buddhist countries is traditionally observed as a retreat. This was my period of seclusion and reflection, and I didn't step outside the vihara for three or four months.

It is very difficult to describe the effect the rainy season has upon the mind. The rain falls steadily, day after day, night after night, with a gentle and soothing sound which muffles every other noise, so you naturally feel in a very reflective mood. Shut up in my vihara, with the rain falling all around, no visitors, just my few books, meditation, study, and reflection, I used to reflect upon all sorts of problems – not psychological problems but questions which required examination, especially questions about the history of Buddhism, Buddhist doctrine, and the spiritual life generally. Sometimes I would succeed in resolving a problem, but there was one that kept coming up rainy season after rainy season to which there appeared to be no solution. It wasn't anything profoundly philosophical or deeply metaphysical, but a historical, almost a sociological question, with all sorts of philosophical and spiritual implications. It was a question which arose in my study of the history of Buddhism, and which people often used to ask me: why did Buddhism disappear from India?

Buddhism began in about the year 500 BCE, and it flourished in India for upwards of 1,500 years. At the height of its development and influence, from around 200 BCE to around 400 or 500 CE, it spread all over India and produced some of the greatest spiritual teachers and thinkers that the world has ever seen, and some of the greatest spiritual art and literature. But after that glorious efflorescence we see a gradual, as though inevitable, decline and disappearance, something almost unprecedented in the history of the religions in the world, and by the eleventh or twelfth century CE it had completely disappeared. Why? As I reflected on this question, I saw that there was no simple answer. No one factor was responsible for the disappearance of Buddhism from the land of its origin. All sorts of reasons were involved, some more important than others. Not only that. As I tried to go more and more deeply into this question, I saw that its ramifications extended far beyond the history of Buddhism, far beyond Buddhism itself. It was out of a consideration of some of these ramifications that I was led eventually to recognize the importance of the distinction between ethnic religion and universal religion, our subject tonight. How it fits into the general evolutionary scheme of things we shall see a little later on. For the moment, I want to deal briefly with the main reasons for Buddhism's disappearance from India. This will help us to establish the nature of the distinction and relationship between ethnic religion and universal religion, and this in turn will pave the way for a consideration of the characteristics of these two kinds of religion.

Why, then, did Buddhism disappear from India? We can list four or five main reasons, all of which are interconnected. The order in which we deal with them is not important, so I shall take them just as they come. First, the centralization of monastic life. It may come as a surprise, but originally in Buddhism there was no such thing as cenobitical monasticism, monks living permanently in monasteries. There were no monks, in fact, in that sense. There were only *parivrājakas*, people wandering from place to place and living on alms, going to people's doors every day and accepting whatever food was offered to them. In India you can't go roaming around during the rainy season, because the rains are far too heavy, so then the wanderers stayed in some mountain cave, or a hollow tree, or a hut in somebody's garden, and practised meditation. Then, when the rains were over, they would start wandering again. They memorized simple sayings of the Buddha, often in verse form, and as they roamed about they would recite these to themselves. If two or three of them were going along the road together they would chant the verses as they went along. Sometimes groups would congregate, especially on the day of the full moon, and they would chant whatever verses and sayings they had memorized, and then sit in meditation. In this way, you had these little bands of wanderers, and individual wanderers too, living in this simple, unpretentious way. Of monastic life as we have known it in the West there was nothing at all. There wasn't even any specifically monastic dress. The wanderers used to take ordinary Indian lay dress, two single pieces of cloth, one to put round the waist and the other over the shoulder, and discolour the cloths with brown earth so that they weren't of any use to anyone else, and that's what they wore.

After the Buddha's death, some wanderers got into the habit of returning to the same spot for the rainy season retreat every year. Then some of them stopped wandering altogether, and once they were staying in one place all the year round, they found that a temporary shed or hut was no longer enough, so they started putting up permanent buildings. As more and more people settled they needed bigger and bigger buildings, so they started enlisting the support of kings and other wealthy people and obtaining grants of land. In this way something more closely resembling Western monasticism developed. During this period, two or three hundred years after the death of the Buddha, the spiritual life became more and more identified not so much with the life of the lay community, or even with the life of the wanderers, but with monastic life in this cenobitical sense, and there was a tendency for the monasteries, the *mahāvihāras* as they were called, to become bigger and bigger. From sheltering just a few monks, they came to shelter thousands. The biggest and grandest of them all was Nālandā in Bihar, where in its heyday 14,000 monks lived in a great complex of monastic buildings. We know a lot about life at Nālandā during the early Buddhist Middle Ages because the great Chinese pilgrim Xuanzang became a professor there in the sixth century, and he wrote memoirs giving a detailed, vivid picture of the life of Nālandā during his stay.[167] By this period, Buddhist monastic life in India had become highly centralized. There weren't lots of little hermitages and monasteries dotted all over the country, but just a few very big ones containing practically all the monks. Whoever became seriously interested in Buddhism, especially during the later period, tended to become a monk, and whoever became a monk joined a big monastery. Buddhism thus became centralized in these large monastic institutions which were dependent upon royal patronage, and the monks became more and more cut off from the life of the people. We shall see the consequences of this in a minute.

A second reason for the disappearance of Buddhism from India was dependence on and eventual failure of royal patronage. The individual wanderer could go to someone's house and get enough food for the day, and that was that. Even when small hermitages were established in the vicinity of a village or town, they could depend for support on the village community. But if one wanted to establish a large monastery, to whom could one turn? Only to the king, for only he had enough money to support ventures of this kind. From the beginning, Buddhists tended to enlist the support of kings. Very often they succeeded brilliantly, and there were kings who were celebrated for the munificent support they gave Buddhism, especially in the way of endowing and maintaining huge monasteries: Aśoka, Kaṇiṣka, Harṣa, and so on. Sometimes Buddhism succeeded in gaining the support of whole dynasties, like the Gupta dynasty, and the Pāla dynasty in north-eastern India, and the Sātavāhanas in the south. This support was not always exclusive; many kings supported other religions as well. The example of the king was followed by lesser folk, so if he supported Buddhism, other people would also tend to support it, but this strength of Buddhism was also its weakness. Kings are fickle creatures – 'Put not your trust in princes.'[168] Sometimes they changed their religion for political reasons; they would suddenly become Shaivites or Jains, and withdraw support from Buddhism, or even start persecuting it, or sometimes a Buddhist dynasty just dwindled away. However it happened, support was withdrawn, and monastic Buddhism suffered.

The third factor in Buddhism's disappearance was the hostility of the Brahmins. The Brahmins were the hereditary priesthood of orthodox Hinduism, and they were in existence in India long before the time of the Buddha. They traditionally claimed the exclusive right to teach both religious and secular subjects. One of the things for which they criticized the Buddha was that being a Kshatriya, a warrior, he dared to teach religion. The Brahmins had very strong notions indeed about their own superiority to everybody else. We find them claiming that they were born at the very beginning of things, at the dawn of creation, out of the head of the god Brahmā, whereas the Kshatriyas, the fighters, were born from his shoulders, the Vaishyas or traders were born from his thighs, and the Shudras, the workers (that is, the vast majority) from his feet.[169] Throughout the history of India, the Brahmins have been a proud, exclusive, haughty, and powerful body of men, claiming social precedence and a deciding voice in all political affairs. In ancient India they considered themselves above the law. A Brahmin could not really be punished, and certainly could not be put to death, regardless of the crime committed. This law was in force in Nepal until quite recent times.

It is not surprising that the Brahmins were hostile to the Buddha, because the Buddha didn't agree with the caste system, didn't agree that some people were superior and others inferior by birth, but taught unmistakably that your worth depended not on your birth but on your deeds, your character, your spiritual attainments.[170] So the Brahmins were not very happy with the Buddha or his teaching. Sometimes they used to come to him with tricky questions. The Pāli scriptures represent them as plotting among themselves, saying, 'Let's go to him and put such and such a question. There are only two possible answers. If he answers in this way, we'll catch him out like this. If he answers in that way, we'll catch him out like that. He won't be able to escape.' Then they would come before the Buddha, very often with mock humility, as if to learn something, and put these questions. But the Buddha invariably answered the questions in a way they weren't expecting, and the Brahmins were invariably discomfited.[171] It's rather like the scribes and Pharisees coming to Christ with their questions and expecting to catch him out. The fact that the Buddha wasn't ever caught out didn't make him any more popular with the Brahmins, but even they had to recognize his great superiority, intellectually and spiritually, and they could do nothing about it during his own lifetime or for a long time afterwards. But they bided their time. It is characteristic of hereditary priesthoods that they have a very long memory, and the Brahmins of India certainly never forgot or forgave Buddhism.

The Brahmins were householders, not monks. They lived at home with their wives and families, and officiated at social and religious ceremonies for other lay people. In orthodox Hinduism your whole life is marked out by ceremonies. As soon as you're born, there's a ceremony of purification, then there's a name-giving ceremony, and another ceremony when you're given rice for the first time. Every time there's a ceremony, the Brahmin priest is called, because only he has the right to pronounce the sacred words, and you have to pay him for that. Even after death you're not free from the Brahmin; he has to be called in to perform the after-death ceremonies which ensure that the person who has died will go to heaven. If you go to Benares (Vārāṇasī) even now, you see the Brahmins sitting under magnificent umbrellas and people coming to them on the steps of the ghats and paying them to perform these ceremonies. So the Brahmins were in close touch with the lay community from birth until death and after death, and they gradually became dominant in the social and religious life of the community, while the Buddhist monks remained confined to large monasteries, supported by kings.

The fourth reason for the disappearance of Buddhism from India was the partial absorption of Buddhism by Hinduism. Really, there is no such thing as Hinduism. It has no one single founder. It is simply the sum total of the cultural and religious beliefs and practices of the Indian people, from prehistoric times right down to the present day. Gautama the Buddha, the founder of Buddhism, lived and taught in a

Hindu environment. By virtue of the fact that he was the Buddha, and that his Enlightenment was not just wisdom but also compassion, he had something that he wanted to share with the people around him, but how was he to communicate it? Even though his experience of reality was unprecedented, new, unique, he still had to use the old language, not only in the linguistic sense but in the sense of the language of thought, ideas, concepts, and attitudes. To put it simply, Buddhism had to speak the language of Hinduism.

It is important to understand that much of what we think of as Buddhist is actually Hindu, or simply Indian. There are all those long lists of doctrinal terms in the Buddhist scriptures: the five of this, the eight of that, the twenty-four of something else. Sometimes Buddhist literature seems to consist entirely of lists, and lists of lists. One might think this is just how Buddhism is, but it has nothing to do with the Buddha's Enlightenment experience. It's just the Indian mind at work. The Indian mind loves tabulation, and it got busy on Buddhism. It was a useful way of remembering things, but it is really Buddhism speaking the language of Hinduism. In the same way, much of what we think of as Zen – a certain way of sitting, cushions of a certain shape and size, a particular way of chanting – is merely Japanese. To come nearer home, much of what we think of as Christianity has nothing to do with the teaching of Christ. It is Mediterranean paganism or Roman imperialism.

But when Buddhism used the language of Hinduism, Hinduism itself changed. It is very important to notice this. It's similar to how Shakespeare's use of the English language permanently enriched the language. The fact that in modern English we can interchange all the parts of speech is due mainly to the poetic genius of Shakespeare, who did it on a grand scale, and made the English language more elastic and expressive than it had ever been before.[172] In the same way, when Buddhism speaks the language of Hinduism, Hinduism itself is changed. The Buddha and his teaching profoundly influenced Hinduism, in fact transformed it. Hinduism as we know it today is quite different from the Vedic Hinduism of the time of the Buddha, and it developed largely as a result of the stimulus given to it by Buddhism over the course of 1,500 years. This is well illustrated by the history of Indian logic – a classic case because it is so clear. Hindu logic was originally a primitive affair, but the Buddhist logicians criticized it and the Hindu logicians responded, the one sharpening and refining the other and provoking it to greater and greater subtlety. This went on for a thousand years, a ding-dong battle between rival schools of logicians, right down to the time of the disappearance of Buddhism from India. The battle of logic continues in Tibet, and between Buddhist and Marxist logicians, right down to the present time. This happened in practically all other fields of knowledge as well. The process was sharpened by Brahminical rivalry and when they saw which way the wind was blowing, they started deliberately borrowing from Buddhism, though it was only a partial absorption, because the real spirit of Buddhism was not assimilated. The caste system with all its inequalities and injustices remained intact and thus the supremacy of the Brahmins was ensured.

So this was how things stood. Buddhism had become centralized in the large monasteries and was dependent on the support of a dwindling number of Buddhist kings. It was cut off from the lay community, which was itself increasingly under the influence of the Brahmins. The Brahmins had succeeded in borrowing more and more from Buddhism. It's obvious that the Buddhists in India were heading for trouble, and trouble came. It came with the fifth factor, the Muslim invasion of India. Muslims are great iconoclasts. When I was in Pune once, I was staying with friends whose Muslim servant told me about the Hindu–Muslim riots in his home town in Bihar, and described how he and a party of friends had entered a Hindu temple and destroyed its images. From the gleeful way he said, 'We smashed them to pieces,' I could tell the strength of feeling against the image of the Muslim. When a Muslim sees an image, whether it's a Buddha, a Hindu god or goddess, or a Christian image of the Madonna or a saint, feeling that God is being affronted, he may have an irresistible urge to tear the image down, rather as the Puritan iconoclasts did in England in the seventeenth century. When the Muslim hordes poured down into India, they saw temples and monasteries full of images, and they indulged in a frenzy of destruction, smashing images and desecrating temples wherever they found them, Buddhist and Hindu alike. It is one of the saddest sights in India to go from one ancient Buddhist site to another and see the beautiful images which have been dug up from the earth all mutilated. The Buddhists were particularly vulnerable to the Muslim iconoclasts' fury because they stood out in the landscape. India is a flat country, especially the great Gangetic valley, and from miles away you could see these many-storeyed buildings looming up, and they were all destroyed. Nālandā itself was sacked in the year 1197. According to a Persian historian, thousands of monks were burned alive, thousands were beheaded, and the burning of the great library at Nālandā, which was famous all over the Buddhist world, continued for several months together.[173] In this way Buddhism disappeared from India, and the Brahmins were left in possession of the field, though not exclusive possession, because Islam also took root.

This story illustrates the nature of the distinction and the relationship between ethnic religion and universal religion. To explore this subject, our main point of departure will be the fourth factor in the disappearance of Buddhism from India, the partial absorption of Buddhism by Hinduism. Let's consider the general characteristics of ethnic and universal religion. I am not going to define the word religion itself, but perhaps a definition will emerge as we proceed. As the term suggests, ethnic religion is the religion of an ethnos, a race – that is, a group of people related, or at least originally related, by blood. This ethnic group is usually tied to a particular geographical area, and ethnic religion tends to be identified with that locality, and especially with its culture. An ethnic religion does not pertain to the individual as such but to the human collectivity, and this collectiveness is the basic characteristic of ethnic religions. Ethnic religion is the religion of the group as group, and of the individual only indirectly. It is the religion not of the free individual, but of the group member, only in so far as he or she is a member of the group – the family, the tribe, the clan, and so on. Ethnic religions have no one single founder, and there are no individual followers. You don't follow an ethnic religion as an individual, but only as a member of the group. Another characteristic of ethnic religion is that you have to be born into it, so there is no such thing as conversion. An ethnic religion affirms the collective values of the group, not individual values. Exalting values that ensure the survival of the group as a biological, anthropological entity, it emphasizes and indeed consecrates such things as marriage, family and tribal relationships, and submission to the group, to the elders, and to authority. There are other characteristics of ethnic religion, but these will suffice for our present purpose.

The characteristics of universal religion are the exact opposite. Universal religion is not the religion of the group, the human collectivity, but the religion of any individual, anywhere, at any time – at least potentially. A universal religion is never tied to any particular locality or identified with any particular culture. It may embrace cultures, work through cultures, express itself in cultures, but it is never in principle identified with any of them. Above all, universal religion is individual. One follows a universal religion as an individual, for oneself alone, by oneself alone. Others may happen to be following it too, but one does not follow it because they are following it or because one belongs to a group that follows it. One follows it on account of one's own decision. Universal religions all have individual founders. At the very source of the tradition they represent there stands one who has become a true individual and encourages others to become likewise. You can't be born into a universal religion. You must be personally converted to it by virtue of a change of life. Universal religion affirms individual values, and it negates collective values – such things as marriage, tribal relationships, ties of blood and soil – and passes beyond them. Negating the idea of submission to the group or to other more powerful members of the group, negating authority, universal religion exalts whatever enhances individuality, emphasizing freedom, independence, and individual responsibility.

What place do ethnic religion and universal religion occupy in the total scale of human evolution? This isn't difficult to see. The basic characteristic of ethnic religion is that it is collective, so it belongs to the lower evolution, though it has branches in the ultra-human stage of the higher evolution. The basic characteristic of universal religion is that it is an individual affair, so it belongs to the higher evolution, though it has roots deep in the lower evolution, specifically in the stage of humanity, both primitive and civilized. There is also a correspondence between folk art and ethnic religion, and between the fine arts and universal religion, but we have no time tonight to pursue this question further.

HINDUISM

Hinduism is very obviously an ethnic religion. The sum total of the beliefs and practices of the people of India, it is confined to that subcontinent, and found elsewhere only where Indian culture has been transplanted. Hinduism is so closely identified with Indian culture that one can hardly say where the one ends and the other begins. It is the religion of all the Indian people, with the exception of those who have been converted to one of the universal religions, and it is collective. It has no single founder, though a large number of great personalities are revered within Hinduism, and one has to be born a Hindu. This is illustrated by the story of the great emperor Akbar. He was of Muslim descent, and a liberal-minded man, and he decided that he ought to become a Hindu. The majority of his subjects were Hindus, and he probably thought it would be a good thing to do politically. So he invited the pundits of Benares, the most learned, scholarly, and orthodox of all the Brahmins of India, to meet him at Agra, and he said, 'I would like to become a Hindu. Please tell me how it is to be done.' The pundits of Benares clearly had a sense of humour. They went away and returned with a donkey, and said to Akbar, 'Your Majesty, please make this donkey into a horse.' So Akbar said, 'But that's impossible. He's been born a donkey. How can he possibly become a horse?' And they said, 'Your Majesty, you have been born a non-Hindu. How can you possibly become a Hindu?' So Akbar remained a Muslim and India continued to be ruled by his Muslim dynasty.[174] You can't be converted to Hinduism.

Hinduism affirms group values and stresses caste solidarity and the performance of caste duties. In the eyes of orthodox Hinduism you are not an individual, but the member of a caste, and you can't get away from that caste. In India, it is practically impossible not to have a caste, even if you are not a Hindu. In my own wandering days in South India, the question I was asked by every person I met was 'What is your caste?' I would say, 'I'm a Buddhist, and Buddhists don't believe in caste; and also I'm English, and we don't have a caste system. So I have no caste.' They would always say, 'That's impossible. Everybody must have a caste.' They used to think that I must be very low caste and I was concealing it because I was ashamed. They would sometimes become upset that I had tried to escape from the net of the caste system and become a free individual. Even Christians, who don't belong to the caste system as they are not Hindus, have been given a caste in India. The Anglo-Indians have been given a caste, and so have the Jains. This is the tendency in Hinduism. You can't be an individual, you are a member of a group. You have your existence only through the group, and Hinduism affirms group values.

In Hinduism it is a sin not to propagate the human species. Here again, group values are being affirmed. We are told in some of the Hindu religious books that if a Brahmin leaves his daughter unmarried, he is guilty of as many murders as potential children she might have had. This was one of the reasons for marrying girls off as soon as they reached puberty. Hinduism also lays strong emphasis on worldly prosperity. In the Vedas, the main scriptures of ancient Hinduism, there are scores of prayers for cows, which represented wealth, and there are stories of Brahmins asking for a thousand cows as reward for their services to the king. All this goes to make Hinduism very much an ethnic religion.

BUDDHISM

It is equally clear that Buddhism is a universal religion, because the truth taught by Buddhism is to be experienced by each person for himself or herself individually, and this can be done at any place, at any time. Buddhism didn't remain confined to India, but spread all over the East and is beginning to spread in the West. It isn't identified with any particular culture. One can't be born a Buddhist. One becomes a Buddhist only by practising the teaching, and this finds outward expression in the act of Going for Refuge to the Three Jewels. And Buddhism negates collective values, encouraging one to go forth from home, from the family, the tribe, even the nation. It stresses individual values like mindfulness, awareness, and self-responsibility, and has no time for authoritarianism. Sometimes friends ask me, 'Who tells you what to do? Who sent you to London?' They imagine that there is some great superior sitting somewhere in the East, rather like the pope in Rome, ordering us all to go here and go there, do this and do that. But I say, 'Nobody ordered me to do this. It is my own free decision.' This is the way Buddhism is organized, or rather isn't organized. As soon as you have had your training, ten years of it, or even five years will do at a pinch, you're free to go out and do what you want to do. You've no one breathing down your neck. You have your elders and your teachers, whose advice you will ask from time to time, but they never attempt to control you or dictate to you. Whether you want to go and meditate in the jungle, or study, or preach, or paint pictures of the Buddha, you are free to do that. So long as you are occupied with Buddhism in some way, everybody is happy. You are not shifted around like a pawn on the ecclesiastical chessboard. There is no time for authoritarianism in Buddhism, and it is certainly not concerned with the propagation of the race. It leaves that to the ethnic religions. So Buddhism represents universal religion in a very pure form, just as Hinduism represents ethnic religion in a very pure form.

CONFUCIANISM

Confucius was undoubtedly a true individual, if perhaps not of the very highest type. His teaching, so far as it is recorded, has ethnic characteristics, and it is confined to China and identified with certain important aspects of Chinese culture. Confucianism stresses group relationships and responsibilities, especially filial piety, so that from your own birth to the time of your parents' death you are under their control. In a sense you never really grow up. Confucianism also stresses loyalty to the ruler, and civic duties and responsibilities. Confucius did inculcate some individual values, such as self-respect, mindfulness of one's actions, and mindfulness of and for other people, and he also stressed independence of judgement. You were not bound to serve a bad ruler, for instance. But on the whole, Confucianism is an ethnic religion and perhaps in time it became even more ethnic than it was originally.

DAOISM

Daoism is a rather curious case. It is confined to China and identified to some extent with Chinese culture, but it is potentially a universal religion, though unfortunately it quickly degenerated. It is highly individual, or even individualistic, as expressed in the text known as the *Dao De Jing*. One might even say that Daoism in its original primitive form is anarchistic. It is opposed to the collective. It wants to give up the refinements of civilization and go back to primitive simplicity. It preaches a return to nature. Sometimes it seems to advocate a return from the collective to the pre-collective, to primitive human existence before the time of the River Valley civilizations, rather than an advance from the collective to the individual, but nevertheless its cosmic insights are of value at all levels of human evolution, whether lower or higher. We could probably regard Daoism as a quasi-ethnic system which teaches advance to the new in terms of retreat to the old. For this reason perhaps, Daoism never really got started. If we want to characterize it at its best, we can call it a transcendental primitivism, and it remains the solace of the lonely individualist.

SHINTO

Shinto literally means the way of the gods, and the gods are those of Japan, the Land of the Rising Sun. According to Japanese mythology, the gods created Japan first, before the rest of the world. So Shinto is very definitely an ethnic religion. Its relationship with Buddhism is a very interesting and instructive chapter in the history of comparative religion, but we have no time to discuss it now.

ZOROASTRIANISM

Zoroastrianism is a universal religion with some ethnic features. It never spread much beyond the boundaries of the Persian empire, but it had a single founder, Zarathustra Spitama, who on the whole stressed individual rather than collective values. It is perhaps significant that he was strongly opposed by the Magi, the hereditary priests of the old Persian ethnic religion, just as the Buddha was opposed by the Brahmins.

JUDAISM

Judaism is an ethnic religion, although later on in its history it developed some universal features. It is confined to a single, blood-related (in principle) group, the Jewish people, and it has a strong identification with a particular area, Palestine. It is significant that after 2,000 years at least some Jews returned to Palestine. No Western Buddhist would be likely to think of returning to north-eastern India just because that was where Buddhism originated. Here we can begin to see the great difference of perspective between an ethnic and a universal religion: an ethnic religion is identified with a particular geographical area, and a universal religion is not. In Judaism, Moses and the prophets are revered but there is no one single founder of the religion, and Judaism, like Hinduism, stresses collective values and the importance of the family. Traditionally you can't be a rabbi, a religious teacher, unless you are married and have at least one child. On the whole there is no such thing as conversion to Judaism, though that seems to be changing now, especially in the United States and among what are called Reformed Jews.

CHRISTIANITY

This is obviously a universal religion so far as the actual teaching of Christ is concerned. Christianity addresses itself to the individual. It is not confined to any particular area or culture and it has spread over practically the whole earth. It has a single founder, Christ, and one can't really be born a Christian. One becomes a Christian, strictly speaking, by virtue of a spiritual rebirth, and the rite of baptism is a symbol of this process. The teachings of Christ affirm individual values and attack group values even more vigorously than Buddhism does. We find Christ saying that if a man is not ready to give up mother and father then he is not worthy to be his disciple, and there's that well-known episode when Christ said to his mother, 'Woman, what have I to do with thee?'[175] He cut off contact completely from family, and tribe, his true family being those who were following his teaching, his spiritual brothers and sisters, sons and daughters. No need to insist on these points. Christianity is clearly a universal religion in the fullest sense of the term. What has been made of it over the centuries is a different matter.

ISLAM

This is a universal religion with some ethnic features. It has a single founder, Mohammed, and it has spread practically all over the world. On the whole, Islam stresses individual values, though the individual is not entirely emancipated from the group, and especially not from the family. There is no monastic life in Islam, for instance. In Islam, the head of the family enjoys freedom to the extent that the family submit to him unconditionally, but this is not true freedom because it is based upon the submission of other people, not on one's own free individuality.

There are many other religions that I would like to comment on, especially Manichaeism, but there is no time. I must just briefly mention the religions of Ancient Greece and Rome and of the Teutonic and Celtic peoples. None of them have special names but they are all ethnic religions. But it is time we started drawing a few conclusions. First of all, a universal religion never appears out of the blue among primitive people, but appears in the context of a fairly well-developed ethnic religion. Buddhism arose in the midst of Hinduism, and even when it went to China it grafted itself onto Confucianism and especially Daoism. It did the same thing with Shinto in Japan. Christianity arose in the context of Judaism, and so did Islam, though it was also influenced to some extent by Christianity. Zoroastrianism arose in the context of Magian religion. The general principle is that an ethnic religion may or may not give birth to a universal religion, but a universal religion always arises on the basis of an ethnic religion, and the religions making up each pair are continuous with each other, just as the higher evolution is continuous with the lower evolution. This is illustrated very clearly in the case of Christianity. We find the Old Testament, representing Judaism, bound up with the New Testament, representing Christianity, in one and the same Bible, the latter continuous with the former even though it goes quite beyond it.

At this point, a number of lines of investigation open out. We can't pursue them all and we can't pursue any of them very systematically, but I want to touch on at least a few of them, because they disclose insights and perspectives of great importance. First of all, as we saw, universal religion speaks the language of the ethnic religion in the midst of which it was born. Buddhism speaks the language of karma and rebirth, of Hindu cosmology and psychology, and Christianity speaks the language of Messianism, Jewish eschatology, angelology, and demonology. In speaking the language of the ethnic religion, the universal religion expresses its own content and at the same time refines the language, and the ethnic religion itself. But herein resides a danger, because the process can work the other way round. A universal religion can become coarsened if it speaks the language of ethnic religion too much or for too long, especially if the followers of the universal religion start taking that language too literally or if the universal religion incorporates too many unassimilated ethnic aims.

As a general rule – and this has never been pointed out before, as far as I know – a universal religion in time tends to be transformed into an ethnic religion, to become not individual but collective. This is a great betrayal, and a terrible degeneration, but it is happening to all universal religions in differing degrees. It tends to happen especially as the universal religion becomes more popular, less concentrated, and more thinly spread out. We have to recognize that the universal religion belongs to the higher evolution. It goes beyond the ordinary human being even at their best, aiming at the production of the true individual.

It insists on the development of mindfulness, awareness, responsibility, and freedom. Very, very few people are capable, in any age, of truly following a universal religion, because they are not capable of pursuing the higher evolution. They may pay lip service to its ideals, but in practice they tend to bend the universal religion to serve the needs of the group, the collective, the lower evolution. That great existentialist thinker Søren Kierkegaard has some devastating things to say in this connection. He says them of Christianity but his remarks are of general application, so I shall quote from a work called *The Present Moment.* Bear in mind that he was himself a Christian in the true sense.

> The intention of Christianity was to change everything. The result, the Christianity of 'Christendom' is: everything, literally everything, remained as it had been, with just the difference that to everything was affixed the attribute 'Christian' – and for the rest (strike up, fiddlers!) we live in Heathendom – so merrily the dance goes around; or, rather, we live in a Heathendom made more refined by the help of Life Everlasting and by help of the thought that, after all, it is all Christian! Try it, point to what you will, and you shall see that I am right in my assertion. If what Christianity demanded was chastity, then away with brothels! But the change is that the brothels have remained just as they did in Heathendom, and the proportion of prostitutes remains the same, too; to be sure, they became 'Christian' brothels! A brothel-keeper is a 'Christian' brothel-keeper, he is a Christian as well as we others. Exclude him from church membership? 'Why, for goodness sake,' the clergymen will say, 'what would things come to if we excluded a single paying member?' The brothel-keeper dies and gets a funeral oration with a panegyric in proportion to the amount he pays. And after having earned his money in a manner which, from a Christian point of view, is as filthy and base as it can be (for, from a Christian point of view it would be more honourable if he had stolen it) the clergyman returns home. He is in a hurry, for he is to go to church in order to deliver an oration, or as Bishop Martensen would say, 'bear witness'.
>
> But if Christianity demanded honesty and uprightness, and doing away with this swindle, the change which really came about was this: the swindling has remained just as in Heathendom,

> 'everyone (every Christian) is a thief in his own line'; only, the swindling has taken on the predicate 'Christian'. So we now have 'Christian' swindling – and the 'clergyman' bestows his blessing on this Christian community, this Christian state, in which one cheats, just as one did in Heathendom, at the same time that one pays the 'clergyman', that is, the biggest swindler of them all, and thus cheats one's self into Christianity.[176]

This is Kierkegaard's famous attack on Christendom, but it is an attack in principle on all universal religions that have become corrupted into ethnic or pseudo-ethnic religions. Exactly the same thing has happened in Buddhist countries. After all, everybody there is a Buddhist. Think of that! Sometimes people add up statistics and say, 'In the world there are 600 million Buddhists and 500 million Christians, etc.' If that was true, it would be heaven on earth, but it assumes that one can be born a Buddhist. I have met so many Buddhists in the East who have asked me, 'Are you a Buddhist?' When I said 'Yes', they said 'How long have you been a Buddhist?' 'Twenty years.' 'Ah,' they would say, with an air of superiority, 'I'm a born Buddhist.' But in most cases this just means that you go on exactly as you would have done without Buddhism, except that every now and then you call in the monks to chant a few *sūtras*. I have seen photographs of Thai monks sprinkling holy water on guns destined for Vietnam. Why? Because the Thai government had ordered them to do so. In all the Buddhist countries of the East nowadays Buddhism is closely identified with the national culture, and very often even the monks are unable to tell which is which. Very often they don't know what Buddhism is; they only know their own national customs and traditions, and those are what they want to spread abroad. It was similar with the Christian missionaries in India in the days of the Raj. They got hold of some poor Indian villager, put him in a pair of trousers and a shirt and a jacket with brass buttons, made him sit on a chair and use a knife and fork, instead of his 'dirty fingers', as they thought them to be, and then they would tell him, 'John,' (because they had given him a Christian name) 'now you really are a Christian.' And if we're not careful, we do the same thing in Buddhism. We take on all sorts of cultural customs from the East, and we think that this is Buddhism, and that we become Buddhists by learning these things. Some years ago I heard that some Burmese monks had come to Assam and were spreading

Buddhism there. I was told they were very successful, but when I asked some 'converts' what they had been taught, they said, 'They taught us two things: to eat dried fish and to write the Burmese alphabet.' And those monks really thought they were spreading Buddhism. One might think it would be impossible for this to happen, but it does.

But why does a universal religion tend to become an ethnic religion? It's the result of what I call the gravitational pull, an expression I've borrowed from physics. We all know that the earth has a gravitational field and that any object within this field will be pulled down towards the earth. In order to escape that pull, you have to go beyond the gravitational field of the earth, then you can swing free into space and lose yourself among the stars. It's the same with universal religion and ethnic religion, the higher evolution and lower evolution. The true individual struggles to emerge in the midst of the group, feeling all the time the pull of the group. This happens in the case of the artist too. The artist wants to be an individual, wants to be free to follow their own path, paint their own pictures, compose their own poems. But what does society say? What does the group, the herd, say? Conform! Sometimes, conform or perish. The person who is struggling to emerge may have no alternative but to submit. And this pull is not just outside yourself, but inside too, because you are still partly a group member, you still belong partly to the lower evolution. You are only free of this gravitational pull after reaching a certain point rather high up in the higher evolution: Stream Entry, also called the point of no return.

But we should not conclude that universal religion should or can cut itself off from ethnic religion. That would be going to the other extreme. Just as the ethnic has branches in the universal, so the universal religion has its roots in the ethnic. This is a special aspect of the continuity of the whole evolutionary process, ever advancing in one continuous process from lower to higher levels of being and organization. Unfortunately, the continuity of our religious life in the West was disrupted by the advent of Christianity. Wherever Christianity went in these islands, pagan images were smashed, stone circles were damaged, sacred groves were cut down, and priests were killed. Paganism was practically destroyed, root and branch, and if it survived at all, it was only in rather negative and distorted forms such as what is popularly called witchcraft. The result is that today we can only look back through 1,500 years of religious history: the Oxford Group of the nineteenth century, the Methodist revival before that, Puritanism before that, the medieval church, and the beginnings of the Church in this country, back to the introduction of Christianity. Before that we can see only an abyss of darkness in which hideous shapes vaguely swarm, a pagan abyss from which we have been conditioned to shrink back in horror. So we can't feel our own roots deep down. There is no continuity with the past, though we are not aware of this and don't know that we have been deprived of it.

But in India, people can look back into the past for thousands of years, back to the great saints and reformers of the nineteenth century, the medieval mystics, the early medieval philosophers, back to Buddhism, Brahmic Hinduism, Vedic Hinduism, all the way back to the primitive cults before that, one single uninterrupted process right back into the dawn of history and beyond until that line of evolution loses itself in the mists of the past. The modern Hindu can feel their continuity with the Vedic rishis living thousands of years before Christ. It's surely a wonderful feeling to be able to feel that one's religious roots go so far back, so deep down, like a flower looking down into the earth and feeling its roots. In the West it's like a flower in a glass of water, or even an artificial flower. Continuity with our religious past and our own special brand of paganism has been lost. I feel that this link must be restored as far as possible. As many people are beginning to recognize, it is important that the old myths and legends, beliefs and practices should be studied, not as grist for the academic mill, but so that we can feel our way back into the ancient religion of this country. Once at a meeting at an art college in Portsmouth someone asked me, 'What must happen before Buddhism can flourish in this country?' I replied, feeling in a rather jovial mood, that first there must be a revival of paganism. Everybody thought I was joking, and they had a good laugh, but one young man came to see me afterwards and said, 'Did you really mean that? And what did you mean by it?' So I said, 'By paganism I meant freedom from Christian conditioning in moral matters, especially with regard to sex.' But I meant much more than that. I meant that we must re-establish contact with our religious roots.

As I started with a bit of autobiography, I will finish with another bit. I came back to this country after twenty years in the East in 1964. For a while I was very busy with lectures, meetings, and classes, but one day a friend offered to take me out for the weekend and asked me where I'd like to go. I thought it over and said eventually, 'Let's visit Stonehenge.'

It's a very impressive sight, that great circle of stones that have stood there on Salisbury Plain for 4,000 years. But they are just stones, just archaeological monuments. We don't feel any real continuity with the religious and cultural life of the people who placed them there. I feel it is important that people, including Buddhists, should try to establish contact with their pre-Christian past. One might even say that Buddhism will have to put down roots in this country before it can start producing flowers. Personally, I wouldn't mind seeing a combination of Celtic paganism and Buddhism, the one for the majority and the other for the minority, and each perfectly tolerant towards the other, so that it would be easy for those who wished to pass from the one to the other, from the ethnic to the universal, from the lower evolution to the higher. This was the situation in India in the Buddha's time. On the whole people followed the old ethnic cults but the Buddha, the true individual, was free to recruit other potential individuals from their midst. I feel that the days of pseudo-universal religions, universal religions that have become corrupted and now function as ethnic religions, are over. Society is becoming day by day more secular and more pagan. The fashionable word is 'permissive'. It's a dirty word in some quarters but it probably represents a very healthy development. I think that in the future, in the midst of this secular and pagan society, universal religion will be found by those who really want it.

THE 1970S

FROM ALIENATED AWARENESS TO INTEGRATED AWARENESS

From the series 'Aspects of the Higher Evolution of the Individual', 1970

At present we are engaged in the study of the higher evolution of the individual,[177] not in the abstract but very much in the concrete. The process of the higher evolution is arduous, involving a great deal of effort, determination, strain, and even a measure of suffering. We may even go so far as to say that this type of effort is by far the most difficult thing that any human being can attempt. But although it is the most difficult, it is also the most worthwhile. And in this higher evolution of the individual, being arduous, demanding everything we've got, every aspect of our nature, and a great deal of self-knowledge and coming to terms with ourselves in various ways, all sorts of problems arise which must be resolved if further progress is to be made. It is some of these problems – not just ordinary difficulties, pressing as these sometimes are, but problems arising directly out of our effort to grow – that we shall be exploring today.

In the course of the lower evolution we recapitulate the process of human evolution, but it takes us so far and then leaves us to struggle on by means of our own efforts. Further development depends not on nature, nor even on nurture, but on our own individual efforts. The immediate task before us is to develop rudimentary self-consciousness to perfection and at least the beginnings of transcendental consciousness. Only if we are doing this, or trying to do this, can we be said to be leading truly human lives. So now we come to the first of our problems, one that, at least in the West, tends to arise quite early in the spiritual life. It is very important that we solve this problem, especially as it arises in connection with awareness. Awareness is the growing point of the whole process of the higher evolution, so if there is any misunderstanding about developing it, one's growth may be affected, or even made impossible, just as if the bud is damaged the flower will not be able to unfold to full perfection. This is not to say that awareness itself is a problem – indeed, awareness is the resolution of many of our problems. The problem comes if we confuse what I term alienated awareness with what I term integrated awareness, and tonight we are primarily concerned with this question. We are going to proceed slowly, step by step, first considering awareness in general, and especially the way it is to be cultivated according to the traditional Buddhist teaching. Here many of us will find ourselves on familiar ground. After that, we shall be striking out in a new direction, exploring comparatively unfamiliar territory.

There is a detailed account of awareness (or mindfulness, as it is often termed in writings about Buddhism) along traditional lines in the first chapter of my *Survey of Buddhism*.[178] I also dealt with perfect awareness in the seventh lecture in the series on the Buddha's Noble Eightfold Path,[179] and awareness is approached in a more contemporary and comprehensive manner in a talk I gave on dimensions of awareness.[180] This evening we have only time for an outline of the subject of awareness in general. Altogether there are four main kinds or dimensions of awareness: awareness of things, awareness of self, awareness of people, and awareness of reality.

Awareness of things means awareness of the world around us, our material environment, nature. If we want to be aware of the world around us, we have to learn to look at and listen to it, although very few people ever do this, most people saying that they have no time. We need to learn to look at the things that are around us all the time, but which we never really see: at the sky, at mountains, at trees, at flowers, at rocks, at water, at fire, and at less poetic things like brick walls and unemptied dustbins. And awareness is not only a question of using our eyes. No doubt the highest degree of perceptual awareness is possible through the sense of sight, but we also have to learn to hear, to taste, to smell, to touch. We need to learn to look not only at natural objects and household things, but at works of art, things we may take for granted as part of our cultural heritage. We know they are there in the museums and art galleries, and maybe as reproductions on our walls, but we don't really look at them. We should also learn to listen to music. Lots of people have music on as a background noise, a running rivulet of sound to which they never listen. Whether it is Bach or the latest popular song they don't know. But if we are going to develop awareness, the first thing we need to do is to become more aware of the material environment, of nature, and of human handiwork.

Secondly, we need to become aware of self. By this I don't mean anything metaphysical, but simply awareness of the changing empirical self, which is in any case all that we usually experience. Traditionally in Buddhism awareness of self is of three kinds, of increasing degrees of subtlety. First, there is awareness of the body and its movements, including the breathing process, on which a whole concentration technique is based. Traditionally it is taught that as you move about, you should be aware of how you are moving. If you are standing, be aware that you are standing. If you are sitting, experience yourself sitting. If you move your hand, be aware you are moving your hand. If you close the door, be aware that you are closing the door. If you are talking, be aware that you are talking. If we try to practise in this way, even for a little while, we quickly become aware that we have lapses of awareness. There are whole tracts of time when we quite literally don't know what we are doing. We don't know what we are doing with our bodies, if we are doing anything with them. We don't know where our hand is or what it is doing. We don't even know where our own head is, sometimes.

Being aware of the physical body is the simplest form of self-awareness, but it is still very difficult, and it is the foundation of all the other forms of awareness of self. It is traditionally held that if you can't practise this, it is not much use trying to practise any other more advanced form of awareness. From Japan there comes a little story to illustrate this point. It's about a young monk who wanted to learn meditation, so he decided to seek out an old monk who was a great meditation teacher. He made a long journey to the monastery where the master lived, and at last he presented himself at the gate and was admitted. He folded up his umbrella and took off his shoes, and then he was ushered into the presence of the master. He made his three prostrations, and the master asked him, 'What have you come for?' He said, 'Enlightenment.' The master said, 'That is very good. Let me ask you a few questions.' So the young monk sat back, getting ready to answer questions on Buddhist philosophy, logic, his spiritual experiences and so on, but the master asked, 'When you came here just now, what was the weather like?' The young monk, rather surprised, said, 'It was raining.' The master said, 'And did you get wet?' 'No, I had an umbrella.' 'Where is the umbrella?' The young monk thought, 'This conversation is getting more and more ridiculous,' but anyway he politely answered, 'I left it outside with my shoes.' The old master thought for a minute, and then he said, 'Tell me: on which side of the door did you leave your umbrella?' The young monk thought and thought, but he couldn't remember. So the old master said, 'That won't do. If you can't even practise mindfulness, how do you expect to practise meditation? How do you expect to gain Enlightenment? You had better go away. This is not the place for you.' So the poor young monk had to depart.[181]

But suppose you pass the test; suppose you know where your umbrella is. Then you can go on to practise awareness of feeling, awareness of whether your feeling tone is pleasant or painful or whether you are experiencing a grey, neutral state. From there you can go on to being aware of your emotions, of whether you are experiencing love or hate, fear or anxiety, desire or hope, jealousy or delight, expectation or disgust, or any other emotional state. If you can do this – if you can be aware of your whole emotional life – you will find that this has a twofold effect. Your negative emotions will tend to be dissolved, or at least brought under control, and your positive emotions will tend to be refined.

Thirdly, there is awareness of thoughts. Very few people are masters of their thoughts. In most cases, thoughts just drift through our minds and take possession of us. We don't know why they have come or where from; they just come, and very often there seems to be little we can do about it. Even if we want to meditate and keep our minds free from thoughts, we have to watch the thoughts rioting in the playground of our mind, and it seems we are powerless to chase them away. So we have no control over our thoughts. They are not our own thoughts, really. All that is happening is that we are subject to a loose association of ideas which is easily interrupted or redirected. But if we become aware of what is happening, if we cultivate awareness of our thoughts, then thinking becomes more purposeful. In a sense, our thinking becomes our own. It becomes an active rather than a passive process. Wandering thoughts are gradually eliminated and we experience a more peaceful and harmonious state of mind.

This is the traditional classification of awareness of self: awareness of the body and its movements, awareness of feelings and emotional states, and awareness of thoughts. But other classifications are possible. We can speak, for instance, in terms of various kinds of psychological conditioning, by which I mean the tendency of our actions to be determined, without our realizing it, by previous patterns of experience – in many cases, patterns laid down very early in life. This conditioning is of various kinds. We are conditioned by being humanoid as distinct from non-humanoid mammals, by being male or female, by the place where we were born, by our race, our nationality, the social group to which we belong, caste, class, profession, party, church, and even religion. Such conditioning is also resolved by means of awareness of self. To the extent that we become aware, really aware, that we are psychologically conditioned in all these ways, to that extent we become free from that conditioning.

Thirdly, we practise awareness of people. Strange to say, this kind of awareness is comparatively rare. Usually we are aware of people not as people but as things, objects, bodies 'out there'. The extreme case is that of the infant. In the early months of life a baby is not aware of mother as a person. She is just an object that gives warmth and nourishment, just a breast. We like to think we grow out of this attitude towards people, and to some extent we do, but unfortunately only too often we treat other people not as persons but as objects. We can't be aware of people unless we look at them, and only if we are aware of people can we love them.

The fourth dimension is awareness of reality, which is the highest kind of awareness – not that this and the other dimensions of awareness are mutually exclusive. You can have glimpses of reality through all the others, indirectly at least. But here, our awareness of reality is direct. In what it consists it is very difficult to say, because it is beyond words, but we can perhaps say that it is synonymous with meditation in the highest sense, meditation as contemplation.

The four kinds or dimensions of awareness – awareness of things, of self, of people, and of reality – are connected with the four kinds of consciousness. Awareness of things is connected with simple consciousness, awareness of self and awareness of people are connected with self-consciousness, and awareness of reality is connected with transcendental consciousness and absolute consciousness. We shall be dealing with the question of personal relationships and the higher evolution later on in this series.[182] For the present, we will confine ourselves to the more subjective side of self-consciousness. Here we come to the heart of our subject: the distinction between alienated awareness and integrated awareness.

This is not a traditional distinction. It is not found in Buddhist texts, or referred to in Buddhist circles in the East. The phenomenon of alienated awareness certainly does occur there, as I have witnessed myself, but it is more characteristic of the modern West. We shall try to understand why a little later on. But let's start by investigating the difference between alienated awareness and integrated awareness. Integrated awareness is in principle identical with awareness in general, especially awareness of self. But what is alienated awareness? What is it alienated from? What is integrated awareness? What is it integrated with? Briefly, alienated awareness is being aware of ourselves, especially of our feelings and emotions, without actually experiencing ourselves. In its extreme form alienated awareness is awareness of one's non-experience of oneself, even awareness that one is 'not there', paradoxical as that may seem. This is obviously quite a dangerous state to be in. Alienated awareness may be accompanied by physical symptoms which may include severe pains in the head, especially if one is increasing alienated awareness under the erroneous impression that one is thereby practising mindfulness. I am not saying that all pains in the head encountered in meditation are due to alienated awareness, but such pains are one of the physical symptoms of alienated awareness. Integrated awareness is awareness of ourselves while at the same time experiencing ourselves. Our experience of ourselves may be positive or negative, but even if it is negative, the negativity will eventually be resolved by the fact that we are aware of it besides actually allowing ourselves to experience it.

The nature of the distinction between alienated awareness and integrated awareness should now be clear conceptually, but perhaps it is still difficult for some of us to recognize it in a way that accords with our experience, so let us approach it in a different way. Let us imagine three levels of awareness. First of all, there is experience without awareness. This is what we have most of the time. We feel happy or sad, we experience pain or joy, love or hate or fear, but we don't really know that we are experiencing these emotions. There is just the bare sensation, the bare feeling, the bare emotion, but no awareness. We are lost in the experience, immersed in the experience. We forget ourselves – as when, say, we become very angry. When we recover and survey the damage, we say, 'I didn't know what I was doing, I forgot myself.' In other words, while we were under the influence of that emotion, possessed by that emotion, identified with that emotional state, there was no awareness. Secondly, there is awareness without experience. This is alienated awareness. We stand back from our experience. It is not our experience, it is going on 'out there', so we are not really experiencing it, not really feeling our feelings, not really emoting our emotions. We love but we don't really love, we hate but we don't really hate. And the third level is integrated awareness, which is experience plus awareness. Here we have the experience but alongside the experience – well, not even alongside it, but saturating it, in a sense identical with it – we have awareness. The awareness gives clarity to the experience, the experience gives substance and body to the awareness, and the two coalesce. You are fully immersed in the activity, and even if the emotion is accompanied by activity you are fully immersed in the emotion in the sense of actually experiencing it, but at the same time, together with it, without being different from it, you have got awareness. It is very difficult to have any idea about this state if you haven't experienced it yourself: not so much awareness *of* experience, but awareness *with* experience, awareness in the midst of experience.

How does alienated awareness arise? How do we come not to experience ourselves? This is due to some extent to the nature of the times in which we are living, especially in the West. We are often told that we are living in an age of transition, and this is very true, but sometimes we don't realize how abrupt, even violent, and also how potentially valuable, the transition is. Many of the old values are breaking up. People are no longer sure what is right and what is wrong, what we ought to do or not do, how we ought to live, what role to adopt, what part to play. We are no longer sure who or what we are. Our sense of identity is weakened, and on this account there is widespread anxiety. But I don't want to attach too much importance to the times in which we live. I want to look more closely at some of the more immediate factors. I have spoken of three levels of awareness of self: awareness of body, of feelings and emotions, and of thoughts. In the same way, we can speak of three levels of the non-experience of self.

First of all, there's non-experience of the body. There are several reasons for this, one of the most important of which is the refusal to allow ourselves to experience bodily sensations, especially those connected with sex. This refusal is often connected with wrong early training. People are brought up with the idea, or the vague feeling, that the body is shameful, or at least not so noble or respectable as the mind, and that sexual feelings are sinful. These ideas and feelings are attitudes left over from Christianity. Though we may have outgrown Christian dogma and ecclesiastical supervision, these attitudes are widespread and still do a lot of harm. It is one of the great merits of the work of Wilhelm Reich that he has gone into this subject so thoroughly and has shown clearly how inhibition of pleasurable bodily sensations early in life can lead to a crippling negation on the part of the adult person of his or her whole life force.[183]

Non-experience of feelings and emotions comes about in various ways. We may be brought up to believe that certain emotions are wrong and should not be indulged in. For instance, we are taught that anger is wrong, so we feel guilty if we become angry for any reason, and sometimes when we are angry we try to pretend that we are not. We repress the feeling, we refuse to experience it, and it goes underground. Alternatively, we experience an emotion, but we are told by someone in an authoritative position that we do not in fact experience it. Mother tells the small boy that he is not afraid of the dark, because brave little boys are never afraid of the dark. You want to be considered a brave little boy, so you repress your fear of the dark and cease to experience it consciously, but it may come out in terrible nightmares. Or perhaps it happens that you don't like your little sister. That is a very common family situation. But you are told by Mother or Father that you like her because she is your little sister, so you don't know where you stand. You experience a feeling but you are told you don't experience it; not even that you ought not to, but that you don't, you can't, it's impossible. It's like when the little boy blurts out, 'I want to kill Daddy', and Mother says, 'Of course you don't. No one would ever want to kill Daddy.' So it is repressed. You cease to experience it. To take another common example, the child doesn't like brown bread, but Mother says, 'Of course you like it, because it's good for you.' Once again, there's confusion and repression. In this way the child becomes very confused indeed, and alienated from his or her own feelings, and the effects of this may continue throughout life, and be powerfully reinforced in other ways. When we are adolescent, we discover we dislike going to parties, but we convince ourselves that we like going because everybody likes going to parties. Or we discover that we are not in the least moved by the work of a certain famous artist, but all our most intelligent friends are very much moved by the work of that artist, in fact highly excited by it, so we have to be highly excited too. I need not multiply examples, but the end result is that we become alienated, to a greater or lesser degree, from our feelings and emotions.

With non-experience of thoughts, it's not so much that we fail to experience our thoughts; more that we fail to have any thoughts at all. Nowadays so many agencies tell us what to think, tell us, in fact, what we think. The problem isn't that we're fed with information, but that value judgements are also imparted: this is right and that is wrong, this is good and that is bad. The media give us very slanted, selective information and make up our minds for us, although we are not usually conscious of that.

So most of us are in a state of alienation from ourselves: from our bodies, from our feelings, from our emotions, and from our thoughts. We don't experience ourselves. This is something that we have to recognize, accept, and come to terms with. We can think of the iceberg: the tip protrudes above the waves but there's a whole mass below. Our self is relatively extensive, like the iceberg underneath the water, but that part of our self that we allow ourselves to experience is relatively small, in some cases infinitesimal. This is the state into which the world has got us, society has got us, our parents have got us, our teachers have got us – and we ourselves have continued the work. So what happens next?

In the case of some of us, we come into contact with Buddhism. Among all the wonderful things we hear, we learn all about mindfulness or awareness, and what we hear about it seems to say that what we have to do is stand aloof from ourselves, especially from our negative emotions, and just watch ourselves, as though we were watching another person. We are very much impressed by this, and in our alienated state we can't help thinking that this seems just what we need. So we start practising awareness, or what we think is awareness. We stand back from our thoughts, from our emotions and our feelings. We just look at them, push them 'out there'. And what is the result? In nine cases out of ten, we simply succeed in intensifying our experience of alienated awareness.

Not only that. From Buddhism we also learn that craving, desire, anger, and so on are unskilful mental states. We're told we mustn't call them sins because in Buddhism there aren't any sins. We should call them unskilful states, but they are just as bad as sins – if anything, they are worse, and we have to get rid of them. We are very glad to hear – well, we *think* we are glad to hear, because we can't even really feel glad at this stage – that craving, desire, anger, and fear are unskilful states, because this means we can go on sweeping them all under the carpet and pretending they aren't there. This too increases our alienated awareness.

Later still, when we start studying Buddhist philosophy, we come across the *anattā* doctrine, the doctrine of no-self. At this stage, some smiling Eastern monk may tell us that according to Buddhism the self is pure illusion. If we could only see clearly, we would see that we haven't got a self, and thinking we have is our big mistake. We like the sound of this teaching too, because as a result of practising so-called mindfulness and increasing our alienated awareness, we have begun to feel rather unreal. To us it seems, in our experience of the unreality of ourselves, as though we have begun to realize the truth of *anattā*, to have some experience of that great spiritual truth that there is no self. We start thinking that we have developed insight in the transcendental sense, and maybe the same smiling monk, not knowing anything about the mistakes Western people can make, encourages us to go on thinking this. The result is that we get more and more alienated and start feeling pains in the head. The way some people have described it to me, it feels as though there is a great iron band around the head that is getting tighter and tighter. This is because one is getting more and more alienated. In some extreme cases, people even have a complete mental breakdown, and then a very serious situation develops.

This is the kind of thing I encountered when I came back to England in 1964. During the twenty years that I was in India, I had kept up communication with some Buddhists in this country and I knew roughly what was going on. I was very pleased to hear that there were one or two meditation centres and people were practising meditation, but when I started seeing things for myself, I got quite a shock. On one occasion I was taken to a meditation centre where I encountered some people who had been meditating for several weeks and they seemed to me just like zombies. They just weren't there at all, they were so completely alienated from themselves. They had made themselves mentally ill, and some of them ended up in mental hospitals. They had been not meditating but developing alienated awareness.

This can happen to those who take up other forms of Eastern tradition in the wrong way too. An alienated person may come in contact with Vedānta, which tells you that you are not the body, not the emotions, not the mind; you are God with a capital G, Brahman, Reality itself. You have just got to wake up to this fact. You take that on board, and you end up alienated from yourself. This is not to say that the Vedāntic teaching is wrong, or that the Buddhist teaching is wrong. The trouble is that we apply it wrongly, or sometimes Eastern teachers, unacquainted with the Western mind, apply it wrongly. The teaching is metaphysically true. In a metaphysical sense, there is no individual self. In a metaphysical sense, you are God. But we don't take it metaphysically, we take it psychologically, and in this way the misunderstandings begin. In some Buddhist circles you find that people are on the whole quite mindful. They shut the door quietly and wipe their feet before they come into the house, and they don't get angry, or at least they don't show anger. They are very controlled and very quiet. But they don't seem really alive, because they have not developed integrated awareness; they have not merged their awareness and their life principle, their aliveness. They suppress, they repress, their life principle and they develop cold, alienated awareness instead of true, integrated awareness.

So how can integrated awareness be developed? First we have to understand, at least theoretically, what has happened. Coming to understand the distinction between alienated awareness and integrated awareness, we have to retrace our steps and undo the harm we have done, or that has been done to us. If alienated awareness has developed to any degree, we have to go back to square one and allow ourselves to experience ourselves. We have to experience our own body, and our repressed feelings and emotions, and we have to insist on thinking our own thoughts. This will not be easy, especially for those who are comparatively advanced in life, because some feelings are deeply buried and very difficult to recover. We may even need professional help. We may have to act out our feelings, not only experience them but express them, even the negative ones. This does not mean that we should indulge them, but slowly and with awareness we should start letting them out and allowing ourselves to experience them while remaining conscious of them. If we do this, we shall begin to experience the whole of ourselves – the so-called good and the so-called bad, the so-called high and the so-called low, the so-called noble and the so-called ignoble, experience it all as one living whole which is our self. When we have done this, when we really experience ourselves in this way, fully and vividly, then we can begin to practise mindfulness; and then, when we practise mindfulness, it will be the real thing. It will be integrated awareness, not alienated awareness.

I hope it is clear now how alienated awareness arises and how integrated awareness can be developed. The whole subject is of great practical importance. Awareness is the growing point of the higher evolution of the individual, but it is only the right kind of awareness, only integrated awareness, that constitutes this growing point. If we develop integrated awareness – awareness in the true sense – and if we continue to develop it on ever higher levels along with our experience on ever higher levels, then the higher evolution, so far as we individually are concerned, is assured.

THE QUESTION OF PSYCHOLOGICAL TYPES

From a series on 'The Higher Evolution of the Individual', 1970

In our lives we come into contact with all sorts of men and women, and if we are observant we will begin to notice various things about the people we meet. We will notice that although they're all physically different, in many ways they're very much alike. In fact, people seem to fall into groups, the members of which have certain characteristics in common, as though they are related to one another. We've all had the experience of reading a novel and finding that one of the characters reminds us exactly of someone we know. They not only look like the person described; they behave in the same way as the character does in the novel. Sometimes when we meet someone for the first time they seem familiar, and we realize that they resemble someone we know. Sometimes the resemblance is not just trivial, but extends to the whole character structure. If we are particularly observant we may notice that some types turn up again and again, in fiction and also in real life, almost as though there's a limited number of relatively fixed types. This understanding can be of great practical use. If we know from certain little indications the type to which people belong, we can judge how they are likely to respond to what we say, or when something happens to them, and then we will know how to avoid treading on their toes, how to put things across to them, and how to anticipate their difficulties or objections.

In view of all this, it isn't surprising that the question of psychological types should have been studied with considerable interest from very early times, or that it is relevant to the higher evolution of the individual.

I want to begin by describing some of the theories that have been put forward, and some of the lists of psychological types that have been drawn up by different people at different times. The expression 'psychological types' has been popularized by Jung, but there are several others: personality types or character types, psychosomatic types, and temperaments. All these expressions have their own shades of meaning, but for practical purposes they approximate to the same thing.

So far as I've been able to discover, in classical times there was to all intents and purposes only one theory of psychological types, the theory of the four humours. Humour in this context means simply a fluid, and according to this theory the four humours are blood, phlegm, yellow bile (also known as choler), and black bile. There was originally a medical theory according to which these four humours make up the constitution of the human body, and their relative proportions determine not only physical health and strength but also temperament. A person with a predominance of blood is said to be of sanguine temperament, has a ruddy complexion, and looks healthy and vigorous. By nature they are cheerful and optimistic, always hoping for the best, like Mr Micawber, always sure that something will turn up.[184] But this type of person, though cheerful and optimistic, is not always very persistent. They may get discouraged and give up if their efforts do not immediately result in success. A person with a predominance of phlegm in their system is said to be of phlegmatic temperament and they are described by the ancient sources as being sluggish, not easily aroused or moved, apathetic, but also calm and composed, so there's a positive as well as a negative side. One with a predominance of yellow bile is said to be of choleric temperament and we're told that they tend to be brunette in colouring, with strong muscular physique. Such a person is hot-tempered, irascible, and passionate. I can see a few people smiling as if they recognize themselves. Then we've got the person with a predominance of black bile, a rather unpleasant fluid, acrid and evil-smelling. This person is said to be of a melancholic temperament; they tend to be unhappy, gloomy, and dejected, but serious, thoughtful, and even meditative. We can see at once that, bizarre though it may seem from a medical point of view, psychologically there's a great deal of truth in this classification. It does correspond to at least some of the facts, and we might even be able to classify not only ourselves but some of our friends. The theory of the four humours is no longer accepted as scientific physiology but the terms used – sanguine, choleric, phlegmatic, and melancholic – are still in general use, especially in literature.

In more recent times there have been many theories of psychological types, most of them associated with psychology or psychoanalysis. Some of them are rather sketchy, more of the nature of bright ideas, but others are worked out in considerable detail. As I've mentioned psychoanalysis, let's begin with Freud, its founding father and perhaps the greatest name in the field of modern psychology. He classifies individuals according to the stage of their sexual development, distinguishing three stages: the oral stage, the anal stage, and the genital stage. According to Freud, in the oral stage it is the mouth, of all the parts of the body, which is the principal source of sensuous pleasure, in the anal stage the principal source of sensuous pleasure is the anal region, and in the genital stage it's the sexual organs. According to Freud, a psychologically and sexually mature adult has passed through all these three stages. But Freud points out, and this is one of his distinctive contributions, that the development of the individual can be arrested at any stage, so that one might be an oral type, stuck in the first stage, or an anal type, stuck in the second stage. In this way the three main types of his classification emerge.[185] It could be objected that these are not true psychological types, and I'm not sure if Freud referred to them as such, but it is well-known that Freud regarded sex as being of great importance in the emotional and psychological life of the individual, and he pointed out in a scientific manner, perhaps for the first time in history, that it is responsible for a great deal of human happiness and misery, so that the effects of adjustments and maladjustments in this sphere extend to almost every other aspect of the total psyche. According to Freud sexual development proceeds with the development of the total personality, so that one can't have an infantile sexuality and a mature adult personality in the psychological sense. It may be concluded that one is justified in regarding the oral, anal, and genital types not just as types of sexual development but as psychological types.

A number of Freud's followers have put forward their own theories. Some of them have exemplified his teaching about the Oedipus complex and turned against their founding father, rejecting some of his theories to put forward theories of their own, sometimes giving a rather broader – or sometimes a rather narrower – context for their theories of psychological types. For instance, Karen Horney's classification is bound up with her theory that conflict is an essential feature of neurosis. Her theory rests upon recognition of the importance of human relationships and she points out that not only during infancy but during the whole of our lives, it's possible for us to take three distinct attitudes towards other people: moving towards them, moving against them, and moving away from them. We learn all three of these attitudes very early in life, and Karen Horney points out that it should be possible for us, whether as child or as adult, to adopt any one of these attitudes according to the nature of the situation. We should be able freely to decide to move towards, or away from, another person, but usually as we grow up, one or another of these three attitudes predominates, and we become fixed, not moving as circumstances require, but mechanically reacting to all situations with the same response, and in this way the three main types develop. Karen Horney calls the person who invariably moves towards others the compliant personality, the person who moves against people the aggressive personality, and the person who moves away the detached personality, and according to her, neurosis is due to conflict between these attitudes.[186] When you're confronted by a certain person or situation, two contradictory attitudes are activated at the same time, and you don't know what to do about it.

Coming to another former follower of Freud, Wilhelm Reich's theory is connected with his concept of character armour, by which he means the totality of neurotic character traits inasmuch as these traits make themselves felt as a defence mechanism against the therapeutic endeavours of the analyst. He describes three character types, all of which are neurotic in varying degrees: the hysterical character, the compulsive character, and the phallic narcissistic character.[187]

Perhaps the best known of all the modern theories of psychological types is that of Carl Gustav Jung. Jung distinguishes between two different attitudes towards the world and four different psychic functions. The two attitudes are those of the extrovert and the introvert, the extrovert being one who goes out towards the visible world whereas the introvert remains within themself. The extrovert wants to explore the universe without whereas the introvert prefers to explore the universe within. The terms extrovert and introvert have become so popular, though they are sometimes misunderstood, that perhaps we need not dwell upon them further. The four psychic functions are those of thinking, sensation, feeling, and intuition. Jung tends to use these terms in his own way. By thinking he means our capacity for seeing how things fit together logically; by sensation he means direct perception of phenomena by means of the physical sense organs; by feeling he means not pleasurable and painful feeling, but the capacity to make accurate and coherent value judgements about the worth of things; and by intuition he means one's capacity for seeing beyond the bare facts and sensing the intangibles of a situation. The thinking and feeling functions, Jung points out, are opposite and complementary, and so are the sensation and intuitive functions. According to Jung, most people have one or another of these four functions particularly well developed and the complementary function moderately well developed, but the other two functions exist in only a comparatively rudimentary form. By combining the two possible attitudes towards the world, the extrovert and the introvert, with the four psychic functions, Jung ingeniously arrives at a total of eight psychological types.

First of all, there's the extroverted thinking type. People of this type collect data, ideas, and thoughts. They are always observing, learning, reading, discussing, and accumulating facts. But they rarely work up all these facts into a coherent whole or understand their total meaning. Just like a child who goes to the beach and collects beautiful pebbles but never sorts them out, so there's just a heap of stones, the extroverted thinking type collects heaps of facts and ideas, but never builds them into a coherent structure or makes sense of them. Secondly, there's the introverted thinking type. People of this type are the complete opposite. They have a passion for synthesis, for bringing facts together and forming them into patterns. Sometimes unfortunately this type has the pattern or theory ready, then looks around for facts to fit it. It was said of Herbert Spencer, the great scientific philosopher, that his idea of a tragedy was a theory killed by a fact.[188] He must have been an introverted thinking type.

Thirdly, we come to the extroverted feeling type. This is the adventurer, always seeking new experiences, new friends, new relationships. They are usually socially very capable, but though having many acquaintances, they sometimes have hardly any friends. They don't give themselves time to go very deep or get very far with anybody. With them it's perhaps a question of quantity rather than quality. Fourthly, there's the introverted feeling type. He or she tends to be shy and withdrawn, but underneath there's great intensity of feeling. Still waters run deep. On the surface they're so quiet, so gentle, that you'd think a ripple never disturbed that placid surface, but underneath there are all sorts of powerful currents of feeling. This type tends to hold certain values and ideals very strongly, but unfortunately is often unable to give them outward expression.

Fifthly, there's the extroverted sensation type: the explorer, the globetrotter. They are always eager for new sights and sounds, people and places. The extroverted sensation type is not unlike the extroverted feeling type – perhaps a rather cruder version of the same thing. And the sixth type, the introverted sensation type, is the perceptive connoisseur, the man or woman who cares not for quantity but for quality in all things. They may spend a long time sniffing the bouquet of the wine, or be a connoisseur of paintings, knowing all about different schools and periods. This type can easily degenerate into the dilettante and the aesthete.

Seventhly, the extroverted intuitive type is always in search of new possibilities in the outside world, to get new things done, to set new movements going, but once things are under way, this type wants to leave them and start up something new. You sometimes meet people like that in religious societies. They get something going and it's all functioning nicely, but they can't stay with it and consolidate it, they have to go somewhere else and start up something new. I knew a man in India who in three or four years started some twenty different organizations in different places, from Kalimpong to Bombay, but none of them lasted very long. That's the extroverted intuitive type. And lastly, the introverted intuitive type is concerned more with the possibilities hidden in the depths of the psyche, and they often get lost. For a person of this sort, the external world hardly exists at all. They're busy exploring those inner depths, finding their way through the murk deep down in the depths of the psyche, and like a person exploring the bed of the ocean, they are hardly able to remember what the world is like above the waves. Some people think that Jung himself was an introverted intuitive type.

This short summary is just the bare bones of Jung's theory. His own account in his book on psychological types is extraordinarily rich and complex but I've no time to say anything further about it.[189]

Another very interesting theory of psychological types is that of Erich Fromm. It isn't nearly so well known as Jung's but in some ways it's even more elaborate and thorough. Fromm's theory is based on the idea that for a human being living means relating. He points out that humans relate to the world in the first place by acquiring and assimilating things, e.g. food, and in the second place by relating to people, including themselves. The first of these Fromm calls the process of assimilation, and the second, socialization. According to Fromm, character consists in the relatively permanent form in which energy is channelled in the process of assimilation and socialization. He says that the individual can relate to the world, or can channel energy, in five different ways, which he calls orientations.

First, there's the receptive or accepting orientation. If you are of this type, you believe that the source of all good, happiness, welfare, and true being is outside yourself, and that the only way to get what you want is to receive it from outside. This applies to material things and also to love, knowledge, and pleasure. If you are of this type and you are religious in any way, you tend to believe in a personal God situated out there in a literal heaven or a metaphysical, transcendental outer space, and you expect that all happiness, knowledge, power, salvation, and enlightenment will come from this external source, because nothing can come from yourself. You yourself are nothing, have nothing.

Secondly, there's the exploitative or taking orientation. Fromm says that people with this orientation also believe that the source of all good is outside and that they can't produce anything themselves, but believe that what they want must be taken by force or by stealth. In personal relationships they try to grab affection and rather enjoy taking or luring one person away from another, and on the intellectual plane they delight in using other people's ideas and even passing them off as their own. I got a shock some years ago when I was looking through a book on Buddhism and noticed that some pages seemed rather familiar. They seemed to be in a different style from the rest of the book, but there were no quotation marks. I eventually realized that I'd written those pages myself. The person who wrote that book must have had this exploitative orientation of character. Of course, many of us do this a lot in conversation.

The third type is what Fromm calls the hoarding or preserving orientation. This person doesn't expect anything from outside; their security is based on hoarding and saving. They don't like to part with anything, and in emotional life they think very much in terms of possessing people, having them under lock and key. They like to treasure up memories and mementoes, and tend to idealize the past.

If a painting is old, even if it has no artistic merit, they like to keep it, and even though some books are just so much waste paper, they can't bear to throw them away.

Fourthly, there's what Fromm calls the marketing or exchanging orientation. This is more difficult to describe and understand, and I must confess that I can't make much sense of it, but briefly, this person's qualities come to be alienated from them and experienced not as parts of them but as commodities, detachable things with a certain value, even a certain price. If you are of this type, you experience yourself as a thing and you treat others as things too. Your value depends not upon what you think and feel about yourself but on your price in the market, what others will pay for you. Your value isn't in yourself but in what you are and what you do, and this is determined by other people. Your identity is determined by what others think of you too. Fromm says that this orientation is particularly characteristic of the modern age. He doesn't say so, but from his other writings I gather that Fromm links this up with the early thought of Marx, which follows on from the later thought of Hegel.

Fromm says that these four orientations all have both positive and negative aspects. On the positive side, the exploitative orientation is active, able to take the initiative, proud (it's interesting that Fromm regards pride as positive), impulsive, self-confident, and captivating. But on the negative side, this type is exploitative, aggressive, egocentric, conceited, rash, arrogant, and seducing. In this way Fromm tabulates the positive and the negative aspects of each of these orientations, and this gives his study of the subject great richness and complexity of detail.

Whereas there are four non-productive orientations there's only one productive orientation, according to Fromm, and he says that a person with this type of orientation aims at the growth and development of all their potentialities, all their powers. He says that by power he does not means 'power over': power over things or people or situations or events, which he says is a perversion. He means 'power to': power to do, power to feel, power to act, power to think, power to develop.[190]

All the theories of psychological types I have mentioned so far have been taken from the West, and most of them are quite modern. A theory from the ancient East is to be found in that well-known Hindu text the *Bhagavad Gītā*. The *Bhagavad Gītā*'s theory of psychological types is based on the Sāṃkhya philosophy, which is one of the six systems of orthodox Hindu philosophy. Most schools of Indian thought are either monistic, meaning that they recognize one ultimate principle, or pluralistic, meaning they recognize a multiplicity of ultimate principles, but the Sāṃkhya is dualistic, recognizing two ultimate principles beyond which you can't analyse, which are irreducible: the *puruṣa* and the *prakṛti*. Very roughly, by *puruṣa* is meant pure spirit and by *prakṛti* is meant nature or matter. *Prakṛti* is said to consist of the three *guṇas*. The word *guṇa* literally means a strand, but it's usually translated as attribute or quality or element, and the three *guṇas* are *sattva*, *rajas*, and *tamas*. These terms are not easy to translate, but we could say that *sattva* is the quality of light, purity, peace; *rajas* is the quality of fire, passion, activity; and *tamas* is the quality of darkness, sloth, inertia. According to the *Bhagavad Gītā* all three are in every individual, but one or another will predominate and it's according to the predominating quality that the psychological type is determined. The *Bhagavad Gītā* says that one in whom the quality of *sattva* predominates is calm, peaceful, religious-minded, gentle, wise, and compassionate; one in whom *rajas* predominates is fiery, noble, high-spirited, and active; and one in whom *tamas* predominates is dull, slothful, ignorant, stupid, and brutal.[191] Of course this classification is linked, as everything in India has to be sooner or later, with the caste system, devised by those brilliant people the Brahmins. According to their classification the Brahmin is the *sattvic* type, the holy man with all the good qualities. The Kshatriya, the warrior, is a person in whom there is both *rajas* and *sattva*. The Vaishya is the trader, the merchant, the peasant, the agriculturalist, and in him there's a mixture of *rajas* and *tamas*. And the poor Shudra, the serf, including the untouchable, is composed entirely of *tamas*.

There are other theories of psychological types known in the East but I'll deal tonight with the one that is the most important and relevant because it will give us a valuable clue to the nature of the connection between psychological types and the process of the higher evolution. This ancient Eastern theory is a Buddhist one, found in a famous work of Theravāda Buddhism called the *Visuddhimagga*, which was written about 1,500 years ago in Ceylon by the great *ācārya* Buddhaghosa. In principle its theory is quite simple. It posits three main psychological types, the greedy type, the angry or hate type, and the bewildered or deluded type (in the original Pāli, *lobhacarita*, *dosacarita*, and *mohacarita*). According to the *Visuddhimagga*, these three types are linked with three kinds of experience of the world. A person who experiences the world as predominantly pleasurable will develop into the greedy type of character. For some people the world is predominantly a painful place, and in this way the angry or hate type of character develops. And the bewildered type isn't sure. Sometimes the world seems a very pleasant place but at other times it's just awful.

Buddhaghosa gives many interesting details about how these three types can be recognized. The *Visuddhimagga* is rather dull and scholastic in parts, but when Buddhaghosa comes to this part of the work (whose title means 'Path of Purification') he really lets himself go, and you start thinking he might have made a good novelist. He says that in the first place you can recognize the different character types by the way they walk. The greedy type of person walks along very smoothly and gently and evenly, but the hate type walks along roughly, digging their heels into the ground and striding along, and the deluded, bewildered type sometimes walks in one way, sometimes the other. If you watch someone long enough, you will find out which type they belong to. You can also recognize these types by the way they eat. Thinking in terms of eating rice with the hand, Buddhaghosa says that greed types make the rice into neat little balls of just the right size and gently put them into the mouth. They keep their fingers very clean and don't scatter a lot of mess around their plate. Angry types make big unshapely balls of rice and toss them into the mouth, scattering lots of bits and pieces around, and their hands are rather dirty. And poor old deluded or bewildered types act in either way according to circumstances or the whim of the moment. The types talk differently too. The greedy type speaks agreeably and smoothly, but the angry type speaks harshly, loudly, and rudely, and as for the poor bewildered type, what I said before goes here too. You can also recognize the types by the way they wear their robes and colours they choose. (Buddhaghosa is talking about monks.) There are various rules about wearing the robe – the hem of the upper robe must be four inches above the hem of the lower robe and so on – and the monk with the greedy temperament will pay strict attention to all this, so he'll look very neat and smart, and his robe will be bright yellow, like a buttercup. But the angry or hate type will just throw his robes around himself, and he'll tend to choose dark hues, a dark brown or deep saffron. You can even tell the different types by the way they sweep the floor. When they join the monastery, novices are given this job to do and all the other monks watch them to see how they sweep. If the young novice has a greedy temperament he'll sweep with smooth, rhythmical strokes, but if he is of the hate type, he brushes quickly and unevenly, and leaves lots of dust in the corners or even tries to sweep it behind the door. And again the deluded type just acts anyhow.[192]

Buddhaghosa correlates these three temperaments with the forty *kammaṭṭhānas*, and it's this part of his account that gives us our clue to the connection between psychological types and the higher evolution. *Kammaṭṭhāna* literally means place of work, and the work is that of concentration and meditation, so the forty *kammaṭṭhānas* are the forty methods of concentration and meditation. You might have thought that there are just two or three ways of meditating but according to the Pāli canon alone there are forty, and there are many other methods too. In the second section of the *Visuddhimagga*, Buddhaghosa describes the forty methods in some detail, and then goes on to say which methods of concentration and meditation are suitable for which temperament. He says that if you are of a greedy type, you should meditate upon the ten stages of the progressive decomposition of a corpse, going to a graveyard or a burning ground for the purpose, and you should also practise recollection of the loathsomeness of food. In this way you will overcome your greedy tendencies. The angry or hate type should practise the *mettā bhāvanā*, the development of universal love. And if you are a bewildered type, you are especially advised to practise the mindfulness of breathing, to steady your mind a bit and learn to concentrate on one thing. Buddhaghosa says that some of these forty methods are equally suitable for people of all three temperaments.[193]

For Buddhaghosa concentration and meditation represent the standard spiritual practice, so he is saying two very important things in correlating meditation methods with temperaments. He's saying that so far as the individual is concerned the spiritual path, the higher evolution, is not a vague, general process but a specific action here and now, and also that the steps of this path are determined by a person's temperament or psychological type. We tend to think it's enough if we engage in some spiritual practice which we hope will somehow bring us to the goal in the end, though we've no clear idea exactly how, but Buddhaghosa says that we must be much more specific than that. We must know from day to day, almost from hour to hour, which particular method will help us to go forward, and that means knowing what in us has to be corrected, what has to be developed, and what has to be removed, where our weaknesses and strengths are. All this means knowing ourselves: knowing our own patterns of behaviour, our particular conditioning, and the psychological type to which we belong.

We'll be able to understand all this much better if we refer back to the theories of psychological types I have mentioned. The list is by no means complete – for instance, I haven't made any mention of Sheldon's well-known classification of human types – but it's complete enough for our present purpose.[194] If we examine these theories, we find that they are mainly of two kinds, based on two different principles of differentiation. They're differentiated in the first place according to stage of overall development: if you are at this stage of development, you belong to this type, if you are at the next stage of development you belong to another type. Freud's theory of oral, anal, and genital types is a theory of this kind. In the other kind of theory, the types are differentiated according to the faculty in the individual which happens to be most strongly developed. The most prominent example of this is Jung's theory of the extroverted and introverted, thinking, sensing, feeling, and intuitive types.

If we classify them in this way, we can see at once how useful both these kinds of theory are, because they show us where we stand, at least after a reasonable amount of self-analysis, and what our next stage of development should be. We see which faculties are quite well developed already and which still need to be developed, and having seen this, we can see what steps we need to take next. For instance, if after studying Freud's classification we discover, somewhat to our astonishment, that we happen to be an anal character, then we understand that we have to take active steps to develop full genitality. If after a perusal of Jung's classification of types we discover that we happen to be an introverted thinking type, we have to take steps to develop our extroverted feeling function. In this way the whole business of the higher evolution becomes more specific, more concrete, more particular – not just some vague beautiful dream but a matter of actual detailed practice.

Having heard about all these theories, and perhaps feeling a bit bewildered, you might wonder which theory is most true or at least most helpful, but there's no answer to that question on those terms. All the theories represent a cross-section of the individual from a particular point of view, and therefore they all help us to understand ourselves and know what we must do in order to evolve. Understanding of the kind they represent is very necessary to us in the whole process of the higher evolution.

Other questions may arise. For example, is there a religious type? Sometimes someone says, 'I'm not interested in religion, I guess I'm not the religious type.' They may say it defensively, as if apologizing, or aggressively, as if being religious was a weakness. Either way, what they're trying to convey is that since they're not the religious type it's no use expecting them to be interested in religion. But what does one mean by the religious type? Indeed, what does one mean by religion in this context? Here we can take the word religion in two senses. It can mean the whole process of the higher evolution, the evolution of consciousness from simple consciousness to self-consciousness to transcendental consciousness to absolute consciousness. Alternatively, we can take religion in the much narrower, more limited sense of conventional pious belief and observance. If we take the word religion as synonymous with the higher evolution, there's no such thing as a religious type. All psychological types are religious types, all are cross-sections of individuals, and all individuals are capable of higher development. It's a question of being aware of oneself and wanting to evolve. But if we take religion in the narrower sense of conventional pious belief and observance, it may be possible to speak of a religious type, and it may be that this religious type is more or less identical with Jung's introverted feeling type or possibly the introverted intuitive type. But if we take religion in this narrower sense, we must make it clear that both the so-called religious types and the so-called non-religious types are capable of the higher evolution.

Is there a meditating type? This question is similar to the first one and the answer is pretty much the same. It depends what you mean by meditation. If you mean the development of a higher stage of consciousness, all psychological types are meditating types. If by meditation you mean introversion, obviously there are meditating types, because there are introverted types. But if you take meditation in the narrower sense you will have to say that both meditating and non-meditating types are capable of the higher evolution, regardless of whether or not they practise meditation in the narrower sense.

Do the two sexes represent different psychological types? To answer this question properly one would have to go into the matter very thoroughly indeed, but one thing is clear. Sex, which is a very mysterious thing that no one has really explained, is not just a matter of physical differences. It is closely, perhaps inseparably, associated with different kinds of mental outlook, different kinds of psychological conditioning. It's well known that the feminine mentality is in many ways very different from the masculine mentality and it's possible to speak therefore of a masculine type and a feminine type. Whether these constitute different psychological types in the sense I've been using that term is another matter. At present we're concerned with one practical corollary, which is that if men and women as such have different kinds of psychological conditioning, they will need to have recourse to different methods of undoing those psychological conditionings, which means that they may have to take up different, possibly complementary, spiritual practices. We usually assume that all spiritual practices are equally suitable for both men and women but it may turn out not to be so, and we may have to consider separate provision in certain respects for the two sexes.

Lastly, should one be an all-rounder or a specialist? This question arises particularly within the context of the second kind of theory, the type that differentiates according to the predominance of a particular psychic function, for example Jung's theory. Let's suppose that someone is extremely intellectual, very good at abstract thought, manipulating concepts, philosophy, and so on, but has very little emotional life. If such a person takes up the spiritual life, how should they proceed? Some people would advise following the line of least resistance and going all out for philosophical development, trying to reach truth with your mind. The Hindus would say, be a *jñāna-yogi*, one who tries to know the truth by sheer force of intellectual understanding, by means of dialectics, as Plato would say. But someone else would say, 'No, your intellect is already well developed. You need to develop in a balanced way and your emotions are under-developed, so you've got to develop your emotions. Do devotional practices, chant, bow before the image of the Buddha, offer flowers, read devotional books. Try to develop your emotions to the point where they are as well developed as your intellect.' This second view is on the whole the Buddhist view, exemplified by the teaching of the five spiritual faculties: faith which must be balanced by wisdom; meditation which must be balanced by vigour; and all four held in equilibrium by the all-important faculty mindfulness or awareness.[195] This is how Buddhism sees the spiritual life, in terms of a complete harmonious unfoldment of all the aspects of the individual human being.

So we can now see the importance of the question of psychological types to the process of the higher evolution of the individual. We are individuals, but we're individuals of a particular type, we follow a particular psychological pattern, and if we know to which type we belong, we'll have a rough and ready map, a crude chart with the help of which we can find our way around the maze which is ourselves. If we know ourselves better, including the type to which we belong, we'll know what step needs to be taken next. And if we take that step, then, and only then, we shall evolve. Otherwise all our talk of the higher evolution will remain simply a beautiful dream.

PADMASAMBHAVA, TANTRIC GURU OF TIBET

Pundarika, Archway, North London, 1972

Darjeeling, whose name means the place of the thunderbolt or diamond, is a small town in the foothills at the eastern end of the Himalayan range, about 7,000 feet above sea level, and it's inhabited by all sorts of people, especially by the Nepalese, mainly Gurkhas, but also by Sikkimese, Indians, Bhutanese, and all sorts of tribes speaking various languages and dialects. Amongst all these people there are quite a number of Buddhists, so there are a number of Buddhist temples and monasteries, large and small. On a visit there years ago, one morning, almost by accident, I found myself standing on a little spur of land in front of a three-storey pagoda-like building. I couldn't help wondering what it was, and as the door was open, I went in. At first I couldn't see much – there weren't any windows, so the only light came from the open doorway – but as my eyes became accustomed to the gloom I started to make out the outline of an enormous image, perhaps fifteen or twenty feet tall, so big that it seemed to fill practically the entire chamber. This figure, seated cross-legged on an enormous lotus-throne, was clad not in the yellow or orange robes of the Buddha, but in richly decorated princely robes of a deep red colour. In his right hand was resting a golden *phurba* (demon dagger) and his left hand, which rested in his lap, held a skull cup. In the crook of the left arm, resting against the shoulder of the figure, there was a long staff surmounted by a trident, below which I could just discern what seemed to be three human heads in various stages of decomposition. Raising my eyes a little, I saw that on his head he wore a red lotus-cap surmounted by a *dorje*, above which was a long white vulture's feather. But the most remarkable and impressive thing about this great figure was his face. His features were half Indian, half Tibetan, he had a thin black moustache, and his brows were slightly knitted, almost as though in anger. His expression was extremely intelligent and penetrating, powerful and commanding, even fierce. On either side of the main figure were two tiny female figures, one in Indian dress and the other in Tibetan dress, including a multicoloured rainbow apron.

Who was this figure I encountered in the gloom of that pagoda all those years ago? It was Padmasambhava, the great Tantric guru of India and Tibet whom we are celebrating this evening, following the Tibetan tradition. From a historical point of view it is not easy to speak about Padmasambhava. We don't know the exact dates of his birth and death. All that we know for certain is that he lived in the eighth century, and that he was born in India and spent the greater part of his life there and in adjacent countries. He visited Tibet during the reign of King Trisong Detsen, who according to the Tibetan annals reigned from the year 755 to the year 797. According to some accounts Padmasambhava spent some eighteen months in Tibet, and according to others he spent forty years there; as far as we can judge, the former is the more likely. All our information about Padmasambhava comes from Tibetan sources. In India, unfortunately, he seems to have been completely forgotten. This is not surprising. After the revival of orthodox Hinduism and the destruction of the Buddhist monasteries at the hands of the Muslim invaders, the Buddha himself was forgotten for more than 500 years, so it is not surprising that the great guru Padmasambhava should have been forgotten too.

There exist in Tibetan literature a number of biographies of Padmasambhava, the oldest of which appeared in the thirteenth century, attributed to Padmasambhava's Tibetan consort Yeshe Tsogyal; there is a short summary of this important biography in Evans-Wentz's *Tibetan Book of the Great Liberation*.[196] The biographies contain a great deal of valuable material, but they are not very helpful historically speaking. In the first place, the biography of Padmasambhava has somehow been mixed up with the biography of the Buddha, though the Buddha lived some thirteen centuries before Padmasambhava. It is rather as though the biography of St Francis had got mixed up with the biography of Christ. Another difficulty is that in his career Padmasambhava was known by many different names and titles and epithets, according to what he was doing, initiations he received, and so on. In the biographies he is referred to by so many names that we are not always quite sure with whom we are dealing, especially as some of the names he bore were also borne by other people. Thirdly, the biographies include a great deal of what modern Western scholars would dismiss as legendary material. Like the traditional biographies of the Buddha, they are not just concerned with stating historical fact, but also incorporate myth and legend, symbol and parable, all of which shed light on the inner significance of the life from another dimension.

This legendary material is of various kinds. There are episodes which, though represented as having occurred historically, are not historical at all, but symbolize spiritual truths and experiences. One of the more obviously symbolical episodes is that of Padmasambhava's initiation by a *ḍākinī*. In this episode, which is recounted as though it actually happened, some very strange things occur. Padmasambhava enters a *ḍākinī*'s palace and after a few preliminaries, she transforms him into the mantra *hūṃ* and proceeds to swallow him. We are told he receives the secret Avalokiteśvara initiation inside her stomach. Lama Govinda gives an explanation of this episode in his book *Foundations of Tibetan Mysticism*.[197] There are also episodes whose purpose seems to be to emphasize Padmasambhava's greatness. Some represent him more as a cultural hero than as a spiritual teacher, and some incorporate indigenous Tibetan folklore. All this constitutes a very rich body of material, and it is not easy to sort out what is historical and what is not. Some preliminary work has been done by Western scholars, to give a clearer idea about Padmasambhava's career, but there are still a number of unanswered questions.

This evening I am going to try to do three things. In the first place, I am going to give a brief account of what appear to be the main facts of Padmasambhava's career in the present state of our knowledge. Then I will deal with the central episode in his career, historically speaking, his visit to Tibet. This episode is very well attested historically, and it contains legendary elements which are of special significance to us today, and even have some bearing on our own movement here and now. And thirdly, I will give a short account of Padmasambhava's teachings in the Tibetan spiritual tradition of which he is regarded as having been the founder.

But before we start dealing with historical facts I will tell you the legend of Padmasambhava's birth, which illustrates the symbolism that over the centuries has clustered about the events of his life. This legend begins not on the earth at all, but in a higher world, in a sense in the highest of all worlds, the purely transcendental world of the Buddha Amitābha, the chief Buddha of the Nyingma tradition. 'Amitābha' means Infinite Light, so Amitābha is the Buddha of Infinite Light, usually represented in the posture of meditation with his eyes half closed and his hands together in his lap. The legend says that as Amitābha sat in profound meditation there came forth from his tongue a ray of pure red light which shone down to earth, to the centre of a certain lake in north-west India. At the spot where the ray penetrated the water of the lake, there arose a small island which was completely covered with golden grass, in the midst of which flowed three springs of pure water the colour of turquoise. From the centre of the island sprang forth an enormous lotus blossom, and as it sprang forth, the Buddha Amitābha emitted from his heart a golden dorje with five points which fell into the centre of the lotus. Later, people found seated in the lotus a boy of about eight years of age who looked just like an infant Buddha. In his right hand he held a tiny lotus blossom, in his left hand a tiny vase of the kind that are used for Tantric initiations, and in the crook of his left arm was a tiny trident. This was Padmasambhava, whose name means the Lotus Born, the one born from the lotus.[198]

Leaving aside the significance of the legend, the historical facts are that Padmasambhava was born at the beginning of the eighth century in north-western India in the kingdom of Uḍḍiyāna, at that time a famous centre of Tantric practice, and especially esoteric meditation. As a boy Padmasambhava was adopted by the king of Uḍḍiyāna, Indrabhūti, a great Buddhist scholar and yogi some of whose writings on the Tantra survive in Tibetan translation even today. Padmasambhava was given the education and upbringing of a young prince, and in due course he was married to the daughter of a neighbouring king. But despite this, like the Buddha so many centuries earlier, and so many other great masters, teachers, and yogis, he was not satisfied with the household life, not satisfied with high status, position, wealth, domestic felicity, and so on. He left home and became a monk, and over a number of years he studied all the forms of Buddhism then known in northern India and practised meditation, especially Tantric meditation. He visited practically all the Buddhist kingdoms of north-western India and central Asia, and according to some scholars it is probable that here he came into contact with Nestorian Christians and Manicheans, central Asia being at that time a melting pot of religions and cultures of every kind. He also visited Eastern India, Bengal, and Assam, and it is highly likely that he went to Java and Sumatra, which in those days were great centres of Sarvāstivāda Buddhism.

Above all, Padmasambhava spent a great deal of time meditating in cremation grounds. This may seem odd but in India even today Tantric yogis are fond of meditating in cremation grounds. I have visited a number of these places and I have always found them to have a very strange atmosphere. So many bodies are burned there, and the burning ground is regarded as a door from this world into the next. Especially at night, you can almost see the air quivering with a strange vibration. Yogis believe that the intense atmosphere is especially favourable to meditation. When I lived in Kalimpong I heard that there was a Bengali Tantric yogi living in a burning-ground just outside Darjeeling and some of my friends went to visit him there. He stayed there for some weeks and meditated sitting on a very strange seat: the mummified body of an 8-year-old girl. Whether Padmasambhava did anything like this we don't know, but he certainly engaged in a number of highly esoteric occult meditation practices during this period, and had spiritual experiences of various kinds. He mastered the occult arts and sciences and eventually became Enlightened.

After many years he paid a visit to the kingdom in which he was born, Uḍḍiyāna, and at once he got into trouble with the king, perhaps the king who had adopted him or a successor of the same name, Indrabhūti. The trouble came about because while Padmasambhava was in Bengal he had become acquainted with a yoginī, or even *ḍākinī*, called Mandāravā, and she became a devoted disciple of his, and indeed his constant companion. They used to meditate together in the cremation grounds. But you know what people are like. Some people thought Padmasambhava, who was still young and handsome, and Mandāravā were living together as man and wife. They were wrong, but this is apparently what King Indrabhūti thought, and as good people often do on such occasions, he became very indignant – so much so that he ordered that they should both be burned at the stake. But according to the biography they escaped. Many legends have gathered around this remarkable episode.[199]

Having had enough of Uḍḍiyāna, Padmasambhava went to Bodh Gaya, where the Buddha had gained Enlightenment so many centuries earlier, and there he engaged in a great debate with various Brahminical teachers and succeeded in defeating them all in argument. After that he went to Nepal, where he spent quite a long time meditating in a cave, and it was while he was living there that he received the invitation to visit Tibet. He did not delay, and helped the great teacher Śāntarakṣita, who was the head of the Nālandā Buddhist monastery, to establish Buddhism in Tibet. Having done that, we are told that Padmasambhava left for the country of the Rākṣasas (no one knows quite where that is), flying through the air on a winged horse. And so he disappeared from history. These, so far as we know at present, are the main facts of Padmasambhava's career, and you will probably agree they are quite extraordinary enough even without any legends that might have been incorporated with them.

So let's go back to the central episode of Padmasambhava's life, his visit to Tibet. This is one of the most famous and fateful visits in the whole of Buddhist history, comparable to Xuanzang's visit to India and Bodhidharma's visit to China. But how did Padmasambhava come to be invited to Tibet at all? To understand this we have to go back a little. At this time Buddhism had been known in Tibet for only about a hundred years (about as long as Buddhism has been known in England now), since the time of the great king Songtsen Gampo, but the Dharma was by no means well established. A few temples had been built here and there, mainly in the capital, and a few scriptures had been translated, but there were no monasteries, and no Tibetan monks or nuns. Not only that; some of the king's most powerful ministers were for various reasons, some political, some religious, very much opposed to the introduction of Buddhism. But the fourth king after Songtsen Gampo, whose name was Trisong Detsen, was strongly inclined to Buddhism, though we don't know why, and eventually he managed to invite Śāntarakṣita, the head monk of Nālandā, to visit Tibet, although he met much opposition and had to counter many intrigues, even having to get rid of his chief minister, which he did in a rather unpleasant way.

Śāntarakṣita was one of the greatest Indian scholars and teachers of his day, and a number of his works have come down to us in Tibetan translation, as well as one in the original Sanskrit, a work called the

Tattvasaṃgraha, which means 'Compendium of Principles'. A large work in two thick volumes, it is rigorously logical in form, criticizes all rival schools of thought, and establishes the author's own tantra, which is known as the Tantra Yogācāra.[200] On his arrival in Tibet, Śāntarakṣita set to work with a will. He taught in the king's palace for four months, with a Kashmiri monk as his interpreter, and the king, the courtiers, and other interested people listening. The chronicles give us a detailed account of his teachings, and it seems that he taught mainly three things. He started with the ten principles of skilful action, the ten *upāsaka* precepts: abstention from taking life, from taking what is not given, from sexual misconduct, from false, abusive, frivolous, and slanderous speech, and from mental states of craving, aversion, and wrong views. Then he went on to teach the eighteen *dhātus*, the eighteen elements of the perceptual situation: the six senses, the six sense organs, and the six associated consciousnesses. There is a great deal of Buddhist psychological teaching with regard to these things. And thirdly, he taught the twelve *nidānas* or links, the twelve successive stages in the process of birth, death, and rebirth, as illustrated in the outermost circle of the Tibetan wheel of life. In other words, he gave the king and other interested Tibetans an elementary course on Buddhist ethics, Buddhist psychology, and Buddhist metaphysics. This is what he did to establish the Dharma in Tibet.

But the result, we are told, was that the gods of Tibet became very angry. One of the king's palaces was struck by lightning and another was swept away by a flood. The harvest was badly damaged and there was a great epidemic. So terrible in fact was the reaction of the gods that Śāntarakṣita had to leave Tibet. Before he left, he took the king aside and quietly gave him some good advice. He said, 'The situation is beyond me, but in India there is a great spiritual master called Padmasambhava. He will be able to overcome the gods of Tibet. Send for him. I shall also write to him, but you extend an official invitation.' In this way Padmasambhava came to be invited to Tibet around 750 CE. On his arrival, he too set to work with a will, but in a different way. He didn't give any discourses. He didn't hold any seminars. He said nothing at all about the eighteen *dhātus* or the twelve *nidānas*. He just devoted himself to overcoming the gods and demons of Tibet. As you can imagine, there are many colourful legends about this, and they all end by telling us that Padmasambhava not only overcame the gods and demons of

Tibet, but converted them to Buddhism, initiated them, and entrusted to them the task of protecting the Dharma in Tibet. They all became guardian deities.

When the gods and demons of Tibet had been overcome by Padmasambhava, Śāntarakṣita returned, and with the help of the king a great monastery was built in south-eastern Tibet. We are given a detailed description of this monastery. Its ground plan was highly symbolical. Right in the middle there was a three-storey temple to the great bodhisattva Avalokiteśvara, the Bodhisattva of Compassion. This temple represented the central mountain of existence according to Buddhist symbolical cosmology, and at each of the four cardinal points there was a large temple and a small temple, representing the traditional four continents. There was a temple for the sun and a temple for the moon, and there were four stupas of different colours as well as various other buildings, and the whole complex was enclosed by an enormous circular wall. This was the first Buddhist monastery in Tibet, known as Samye, and it is still standing almost intact.[201] The consecration ceremony was performed jointly by Śāntarakṣita and Padmasambhava. Twelve monks were brought from India to live in the monastery, and seven young Tibetans volunteered to become monks. Up to that time no Tibetan had ever been ordained, and Śāntarakṣita thought, 'We don't know what these Tibetans are like, whether they can live the life of a monk. Let's take it cautiously.' He put them all on probation for a while, so they are known in Tibetan history as the 'seven men on trial'. But apparently Śāntarakṣita was satisfied with them in the end, so they were ordained, with Śāntarakṣita himself acting as their preceptor, and a number of the seven subsequently became very well known in Tibetan religious history, especially one called Vairocanarakṣita, who was a great translator. In this way Buddhism came to be properly established in Tibet for the first time.

So Padmasambhava played a very important part in the establishment of Buddhism in Tibet, but the exact nature of the role he played is not clear. The Tibetan people say that he overcame the gods of Tibet, and they are happy to leave it at that, but for us it isn't quite so easy. We can't help wondering, what does it all mean? Who or what are the gods of Tibet, why did they become angry when Śāntarakṣita started teaching Buddhism, and what is meant by Padmasambhava's overcoming them? Let's go into this a little, because it's of interest and also of some significance to our Western Buddhist movement. Let us begin by taking a closer look at Śāntarakṣita's teaching, which so upset the gods of Tibet. He taught mainly three things: elementary Buddhist ethics, elementary Buddhist psychology, and elementary Buddhist metaphysics. Apparently he said nothing about meditation or symbolic ritual, and he didn't tell the Tibetans any parables or stories or legends. It seems clear that his approach was predominantly, or even exclusively, rational. His great work the *Tattvasaṃgraha* is highly intellectual. So we can conclude that although Śāntarakṣita was a great bodhisattva – in fact he is known in Tibetan history just as 'the bodhisattva' – his approach to teaching Buddhism was predominantly intellectual.

This is confirmed by an incident that occurred soon after Śāntarakṣita's arrival in Tibet. In those days all sorts of people were going about saying that they were great teachers of Buddhism, but some of them weren't really teachers at all; they were just wandering here and there exploiting people. The king had heard of this, so he wanted to test Śāntarakṣita before he allowed him to start teaching. He sent three ministers to interview him, and they asked various questions, including 'What is your doctrine?' – a very straightforward question. Śāntarakṣita replied, according to the chronicle, 'My doctrine is to follow whatever is proved correct after examining it by reason and to avoid all that does not agree with reason.'[202] So perhaps we can begin to see why the gods of Tibet were displeased. It's as though they weren't so much displeased with Buddhism itself, or that it was being preached. They were displeased with Śāntarakṣita's one-sidedly rational approach.

But why should the gods of Tibet, or any gods, dislike rationalism? Well, who or what are the gods of Tibet? What do they represent? If we are not going to dismiss them as sheer fiction, as scholars often do, we can say that they represent the non-rational forces of the Tibetan psyche, the Tibetan collective unconscious, and these forces were threatened, even repressed, by Śāntarakṣita's rationalism. In fact, Śāntarakṣita doesn't even recognize the existence of the gods. He just goes on preaching the ten ways of skilful action, the eighteen *dhātus*, and the twelve *nidānas*. To him, irrational forces don't exist. The gods aren't going to take this lying down; they react. They get angry. They create havoc in the national life. They demand to be recognized. So Padmasambhava has to be called in.

Like Śāntarakṣita, Padmasambhava is a great scholar, and he knows all the texts, the philosophy. But he is much more than an intellectual. He is a supreme yogi, a meditator, a master of the occult arts and sciences. He has spent much time in the cremation grounds with the *ḍākinīs*. So who are the *ḍākinīs*? We have to ask that too, because it throws a great deal of light on the character and the approach of Padmasambhava. Broadly speaking, the *ḍākinīs* are a Buddhist equivalent of the Tibetan gods and goddesses. They are the forces of inspiration that arise in the depths of the Enlightened mind. The word *ḍākinī*, like *ḍāka*, which is its masculine counterpart, comes from a root meaning space or sky, so the *ḍākas* and *ḍākinīs* are those who belong to the sky, travel through the sky. And what is the sky? It is not the literal blue sky we see with our eyes. It is the sky of the One Mind, the sky of the Absolute. It's not empty or inert, but full of life, with all sorts of currents of energy flowing through it, all sorts of forces arising within its immaculate depths. These currents, these forces which disport themselves freely in the sky of the Absolute, are personified by the *ḍākinīs* and *ḍākas*.

Padmasambhava has spent much time in the company of the *ḍākinīs* in the burning grounds. He is acquainted with these great spiritual forces, even their master. So on his arrival in Tibet, his approach is very different from Śāntarakṣita's. He begins by recognizing the gods, by seeing that there are gods. Not only that; he establishes contact with them, converts them, transforms them into protectors of the Dharma. In other words, Padmasambhava starts off by acknowledging the irrational, non-rational, even supra-rational forces in the Tibetan psyche, and he succeeds in integrating them into the great current of the spiritual life of Tibetan Buddhism. He doesn't go against them, he carries them along with him, harnesses their energy. Once he has done this, Śāntarakṣita the intellectual and Padmasambhava the yogi together build and consecrate Samye, the great monastery. There is no antagonism between the two approaches. The rational and the non-rational are complementary. Śāntarakṣita and Padmasambhava each recognize the greatness of the other. When Samye has been consecrated through their joint efforts, through the collaboration of the intellectual and the yogi, monks are brought from India, young Tibetans are ordained, and the Sangha is founded. The spiritual community comes into existence.

The significance of all this for Buddhism in the West, even for our own movement, is so obvious that I need not spell it out. It's clear that it's not enough to appeal just to the rational mind. One must appeal also to the unconscious depths. It's not enough just to read books on Buddhism, to listen to lectures. One must also meditate, one must plumb the depths within oneself. One must chant, perform pujas, engage in symbolical ritual. It's not enough just to think, even to think about Buddhism; one must feel. One must respond with one's whole being. Only when a sufficient number of people can do this shall we have a genuine authentic Buddhist spiritual movement in this country, as distinct from a little wave of intellectual interest. Only then shall we have a true spiritual tradition.

The situation here is much more complicated than the situation a thousand years ago in Tibet. To begin with, we don't have any gods of our own. There are no indigenous British gods. What happened to them? I'm afraid we have to confess, sadly, that long ago Christianity turned the gods into devils. Christianity has tended to regard the gods of the countries to which it has spread as evil, and it has therefore tried to destroy them, stamp them out, abolish even the memory of their names. Wherever it went in this country, Christianity smashed images, cut down sacred groves, killed priests. But it couldn't destroy the gods because they had life and energy of their own. It could only repress them. A repressed god becomes a devil – '*Diabolus Deus inversus est*'[203] – and these repressed gods that have been transformed into devils trouble us still. It is time we recognized them, made contact with them, transformed them back into gods. Perhaps if we can do that, they will protect the Dharma in this country.

As I realized from the moment I saw that image of Padmasambhava, and increasingly as I had more and more contact with Tibetan Buddhists, Padmasambhava exerts a tremendous impact on the imagination of the Tibetan people. He is the most distinctive and colourful figure in the history of Tibetan Buddhism, and it is impossible to mistake him for anybody else. It is very difficult to say much, or even anything at all, about his teachings, partly because Padmasambhava, being a yogi above all, was much more important for what he was than for what he said, and partly because the teachings he gave are predominantly Tantric in character, and esoteric Tantric at that. In addition, according to Nyingma tradition, after the consecration of Samye he came to the conclusion that the Tibetans were not spiritually advanced enough to understand his teachings, so he wrote them down and hid them in caves and under rocks. The Tibetans believe that they were discovered many centuries later; they are known as *termas*, which means treasures.

Although Padmasambhava's teachings were predominantly Tantric, he by no means rejected the earlier forms of Buddhism. He regarded them all as successive stages on a single path to Enlightenment. This idea is common to all forms of Tibetan Buddhism, but Padmasambhava went further. He divided the path to Enlightenment not just into three *yānas* but into nine *yānas*, the culminating one being the *ati-yoga yāna*, which was his own special contribution, his own distinctive teaching. I will enumerate these nine *yānas* briefly, to give you an idea of the type of Buddhist tradition that Padmasambhava introduced into Tibet.

First of all, there's the *śrāvakayāna*. *Yāna* means path or way, or stage, or even vehicle or method, and the *śrāvaka* is the disciple, literally 'the one who listens'. It's supposed to be the first characteristic of a good disciple that he listens. He doesn't start asking questions before he's heard what the teacher has to say. So the *śrāvakayāna* is the path of the disciple, the listener. In this *yāna* you go for Refuge to the Buddha, the Dharma, and the Sangha, you take the precepts, whether five or eight or ten or more, and you strive to understand, to realize, the four noble truths, and at least begin to develop insight into the truth of *anattā*, the truth that there is no separate, unchanging ego. If you do these things successfully, you traverse the *śrāvakayāna*.

Secondly, there's the *pratyekabuddhayāna*, the path of the privately or solitarily Enlightened one. At this stage, in addition to what the *śrāvaka* does, you develop an understanding of the law of conditionality, especially the twelve *nidānas*, and some insight into the truth of *śūnyatā*, the voidness.

And thirdly, there's the *bodhisattvayāna*, traversing which you develop the will to Enlightenment, the aspiration to become Enlightened so that you may help all living beings. You observe the special bodhisattva precepts, you practise the six perfections – generosity, ethics, energy, meditation, patience, and wisdom – and you have a spiritual experience to the effect that everything is like a magical illusion, like the reflection of the moon in water. It's neither real nor unreal, both real and unreal. It's difficult to evoke this in a few words, but it is one of the principal insights developed by the bodhisattva.

Fourthly, there's the *kriyāyogayāna*, the *yāna* of Tantric yoga, which consists mainly in symbolic ritual with some meditation. You purify, at least to some extent, all sorts of subtle inner defilements, you repeat mantras hundreds of thousands of times, and you visualize one or another of the three family protectors: the Bodhisattva of Compassion, the Bodhisattva of Wisdom, and the Bodhisattva of Power. You meditate upon them as distinct from yourself: you look up to them, you see them clearly, you have a definite spiritual relationship with them, but you are separate from them.

We come fifthly to the *ubhayacariyāyogayāna*. *Ubhaya* means 'both sides' and *cariyā* means 'practice', so it's the practice of both sides, the practice in which the inner and outer aspects of practice are equalized and harmonized. In this *yāna* you are initiated into the mandala of the five Buddhas, and your relationship with your particular family protector becomes much closer. You practise two kinds of yoga, the yoga with signs and the yoga without signs. There is no time to explain all this now, but the result of practising this *yāna* is that you are gradually transformed into Vairocana, the Buddha of Light, who occupies the centre of the five Buddha mandala.

Sixth is the *yogayāna*. *Yoga* here means the union between wisdom and compassion, and the principal practice in this *yāna* is to achieve this union. There are many different initiations and four esoteric practices called the four *mudrās*. The word *mudrā* means a sign or gesture, but that tells you nothing about the practices at all. Here again you practise the yoga with signs and without signs, and your practice becomes very much deeper. In the end you realize the five knowledges which are associated with the five Buddhas: the knowledge of the absolute, the mirror-like knowledge, the all-performing knowledge, the knowledge of sameness, and the discriminating knowledge.

Seventhly comes *mahāyogayāna*, the great yoga, and here the real esoteric tantra begins. One can't really say anything about this at all, but perhaps one thing I can say is that in this stage you do visualization exercises of a very advanced, complex kind. You visualize Buddhas and bodhisattvas, but in this *yāna* they are always visualized in *yab-yum* ('father-mother') form – that is, a male Buddha and a female Buddha are visualized in sexual union.

Eighth is the *anuyogayāna*. *Anu* means 'following after', and this *yāna* follows after the *mahāyogayāna*. Here the main practice is the development of *tummo* or psychic heat, which isn't to be taken literally, but is a spiritual experience, as described in one of the texts translated in Evans-Wentz's *Tibetan Yoga and Secret Doctrines*.[204] In this *yāna* you also get various practices which Western writers sometimes call sexo-yogic practices, although they have nothing at all to do with sex in the ordinary sense of the term.

And ninthly and lastly, we come to *atiyogayāna*, the *yāna* of supreme *yoga*. This consists in the direct, immediate recognition and realization of the One Mind, the *dharmakāya*, by means of various highly advanced and esoteric meditation practices. This *atiyogayāna* is the special teaching of Padmasambhava.

This nine-*yāna* teaching is the spiritual tradition which Padmasambhava took to Tibet from India, and which is still continued, especially in the Nyingma tradition, which was founded by Padmasambhava himself. Nyingmapa means an 'old style' one, someone who follows the old ways, if you like an 'old timer', even a conservative, and the Nyingmapas are those who follow the traditions introduced into Tibet by Padmasambhava and do not follow, perhaps do not even recognize, the later reform movements started some centuries later by Atiśa, Tsongkhapa, and other teachers. Sometimes the Nyingma tradition is known as the 'Red Hat' tradition, because for ceremonial purposes their lamas wear tall red caps, whereas the Gelugpas wear yellow ones. The Nyingma is one of the four main schools of Tibetan Buddhism, the others being the Gelug, the Sakya, and the Kagyu. The Nyingma school is the second largest (after the Gelug) and in the centuries since the time of Padmasambhava right down to the present day it has produced many highly distinguished lamas.

I can say from my own experience of them that Nyingma lamas tend to be a bit unconventional. They tend to be very spontaneous, to do things suddenly as a result of an inspiration that has come to them in meditation or at some other time. When one of my own Nyingma teachers was staying with me in Kalimpong, at breakfast one day he said, 'What do you think I saw in my meditation this morning? I saw this monastery, and on the roof was a great banner of victory.' These banners signify the victory of Buddhism over the three worlds, with coloured silk flounces and so on, but we didn't have one at my vihara. So the lama said, 'We must put one up', and in the next week he got one of these enormous cylindrical banners of victory made, and up it went on the roof.[205] That's a very small thing, but this is how Nyingma lamas operate. They see something in their meditation or they feel something, they get an inspiration, and they act on it. Gelug lamas, though very virtuous and learned, operate in a different way. If they are thinking about doing something they will consult the literature, especially Tsongkhapa's writings, and they will only do what they have in mind if they can find it written down somewhere. They don't trust their inner spiritual inspiration so much as the Nyingma lamas do. Nyingma lamas don't usually live in large monasteries with thousands of monks as the Gelugpas do. Although they have a few large monasteries, the gurus tend to live with small groups of disciples here and there. They are not nearly as highly organized as the Gelugpas. They emphasize meditation, especially *ati-yoga*, or Dzogchen, as they usually call it, which is a special form of *ati-yoga*.

During my stay in Kalimpong I knew a number of highly developed Nyingma lamas, and one of the interesting things I discovered was that although they had a very high regard for the *sūtras*, the discourses of the Buddha, they had just as high a regard for the *termas*, the texts that Padmasambhava hid away during his lifetime and which were subsequently discovered. Nyingmapas believe that these *termas* were discovered or taken out by great lamas, who are called *tertons*, and are partial manifestations of Padmasambhava himself. The *tertons* not only took out the *termas*, but established the spiritual traditions they taught and handed them on to their disciples. The tradition that derives from the *termas* is called by Nyingmapas the 'near tradition', whereas the tradition arising from the *sūtras* is called the 'far tradition'. They call the *sūtra* tradition 'far' because if you follow a practice based on the *sūtras*, you have a guru to teach you that, and he has a guru, who had a guru, and there may be eighty generations of gurus to get you back to the Buddha's time, so there are many possibilities of slips. But with the near tradition of the *termas* you are much nearer the original source, because Padmasambhava wrote the teaching down and hid it, and it was discovered hundreds of years later, maybe only two hundred years ago. Then it was taken out and the tradition was established by someone who was a manifestation of Padmasambhava, so it comes to you after only five or six generations. The Nyingmapas say that the near tradition of the *termas* is therefore more powerful than the distant tradition of the *sūtras*.

There's an enormous number of these *termas*, to be found in a collected edition called the *Rinchen Terdzö*, the 'Treasury of Precious

Termas', in sixty-four volumes.[206] One of the *termas* in the collection is the *Tibetan Book of the Dead*, which according to the Tibetans was written by Padmasambhava, hidden away, and then taken out some centuries later. Of course, the Western scholar will have none of this. He will say, 'Nonsense! Padmasambhava wrote nothing, hid nothing. These lamas who came centuries later just wrote these texts and attributed them to Padmasambhava so that they could circulate them widely and be respected.' Be that as it may, we don't know, and we must be careful about setting limits to what is possible. We have to judge these texts on their own merits, read them, practise the teachings, see what they are like. The *termas* are for the most part highly important esoteric spiritual teachings which exert vast and profound influence. Even today, among Tibetan Buddhists in general and the Nyingmapas in particular, though many of them have had to leave their own country, the spirit and influence of Padmasambhava is still very much alive, and that influence is now extending to other parts of the world. I was very impressed when one of my Nyingma teachers in Kalimpong told me that in Tibet he read a work of Nyingma literature containing some prophecies attributed to Padmasambhava, one of which said, 'When iron birds fly in the sky, my teaching will go to the West.'[207] Perhaps we can say that our commemoration today of Padmasambhava, the great Tantric guru of India and Tibet, is a sign that this has started to happen.

LEVELS OF GOING FOR REFUGE

Order Convention at Padmaloka, 1978

Upāsikās and *upāsakas*: when you heard the title of this lecture, you might have wondered why on earth I chose to speak on this subject tonight. It's certainly an appropriate subject for a convention of Order members. After all, it's because we've gone for Refuge, we go for Refuge, and we will go for Refuge that we are here at all. But you have heard quite a lot about this subject before, and the human mind delights in variety. You may think that you already know very well what Going for Refuge means, not just from books or hearsay, but to some extent at least from your own experience, so the thought may have crossed your mind that it surely isn't necessary to go over this old ground again. You may even have thought that perhaps I was stuck for a lecture and I'm producing an old one to fill the gap. Reminders are always useful, especially about so important a subject, but let me assure you that I'm not going to go over the same old ground. I'm going to speak tonight about an aspect of Going for Refuge about which I've recently been thinking quite a lot, but about which I've so far not communicated anything to anybody, so far as I recollect. I certainly haven't mentioned it in any lecture, or even in any book review.

I'll start by indulging in a few reminiscences about my own experience of Going for Refuge in the formal sense, in the sense of reciting the words of the three Refuges and the five or ten precepts in Pāli. My first reminiscence goes back a long way, and it's hazy, but a few moments stand out like points of colour in the haze. I'm in central London, in a room in a hotel in Victoria or Bloomsbury. The year is 1943 or 1944, and in this room is a short, fat, dark little man wearing thick horn-rimmed spectacles and orange robes. There this part of the reminiscence stops. I'm not sure what he's doing or saying. But I have a recollection that as we entered the room, we were handed little white cards called '*pansil* cards', *pañcaśīla* cards, on which were printed the Refuges and Precepts in Pāli, and we recited the Refuges and Precepts reading from these little cards. I can't remember how many of us were there. Perhaps it was a Wesak celebration. I can't account for the fact that it all made so little impression on me. But one thing stands out sharply in my memory. I was looking at this card, and as I read the Pāli words which we pronounce as *dutiyampi, tatiyampi*, and so on, not knowing anything of Pāli, it didn't seem to me that they sounded like that at all, and this really struck me. I suppose it's my literary turn of mind. So there we all were, reciting the Refuges and Precepts with perfect Pāli pronunciation apparently, but there was no attempt on anybody's part to explain what it all meant. Apparently this was just something that Buddhists did. It strikes me now as rather odd that it didn't occur to me to wonder why so little was explained about what we were doing when we chanted those Pāli words and took, as I suppose one can say, the Refuges and Precepts. So that's my first reminiscence, rather vague and unsatisfactory from a strictly Buddhist point of view, you must admit.

In my second reminiscence I'm in India some years later. The scene is a little vihara, a monastery-cum-temple, in Kusinara in north-eastern India, the place where centuries earlier the Buddha attained what Buddhists call *parinirvāṇa*. I'm wearing orange robes and crouched in a squatting position in front of a very old monk, with my elbows on my knees and my hands together, and I'm repeating the Refuges and the ten *śrāmaṇera* precepts after this old monk, and being ordained as a *śrāmaṇera*. The monk is very insistent about my getting the correct pronunciation of the Refuges. At the ordination ceremony, one has to repeat them according to both Pāli and Sanskrit pronunciation, and I'm having great difficulty with my aspirated consonants, so the monk is coaching me. I just want to get ordained as a *śrāmaṇera*, and here I am having a lesson in Pāli and Sanskrit phonetics! Eventually I got it absolutely correct, every aspirated consonant, every nasalization, my preceptor was satisfied, and I was ordained, but there was no explanation of what Going for Refuge meant. I had a thorough lesson in Pāli and Sanskrit phonetics, but the significance of what I was doing, the importance of the step I was taking from a spiritual point of view, was not explained at all. In justice, I must admit that the precepts were explained – what it meant to abstain from violence, what it meant not to take the not given, and so on – but the real significance of the Going for Refuge was not explained. I just had a vague, though strong, sense that I'd arrived, that I'd joined the Buddhist community. So that's my second reminiscence.[208]

In my third reminiscence I'm in another vihara, a very small one, somewhere in Nepal, some weeks later. I'm sitting near the shrine and around me, kneeling on the floor, are several dozen Nepalese Buddhists, mostly women. They've come to the vihara for a special purpose – to be 'given', as it's called, the Refuges and Precepts. Being a very new *śrāmaṇera*, I'd never had the opportunity of 'giving' anybody the Refuges and Precepts before, and I didn't know what to do, so I had to ask. The people told me that I should recite the Refuges and Precepts, and they would recite them after me, and then I should give a blessing and a little discourse. Once I'd learned to do all of this, these good people used to come along every morning and they'd 'take' the Refuges and Precepts from me, which made them very happy. They knew what the words meant, but they clearly didn't think about it too much. They didn't understand, and perhaps they didn't want to understand, what it really meant to go for Refuge to the Buddha, Dharma, and Sangha. They were perfectly happy to recite the holy words after me and leave it at that. The recitation showed that they belonged to the Buddhist community, and that was what mattered. So this is my third reminiscence.[209]

My fourth reminiscence is a non-reminiscence. I ought to remember reciting the Refuges and Precepts, especially the Refuges, at the time of my ordination as a *bhikṣu* in 1950, but I must confess that I've no recollection of it whatsoever. I suppose I did recite the Refuges on that occasion, but they must have made no impression on me, and that means that they could not have been considered very important – a significant fact, as we shall see later on.

Reminiscence number five is not just one reminiscence but a whole group of them extending over several years and embracing all sorts of places in many parts of India, including hundreds upon hundreds of Buddhist meetings, many of them with thousands of people present. Most of these meetings were held late at night, somewhat to my reluctance, mostly in the open air, sometimes with a cold wind cutting through the place. And at these late-night open-air meetings I was called upon – sometimes at one or two o'clock in the morning, after I'd had a cup of tea to keep myself awake – to 'give' the Refuges and Precepts to thousands of people – ex-Untouchable Mahars, mostly, of Maharashtra – who became Buddhists at that moment. By this time – we're now in the late 1950s or early 1960s – I had some idea as to what Going for Refuge really meant. Nobody had ever told me, but I'd worked it out for myself, more or less, with the help of some of the ancient Buddhist texts. In the talks I used to give at these meetings, I used to try to explain to these new Buddhists what Going for Refuge really meant, what it meant to be a Buddhist. Though it was late and they were tired, though they'd been working hard all day, they used to listen patiently and try to understand, but one could see that a lot of them were not really interested in understanding what Going for Refuge meant in the deeper and more fundamental sense. So far as they were concerned, conversion to Buddhism meant simply, at least to begin with, getting out of the clutches of orthodox Hinduism. It meant escape from the iniquities of the Hindu caste system, at the very bottom of which they were oppressed by everybody else. Having had quite a bit of contact with these people, having seen the way they used to live, the way they were treated by the orthodox caste Hindus, I can't blame them at all for seeing conversion to Buddhism in this way. But clearly that wasn't enough.

In my sixth and last reminiscence, I'm back in London after twenty years in India. It's 1964 and it's Wesak Day (the celebration of the Buddha's Enlightenment), not long after my return. The scene is Caxton Hall, Westminster, and I am on the platform with Mr Christmas Humphreys and other British Buddhist dignitaries whose names I've forgotten. At a certain stage of the proceedings – and Wesak celebrations in those days used to last exactly an hour, not a minute longer – I was asked to recite '*pansil*', the Refuges and Precepts, and when I say recite I mean recite. I was not asked to lead it, but to recite it, the idea being that we should all recite it together. I gathered that at the bottom of this strange practice there was some pseudo-democratic or pseudo-egalitarian idea. I raised a feeble objection, pointing out that this wasn't the custom in Buddhist countries, where the *bhikkhu* or whoever was officiating led the Refuges and Precepts and others repeated them after him, which produced a rather pleasant antiphonal effect, but this didn't go down at all well. My objections were brushed aside and Christmas Humphreys said, 'We've done it this way for forty years and we're not going to change now.' So I recited them and the people present – there must have been about a hundred – tried to recite them with me, but they came straggling along rather in the rear. Very few of them knew the Refuges and Precepts by heart and on this occasion there were no *pansil* cards, so the results were ragged to say the least – in fact, appalling. I realized then, if I hadn't realized it before, having been in England for some months, that something was seriously wrong with British Buddhism.

These are just some of my experiences of Going for Refuge before the Western Buddhist Order was founded. There are others, some of them of a more positive and inspiring nature. But you will have noticed at least one thing that my reminiscences have in common: that real appreciation of the significance of Going for Refuge is rather lacking nowadays. It's certainly lacking in Buddhist circles in the East, and it's also lacking in some of the corresponding circles in the West. More often than not the Refuges are simply something that you recite to show that you are a Buddhist, that you belong to the Buddhist community in a social sense, or even just a flag that you wave on important occasions. When you go to the temple on Wesak Day, you recite the Refuges. If there's a wedding, you recite the Refuges. When a baby is a few days old, it's given a name and you recite the Refuges. When Grandfather dies, there's an after-death ceremony, and you recite the Refuges. If there's a public meeting of the Ratepayers Association, they're all Buddhists, so they recite the Refuges. Reciting them shows that you're a decent, respectable, law-abiding person. This is the significance it usually has nowadays in the East.

There's nothing wrong with reciting the Refuges. It's a wonderful thing. It would be fine if we could chant the Refuges every morning and evening, or three times a day, or every hour, or all day. The trouble is that although people in the East recite the Refuges, which is a good thing to do, that's all they do. They don't think about the meaning. In my experience, it's only the Tibetan Buddhists who have some appreciation, sometimes a very deep appreciation, of what Going for Refuge really implies in spiritual terms, deeply and fundamentally, of its central and basic importance in and for the Buddhist life. Elsewhere in the Buddhist world they seem to have almost entirely forgotten. People recite the Refuges frequently and loudly, but they hardly ever really go for Refuge.

This is surprising when one thinks about it, because the significance of Going for Refuge as the central act of the Buddhist life is clear enough from the scriptures, especially those of the Pāli canon. It wouldn't be too much of an exaggeration to say that there are references to it on almost every page. Typically there's a little group of people somewhere, maybe in the forest or the village, and the Buddha is giving a teaching to someone, maybe a naked ascetic or a Brahmin priest, a king or a householder, a merchant or a sweeper, a housewife, a fisherman, almost anybody. I say that the Buddha is giving a teaching but really he is just talking with the people he happens to meet. The Buddha is just himself, his own Enlightened self, in relation to whoever comes his way. He may give a lengthy discourse or say just a few words. Usually he speaks in prose, but occasionally, when he has something of special importance to impart, something which he feels particularly deeply, he bursts into verse, as when he breathes forth some inspired utterance, an *udāna*.[210] Sometimes he gives a profound philosophical exposition and sometimes he tells a story with a meaning.

But whatever and however the Buddha communicates – at length or in brief, in prose or in poetry, profoundly or simply – the effect is usually tremendous, shattering. Some people are unmoved, because human beings are free not to be impressed even by the Buddha, but usually they are profoundly moved by what he has to say. In fact, his inspired speech is a revelation to them. What he says opens up a completely new world. They see their own life in a completely new light, and see stretching before their feet a new path that stretches to infinity. As they hear the Buddha's words, their whole being is shaken to its foundations. Sometimes their hair stands on end with the shock. They even shed tears, they are so moved. When they try to speak they find that their voice chokes and they can hardly speak for emotion, but when they manage to bring out a few words, in episode after episode they say the same thing. We mustn't allow the fact that these words are repeated so many times to deaden or weaken their impact on us. So what are the words that they manage to get out at last, with their hair standing on end and tears in their eyes? They say, 'It's amazing, Lord, it's wonderful.' Their reaction of awe, wonder, astonishment, reminds me of Plato's statement that 'philosophy begins with a sense of wonder'.[211]

Then, having expressed their wonder, they try to describe what has happened, and usually they give four comparisons. At this crucial moment, when they're on the brink of eternity spiritually speaking, suspended in mid-air – they haven't yet come down and they haven't started flying up – they have recourse to poetry. They speak not in terms of psychological or metaphysical analysis, but in comparisons, and the first thing they say is that it is as though something which had been cast down has now been set upright. Having been downcast and overthrown, they now feel uplifted, stable, strong, secure, firm, erect. Next they say they feel as though something which had been hidden has been revealed. It was there all the time, and now it has been brought to light so they can see it clearly. They feel, too, like a person who had gone astray to whom the way has been pointed out. They see their path clearly now. They know which way to go. There's no doubt, no hesitation, no confusion, no uncertainty. And, they say, it's as though a brilliant light, brighter even than the light of the sun, has shone forth in the midst of the darkness, and now they can see. These are the comparisons they give, this is the poetry they speak, expressing their feelings, communicating their experience.

Next, they say 'I go for Refuge', or to translate strictly, 'For Refuge I go'. I go for Refuge to the Buddha, the Dharma, and the Sangha. Clearly this is not just the recitation of a formula, but the heartfelt response of their total being to the impact of the truth. They commit themselves to the truth, surrender to it, want to devote their whole life to it. For many of those who heard the Buddha's words and felt the impact of the Dharma, Going for Refuge meant Going Forth. They went forth from the group, from the household life, as a single, solitary individual, and sooner or later they were accepted into the spiritual community of others who have gone forth as individuals, the full-timers, as I've sometimes called them. This is what Going for Refuge used to mean, and still means, according to the scriptures.[212]

I've spoken of hearing the Dharma as having a tremendous impact leading to the Going for Refuge, but seeing the Buddha could have the same effect. There's the well-known example of the Buddha's cousin and disciple Ānanda. According to the *Śūraṅgama Sūtra*, Ānanda was not converted, to use that term, by hearing the Dharma, but simply by seeing the Buddha's beauty. He saw in the distance the Buddha's noble, majestic appearance, his golden complexion, his kindly gaze, the light that seemed to radiate from his form, and he felt that he had never before seen anyone so beautiful.[213] As a result of this tremendous experience, Ānanda went forth from the household life and became for many years the Buddha's faithful attendant, looking after him, introducing people to him, running errands. And eventually, after the Buddha's *parinirvāṇa*, Ānanda gained Enlightenment. We should not forget the importance of beauty in the spiritual life. Beauty may or may not be truth, but truth is certainly beauty, and spiritual beauty has a tremendous power of fascination. In later Buddhist iconography the bodhisattvas are depicted as beautiful young princes, representing the fact that Enlightenment – and the bodhisattvas are personifications or embodiments of this or that aspect of Enlightenment – is eternally, everlastingly young, because it's always new, always fresh, never grows old, and is supremely attractive.

There's not only the Buddha and the Dharma, there's the Sangha, and seeing the spiritual community can also have a tremendous effect which leads one to go for Refuge. There are many examples of this. For example, there's the story of Ajātaśatru, who was a king in the Buddha's day. To gain the throne, he'd murdered his father and shut his mother in prison, and his mind was dreadfully uneasy on this account. He consulted with his friend and physician, Jīvaka, who said, 'I'll take you to see the Buddha.' So they set out one night, the whole court, including the ladies of the harem, mounted on five hundred elephants. At the edge of the forest they dismounted, and Jīvaka led the king deeper and deeper into the forest. It was a very dark night, and the branches of the trees were thickly interlaced above their heads. The king with his guilty mind became very suspicious, and he said, 'Jīvaka, you are not leading me into a trap, are you?' Jīvaka said, 'No, your majesty. It's just a little way further on.' They went deeper into the forest, it got darker and darker and quieter and quieter, and the king said, 'Jīvaka, didn't you tell me that the Buddha was staying in this forest with twelve hundred and fifty monks? I can't hear a sound. You're not leading me into a trap?' Jīvaka said, 'No, no, your majesty. You'll soon see.' And soon the king saw a clearing, lit by a single lamp. Just then the moon came out from behind a cloud and the king saw the whole assembly – twelve hundred and fifty *bhikkhus* all seated around the Buddha meditating in the middle of the night, and there wasn't a sound. The king was deeply impressed by this sight. He hadn't heard the Dharma yet; he just saw the Sangha. He had a son called Udāyabhadda and he was so impressed that he said to Jīvaka, 'I only wish that Udāyabhadda could know the peace of mind that these monks enjoy.' He knew that to hope for peace of mind for himself was impossible because he'd committed such a terrible crime, but he wished it for his son. So even this murderous, suspicious king was deeply moved by the sight of the Order, the spiritual community.[214]

Another famous example comes from China's Tang dynasty. Apparently there was a Chinese scholar-poet, a rather strict Confucian, who one day went to visit a Chan monastery. The monks there were so beautifully disciplined, wore their robes so neatly, walked about so sedately, ate in such a refined, mindful fashion, spoke to each other so politely, were so aware, that this strict Confucianist scholar was deeply impressed and exclaimed, in words which have become famous in Chinese Buddhist history, 'Ah, the etiquette of the Three Dynasties is surely embodied here.' Etiquette is a very important thing for Confucianists, so that was the highest possible praise.[215]

There are examples of the same thing nearer home and on a more ordinary level. Visitors to Sukhavati have been very impressed by the way in which the Order members and Mitras there worked together. The visitors didn't know anything about the Dharma, and so far there's no Buddha in the shrine-room, but they saw people working together and they were impressed. The same thing happened when last year a team of six people went to Norwich to help build the centre there. They apparently worked smoothly, efficiently, quickly, and as a team, relating to one another very positively, almost creatively, and this deeply impressed people who came along to see what they were doing.[216]

If you are a Buddhist, it's important to remember that more often than not other people will not see the Buddha, or even an image of the Buddha. They won't hear the Dharma, or read a book on Buddhism. But they may see the sangha, they may see *you*. They may see how you behave, how you work, how you relate to others in the sangha, whether you are positive or negative, inspiring and good to be with, or depressing and drab. You could be someone's first point of contact with the whole Buddhist tradition, the first Buddhist that somebody has ever seen. Almost as though they're seeing some strange new creature in the zoo, they're going to take a good look at you and see whether you look intelligent or stupid, absent-minded or on the ball, warm or distant. If you're thinking, 'Why don't you go away? I've got better things to do with my time,' they're going to see that too. So you've got a tremendous responsibility.

We've seen how important Going for Refuge is, whether as a result of seeing the Buddha, hearing the Dharma, or seeing the Sangha. We've also seen how the importance of Going for Refuge is made clear in the scriptures, even though the greater part of the Buddhist world seems to have forgotten that significance. It's time that we came on to the levels of Going for Refuge. There are altogether six of these: cultural, provisional, effective, real, ultimate, and cosmic. I fully realize that these terms are not very satisfactory, and they may need to be changed when I've had time to think about the matter a little more. Not all of them correspond to any traditional classification, though some do. I should perhaps correlate them systematically with Buddhist tradition. Meanwhile I want to say a few words about each of these levels of Going for Refuge.[217]

First of all there's what I've called the cultural Going for Refuge, but we also could call it the formal or even the ethnic Going for Refuge. In the course of fifteen hundred years, Buddhism spread from India all over Asia, and practically the entire population of those areas is Buddhist, or at least that was the case until the time of Communism. The population of those areas is, or until recently was, as Buddhist as the population of Europe is Christian, and in much the same way. In these countries, people don't generally follow Buddhism as a spiritual teaching. They may be influenced by it in a highly positive manner on the social level, or even on the ethical level, but they make no conscious effort to evolve individually. The majority don't follow Buddhism as a spiritual path. But nonetheless they are very proud of their Buddhism. It's often the most important part of their cultural heritage, or even practically the whole of it, because in some cases they had virtually no culture before Buddhism.

In those areas where, under Western influence, nationalism has become a strong force, the people are proud of Buddhism not only as part of their cultural heritage but also as part of their national heritage. They are what we might call 'ethnic' Buddhists, though that's really a contradiction in terms, and their Going for Refuge is what I've come to call the cultural Going for Refuge. They recite the Refuges in Pāli or some other language as an affirmation of cultural and national identity. They often think that someone who has merely been converted to Buddhism is a rather inferior kind of Buddhist. The real Buddhist is someone whose mother and father, grandfathers and grandmothers, were Buddhists. I must confess I used to take rather a strong line with such people when I met them. I used to tell them that it's completely unBuddhistic to say that you're a born Buddhist. The Buddha criticized the Brahmins for claiming to be Brahmins by birth, saying that you are a Brahmin only if you possess the qualities of a Brahmin.[218] You can't be a Buddhist just because your parents were Buddhists. You are Buddhist only if you follow the spiritual path shown by the Buddha. But these 'born Buddhists' tend to feel that Buddhism is in their blood, even to the extent that they understand it automatically without study, and that whatever they tell you about Buddhism must be correct. Many Hindus think the same thing. Because they were born in India, where Buddhism originated, they take it as axiomatic that they know all about Buddhism. They don't have to study it – they've inherited it! I've also met Buddhists who believed that everyone should remain in the religion into which they were born. They used to tell me it was wrong for a Christian to become a Buddhist.

In our own movement, we don't have any cultural Going for Refuge because we don't have any born Buddhists, but something analogous to it occurs when someone is attracted to the Movement as a positive group because everyone seems cheerful and friendly. They don't bother much about the Buddhist part of it, but they will join in happily. If you ask them to meditate, they meditate. They'll come along to a festival or help you organize a jumble sale. If you ask them to sit in on a puja and join in the Refuges and Precepts, they'll do that quite happily because it's all part of the group activity and they enjoy the friendliness of the group. This is all right as far as it goes, but it just reaches a certain level and doesn't go any further than that.

Then there's what I call the provisional Going for Refuge. That term is not at all satisfactory, but I'll try to explain what I mean. The provisional Going for Refuge goes beyond the cultural Going for Refuge, but it falls short of the effective Going for Refuge. On this level, you may be born into Buddhist surroundings, Buddhist society, Buddhist culture, but you start taking Buddhism seriously and start practising it to some extent. You haven't committed yourself to spiritual development, but you are aware of the possibility and even the desirability of doing so, and you may be thinking of committing yourself later on, even if it's only in the next life. In our own movement this level is represented by the Mitra. As a Mitra, you regard yourself as belonging to the FWBO. You meditate fairly regularly and help out in various practical ways. You might sweep the centre, or run errands for the Order member in charge. Maybe you're thinking about ordination. And when there's a puja you join in the recitation of the Refuges and Precepts.[219]

And thirdly there's what I call – perhaps more happily – the effective Going for Refuge. This is the Going for Refuge described in the scriptures. Effective Going for Refuge means actually committing yourself to the Three Jewels, with body, speech, and mind. All of you present here know very well from your own experience what it means, because it corresponds to the *upāsaka* (*dharmacāri*) ordination or *upāsikā* (*dharmacāriṇī*) ordination in the WBO. Perhaps I should just say more simply that it corresponds to ordination or threefold commitment, because it seems that the traditional socio-religious categories are becoming less and less relevant to our situation and our needs.

In a Vajrayāna context, effective Going for Refuge is twofold: general and specific. General Going for Refuge has for its object the Three Jewels in the ordinary sense, which is extraordinary enough: the Buddha, the Dharma, and the Sangha. But the specific Going for Refuge has for its object the Buddha, the Dharma, and the Sangha in their esoteric forms, as guru, *deva*, and *ḍākinī*. These Refuges are not called esoteric or secret (*guhya*) because they've been deliberately hidden or artificially kept secret. They're secret because they're difficult to communicate, and they're difficult to communicate because they are matters of experience, and experience is difficult to express. Ideas, concepts, and even philosophies are easy to communicate, but your own deep individual, personal experience, which is unique to yourself, ineffable, is very difficult indeed to communicate. You don't want to keep it secret – you may fervently want to share it – but the fact that it is *your* experience and you're trying to talk about it to somebody else who may have a different kind of experience, a different outlook, even a different language, makes it very difficult to communicate. Experience as such is esoteric, secret, *guhya*.

The Vajrayāna – the third of the three *yānas* – is the *yāna* of experience par excellence. The other *yānas* are *yānas* of experience too, but not so thoroughly, deeply, or radically as the Vajrayāna. Because it's the *yāna* of experience, it's also the *yāna* of practice, because there's no experience without practice. The Vajrayāna, in fact, is all practice. It has no theory, no philosophy of its own. The esoteric Refuges are that aspect of the exoteric Refuges, the Buddha, Dharma, and Sangha, which you personally experience, and that may be very little. After all, you don't see Gautama the Buddha. Maybe you experience him indirectly to a limited extent – you read about him in the scriptures, you see his image – but you don't experience the Buddha himself. You would have to have lived 2,500 years ago to do that. You say 'To the Buddha for Refuge I go', but how can you go for Refuge to a Buddha that you have never seen? Can you go for Refuge to an idea, or an image? Are you an idol worshipper, as the Christians sometimes accuse us of being? But you do see the guru, you do experience the guru. So according to the Vajrayāna, for practical purposes the guru is the refuge. If you get into difficulties, if you want advice, if you want teachings specifically related to your needs, you can't go to the Buddha. Even if you read the scriptures the advice is too general, too broad, even too vague. But you can go to the guru and he can give you exactly what you need for your particular situation. This is what is meant when we say that the Guru Refuge is the esoteric, and maybe we should say the experiential, form of the Buddha Refuge.

It's the same in the case of the Dharma. The Dharma is so vast, like an infinite ocean. Sometimes we are told that it consists of an infinite number of teachings, but it's traditionally said to consist of 84,000 independent, or interdependent, teachings. You may know, theoretically, quite a few hundred of these 84,000 *dharmaskandhas* as they're called, but how many have you practised? That's what counts. It's the Dharma we've actually experienced that is the Dharma to which we really go for Refuge. This is the esoteric Dharma Refuge, the *Deva* Refuge. We go for Refuge only to the Dharma that we actually practise in a real, deep, living sense, and for the Vajrayāna this is primarily the Buddha or bodhisattva (the *deva*) on whom we regularly meditate, because we've at least experienced him or her in our meditation. So the *Deva* Refuge is the esoteric form of the Dharma Refuge.

Likewise, we go for Refuge to the Sangha, but the Sangha consists of millions of individuals, both mundane and transcendental, past, present, and future. We can't possibly have contact with all of them. We can't go for Refuge to the whole Sangha. That's inconceivable. We go for Refuge in practice, in our own experience, only to a very limited number of members of the spiritual community, perhaps only to two or three, or even one. One is the minimum, and this is the *ḍākinī*. The *ḍākinī* is that part of the Sangha with which we have a real living spiritual contact, and the *Ḍākinī* Refuge is therefore the esoteric form of the Sangha Refuge. There's some possibility – in some cases even actuality – of misunderstanding here. The word *ḍākinī* happens to be in the feminine gender, so the concept of *ḍākinī* is sometimes interpreted as a female partner, a pseudo-spiritual girlfriend with whom one allegedly practises the Dharma. But the *ḍākinī* (and there is a masculine form, *ḍāka*) is really any member of the spiritual community with whom you are in close personal contact, who sparks you off spiritually, inspires you.

There's an even more profound way of looking at the *ḍākinī*. The *ḍākinī* is not really anyone outside oneself at all. If you are a committed, integrated person, you should be able to spark yourself off. What the *ḍākinī* really represents is the higher, more refined emotional side of your own being. She represents friendliness, befriending, compassion, sympathetic joy, peace and tranquillity, faith and devotion. All these higher, more refined, more positive emotions are to be developed within oneself. Does this mean that the Sangha Refuge can be dispensed with? Does it mean that spiritual fellowship and communication is unimportant? No. What it means is that you can't go for Refuge to the Sangha, to the *ḍākinī*, unless you have your own *ḍākinī* within. *Ḍākini* goes for Refuge to *ḍākinī*, *ḍākinī* communicates with *ḍākinī*. In other words, within the context of the spiritual community we can't communicate just through ideas or concepts, but only with the help of our own higher, more spiritual, more refined emotions, only through our own personal, integrated *ḍākinī*, addressing the *ḍākinī* of the other person.

The *ḍākinī* more or less corresponds to what William Blake calls the emanation. He says something to the effect that in the perfect state – perhaps in the state of eternity – individuals converse with one another through their emanations.[220] Without genuine spiritual emotion there is no communication. If your conversation is merely intellectual, you may talk for ages, but there will be no communication, just words, and by the end you'll feel dry and barren, as though your mouth was full of dust. If you only communicate through the medium of concepts, if you only talk philosophy in this dry, academic pseudo-intellectual way, it's just the dry bones of concepts rubbing up against one another but kindling no spark, no warmth, and leaving you dull, dry, and dissatisfied. Genuine communication is only possible with the help of emotion, warmth, friendliness, and in the context of spiritual community, the higher, spiritual emotions, and this is what is meant by the *Ḍākinī* Refuge. By emotion I don't mean anything soft or sloppy or sentimental, but the Abhidharma sense of positive mental events.

The fourth level is that of the real Going for Refuge. This takes place when you develop insight and wisdom, and in that way enter upon the transcendental path, become a Stream Entrant. In traditional terms, the real Going for Refuge is the transcendental Going for Refuge. The previous refuges, even the effective refuge, are all mundane. This is a sobering thought, because it means that until you have entered the Stream, until you have entered upon the transcendental path, you can fall back. You can go round and round in the wheel of life. Not only can you be born a human being again; according to tradition you can become a titan, or an animal, or a hungry ghost. If you haven't entered the Stream you can fall back. You can leave the spiritual community, you can resign from the Order. You can't be sure, which is why we have to stress the importance of a positive, creative, spiritually supportive environment. This is indispensable until you enter the Stream.

The fifth level is the ultimate Going for Refuge. No need to say much about this, because it occurs only when one is Enlightened, and at this level one doesn't go for Refuge to anything outside oneself. One is one's own refuge. In fact, there's no inside and no outside because there's no self and no other, and one can't say any more than that.

So these are the five levels of Going for Refuge, and I hope I've been able to make them clear. I've been more concerned tonight with basic structure than with details or specific applications. But there's still one more – though it's not exactly a level. Sixthly and lastly, there's the cosmic Going for Refuge. It sounds rather grand, and the word 'cosmic' is quite inspiring, but it's really quite simple. The cosmic Going for Refuge refers to the evolutionary process. To recall our evolutionary studies, the amoeba comes first, then, some time later – I'm paraphrasing! – comes the mollusc, then the fish, the reptile, the bird, the mammal and then, finally, in all our glory and misery, there's *Homo sapiens*. If one looks at this process, one sees a Going for Refuge, because each form of life aspires to develop into the next higher form, goes for Refuge to the next higher form. This may sound impossibly poetic, but it is in fact what one sees. In human beings the evolutionary process becomes conscious of itself, and this is the higher evolution. And when the higher evolution becomes conscious of itself, that's effective Going for Refuge. So through effective Going for Refuge, we're united with all living beings who also, in their own way, on their own level, go for Refuge. All living beings go for Refuge. The flower goes for Refuge. The tree goes for Refuge. The bird goes for Refuge. I don't want to sentimentalize – I'm perilously near that – so let's stop there and just say that the whole cosmos goes for Refuge. So the Going for Refuge is not simply a devotional practice. It's not even just a threefold act of individual spiritual commitment. The Going for Refuge is the key to the mystery of existence itself, and it is therefore most important that we understand, at all its levels, what it means.

THE MANU, THE BUDDHA, THE GURU, AND THE TERTÖN

London Buddhist Centre, Padmasambhava Day 1979

Today we're not only celebrating Padmasambhava Day, but also unveiling our Nālandā crest. There is a connection, because Padmasambhava was associated with the great monastic university of Nālandā. Part of Nālandā's crest is a lotus, symbolizing spiritual rebirth, and the name Padmasambhava means the one who is born from the lotus, the one who is spiritually born, even spiritually reborn. He was born in India in the eighth century into a princely family, he left home like the Buddha, he became a Tantric guru and a great scholar, renowned for his psychic powers and his mastery of yoga, and he was altogether doing very well in the world of Indian Buddhism, when there came one day an invitation from the kingdom of Tibet, which was in those days a very long journey indeed from India. Perhaps he'd never thought of going to Tibet, but he thought seriously about it now, and in the end he decided to go. He was badly needed there, it seems, because efforts were being made to introduce Buddhism into the Land of Snows, but there were obstacles. The great monastery of Samye was being built by someone else who had also been invited to Tibet, the bodhisattva Śāntarakṣita, usually known as the bodhisattva abbot. He was trying to build this great monastery, which was to be a centre for the propagation of the Dharma in Tibet, but he wasn't able to do it. The workmen did a day's work, but mysteriously, in the morning the bricks they'd laid had all returned to the brick pile. Those of you who were until quite recently building, or rather rebuilding, Sukhavati, might almost have thought some mornings when you went back to work that some mysterious agency had undone yesterday's work in the night so that you had to start all over again.[221] That was certainly the case at Samye. According to the legends, the destruction was the work of the *nāgas*, gods, and demons of Tibet, who were for reasons of their own not in favour of the teaching of the Buddha being introduced into Tibet, and opposed it with all their might.

The bodhisattva abbot, Śāntarakṣita, was a very good man, and he explained the Dharma very beautifully, the ten ways of skilful action, the four noble truths, even the twelve links of conditioned co-production. But although the king and the people of Tibet were impressed, the gods and demons of Tibet were not, and they continued to undo his work. The bodhisattva abbot said to the king, 'There is in India, at Nālandā, a great teacher who is not only well versed in Buddhist philosophy and meditation, but also a master of the occult arts and sciences. He will tame the gods and demons of Tibet.' So Padmasambhava was sent for, and he came, and he did tame the gods and demons. He didn't have to spend very long in Tibet, it seems. Some accounts say he was there for only eighteen months, but that was long enough. He subdued those tremendous forces, and the Dharma was eventually securely established in Tibet. And then Padmasambhava departed for the Land of the Rākṣasas, wherever that may be.

This is the story of the life of Padmasambhava as it has come down to us through historical sources. It's not the whole story, but it's the story which is accessible to secular history. I told it some years ago when we celebrated Padmasambhava Day at Archway, at Pundarika, so this evening I want to go in a rather different direction.[222] I'm going to take as my starting point the fact that in Tibet, especially among the Nyingmapas, who regard themselves as his followers, Padmasambhava is often referred to as the second Buddha. That might seem rather extraordinary. How could there possibly be a second Buddha? We all know that the first Buddha is Śākyamuni, and he's called the first because at a time when the Dharma, the path to Enlightenment, was not known, he opened it up again. There had been Buddhas in previous world periods, but they had come and gone. Their teaching had flourished for a while, and then it had disappeared and was not known perhaps for thousands upon thousands of years. That is the tradition. A supremely spiritually gifted individual appears at a time when the path to Enlightenment is not known, and he rediscovers that path and opens it up again for humanity. Because he is the first, because he shows the way and others follow after him, he is known as the Buddha. This is what Buddha means: not just the Enlightened one, not just one who has realized Nirvāṇa, but one who has reached it by his own efforts at a time when it was not known, and by reaching it makes it possible again for other people to follow that path, and to realize that supreme state of Nirvāṇa. There can't therefore be another Buddha until the Dharma has been lost again and has to be rediscovered again. Padmasambhava came at a time when the Buddha's Dharma was still flourishing. He himself studied and taught that Dharma. So why do his followers call him the second Buddha?

Perhaps we can understand this a little more clearly if we use a different word. Padmasambhava is the Guru, and in *The Life and Liberation of Padmasambhava* he is very often referred to as such. So let's speak not of the first Buddha and the second Buddha, but of the Buddha and the Guru, the Buddha being the Buddha in the full sense, and Padmasambhava being the Guru in the full sense, not just the ordinary sense of spiritual teacher. In *The Life and Liberation of Padmasambhava*, there's a chapter that speaks of Buddhas and Gurus appearing in different ages. It says in such and such an age came such and such a Buddha, and just after him there came a second Buddha, a Guru, of that particular period.[223] So according to this text a Buddha appears in every period and every age, and then a Guru follows closely on his heels. What does this mean? That's what I want to go into a bit this evening, because it will help us to understand the significance of the life of Padmasambhava and the part he plays in the Nyingmapa tradition and in the spiritual economy of the cosmos, including our own generation.

I'll start by enlarging the context a bit. I'm going to speak not just of the Buddha and the Guru, but of four personalities or archetypes: the Manu, the Buddha, the Guru, and the Tertön. Manu is a Sanskrit word, and to explain it, I'll go back to my days in India with the ex-Untouchable Buddhists after their mass conversion to Buddhism under the leadership of Dr B. R. Ambedkar, who died six weeks after the conversion ceremony. His followers now called themselves Buddhists, so, realizing that they needed to know what Buddhism was and make some effort to practise it, I went around from village to village and town to town and city to city, sometimes for the whole winter, giving lectures and performing ceremonies of various kinds, especially wedding ceremonies, which were in great demand. On these tours I used to go to Bombay, where I had friends in various communities. One of my friends there was by birth a Polish Jew. He was a little old man, just like a gnome, only about four foot six tall, and with a little bald head. Though he'd been born into a Jewish family, he'd become a Jesuit priest, but eventually he'd given that up, come to India, and become a follower of Mahatma Gandhi. He wore thick white homespun, as Gandhi's followers did, and he eventually became a follower of Krishnamurti. He had rather a caustic tongue and he was very fond of giving me advice. At that time I was still in my thirties and he was about 65, so he considered himself fully qualified and entitled to give me as much good advice as I needed. I once went to stay with him in his beautiful flat, which he shared with a Parsee lady who was even more eccentric than himself; she was aged about 80, and was also a follower of Krishnamurti. I was a bit tired after all that journeying from village to village and all the lectures I'd been giving, so as soon as I'd been given a cup of tea, Maurice said in his fatherly way, 'Sangharakshita, you're wasting your time trying to teach Buddhism to these people. In fact, you're wasting your time trying to be a Buddha for these people. What they really need is a Manu.' I didn't need to ask Maurice what a Manu was, because I knew exactly what he meant, and after thinking it over I was inclined to agree with him.

According to Indian cosmogenetic belief, at the beginning of each world period, when the human race reappears, at the very dawn of history, there also appears a great law-giver who lays down the basis of society, and he is called a Manu. The word *manu* is connected etymologically with *manas*, which means mind, which is also connected with *manuṣya*, human being. A *manuṣya*, a human being, is one endowed with mind and a Manu is the archetypal human being, the one archetypally endowed with mind, the law-giver who guides the whole of society and lays the basis for a positive social life, for the positive group. According to the Indian tradition, at the very beginning of things this law-giver emerges and lays down laws governing society from the ethical point of view, laws which will make it possible for human beings to live in such a way that when a higher, transcendental teaching is proclaimed, they are able to understand it and follow it. The Manu comes right at the beginning for the good reason that humanity needs him. Humanity needs social organization, but it must be on the basis of not just social but moral, ethical, and ultimately spiritual principles. Social life in all its aspects must be so organized as to make the spiritual life possible, or even to prepare people for the spiritual life. This is the function of the Manu. What my friend really meant was that until you've got society organized in such a way that it reflects ethical values, until society can prepare the individual human being ethically, there's not much point in preaching lofty spiritual ideals. You need the positive group, to use our own terminology, before you can have the spiritual community. You need the FWBO before you can have the WBO, at least historically if not in principle. This is what he was getting at and I was very much inclined to agree. In fact, to a certain extent in my work with the new Buddhists I was acting as a law-giver. They used to ask how they should perform the Buddhist wedding ceremony, and I used to tell them what to do and what not to do. It had nothing to do with the spiritual path directly, nothing to do with the attainment of Enlightenment, but it was a necessary basis in social and family life, preparing the way for the emergence of positive, happy, healthy human beings who could then as individuals direct themselves to the spiritual path.

In traditional terms, the Manu prepares the way for the Buddha. If we read the Pāli scriptures, which are the oldest Buddhist scriptures and give us a picture of what India was like in the Buddha's day, we notice what a high standard of cultural life there was in India at that time, how harmonious their social life seems to have been, how dignified their religious life was, with what courtesy they discussed things even when they differed drastically as to their religious opinions. One has the impression that there was a very high degree of social organization, a very pure, noble cultural life, and it was because the way had been prepared, the basis had been laid, that the Buddha was able to gain such a ready hearing. His teaching was very subtle. It presupposed a great social and cultural development.

So the Manu prepares the way for the Buddha. What we mean by the Buddha is much easier to understand. The Buddha is the one who shows the way. Society may be happy, healthy, and human, but the path to the transcendental still has to be discovered and opened up, and that is the work of the Buddha. It's difficult work because sometimes social and cultural development is so refined that people think that they've got everything it's possible to have. They don't realize that there is something far beyond it, something transcending the social, the cultural, the religious, and the philosophical – the nirvāṇic, that which pertains to the Enlightenment experience. It's the function of the Buddha to discover that, to experience it for himself and then to retrace his steps, come back to unenlightened humanity, and show them the way to that experience. This is what our Buddha, Śākyamuni, did. He tried to communicate to other individuals or incipient individuals the content of his experience of Enlightenment, so that they could be liberated just as he was. This goes immeasurably far beyond the social and the cultural and the religious and the philosophical. It belongs to an entirely different dimension, an experience which is *sui generis*, not to be compared with anything else whatsoever.

It's not easy for the Buddha to communicate this because he has to use the terms of the existing culture. He tries to formulate a philosophy, a thought construction, as a bridge between the minds of ordinary human beings and his Enlightened mind, and this results in the Dharma, but it is communicated in very general terms. Gautama the Buddha only lived for forty-five years after his Enlightenment, and that is not long to communicate the truth. Because of the tremendous force of his personality he was able to transform the lives of thousands of people, but the formulation of his teaching is very general, even abstract. The four noble truths, the Noble Eightfold Path, the twenty-four links of the chain of conditioned co-production – all these teachings are abstract, and can be rationally, intellectually communicated. They are aimed at the intelligence because it is the intelligence that is the growing point of humanity. We understand things intellectually, theoretically, and a long time afterwards the rest of our personality, especially our emotions, catches up. This is why the path of vision is short and the path of transformation is long – except that the path of vision is not just theoretical and mental, but the principle is the same.

The Buddha had time to proclaim the teaching only in a general way, and he addressed it mainly to the conscious, rational part of humanity. A teaching which is able to appeal to other aspects takes much longer to develop, longer than any individual teacher, even a Buddha, has at his disposal. A lot must happen after his *parinirvāṇa*. He has made a start. He has touched the comparatively superficial levels, so far as the mass of humanity is concerned, but he hasn't yet touched the deeper psychic levels on a mass scale. That is the work of the Guru with a capital G. In this particular period it is the work of Padmasambhava. He is the one who subdues the demons, particularly the gods and demons of Tibet, and that is his principal work. If we look at the life of Śākyamuni the Buddha, he did subdue a few gods and demons – he took various Brahmās down a peg or two, and he had dealings with *nāgas*, serpent deities – but his emphasis was on communicating the teaching in a clear and rational manner to ordinary human beings. He did not have time to influence on deeper and deeper levels the archetypes of the collective unconscious, to borrow a Jungian phrase. Don't take this too literally, but the Buddha's teaching – and it was still the Buddha's teaching – had to bite much more deeply into the consciousness of humanity, even into the consciousness of the universe.

This is where the Guru comes in. He doesn't add anything, he doesn't teach anything different, but he is concerned with the transformation of the depths, and this is why he figures as the subduer of gods and demons. These are not just mythological figures, but forces within the human mind itself at a very deep level, to be found not only within the individual mind, but where the individual mind ends and the collective mind, the collective consciousness, the collective unconscious, begins. At the same time they influence every individual conscious mind until it has attained a degree of superconsciousness. These primordial forces have to be tackled if there is to be a thoroughgoing transformation of the spiritual life of humanity, and this is the prominent feature in the life of Padmasambhava. He tackles the gods and demons not just of Tibet or India, but of the world, East and West – and in the West we've got a lot of demons which need a lot of tackling. This is one of the reasons why we celebrate Padmasambhava Day, because that is the help that we need to invoke. It's not enough to scratch the rational surface of our minds. We have to penetrate to the depths, drop a depth charge and blow up all the primordial forces that are holding us back.

It's easy to talk about these primordial forces. Jung talks about the archetypes of the collective unconscious at great length. It all sounds so easy and smooth, as though we know all about it, but do we? What are they? What are they like? In *The Life and Liberation of Padmasambhava* there are vivid descriptions of some of them. I'm going to read a few passages to give you an idea of them, because we shouldn't engage in abstract descriptions here. We need to bring ourselves right up against these forces in a vivid and concrete manner. They have various names:

some are called gods or demons, and some are called *ḍākinīs*. The *ḍākinīs*, which appear again and again in *The Life and Liberation of Padmasambhava*, represent these primordial energies in a particular aspect. They're very strange, but they're within all of us and we have to come to terms with them. So let's get to know a few. In some of his early encounters with *ḍākinīs*, Padmasambhava went to cremation grounds, where he practised austerities and meditated, the *ḍākinīs* started gathering around him, and he subdued them. What that means you can perhaps understand for yourselves. The text says:

> There are to be seen countless ḍākinīs:
> some of them have eyes that dart out sun rays;
> others give rise to thunderclaps and ride water buffaloes;
> others hold sabres and have eyes which inflict harm;
> others wear death's heads, one above the other, and ride tigers;
> others wear corpses and ride lions;
> others eat entrails and ride garuḍas;
> others have flaming lances and ride jackals;
> others, five-faced, are steeped in a lake of blood;
> others in the numberless bands carry many generations of living beings;
> others carry in their hands, their own heads, which they have severed;
> others carry in their hands their own hearts which they have torn out;
> there are others who have made gaping wounds in their own bodies and who empty out and devour their own intestines and entrails;
> there are others who hide and yet reveal their male or female sexual organs,
> riding horses, bulls, elephants.[224]

So these are the primordial forces within ourselves that have to be subdued – not crushed or held down by force, but integrated into our conscious attitude, so that our conscious personality can be enriched, so that our spiritual life isn't just some pale anaemic thing, but glowing and throbbing with the energy of the *ḍākinīs*, with the energy of the gods and demons that have been tamed and transformed.

Here's another little passage. The last one described a whole gang of *ḍākinīs*, but this one describes an individual *ḍākinī*, a very interesting character called Adamantine Conqueror of Demons (for demons themselves sometimes conquer demons).

> In the northeast is the ḍākinī Adamantine Conqueror of Demons
> who arouses sexuality and vomits small children.
> She has a cranberry red body and wears trousers of blue cotton.
> She has the beak of a peacock, the eyes of an owl,
> wears the six ornaments of bone on her pure breast,
> a mirror in the middle of her forehead,
> a vajra circle tying a tuft of hair,
> and in her hands are yellow vajras.[225]

So this is the kind of being that Padmasambhava subdued. Padmasambhava, the Guru, represents the Buddha in this aspect of being the subduer of all these primordial energies and forces in the depths of our own unconscious mind, so that they can be integrated with the purer, clearer energies of the spiritual life, so that our spiritual life pulses with life and energy. We're not to cut ourselves off from these forces, these energies, we're not to disown them, we're to incorporate and integrate them, which means subduing them.

There's another powerful description of a god or demon of a much more monstrous, basic, primordial kind, a figure is known as Tarpa Nagpo, who should be one of the classic figures of Buddhist mythology. Actually we're already very familiar with him but we don't realize it. Tarpa Nagpo means Black Salvation, and originally he was a monk, the disciple of a guru in an ordinary sense. Tarpa Nagpo – he wasn't called that originally, but let's call him that – was proud, vain, and conceited. There was once an argument between him and another disciple, and the guru decided that the other disciple was right. Tarpa Nagpo's ego was so affronted, and he was so angry, that he virtually disowned the guru and went his own way. He did all sorts of horrible things, resulting in a long series of unfortunate births, and then he became Tarpa Nagpo, Black Salvation. I'll read the part about the end of that particular life and then we'll go through those rebirths, to his existence as Tarpa Nagpo.

Then the monk Tarpa Nagpo,
turning himself to the activities of the hunt and other worldly ways,
incapable of reciting the Formulas for the contemplation of the gods,
violated in his savage soul his vows to superior and brother.
He enlarged and multiplied endlessly the doors of the Dharma:
instead of weighing the Two Doctrines [i.e. the *Sūtra* and the Tantra] as he should have,
Tarpa, following the inclination of the logic [mind you, the logic] dear to himself,
led everyone astray on an evil path.
In his aberration, he freed the male demons,
and gathered the female demons under his power.
And he took the dead into charnel-houses in order to have his fill of them;
he put on human skins which caused him to have scabs.
Instead of cattle he raised
bloodhounds and other beasts with rapacious instincts.
Assembling the courtesans he consecrated them and took sport in luxury.
The nature of the four substances was transgressed.
Among the ten iniquities he presided over evil hangings,
and the lords and the army resembled brigands.

When he had for twelve cycles practiced the black doctrine,
incarnations followed each other:
he had five hundred existences as a black jackal,
five hundred as a wandering mastiff,
five hundred as a carnivorous mongoose,
five hundred as a bee with a poisonous sting,
and five hundred as a nimble worm.
Still more he had as a ghost, a sucker of feet, and other inconceivable things.
Then five hundred as an eater of vomit
and others lower than the rank of animals.
After various births lower than the rank of ghosts,
he received a new form as a flesh eater, gnawer of bones.

Again he was reborn with neck and shoulders rotten,
[a] pus-ghost named Eager to Make Inquiry.

Then at the end of twenty thousand existences,
after the teaching of the Buddha Dīpaṅkara,
that of Śākyamuni not having yet appeared,
and in this interval many years having passed in the absence of the Teaching,
in Laṅkāpura, the land of the ogres,
a courtesan, Kuntugyu, Wandering Everywhere, mated with
a māra of the twilight and a demon of midnight.
And a genie of the dawn also mated with her, and she conceived.
The fathers being three fierce spirits,
there was born at the end of eight months a child with three heads.
It had six hands; it had four feet;
it had two wings which pushed into its body;
it had nine eyes, three on each head;
it presented multiple appearances.
As soon as it was born calamity announced itself;
sickness filled the Lands of Laṅkā,
the amount of merits done declined,
famines, wars, epidemics, and the three scourges increased
and there were nightmarish dreams of many deadly beings.

Nine months after his birth the child fell ill,
and Kuntugyu herself died.
The people of the land said: 'This bastard of ill omen
must be disposed of secretly.'
In the root of the funerary tree was a poison, 'nalbyi';
there was the black swine of the tombs, a lair of error,
in the middle of which was the venomous serpent, the container of hate;
and at the peak was the nest of the kite of desire.
The ogres bring their dead to this place –
it is the haunt of the elephant and the tiger,
and here reptiles instill their poison.
It is also here that the ḍākinīs convey the corpses,

and here at the root of the tree that the ogres build their tombs.
The child was buried with the dead mother.
Now, embracing his mother, the child nursed her breast,
with the result that he sustained life for seven days with the
yellow fluid.
Then by sucking her blood he lived seven days;
then by eating her breasts he lived seven days;
then by eating her viscera he lived seven days;
then by eating her flesh behind he lived seven days;
then by eating her bone marrow, the corrupted spine marrow,
and by eating the brain, he lived the span of seven days.
For forty-two days his body grew.
And when he no longer had anything to eat he shook and made
the tomb collapse.
On looking inside, the ḍākinīs saw that the cadaver had been
devoured:
having eaten her flesh and drunk her blood, he had also taken her
skin as a tunic
and her skull as a cup of bloody libations.
Seeing a serpent he made himself an anklet for his foot, a bracelet
and a necklace.
Finding a dead elephant he ate its flesh and stretched out its skin.
He drank the blood and ate the flesh of a tiger, and used its pelt
as a cloak.
Then from his mouth he produced the fixed form of a curd of
blood,
and from his body he disposed of a small pile of ashes.
And he who had eaten his mother for nourishment and dressed
himself in her raw skin,
who in his thirst had drunk her blood, and who in action had
perpetrated crime,
who, to live, had lived off the dead, had a complexion which
shone with light.
White on the right, red on the left, blue in the middle, his faces
were fierce;
his giant body was of a pale ash color;
his face was maliciously gracious with coarse muscular bundles
of rough flesh.

He attached on one side of himself a row of withered heads,
and hung fresh heads about him.
He made himself a garland of three fringes dangling with skulls,
and he oiled all his cheeks with red semen.
On his body a swine's skin grew. His mouth and eyes were scarlet;
his mop of hair, red with the mud of hanging curls,
he tied a knot of half-length with five kinds of asps.
Armed with bird claws on all his limbs,
he tied to these in turn the serpents of five species.
He swallowed voraciously, flesh and blood, every prey which he could seize.
Boar spears and whatever could serve as a weapon, he carried.
From his left hand he drank from the skull filled with blood.
His breath gave rise to all contagions of heat,
his nose to the various kinds of cold illnesses.
From his eyes, from his ears, and from his lower orifices
issued the four hundred and four sorts of typhus maladies.
Evils of air, earth, water and fire,
acute quinsies, stomach spasms, malignant gastritises,
the ulcers of leprosy, the scabs of smallpox, great plagues, dropsies,
abscesses, erysipelas, cow-lickings, abscessed kidneys,
manifold and terrifying ravages were spread abroad.
By name he was called The One Who Devours His Mother, Mātaraṃgara.

At this time twenty-four countries had formidable and irresistible masters:
the countries of Pulliramalaya, Jālandhara, Uḍḍiyāna and Arbuda were seized by the gods;
Godāvarī, Rāmeśvara, Devīkoṭā, and Mālava, all minor countries, were seized by the gandharva.
All eight which the gods and gandharva seized were of celestial rank, because they had been seized by those from heaven.
Kāmarūpa and Oḍiviśa were seized by the yakṣa;
Triśakuṇa and Kosala, minor countries, were later seized by the yakṣa;

Kaliṅga, Lampāka, and Chandoha were seized by the ogres;
Kāñcī, the Himalaya, and Upacchandoha were seized by the ogres, and constituted the earthly empire;
Pretapurī and Gṛhadevata were places of assembly seized by the nāgas;
Surāṣṭra and Suvarṇadvīpa were minor places seized by the nāgas;
Nāgara and Sindhu, cemeteries, were seized by the asuras;
Maru and Kalūta, also minor cemeteries,
were seized by the asuras, nāgas of the Nāgaloka,
and titans of the crypts of Meru –
these were said to be of the lower domain.

The haughty masters of the world,
taking life from the inhabitants of the earth
with battle axes, pitchforks, boar spears, swords,
wore eight macabre suits of bones,
and told their wives at the time of marriage:
'We who are happy and without rivals
will fall into civil war for lack of a chief,
lose our means of eating and drinking,
and find ourselves enmired in quarrel and battle.
The very strong one, great lord, great god,
magic coffer who commands all through action,
Mātaraṃgara: this is the chief to take.
And to make deeds conform to principles,
we and the bhūta, devourers of life,
whether it be of the body, speech, or mind,
promise never to tremble at his orders.'
Thus Mātaraṃgara became chief of the entire world of the genies.

All were eager for the magic coffer;
the vighnas, day and night, perpetually guarded their sinister chief.
A multitude of bhūtas, the nonhuman beings, crowded around,
battering everyone, seizing living human beings,
and making slaves of each one, or slaves of slaves.

The great strength of the Formidable One crushed his adversaries
and at that time all who died went to hell,
Now he said: 'I now must announce
the Renowned of the World according to merit.
Who is greater than I? Who surpasses me?'
In a frenzy of pride he talked such nonsense:
'We need an army of burning fire; I will create it;
I am the lord of all the bhūtas
and if any other lord excels me,
to that one will I submit.'
Pride, thus proclaimed him to the ten points of space,
obscured his mind.[226]

What a tremendous demoniacal figure! It's this that Padmasambhava was up against, and it's this that we're all up against, because this great figure, Mātaraṃgara, is lurking in the depths of all our minds, lurking in the depths of the collective unconscious, lurking in mundane existence. In a sense he doesn't even lurk; he *is* mundane existence. Later on in the story, this great Rudra, this great fierce one, Tarpa Nagpo, Black Salvation, is subdued by an incarnation of Padmasambhava in a strange and dramatic way, and, remarkably, transformed into a protector of the Dharma. From these strange figures – the gods and demons, the *ḍākinīs*, this cosmic figure, Black Salvation – we can get some idea of what the Guru has to transform, and what in a sense we too have to transform.

Mātaraṃgara reminds me of a few similar figures in our own tradition in the West, perhaps not quite so extraordinary or dramatic or powerful, but of much the same kind and spelling out much the same kind of message. For example, Blake's Urizen is the same kind of figure from a somewhat different point of view. Urizen – 'your reason', according to some commentators – was originally the Prince of Light, the illumined intelligence, but he falls. He falls into duality, he limits himself, he contracts and starts seeing the world in a narrow, limited way, just with his reason and through his senses. He explores this constricted, confined existence all the time in the dark, and tries to bring everything under his own rational control. He prescribes laws. He's the God of the Old Testament. He tries to hold everything down, limit everything, constrict everything. He doesn't want anything to be free or spontaneous, he wants to have it all bound down and reduced to order, which is actually disorder, because the disorder he wants to reduce to order is not disorder at all, but richness and creativity.[227] Another figure that comes to mind is Sauron in Tolkien's *The Lord of the Rings*, an almost cosmic principle of evil who is trying to destroy everything good, trying to gather power to himself. He's evil personified, he's destructive, negative, death, poison, for he's trying to bring everything under his control with the help of the One Ring. It isn't enough to skim the spiritual surface and ignore these forces, because the flames are licking at your heels and you have to do something about them. You can't just soar above them. You've got to descend into the flames, as Blake would have said, and transform them. You've got to delight in the flames, not run away from them into some vague, ambiguous light. We see in *The Life and Liberation of Padmasambhava*, and reflected also in Western tradition, these vast, primordial, archetypal forces as something to be transformed, something to be brought within the sphere of the spiritual life, and this is what Padmasambhava represents.

We've explored the Manu, the Buddha, and the Guru. The fourth figure is the Tertön. This is not a Sanskrit word as the others were, but a Tibetan one. Tertön means a taker-out of treasure, *ter* meaning treasure or what is hidden and *tön* meaning one who takes. So what is this treasure? The Tibetan legend is that Padmasambhava gave many Dharma instructions in Tibet, as well as subduing the demons and the gods, but he foresaw a time when other teachings would be needed, teachings which if he gave them at that time would have been misunderstood. So according to tradition he hid treasures in different parts of Tibet, and India too. There's a very interesting chapter in *The Life and Liberation of Padmasambhava* which deals with the *termas*. Apparently they're not just books, or even just material objects. You can have mind *termas*: *termas* which are hidden in the depths of the mind. You can have *termas* of kings, of males, of females, of hermaphrodites. So *terma* begins to mean something very mysterious. It isn't just a book tucked away in a cave, though it can include those. In fact, we are told that there are eighteen kinds of *termas*.[228] But whatever they are, Padmasambhava, the Guru principle, this transforming and transfiguring principle, hides away teachings, catalysts, inspirations, in places or dimensions where they can remain for hundreds or even thousands of years until they are needed, and then they'll be taken out. And those who take them out are the Tertöns, who are believed to be emanations of Padmasambhava himself.

This is the tradition. What does it mean? It means that even Padmasambhava can't do all the work. The Buddha proclaims the teaching in a general way, and Padmasambhava causes it to penetrate into the depths of the psyche, to transform the archetypes of the collective unconscious, but even he can't do it once and for all. Circumstances change, and new versions of the teachings need to be adapted to new circumstances. This is what the *termas* represent: the transforming principle adapted to specific circumstances in the here and now, inspirations which come to us for our guidance in accordance with the general principles of the teaching in both its visionary and its transforming aspects.

We can go further than that. Tarpa Nagpo is huge, many-sided, multidimensional. He doesn't just exist as an archetype in our collective unconscious; he's much more in evidence than that. He can be regarded as this world itself, certainly the world as we perceive and experience it. It's a self-centred world. That's the world we're up against. That's the world we have to grapple with. This chapter of *The Life and Liberation of Padmasambhava* says that the treasures are hidden away in caves and among stones, but what does that mean? They're hidden in the body of Tarpa Nagpo. There's one treasure hidden in his kidneys, another in his veins, another in his lungs, another in his foot. So what does this mean? Well, to express it in a few words, you find the remedy where you find the disease. If you understand the disease, you arrive at the remedy. If you plunge deeply into the body of Tarpa Nagpo, you can take out the treasure. You don't have to go outside the world to find the transcendental. You go very deeply into it. You utilize all its forces, all its energies, integrate them with yourself, and that is your spiritual life. You dig deep within the body of Tarpa Nagpo himself, this gigantic, festering, foul body, because that's where you'll find the treasure. And that's you, anyway.

Quite a few years ago, shortly after I started the FWBO, a friend was driving me through the City of London. I'd not been to the City since my return to England – I mean the City with a capital C, where the Stock Exchange is, and all the banks. As I looked from side to side at all these ponderous buildings, all connected with high finance, I said to my friend, 'This is what we're up against.' This is one of the demons:

this money, this form of power which has got out of the control of the spiritual principle. There are economic demons, sociological demons, political demons, even religious demons and philosophical demons, all of which need to be brought under control. We mustn't think of demons as just mythological. Don't imagine they're things you read about in fairy stories but could never meet. You're meeting demons of one kind and another all the time. You're living in a world of demons. You yourself are half demon. It's a good thing, provided you can subdue your demon half, or two-thirds, or nine-tenths or whatever it is, or your *ḍākinī* half. This is what we're up against and this is what we have to do. It's not simply that we're in the midst of demons. It's all a demon. The world is a demon. The god of the world is a demon. And that is Tarpa Nagpo.

So we've got these four great figures. We've got the Manu, the law-giver, the founder of the positive community. We've got the Buddha, the opener of the path to the transcendental, who proclaims the Dharma in a general, philosophical way. We've got the Guru, who brings it right down into the depths, who overcomes the forces of the archetypes of the collective unconscious and brings them into harmony with the Dharma, makes them subserve the purposes of the spiritual life. And we've got the Tertön, the person who digs deep into the body of Tarpa Nagpo and finds the exact remedy for the concrete situation within the situation itself. If we look at the figure of Padmasambhava within this wider framework, we can get a much better idea of what he really represents. He's the transforming principle which must follow in the wake of the illumining principle. If we take the Buddha as the personification of the path of vision, Padmasambhava is the personification of the path of transformation. This is why he's very much needed today, because we've got a lot to transform, not only within ourselves, but also outside ourselves. We have to transform ourselves and the world. Padmasambhava represents that powerful principle of transformation, which is even more powerful than what has to be transformed. He's the subduer of Rudra, Tarpa Nagpo, Black Salvation, and that's why we're celebrating Padmasambhava Day today.

It's also why we've got these emblems of Padmasambhava on the shrine. There's the lotus cap, surmounted by the *vajra*, which is surmounted by a vulture's feather, the vulture being the highest flying of all the birds. Sometimes it's an eagle's feather; many different explanations are given. And somewhere there should be a skull cup, and strictly speaking it should be filled with blood, or at least red wine, to represent the bliss you drink when you experience the voidness and you have renounced everything. That renunciation is bliss, and that bliss is drunk from the bowl of your renunciation. And then there's Padmasambhava's staff, with the same trident we see at the top of the Nālandā crest. According to some interpretations this symbolizes Buddha, Dharma, and Sangha, and according to others it symbolizes the three *kāyas*, the *dharmakāya*, *sambhogakāya*, and *nirmāṇakāya*. Then there are the three heads, which some say represent the three poisons and others say stand for the three *kāyas*. You've got the two *vajras*. Padmasambhava holds the staff in the crook of his arm, so it represents the subjugated *ḍākinī* principle, or even all the gods and demons and *ḍākinīs* which Padmasambhava has subjugated and which have been integrated into his being.

This celebration is primarily about the integration of all the basic primordial energies, which take so many negative forms in ourselves and in the world outside us, into our spiritual lives and into a more positive, more creative society, in fact the spiritual community ultimately. The London Buddhist Centre is ideally a centre of transformation, so that whatever comes in contact with this place starts being transformed. The place itself, and the people who belong to it, should be strong and powerful enough to transform whatever comes into contact with them. Let the demons come! Let all the gods and demons of the City of London and the West, and the whole world, come and be transformed. One shouldn't be afraid of the gods and demons, or of the *ḍākinīs*, even if they do ride upon buffaloes. Let them come! But let them be transformed, and let them contribute their energy to the spiritual life, not be alienated from the spiritual life so that there's a constant struggle between the two. To begin with we have an idea, a vision, of the spiritual life, and in the light of that vision we try to grow, but sooner or later we have to contact all the deeper, more primordial energies within ourselves and incorporate them into our spiritual quest. Only then will our spiritual life be rich and growing, not based upon tension and struggle. And we need to do much the same thing with the world. It's not that the world is bad, or evil, or wrong; it's simply that the world's energies, or the energies which are the world so-called, are misguided, and they've got to be guided in the right direction. Transformation of self, transformation of world, as we saw in those talks some time ago on the *Sūtra of Golden Light* – that's an aspect of the message of Padmasambhava.[229]

So today, as we celebrate Padmasambhava Day, let's try to realize that the spiritual life is essentially a process of the subjugation and integration and transfiguration of all the gross but powerful and potentially very rich energies of our own consciousness, the collective unconscious of humanity and of the world in general. Living a spiritual life means not running away from but facing these energies, these forces, these processes, subjugating them, transforming them, even dragging them along the path by the hair. But eventually you won't need to drag them, they'll willingly go along with you and melt into your being and reinforce your energies with theirs, because ultimately they are you and their energies are your energies. We have to think of ourselves as living in a world of scattered energies which we have to claim and collect and bring together and incorporate into the spiritual life, so that our individual spiritual lives and the collective spiritual life of the spiritual community can be reinforced. Our centres, our communities, and our co-ops are all ways of contacting different aspects of life and transforming them, because this is essentially what our movement is about. It's not simply a Buddhist movement in the narrow sense, or even a spiritual movement in the narrow sense. It's a stream of spiritual energy that deeply transforms and transfigures everything and everyone with which and with whom it comes into contact. Padmasambhava encountered gods, demons, and *ḍākinīs*, and transformed them, and this is what we must do, if we're strong enough. We should not flee from these energies but allow ourselves to be in contact with them within our own selves, transform them, and go forward along the path with renewed energy, strength, and inspiration. I hope that everybody who has participated in the celebration of Padmasambhava Day, listened to the readings of *The Life and Liberation of Padmasambhava*, taken part in the pujas and meditations, and seen the unveiling of our new Nālandā crest, will feel inspired to do this. We've got to transform everything with which we come into contact, especially everything with which we come into contact within our own selves. In this way we shall all go forward together and our spiritual movement will flourish more and more, involve more and more people and do more and more good to the whole world, or at least to that section of it with which we come into contact.

THE 1980S

BUDDHISM, WORLD PEACE, AND NUCLEAR WAR

1984

Gautama the Buddha gained Enlightenment at about the same time that Cyrus the Great captured the city of Babylon and founded the Persian Empire. Five years later the Buddha paid a visit to his home town, Kapilavastu, just inside the modern state boundary of Nepal. It was fortunate that he did so. A dispute had arisen between the Śākyans of Kapilavastu and their neighbours the Koliyans of Devadaha, to whom the Buddha was related through his mother, and as a result of this, war was about to break out between the two peoples. The original cause of the dispute was comparatively trivial. Both the Śākyans and the Koliyans were accustomed to irrigate their fields with water from the River Rohiṇī, which flowed between their respective territories, but that year it was obvious that there would not be enough water for them both. The Koliyans proposed that they should have the water, on the grounds that their crops would ripen with a single watering, but the Śākyans flatly rejected this proposal, saying that they would have no mind to beg food from the Koliyans later on in the year and that in any case their crops too would ripen with a single watering. Neither side would give way, the dispute became very bitter, and eventually blows were exchanged. To make matters worse, the Koliyans started casting aspersions on the origins of the leading Śākya families, saying that they had cohabited with their own sisters like dogs and jackals, while the Śākyans cast aspersions on the leading Koliya families, saying that they were destitute outcastes who lived in the hollows of trees like animals. Reports of these aspersions soon reached the ears of the leading families themselves, who immediately came forth armed for battle, the Śākya warriors shouting, 'We will show the strength of those who have cohabited with their sisters!' and the Koliya warriors shouting, 'We will show the strength of those who live in the hollows of trees!'

Thus it was that, one fine morning, the Buddha came to know that war was about to break out between his paternal and maternal relations. Realizing that unless he intervened they would destroy each other, he at once went to the place where the two armies were gathered. As soon as they saw him his kinsmen on both sides threw away their weapons and respectfully saluted him. When the Buddha asked them what the quarrel was all about, however, they were unable to tell him. Eventually, after cross-examining various people, the Buddha succeeded in establishing that the cause of the quarrel was water. Having established this, he asked, 'How much is water worth?' 'Very little, Reverend Sir.' 'How much are warriors worth?' 'Warriors are beyond price, Reverend Sir.' 'Then,' said the Buddha, 'it is not fitting that because of a little water you should destroy warriors who are beyond price.' And they were silent.[230]

Some features of this incident are only too sickeningly familiar to us today. They are in fact characteristic of disputes and wars from the Stone Age down to modern times. There is the same clash of vital interests between different groups of people, the same unwillingness to compromise, the same dreadful escalation from harsh words to isolated acts of violence, and from isolated acts of violence to preparations for full-scale war. There is the same fatal spirit of belligerence, the same readiness on the part of large numbers of people to fight without really knowing what they are fighting for. There is even, we note, the same irrelevant mutual vilification, suggestive of antipathies that have long lurked beneath the surface and now have an opportunity of breaking out. But there is also – and this is more encouraging – the same solitary voice of sanity and compassion that, if only we listen carefully enough, we can hear even today. There is the same appeal to reason, the same reminder of what is truly most valuable, that has been heard if not from the Stone Age then at least from the Axial Age, and heard, perhaps, with increasing frequency, regardless of whether people listened or not.

But although there are similarities between the Rohiṇī incident and the situation in which we find ourselves today, there are differences too. The quarrel between the Śākyans and the Koliyans involved the inhabitants of two small city states living side by side at the foot of the Himalayas, whereas the quarrel between the superpowers of the twentieth century involves hundreds of millions of people occupying continents separated by vast oceans and affects the whole world, directly or indirectly. Like the heroes of Ancient Greece, the Śākyans and the Koliyans were armed with swords and spears and bows and arrows, and they fought either on foot or from horse-drawn chariots. The superpowers are armed with a variety of nuclear weapons, capable of destroying life on a scale unprecedented in history and unimaginable before the present century. The Śākyans and Koliyans could actually see each other across the waters of the River Rohiṇī. They spoke the same language and worshipped the same gods, and it was possible for one man to make himself heard by the warriors on both sides. Now it is possible for hundreds of millions of people to quarrel without actually seeing one another, and even to prepare to destroy one another without knowing, humanly speaking, who it is they are preparing to destroy. They speak the same language neither literally nor metaphorically, they certainly do not worship the same gods, and despite our marvellously improved facilities of communication it is not really possible for one man to make himself heard by them all. Indeed, these marvellously improved facilities of communication are used only too often either for the exchange of insults or for the reiteration of positions known to be unacceptable to the other side. Thus facilities of communication are used for purposes of non-communication.

Highly significant as these differences are, there is one difference between the Rohiṇī incident and the situation in which we find ourselves today that is more significant than any of the others. Had war actually broken out between the Śākyans and the Koliyans, there would have been the possibility of one side winning. No such possibility exists in the case of nuclear war between the superpowers. Even limited nuclear war would be so destructive of human life, and do so much damage to civilization and to the earth itself, that neither side could be victorious in any meaningful sense of the term. Limited nuclear war must therefore be regarded as an absolutely unacceptable option. Full-scale nuclear war is even more unacceptable, if that is possible. Full-scale nuclear war is a prospect so frightful that no one with the slightest imagination can even contemplate it without an effort of will. All the deepest instincts of humanity recoil from it in utter horror. Full-scale nuclear war means nuclear holocaust, with hundreds of cities reduced to rubble, hundreds of millions of people burned or blasted out of existence, and millions more doomed to an agonizing death from the short-term or long-term effects of nuclear radiation. Full-scale nuclear war means firestorms and 'black rain'. It means the destruction of the ecosphere. It means the death of the earth. It means the suicide of humanity.

Nuclear wars are fought with nuclear weapons. If even limited nuclear war is unacceptable it follows that nuclear weapons are unacceptable too, and they must be abolished. They would still have to be abolished even if there was at present no intention on the part of the superpowers and others who have produced them ever to make use of their dreadful destructive capacity. So long as nuclear weapons exist in the world there will always be the risk of accidental nuclear attack due to mechanical failure or human error – not to mention sudden insanity in one or other of the seats of power – and so long as there is the risk of accidental nuclear attack there will be the risk of full-scale nuclear war. We are thus obliged to regard the very existence of nuclear weapons as being tantamount, in the long term at least, to the actual use of those weapons. Control of nuclear weapons is therefore not enough. There is no way of ensuring that nuclear weapons are not used, and that a nuclear holocaust does not take place, other than by making sure that nuclear weapons no longer exist. So long as the superpowers and the small powers have their stockpiles of nuclear weapons, prevention of nuclear war is no more than a pleasant dream. Indeed, it is a dangerous dream, since it tends to make us oblivious to the very real threat to humanity that the mere existence of such stockpiles represents. There is no one in the world, perhaps, who does not want peace (what peace really is I shall try to explain later on), but it is important to realize that even in the very limited sense of the absence of nuclear conflict, peace is impossible without the total abolition of nuclear weapons. Working for peace therefore involves working for the abolition of nuclear weapons, and working for the abolition of nuclear weapons involves working for peace.

Peace of course means world peace. Even if the Rohiṇī incident had led to war, and Śākyans and Koliyans had been killed by the thousand, hostilities would have remained confined to that particular stretch of the Terai. For thousands of years it was possible for some parts of the world to suffer all the horrors of what we now term 'conventional war' while others remained profoundly at peace. It is highly unlikely that anyone in Magadha knew that Cyrus the Great had captured Babylon until many years after the event, and equally unlikely that anyone in the Persian Empire knew that King Ajātaśatru had, shortly after the demise of the Buddha, defeated the Vajjī confederacy until long after that unscrupulous monarch had achieved his purpose. Even during the First and Second World Wars there were countries that were not affected to any serious extent by the events that were convulsing the rest of the globe. On the contrary, in some cases they even profited from them. But peace is no longer divisible in this kind of way. Peace has become a seamless garment, and the world has to wear the whole garment or go naked to destruction. There can no longer be any question of a scrap of peace covering one part of the world's nakedness and not another.

This makes it impossible for us to think in merely geopolitical terms. We have also to think in geo-ethical, geo-humanitarian, and geo-philanthropic terms. Since peace is indivisible, the stark choice before us is either world peace or no peace, one world or no world. We shall be able to achieve peace only if we realize that humanity too is indivisible, and if we consistently act on that realization. In other words, we shall be able to achieve peace only by regarding ourselves as citizens of the world, and learning to think not in terms of what is good for this or that nation state, this or that political system, this or that ideology, but simply and solely in terms of what is good for the world, or for humanity, as a whole. There can be no world peace so long as the governments of sovereign nation states insist on regarding their separate, sometimes mutually exclusive, interests as paramount and to be pursued at all costs. Nationalism is the curse of modern history. It is nationalism that was responsible for the rise of sovereign nation states, and it is sovereign nation states that produced nuclear weapons in the first place, that produce and possess them now, and that have the power to unleash their destructive capacity upon mankind. Peace and nationalism are therefore incompatible. Nationalism is not, of course, the same thing as patriotism. Nationalism is an exaggerated, passionate, and fanatical devotion to one's national community at the expense of all other national communities and all other interests and loyalties. It is a pseudo-religion, an idolatrous cult that demands bloody sacrifices. Patriotism, on the other hand, is simply love of one's country, in the sense of an attachment to, and a desire to care for and protect, the place where one was born and grew up, and it does not exclude smaller or larger interests and loyalties, or honest pride in such things as one's own history and culture. Thus patriotism, unlike nationalism, is not incompatible with peace, even though peace goes beyond patriotism, which, in the famous words of Edith Cavell, is 'not enough'.[231] This does not mean that in order to achieve peace we have to stop loving our own village or city, our own province, our own country, or our own continent, but rather that we have to love them because they are all part of the world and because we love the world. It means that we have to identify ourselves with humanity, rather than with any particular section of it, and love humanity as ourselves. We have to feel for the different national communities, and the different ethnic and linguistic groups, the same kind of love that we feel for the different limbs of our own bodies.

Of this kind of love the Buddha, as he stands between the opposing Śākya and Koliya forces, is the supreme exemplar. The Buddha identified himself with both the Śākyans and the Koliyans, so he could love them both. After all, even apart from the fact that he had attained Enlightenment and thus identified himself with all living things not in any abstract, metaphysical sense, but in the sense of experiencing the joys and sorrows of others as his own, he was related by blood to both parties in the dispute. Through his father he was related to the Śākyans, and through his mother to the Koliyans. Among the warriors on both sides he had uncles, cousins, and nephews, besides old friends and childhood companions. Thus the Buddha's position was similar to our own. We too stand between opposing forces, though the forces with which we have to deal are as much superior to those of the Śākyans and Koliyans as the Buddha's sanity and compassion are superior to ours. Moreover, in our case we do not stand unambiguously between these forces but only too often identify ourselves with one or the other of them and are perceived so to identify ourselves. If peace is to be achieved, however, we have to identify ourselves with both parties, just as the Buddha identified himself with both the Śākyans and the Koliyans. Though we may not be related to them by blood in the way that the Buddha was related to his embattled paternal and maternal relatives, nevertheless we are related to them, inasmuch as we all belong to the same organic species, *Homo sapiens*, and it should not be necessary for us to attain Enlightenment in order to realize this fact. If we identify ourselves with both parties and with humanity in this manner, then we shall be able to stand cleanly and unambiguously between the 'fell incensèd points of mighty opposites' of our day.[232] We shall be able to speak as the Buddha spoke, because we shall love as the Buddha loved. We shall be a voice of sanity and compassion in the world. We shall be able to appeal to reason. We shall be able to remind humanity, in its own name, what things are of greater value and what of less. We may even be able to remind it what is the most valuable thing of all.

Between the Rohiṇī incident and the situation in which we find ourselves today there are, as I have pointed out, both similarities and differences. Some of those differences are very great, even if only in terms of scale. Though the implications of the incident are of universal significance, and although that significance has already emerged to a limited degree, it will have to be explored much more deeply if we are to appreciate the full extent of its applicability to the issue of world peace and nuclear war. In exploring the significance of the Rohiṇī incident in this way we shall naturally have to go beyond the immediate context of the incident itself. We shall even have to go beyond the issue of world peace and nuclear war, though not beyond Buddhism, and at least touch upon closely related issues of even greater consequence to every individual human being and, in fact, to humanity as a whole. We shall have to touch upon issues on account of which the issue of world peace and nuclear war itself is of such overwhelming importance. In other words, we shall have to touch upon questions of ultimate significance for all of us.

What I have already said on the subject of Buddhism, world peace, and nuclear war, as well as what I am going to say, all rests on a single assumption. Some people would regard it as a very big assumption indeed, but I nevertheless hope it is one you share with me, since otherwise it will be difficult for us to explore together the significance of the Rohiṇī incident in the way that I have proposed. Indeed, it might even be useless for us to do so. This assumption is that nuclear holocaust is not inevitable, that nuclear weapons can be abolished and world peace, in the sense of the absence of nuclear conflict, achieved. If that was not my assumption I would not be wasting my time and yours by talking to you this evening. Admittedly the risk of nuclear war is very great and world peace is very difficult to achieve. But as we contemplate the increasing possibility of nuclear holocaust we should not allow the sheer horror of the prospect to reduce us to inaction, like frightened rabbits mesmerized into immobility by the headlights of an approaching car. Neither should we allow ourselves to be seduced by the siren voices of fanaticism, fundamentalism, and fatalism as they seek to assure us that nuclear holocaust is the prophesied Armageddon and that instead of trying to avert it we should welcome it as the righteous judgement of an angry God on sinful humanity. Whatever other religions may teach, Buddhism, like secular humanism, teaches that ills created by human beings – and many not created by human beings – can be remedied by human beings. This does not mean that Buddhists underestimate the difficulties involved, least of all those that stand in the way of the achievement of world peace through the abolition of nuclear weapons, and it certainly does not mean that Buddhists subscribe to the shallow optimism of which some forms of secular humanism have been guilty.

But let's return to the figure of the Buddha, as he stands between the opposing Śākya and Koliya forces, and begin our deeper exploration of the significance of that sublime incident as it applies to the situation in which we find ourselves today. One of the things that strikes us as we look at the pro-peace, anti-nuclear movement is that it is not a strong and unified body of opinion speaking with one voice about what has to be achieved and how it can be achieved. It is not a movement at all, but a motley collection of forces eddying more or less confusedly about matters of growing popular concern. Some of these forces even seem to be moving in contrary directions, as we can see in the case of the debate as to whether nuclear disarmament should be unilateral or multilateral. All such differences are, of course, differences about means rather than ends. The solitary figure, the solitary voice, of the Buddha serves to remind us that if we are to speak to the opposing forces of our own day with any effect, we will have to speak to them as one person. We will have to speak with one voice: we will all have to say the same thing. At present our energies are divided. Time that should be spent impressing upon the authorities that what we desire above all things is the total abolition of nuclear weapons is spent arguing with one another about the exact way in which they should be abolished, thus letting the authorities off the hook. The authorities in question are, of course, the governments of the various sovereign nation states that possess, or are about to possess, nuclear weapons, including the government of this country. The way in which nuclear weapons are abolished is a matter of secondary importance, and one that can be finally settled only at international level, when the governments of nuclear and non-nuclear powers alike meet together and, in response to the irresistible pressure of world opinion, apply such wisdom as they collectively possess to the question of how best to lift the shadow of nuclear weapons and nuclear war from humanity. Until then we must keep up the pressure on our own government and on the governments of other countries to whatever extent we can. Such pressure should be massive, unanimous, and unmistakable, and we should keep it up until we see governments in general, and the governments of the nuclear powers in particular, making the total abolition of nuclear weapons their top priority. We should keep it up until we see the nuclear stockpiles dwindling. We should keep it up until the abomination of nuclear weapons disappears from the face of the earth, and we can breathe freely once again.

There are a number of ways in which we can bring pressure on a government to take steps towards the abolition of nuclear weapons, but which ones we adopt will depend on the kind of government with which we are dealing, as well as on the political and cultural history of the country concerned, and even on the psychological make-up of its people. Where parliamentary democracy prevails and governments are elected by popular vote, it will be possible to bring pressure to bear simply by refusing to vote for any party, or any candidate, not unambiguously committed to working for the total abolition of nuclear weapons. Pressure can also be brought to bear by the persistent lobbying of members of parliament, by the presentation of petitions, by public meetings, marches, and demonstrations, by fasts and solemn vigils – even by 'love-ins' and 'be-ins'. By these and similar means the government should be left in no doubt as to what the wishes of the electorate really are. If it remains unresponsive to those wishes, or not sufficiently responsive – and the situation is one of extreme urgency, where every day is precious – then more serious measures should be taken and pressure brought to bear on the government by means of mass civil disobedience along Gandhian lines.

About one thing, however, we must be quite clear. In whatever way pressure is brought on a government to make the abolition of nuclear weapons its top priority, that pressure must be brought non-violently. Violence of any kind would be totally out of place on a march, or at a demonstration, or in connection with any other expression of public opinion the purpose of which was ultimately the achievement of world peace. The dove is not a bird of prey, and should what purports to be a dove be seen with bleeding flesh in its beak and claws one would rightly suspect that it was not a dove at all but belonged to some more ferocious species. We should also avoid wasting time and energy on empty gestures whose only purpose is to give expression to purely personal feelings of resentment and frustration – feelings which have, more often than not, no real connection with the issue with which we are supposedly concerned. Similarly, we should resist any temptation to use pro-peace, anti-nuclear activities for the furtherance of any sectional interests, however important to us personally those interests may be, and regardless of whether they are of a social, a party political, or an ideological nature. There must be no attempt to hijack the peace express. The abolition of nuclear weapons is of such transcendent importance for the future of humanity that whether the pressure we are able to bring on governments is great or small, we cannot allow it to be weakened by any doubts as to the true nature of the interests on behalf of which it is being exerted. To weaken it in this way would be in the highest degree irresponsible, and a betrayal of the trust of mankind.

Keeping up the pressure on governments until nuclear weapons are abolished is not the only thing that must be done, though it is probably the most crucial thing. Indeed, it is not only on governments that pressure must be brought to bear. We also need to bring it to bear on our fellow world citizens, and in particular on other members of our own national community. Here too pressure can be brought to bear in a number of ways, mainly by disseminating information about the danger of full-scale nuclear war and by helping people to develop a more positive attitude towards other national communities – especially if they too happen to possess nuclear weapons. Information about the danger of nuclear war, and about what the consequences of nuclear war would be for civilization, for the human race, and for life on this planet, should be disseminated as widely as possible and by whatever means. Such information is now readily available. It can be disseminated by means of the written or spoken word, as well as audio-visually. More specifically, we can write books and articles, make speeches, show films, hand out leaflets, put up posters, and buttonhole friends, acquaintances, and perfect strangers in pubs and at parties, on buses and trains, at our places of work, and even in the street. Those of us who have access to press, radio, and television are particularly well placed to disseminate information and have a special responsibility to do so. People can be helped to develop a more positive attitude towards other national communities by being encouraged to learn more about them. Knowledge will lead to understanding, understanding to sympathy, and sympathy to love. To be more specific, we can encourage people to study the history and culture of other countries, to read translations of their literature, and to learn their language. We can encourage them to visit those countries for business or pleasure, or for the sake of cultural exchange, and to develop personal friendships with as many of their nationals as circumstances permit. Above all, perhaps, we can teach people to practise the *mettā bhāvanā*, the development of universal friendliness, a traditional Buddhist method of developing an increasingly positive attitude towards all other living beings, including those with whom ordinarily we do not get on very well, or whom we may dislike or even hate. It is one of the fundamental postulates of Buddhism that the individual is responsible for their own mental and emotional states. This means that we can change those states – provided we really want to do so and know the right way to go about it. If people were to take up the practice of the *mettā bhāvanā* in sufficiently large numbers it could result in the development of a more positive attitude towards other national communities not only on the part of private citizens but on the part of governments too, and this would undoubtedly contribute to the reduction of international tension and thereby to the eventual abolition of nuclear weapons. Those of us who are Buddhists should perhaps give serious consideration to the possibility of teaching the *mettā bhāvanā* on a nationwide scale.

In bringing pressure to bear on governments and on our fellow world citizens we should not, of course, forget to bring pressure to bear on our own selves. We can hardly expect others to disseminate information about the danger of nuclear weapons or develop a more positive attitude towards other national communities unless we ourselves are prepared to do likewise. Those who take any sort of initiative, or give any sort of lead, should in fact be prepared to do more than they ask others to do. It is not enough simply to take the initiative, or give a lead. One must also set an example (setting an example indeed is the best way of taking the initiative, or of giving a lead), and in the present instance the example that is set has to be a very lofty one. It has to be an example of impartiality and detachment, an example of love for humanity as a whole, an example of genuine devotion to the achievement of world peace by non-violent means. It has to be an example of a sanity and compassion which, though it may fall far short of the sanity and compassion of Enlightenment, is yet more nearly commensurate to the strength of the opposing forces between which we stand, and with which we have to deal, than is at present the case.

This brings us back to the figure of the Buddha, and to another turning in our deeper exploration of the significance of the Rohiṇī incident in relation to the situation in which we find ourselves today. Besides the fact that it does not speak with one voice, what strikes me about the pro-peace, anti-nuclear movement is that its many different voices do not always speak the same language. When the Buddha asked the Śākya and Koliya warriors to tell him what the quarrel was all about, they could understand the meaning of his question, and were eventually able to give him a reply. He in turn could understand their reply, and when he went on to ask them how much water was worth and how much warriors were worth they knew exactly what he was talking about and could reply accordingly. Similarly, they knew exactly what he was talking about when he told them it was not fitting that because of a little water they should destroy warriors who were beyond price. There was no problem of communication, as we call it nowadays. The Śākyans and the Koliyans, and the Buddha himself, all spoke the same language, both literally and metaphorically. When the Buddha wanted to know what the quarrel was about, neither the Śākya nor the Koliya warriors denied that they were quarrelling. Neither protested that *they* had simply staged a peaceful demonstration on which the warriors on the other side had proceeded to launch a vicious and entirely unprovoked attack. In the same way, neither the Śākya nor the Koliya warriors attempted to argue that 'water' could mean 'earth' or that in the case of the warriors on the other side 'beyond price' really meant 'worthless', or that there was in any case no question of destroying warriors but only of *eliminating* them. Thus the Rohiṇī incident could be dealt with much more easily than the situation in which we find ourselves today, when the superpowers, unlike the Śākyans and Koliyans, do not speak the same language either literally or metaphorically and when, therefore, there is a problem of communication. In extreme cases, one superpower will even insist that the other superpower is saying no to a proposal when that superpower no less emphatically insists that it is saying yes. Such mutual miscomprehension would be laughable if it were not so tragic, and it is tragic because miscomprehension as chronic as this between superpowers armed with nuclear weapons could well cost us our lives.

Since they do not speak the same 'language' it is difficult for us to speak to the opposing forces of our day in the way that the Buddha spoke to the Śākyans and Koliyans at the time of the Rohiṇī incident. It is even difficult for all those who are involved in the pro-peace, anti-nuclear movement to speak with one another, since what for one is 'pro-peace' and 'anti-nuclear' for another may be 'anti-peace' and 'pro-nuclear'. There is no agreement even about basic terms and therefore no real unity and of course no really united voice. Thus there is a serious problem of communication, not only between the superpowers, and between the sovereign nation states both large and small, nuclear and non-nuclear, but also within the peace movement itself, as well as between the superpowers and other sovereign nation states on the one hand and the peace movement on the other. There is also, of course, a problem of communication between the different races and religions of humanity, and sometimes this problem adds to, and complicates, that of communication between the superpowers. So chronic, indeed, has this problem of communication between the superpowers become that one is now faced by an actual failure of communication (in the sense in which one speaks of a failure of electricity) between large and important sections of the human race, and unless this failure can be overcome and communication restored – unless humanity, especially the superpowers, can learn to speak a genuinely common language – world peace will be very difficult to achieve and nuclear war very difficult to avoid.

We shall be able to overcome this failure of communication, however, only if we can understand on what it is really based. There is a lot that could be said on this topic, as well as on the topic of communication in general, but let us go straight to the heart of the matter without wasting time either on the commonplaces of the encounter group or the subtleties of the communications theory seminar. The failure of communication which is so striking a feature of our times is ultimately based on a breakdown of the notion of objective truth, that is to say, on a breakdown of the notion that truth is truth regardless of our subjective feelings about it and the way in which it affects our personal interests. That people do not in practice exhibit total loyalty to the notion of objective truth, even though they may uphold it in theory, is of course well known and widely accepted. Indeed, in the ordinary transactions of life due allowance is generally made for this fact. We no more expect the used car dealer or the estate agent to dwell on the less favourable features of the car or the house he is trying to sell us than we expect him to tell us a deliberate, downright lie. But even if people do not in practice exhibit total loyalty to the notion of objective truth, it is important that such loyalty as they do display to it is not allowed to fall below a certain point, since otherwise the transactions of ordinary life will become impossible.

Unfortunately, it often does fall below that point. Loyalty to the notion of objective truth becomes *selective*. Actual lies may not be told, but those facts that are not in accordance with the feelings and interests of this or that individual or group are increasingly ignored, misrepresented, distorted, and suppressed. In extreme cases such facts are not acknowledged ever to have existed at all. From the stage where loyalty to the notion of objective truth becomes selective – that is to say, becomes that which is in accordance with certain personal or sectional interests – it is not a very big step to the stage where that which is in accordance with those interests becomes the truth. At this stage, there is a breakdown of the notion of objective truth. 'Truth' is whatever happens to be in accordance with the interests of a particular class, sovereign nation state, or ideology. Since there are many classes, sovereign nation states, and ideologies, and therefore many different, even conflicting, interests, there will be not one truth but many truths. Thus there is not only a breakdown of the notion of objective truth but also a substitution of the notion of objective truth by the notion of subjective truth. Subjective truth in effect becomes, for a particular group, objective truth, and since there can be only one objective truth the objective truth of all other groups – including what might be termed objectively objective truth – necessarily becomes untruth. Under these circumstances, communication is impossible. Words no longer have the same meaning for everybody, and what one group regards as facts another regards as non-facts. There is a failure of communication. Indeed, those whose views and attitudes are not in accordance with the interests of a particular group are treated as non-individuals in the same way that facts that are not in accordance with these same interests are regarded as non-facts. Such an individual is not so much wrong as, in theory, non-existent, and since he is non-existent in theory it is only natural that he should very quickly become non-existent in practice too. Thus we arrive at a state of affairs such as is characteristic of the nightmare totalitarian world of George Orwell's *Nineteen Eighty-Four*, where the three slogans of the Party are 'War is Peace,' 'Freedom is Slavery,' and 'Ignorance is Strength', where Newspeak is fast replacing Oldspeak, where history is being continually rewritten, and where a word from Big Brother can turn a person into an unperson overnight.[233]

Fortunately, the 1984 which has come to pass is not wholly that of Orwell's grim foreboding. The nightmare has not yet come true to more than a limited extent. Nevertheless, the situation in which we find ourselves today is sufficiently alarming, and one of its most dangerous features is that we are faced by a failure of communication between large and important sections of the human race, particularly between the superpowers. As I have tried to show, this failure is based, ultimately, on a breakdown of the notion of objective truth, so that if communication is to be restored, and if the superpowers are to learn to speak the same 'language', the notion of objective truth will have to be reinstated to its former central position in human affairs. Only then will we be able to speak to the opposing forces of our day as the Buddha spoke to the Śākyans and Koliyans, because only then will it be possible for us really to communicate with them. Only then will it be possible to ascertain the facts of the situation. Only then will it be possible for the voice of sanity and compassion to make itself heard at last. Only then will it be possible to appeal to reason. Only then will it be possible to come to an agreement as to what things are of greater value and what of less. Only then will it be possible to achieve peace and avoid nuclear war by the total abolition of nuclear weapons. Until the notion of objective truth has been reinstated in its rightful position all our attempts to communicate, whether with one another or with the superpowers, are doomed to end in frustration. Though people may visit foreign countries by the score, and develop personal friendships with the nationals of those countries by the thousand, in the absence of a common reverence for the notion of objective truth all this will be of little avail. The reinstatement of the notion of objective truth to its rightful position therefore ranks as one of our most urgent tasks. To work for the reinstatement of the notion of objective truth is, in the long run, to work for the achievement of world peace, for it is one of the most important conditions upon which the achievement of world peace depends.

But even if world peace in the limited sense of the abolition of nuclear weapons is actually achieved, and the shadow of nuclear war is lifted, this will not mean that we have solved all our problems. If I have so far spoken of the achievement of world peace and the abolition of nuclear weapons as though the two things were practically synonymous this was only because the avoidance of nuclear war is our most immediate and pressing concern. Though there can be no world peace without the abolition of nuclear weapons, the abolition of nuclear weapons is far from being synonymous with world peace in the full sense of the term. Nuclear weapons are not the only weapons in the arsenals of the sovereign nation states. There are many others, some of them hardly less horrible than nuclear weapons themselves, and even if nuclear war ceases to be a possibility these could still do irreparable damage to civilization and inflict untold suffering on humanity. If peace in the full sense of the term is to be achieved we shall therefore have to work not only for the abolition of nuclear weapons but also for the abolition of conventional weapons. We do not want to abolish nuclear weapons only to find ourselves in the same kind of situation that we are in today, minus nuclear weapons. Neither do we want to abolish them only to find ourselves in the same kind of situation that we were in yesterday, or even the day before yesterday. Though it will undoubtedly be a tremendous blessing and an infinite relief, the abolition of nuclear weapons is by no means enough. Even the abolition of both nuclear and non-nuclear weapons is by no means enough. Peace in the full sense of the term will be achieved only when disputes between sovereign nation states, as well as between smaller groups and between individuals, are settled entirely by non-violent means.

In order to achieve world peace in this fuller sense we shall have to deepen our realization of the indivisibility of humanity, and act on that realization with even greater consistency. We shall have to regard ourselves as citizens of the world in a more concrete sense than before, and rid ourselves of even the faintest vestige of nationalism. We shall have to identify ourselves more closely with all living things, and love them with a more ardent and selfless love. We shall have to be a louder and clearer voice of sanity and compassion in the world. We shall also have to bring to bear on the governments and peoples of the world, and on ourselves, the same kind of pressure that was required for the abolition of nuclear weapons but to an even greater extent. Above all, we shall have to intensify our commitment to the great ethical and spiritual principle of non-violence, both in respect to relations between individuals and in respect to relations between groups. Ever since the dawn of history – perhaps from the very beginning of the present cosmic cycle – two great principles have been at work in the world: the principle of violence and the principle of non-violence or, as we may also call it, the principle of love – though love in the sense of *agape* rather than in the sense of *eros*. The principle of violence finds expression in force and fraud, as well as in such things as oppression, exploitation, intimidation, and blackmail. The principle of non-violence finds expression in friendliness and openness, as well as in such things as gentleness and helpfulness, and the giving of encouragement, sympathy, and appreciation. The principle of violence is reactive, and ultimately destructive; the principle of non-violence is creative. The principle of violence is a principle of Darkness, the principle of non-violence a principle of Light. Whereas to live in accordance with the principle of violence is to be either an animal or a devil or a combination of the two, to live in accordance with the principle of non-violence is to be a human being in the full sense of the term, or even an angel. So far, of course, human beings have lived in accordance with the principle of violence rather than in accordance with the principle of non-violence. We could do this because it was possible for us to live in accordance with the principle of violence without destroying ourselves completely. But this is no longer the case. Owing to the emergence of superpowers armed with nuclear weapons it is now virtually impossible for us to live in accordance with the principle of violence without sooner or later annihilating ourselves. We are faced with the necessity of either learning to live in accordance with the principle of non-violence or not living at all. The possibility of nuclear holocaust has enabled us to realize the true nature of violence by showing us what the consequences of violence on the biggest conceivable scale would be, and it has also given us a much deeper appreciation of the real value of non-violence.

It is because of this deeper appreciation of the real value of non-violence that we are able to realize what peace in the full sense of the term would really mean, as well as how the problem of its achievement is to be solved. World peace is something we can hardly imagine today.

We can hardly imagine a state of affairs in which disputes between groups and between individuals are settled entirely by non-violent means because all of us are committed to the principle of non-violence and live in accordance with its precepts. A world in which the principle of Light had overcome the principle of Darkness to so great an extent would be a world that surpassed More's Utopia, Bacon's New Atlantis, Campanella's City of the Sun, and Morris's Nowhere as much as these dreams of an ideal world surpassed the real worlds of their respective days.[234] Such a world would be a heaven on earth. It would be a world of the gods.

But even the gods have their problems. Even if we achieved world peace in the full sense of the term we still would not have solved all our problems by any means. One problem that the gods have to face is the problem of leisure, the problem of what to do with their time, and although we have less leisure than the gods this is the kind of problem that faces us too. Indeed, it faces us in the still more acute form of what we are to do with our lives. It would be a thousand pities if, having achieved world peace in the full sense of the term, we were to make no better use of our time, or of our lives, than many of us do at present. In Tennyson's 'The Lotos-Eaters' the gods of Homeric Greece are imagined as lying beside their nectar and looking over lands wasted by plague, famine, earthquake, and war, and on a human race subject to the painful necessity of wringing a laborious subsistence from the cultivation of the soil.[235] It would be a thousand pities if when we had solved the problem of world peace, the gods were to look down on a world that in many respects resembled theirs only to see us playing bingo or watching third-rate television programmes. Idealists or cynics might even be tempted to wonder whether it was really worthwhile delivering humanity from the horrors of nuclear war only that it might fall victim to trivial interests and worthless pursuits. Even if we succeed in solving the problem of peace in the full sense of the term we shall still be faced – as we are now faced – with the even greater problem of what to do with our lives.

But even if that problem too had been solved and we were living in a manner that was truly worthy of a human being, there would still be one problem that we had not solved. It would not be strange that we had not solved it, for it is a problem that the gods themselves, despite their nectar, are unable to solve. Indeed, it is a problem that no form of sentient conditioned existence is able to solve so long as it remains merely conditioned. As we know from Tibetan Buddhist scroll-paintings of the wheel of life, there are six main forms of conditioned existence, or six main classes of sentient beings: gods, anti-gods, men, animals, hungry ghosts, and beings in states of torment. These six classes occupy the six 'worlds' or 'spheres' depicted as occupying the six segments into which the third and widest circle of the wheel of life is divided. The innermost circle is depicted as being occupied by a cock, a snake, and a pig, symbolizing greed, aversion, and delusion: the three unskilful mental states that keep the wheel of life turning. The second circle is divided into two segments, one representing the path of light, the other the path of darkness, and the outermost circle is divided into twelve segments representing the twelve 'links' that make up the entire process in accordance with which one passes from one form of sentient conditioned existence to another. All four circles, and thus the wheel of life in its entirety, are supported from behind by a dreadful monster, whose four sets of claws are seen curving round the edge of the wheel, while his scaly reptilian tail protrudes below and his bared fangs project over the top of the wheel beneath fiercely glaring eyeballs and locks crowned with skulls. This dreadful monster is the demon of Impermanence, the demon of Death, who holds in his inexorable grasp not only the six worlds but the whole of conditioned existence, from the electron spinning about its nucleus to the extragalactic nebulae receding from us at an unimaginable rate. He holds in his grasp the highest as well as the lowest heavens, the least evolved as well as the most highly evolved forms of earthly life, from the amoeba to *Homo sapiens*. Even if we succeed in abolishing nuclear weapons, even if we achieve world peace in the full sense of the term, even if we live in a way that is meaningful and purposeful, we shall still have to face the problem of death. Whether we live in a hell or in a heaven on earth, we shall still see the demon of Impermanence, the demon of Death, glaring down at us over the edge of the wheel.

More than that. The demon of Death glares at us not only individually but collectively. He glares not only at you and at me but at the whole world, the whole earth. Whether or not nuclear war is averted, we shall still have to die, each one of us. The human race will still have to go the way of the dinosaurs. Civilization will still have to collapse. The earth itself will still have to come to an end, even if after thousands of millions of years. Indeed, the very solar system to which the earth belongs will come to an end, as will the galaxy of which that solar system forms part. All conditioned things are impermanent. Whatever comes into existence must one day cease to exist. Thus the solution of the problem of world peace and nuclear war does not really solve anything at all. We still have to face the problem of death. Even though the Buddha was able to prevent the Śākyans and Koliyans from destroying each other on that morning twenty-five centuries ago, he could not save them from death itself. In the case of the Śākyans, he could not even save them from an untimely death at the hands of their enemies. So thoroughly had his paternal relations been converted to the principle of non-violence that when, some years later, they were attacked by the King of Kosala, they decided to offer no resistance and were massacred to a man – thus giving us, for the first time in history, an example of personal – as distinct from political – pacifism.[236] It was not fitting, they declared, that the relations of the Enlightened One should commit the sin of taking life.

Not only could the Buddha not save the Śākyans and Koliyans from death, he could not save himself from death. Truth to tell, he did not wish to do so, or even to prolong his earthly existence to the extent that, according to tradition, he could have prolonged it had he been requested to do so. Forty years after the Rohiṇī incident, therefore, when the Śākyans themselves were dead and when the ashes of his two chief disciples, Śāriputra and Maudgalyāyana, lay beneath their memorial mounds, the Buddha came to the little wattle-and-daub township of Kusinārā and lay down between the two *sāl* trees in the *sāl* grove of the Mallās to die or, in traditional Buddhist phrase, to enter into *parinirvāṇa*, a state as much beyond non-existence as it is beyond what we call existence. And having lain down between the twin *sāl* trees, with his head to the north and his feet to the south, he did, at the age of 80, die. No miracle intervened to save him. Having traversed all eight *dhyānas* or meditations his consciousness came down to the first *dhyāna*; having come down to the first *dhyāna* it traversed the first four *dhyānas* a second time and then, as it passed from the fourth *dhyāna* and entered *parinirvāṇa*, the Buddha died. His body was cremated, and the ashes placed beneath a memorial mound. The Buddha had to die, as we all have to die, and there was no resurrection, whether on the third day or any other day. In connection with the sublime scene in the *sāl* grove the notion of a bodily resurrection indeed appears, if I may say so, a little cheap, as indicating an inability to accept the fact of death, or a clumsy attempt to negate the fact of death on its own level instead of transcending it. The Buddha had to die, as we all have to die, because he had been born, and because even for him there could be no exception to the rule that, birth having taken place, death must inevitably follow. Even his Enlightenment could not save him, any more than our knowledge, or virtue, or riches, or friends and relations, can save us. When the messengers of death come, willing or unwilling, ready or unready, Enlightened or unenlightened, we have to go.

Only too often we try to ignore this fact. We refuse to face the problem of death, as though we hoped that if we don't look at the monster with the fiercely glaring eyeballs he won't look at us. We may even try to convince ourselves and others that it is morbid to think about death. But the truth of the matter is that it is morbid *not* to think about death. Not only do we know that we must die, but it is the one thing about ourselves that we really do know. However unsure we may be about other things, we can at least be quite sure of this. Not to think about death is therefore to deprive ourselves of the most certain knowledge that it is possible for us to have, the one thing on which we can rely absolutely. Not to think about death is to deprive ourselves of the possibility of knowing what we really and truly are. It is to deprive ourselves of our very humanity. All conditioned things are impermanent. All sentient beings are subject to death. We are the only beings (in the sense of the only form of terrestrial life) who are not only subject to death but also aware that we are subject to death. We are the only beings for whom death is a problem. Indeed, a human being may be defined as one for whom death is a problem. For us to ignore the face of death, or to refuse to face the problem of death, is therefore to be untrue to our nature. It is not to be a human being in the real sense of the term.

The Buddha certainly did not refuse to face the problem of death. He faced it, in fact, quite early in life. According to what became the standard traditional account, he faced it when, as a young Śākya warrior of the ruling class, he drove out from the luxurious mansion in which he lived with his wife and infant son and saw, for the first time in his life, an old man, a sick man, and a corpse. On seeing them he realized that although young, healthy, and very much alive, he too was subject to old age, disease, and death. He also realized that being himself subject to birth, old age, disease and death, sorrow and corruption, he sought what was subject to birth, old age, disease, death, sorrow, and corruption, and thus lived an unethical and unspiritual life. In other words the Buddha, or Buddha-to-be, became aware of the fact of death. He faced the problem of death. But there was another sight that he saw for the first time, and that was a yellow-robed wandering 'monk' who had gone forth from home into the homeless life. On seeing him the Buddha-to-be realized something else about himself. He realized that although he was subject to birth, old age, disease, death, and corruption, and sought what was of like nature, he could change; he could seek, instead, what was *not* subject to birth, old age, disease, death, and corruption, and thus lead an ethical and spiritual life. He could seek Nirvāṇa. He could seek the Unconditioned.[237] In other words, he became aware of the possibility of there being a solution to the problem of death and that the finding of that solution was somehow connected with the homeless life. Accordingly he left home, sat at the feet of various teachers, none of whom could satisfy him for long, practised extreme self-mortification and realized the futility of that, adopted a middle way, refused a half share of a kingdom, and eventually, at the age of 35, sat down under a peepul tree at what afterwards became known as Bodh Gaya. While meditating he realized that death arises in dependence on birth, and that birth, i.e. rebirth, arises in dependence on craving, i.e. craving for continued existence on this or that plane of conditioned being. He realized that when craving ceases birth ceases, and that when birth ceases death ceases. With the cessation of craving one attains Nirvāṇa, or the Unconditioned. One attains a state of irreversible spiritual creativity in which there is no birth and no death because in passing beyond the cyclical and entering upon the spiral order of existence one has transcended all such pairs of opposites. Paradoxically, though the Buddha had solved the problem of death, he still had to die beneath the twin *sāl* trees forty-five years later. But it did not really matter that he had to die. Because he had eradicated craving and the other unskilful mental states that make for rebirth, he had solved the problem of birth, and because he had solved the problem of birth he had solved the problem of death in the sense that he would not have to die again.

The Buddha faced the problem of death when he saw his first corpse, and because he could face it – because he could look at the monster with its fiercely glaring eyeballs without shrinking – he could also find the solution to the problem of death. In our case it usually takes much more than the sight of a single corpse to make us realize that we too are subject to death and to convince us that death is a problem. We are usually able to ignore any number of corpses, especially if we only read about them in the newspapers or see them on television. Even if we do become vaguely aware of the problem of death we usually hope, no less vaguely, that we can somehow solve it without having to solve the problem of birth, just as we usually hope, with the same vagueness, that we can somehow achieve peace without having to give up violence. In other words, we usually become aware of the problem of death only to the extent of hoping – or perhaps praying – for the impossible. So far as the problem of death, at least, is concerned, it is a true saying that 'What men usually ask of God when they pray is that two and two should not make four.'

But now all that has changed. We have begun to realize that we cannot have peace without abolishing war. We have begun to realize that we cannot have birth without also having death. We have, in short, woken up to the problem of death. In fact, we have woken up to it to a greater extent than ever before in history. The reason for this is not far to seek. The reason is that we, the human race, are now faced by the possibility of full-scale nuclear war. We are faced by the fact that each one of us may at any time meet with a premature, painful, and horrible death, and that the whole human race may be destroyed. It is the realization of this frightful fact that has had, upon some of us at least, the same kind of effect that the sight of his first corpse had upon the Buddha. It has made us aware of the problem of death. It has made us aware that the fundamental problem is not the abolition of nuclear weapons, or even the achievement of world peace in the full sense of the term. The fundamental problem is not living in a way that is worthy of a human being. For a human being worthy of the name, the fundamental problem is the problem of death, and the real significance of the possibility of nuclear holocaust that now confronts us is that it sharpens our awareness of this problem to a greater extent than has ever before been the case. The possibility of nuclear holocaust thus represents not only the greatest threat that humanity has ever faced but also the greatest opportunity. Formerly it was possible for some people to dwell in peace while others were at war, for some people to live in accordance with the principle of non-violence while others lived in accordance with the principle of violence, for some people to face the problem of death while others ignored it. This is no longer the case. The possibility of nuclear holocaust means that we must all dwell in peace, learn to live in accordance with the principle of non-violence, and become more aware of the fundamental problem of death. We must all rise to our full stature as human beings, or perish.

What, then, are we to do? Once again we look at the figure of the Buddha, not only as he stands between the Śākyans and the Koliyans but as he stands beside – and above – the wheel of life. In some Tibetan Buddhist scroll-paintings the Buddha is depicted in the top right-hand corner, well outside the wheel, with one arm raised and pointing in an upward direction. He is pointing the way – the way to Nirvāṇa, the state where there is no death because there is no birth. What we have to do is to realize not only the significance of the Rohiṇī incident, and the meaning of the Buddha's exchange with the Śākyans and Koliyans, but also the significance of that solitary wordless gesture. We have to solve both the problem of world peace and nuclear war *and* the problem of death. The very enormity of the problem of world peace and nuclear war indeed serves to make us – if we have any imagination at all – more aware than ever of the problem of death, and unless we can solve the problem of death even the solving of the problem of world peace and nuclear war would, despite the unexampled magnitude of such an achievement, be only the most magnificent of our failures. We must therefore not only abolish nuclear weapons, achieve peace in the full sense of the term, and learn to live in accordance with the principle of non-violence, as well as deepen our realization of the indivisibility of humanity and restore communication by the reinstatement of the notion of the objectivity of truth, but we must also eradicate craving, transcend both birth and death, and attain Nirvāṇa, or the Unconditioned.

The situation in which we find ourselves today is dangerous in the extreme, perhaps more dangerous for humanity than at any other period in history, and time is running out. Whether we shall be able to achieve world peace and avert nuclear war we do not know. We can only do our best in a situation which, to a great extent, is not of our own personal making. But whether we succeed in achieving world peace and averting nuclear war or not we shall still have to die. If we can solve the problem of death it will not, in the most fundamental sense, matter whether we solve the problem of world peace and nuclear war or not – though, paradoxically, if we do succeed in solving the problem of death then we shall, in all probability, succeed in solving the problem of world peace and nuclear war too. In any case, if we solve the problem of death, the problem of birth, the problem of craving, then we shall be able to live in the world as the Buddha and his disciples lived. We shall be able to join them in chanting those celebrated verses of the *Dhammapada*, the first three of which the Buddha, according to tradition, recited to the Śākyans and Koliyans by way of admonition immediately after he had prevented them from destroying each other:

> Happy indeed we live, friendly amid the haters. Among men who hate we dwell free from hate.
> Happy indeed we live, healthy amid the sick. Among men who are sick we dwell free from sickness.
> Happy indeed we live, content amid the greedy. Among men who are greedy we dwell free from greed.
> Happy indeed we live, we for whom there are no possessions. Feeders on rapture shall we be, like the gods of Brilliant Light.
> Victory begets hatred, (for) the defeated one experiences suffering. The tranquil one experiences happiness, giving up (both) victory and defeat.[238]

If we can chant these verses from the very depths of our hearts then we shall be living in accordance with the teachings of Buddhism and working together for what we all most ardently desire: the achievement of world peace and the avoidance of nuclear war.

A BUDDHIST DAWN IN THE WEST

London, April 1986

Order members, Mitras, and Friends: In his introduction Kulamitra referred to 'The Glory of the Literary World' as my most recent public talk in London, but in fact it wasn't so much a talk as a paper.[239] I have given thousands of talks, lectures, sermons, discourses, and addresses, but nowadays – having rather gone off giving talks, to be frank – I prefer to prepare and read papers. I thought 'The Glory of the Literary World' rather a good paper, and I got some appreciative feedback, but I also got, indirectly, a bit of criticism. I gather that some people felt that a paper of that sort was rather too much to expect the average person, even the average Order member, to take in in the course of an hour. The diet was perhaps – to put it nicely – a bit too rich, concentrated, even indigestible. I must admit that when I read that paper I did notice a few people, even Order members, stifling their yawns.

So I decided that today I'd give one of my old-fashioned talks, just preparing a few words and speaking more or less off the cuff. But my hand really wanted to write a paper, and I found that instead of having two pages of notes I had four, then five, then six. I thought, 'Oh dear. I'm starting to write a paper, and I really mustn't. People are coming along to celebrate the anniversary of the FWBO. They want to have fun, they don't want to listen quietly, carefully, and attentively to a paper that needs a lot of concentrated thought.' So I tore up those pages and started again. I started five or six times, and ended up with two or three pages of rough notes. I may not even stick to those very closely.

I'm already introducing my topic in a completely different way from how I intended. But it does seem appropriate that on an occasion like this I should let myself go a little and not stick too closely to my text.

The occasion, of course, is the nineteenth anniversary of the Friends of the Western Buddhist Order. As I sat at my desk in my study at Padmaloka, looking out across the lawn, I tried to allow this fact to sink in, but it's very difficult to believe. Sometimes I don't feel 19 years old myself. As I sat there at my desk trying not to write a paper, I couldn't help thinking back to those early days. Nostalgia is in fashion, so why not be a little nostalgic? So, as my mind goes back, what do I see? Well, frankly I don't see much. Mainly I see just me. Right at the beginning, even before the time of Sakura, our first tiny centre, it was just me.

I can remember the very moment when the FWBO was conceived – in Calcutta, of all places – and to explain that, I will have to go a little further back, and indulge in a little more nostalgia. I spent twenty years in India, quite a large slice of anybody's life, and I had no intention of returning to the West. But then a call came and I felt that I had to respond to it, so I came back to England at the invitation of the English Sangha Trust and the Sangha Association. For two years I worked mainly in London, but also around the country in the various little Buddhist centres and groups that existed in those days. I functioned partly under the auspices of the Sangha Association, partly under the auspices of the Buddhist Society, and partly independently, giving talks, teaching meditation, and leading study and retreats. At the end of two years I felt that I ought to stay longer, because there was a field ready and waiting in Britain for the seed of the Dharma. My Buddhist work had in any case reached a sort of impasse in India, and I had been feeling a little frustrated for some time, for various reasons that I won't go into now. So I decided to transfer my activities to England.

I wanted to go back to India for a few months to visit my teachers, especially Dhardo Rimpoche, to explain what I wanted to do and seek their blessing. I also wanted to visit my friends among the Ambedkarite Buddhists, especially those in Pune and Nagpur. I told my friends at the Sangha Association and the Buddhist Society my plan, and they bade me farewell, urging me to come back as quickly as possible. I promised I would, and off I went to India. I visited Delhi, Pune, and Nagpur, and then in Calcutta I received a letter from the trustees of the English Sangha Trust, the gist of which was that they didn't want me back. They suggested that although I had promised to come back, I should announce that I'd changed my mind. When I received that letter I understood its significance at once, and said to the friend who was with me, 'Do you know what this means? It means that there's going to be a new Buddhist movement in Britain.'

When I got back to England, I found that indeed the trustees of the English Sangha Trust didn't want me back, and neither did the Buddhist Society. The doors of the existing Buddhist groups and societies were closed to me for several years. So, with faithful friends and followers who had been attending my talks and classes at the Hampstead Buddhist Vihara, many of whom belonged to the Sangha Association, I started up the Friends of the Western Buddhist Order. One day I hope to write a volume of memoirs giving the circumstances leading up to the setting up of the FWBO.[240] I've given you the merest sketch.

So how did we start? Where did we start? We started in central London, because if one is going to do anything in Britain, one might as well start in the centre of things. We started in the basement underneath a shop called Sakura, which sold Japanese things, in Monmouth Street, which is roughly between Charing Cross Road and Drury Lane, and is quite a well-known street in English literature. I've found references to Monmouth Street going back to the seventeenth century, and in Charles Dickens' time the street was famous for shops selling second-hand clothes and shoes.[241] It's to the tiny basement under Sakura that my thoughts go back this evening. I think I functioned there for about five years. In two days' time, on 7 April, it will be the nineteenth anniversary of our dedication ceremony, and I remember the occasion very well.

The owner of Sakura, Emile Boin, and a few other friends set to work and turned this little basement (it was only about twelve feet by fourteen) into a Japanese-style Buddhist shrine with a little image, a little altar, and some very small chairs. They had to be small, and even so we could only accommodate about twenty people. In those days people didn't sit cross-legged for meditation. Chairs have only disappeared from FWBO meditation centres comparatively recently, and even now we keep a few chairs at the back for those who don't want to sit on the floor. I remember sitting cross-legged on my raised seat at the far end next to the shrine. I'd have people sitting right in front of me because it was so small, and I had to be very careful not to bend over because behind me there was a curtain, behind which was a hole which led into another little space underneath the road into which coal used to be tipped in the old days. For the dedication we invited our friends, those who were to form the nucleus of the FWBO, and squeezed into that tiny room. Just a few days before the opening I'd composed a special dedication ceremony – the one we still use – and on the opening evening, I recited it and the others recited it after me. In this way our Triratna meditation centre and shrine, as we grandly called it, was established: so the new Buddhist movement was associated with the name Triratna from the beginning. We used to go into the basement down a winding staircase. There was a curtained-off space about three times the size of this lectern where we used to keep the cups and saucers and where I used to give private interviews. We had to pretend that the interviews were private, although every word that was spoken behind the curtain could be heard all over the basement. People coming to see me before or after the class used to pour out all their troubles while other people pretended they couldn't hear.

I started a couple of weekly meditation classes, one for the people who had been meditating with me at the Hampstead Buddhist Vihara and one for completely new people, and these went on steadily week after week. Quite a lot of people passed through, and after a few weeks or months I started giving courses of lectures. The very first course of lectures I gave under the auspices of the FWBO took place at Kingsway Hall in Holborn, and it was on aspects of Buddhist psychology.[242] Psychology was very popular in those days, and those who thought of themselves as Buddhists used to read mainly psychological literature – Freud, Jung, Stengel, Sullivan, Erich Fromm – so we decided to lure them in with the magic word 'psychology'. But under this heading we had the analytical psychology of the Abhidharma – good tough material to begin with – and the depth psychology of the Yogācāra, which brought in lots of Buddhist metaphysics, and even the archetypal symbolism of the life of the Buddha, because archetypal was another word that really attracted people. We also had a talk about the *Tibetan Book of the Dead*, and to my surprise people came flocking to that lecture, which was the most successful one of the whole series. So under the banner of psychology I was able to put across a lot about Buddhism. The second series of lectures I gave, at Centre House, was on the Buddha's Noble Eightfold Path. Here we came to really basic Buddhist material. The edited transcripts of those tape-recorded talks are still very much in circulation in the FWBO, and were recently printed in our *Mitrata* series with all sorts of comments and explanations taken from seminars.[243] I'm pleased to know that those early lectures are still so useful. Incidentally, they are also being published by Buddhist friends of ours in Malaysia, and they're going to give us 4,000 copies for free distribution, mainly in India. It's really interesting to think that lectures I gave at Centre House in Kensington nearly nineteen years ago are proving useful all these years later to Buddhists in faraway Malaysia.

In addition to lectures we started having retreats out in the countryside. We went to some retreat centres belonging to the Ockenden Venture on the outskirts of Haslemere. The first place we used was Quartermaine, and our first retreats were very experimental, just a couple of dozen people with a loosely organized programme – some meditation, a few talks by me, sometimes two a day, and communication exercises, which we found very useful in removing people's inhibitions and blockages.[244] On those early retreats I had to do everything myself, including leading the communication exercises and the concluding puja. Our meditation classes were still going on at Sakura, so immediately after I'd taken the afternoon meditation class someone would rush me by car to Waterloo Station, and I'd get back to Quartermaine in time to take the concluding meditation. On one occasion, after we'd been going for a year and a half or so, I entrusted the leading of the evening puja to Dharmachari Ananda. I remember very clearly arriving back at Quartermaine and entering the hallway. The shrine was just next to the hall and I could hear Ananda leading the puja, and I thought to myself, 'They've got on all right without me.' That was the first time that anybody had done anything of that sort. Now, of course, Sevenfold Pujas are led all over the world by Order members, and Order members lead retreats, take classes, give lectures, write books, go on solitary retreats, and spread the Dharma far and wide.

This is the way we carried on for our first year: twice weekly meditation classes in our little basement in Monmouth Street, the two series of lectures, spring and autumn, and our Easter and summer retreats. That was the FWBO, just a very small group of people. Then at the end of that first year something quite important happened: the first batch of ordinations. The private ordinations took place as convenient in the course of the previous week – not everybody received their private ordination at the same time – and the public ordinations took place at

Centre House exactly eighteen years ago. I remember that all the twelve people being ordained – there were some men and some women – wore for the occasion either a dark suit or a dark dress. I don't think you'd find that happening now.

With these ordinations things really began to get under way. We had not only the Friends of the Western Buddhist Order, but also the Western Buddhist Order, and that was the Buddhist dawn in the West. If that moment in Calcutta was the conception, the one-year period was the gestation, and our movement was fully born eighteen years ago with the founding of the Order. But wasn't there Buddhism in the West before the Western Buddhist Order? Well, in a sense there was. There had been a Theravāda dawn, and a Zen dawn, but there hadn't really been a Buddhist dawn, because the Buddhism taught was according to the teachings of a particular tradition. Buddhism as such, the Dharma as such, was not transmitted at all. This is why I emphasize the fact that we are just a Buddhist movement, plain and simple, in the sense that we derive inspiration from the whole of the Eastern Buddhist tradition.

This is very much the case when it comes to the study of scriptures. Sometimes you'll find us going through them word by word, and referring to the original text. Quite a few Order members and Mitras have learned to consult their Pāli–English dictionary, which is giving a certain amount of backbone to the study of Pāli texts like the *Udāna*, the *Dhammapada*, the *Sutta-Nipāta*, and the *Majjhima Nikāya*. We also study some of the great *sūtras* of the Mahāyāna tradition – the *Sūtra of Golden Light*, the *Diamond Sūtra*, the *Heart Sūtra*, the Perfection of Wisdom *sūtras*, the *Vimalakīrti-nirdeśa*, and the *White Lotus Sūtra*, especially its beautiful parables and myths. And turning to the Zen tradition, a text which influenced me very much in my early days is the so-called *Sūtra of Wei Lang* or *Sūtra of Huineng*. This was one of the two texts – the other being the *Diamond Sūtra* – the reading of which made me realize I was a Buddhist. Then there's the 'Song of Enlightenment' by Hakuin, a great Rinzai Zen master, which we often read in the context of a puja. Then, turning to Tibetan Buddhism, there's a work by Geshe Wangyal called *The Door of Liberation* and Gampopa's *Jewel Ornament of Liberation*. There are many Order members and Mitras who take *The Hundred Thousand Songs of Milarepa* with them wherever they go, especially on solitary retreat. We derive guidance and great inspiration from all these sources.

I think this is the only intelligent approach possible. I don't think it's possible for us in the West to say, 'I shall limit myself to the Pāli canon, only that is the Buddha's real teaching', or 'I shall limit myself to the Mahāyāna *sūtras*', or 'I shall confine myself to Zen literature, that's what it's really all about, the rest isn't worth wasting time on.' In the FWBO we accept the whole Buddhist tradition, and all the Buddhist scriptures. That is not to say that we derive inspiration from all of them equally, or that we even know all of them, but we don't limit ourselves to any particular tradition or set of scriptures. I think this is becoming increasingly the tendency in Buddhist movements throughout the West: to recognize, honour, and derive inspiration from the teachings of all the great schools of Buddhism.

Then again, we're Buddhist in the sense that we're just Buddhist. I don't believe in trying to mix Buddhism with the teaching of other religions for the sake of a purely theoretical syncretism. We go for Refuge to the Buddha, Dharma, and Sangha, and the teaching of the Buddha represents our major source of inspiration, so we don't try to produce a mixture of Buddhism and Hinduism, or Buddhism and Christianity, or Buddhism and theosophy, or Buddhism and the teachings of Gurdjieff. We are just Buddhist. But I don't mean that in a narrow sense. After all, what does being Buddhist mean? The Buddha himself said that the Dharma is whatever helps the individual to grow and develop.[245] If a teaching from some other tradition, or some other literature, helps us to grow and develop, we are quite free as Buddhists to accept that, as long as it is in accordance with the Buddha's teaching. Some of us derive great inspiration from the writings and sayings of William Blake, or Goethe, or Plato. All of these we are free to weave into the Dharma, because they also help us to grow and develop.

But how do we know what is going to help us grow? As I said, it's not a question of any sort of superficial, purely theoretical syncretism. We refer to our own experience. If we are actually making an effort to develop in the direction of Enlightenment, we shall very quickly find out whether a teaching or practice helps us to grow in that direction or not. But we cannot find this out in a theoretical way. We have to find it out in the context of our own practice. You can't decide what is going to help you develop spiritually unless you are trying to develop spiritually. It's no use just reading books and saying, 'I think this would help, and I think that wouldn't help.' You have to actually start living the spiritual life, trying to develop, trying to reach Enlightenment, or at least trying to become a Stream Entrant. Only then will you be able to tell what helps and what doesn't, perhaps not just by yourself but in consultation with your spiritual friends. So you can't really apply this criterion unless you commit yourself to the Three Jewels. We therefore find in practice that the Friends of the Western Buddhist Order is not just Buddhist. It also has an order at the heart of it, a spiritual community of people committed to trying to become as the Buddha was, trying to gain Enlightenment, or at least to attain Stream Entry in this life.

The Western Buddhist Order, the nucleus, now has nearly 300 members who are committed to the Buddha, Dharma, and Sangha, who are making an effort to reach Enlightenment. The Order is known in India as the Trailokya Bauddha Mahasangha, the Buddhist sangha of the three worlds. *Trailokya* is a Sanskrit word. (The Pāli equivalent would be *tiloka.*) In case anyone is a bit puzzled by this three-world business, let me offer a few words of explanation. What are these three worlds? One can look at it in two ways. There's the *kāmaloka*, the world of sensuous experience, the *rūpaloka*, the world of higher, archetypal experience, with which we come into contact through our meditation and to some extent through our experience of the fine arts, and beyond that there's the *arūpaloka*, the so-called formless world of infinitely more refined spiritual experience, beyond which is Nirvāṇa, or Enlightenment. The Trailokya Bauddha Mahasangha is the sangha, the spiritual community, of those people who have committed themselves to the Buddha, the Dharma, and the Sangha, with a view to transcending the *kāmaloka*, the *rūpaloka*, and even the *arūpaloka*, and gaining Enlightenment, to become *trailokya vijayin*, conquerors of the three worlds. This is why the Buddha is called the Jina, or conqueror. He conquered the three worlds, transcended the mundane in its most refined manifestations, and achieved Enlightenment. So this is the first meaning of *tiloka* or *trailokya*. The other one is more up to date. In modern parlance we've got the developed world, the undeveloped world, and the developing world, and we hope to function in all those worlds, so the sangha in India is *trailokya* in this sense too. We are *trailokya* not only in traditional spiritual terms but also in modern secular terms. Incidentally, some of us have been thinking that even in the West the term 'Western' may not be altogether appropriate for our Order, so we are thinking about changing the name in the future, but that's another story.[246]

I mentioned the day on which the first public ordinations were given, eighteen years ago. Consulting my notes, I find that I gave two talks on that occasion, one on the *upāsaka* ordination in the Western Buddhist Order and the other on the bodhisattva vow. In the first of these talks I referred to the four grades of ordination, because that is how I was thinking in those days. I spoke of the traditional ordinations, the *upāsikā* and *upāsaka* ordination, the *mahā upāsikā* or *mahā upāsaka* ordination, the bodhisattva ordination, and the *bhikkhu* ordination, because at that time I was thinking of having an order in which you moved up through these grades. But we changed that quite soon as a result of our growing and deepening experience of the real meaning of spiritual community, the real meaning of Going for Refuge. What started to become clear was that the main thing was Going for Refuge to the Buddha, Dharma, and Sangha. That was the absolutely central act that made one a Buddhist, and everything else – whether you were a monk or a layman, a nun or a laywoman, whether you were living in the forest alone or at home with your wife or husband and your family – was secondary. The main thing was that you went for Refuge to the Buddha, Dharma, and Sangha, and the spiritual community consisted of all those who went for Refuge in this way. That was the most important thing anybody could do in their life. As the years went by, the Going for Refuge seemed to us of such overwhelming significance that we could only really speak in terms of one ordination, that occasion on which you commit yourself to the Buddha as the ultimate spiritual teacher, to the Dharma as his teaching of the path to Enlightenment, and to the Sangha, the spiritual community of his Enlightened followers, and all those who are treading that path. That seemed to us to be what Buddhism was all about. There was no question of a lower ordination or a higher ordination. There was just ordination, just Going for Refuge to the Buddha, the Dharma, and the Sangha.

But although we dropped the idea of different grades of ordination, there are different levels of Going for Refuge, and this was also something that we discovered quite soon. You can go for Refuge with more or less energy, more or less force, more or less conviction, more or less experience both mundane and spiritual, so we came to distinguish different levels of Going for Refuge, in particular what we called effective Going for Refuge and real Going for Refuge. Effective Going for Refuge means wishing to become Enlightened, wishing to follow the path of the Buddha with total sincerity, committing yourself to the Buddha, the Dharma, and the Sangha as fully as you possibly can, wishing to make the Three Jewels absolutely central in your life, wishing to place them in the very centre of your mandala, as we say. But inasmuch as you are not Enlightened, nor in a sense even on the path to Enlightenment, the higher path, if you're not careful you can withdraw, and in the very early days of the Western Buddhist Order some people did. They found that they had bitten off more than they could chew. On the occasion of that first public ordination ceremony twelve people were ordained, but most of them didn't last more than a couple of years, and there is only one who is still effectively with us, and that is Ananda. He is therefore the only person who can share with me nineteen years of memories of the FWBO.

Someone who stayed with us right up until the time of his death three or four years ago, was Vangisa. It was a great blow to the whole movement and especially to the Order when we lost Vangisa. He was one of those who came along to my lectures at the Hampstead Buddhist Vihara and helped me to set up the FWBO. He was with us through all sorts of personal difficulties and illnesses until almost the hour of his death; in fact he led his last meditation class just a few hours before he died.

Many people were not able to maintain that original commitment, but as the years went by the Order became stronger, and more support could be given to those who were having difficulties in following the spiritual path. Effective Going for Refuge, though utterly sincere at the time, is not permanent. Insight, transcendental experience, has not arisen, so you can slip back. Obviously most Order members are still in that position, so they need to be very careful, and that's even more the case for Mitras and Friends who are just beginning to set their feet upon the path. But real Going for Refuge is that Going for Refuge which you experience after you have entered the Stream. I am not going to say any more about that now, but if anyone is interested, there is my lecture, now published as a booklet on Going for Refuge, in which I distinguish four different levels of Going for Refuge.[247] Once one has gone for Refuge effectively, one's main object must be to go for Refuge in what I call the real sense, the sense in which you can no longer not go for Refuge because insight into the true nature of existence has arisen and you can only go forward. You've passed the point of no return.

We've got one ordination for everybody, but there is still a trace of grades of ordination in an informal way. We sometimes speak of senior and responsible Order members, and they roughly correspond to *mahā-upāsakas* and *mahā-upāsikās*, though not in any formal way. We've also got *anagārikas*, those who change the third of the ten precepts taken by all *dharmacāris* and *dharmacāriṇīs* from abstention from sexual misconduct to abstention from non-celibacy; in other words they take a precept of chastity. There aren't many of those in the Order but I hope that before long there will be a few more. They in a sense correspond to *bhikkhus* and *bhikkhunīs*.

But what about the bodhisattva ordination? This shouldn't be considered as a separate ordination, for it represents the altruistic aspect of the Going for Refuge. You go for Refuge not just for your own sake, but for the sake of all. You seek to attain Enlightenment not for personal gratification, but so that you can be of greater service to other people. More than that, you see that you can't separate your own development from that of other people. One can't really adopt a purely self-regarding attitude to the spiritual life. It has a self-regarding aspect and an other-regarding aspect, and these two have to be combined. You are trying to develop yourself, but you're trying to do so in association with other people. You can't separate yourself and devote yourself exclusively to your own spiritual welfare. One might regard the Going for Refuge as representing the self-regarding aspect and the bodhisattva vow as representing the other-regarding aspect. This may seem a little obscure, but it is spelled out in the booklet I mentioned earlier.

We are the Friends of the *Western* Buddhist Order. There is an emphasis on Western, at least initially. We are committed to the Buddha, the Dharma, and the Sangha under the conditions of modern Western life. We can't pretend that we are living in fifth century BCE Magadha, or twentieth-century Ceylon, or medieval India, or Japan or Tibet. The conditions under which we practise Buddhism here in the West are different from those under which people have tried to follow that same path in the East, and we can't escape that fact. This is why we call ourselves the Friends of the Western Buddhist Order. We are not following a particular kind of Buddhism called Western Buddhism, or trying to adapt Buddhism to any particular Western point of view. We commit ourselves to the same Dharma to which all true Buddhists have committed themselves through the ages, but we have to practise that

Dharma in our own conditions. More recently the FWBO has spread to the East, which is rather interesting, because culturally speaking the East is being invaded by the West, being Westernized. There are many people in Eastern Buddhist countries whose outlook is quite Western and some of those people are intrigued and attracted by the way in which we try to present and live Buddhism, because the conditions under which we are trying to do that are being to some extent duplicated in their own countries.

We're called the *Friends* of the Western Buddhist Order, which signifies that we don't have an ordinary membership. You can't join the FWBO by paying a subscription, and much less still can you join the Western Buddhist Order in that way. In 1952, I attended a meeting at Sanchi which was also attended by an Indian gentleman who had recently established a Buddhist order of his own.[248] He was going around propagating this order in grand style. He was dressed in a beautiful satin saffron suit – don't laugh, we may be wearing these things ourselves one day – and he was enrolling members of his sangha. He tried to enrol me. He told me that there were four classes of membership, and the higher the grade of membership the larger the subscription you'd have to pay. There were Stream-Entrant members, non-returner members, once-returner members, and of course *arhant* members, and if you wanted to be an *arhant* member you'd have to pay five hundred rupees. You might be able to join a society devoted to the study of Buddhism in that way, but I feel very strongly that you can't join a Buddhist movement in that way. You can only join a real live Buddhist movement by being actively involved in it.

In the FWBO we have different degrees of involvement. First of all there are the Order members, the *dharmacāris* and *dharmacāriṇīs*. They are people who have committed themselves wholeheartedly, body, speech, and mind, to the Buddha, the Dharma, and the Sangha. Then we've got Friends, with a capital F. They are not committed, just interested. Perhaps they just come along once a year to Wesak or to the anniversary of the FWBO, but they're also part and parcel of the Movement. Then in the middle there are Mitras. They are involved, but not yet committed, though some of them may be thinking about commitment, and they're certainly more than just interested.

The Buddhist dawn in the West began just nineteen years ago, and since then I think I may say that it has been gradually growing brighter and brighter. In the course of those nineteen years all sorts of things have happened. We started off in that tiny basement in Monmouth Street, but now you'll find large FWBO centres and communities and co-ops in at least a dozen countries. There are nearly 300 Order members, a large proportion of whom are working full-time for the Movement in one way or another. There are double that number of Mitras and if we include India there are several hundred thousand Friends. We've got communities and retreat centres, including Vajraloka, the men's meditation centre in Wales, Aryaloka, which was started about a year ago in the United States, and our retreat centre in India at Bhaja near those ancient Buddhist caves. We've produced many publications. So quite a lot has happened.

I'd like now to speak briefly about what I would say are the three main events of the last year, to give some idea of the directions in which the FWBO is expanding and progressing. The first of these events is the establishment of the women's retreat centre in Shropshire. There was quite a bit of discussion as to what it should be called but the Order members who founded it eventually came up with the name Taraloka, and when it was announced everyone felt that it was a really appropriate name. Tārā is the great female bodhisattva, or rather, since bodhisattvas are neither male nor female, she is a bodhisattva appearing in female form. The name Tārā means 'she who ferries across' – ferries across the ocean of birth, old age, disease, and death. In the Buddhist East, especially in China and Japan and Tibet, all sorts of beautiful associations have gathered around the figure of Tārā. Her name also means star, and just as you guide yourself by the stars, the spiritual ideal represented by Tārā guides you, inspires you, ferries you across, even in a sense saves you. *Loka* means world or plane, so Taraloka is the world or the plane or the dimension inhabited by, ruled over, inspired by, the bodhisattva Tārā. The women creating the retreat centre are trying to create a world of Tārā, where the Tārā principle reigns supreme, and I am sure that when they've succeeded in doing that, Taraloka will exercise an enormous influence throughout the Movement. I also hope that it will help speed up the process of ordination for women. Going for Refuge is an individual act, so ordination is a personal thing, but facilities like meditation classes, study groups, and retreat centres can greatly help people in their progress towards Enlightenment, in their committing themselves to the Buddha, Dharma, and Sangha, in their becoming ready for ordination. I hope that as soon as the women's retreat centre is fully established we shall see many more women preparing themselves for ordination more quickly than has usually been the case in the past. Not that I want to hurry anybody, but sometimes improved facilities can help. I particularly want to see chapters of the women's wing of the Order in places like Brighton, Manchester, and Glasgow, where we don't at the moment have them, and where therefore a certain imbalance exists. Perhaps when the anniversary comes round next year we may have a different story to tell.

I don't often speak about the women in the Movement as distinct from the men, and some people might say that this is a rather controversial topic, but to walk in where angels fear to tread, I think that conditions and facilities for women in the FWBO are particularly good as compared with at least some other Buddhist groups. My sense is that in some Buddhist groups, the women are rather under the shadow of the men, and the nuns are very much under the shadow of the monks and can't do anything without their permission. There's nothing like that in the FWBO. Whether women are Mitras, Friends, or Order members, they are at least as independent as the men are. They no more need the permission of the men than the men need the permission of their female counterparts. I hope that is quite clear. I've given quite a bit of thought to this, and I really think that in our movement women probably have far better facilities for personal growth and development in the direction of Enlightenment than any other Buddhist group in the West at this time. It would be well if we were more mindful of this, and spread the word around a bit more than people sometimes do.

The second of the three main events of the last year was the ordination retreat that took place last December in India. Ordination ceremonies have been taking place there ever since we started in 1979, but what was special about these ordinations was that I did not confer them. This was a historic occasion. I've ordained nearly all of the 300 Order members we have at present, which has meant quite a lot of preparation, personal contact, assessment, and exchange. I have talked with some people and been with them on retreat many, many times before they were ordained, so I've had very close contact with them. But the Movement has been expanding into a number of countries, and it is becoming more and more difficult for me to get around all of them. In fact, the Movement had hardly begun before I started handing over whatever responsibilities I could, because I saw that this was the only way in which the Movement would grow. Some people have now been Order members for ten, twelve, or fifteen years, and quite a few of them can do all kinds of things about which I know absolutely nothing. Some of them can operate word processors, a lot of them can drive motor cars, and some of them are beginning to give lectures which are nearly as good as mine. I really look forward to the time – it shouldn't take more than five years – when some of them will be able to give better lectures than me. When that day comes I will congratulate myself on a job well done. I know it's possible because I can remember the days when some of our most accomplished speakers, who could now hold you spellbound for a whole hour, could barely stammer their way through a ten-minute speech in our speakers' class. I'm delighted when I hear them holding forth with such confidence and knowledge and inspiration, and I don't think it's expecting too much to think that in five years' time they'll be able to do better than me.

This brings me to an important principle that I formulated some years ago: that if your disciples don't do better than you, you haven't succeeded. After all, they're able to stand on your shoulders. Think of my position when I started on my Buddhist career at the age of 16. In London at that time there was a Buddhist Society, but that was all. There were a few books and translations, weekly meetings, and an annual Wesak celebration. I was the youngest person around at the Buddhist Society. There was no spiritual guidance, no one to whom I could turn. I met many spiritual teachers in India, and many Buddhists in Sri Lanka, Singapore, and other places, but I had to discover for myself all sorts of things about which people in the FWBO now get help and guidance.

People coming into contact with the FWBO these days have all sorts of wonderful facilities available to them. Sometimes I think that people don't recognize their good fortune. You've only got to walk in the door of the centre and there it is, all laid on for you. There are Order members hovering around waiting to explain that the image is not an idol and we don't indulge in idol worship, and that meditation doesn't mean going into a trance. If you want to meditate there's a meditation class. If you want to learn the Dharma, there are study groups and Mitra study classes. There are large retreats for men and women if that's what you want, and if you prefer to go on a single-sex retreat, they are available too. If you want to go on a meditation retreat or practise hatha yoga, you can. I can honestly say that the facilities available are such that if you took full advantage of them, within ten or fifteen years you could be a Stream Entrant. That's a tremendous thing to say, but it's true. You could be enjoying a state of completely positive emotion and very nearly complete mental clarity all the time. You could always be full of energy and joy. You could be free from delusion. You could help other people and be a source of inspiration to them. All you would have to do is to take full and sincere advantage of the opportunities that are available to you in an FWBO centre. I didn't have all these facilities but they are now at your disposal, so you should be able to do better than I've done, and I will have done my duty if at the time of my departure at least fifty or sixty of you are able to do quite a lot better than I have done.

Until a few months ago I wasn't able to hand over the great responsibility of conferring ordination, but I've now made a start even with this. In December, three *dharmacāris*, Subhuti, Kamalashila, and Suvajra, went to India on my behalf – I couldn't go for one reason or another – and in the context of an ordination retreat in our beautiful retreat and meditation centre at Bhaja they ordained some seventeen people. I was so glad when I heard that they'd arrived safely (though one of them was sick), that they were on the retreat and had conferred the ordinations, and that there were now seventeen more Order members in the world, all without my having done anything. I've never even seen some of the people who were ordained, because they've started coming along since my last visit to India, so six or seven Order members now in the world have been ordained without any personal contact with me at all. This is an enormously important step, the most important step taken by the Order since its establishment eighteen years ago, because it ensures the continuation of the Order. It is no longer dependent on me, which is a great relief. I sometimes used to think, 'Suppose I'm involved in an air accident before I've handed over this responsibility. What will happen to the Order?' But now, even if I was to be involved in an accident next week or if I was to have a heart attack in the middle of this talk (let's hope I don't), the Movement and the Order as the heart of the Movement would be able to continue. So I felt not only great joy but great relief when I received the news of the ordinations in India.

Even if I manage to hand over all my responsibilities, I'm certainly not going to retire. I still have quite a lot of work to do. As I hand over more and more organizational responsibilities, I hope to be able to devote myself more and more to literary work. I hope that at least some of the things that I'm able to produce will be of use to the Movement, but I've even started handing on the responsibility for writing books. Subhuti has produced a couple of books, and Nagabodhi, Kamalashila, and Ratnaprabha are all writing books, so we are creating more and more literature which will introduce people to Buddhism in a manner that they can understand and provide them with a basis for practice. I'd be very happy if I didn't have any responsibilities at all, but of course people have to be ready to take them on, so it is one of my responsibilities to hand over my responsibilities only to those who I feel sure are able to take them on. Fortunately, Subhuti, Kamalashila, and Suvajra were genuinely able to take on the responsibility for conferring those ordinations in India, and I know from the reports I received from people who were there that there was no difference between the way in which they conferred the ordinations and the way in which I would have conferred them. In a way people missed me but in a way they didn't. The ordinations were conferred, and that was the main thing.

There are very few other Order members who could have taken on that responsibility, though, so another question arises. Why aren't more people ready to take on responsibilities? Well, it's because people are not sufficiently 'active'. I put 'active' within quotation marks because I don't mean just busy. What I mean is a certain lack of motivation. People are not sufficiently alive in the spiritual sense, and not sufficiently mature, because one of the signs of maturity is that you can take on responsibility. I've been thinking a lot about the question of what motivates people, and although my thoughts are not fully formulated yet, I'll share with you some of my ideas. I'll start from the standpoint of survival. We're all alive. There are lots of living things on this earth, not only human beings, but animals, insects, and plants, and the one thing we all have in common is that we all want to survive, and we have to struggle to do so. This was certainly true of human beings in the earlier stages of evolution. Perhaps life was easy in some remote mythological golden age but it wasn't in any age of which we have any real knowledge. You had to gather food, fend off wild beasts, and protect yourself from natural calamities, so people were kept on their toes by the need to survive. Until very recent times the vast majority of human beings had to spend much of their time and nearly all of their energies just surviving, or in more recent times just earning a living, otherwise they would starve, so they were motivated to be active. But in modern times, in some favoured parts of the world, people can survive without doing anything at all. In our own part of the world there's the welfare state – the 'dole' – and people can survive without making any effort. So what motivates them? Now that people can survive without working, now that they can drift and become lazy, what happens to their energies? Not having any proper outlet, their energies may turn negative, even destructive, so you get vandalism, hooliganism, and violence. This has increased in the last few years, and there have been all sorts of horrific incidents. I think the reason is that people no longer have to struggle to survive, and perhaps their energies are too crude as yet to find employment in any other way, although some people are able to channel their energies into the arts and creativity and a very few people manage to channel them into spiritual life.

I think a lot of people in our own movement are in an intermediate position. Many of them don't have to work – some of them may be quite literally living on the dole – so their energies are not stimulated by the need to survive or earn a living. Their energies are engaged in cultural and spiritual activities to a limited extent, but they haven't yet completely shifted their energies out of the survival gear into a higher cultural and spiritual gear. Some of the best known and most spiritually successful Order members have succeeded in transferring those energies which ordinarily would have gone into the struggle for survival into purely cultural and Dharmic channels, and all their energies are therefore behind everything they do. We all know people who can go from one activity to another. After they give a talk they can help to lead a meditation class, and if after that you want them to spend some time with you and give you some advice, they can do it. All their energies are available for the Movement, for the Three Jewels. But a lot of people in the FWBO are in an intermediate position. They've not yet been able to transfer all their energies, disengaged though they are from the struggle for survival, into purely cultural and spiritual channels, so they remain half alive. They're not very active and therefore it's not possible for anyone to give them very much in the way of responsibility.

To be frank, I sometimes wonder why people don't do more, because there is so much to be done. There are so many people in this world of ours who could benefit from the Dharma, but it seems that not many people in our movement feel a real urge to go out and communicate it to them, even though they know it could benefit them so much. You read in the newspaper and hear on the radio all sorts of terrible stories of people committing suicide, becoming alcoholics, becoming dependent upon drugs. If we have any spark of *mettā* and *karuṇā* within us, we should want to communicate with these people and bring to them the awareness that there is another way. They don't have to indulge in all these dreadful things; it is possible to grow and develop as a human being. It is tragic and extraordinary that in our welfare state, where so many facilities are provided, so many people have recourse to alcohol and drugs and violence. Something has gone seriously wrong somewhere, and we could help to put it right if we were more outward-going in communicating the Dharma. We could have a greater impact than the FWBO has as yet had.

So we have to strengthen our motivation. I ought to be able to hand over responsibility for conferring ordination to every Order member who has been ordained say for ten years. Some Order members are already very busy, but they could be relieved from some of their responsibilities if Mitras were more active, and Mitras could be relieved of some of their responsibilities if Friends were more active. One just needs a stronger motivation, a more effective channelling of one's energies away from the need to survive into definitely cultural and spiritual channels instead of leaving them stagnating somewhere in between. So how are we to strengthen our motivation? I am going to conclude with a few hints on how we could do this.

First of all, avoid distractions. These words should perhaps be written in letters of gold above the entrance to every city centre. London, as we know, is the distraction capital, and if you allow yourself to be distracted, you'll never be able to direct all your energies into cultural and spiritual channels.

Secondly, lead a regular lifestyle, with regular meditation, regular study, regular retreats, including solitary retreats, and regular communication with spiritual friends. You need these constant reminders of what your real goal is, where your true interest lies.

Thirdly, make sure that you have *kalyāṇa mitratā*, good regular contact with your spiritual friends. It's so easy to get out of touch with spiritual life, it's so easy to forget. This is what people very often tell me, sometimes in person, sometimes in writing. If they don't go to a class, or a chapter meeting if they're an Order member, for a few weeks or months, they get right out of touch, and they can feel strangely alienated. You need to keep in contact with your spiritual friends, because only they will reach out to you and rescue you and gently draw you back when you get out of touch. Have as much contact with your spiritual friends as you possibly can, especially what I've called vertical *kalyāṇa mitratā*, spiritual contact with others who are more experienced than you are yourself, with more emotional positivity, more insight, greater clarity, greater freedom, greater spontaneity, and more energy. This is a very important way of strengthening your motivation.

Fourthly, keep up your spiritual practice, especially your meditation, your mindfulness of breathing and your *mettā bhāvanā*. These will help you to strengthen your motivation.

Fifthly, keep up your Dharma study. Dharma study is a wonderful thing. We've got all these texts – the Pāli scriptures and the Mahāyāna *sūtras*, and the great Tibetan works. There's a wonderful fund of inspiration in them. Unless you're someone who objectively needs to keep in touch with the outside world – the chair of a centre, for example – why bother to read newspapers? Why bother to read *Time Out*, or *Woman's Own*, or *Motor Cycle News*? Soak yourself in the scriptures. They're tremendous sources of inspiration.

And sixthly, I've become a bit concerned in the last couple of years about the comparative lack of mindfulness in the FWBO – not in the context of meditation but in the affairs of daily life. When someone forgets to shut a door, or doesn't wash up their own cup and saucer, apparently at the back of their mind is an unconscious idea that Mother is still around to do it, but in a spiritual community you should do things yourself. There was a time at Padmaloka a couple of years ago when people kept slamming doors. My study is situated immediately above the front door at Padmaloka and I used to wonder why when people went out through that door they always slammed it violently behind them, so that the front of the building shook. I used to ask people not to do it, but they just couldn't remember. There were all sorts of other little incidents of this kind and I became more and more conscious that the level of mindfulness in this ordinary basic sense is quite low. This is something to which everybody, including Order members, I'm afraid, should give very serious attention.

If you can strengthen your motivation in these ways, more and more of your energies will flow into cultural and Dharmic channels. Mitras will be able to hand over more and more of their responsibilities to Friends, Order members will be able to hand over more and more of their responsibilities to Mitras, I will be able to hand over more and more of my responsibilities to senior and responsible Order members, and then there really will be a Buddhist dawn in the West.

The third great event of the past year is the launching of *Golden Drum*, our new magazine.[249] I must say it gives me very great satisfaction to see the first issue of *Golden Drum* being launched. I have wanted a magazine for the FWBO for years, but I felt we had to be ready. We had to have the resources, not just finance, but a certain degree of intellectual and spiritual maturity in our contributors before we could effectively communicate the message of the FWBO through a magazine. I hope that *Golden Drum* will make what the FWBO stands for more and more widely known, and then there will be a Buddhist dawn not only in the West but perhaps in many other parts of the world.

Just a week ago I was in Spain, staying with some friends in the Alicante area. For the whole week the sky was absolutely blue – not a fleck of cloud – and it was beautifully hot. I was given a lovely room on the first floor of a villa, and I used to go out on the little wrought-iron balcony early in the morning. Below me were orange groves, olive groves, farmhouses, and cactus bushes, and in the distance (ignoring the towers of Benidorm) was the sea. During the day it was a brilliant blue, but I used to sit on the balcony early in the morning before the sun rose, and at that time of day the sea was gun-metal blue. I would see a dot of fiery orange rising in the East above the sea with remarkable speed. I'd see a third of the disc of the sun, and then a half, and then the whole sun. Due to the morning mist, though it was so bright I could actually look at it. It was a beautiful rosy red, quite soft at that time of day, almost more like a full moon than a sun. But as it rose higher and higher into the heavens it became more and more brilliant, more and more like a disc of burnished gold, and soon it became difficult to look at it.

As I watched the sunrise from my veranda, I thought about this talk. I didn't have much idea of what I was going to talk about, but I'd already given it the title 'A Buddhist Dawn in the West'. I thought as I watched that rising sun that in some ways it was like the Buddhist dawn in the West and in some ways it wasn't. At dawn in Alicante there were no clouds, just a pure blue sky and the sun rising out of the sea, but the dawning sun of Buddhism in the West had to rise from amidst quite a few clouds, as I indicated at the beginning. But now, though perhaps there are still one or two clouds in the sky of Buddhism in the West, I think we can say that the sun of the FWBO has risen above them and is shining more and more brilliantly. One can see that golden disc not just as a sun but as a golden drum. In the *Sūtra of Golden Light*, the golden drum is compared to the sun,[250] and in one of the Upanishads, to quote a non-Buddhistic source, a sage speaks of the sun as a sort of golden door which you have to open by means of your spiritual practice, a golden door through which you pass into a higher spiritual world.[251] So that's one way in which we can think of that golden disc. You may remember that at the beginning of the *Sūtra of Golden Light* a figure is described who beats upon that great golden drum. That's what I've been doing this evening, beating upon the drum and trying to rouse you a little bit. Now that I've started handing over my responsibilities, the FWBO is less and less 'my' movement every day, and I'm very happy to see that. It's *your* movement. For me this has been a very enjoyable occasion, in a sense nostalgic but also very inspiring, because I'm beginning to hear the golden drum which is the FWBO sending forth quite a vigorous note without my even touching it, and I like just sitting and listening to the sound of that beautiful music.

TWENTY YEARS ON THE MIDDLE WAY

London Buddhist Centre, 1987

While thanking Dhammarati for his introduction, I have to make one little correction. I founded the Triyana Vardana Vihara seven years after my arrival in Kalimpong. It was the Young Men's Buddhist Association that I established a year after I arrived in Kalimpong. It's nice to get the biographical facts exactly right, because I sometimes find it necessary to check the growth of what might be called the Sangharakshita Legend. I have heard it said, and even seen it in print, that during the war I was a fighter pilot in the RAF. I can assure you that I have no such pretensions; my style of pilotry is of quite another nature. Facts are facts, and legends are legends.

Whether it may be considered a fact, a legend, or a mixture of the two, this evening we're celebrating the twentieth anniversary of that legendary body, the Friends of the Western Buddhist Order. In terms of the average lifespan twenty years is not long, but in that time quite a lot can happen. In the last twenty years FWBO centres have sprung up in many parts of the world, as have spiritual communities and team-based right livelihood businesses, and in this way there has come into existence the nucleus of the new society, to borrow that expression, or at the very least the nucleus of that nucleus. Compared with some other new religious movements the FWBO is not very big, but it has grown more quickly than some of us expected, especially when we consider the nature of our ideals and how difficult those ideals are to implement, as most of us find almost every day.

As we look back over the last twenty years, we may experience a variety of powerful emotions. We may experience thankfulness that a spiritual and cultural movement like the FWBO exists, that there is a situation in which we can develop as human beings, become true individuals, form spiritual friendships, and deepen our spiritual experience. We may feel thankful that we can put all our old problems well and truly behind us. We may experience a certain amount of pride in the positive sense: pride that we could help build up something like the FWBO, that we could be the means of bringing the teaching of the Buddha to other people with whom we come into contact. But that pride may be mingled with disappointment that we have not been able to do more, disappointment that the FWBO is not bigger and better than it is, and that it has not been able to exercise a deeper and more extensive influence than it does, especially when one considers how badly the world needs the kind of influence that the FWBO represents.

As I look back over the last two decades, my own emotion is more of wonder than anything else: wonder that the FWBO should have come into existence at all, because only I know how very nearly it didn't, and wonder also that having come into existence, it has survived and grown. Someone referred to it this afternoon as a sapling, but it certainly wasn't a sapling to begin with, just a tiny shoot with all sorts of cold and discouraging blasts blowing upon it. Or, to change metaphor, it was like a little flame which I was trying to shelter with my two hands from the discouraging blasts trying to blow it out. But they didn't succeed, and it is now a moderately big flame. To drop the metaphors altogether, the FWBO started in a very small and insignificant way in a tiny basement room in Monmouth Street in central London. I'm sure no one is in any danger of forgetting it. I believe we've even got a photograph or two in this hall this evening to remind us. I'm not going to start reminiscing about the good old days as some of our friends call them – the days when I had to do everything myself. I'm quite happy to live in the bad new days, when lots of other people are doing the things that I used to do and I can sit back, relatively speaking.

Instead of reminiscing, I'm going to consider what the FWBO has been doing these last twenty years, not in detail but in principle. In the name 'Friends of the Western Buddhist Order', we have two nouns and two adjectives. They are probably all of equal importance, but so far as this evening's talk is concerned, the emphasis falls on one of the adjectives:

'Buddhist'. The FWBO is a *Buddhist* organization. It belongs to the great spiritual tradition which in the West we call Buddhism, but in the East they simply call the Dharma, or just Dharma, or Dhamma, or *chös* in Tibetan. That great spiritual tradition looks for its ultimate inspiration to Gautama the Buddha, the founder of Buddhism, the discoverer or rediscoverer of those spiritual truths which we call the Dharma. What is Buddhism? In the last forty years I've given a number of answers to this question, but the answer I'm going to give this evening is quite short and simple. Buddhism is the teaching of the middle way. The Buddha followed this middle way himself, exemplified it, embodied it, and taught others to follow it. And since the FWBO is a Buddhist movement, the FWBO is on the middle way, and has been on it for twenty years. *We* have been on the middle way for twenty years, because the FWBO doesn't exist apart from its members.

So what is the middle way? During my twenty years in India I gave quite a number of lectures on this topic, and usually I spoke of it as having three aspects or levels of application: ethics, psychology, and metaphysics. The middle way in ethics is the avoidance of the extremes of self-mortification and self-indulgence, asceticism and hedonism. The middle way in psychology is not quite so well-known, but here also there are two extreme views. According to one of these, we have an unchanging soul which survives bodily death, but according to the opposite view we possess no soul, unchanging or otherwise, and there is therefore nothing of us that survives bodily death. These two extreme views were well represented at the time of the Buddha by different thinkers.[252] Here the middle way is the view that there is not an unchanging but a changing soul, and that this changing soul continues to exist after death in the same way as it existed during life. After death it may again become connected with a physical body, whether gross or subtle, and this is what is popularly known as rebirth or reincarnation. The middle way in metaphysics is more abstruse. One may think, as some of the thinkers in the Buddha's day did, of ultimate reality in terms of existence, being, or in terms of non-existence, non-being. The middle way consists in thinking of it in terms of becoming, and in terms of *śūnyatā* or voidness. In India this threefold explanation of the middle way was very popular with my audiences, both Buddhist and non-Buddhist, and it forms part of our standard FWBO teaching, but this evening I'm not going to enlarge on it. I'm going to speak instead of our being on the middle way in more directly practical terms which have particular relevance to us here in the West.

The FWBO was established twenty years ago with a view to the establishment of the Western Buddhist Order, which came into existence almost exactly a year later. As a Buddhist order, the Western Buddhist Order is naturally on the middle way, but in what way specifically? To understand this we shall have to take a look at the Eastern Buddhist world as it exists today, and especially at the Theravādin Buddhist world – Sri Lanka, Thailand, Burma, and so on. In the East the Buddhist community is sharply divided into two sections: on the one hand there are the monks, and on the other, the laymen and laywomen. There are no nuns; *bhikkhunīs* only exist in some of the Mahāyāna countries, and even there only in very small numbers. In the East it is usually only the monks who are regarded as being the real Buddhists, so if you really want to practise Buddhism, you have to become a monk. The function of the laity is generally considered to be to support the monks. In other words, though there are exceptions, the laity tend to practise Buddhism at second hand. In a way the monks practise it for them. From a Buddhist point of view this is self-contradictory, and quite opposed to the fundamental teachings of the Buddha. According to the Buddha, the Dharma is something that you have to practise yourself, because only then will you develop, just as you'll only be nourished if you eat food yourself.

In the Mahāyāna countries the sharpness of the division between monks and laity has been modified in varying degrees by the emphasis on the bodhisattva ideal, which can be practised by both the monks and the laity, and thus has a unifying effect. Nonetheless, the division remains, at least to some extent, and in the Theravādin countries it is very sharp, since the bodhisattva ideal is not emphasized. So how did this division come about? How did the monks come to be regarded as the real Buddhists, and laymen and laywomen mainly as the supporters of the monks? To understand this, we have to make an important distinction with which we in the FWBO have become familiar but which is not always recognized by other Buddhist groups. This is the distinction between commitment and lifestyle. By commitment I mean commitment to the Three Jewels, to the Buddha, the Dharma, and the Sangha, and by lifestyle I mean the specific way in which we express that commitment in our ordinary daily living.

Being a monk or a lay person is a matter of lifestyle, and in neither case does the lifestyle necessarily express spiritual commitment, although it may do so. In most of the Eastern Buddhist world, the monastic lifestyle has come to be identified with spiritual commitment. If you are a monk you are automatically committed, and if you are committed you are automatically a monk. But as we see things in the FWBO, whether you are a monk or a layman or a nun or a laywoman is of secondary importance. What really matters is whether you are committed to the Three Jewels, to the path to supreme Enlightenment. This attitude has found expression in a little saying: commitment is primary, lifestyle is secondary. This does not mean that lifestyle is not important. It is very important indeed, but it is important only as an expression of commitment. So here the Western Buddhist Order follows the middle way in the sense that it avoids the extreme of rigid, formalistic monasticism and lax laicism, to coin a phrase. A member of the Western Buddhist Order is first and foremost simply a Buddhist, simply one who is committed to the Three Jewels. Whether he or she lives more or less as a monk or nun or more or less as a member of the laity depends on the nature of his or her spiritual needs, and those needs are not necessarily the same from one year to the next.

It's not easy to be simply a Buddhist. It's not easy to be committed to the Three Jewels. In the East one who has been ordained as a monk often assumes himself to be leading a spiritual life simply because he's shaved his head, wears the yellow robe, and observes various rules. Similarly, the layman often assumes that he is not committed because he is not doing any of those things. Thus, most so-called monks and most so-called laymen are able to evade the demands of the spiritual life. But for a member of the Western Buddhist Order no such evasion is possible, or at least not for long. In one way or another he or she is constantly being brought up against the question: 'Am I deepening my commitment to the Three Jewels, and is my lifestyle giving adequate expression to that commitment?' It is thus not easy to be simply a Buddhist, not easy to be a member of the Western Buddhist Order. In fact, it's not even easy to be a Mitra. If you went to almost any Eastern country this week, probably next week you could be a monk – that is, if you are a man. For a woman to become a nun would be much more difficult. But it might take years before you were considered to be ready to become a Mitra in the FWBO.

Even though it's not easy to be a member of the Western Buddhist Order, or even to be a Mitra, nevertheless quite a number of people are making the effort, not only here in England but in a number of other countries as well. Because they are making that effort, because they are trying to deepen their spiritual commitment and bring their lifestyle into harmony with that commitment, they change. They develop, they grow spiritually, and sometimes they change a great deal, and very quickly. I have certainly seen this in the last twenty years, and it's one of the most rewarding aspects of my personal association with the FWBO. One concludes that the Buddha's teachings really do work – if you practise them. I've absolutely no doubt about that, and the evidence is here before me. I'm sure that each and every one of you has changed for the better due to your contact with the Dharma.

This is a very imperfect world, in which even change for the better may bring its own problems. When you develop spiritually, even to a small extent, you not only grow, you grow away from. You grow away from your old friends and relations because you no longer share their ideas and attitudes. You don't necessarily want to grow away from them; it's the inevitable result of the process of development. In particular, perhaps, you grow away from your parents. In any case, in modern Western society, relations between parents and children are often strained, difficult, and painful. Here too the FWBO follows the middle way between two extremes, which could be called submission and rejection, or perhaps conformity and rebellion would be better. By submission I mean accepting your parents' point of view in practically all things and not doing anything of which they would disapprove. When I was in my teens I heard about a married woman with a family who didn't dare to mend a stocking on the Sabbath because her old father, who was living with them, disapproved of that sort of thing. This kind of submission is becoming increasingly rare, but there is also what we may call the internalized parent, who is often more powerful than the actual parent ever was. The mere fact that we are changing means that we are moving away from our parents, so there is no question of our submitting to them. Indeed, we may have moved away from them both literally and metaphorically long before we came into contact with the FWBO, so we are not in much danger of falling into the extreme of submission.

We're in much greater danger of falling into the extreme of rejecting our parents. Society often seems to encourage us to do so, seems to accentuate the differences between us. There are some extreme religious groups which encourage people to reject their parents and cut off all contact with them. But this most emphatically is not the attitude of the FWBO. We encourage people to keep up contact with their parents and improve their relations with them, though without compromising their own independence. The reason for this is very simple, and it is a Buddhist reason: when you reject your parents, in fact when you reject anybody, the rejection is almost always the expression of a negative emotional attitude. In plain English, it's an expression of anger or ill will or even hatred, and negative emotions are one of the biggest obstacles to the leading of a spiritual life. Hatred is one of the five mental hindrances that prevent us from meditating properly, from entering into higher states of consciousness. It is thus of the utmost importance that we get rid of our negative emotions, and particularly any that we have towards our parents.

I think the reason is obvious. Under normal circumstances it is our parents who bring us up, so we have a longer connection with them than with any other human being, with the possible exception of our siblings. Because we are so closely associated with our parents from the beginning, our emotional ties with them are naturally very strong – sometimes we don't realize how strong. They are probably stronger than our emotional ties with anybody else, and may determine the pattern of all our subsequent emotional relations. A great deal of emotional energy is thus invested in our relationship with our parents, even though we may not be aware of that. If our attitude towards our parents is negative, our whole emotional life is disturbed, even distorted. We may have difficulty in relating to other people in a positive manner, and it may be more difficult for us to develop spiritually. It is therefore of the utmost importance that we should get rid of any negative feelings towards our parents and establish positive, friendly relations with them. This may not be easy, either for them or for us, but we should be patient. What has taken a long time to do will probably take a long time to undo. Your parents may disapprove of your way of life. They may be disappointed that you're not living up to their expectations. They may not be able to understand why you have given up a good job for the sake of what they see as a passing whim, namely Buddhism. All this may make your task more difficult. But you should persevere. If you explain to your parents what you're trying to do, communicate yourself as fully as possible, in the end usually they will understand, at least to some extent. At least they will come to understand that Buddhism really is important to you. Perhaps they'll even see that you've become a better and happier person. But even if they don't understand, you will have cleared the air so far as you are concerned. Your attitude towards them will be positive, whatever their attitude towards you may be. You will feel *mettā* for them, and in this way you will avoid the extreme of rejecting your parents, even as you avoid the extreme of submitting to them. You will be following the middle way so far as relations with your parents are concerned.

Though parents loom so large in our life, especially when we're young, they're only part of a larger society, and that society has its own customs, traditions, and culture. What should be our attitude towards these? Once again we find ourselves, I hope, on the middle way. According to a modern dictionary, the word culture has ten distinct meanings. This evening, we're concerned with the fourth of these: 'The artistic and social pursuits, expression, and taste valued by a society or class.'[253] Culture in this sense finds objective embodiment in works of art: paintings, sculptures, musical composition, poems, plays, novels, and so on. It finds embodiment in the masterpieces of Turner, Michelangelo, Mozart, Shakespeare, Milton, Tolstoy, to name only a few of the very greatest. These are among the supreme achievements of Western culture and are an integral part of our heritage. What should our attitude to them be?

Here too we have to distinguish between two extremes: unthinking acceptance, and unthinking rejection. These terms are not very satisfactory, but what I mean by them should emerge as we proceed. Unthinking acceptance of Western culture by a Western Buddhist consists in the acceptance of it in the same way, and for the same reasons, as it is accepted by non-Buddhist Westerners. It is unthinking because it makes no attempt to link Western culture to the Dharma. This was very much the attitude when I returned to England in 1964. Culture in the higher sense did not usually come into the picture. It was as though Western Buddhists in those days divided their lives into two separate compartments, keeping their Buddhism, such as it was, in one and everything else in the other. When you attended a Buddhist meeting or read a Buddhist book you were a Buddhist, but on all other occasions you were just like everybody else of your social class and educational background, and perhaps you were proud of that. People used to say to me, 'Yes, I'm a Buddhist, but I'm really just like everybody else.' You lived in the same kind of house, worked in the same kind of job, had the same kind of family, went to see the same films, and hung the same kinds of pictures on your walls. Your acceptance of Western culture was unthinking because you made no attempt to relate it to Buddhism. This attitude is still common among Western Buddhists outside the FWBO, especially when their connection to Buddhism is tenuous or predominantly theoretical.

What about the other extreme, the unthinking rejection of Western culture? Those Western Buddhists who reject Western culture tend to be of two kinds. There are those who reject it because they reject all culture. They believe that all one has to do is follow the Noble Eightfold Path, or practise *vipassanā*, looking neither to right nor left, never visiting an art gallery, never looking at a picture, never listening to music. And then there are those who reject Western culture but replace it by some form of Eastern culture. In the early days of the FWBO, Japanese culture was in favour, but nowadays I think Tibetan culture is the most popular. The extreme attitude of rejecting Western culture root and branch, even in its sublimest manifestations, as totally irrelevant to the practice of Buddhism in the West, was exemplified recently by a Western Theravādin monk who declared that he saw no point in visiting art galleries, since the paintings were simply the products of greed, hatred, and delusion. Here Buddhism and Western culture are not just kept separate but seen as completely opposed to each other, and being a Buddhist therefore means giving up Western culture. But that is an unthinking rejection based on pure assumption, even prejudice. The person concerned does not actually experience individual works of art and ask, 'What effect does this painting (or poem, or piece of music) have on me?' Interestingly, the monk in question, when asked whether the works of Michelangelo and William Blake were the products of greed, hatred, and delusion, replied that they were only of peripheral importance. One can't help wonder how close his acquaintance was with the culture he so confidently rejected. The unthinking rejection of some of the loftiest products of the human spirit is unpleasant to contemplate, and unnecessary. Here as elsewhere we can apply the great criterion that the Buddha gave Mahāprajāpatī Gautamī, his aunt and foster-mother and faithful disciple.[254] We can ask ourselves if this or that painting or poem helps us to practise the Dharma or hinders us. Does it help us to develop spiritually or not? If it helps, we're free to accept it, look at it, read it, expose ourselves to its influence. And if it does not, we can reject it, or at least put it to one side.

But how can a work of art help us to develop spiritually? A clue is found in the fifth of the ten definitions of culture to which I referred: 'The enlightenment of refinement resulting from these pursuits' – i.e. from the artistic and social pursuits mentioned in the preceding definition. Culture refines us, and in particular it refines our emotions and makes our emotional life more positive, and without positive emotion there is no spiritual life. In this respect too we have been on the middle way for the last twenty years.

Western culture is part of world culture, and culture is part of social and public life, part of the world, part of what Buddhism calls the *saṃsāra*. What then is the FWBO's attitude towards the world? Once again we follow the middle way, avoiding two extreme views. The first extreme consists in accepting the world on its own terms, in immersing ourselves in the existing social, political, and economic order, even in the existing cultural and religious order. In this case we experience ourselves as wholly belonging to the world, as being part of the world with nothing left over for ourselves as individuals. Indeed, there is no self, no self-conscious, responsible, autonomous individual. We are simply a member of the group, whether the group is small or large. We don't question the values of the group, or of the world.

The other extreme is the exact opposite. Here we reject the world – not only reject it, but try to escape from it, at least for the time being. Some try to escape into rural life. That was the dream of the Sixties – to get away to a beautiful little stone cottage in Wales and have wood fires, and smoke dope, and grow your own food, and make your own shoes, and weave your own cloth. Others escape into mystical or aesthetic experience, like the hero of Tennyson's poem 'The Palace of Art'.[255] Others again escape into daydreams, fantasies, even madness. But though they do their best to ignore the world, usually the world refuses to ignore them, and that is another story, often quite a sad one.

How does the FWBO avoid these two extremes? In what way do we follow the middle way where the world is concerned? The answer is to be found in a single word: transformation. Our attitude is that we want to transform the world. We do not accept it on its own terms, and at the same time we don't reject it or try to escape from it. In the long run, indeed, it's impossible to escape from the world. We therefore seek to bring the world more and more under the influence of the moral and spiritual principles signified by the word Dharma, more and more under the influence of what we've come to refer to as the golden light.[256] We seek to create a new society, a society that is conducive to the spiritual development of the individual in the fullest sense of the term. The nucleus of that society is to be found in the FWBO centres, spiritual communities, and team-based right livelihood businesses that have sprung up in the last twenty years. In this respect too we can speak of twenty years on the middle way.

In the last twenty years the FWBO has been on the middle way in many different respects, and this evening I have mentioned only some of the more important of them. We're on the middle way inasmuch as we avoid the extremes of formalistic monasticism and lax laicism. We emphasize that commitment to the Three Jewels is primary, lifestyle secondary. Our attitude to our parents is neither one of submission, nor one of rejection. We try to relate to our parents as one human being to another, and develop a positive attitude towards them. We neither unthinkingly accept nor unthinkingly reject our Western cultural heritage; we accept and utilize that part of it which helps us to develop spiritually, and that part of it which does not help us we put aside. And we neither accept the world on its own terms, nor seek to escape from it into a private world of our own. Instead we seek to transform the world. I am glad that we have been on the middle way together for so many years, and I hope we shall continue to tread it for many more years to come. I hope that one day the FWBO will be able to look back not just on twenty, but thirty, forty, fifty, even a hundred and more years on the middle way.

THE NEXT TWENTY YEARS

Twentieth anniversary of the Western Buddhist Order, 1988

Dharmacāris and *dharmacāriṇīs*: The Western Buddhist Order has been in existence for twenty years: twenty years of meditation classes, lectures, Dharma study, retreats, team-based right livelihood, work, play, triumphs, disappointments, heartache, disillusionment, and through them all the Order and the Movement steadily growing. I can't help reminiscing about the meditation classes at our old Sakura basement, followed by walks with Ananda along the Victoria Embankment, sometimes in the late spring sunshine, sometimes in the snow, talking about poetry, Buddhism, the arts, the novel on which Ananda was working.[257] There have been twenty years of spiritual friendship, and twenty years of commitment to the Buddha, the Dharma, and the Sangha.

But what about the next twenty years? What do they hold for us, individually and collectively? I must confess straightaway that I'm unable to see into the future. I can't give you any clue as to what is going to happen in the next twenty years. I don't know any more than you do. But perhaps there is just one thing I can be sure of. I'm almost sure that twenty years from now some of us will be dead. The only thing we can be sure of in this life is death. In his introduction Ananda spoke about the paradox of time and eternity, but there's also the paradox of life and death, the paradox that the only thing that we can be utterly certain about with regard to life is that it will end.

The day after tomorrow I shall be reading a paper on the history of my Going for Refuge.[258] This is something to which I've given a great deal of thought, something I've composed very carefully. But I haven't prepared a lecture for this evening. It's going to be more of a semi-impromptu talk on the basis of some rough notes. I'm not going to try to predict what's going to happen, because there are so many unknowns. What I'm going to do is simply share with you some of my hopes and fears with regard to the next twenty years. I can't resist just a little formality, so there are going to be three headings: self, the Order-cum-movement, and thirdly, rather grandly, the world.

SELF

By self I don't mean anything abstract or philosophical this time – I'm just going to talk about myself. So what about me? What's going to happen to me in the next twenty years? Well, very probably I'm going to die. I might linger on a few more years, who knows? I might even hit my century. But if I do come to an end so far as this physical body is concerned in the next twenty years, I hope nobody will be surprised because, as I said, the fact of death is the one thing we can be sure about. I have to face up to the fact that in the next twenty years I may disappear from the scene, and even if I'm still here, I probably won't have the energy and robustness to carry on doing what I have been doing for these last twenty years and more. This raises an important question about my responsibilities with regard to the Order and the Movement. In the last few years I have been making some effort to hand them over, but I'm quite surprised to find how many I still have. It sometimes seems as though they are not diminishing, but growing. But I hope that within the next four or five years I will be able to hand over all my remaining responsibilities to the more senior and experienced members of the Order.

Then what am I going to do? Am I going to sit under a shady tree somewhere or lie in a hammock? Am I going to devote myself to reading the collected works of Dr Samuel Johnson, or the *Encyclopædia Britannica*? Am I going to start learning Chinese or retire to a cave in the Himalayas, visa permitting, and devote myself to meditation? The answer is quite simple. If I succeed in handing over my organizational-cum-spiritual responsibilities, I would like to do more writing, which I hope will benefit not only myself but the Movement, and perhaps people beyond the Movement too. I have been struggling to finish a second volume of memoirs for nearly ten years, and when I've finished that I'd like to write more autobiographical material. I want to devote more time to literary work, and perhaps to the editing of some of the transcripts of my seminars and lectures as well, though I rather hope that some of you will be able to give me a helping hand with that. There are quite a few people within the Order who are able to edit seminars quite successfully, and I hope that in the next twenty years they will be able to edit and publish the bulk of the seminar transcripts and the earlier lectures.[259] I must also confess that I wouldn't mind being able to spend some of my old age, even as I spent quite a lot of my youth, writing the poems that come to me when I'm quiet and undisturbed.

I would very much like to carry on my literary work at Guhyaloka, at least for some months of the year.[260] I hope to be able to spend four months there this year, and while I'm there, as well as taking part in the men's ordination retreat, I hope to write a few more chapters of my memoirs. But I won't be taking my office with me. I want to have a modest collection of a thousand or so books there, which I will need in connection with my literary work, but I don't intend to take all those filing cabinets and archives we're accumulating at Padmaloka. In the last few years we've built up a reasonably efficient infrastructure, upon which the successful running of the Movement depends. Even if I withdraw from active participation in the running of the Movement, that infrastructure will have to continue and will need to be supported. I see a picture emerging in the next few years, if I'm spared, of spending four or five months of the year at Guhyaloka engaged in literary work and the rest of the year either at Padmaloka or visiting centres in Britain and elsewhere. I hope that by the time we're halfway through the next twenty years, I shall be spending rather more time at Guhyaloka than at Padmaloka and engaging myself more and more deeply in literary work.

My most important responsibility, and one which I've only just begun to share with a few senior Order members, is that of conferring *dharmacāri* and *dharmacāriṇī* ordination, and in that way accepting people into the Order. But when I hand over that responsibility, what exactly will be handed over? I won't be giving anybody a certificate or a title, so what will I be giving them? Will I be giving them anything in the literal sense? Let's get down to basics. We are human beings who go for Refuge to the Buddha, the Dharma, and the Sangha. To begin with, so far as our own movement is concerned, there was only me Going for Refuge, but gradually other people came along, practised meditation, studied the Dharma, started communicating with one another, started going on retreat, started becoming friends with me. After a while I started to feel that other men and women around me were Going for Refuge in the same way I was, so I ordained them. They were going in the same direction as me, or, to change the figure of speech, they were learning to dance in the same way that I was dancing, and then we danced together, two or three of us to begin with, then ten, twelve, and later hundreds. Basically, I went for Refuge, others went for Refuge, I saw that they were Going for Refuge in the way that I was, and that recognition was their ordination within the Western Buddhist Order.

This is what I mean by handing over my responsibilities for conferring ordination. We go for Refuge in the same way, we all take Going for Refuge as the central and essential act of the Buddhist life. You come into contact with people, just as I did and continue to do. You teach them meditation, discuss the Dharma with them, go on retreat with them, develop spiritual friendship with them, and after a while it dawns upon you that this man or this woman is Going for Refuge in the same way as you, and you feel they're ready to be ordained. Sometimes people aren't sure whether someone is ready for ordination, and sometimes there's even a difference of opinion between Order members. It's difficult to know other people. But if you are unsure whether someone is ready for ordination or is beginning to go for Refuge, ask yourself, 'How sure am I about my own Going for Refuge?' If that is unmistakably clear and strong, it won't be difficult for you to know whether it resonates in another person you know well.

Ideally each and every one of you will be in the position that I was in when the Order was started. You will recognize that other people go for Refuge or are beginning to go for Refuge, just as I recognized it in the early days and have been recognizing it ever since. When you can do that, there will be a handing over of responsibility for ordination without anything being handed over at all. It won't be a question of me giving it to you because you will have it already, you will have developed it by virtue of your own Going for Refuge. Because your own Going for Refuge is strong, powerful, clear, direct, and unambiguous, you will be able to recognize whether others go for Refuge or not. And when a sufficient number of you recognize that, then you will be in the position of conferring ordination within the Western Buddhist Order. That's the principle. I haven't yet worked out the mechanics, though I hope to do that fairly soon, but it's not just a question of authorizing in a purely formal way what I've spoken of as the responsibility for conferring ordinations. It's to be handed over only if within each and every Order member, or at least within the senior, more experienced Order members, there is a Going for Refuge sufficiently clear and strong to recognize Going for Refuge quite unmistakably in others.

Each and every one of you ought to be able to do what I've done. Especially if you've been ordained for seven or more years, it ought to be possible for me to put you down in the jungles of Brazil or the deserts of Australia and say, 'Start up the FWBO, start up the Order.' In principle, ideally, every single one of you, in the course of your lifetime, should be able to do more or less what I've done, except that you have the advantage of belonging to an existing order. You are not only included in the mandala of the Order; you are also the nucleus of an order which could develop from the Order as we have it now. Each of you could become the centre of another spiritual community of members of the Western Buddhist Order. In the last twenty years, doing my best, I have been able to produce, not counting some who have dropped out, the 337 Order members who are in the Order at present. I'm quite sure there are people sitting here who, if not in the next twenty years, certainly in the next forty years, if the world doesn't come to an end and they don't die prematurely, will have ordained far more people than I have. Don't think, 'Well, Bhante's ordained 337 Order members, so maybe in my lifetime I'll ordain five or ten.' We've got to grow, we've got to expand. There's no reason why some of you shouldn't, in association with other Order members, ordain five hundred or even a thousand other people.

At present our movement is very small, but I'm sure it can grow. In my lifetime I've seen so many changes which I could not have dreamed of, both for better and for worse. For instance, when I tried to visit Tibet in 1950 or 1951, I wasn't allowed in. No one was. Tibet was a theocracy. There were thousands of monasteries and tens of thousands of monks, and without idealizing the state of affairs then, virtually the whole population was devoted to the Dharma. But sadly, we all know what the position is now. During my lifetime changes have taken place in China too, and in Vietnam and Cambodia. That's the debit side of the balance sheet. But when I arrived in India, how many Buddhists were there? At a guess, not more than 100,000, mostly in places like Sikkim, Darjeeling, and Ladakh, and just a few thousand scattered over the plains of India. Now there are at least four million Buddhists in India, some people say twenty million. Look at that tremendous change, due mainly to the efforts of Dr Ambedkar. I certainly would not have thought that there would have been this tremendous expansion of Buddhism in India during my lifetime. So I don't see it as impossible that there will be a tremendous expansion of the Order in the next twenty, thirty, or forty years. I haven't done much more than plant a few seeds; it'll be up to all of you and those who come after you to water those seeds, nurture the plants that spring up, and plant more seeds. I'm quite sure that most of you can do much more than you think you can. Some of you have discovered that recently, especially those who have done things like door-knocking or going to America to raise funds for Aid For India.[261] You probably wouldn't have thought seven or eight years ago that you could have done that, but you've done it, and I'm sure that you can do a lot more. We have to think big, not in a megalomaniacal way, but because we have faith in the Dharma and confidence in our own Going for Refuge. If we have that, there will be a network of chapters spreading far and wide.

I think I can say that my share of the work will be complete only when the Order is no longer dependent on me personally. I no longer have to lead all the meditation classes, give all the lectures, or lead all the retreats, but there are still a lot of things I have to do, including the conferring of ordinations. I shall consider that I have really done my work for the Dharma in this lifetime when I am able to hand over all my responsibilities and see the whole Movement, and the Order especially, functioning well and happily and effectively without me. My biggest hope is that in the next twenty years the Movement will become quite independent of me, so that it won't matter whether I spend my time at Guhyaloka or Padmaloka, whether I write prose or poetry, or whether I do absolutely nothing at all, whether I just put my feet up, assuming I've got somewhere to put them up and they're not too stiff.

THE ORDER AND MOVEMENT

It's obvious in view of what I've already said that I hope that in the next twenty years the Order and the Movement will grow. Barring untoward circumstances, barring something like a major conflict or even a nuclear war, I'm confident that it will. But I'd like to express a few hopes and preferences. I must confess that I would like to see proportionately more women Order members. For years I've lain awake at night wondering why we don't have more women Order members. We've got plenty of women in the Movement. Is it because they're naturally slower, or more thorough in their preparation, or more cautious? I've not been able to come to any definite conclusion, but I can't help hoping that in the next twenty years the proportion of women in the Order throughout the world will increase.[262]

I'd also like to indulge the hope that we will have more *anagārikas* and *anagārikās*. First of all, I think that if one can subsume and sublimate one's sexual feelings and live a naturally, happily celibate life, that is really best. Also, if we have more men and women who are *anagārikas* and *anagārikās*, I think they will hold the two wings of the Order together a little more closely. We have found from experience that single-sex communities, retreats, and right livelihood situations are excellent things, conducive to growth and development, but we don't want the two wings of the Order drifting too far apart, because we do after all constitute one order. I'm sure that if we have a sufficient number of *anagārikas* and *anagārikās* and especially if they're a little on the elderly side, mature, above the emotional conflict and turmoil that younger people are sometimes subject to, they will form a solid body in the middle, holding the balance between these two wings.

In a sense I don't want to encourage people to become *anagārikas*, because you mustn't take this vow of celibacy, to call it that, prematurely. You must be ready for it and I doubt very much whether young people are usually ready for it. It suits older people who have been through all that, perhaps through their family life, and have come out at the other end and dedicated themselves to celibacy. I have mentioned in the past the age of 40, but let's make it 45, to give you a few more years of grace – or disgrace. By the time you're 45, and especially if you've been an Order member for some years, you should be prepared seriously to consider celibacy – not because Bhante said it once upon a time in a lecture, but because you start naturally feeling that way inclined. When your energy starts naturally employing all of you along purely cultural and spiritual channels, when you're naturally sublimating your lower instincts or impulses, you can start giving serious thought to the question of living a celibate life and becoming an *anagārika*.[263]

That leads on to something which is quite closely connected: the precepts. A few years ago I gave a paper on the ten pillars of

Buddhism.[264] I don't know the extent to which Order members have studied this paper, but clearly the ten precepts are absolutely basic. The observance of the ten precepts represents a natural application of one's Going for Refuge to every aspect of one's life. In the next twenty years I'd like to see people taking the precepts more seriously and scrutinizing their behaviour, their thoughts, and their words in the light of those ten ethical principles. Perhaps I could draw special attention to the speech precepts. We're talking so much of the time, and it's so easy to break or at least fracture one or other of the speech precepts. In particular people need to avoid rough or harsh speech. I must admit I'm surprised by the rather rough way in which Order members sometimes address one another. We need to make a much more constant effort to speak gently, kindly, thoughtfully, at the right time, and in the right manner. I'm afraid that even within the Order, and especially perhaps within the men's wing, there's still a great deal of room for improvement in this respect.

I'd also like to see more mindfulness. There's a book by a Vietnamese monk which is very popular at the moment: *The Miracle of Mindfulness*.[265] He probably calls it a miracle because mindfulness is so rare. If you practise mindfulness it's a real miracle. As Buddhists we're not supposed to perform miracles in the literal sense, but let me assure you, we are allowed to perform the miracle of mindfulness. So don't hesitate. The more people who read that little book, the better. It's not about straining and struggling to be mindful while you're meditating or while you're in the shrine-room; you need to be mindful all the time, aware all the time, conscious all the time, in the fullest sense. Also, maintain your continuity of purpose. We can get so easily distracted, forgetting what we're supposed to be doing in even the most ordinary sense. I've given all sorts of illustrations of this before, but still it seems that mindfulness is a very difficult lesson for us to learn. But in the next twenty years I would like to see an increase in the practice of mindfulness in ordinary everyday life.

I'd also like to see an improvement in people's manners. Some people think that good manners are very middle class, very Victorian, and that being rude and ill-mannered shows how free and spontaneous and individual you are, but it really just shows how crude and uncultured you are, and how lacking in sensitivity to other people's feelings. I'm not suggesting that manners should become very formal. During the war the Polish officers won the heart of many a British maiden with their smart clicks of the heel and little bows from the waist. Some of my English friends tried to imitate it but they couldn't do it like the Poles, especially when the Poles were handsome and had moustaches that they could twirl. I'm not speaking of manners in that sense, but just genuine politeness. When the doorbell rings and you go to answer it, don't just say 'Uuur?' I've seen it! I've heard people answering the phone just with 'Yes?' If your mother and father didn't teach you good manners, teach yourself. Courtesy paves the way for friendly communication, not only among ourselves but with the outside world. You may be the first Buddhist that someone has ever met, so don't let people think that Buddhists are rude or ill-mannered or thoughtless. This is all very basic stuff. Ananda spoke of the magical mystery tour of the future, but I'm afraid I'm simply reminding you of some basic things and expressing my hope that they will be given greater attention in the next twenty years. Connected with this question of better manners is the question of mutual kindness. I've been rather surprised sometimes to see that Order members aren't always very kind to one another. They don't always speak kindly to one another or treat one another very considerately. I'd like to see a great improvement in this area too.

I'd also like to see more vision. I'd like to see more imagination, I'd like to see people taking a broader view. I know that's difficult if you're bogged down in the day to day work of running a co-op, or if you've got classes to take every day. If you're not careful, you can lose your wider vision of Buddhism and the Movement and the spiritual life. But we must retain that vision, retain that imagination, retain even that transcendental insight, so that it illumines everything that we do.

Here we come to a mixture of fear and hope for the next twenty years. I hope that we can keep the Dharma free from non-Buddhist admixtures. There are always temptations to mix the Buddha's teaching with something else, or interpret it in a way that is not in accordance with that teaching. For example, we quite rightly talk about our development as human beings, our spiritual development, our emotional development, our development from a lower to a higher level of consciousness, but if we're not careful we can introduce a subtle misunderstanding and start looking at things in terms of whether they're good for our development in a very narrow, almost precious way. Someone may ask you to work in a co-op and you say, 'Well, I'm feeling a bit sensitive these days – I don't think it would be good for my development.' Or they suggest that you should meditate a bit more, and you say, 'Well, I'm not really into meditation, and if I were to force myself it wouldn't be good for my development.' Or you might say, 'I think it would be good for my development if I had a holiday, if I let myself go for a bit, if I wasn't so mindful, and maybe if I gave up meditation for a while.' Or maybe someone in difficulties asks you to help them, and you say, 'I don't think it would be good for my development to bother about that. I really need to stay quiet for a while.' In that way the idea of spiritual development becomes self-centred, even selfish; you twist the whole idea in a quite unBuddhistic way. I detect within the Movement a tendency of that sort. I'm not saying we shouldn't think in terms of self-development – it's very valuable – but we should also see the altruistic dimension of Going for Refuge much more clearly. We need a much greater emphasis on the bodhisattva ideal. I've even been wondering whether we should recite or read the bodhisattva precepts in the Sevenfold Puja, to remind ourselves of that other dimension.[266] It's not just a question of Going for Refuge ourselves; it's also a question of making the Dharma available to other people and helping them, especially other Order members, in whatever way we can. From time to time I invoke the image of the eleven-headed, thousand-armed Avalokiteśvara as an embodiment of the Order, and the whole movement. At the highest level, the Order is an embodiment of the *bodhicitta* in the world. There's no place for 'development' in a narrow or self-centred way. We perhaps need to emphasize the bodhisattva ideal as the altruistic dimension of Going for Refuge much more than we've done in the past.

I've sometimes wondered too whether the Order should change its name. It has really ceased to be 'Western' because now we have many Order people who are not Westerners. The 'Western Buddhist Order' is well known, but perhaps this is something that we may have to consider in the next twenty years.[267]

On a wider front, I'd like to see more emphasis on cultural activities, on the arts, because these do help very much to engage, sublimate, and direct our emotions, as well as our intellectual understanding, along the spiritual path. In the last year I've been thinking very seriously that we need to connect more with our Graeco-Roman philosophical heritage and tradition. I've begun to feel that we can regard the Christian centuries as a bad dream from which we've woken up. I've been rereading Plato and Plotinus and Pythagoras and the other great sages and thinkers of Greece and Rome, and there's an amazing wealth of ideas and inspiration there. One finds philosophy taken seriously, being understood not just as an academic discipline, but as a whole way of life that is very congenial to Buddhists. I'd like people to read things like Plato's *Symposium* and Aristotle's *Ethics*, the thoughts of Marcus Aurelius, the letters of Seneca, and the dialogues of Cicero. There are literary classics too: the plays of the great Greek dramatists, the *Iliad* and the *Odyssey* and the *Aeneid*. These are the connections we should be making. If we can point out parallels between the Graeco-Roman philosophical, religious, and spiritual traditions and the Indian Buddhist traditions, that will help us feel that Buddhism isn't so foreign, isn't just something brought to us from the East, but has parallels and even roots in the classical West. This is something I would very much like to see developing in the next twenty years. A few Order members have been studying Greek and Latin. I'd like to see more people reading the classics in translation and taking them seriously. Something like Cicero's dialogue on friendship says so much, it's so useful to us. There's a lot that we can learn, a lot with which we can feel very much at home in a way that we perhaps can't in Christian literature.

An allied topic is that of ethics in society. Nowadays we read a fair amount in the papers about the need for morality in society, and there certainly is that need, but society is not going to be held together by the police force and the law courts, or by the army as is the case in some countries. Society is held together by a generally accepted system of social and cultural ethics. Dr Ambedkar gave a great deal of thought to this area of life, and stated very clearly that society can't be held together by force, but only by morality, by feeling.[268] The great mistake that the politicians and commentators make is in thinking that because we need more ethics in our social life, the ethics have to be Christian. They point us in the direction of the dear old Church, which in fact has failed to provide an ethical basis for our society. As a movement, as an order, it is our duty to go out as much as we can into society and make clear the Buddhist conception of ethics, which is healthy, positive, and creative in a way that Christian ethics is not. We don't want an ethics of guilt and fear, but an ethics of growth and development, which is what we have in Buddhism. So we need to try to fill this gap. We accept the need for more ethics in our social life but we reject the notion that those ethics have to be Christian. This is a topic on which we have a lot to say and we should say it loud and clear whenever we get the opportunity.

Closely linked to this is the question of team-based right livelihood. I've sometimes said that this is one of the most difficult things we've undertaken. It's not very difficult to set up a centre, and it's not much more difficult to start a community, but it seems to be ten times more difficult to set up a successful right livelihood structure. I think some Order members are beginning to have doubts, if not about team-based right livelihood, at least about the cooperative structure. I don't want to insist on that structure, but I do want to insist on the importance of team-based right livelihood. I hope that in the next twenty years there will be more and more emphasis on it, that we shall see not just Mitras directed from a distance by Order members, but teams of Order members working together creating wealth to donate to those sections of the Movement which are devoting themselves to things other than the accumulation of wealth. In some cases we need to alter our attitude towards money. The Movement doesn't run on money but it's going to be very difficult for it to run in any practical way without it, and some of us are beginning to realize that. I didn't realize it fully myself until comparatively recently. After all, for twenty years in India I got by more or less without money. I certainly didn't start up a business, unless my production of reviews and articles could be described as a literary industry. I did occasionally get paid for them, but whatever I earned didn't bring in much more than a few rupees to buy a few more books. But since then I've given a great deal of thought to the question of right livelihood, and I think it is, and will be, one of the great planks of the FWBO and of the Order, so I hope that more attention will be given to it in the next twenty years.

I would also like to see the Order and the FWBO engaging in more effective publicity. I think we still hide our light under a bushel, in the biblical phrase, far too much. We really must make ourselves better known. I'm quite sure that around the world, in so many countries, there are people who, in the Buddhist phrase, have their eyes covered with just a little dust, and who are perishing for not hearing the Dharma. We're just starting to publicize ourselves a bit more. Almost every few days I get a letter from someone, or someone comes to see me, and they say, 'Thank you for establishing the FWBO.' I ask, 'How did you hear about it?' and they say that they saw a poster, or an advert, or someone in the office told them about it. People who would love to be in contact with a movement like the FWBO are not going to be able to do so unless we make ourselves known to them. In the next twenty years I would like to see the Movement making itself much better known so that more and more people can benefit from what we have to offer.

THE WORLD

I must say that, looking at the world, or at least reading the newspapers from time to time, although by nature I'm optimistic, I don't feel all that optimistic about the world. In the last year or two perhaps there's been some slight change on the international front, politically speaking, but not much, and that change could easily be undone. There could be an atomic explosion at any time, even by accident, and I'm still very aware of the possibility of an atomic war. We banish these things to the backs of our minds, but they are still possibilities. I spoke about this in my lecture some years ago, 'Buddhism, World Peace, and Nuclear War', so I'm not going to dwell on it now.[269] I just want to touch on three topics of national and international concern to which I think we ought to give more thought.

First of all, there's AIDS. We all know about it, but I wonder whether every Order member and every Mitra is sufficiently careful about it. So far the Movement seems to have remained almost free from AIDS, but there are two Friends who have it, one in the United Kingdom and one in New Zealand, so it's beginning to come close. I really hope that in the next twenty years not a single Order member or a single Mitra catches AIDS. I know that occasionally people catch it through no fault of their own, for instance by way of blood transfusion, but leaving aside matters of that sort, I hope and expect that in the next twenty years AIDS won't touch the Order and movement, and that depends upon the mindfulness, the thoughtfulness, of individual Order members. I'd like you to give serious thought to this matter. I know that a few of you are very aware of this problem, but it's very easy to forget, and all those who are not leading celibate lives need to bear it in mind all the time.

Something else about which I've felt quite concerned and pained recently is the question of racial prejudice and discrimination. If you had asked me a few years ago whether racial prejudice and discrimination was on the decline in Britain I would have said, 'Yes, it certainly is, and it won't be many years before it disappears altogether', but I don't think I could say that today. In the last few months I've read in the newspapers so many reports of cases of harassment that I've come to the conclusion that as a movement, and especially as an Order, we need to take a much more active part in combatting prejudice and discrimination of that sort. I'm quite sure that within the Order, and perhaps within the Movement as a whole, there is no racial prejudice or discrimination of any kind, but there's certainly a lot of it in Britain and I think we have to try not just to ensure that it doesn't exist in our midst, but to do whatever we can to remove such prejudice from the society in which our movement functions. We can't just look the other way and content ourselves with the fact that we ourselves don't personally practise that discrimination or indulge in that prejudice. I'm not suggesting we take a militant attitude – that is often counter-productive – but in a gentle and kindly and non-violent way we must do everything in our power to counteract this menace, which is obviously quite opposed to the whole spirit of the Dharma.

Another matter that I've felt quite concerned about recently is the environment. It does seem that human beings are destroying our own environment, and it may be that in the next twenty years very serious damage will be done to the total environment of life on earth. One reads dreadful things about the destruction of rainforests, and of all sorts of species of living things. To me it seems dreadful that thousands of beautiful species of animals, fish, birds, and butterflies are just being wiped out each year. We need to take a much stronger stand on such issues, and perhaps play a more active part, at least in our individual capacities, in the environmental movement. This is completely in accordance with the principles of Buddhism. As Buddhists we are urged to direct *mettā* towards all living beings, and that doesn't just mean all human beings, but all animals, insects, plants, birds, and life of every kind, so this is the basis of our ecological concern. We wish all living beings well. It's in our own interests to do so because we can't live on a naked planet. We can't live on rock and sand; we depend upon vegetation and animal life. We're all interconnected, another great lesson from Buddhism. In the next twenty years I would like to see the Order developing an ecological dimension, and I would like to see some Order members working in this field on the basis of their Buddhist commitment, perhaps in some cases working alongside non-Buddhists who share this concern.

There's a lot more that I could say. Don't think that because I haven't mentioned something, I don't consider it important. I couldn't possibly have mentioned everything in a mere hour and a half. But these are at least some of my reflections, some of my hopes and fears. In conclusion, I think I have to say that in some ways the next twenty years will be more difficult than the last twenty, because they are going to be a period of transition, a period of the handing over of responsibility, and especially responsibility for ordination, from me to all of you. That presupposes that you will be able to take over that responsibility, both individually and collectively. I have every confidence that you will be able to do that. In the last twenty years I've at least to some extent shown the way. The rest, in the next twenty years and beyond, is up to you.

FIFTEEN POINTS FOR NEW – AND OLD – ORDER MEMBERS

Guhyaloka Ordination Course, 1988

I'm not sure what everybody is expecting, but this isn't going to be a lecture, or even a talk – just a reminder, or rather fifteen reminders. They are not exhaustive, just points that have occurred to me as I've had contact with people on the retreat and called up memories of past retreats, especially thinking about what it's like going back into the world after a retreat. These reminders are mainly for the nine people who have just been ordained, though they will be of value for others too, whether they have been ordained for a long or a short time. The reminders are not arranged in order of importance. Perhaps you could think of them as arranged in a circle. They all hang together, they are of virtually equal importance, and they more or less reinforce one another.

1. KEEP UP CONTACT WITH ME

The first point I want to make is that I hope that those who have been newly ordained will keep up contact with me in the days, months, and years to come. This might sound obvious, but I can assure you it doesn't always happen. Sometimes I've had the experience of being on an ordination retreat for three months with somebody. We've had a very good time together, studied together and meditated together, but then he goes back to his centre and I don't see him again for a whole year. Maybe he doesn't even write. Before he was invited on the ordination retreat he might have been writing to me every month, even every week, but after he's been ordained I don't get so much as a birthday card or a Wesak greetings card. So do your best to keep up personal contact with me. I know that when you go back to your own centre you're going to be very busy, but I haven't forgotten you and hope that you haven't forgotten me. Occasionally come to see me, or write a letter, or at least send a picture postcard from the nearest museum or art gallery. Sometimes people genuinely think that I'm too busy to answer or even read letters, but I can always make time for Order members, especially those who have been recently ordained. Sometimes people think that they've nothing very interesting or important to say, but that seems to be to do with not valuing oneself sufficiently, having a poor self-image, as the psychologists say. Whatever you've been doing, even if you haven't been doing very much, I would like to know. If you haven't been doing very much and should have been doing more, I would then have the opportunity to write and tell you so. So please do keep up personal contact in whatever way you can.

2. BE REGULAR IN YOUR ATTENDANCE AT CHAPTER MEETINGS

You will have heard that there are these weekly gatherings of Order members living and working in the same area. They are extremely important. We all know what the Buddha said about his disciples needing to meet together regularly and in large numbers in order that the unity of the Sangha should be preserved.[270] The same Order members may meet on other occasions for other purposes, but when you meet as a chapter you meet just because you are Order members and appreciate being together, though not just in a social way. I've spoken of chapter meetings as spiritual workshops. I know they are not always that, but that is definitely what they should aspire to be. Being together on the occasion of a chapter meeting should mean having a vivid, lively spiritual exchange on the basis of your common commitment to the spiritual life and the Three Jewels. I know that chapter meetings sometimes become a bit dull, and sometimes Order members wonder why on earth they bother. But fortunately, especially for those of you who are going back as new Order members, in the last couple of years things have improved considerably, and many chapters are real spiritual workshops in which people get to grips with one another, with the Dharma, with their mutual communication, and with any problems that may arise in their midst. So be regular in your attendance at chapter meetings and try to contribute to them as real spiritual workshops, which is why they are there.

3. ATTEND ORDER WEEKENDS

Order weekends occur less frequently than chapter meetings, and they should be a real event for every Order member. Whatever the current arrangements are, make sure you know when the next Order weekend is and plan accordingly. Sometimes I ask someone, 'Why weren't you at the Order weekend?' and he says, 'Oh, I'd forgotten about it,' which seems quite extraordinary. Or he says that he'd arranged to go sailing, or go away with his girlfriend, or visit his parents. That is carelessness, a lack of organization. As soon as it is known when the national Order weekends are going to be held, make a note in your diary and organize the rest of your programme around that. Sometimes I've felt a bit suspicious in the case of Order members who seem to have arranged to do something else every time an Order weekend comes up. One can't help wondering whether there is an unconscious wish to avoid Order weekends, though why that should be one can't imagine. So plan your year well ahead, so that you are able to attend Order weekends.

Also, try to make sure that you arrive fresh. Arrange your work during the days leading up to the Order weekend so that you don't arrive so tired that you can't join in with things. Try to arrive in good time so that you can join in with the opening puja or meditation, and don't hurry away before the weekend is over unless it is absolutely necessary. It is very disheartening to find people arriving on Saturday just in time for lunch and going away on Sunday straight after lunch, after a very short weekend. Occasionally it can't be helped, but don't make a habit of it. Try your utmost to be present for the whole of the event.

4. REPORT IN TO *SHABDA*

You have all heard about *Shabda*, and you may even have read an issue of it by this time, so you will know that it contains reports from Order members in which they describe what they have been doing the previous month – anything of general interest, anything positive they have to contribute. If you've read that first issue of *Shabda*, you may have been a bit disappointed to find that there was no report from your favourite Order members back home. Where are they? What have they been doing? Are they all asleep? Are they all away on solitary retreat? I myself have often felt disappointed to open *Shabda* wanting to know what somebody is doing in some distant part of the globe only to find that there's not a word. Occasionally one finds a whole chapter not reporting in. It's as though they had dropped out of the Order for a while.

So if you possibly can, report in to *Shabda* every month, or nearly every month. Let other Order members know where you are and what you're doing, what you're thinking and feeling, how your meditation has been going, what you've been reading, whether you've been travelling, whether you've had any interesting experiences, whether any insight has come to you which may be of value to the Movement as a whole, whether you've read a book that you would recommend to other Order members, or you've discovered a new meditation technique that you'd like others to try. Contributing to *Shabda* is a means of communicating with the whole Order. Sometimes you may like to contribute an essay on some topic. Occasionally, subject to great self-criticism, you might even like to contribute a poem – though not too often, even if you're a very good poet. If you're as good as all that, you should be collecting your poems together and publishing them in booklet form at your own expense. When someone doesn't report into *Shabda*, it can be very disappointing. It's rather like phoning somebody up and nobody answers, or, worse still, you hear a voice saying, 'This – is – an – answering – machine.' Please do communicate through *Shabda* as much as you possibly can.

5. REALIZE THE UNITY OF THE ORDER

You all know that the unity of the Order is symbolized by the figure of the eleven-headed and thousand-armed Avalokiteśvara. One could say that each of those eleven heads symbolizes a chapter or, as we've got more than eleven chapters, eleven regions throughout the world. The heads represent a degree of unity, and then there are the thousand hands, each holding an implement – a flower, a wheel, a vase, a bow and arrow – representing the particular activity of each Order member, the particular gift they bring to the Order, to the Movement, to the world.

All those symbols and implements, all those hands, all those heads, are integrated into this one figure, Avalokiteśvara, which is the Order, or even, in the widest possible sense, the Movement. It is very important that as an Order member one feels oneself to be one of the hands of Avalokiteśvara.

6. IDENTIFY WITH THE ORDER AS A WHOLE

Your identification with the Order as a whole should be very strong indeed – sufficiently strong, at least, to enable you not to over-identify with your own chapter or centre. When you are spending almost your whole life within a particular chapter and a particular centre, it is easy to lose sight of the Movement as a whole. It is easy to lose sight of the whole figure of Avalokiteśvara and focus on one head, or even two or three hands. Try not to do that. Be loyal to your own centre and work for it wholeheartedly, but see that it is only part of something which is much greater, much more important, than any one centre. This should be a real feeling, and you should feel it very strongly.

7. OPERATE IN ACCORDANCE WITH THE LOVE MODE

Avalokiteśvara is the embodiment of compassion, just as Mañjughoṣa is the embodiment of wisdom and Vajrapāṇi is the embodiment of energy or strength, so if you are yourself a hand of Avalokiteśvara, you should be operating in accordance with compassion, with the love mode or *mettā* mode, not with the power mode. This should especially be the case when you are communicating with fellow Order members. Unfortunately, when one operates in relation to people, organizations, and institutions outside in the world, it may not always be possible to operate purely in accordance with the love mode, but one should be careful to do so when it comes to communicating with fellow members of the Order. Of course, this is very difficult to do. Usually our tendency is to try to coerce other people, however subtly, to give them a nudge, or even a push, in the direction in which we want them to go or think they should go, but in the case of fellow Order members, we should simply not do this. We should act entirely and exclusively in accordance with the love mode. Otherwise, we are not really relating to other Order members as Order members, as individuals.

8. PRACTISE KINDLY SPEECH

I would like to draw special attention to an expression of the love mode that I've been concerned about in the last year or so. We have to practise kindly speech. I have been struck from time to time by the amount of rough or harsh speech that goes on within the Movement and within the Order, and even when Order members are speaking to Mitras. It is very important that we should make a special effort to practise kindly and affectionate speech. Be careful not to speak in a rough, harsh or abrupt way, or in any way that is not an expression of affection. Especially if you spend part of your time in a masculine world outside the FWBO for any reason, it is easy to forget that the type of relating that may be appropriate in the outside world is not appropriate within the Movement, and within the Order in particular. Make a point of practising kindly and affectionate speech. You have probably been doing it here, but when you get back into the world, there may be temptations to speak in another way.

9. BE KIND TO MITRAS

Unfortunately, Order members don't always speak to Mitras in a gentle, kindly, and encouraging way. Sometimes this is the result of a misunderstanding of fierce friendship.[271] Fierce friendship doesn't involve bullying, or using harsh or aggressive speech. Please be kind to Mitras. Don't forget that you were a Mitra once. Believe it or not, people do forget very quickly. I'm thinking of an experience I had when I was in the army – yes, sometimes even my experiences in the army are relevant to my life in the FWBO! One of my friends, who was called up at the same time as I was, was a very little man, very meek and very talkative. His name was Harry, and we called him Harry the Ticker because he was always going tick-tick-tick-tick-tick, just like a watch or a clock, nattering away. Anyway, one day this nice, quiet, inoffensive little chap was given a stripe and became a lance-corporal, and overnight he became bossy, cocky, aggressive, and authoritative, always ordering people around, well on his way, obviously, to becoming a sergeant.[272] That one little stripe on his arm made that tremendous difference. I hope this doesn't happen when Order members get their kesas round their necks, but something a bit like it does seem to happen with some Order members in relation to their unfortunate Mitras. If you're not careful, you will feel that by becoming an Order member, you have not only made a spiritual commitment but been promoted to spiritual corporal, or even spiritual sergeant.

Be very careful when you get back to your centre that you are not behaving towards the Mitras – and you were a Mitra yourself just a few months ago – as though you have had a promotion and are now in a position to order them around or give them advice. Sometimes I have come across shocking cases of Order members handing out advice to Mitras that was quite unsuitable and didn't do the Mitra any good at all, just out of over-confidence that they as an Order member know all about what is good for Mitras. I don't want to exaggerate, because the Order, even at its worst, is not quite like the army, but human nature is human nature, and sometimes that tendency does creep in to feel that you have been elevated to a higher position and have been invested with authority. Don't let that happen. Remember that you were a Mitra once, and try to relate to Mitras in a kindly, gentle, and encouraging fashion. Fierce friendship may be needed one day, but for now make sure you give them lots of gentle and kindly and affectionate and sympathetic friendship. Starting off with fierce friendship can be very discouraging for the poor Mitra, who may feel as though he has been hit over the head with your friendship. You may think this is a bit of a joke, but believe me, it's very easy to forget what you were like before. It is not just a failure of memory, but perhaps a failure of empathy as well.

10. KEEP UP YOUR *SĀDHANA*

Now we come to something you may have been expecting me to mention. Keep up your *sādhana*. I am quite sure that all of you who are newly ordained have decided – are quite sure, in fact – that you are going to keep up your *sādhana*, that nothing is going to deflect you from it. I don't want to undermine anybody, but it is not as easy as you might think. Once you get back, there will be all sorts of things to do, all sorts of things to think about, all sorts of distractions, and if you want to keep up your *sādhana* on a daily basis, you will have to be very determined indeed. For instance, if you do your *sādhana* in the morning, especially the early morning, you will have to be very careful you don't stay up half the night watching television or doing anything else, because then you won't be able to get up in the morning, and if you don't get up in the morning you probably won't do your *sādhana* that day. Make a very determined effort to do your *sādhana*, and watch very carefully for anything that might get in the way of your doing it.

11. KEEP UP DHARMA STUDY

Here at Guhyaloka you have done a lot of Dharma study – more than you ever did before, probably, certainly within a three-month period. Perhaps you're going to need quite a period for digestion. Don't forget to think about what you've been studying, go through the texts you've studied and the notes you've made on them, and in this way gradually make the material a part of your overall experience, a part of your being. Also, keep up study in the sense of studying new things, new texts, new *sūtras*, new works on the Dharma. But be selective in your general reading. Some people are greater readers than others, but always ask yourself what effect what you read will have on your mind. There are so many good things to read. Leaving aside the *sūtras* and Buddhist texts, there are all sorts of classics of world literature. Some years ago at Padmaloka, we used to keep a portion of the library in what is now the lounge, and I made a little study to find out which books were taken down from those shelves most frequently. There were two winners: a book on Hitler and the Third Reich, and a book on black magic. It could be that people were floating up into spiritual realms and wanted to take on board a little ballast to keep them nearer to home, but for whatever reason those two topics seemed to exercise a great fascination. Even a copy of the *Kāma Sūtra* didn't achieve anything like the same popularity. So be selective, be conscious in your reading, and try to get through, little by little, not just the Buddhist *sūtras* and standard works on Buddhism, but the great classics of world literature. Try to read some Shakespeare or Milton, Keats or Shelley, Homer and the Greek myths and legends, some of the Chinese and Japanese poets, some of the Zen poets. Be selective in your reading; don't read just anything.

12. TRY TO HAVE AN ANNUAL SOLITARY RETREAT

I hope you have all been on solitary retreat at some time or other, if only for a week. From the very early days of the Movement I have always suggested that everybody should try to have a solitary retreat every year, at least for a week, and preferably for two or three weeks or even longer. It does give you a chance to reassess, and to be yourself more. When you're living in a community, working in a centre or co-op, or even just living and working and functioning in the world, other people are impinging on you all the time. It's sometimes very difficult to tell where other people end and you begin, because you're thinking their thoughts, being influenced by their emotions and feelings, tuning into their wavelength, just as they are tuning into yours, and it is very difficult to sort out what really belongs to you, what thoughts and feelings are really yours. Very often when people go on a solitary retreat, their first experience is one of relief. They are just on their own, not being impinged on by other people, not even psychically. They are breathing their own air, moving about in their own space. They are just experiencing themselves, and perhaps nature, and that can be a great relief, a real holiday. So try to have at least a short solitary retreat, at least a week, every year.

13. TAKE PART IN THE POST-ORDINATION PROCESS

This is something of a new development. Subhuti's memo to me reads:

> Can you please stress to those ordained at Guhyaloka this year that they still need to keep working on themselves when they are ordained? In the first year or so, they may find that they come up against many difficulties, and they will need to recontact the inspiration that they will have experienced at Guhyaloka. The ordination process team at Padmaloka are arranging a retreat for them in February. It is quite important that as many as possible of them come.

These wise words are based on experience: not just Subhuti's but mine too, and the experience of many others who have had to do with the ordination process. You still need to keep working on yourself once you are ordained.

The fact that you have been ordained means that you have already done quite a lot of work on yourself. You may have changed quite remarkably over the years of your association with the Movement, and you have therefore been ordained. You have gone for Refuge to the Three Jewels. But sometimes it happens that people have made such an effort in the few years before ordination and during the ordination retreat, and they're so happy to be ordained, that they feel that now they've reached the goal. You have reached the goal only very relatively speaking, but there is the danger that your happiness at having achieved your immediate objective is so strong that it's difficult to think in terms of further effort, to think of ordination as the beginning of a process rather than the culmination of a process. It *is* the culmination of a process, but it is also the beginning of an infinitely greater process, and you mustn't forget that. You mustn't rest on your Guhyaloka laurels. You mustn't think that the investment of energy that you have made in the last few months is a capital fund on which you can go on drawing indefinitely without investing any further. When you get back home, you need to keep working on yourself even though you have been ordained – or rather, you should keep working on yourself all the more *because* you have been ordained.

I have begun to think that the post-ordination process is no less important – perhaps, in some cases, even more important – than the pre-ordination process. At the end of an ordination retreat, people naturally find themselves in a very positive frame of mind. They are full of energy, enthusiasm, devotion, and determination. Everything seems so easy. They have lived under these ideal conditions for so many weeks. They go back to their original situation, or perhaps a new one, and they feel they can conquer the world. At a council meeting or a chapter meeting, when someone asks, 'Who is ready to do this?' the new Order member pipes up, 'I will.' Every time a volunteer is asked for, he volunteers; he feels he can do it all. But after a few weeks, he finds that he has taken on too much in his over-confidence and over-enthusiasm. He hasn't understood his own resources. He hasn't realized the extent to which his positive mental state was due to the very positive conditions in which he was living for all those weeks. Alternatively, he may come up against unexpected difficulties. He may find that other Order members, instead of appreciating his wonderful qualities, seem to be getting in his way, not letting him do what he wants, not appreciating his insights, ignoring his suggestions – or at least it may seem like that – and he may start feeling very downhearted. Or he may meet up with an old girlfriend, or go home when his parents are in the middle of a row, and that will bring him down emotionally. In this way, he begins to have a difficult time. When that happens, the real recourse, the practical refuge, is fellow members of the sangha. Here, keeping up contact not only with me but with fellow Order members, especially those whom you regard as *kalyāṇa mitra*s, takes on extra importance.

To cut a long and sometimes unfortunate story short, after a few months the new Order member may start losing his initial inspiration. This is why Subhuti has thought up the post-ordination process, a short retreat at Padmaloka where people will be able to recontact the inspiration they experienced at Guhyaloka. Even if you haven't lost contact with that inspiration, come anyway; living and working in the world, as most of you will be doing, any inspiration that you can get from any source will be very useful. It may be that in the future, ordination doesn't represent the end of a process but the middle, and there will be a lengthy post-ordination process for all new Order members. What we are going to do about the old Order members I'm not sure, but perhaps we will find some means of rehabilitating even them! But yes, it is very easy to lose contact with one's original inspiration, as experienced especially at Guhyaloka.

14. AVOID DISTRACTIONS

Here you are free from distractions, except for the occasional aeroplane flying overhead, or maybe a change in the weather. On a retreat like this most distractions come from within, from one's own thoughts. But when you get back into the world, as I am sure you know, the distractions will begin, and they will go on increasing and increasing, thickening and thickening, becoming more and more obvious, crowding in on you more and more, until you get back to your centre or your community. You may even find some distractions there. You may find that in your absence a great big television has been installed and is glaring at you, the monster in the sitting room, and you may find your spiritual friends sitting round with their eyes glued to it. Perhaps they will be so fascinated by the programme they're watching that when you enter they don't take any notice. That is the nature of television, as I have observed: it is very, very distracting.

For Order members living in big cities, there are all sorts of distractions. You flip through the pages of a listings magazine, and there's this film and that film, and this event and that event, and you want to see so many things. Even though some of them might be interesting or useful, taken all together they constitute a terrible distraction. Trashy literature is also a distraction. And I hardly need add – in fact, I don't even like to mention the subject in a place like Guhyaloka – that members of the opposite sex can also at times be distractions, and they are to be avoided as much as is humanly possible. They are very big distractions indeed.

15. KEEP BEGINNER'S MIND

I won't say that the last point is the most important, but it runs through all the other points that I have made. Make sure that you keep beginner's mind. Beginner's mind is a Chan or Zen expression which refers to a mind that approaches even apparently familiar things in a fresh way, as though for the first time. You can probably remember your first experience of meditation, the first time you came along to an FWBO centre, your first experience of spiritual friendship. That first experience, in many cases, is very strong, very fresh, just because it is the first. It makes a very deep impression, perhaps so deep that you never forget it. I have known people who have told me that although they have been doing the *mettā bhāvanā* or the mindfulness of breathing for years, their best experience of it was the first, presumably because they approached it with beginner's mind. When you do it for the second, third, or fourth time, it is not quite so fresh, and you don't appreciate it quite so much. If you are not careful, it becomes that old *mettā bhāvanā*, that old mindfulness of breathing, or even that old meditation class. It all becomes rather dull and unstimulating. But try to think each time that you've never done it before. You don't step into the same river twice, as Heraclitus said. Everything you do is done for the first time, because you are different, the situation is different, the time is different, perhaps the place is different.

Keep alive that experience of freshness and newness, and what one might call first-timeness, especially with regard to your meditation practice. If you don't, in the end you might start thinking in terms of that old Order or that old movement or that old FWBO. You have done so many things so many times before that it all becomes a bit dull and stale, and then you start becoming dissatisfied and start looking out for something else, usually some distraction, something that will give you a bit of stimulation, something that will make life seem interesting and exciting. You may even start looking around for another spiritual practice. You may think, 'The mindfulness of breathing doesn't seem to be giving me very much, and neither does the *mettā bhāvanā* or my visualization practice. Maybe I made a mistake. Maybe it wasn't Mañjughoṣa after all, maybe it was Tārā. Maybe I'd better change my practice. Or maybe I need a complete change. Maybe I'm being too spiritual. Maybe I ought to go back and experience the world again.' Thus you give way to distractions or start indulging in carping criticism of the Movement, and your own centre or your own chapter, or other centres and other chapters, as an expression of your disgruntlement. It is very important that you maintain that beginner's mind, that fresh approach, as though everything was happening for the first time, because in truth it *is* happening for the first time. When I was a child I used to sing a hymn in church, beginning:

> New every morning is the love
> Our wakening and uprising prove.[273]

The love is God's love, but ignore that! It is not the same old day, the same old sun. It is new every time. It is not the same old meditation, the same old chapter meeting, the same old movement. It is not the same old Bhante making his tiresome points again and again. It is all new; you have never heard it before. You approach it with a fresh mind, and therefore you appreciate it and enjoy it. You rejoice that you have the opportunity to practise the *mettā bhāvanā* and the mindfulness of breathing, the opportunity to enjoy spiritual friendship. If you lose your beginner's mind, you start not appreciating what you have got. You even start not appreciating the Three Jewels. Even they can start becoming dull and ordinary and uninspiring. So try, above all things, to keep your beginner's mind with regard to everything that you do.

If you bear at least some of these points in mind – because they are all interconnected – you should continue to make good progress. In fact, if you bear some of them in mind, and much more still if you bear all of them in mind, one might even go so far as to say that Stream Entry will be within your reach, and that your having been ordained will be what the Buddha in the Pāli scriptures called a rich and fruitful growing thing.[274]

THE 1990S

MY EIGHT MAIN TEACHERS

Aryaloka, November 1990

All my life I've been a great reader, and in my teens I read a work called *The Philosophy of History* in which Hegel says that history moves from east to west.[275] I may not exactly embody history, but I can say that in recent decades I have moved from east to west. Forty years ago today I was in India, receiving my *bhikkhu* ordination, and twenty years ago I was back in England. Manjuvajra's reminiscences in his introduction reminded me of that retreat twenty years ago at Keffolds in Sussex – not, I'm afraid, because I met Manjuvajra then (I must admit I can't remember that), but because that retreat, for which I came back specially from the States, was overshadowed by the fact that I was very ill. In fact, I'm told I nearly died. I recovered and went back to the States to do whatever I was doing, and now, twenty years later, I'm back here again and giving my very first talk under the auspices of our very own FWBO, which I'm very happy to see flourishing here at Aryaloka and beginning to flourish in several other centres across this vast continent.

In the last week you've had a talk on the meaning of spiritual friendship, which is absolutely central in Buddhism as envisaged by the FWBO. You've had a talk on the Buddha, a talk on some of the great Buddhist teachers, and there's even been a talk on me. Tonight I'm going to talk about my own teachers, not through systematic biographies, but mainly by way of personal reminiscences. In my life I have had many teachers, and not only Buddhist ones. In the earlier phase of my career in India I had Hindu teachers, and before that there were secular teachers. According to Buddhist tradition, your very first teachers are your parents – they're called the *ācāryas*, the old or original teachers. In fact, one learns something from every single person one meets in the course of one's life.

Obviously limits have to be imposed, and I certainly can't talk about all my teachers, so tonight I'm just going to reminisce about my eight most important Buddhist teachers and try to give you a glimpse of what they were like, what they mean to me, and perhaps what they might come to mean to some of you.

JAGDISH KASHYAP

I'm going to start at the beginning, chronologically speaking, with Bhikkhu Jagdish Kashyap. Kashyapji as he was usually called (-ji being an honorific suffix) was from Bihar, the state in India in which Bodh Gaya, where the Buddha gained Enlightenment, is situated. He came of respectable peasant or small landholding stock and seems to have been a rather religious-minded youth. He was born as a Hindu, into the Kayastha caste, and while he was still in his teens he joined a Hindu reform organization called the Arya Samaj. This organization was founded by Swami Dayananda Saraswati in the nineteenth century, and it opposed image worship, was not very much in favour of the caste system, and strongly emphasized Vedic as opposed to Puranic Hinduism. Kashyapji became a sannyasin and embarked upon the study of the Vedas, the most sacred scriptures of the Hindus, because these were the texts the Arya Samaj strongly emphasized. All Hindus believe that the Vedas are the foundation of their faith and practice, and contain all possible mysteries. Some even believe that the formula for the manufacture of the atom bomb is to be found in the Vedas. Kashyapji was thrilled to be able to embark on the study of the Vedas, to do which he had to learn Vedic Sanskrit, which is rather different from classical Sanskrit. But he was very disillusioned. He didn't find any wisdom or any philosophy in the Vedas, he told me, but just hymns to this god and that, especially hymns to Indra, the thunder god, who was quarrelsome and fond of fighting, and often got drunk, a rather unedifying god. He found all sorts of rituals, all sorts of chants and magic spells to destroy your enemies and attract love, and he wondered, 'Where is the sublime philosophy that I was promised?' He used to say to me that the best way of weaning a Hindu away from Hinduism is to get them to study the Vedas. Normally they're not studied, and you rarely find even a Brahmin who possesses a copy. You tend to find them in the libraries of scholars in the West.

To cut a long story short, he became very disillusioned with Hinduism, so he started exploring other faiths: Sikhism, Jainism, and Buddhism. When he came upon Buddhism, which had been dead in India for hundreds of years, he decided that this was the religion for him. He went to Sri Lanka and became a *bhikkhu* there, and studied Pāli at the Vidyalankara Pirivena, the institute of higher learning for Buddhist monks. He studied the whole of the Pāli canon in the original language, which is some forty-five volumes in the Royal Thai edition, and was eventually granted the title of *Tipiṭaka-ācariya*. But he did not have a very high opinion of the Sri Lankan *bhikkhu* sangha. He used to tell me some amusing stories which rather illustrated their formalistic approach to the Dharma.

For example, among the *bhikkhus* in Sri Lanka there are three main sects, and you can tell them apart because they dress a little differently. When they go out of the monastery, the Rāmañña Nikāya and the Amarapura Nikāya *bhikkhus* cover both shoulders with their robes, but the Siam Nikāya people leave the right shoulder bare. There's a difference of umbrellas too. Siam Nikāya *bhikkhus* carry a black umbrella, Rāmañña Nikāya *bhikkhus* carry a Burmese-style parasol-type umbrella, because they originate from Burma, and the Amarapura Nikāya *bhikkhus* are very strict and make do with a big plantain leaf. In Sri Lanka it's very important, apparently, to know which Nikāya a *bhikkhu* belongs to. Kashyapji was always being asked this question. Kashyapji, who after all was not a Sri Lankan, used to say, 'I belong to Buddha Nikāya', but that didn't satisfy them, so they used to ask, 'Well, when you go out, do you cover one shoulder or two?' Kashyapji used to say, 'When it's hot I cover two shoulders, when it's very hot, I cover only one, and when it's very very hot I don't cover either.'

One day he was invited to give a lecture on the *anattā* doctrine, the doctrine of no-self, and he started off by saying that you can't understand what is meant by *anattā*, or no-self, unless you first of all understand what is meant by *attā*, or self, but as soon as he said that, the Sri Lankan *bhikkhus* got to their feet and shouted, 'We don't want any of that Hindu philosophy here.' Kashyapji tried to explain that he wasn't preaching Hindu philosophy, only trying to clarify the concept of *anattā*, but they shouted him down and forced him to resume his seat. The Pāli scriptures were admittedly preserved in Sri Lanka by the *bhikkhus*, but as I related in my memoirs, Kashyapji said to me, speaking slowly and deliberately, 'Sangharakshita, they are a set of monkeys ... sitting on a treasure ... the value of which they do *not* understand.'[276]

He also told me one or two little stories to illustrate the attitude of the laity. He said that one day he was going for alms with his begging-bowl. He was quite a new *bhikkhu*, and his robe kept slipping down. That tends to happen when you start wearing a robe, but after a few years, in some miraculous way the robe just stays up. If you are a monk of some experience, you can do a prostration and your robe won't fall off. If I had my robe with me I could demonstrate. But anyway, Kashyapji found his robe slipping down, so he put his begging-bowl to one side on the ground while he adjusted his robe. An old woman who saw him doing this started screaming 'What kind of *bhikkhu* is this who doesn't even know how to respect his bowl? He's ignorant of the Vinaya!' – because there is an obscure Vinaya rule that says that *bhikkhus* mustn't put their begging-bowl on the ground.[277] The old woman knew that somehow, so she was abusing him for being a bad *bhikkhu*.

After Kashyapji left Sri Lanka he lived for a while in a Chinese Buddhist temple in Penang. At that time, which was about fifteen years before I met him, he was quite a conservative Theravādin, not quite so liberal-minded as he afterwards became. When he visited Mahāyāna Buddhist temples with his Chinese friends, they used to bow to the Buddha image, and to Guanyin, Avalokiteśvara, and all the other bodhisattvas, but Kashyapji, being a good Theravādin, only bowed to the Buddha. The friend who accompanied him to the temples didn't say anything, but when they got back to the house and lunch was served, Kashyapji found that he'd only been given rice. He didn't like to say anything, but after a while he said, 'Where is the curry?' And his friend said 'Well, the rice is the main thing.' Kashyapji said, 'But the curry is also necessary.' And his friend said, 'It's like that with the Buddhas and bodhisattvas. The Buddha is the main thing, but the bodhisattvas are also necessary.' Kashyapji said he learned his lesson – he was someone who could take a point – and whenever he went to the Mahāyāna temples thereafter he bowed to the bodhisattvas too.

He came back to India, and when I came to know him in 1949 he was professor of Pāli and Buddhist philosophy at the Benares Hindu

University. He'd held that post for twelve years, but he was feeling frustrated because he had very few students. The university had been founded by orthodox Hindus, and while they were very keen on Sanskrit, they weren't keen on Pāli. The only reason they had the department of Pāli was that one of their great benefactors, whom they didn't wish to offend, had insisted on it and offered to pay all its expenses. He happened to be a patron of Kashyapji's, a wealthy merchant from western India. So the university made a rule that you could study Pāli, but only if you also studied Sanskrit. Very few people were so eager to learn Pāli that they were also willing to learn Sanskrit, which is much more difficult.

I found Kashyapji to be an excellent teacher, extremely well-versed in the subjects I studied with him: logic (both Buddhist and Western), Abhidhamma, and Pāli. He often knew the texts by heart. I stayed with him for nearly a year, and after that he took me on pilgrimage in Bihar, to places like Nālandā and Rajgir, and then up to Kalimpong, which I'd never heard of before. To cut a long story short, he left me there with the parting injunction 'Stay here and work for the good of Buddhism', which I tried to do. I was then 24 years old. Subsequently Kashyapji left Benares Hindu University and founded a Pāli Institute in the vicinity of the ancient Nālandā *mahāvihāra* or monastic university. I believe the institute has now been raised to university status by the government of Bihar.[278] Kashyapji also edited in *devanāgarī* characters the entire Tipiṭaka, writing prefaces in English to every volume and summaries of all the *suttas*.[279] He told me he'd gone through the entire Tipiṭaka so many times that he felt that he had it in the palm of his hand. He both spoke and wrote Pāli and Sanskrit, and it was his intention to write a *Tipiṭaka sāra*, an essence of the Tipiṭaka, which would give you the essence of the Buddha's teaching as recorded in the Pāli scriptures, but I'm afraid he never got round to it.

The last time I saw him was in 1966 at the Nalanda Pāli Institute, which was then flourishing. I took a picture of him feeding his peacocks. He was very fond of these peacocks. He used to come out of his residence every morning with some grain, and the peacocks would come flying through the air and he'd feed them. So that's my last memory of Kashyapji. He died some years ago, but I'm delighted to say that his work for the Pāli language and literature is being continued by his nephew, Professor A. K. Narain, who is also a scholar in Pāli and Buddhism, specializing in numismatics. He taught for a while in the

States, and I was very interested to learn that Alan Sponberg had been one of his students. Professor Narain is now retired and living in India, in Sarnath. He has founded an institute of Pāli and Buddhist studies in memory of his uncle Jagdish Kashyap, and has invited the cooperation of the FWBO, which obviously we will be very glad to give.[280]

Kashyapji was of medium height, very dark in complexion, and very, very fat. He told me shortly after I met him that had I come a year earlier he would have been unable to go out for a walk with me, because he was so fat he couldn't walk and used to go everywhere by cycle rickshaw, giving the rickshaw wallah double the fare. He was very humble and unassuming. Despite his vast learning he never arrogated anything to himself. He was in some ways quite a childlike person, very simple in his way of life with regard to dress and accommodation. He was a terrific worker – he could work day and night without food or sleep – but if he had no work to do, he'd simply lie on his charpoy (an Indian-style bed) and sleep, hour after hour. I would be studying in the next room and if I came to some knotty point of grammar or logic or Abhidhamma, I'd go to the open door of his room. He'd open one eye when I put my question, and answer with a yawn, but he knew exactly where that verse or passage came in a text, and he could explain it without opening more than one eye. His answer was always clear and to the point. 'Thank you, Bhante,' I'd say, and he'd close his eye and go back to sleep. So that was Jagdish Kashyap, and I have very fond memories of him. Although I very much regarded him as my teacher, he used to say that I was his friend and he learned a lot from me, which I appreciated even though I didn't agree with him.

DHARDO RIMPOCHE

From Bhikkhu Jagdish Kashyap let's move to Dhardo Rimpoche, so-called because he was a Rimpoche, an incarnate lama, of Dhartsendo, a town on the border between eastern Tibet and China. His father was Chinese and his mother was Tibetan. I knew his mother, who lived with him in Kalimpong, and died at quite an advanced age. I'm afraid she gave Rimpoche quite a lot of trouble; she was a very hot-tempered old lady. But that's another story.

Rimpoche was born in 1918. Once I asked him if he remembered any of his previous lives, and he said that up to the age of 7 he had some recollection of his previous life, but then the memories faded away. He told me this was quite common among incarnate lamas. But there was one incident that he could still remember. When he was 4 or 5, and had been recognized as the incarnation of his predecessor, an elderly woman came to the monastery and invited him to take a meal at her house. He said no, and she was quite upset, but he said to her, 'Why should you be so upset? After all, I've come to your house many times before' – which indeed he had, in his previous life.

When he was still quite young he left Dhartsendo and studied at one of the great monastic universities in Lhasa, one of the Gelugpa or yellow cap establishments. The line of the Dhartsendo rimpoches was Nyingmapa, but I gather that the thirteenth Dalai Lama was apt to send Nyingmapa reincarnations to study at Gelugpa colleges, and insisted on Dhardo's predecessor being educated as a Gelugpa lama. Rimpoche pursued his studies, became a *geshe*, and went to one of the two Tantric colleges, but he was unable to study there for more than a year because his health was very frail and the life there was very rigorous. Some people in the West think of Tantric Buddhism as self-indulgent, or even transcendental hedonism, but by Rimpoche's account the life there was very strict indeed. They were only allowed to use one blanket at night, however cold it was, and his health couldn't stand up to it, so he left, although he was in line for the headship of the Gelug order, the position of Ganden Tripa as it's called.

In about 1946 the Dalai Lama sent him to be the abbot of the Tibetan *gompa* in Bodh Gaya, and the Dalai Lama's cultural and religious representative in India. It was in Bodh Gaya that he saw me for the first time, although I only learned this many years later. He didn't tell me the story himself, but told it to one of our Order members who visited Kalimpong a few years ago. Apparently he was standing on the flat roof of the Tibetan *gompa* in Bodh Gaya and looking down onto the nearby Maha Bodhi Society Rest House when he saw a yellow-clad figure. Noticing that this figure was European, he thought, 'That's wonderful! Even Europeans are now following the Dharma!' When we did eventually meet in Kalimpong in 1953, he recognized me as the person he'd seen on that occasion.

To begin with, we didn't become closely acquainted in the ordinary sense, but I became very closely acquainted with his mind and his understanding of Buddhism. There was a young Tibetan in Kalimpong called Lobsang Lhalungpa who had recently made a new translation of the *Life of Milarepa*, and he had been asked by Kenneth Morgan, the editor of a book on Buddhism subsequently published as *The Path of the Buddha*, to write the chapter on Tibetan Buddhism.[281] Lobsang Lhalungpa didn't feel he was qualified to do that, so he consulted Dhardo Rimpoche. Dhardo Rimpoche expounded various aspects of the Dharma, Lobsang Lhalungpa wrote down what he said, and then I went through his notes with him and rewrote the material in what I hoped was decent English. Sometimes Lobsang Lhalungpa's exposition was not clear, so I'd ask him to go back to Rimpoche and write it out again in the light of Rimpoche's further explanation, and we went back and forth in this way for three months. At that time I was writing my *Survey of Buddhism*, so a bit of the information passed into the *Survey*, though not much, as I didn't have much to say about Tibetan Buddhism.[282] In that manner I came into contact with Dhardo Rimpoche's mind and his very deep understanding of the Dharma.

Subsequently I was associated with the school Rimpoche founded for Tibetan refugee children, where half the day is given to modern study, and half to traditional Tibetan study, especially through the Dharma.[283] But it wasn't until 1956 that I got to know Dhardo Rimpoche well. He was not someone who projected himself or went out of his way to make friends, but in 1956 we happened to be thrown together. That was the year of the 2,500th anniversary of Buddhism, and the government of India were sponsoring the celebrations on a grand scale and invited fifty-seven 'eminent Buddhists from the border areas' to take part. Dhardo Rimpoche was invited, and so was I. The government of India gave us a special train which took us around the holy places, as well as factories and dams and things of that sort which the government of India wanted us to see. Among the guests were Theravādin *bhikkhus* from Assam, and lamas and nuns from Bhutan, Sikkim, and Ladakh. Dhardo Rimpoche and I were somehow always together. We always shared the same carriage, we sat beside each other on the coaches, and we got to know each other quite well, and liked each other's company.

Of all the stories I could tell you, I'll tell just one – a story that illustrates Rimpoche's almost supernatural mindfulness. The government train would take us from one holy place to another and we had an official guide. Usually we saw a holy place in the morning and a dam or factory in the afternoon. If we were going to a holy place, we'd always take incense and candles to perform a little puja. One day, I think in Kusinara, the guide said, 'Today we'll be going to the holy place this afternoon,' so we didn't bother to take candles or incense, and off we trooped. But as the result of some muddle, we found ourselves in a Buddhist temple without any offerings. For traditionally-minded Buddhists it's a terrible thing to turn up at a holy place with nothing to offer, so we were all quite upset, except Dhardo Rimpoche. Tibetan monks wear voluminous red robes, and while everybody was expressing their regret, Rimpoche unfolded his robes and pulled out enough candles and incense for everybody. He wasn't just mindful; you never seemed to catch him napping. Lots of people tried, but he always seemed to anticipate what was going to happen, and be ready to meet it. He was very fond of photography and I recently heard that some two hundred negatives of photos which he took on this tour are being made available for us to make prints from.

After that, we collaborated regularly, met quite often, and faced all sorts of problems together. In 1962 China invaded India, and a lot of people were convinced that the Chinese were going to take Kalimpong on their way down to invade Calcutta. There was a great turmoil. Two Buddhist friends of mine, a local businessman and his European wife, had a jeep ready and waiting day and night, stocked with provisions, I was to have a seat in that jeep, and we were going to make a quick getaway if the Chinese did turn up. The Chinese had worked on the local Nepalese people through their propaganda and agents, so they were ready almost to welcome the Chinese if they should come. We heard that the local officials weren't happy about this, and the police in Kalimpong were told that there had to be a spontaneous anti-Chinese demonstration in Kalimpong. The frontier inspector, who was a friend of mine, told me and Dhardo Rimpoche, as the two most prominent and active local Buddhists, that we had to denounce the Chinese for committing aggression against India. That was an order. We said yes, sure, whatever you like, and a public meeting was organized. Up till then we hadn't been permitted to say a word of criticism about the Chinese government. China had invaded Tibet in 1956, but we weren't allowed to criticize China publicly. I certainly wasn't, because I was a foreigner. But now it was different. So Dhardo Rimpoche and I discussed what we were going to say. He would say it in Tibetan, and I would say it in English. A big public meeting was called, and we dealt with the situation in our own way, saying how regrettable it was that China had invaded India, but that it wasn't surprising considering they had already invaded Tibet. We were very happy that at last we were able to say so publicly, and the point was well taken by the local authorities. We were virtually ordered not to leave Kalimpong because we were the two best-known Buddhists there and they said, 'If you two leave Kalimpong, there's going to be a bit of a panic.' The Indian officials were leaving, but we had to stop and reassure the public, or at least the Buddhist public.

From Dhardo Rimpoche I received the White Tārā initiation and also the bodhisattva ordination, and we translated a few Tibetan texts together. The last time I saw him was in 1967, but we kept in touch. Quite a number of Order members and Mitras have visited him over the years, and our charity Aid for India has given substantial funds to his school.[284] Rimpoche unfortunately died earlier this year, and Suvajra is engaged in writing a biography.[285]

Although Dhardo Rimpoche was deeply versed in both the theory and practice of Tibetan Buddhism, he was very critical of certain aspects of it – I won't go into that now. He was also unpopular with Tibetan officials. The officials had the idea that all the Tibetan refugees in India should remain under their feudal control. They wanted almost to create a state within a state. The Tibetans themselves were not at all happy with this, many of them having been dissatisfied with the type of government that had existed in Tibet before the Chinese invasion – not that they had any sympathy with the Chinese. They had the greatest devotion towards the Dalai Lama, but resented the high-handed and autocratic behaviour of the officials, aristocrats, and administrators. Dhardo Rimpoche was one of those who openly criticized the officials and they were so annoyed that they tried to denounce him as a Chinese spy, mainly because his father was Chinese. With his customary dexterity he evaded those difficulties and became an Indian citizen.

Dhardo Rimpoche had a great sense of humour, unusually for a Tibetan – they typically have a sense of fun but not exactly a sense of humour. He was often consulted by Western scholars, and, for example, helped René de Nebesky-Wojkowitz in the compilation of his massive work *Oracles and Demons of Tibet*, which has recently been reprinted.[286] One day a scholar went along to see him with a friend of his, Prince Peter of Greece, who spoke Tibetan fluently, as interpreter. Sooner or later the visiting scholar started asking Rimpoche questions about the Anuttara Yoga Tantra, the highest tantra, the tantra of sex. Rimpoche told me that he told the scholar a little Tibetan story which was the equivalent of the gospel parable of not throwing pearls before swine. The scholar was not very pleased and neither was Prince Peter, but apparently the scholar said, 'Ah well, I don't suppose he knows anything about the Tantra anyway.' When Rimpoche told me this story, he burst out laughing. In fact, he told me the story more than once.

CHATTRUL SANGYE DORJE

Next, Chattrul Sangye Dorje. I met him in 1956 when he was spending a few days in Kalimpong. A Sikkimese friend of mine who was a staunch follower of Nyingma Buddhism urged me to go and meet him. He was only about 35 years old at the time, he was not an incarnate lama, and he had a reputation for eccentric behaviour and utterances, but all the same he was a very famous lama indeed. He was a follower of the Nyingma tradition but he wasn't a monk, though he lived like one, at least at that time. He might have been a *śrāmaṇera*, a novice monk. He didn't wear monastic robes, but an old sheepskin-lined red cloak and not much else. He was the ugliest of my teachers. He had a very unattractive appearance, and no charisma. If you passed him in the bazaar you'd think he was some muleteer or small shopkeeper, or even a cut-throat. Anyway, for some time I'd been thinking I should ask for Tantric initiation. (My reasons for that would make a long story, which I'm not going to tell now.) Perhaps I couldn't find anyone else to ask – there were very few incarnate lamas around in Kalimpong at that time – so I asked him for an initiation and he said, 'Come back tomorrow.' The following day, after a little discussion, he said, 'I'm going to give you the Green Tārā initiation. Many great pandits in Tibet have been given this practice.' So he gave me the practice, explained it, and I've done it ever since. Thereafter I met him a number of times. It wasn't easy to meet him, he was always wandering around and he wouldn't tell anyone what his movements were going to be; he just upped and left, never taking anything with him. Altogether he was quite a mysterious character.

Once I was with him in Darjeeling and he'd just been to Nepal, visiting the ancient stupas. He told me that when he put his hand inside one of these stupas, he pulled out a handful of *ribus* – relics in the form of tiny pearls. He showed these to me, and talked about them in a strange way that I couldn't understand. It was also he who named my vihara the Triyana Vardhana Vihara, although when he did so, I didn't even know I was going to have a vihara. I certainly didn't have the money for one. He told me, 'You're going to have a vihara,' and composed a little verse in which he gave the vihara its name in Tibetan. He is still alive, and one or two of our friends have sighted him, but he's very elusive, always wandering.[287] He's no longer a monk, if he ever was one; he has two wives, all three moving around together. One person who met him some years ago was Thomas Merton, who wrote that of all the lamas he met in India, and he met quite a few, including the Dalai Lama, Chattrul Sangye Dorje impressed him the most.[288] He certainly was a remarkable man, with depths that were difficult to fathom.

JAMYANG KHYENTSE RIMPOCHE

A much more famous figure, certainly more famous in the West, at least by reputation, is Jamyang Khyentse Rimpoche, whom I met in 1956 or 1957 when he was on a visit to Kalimpong. The greatest of all the Nyingma incarnate lamas of the twentieth century, he was a very learned man, and at the same time deeply versed in meditation. He was the head of the Sakya monastery, but belonged mainly to the Nyingma tradition. He also belonged to the tradition known as Rimé, which started in the nineteenth century in eastern Tibet. *Rimé* means 'no boundaries', and a number of lamas who belonged to different traditions, including Jamyang Khyentse, met together and initiated one another into all the practices they had, to create a unified tradition.[289] I've always thought it significant that I have a strong personal connection with Jamyang Khyentse, the representative of what one might call an ecumenical Tibetan Buddhism, because the FWBO tries to be ecumenical with regard to the whole Buddhist tradition.

I met Jamyang Khyentse a number of times, but I'm just going to talk about three incidents that stand out. The first or second time I met him, he looked up from his book and we greeted each other. He was about 55, a grave, dignified, regal figure, and very kind. And he said, 'Do you know anything about dancing?' I had to say, 'No, I'm afraid I don't.' He said, 'That's a pity. In the Tengyur there are fourteen works on dance, and I've been studying them recently.' The Tengyur is the supplement of the Tibetan canon containing the writings of all the great

Mahāyāna philosophers. The Indian works on dance, on *Nāṭyaśāstra*, are the choreographic basis of the Tibetan Lama Dance, and that's why he was interested in them. But this illustrates the extent of his researches. He had read all these fourteen works, and wanted to gather further information on dance if he could, even from Western sources. He was a bit disappointed that I couldn't tell him anything about it.

Some time later I went to Darjeeling and asked him for the Mañjughoṣa practice; I was very keen to do that in addition to the Green Tārā practice. I should mention that he regarded himself as an emanation of a *tulku* of Mañjughoṣa. He said, 'I'll give you four initiations, but I don't have the texts with me. I'll have to get them from Gangtok in a few weeks' time. I'll send for you when I'm ready.' So I went back to Kalimpong. About two weeks later, I received a message saying, 'Come tomorrow, and I shall give you the initiations.' I was ill in bed, with a fever and a raging toothache. The side of my jaw was swollen and I was in very great pain. But I thought, 'There's no choice. I shall have to go.' So despite the fever and the pain I got to Darjeeling – down 4,000 feet from Kalimpong to Chitra Ridge, and up 7,000 feet to Darjeeling – in two hours or less, not very good for the stomach. I arrived feeling a bit groggy, and I went along for this initiation. I can't remember much about it, and it was all in Tibetan anyway, but I do remember vividly that while he was giving the initiation, chanting and invoking Mañjughoṣa, he was looking up with a quite heavenly smile, just as though he could see Mañjughoṣa floating up there and sending down his blessing. He gave me the initiations of Mañjughoṣa, Avalokiteśvara, Vajrapāṇi, and Green Tārā, and then I went back to Kalimpong and back to bed.

Some months later I went to visit him in Gangtok, where he was staying in the Palace monastery. His attendant monk – he was himself a monk, by the way – asked me to wait a few minutes and after a while I was called in. Jamyang Khyentse said, 'Sorry to keep you waiting, but I was performing a ceremony for a lama who died recently.' I asked him what ceremony he'd been performing, and he said that he was reciting the Vajrasattva mantra. Several years later I was in Kalimpong on my farewell journey. After I'd been in the West for two years and I'd decided to stay on there, I went back to Kalimpong to say goodbye to my friends. So I was staying at my vihara. Some years previously I'd had a Western disciple, a rather awful person who had died. He had now been dead for several years.[290] In the middle of the night I woke up. It was pitch dark, but I could see quite clearly. By the side of my bed there was a deep pit, literally a pit, as if someone had dug it. I looked down, and there was this old disciple of mine standing in the pit with his head level with the edge, looking very sorrowful. It occurred to me that he must be in a not very happy state, and I wasn't surprised, knowing how wilful he'd been. I wondered what I could do to help him, and then I remembered Jamyang Khyentse and how he had recited the Vajrasattva mantra for that dead lama. So I started reciting the Vajrasattva mantra, and I saw the letters of the mantra come out of my mouth – there are a hundred of these letters, it's called the hundred-syllable mantra – and go down into the pit like a garland, and my old disciple seized hold of them and hauled himself up out of the pit. I saw this just as clearly as I see you all sitting here. When he hauled himself out of the pit, everything vanished and it was pitch dark, and I heard in the distance the sound of a ram's horn being blown by the Jogis. They are a caste in Nepal who are sent out at certain times of the year by the king to go around the Himalayan area gathering the souls of the dead. People are afraid of them and even the fiercest dog won't go near them. I looked at the clock, and it was two o'clock in the morning. The following morning a Jogi came round for rice and money. They are not poor, they don't do what they do for money, it's just the custom. They're very strange people. People don't like to talk to them, and my servant and my disciples were very afraid of them. I'd say, 'Bring out some rice and money for the Jogi,' and they'd put it down then run away. But I used to ask the Jogi to sit down and I'd start talking with him, because I could speak Nepali. The Jogis looked very strange, almost haunting, not surprisingly. They carried a little bag over their shoulder, and some people believed that the souls of the dead were in that little bag. They came on the night of the new moon when it was very dark. But that's just to illustrate my contact with Jamyang Khyentse, and the efficacy of the Vajrasattva mantra. This is one of the reasons why in the FWBO we always recite the Vajrasattva mantra in connection with after-death ceremonies. Jamyang Khyentse Rimpoche was a very kindly, regal person, like an old Burmese *mahāthera*; he was quite monastic but at the same time he had this regal air. I believe he came from a princely family in eastern Tibet. He died in 1959, after I'd had contact with him for about two years.

All right then, onto Kachu Rimpoche. He was Khyentse Rimpoche's chief disciple, and it was he who suggested I should ask Khyentse Rimpoche for Tantric initiation, saying, 'You'll never get another chance like this, he is the greatest of all the living Nyingma lamas.' Kachu Rimpoche himself was an incarnate lama, or *tulku*, of southern Tibetan origin, I think. At that time he was the abbot of the Pemayangtse Gompa in Sikkim, where they follow the Kagyu and Nyingma forms of Tibetan Buddhism. Pemayangtse Gompa is the chief monastery of the Nyingmapas in Sikkim and also the royal monastery, which used to perform all Buddhist functions for the Maharaja, and Kachu Rimpoche was its *khenpo*, its abbot. It was in that connection that I first heard about him, from a rather eccentric French woman who became a Buddhist nun. We used to call her Ani-la, the polite form of address for nuns in Tibet – it means something like 'reverend auntie'. She'd been ordained by Dhardo Rimpoche, but had become dissatisfied with him, because she thought he wasn't teaching her fast enough. I used to say, 'Look, he knows what he's doing. Be patient,' but patience was one of the last things she was willing to practise. She was about 45, and I was only about 28, but she used to come to me for advice in her voluble, excitable, active way. She was always getting upset, quarrelling with people, and getting dissatisfied, and tearing her hair, except she didn't have any hair. She used to get very red in the face, very irate. One day she said 'Oh Bhante, what should I do?' And I said 'Ani-la, you're doing very well. There's just one thing you've got to learn.' 'Oh yes, what is it? I'll go and do it straight away.' 'You've got to learn to do nothing.' She exploded: 'I've got so much to do, so many books to study, and all these animals to look after. Do nothing?' Oh, she hit the roof.

That's by the way. But it was from her that I heard about Kachu Rimpoche. She was wandering in the jungle in Sikkim in quite a distraught state, and even had thoughts of suicide, as she often did. She came to a clearing, and sitting there was a lama. She was dissatisfied with Dhardo Rimpoche, so she thought, 'Oh, a new guru. How wonderful!' She got into conversation with him, because she could speak Tibetan, and he explained that he was the new abbot of Pemayangtse Gompa, and had just come down from Tibet to take charge of the monastery. According to Tibetan custom he had to enter the monastery on a certain auspicious day, and that day hadn't quite come, so he was staying in a little tent in this clearing, waiting for the day when he could make his official entry. He started asking her about herself: who are you, who ordained you? She said, 'I'm a French woman, ordained by Dhardo Rimpoche.' Then he asked, 'What meditation practice are you doing?' She said, 'I'm doing such and such', and he said, 'No you're not, you haven't done that practice for six months.' And it was true. Of course she was deeply impressed and became his disciple, but in due course she became dissatisfied with him too. But that's another story.

Having heard about him, I was keen to meet him, and when he came to Kalimpong I sometimes used to function as his interpreter, not in Tibetan, which I didn't know, but in Nepali. He knew some Nepali and I sometimes translated when he had European visitors. There was an American couple who wanted to meet him, so I invited him and them for lunch. They asked all sorts of questions, some of them quite tricky, on the subject of Nirvāṇa, and I suddenly realized that he was replying without waiting for me to translate the questions, although he didn't know a word of English. I could only conclude that there was some telepathy going on. That quite impressed me.

He often used to come and stay with me. I think that out of all my teachers – apart perhaps from one I'll mention later on – he was the most committed to meditation, and he relied very much on the inspirations he got from his meditation. Once when he was staying with me at the Triyana Vardhana Vihara, at breakfast he said, 'Sangharakshita, in my meditation this morning I saw a banner of victory on the roof of your vihara.' Having seen it in his meditation, he had to act on it, so he went off to the bazaar, saw the carpenter and got a wooden frame made, went to the cloth merchant and got different coloured silks, went to the tailor and had it all stitched together, then put the banner up on the roof of the vihara with all the necessary ceremonies and offerings. There it was, and there it remained until I left Kalimpong. That was typical of him.

After I'd been given initiation by Jamyang Khyentse Rimpoche, I was as it were handed over to Kachu Rimpoche and he took charge of me. He started me on the four foundation yogas, and gave me the Padmasambhava initiation and various other initiations. But he remained very much a friend. He was a cheerful, lively, unassuming person, very warm-hearted, but a bit rough. He wasn't polished or elegant like some of my other teachers, but he was warm-hearted, generous, communicative, and had a rather earthy sense of humour, and he was deeply devoted to Khyentse Rimpoche and the Nyingmapa tradition. I remained in touch with him until I left Kalimpong. Some of you may have seen his picture in *Life* magazine because the Maharaja of Sikkim, whom I knew, married an American lady, Hope Cooke. There was a big controversy about it, but after the father's death the crown prince became the new Maharaja, his wife became the Maharani, and Kachu Rimpoche, as the head lama of the royal monastery, performed the coronation ceremonies, which were featured in *Life* magazine. I remained in touch with him until he died some years ago in Sikkim.

DILGO KHYENTSE RIMPOCHE

From him we come to Dilgo Khyentse Rimpoche. I should explain that there were five Khyentse Rimpoches, reincarnations, according to Tibetan Buddhism, of the body, speech, mind, *guṇa*, and karma of the previous Khyentse Rimpoche, who is known as the Great Khyentse Rimpoche. Jamyang Khyentse Rimpoche was the chief of the five, and Dilgo Khyentse was his brother *tulku*. I met him in the late 1950s, when he was living in the Bhutanese *gompa* in Kalimpong together with his wife and his two daughters. The whole family were at least six and a half feet tall – they were absolute giants. He was a very gentle, kindly person and a great scholar. He was always reading. Whenever I went to see him he always had a book in his hands which he put aside as I entered. I received many initiations from him. He was a very humble, unassuming person, didn't make much of a splash, didn't look for disciples. He's still living, and he has visited the United States more than once. Where he is now, I'm not sure, perhaps in Nepal. Sometimes messages or greetings pass between us.[291]

DUDJOM RIMPOCHE

And then, last but one, Dudjom Rimpoche, also an incarnate lama, a *tulku*, and perhaps the leading authority on the Nyingmapa tradition. Unlike Dilgo Khyentse he was very short indeed, with rather feminine features. He'd been married a number of times, and he was rather fond of whisky. He lived in regal style in a large house with his current wife and family, and he was not very approachable. Some people said that his wife kept people away, but I don't know about that. Anyway, I managed to approach him and I received quite a number of initiations from him. You'll notice that I received initiations from several different lamas. Three of them were in particularly close connection with one another and formed a group: Jamyang Khyentse Rimpoche, Chattrul Sangye Dorje, and Dudjom Rimpoche. They had a lot of disciples in common, disciples who had different initiations from all three of them. I was told, I think by Kachu Rimpoche, that one day a discussion arose among the disciples as to which of the three was the most spiritually developed. Someone was deputed to go and ask Jamyang Khyentse whether any one of them was more spiritually developed than the other two. So Jamyang Khyentse said, 'Yes, out of the three of us one is definitely more Enlightened than the other two. But you people will never know which one it is.' There's quite a lot in that, if you think about it.

Dudjom Rimpoche died not long ago. He was still working on his great work on the history and teachings of the Nyingma school, which is to be brought out in two fat volumes by Wisdom Publications. It's been on the stocks now for a couple of years and many of us have paid our subscriptions in advance and we're hoping to see it soon. When it does come out it will be a work of paramount value, covering all aspects of the Nyingma school and tradition.[292]

YOGI CHEN

I'm hurrying because there's still quite a lot of ground to cover. We come lastly to Yogi C. M. Chen. He was born in China, and spent quite a few years in eastern Tibet, during which time he was a disciple of Jamyang Khyentse Rimpoche, who was then a comparatively young man. Yogi Chen had practised both Vajrayāna and Chan. He didn't have much time for Zen, which he saw as a Japanese corruption of Chan, which was Zen's Chinese forerunner. When he was in China he read the entire Chinese Tripiṭaka twice, which is a bigger feat than you might think, because there are 1,656 separate works.

I came in contact with Mr Chen in the late 1950s, when he was living in Kalimpong. He hadn't been there long, and he was living as a hermit in a small bungalow on the outskirts of the bazaar area. During the whole time that I was in Kalimpong he didn't go out even once, and generally he did not receive visitors. He spent the greater part of the day engaged in different forms of meditation, and devoted half an hour a day to writing, producing a number of books in both Chinese and English. After getting to know him, I was permitted to spend an evening with him every week for a whole year. He was very communicative and I learned a lot from him, mainly about the Vajrayāna and about Chan and Chinese Buddhism in general. He absolutely refused to consider himself as a teacher, and did not allow anybody to refer to him as their guru. He wouldn't accept disciples in the formal sense, and certainly wouldn't give initiations, but would send people along to the appropriate incarnate lama. This did not, however, prevent him from criticizing the incarnate lamas very vigorously.

He could read almost any English book, but his spoken English was abominable. He had a strong Chinese accent, and very strange ideas about English grammar. Until you'd known him for quite a while, you couldn't make out what he was saying. He was eccentric in various ways, for instance with regard to dress. Sometimes I'd find him wearing a cowboy costume. I don't know where he got these strange costumes from; perhaps they came in the big parcels he used to get from Chinese Buddhists in Hong Kong. Sometimes he wore a formal Chinese scholar's dress. He had a big smile and he was very excitable. I was surprised at first that although he meditated all day, he was so explosive, so emotional, but perhaps lots of energy was generated in his meditation and it spilled over. He became so excited when he spoke that he sometimes shed tears. Once I gave him a book on Zen by Christmas Humphreys, and after reading it he cried 'to think that poor people in the West are being given this stuff instead of the real thing'.

He had all sorts of strange visions and psychic and occult experiences which he'd tell me about, but what impressed me the most about him was that he had a very good understanding of Buddhist doctrine. I used to ask him all sorts of questions, and he gave me the clearest replies that I got from any of my teachers. In the midst of all his eccentricity, there was absolute clarity of understanding. He eventually left his hermitage and settled in California, and that's where he died. He used to send me photographs of himself performing various activities. He was very camera-conscious. I'm sure it was very altruistic, but the photographs were of him packing up boxes, performing ceremonies, and all sorts of things. He used to drive a little van. People were completely devoted to him. So that was Yogi Chen, of whom I also have very fond memories.

Those were, those are, my eight principal Buddhist teachers. I hope I've been able to give you some glimpses of them and make them seem real to you. They're still very real to me. A couple of them are still alive, but even those who are dead, and in some cases have apparently been reincarnated, are very alive to me and form part of my life.

DILGO KHYENTSE

1991

There are two kinds of lectures: one is the product of perspiration, and the other is the product of inspiration. I have to admit that this little talk is not the product of any perspiration at all, and probably not much in the way of inspiration, but in some ways that's not inappropriate, inasmuch as I'm going to be talking about Dilgo Khyentse, and one certainly doesn't associate perspiration with him, except perhaps in a literal sense. Apparently he had a habit of stripping himself to the waist. I don't remember him ever doing that when I saw him, but Khampas from his part of Tibet, eastern Tibet, used to walk down the high street in Kalimpong in the depths of winter stripped to the waist and perspiring, and perhaps he used to feel the heat like that. But I don't associate Dilgo Khyentse with perspiration because he never seemed to be in a hurry. He was always very leisurely, easy-going, relaxed, and calm. There was nothing dramatic or sudden about him. He was a very unobtrusive person, though he was so big. I think it's because of that quality that I can't remember my first meeting with him. It's as though he gradually came within the sphere of my experience in Kalimpong. I can't remember anything dramatic happening in connection with him. He just imperceptibly hove into view, in the late 1950s or early 1960s. I certainly came into contact with him after I had come in contact with Jamyang Khyentse, probably after Jamyang Khyentse's death, which was in 1959. I assume I must have taken the initiative and gone to see him, because I used to call on any Tibetan lama who had newly arrived in Kalimpong, and in that way made contact with dozens of them, including nearly all the eminent ones who passed through.

My meetings with Dilgo Khyentse in Kalimpong took place in a wooden caretaker's cottage at the entrance to the Bhutanese *gompa*. This was a well-built but neglected and deserted *gompa*, called Bhutanese because it was built by the kings of Bhutan when the Kalimpong subdivision was part of Bhutan and before it became part of British India in the 1860s. It may have been built at about the same time as the old Bhutan palace, which Dhardo Rimpoche occupied. They were fairly close to each other. On my visits I must have taken someone with me as interpreter, and certainly on a number of occasions I took with me Sherab Ngawang or Prajnaloka, a Tibetan disciple of mine. He'd been a monk in Tibet, then gave it up, travelled widely, got married, had all sorts of adventures, and then in his relative old age decided he wanted to become a monk again, but not a Tibetan monk. For some reason he made up his mind that he wanted to be ordained by me, though he was twenty years older than me. With some reluctance, after trying to persuade him to be ordained by Dhardo Rimpoche, I ordained him as a *śrāmaṇera*, and he remained a *śrāmaṇera* for many years. Some years ago, by which time I was in England, he received the *bhikkhu* ordination. I used to use him as an interpreter quite a lot, as his English was good.

I don't recollect that Dilgo Khyentse ever came to my place. He didn't go out and about much. In the case of some incarnate lamas one had to make arrangements to see them, but one could just drop in on Dilgo Khyentse. He didn't seem to have any visitors, he didn't seem to be well known at that time, and I must have dropped in on him at least seven or eight times. The Tibetans have a bed which they use as a seat during the day, and there Dilgo Khyentse would always be, seated cross-legged, reading a book.

I had the impression that he was very poor. His robes were shabby, and he had nothing apart from his books. But he always received me with a smile. There was no great demonstration, just an 'Ah yes, hello', a nice smile, and he'd put his book aside. His manner was kindly, fatherly, gentle, unpretentious, and unobtrusive. It's very difficult to describe it. He had a characteristic sweet smile. I met him thirty years ago, and his smile in recent photographs is exactly the same. The Dhardo Rimpoche I see in recent photographs is an old man and the Dhardo Rimpoche I remember from thirty years ago was young, but Dilgo Khyentse seems hardly to have changed at all. Perhaps his hair is a bit scantier and whiter, and possibly the old Dilgo Khyentse was a bit fuller in the face, but otherwise he's just the same.

I assume he must have asked me who I was and where I came from. I got the impression of someone who was very willing to meet and talk with anybody in a completely natural way. Many of the incarnate lamas, maybe not because of personal predilection but just because of tradition, were very formal. When I first knew him even Dhardo Rimpoche was very formal with all his visitors. But Dilgo Khyentse always seemed very relaxed and to have plenty of time. He had not only a smile, but a twinkle in his eye. When I visited, his wife would appear to bring the tea. At that time he had only one servant – not many for an important incarnate lama. Dilgo Khyentse was enormously tall, at least six foot six, his wife was just as tall, and his two daughters were even taller and quite thin. His wife was in some ways quite like him. I think she was just an ordinary wife, not officially a spiritual consort, but she was also friendly, welcoming, and unpretentious, and the two girls likewise, though they were a bit awkward. They were unmarried at that time – they were still teenagers – but least one of them married and had a son, who subsequently acted as Dilgo Khyentse's translator and travelled around with him.

So I had this friendly, casual contact with Dilgo Khyentse, and I could go along and see him whenever I felt like it. I must have talked about him with Mr Chen, who knew all the incarnate lamas, at least by reputation, and I think it was he who advised me to ask Dilgo Khyentse for initiations. Mr Chen was well aware that I was doing my best to work for the good of Buddhism, as per Kashyapji's injunction to me in 1950, and he knew that working for Buddhism wasn't easy, and that to do it you needed all sorts of things. In some ways Mr Chen took his Vajrayāna quite literally, and I remember him urging me to get the initiations of Jambhala and Kurukullā so that wealth and popularity would come to me for the sake of my Dharma work, because Jambhala represents wealth and Kurukullā represents the Tantric function of fascination.[293] I can't say that I took this quite literally, but I used to take what Mr Chen said seriously, so I asked Dilgo Khyentse for those initiations, and he kindly agreed to give them to me. He was pleased to give me whatever I wanted, and he conducted the initiation in his characteristic way. There was just the usual ritual, quite simple. Each ceremony lasted an hour or two, and he was just his own kindly, fatherly, unpretentious self, and his old wife was hovering in the back room, helping.

Mr Chen was a great believer in the *phowa* practice of Amitābha.[294] I don't think he had had much experience of it himself, but I remember him telling me that his wife practised it very successfully in China. Dilgo Khyentse was well-versed in this practice, he said, and advised me to obtain the necessary initiation and instruction from him. It was an oral tradition and I wrote it down; I still have the notes I made. But though I've done the Amitābha part of the practice, I've never done the transference of consciousness part. Maybe that's something I should keep for my old age, though one mustn't put these things off indefinitely. So these were the three initiations I received from him, though it's possible I received others which I've forgotten.

I remained in contact with Dilgo Khyentse right up to the time of my departure from India in 1964. After two years I returned to India for a farewell visit and spent a week in Kalimpong, where I met Dhardo Rimpoche, Mr Chen, and other friends. I also visited Darjeeling, and at that time Dilgo Khyentse was living there with his wife, somewhere in the bazaar, again in very poor circumstances, so I went to pay him a visit. By then I knew that the trustees of the English Sangha Trust didn't want me back, and Dilgo Khyentse was one of the people I told about this. (I told Dhardo Rimpoche too.)[295] I can't remember exactly what Dilgo Khyentse said, but the purport of it was 'Never mind, don't take any notice, just go back and carry on with your own work' – which is more or less what Dhardo Rimpoche said too. I was quite concerned, but they seemed to attach no importance whatever to anything that the Trust might say, think, or do.

Dilgo Khyentse and his wife wanted to give me something as a parting present. They had little to give, they were so poor, but his wife searched around and found a Khampa knife with a bone handle and a little sheath with a bit of silver mounting, and she gave me that, saying, 'We're very sorry, but this is all we're able to give you. Please accept it.' I still have it in my study. But that wasn't the last time I saw them. From the hills I went back to Calcutta, where I arranged to have my books and other things transported to England. I happened to visit the Bengal Buddhist Association and there in their guest quarters Dilgo Khyentse was staying, with his wife and a servant, so we had a very pleasant, unexpected reunion. My friend Terry Delamare was also there, and I have a photograph of that meeting, with Dilgo Khyentse towering even over Terry, who was a six-footer.

That chance meeting was the last time I saw Dilgo Khyentse, but I used to read about his travels in the West, especially in America, and it's clear from the descriptions that people have given of him when he was famous and had all sorts of luxuries at his disposal that he was exactly the same. The photographs of him in America show exactly the Dilgo Khyentse that I knew, and I can well understand people in the West being very much attracted by him. I can't help wondering though whether they were able fully to appreciate him. Some people seemed to want to build him up in a way that I don't think he would have been happy with. I'm sure in his own way he just didn't permit that.

So yes, I have very positive memories of him indeed. My contact with him was in some ways very ordinary, but I was very impressed by him as a character, mainly because of his lack of pretence, his unassumingness, his friendliness, and his warm, kindly, sweet smile. I don't remember seeing him laughing. You may remember that according to the Pāli scriptures the Buddha said that laughter that shows the teeth is madness and that if you have cause to show your pleasure, it is enough to smile.[296] Dilgo Khyentse fitted that perfectly; he had a really beautiful smile. Since I received the Amitābha initiation from him, I especially associate him with Amitābha, but I did receive those other two initiations, Kurukullā and Jambhala, and I also associate the characteristics of Kurukullā with him. He didn't exactly have a fascinating aspect, that's too strong a word, but he had a subtle attractiveness. You couldn't help liking him, forming a favourable impression at first glance. Jambhala, wealth, came to him quite late in life, and he probably didn't bother too much about it. In my own case I don't think Jambhala is around yet, but there has been a change over the years, and at least I'm now able to buy almost any book I fancy, which is my standard of wealth. I hope that Dilgo Khyentse also, in the latter part of his life, was able to acquire any Tibetan manuscript he fancied, because he was a great reader. I didn't know he was a writer, but it wouldn't be impossible for his writings to be translated, just as Dudjom Rimpoche's great work on the Nyingma school has been translated, so we may be able to read his writings one day.[297] I certainly feel that I've been in direct contact with Dilgo Khyentse himself, and with the essence of whatever he might have written, and he stands out in my memory as one of the most subtly impressive people I have ever met.

THE MESSAGE OF DHARDO RIMPOCHE

York Hall, London, 24 March 1991

Today we're observing the first anniversary of Dhardo Rimpoche's death. Paradoxically, we observe the anniversary of somebody's death on account of their life, because the quality of their life has value for us, because it's worth remembering. That's certainly true of Dhardo Rimpoche. I met him for the first time in 1953 in Kalimpong, though I subsequently learned that he had seen me some four years earlier in Bodh Gaya, and had some definite thoughts on the strange figure of the yellow-robed European monk he saw. I saw him for the last time in 1967, also in Kalimpong, so I was in personal contact with him for fourteen years. Our contact was particularly close and intense in the years 1956 to 1964, and in 1962 I received from him the bodhisattva ordination. I have many memories of Rimpoche's mindfulness, his compassion, and his many other qualities, but this evening I am not going to give you much in the way of personal reminiscences. Instead, I want to say something about what I've called Rimpoche's message. It may be news to some of you that he had a message other than that communicated by his life. He didn't write any books or give any lectures in our formal sense. He gave some discourses in Tibetan, but they weren't recorded or written down, so in a sense they have disappeared. But Rimpoche did found a school. He founded in 1954 what he always used to call in full the Indo-Tibetan Buddhist Cultural Institute school. He was very proud of his school, and fortunately it still exists, thanks in no small part to help given by quite a number of people present on this occasion.[298]

For thirty-six years Rimpoche's life revolved around his beloved school, and he overcame tremendous obstacles to keep it going. On one occasion he even had to sell some of his precious and beautiful *thangkas* in order to pay the wages of his teaching staff. He didn't just love his school as an institution or as a building. He loved his pupils, thousands of whom must have passed through his care over the years, and because he loved them, he dearly wanted them to grow up under the benign influence of the Dharma. He wanted them to grow up as real Buddhists. The school day began with the chanting of the praises of the Buddha, Mañjuśrī, the bodhisattva of wisdom, and Sarasvatī, the female bodhisattva of learning and culture, invocation of whom is believed by the Tibetans, as by Indian Buddhists before them, to assist in the preservation of a good memory. It's because Rimpoche wanted his students to grow up as real Buddhists that in addition to various modern subjects they also studied the Tibetan language and literature, Tibetan Buddhist texts, and even historical texts. And as though to reinforce a point, Rimpoche gave his beloved pupils a message – a message of just seven words in English. It's about that message that I want to speak this evening.

Dhardo Rimpoche's message was intended for Tibetan children, and you may wonder what relevance it can have to us sophisticated people of the West, but Rimpoche saw those children as potential adults, potential real Buddhists, perhaps potential bodhisattvas, and he wanted to give them a message that would hold good throughout their lives, a message that they would never forget, a message that would be true wherever they went, whether they returned to Tibet, as many of them hoped to do, or stayed on in India, though very few of them wanted to do that, or even travelled to the West, as some were anxious to do. The message he gave them is true for all people, especially for all Buddhists, as true for European and American adults as for Tibetan children. After all, we in the FWBO are also Rimpoche's spiritual children or grandchildren, and we still have a lot to learn. We've a lot of spiritual growing up to do. Dhardo Rimpoche's message to us on the first anniversary of his death is to be found in the motto he gave his school and caused to be inscribed on the school flag: 'Cherish the doctrine. Live united. Radiate love.'

The doctrine is the Dharma, in Tibetan *chös*, which has two principal meanings. In the first place, it means law, principle, truth, reality, as in the term *dharmakāya*, and secondly, it means the teaching of the Buddha, the systematic expression in terms of concepts and symbols of the Buddha's transcendental experience of the ultimate reality of things, his vision of things as they really are. This communication is for our benefit, intended to help us realize what the Buddha realized before us. It's a raft, helping us across the stormy waters of *saṃsāra* to the other shore. Obviously there's no question of our cherishing the Dharma in the first sense of law, principle, truth, reality. The Dharma in this sense doesn't need to be cherished or protected by us. We can only worship it, take refuge in it. It's the Dharma in the second sense that Rimpoche is asking us to cherish, the Dharma in the sense of the teaching or doctrine of the Buddha.

How are we to cherish the doctrine? We can cherish it in three ways. In the first place, we cherish it by studying the *sūtras* and *śāstras*. The *sūtras* contain the word of the Buddha, or what tradition regards as such, and the *śāstras* are the explanations of the word of the Buddha given by Enlightened masters who lived at a later date. The *sūtras* and *śāstras* constitute a vast literature, and we don't have to study the whole of it. In any case, it hasn't all been translated into English. But we should have a thorough knowledge of a reasonable number of key texts, which may be of Pāli, Sanskrit, Chinese, or Tibetan origin, because in the FWBO we seek to draw freely from the riches of the entire Buddhist tradition. We don't wish to confine ourselves exclusively to any one tradition, however ancient. If we don't have a knowledge of at least a few key texts, we shall be unable to understand the Buddha's teaching, and in the absence of such knowledge, our thinking about Buddhism will be muddled and confused, and we may even fall victim to wrong views, something which in the Buddhist tradition is taken very seriously indeed. Studying the *sūtras* and *śāstras* doesn't mean just reading them. It means reflecting on them, turning them over in our minds, and discussing them with our teachers and our fellow students.

In the second place, we cherish the doctrine by practising it. Of course, we can only practise it if we have at least some knowledge of it. We practise the doctrine by trying continually to deepen our Going for

Refuge to the Buddha, the Dharma, and the Sangha. We practise it by observing the precepts – five, or ten, or more. We practise it by engaging in right livelihood. We practise it by cultivating spiritual friendship, of the supreme importance of which we are sufficiently apprised. We practise it by meditating and performing puja. We practise it by living in a spiritual community. We practise it by helping to run a Buddhist centre. We practise it by going on solitary retreat. In all these, and a hundred other ways, we should practise the Dharma. To the extent that we practise it, we cherish it, we help to keep it alive. We know very well that it is not easy to practise the Dharma. To do so we have to go against the stream, and ultimately against the whole weight of our mundane conditioning. But if we don't practise it, it will not be cherished, and if it isn't cherished, it won't really live, and we shall have in its place only ideas, concepts, words.

In the third place, we cherish the doctrine by propagating it. Obviously we can propagate the doctrine only to the extent that we understand it and practise it, only if we experience it and realize it ourselves. We can propagate the Dharma in many ways. We can propagate it by giving lectures, or leading meditation classes, or writing books, but not everybody is in a position to do this. Most people will have to help propagate the Dharma indirectly, by transcribing and editing the recordings of lectures, by publishing books, by providing facilities for the giving of lectures and the taking of classes, and by donating money. I need hardly tell you that people in the world need the Dharma. Many of them know they need something, but they don't always know that what they need is the Dharma – hence, very often, their surprise and delight when they happen to come into contact with it, perhaps after many years of searching.

So we should do all we can to propagate the Dharma in every possible way. If we propagate the Dharma, people will come to understand it, if they understand it, they will be able to practise it, if they practise it, it will be cherished by them too, and if it is cherished, it will survive. Nowadays the survival of the Dharma is threatened on every side, by materialism and by pseudo-religious fundamentalism, and it needs to be propagated more vigorously than ever. But – and this is very important – it is the Dharma and only the Dharma that must be propagated. We mustn't mix the Dharma with isms and ologies which are foreign to its spirit, even quite inimical to it. In our work of propagating the Dharma so far as possible we should use traditional Buddhist language. The message of the Buddha can't be delivered in the language of Māra (or in one of his languages, because he has many), not even by bodhisattvas. We have to admit, too, that Māra can on occasion use, or appear to use, the language of Buddhism, but that is another story.

LIVE UNITED

Obviously, people do live united in a sense. Without unity, social life would not be possible. Unifying factors include a common language, common nationality or citizenship, race, culture, and religion, all of which bind people together and contribute to the unity of the group. But when Rimpoche exhorts us to live united, it's not this kind of unity he has in mind. After all, we're already living united, more or less, in that mundane way. We mustn't forget that Rimpoche's exhortation is addressed to potential real Buddhists, to us. So what are the unifying factors in our collective existence? What binds us together as Buddhists? What constitutes the unity of the spiritual community, the sangha? Obviously, the principal unifying factors are the Three Jewels. We're united by virtue of the fact that we all go for Refuge to the Buddha, the Dharma, and the Sangha. We're united by the fact that we observe the same precepts, practise the same meditations, perform the same pujas, study the same *sūtras* and *śāstras*, and so on. At least, these are the things that unite us in principle. But do we in fact live united? Do we put that unity into practice? Is it effective in our actual relations with one another? That is only too often another matter. What Rimpoche is really saying is, 'You are united as Buddhists in principle, but you must also be united in practice.'

What prevents us from being united in practice, from being a spiritual community in the fullest sense? I'm afraid there are quite a number of things. There's personal conflict with other members of the spiritual community. There's competitiveness, jealousy, factionalism, the cherishing of ill will, the harbouring of grudges, unwillingness to forgive, reluctance to clear up misunderstandings. In a word, what prevents us from living united is egotism, or, if you dislike that old-fashioned word, individualism. Only too often we think that we are acting as individuals when we are really being individualistic. When Rimpoche says, 'Live united,' he is also saying, in a deeper sense, 'Live egolessly. Live in a non-individualistic manner. Realize that there is in the ultimate sense no separate unchanging self to defend or to assert. Realize *nairātmya*, realize *śūnyatā*.'

RADIATE LOVE

By love Rimpoche means *mettā* and *karuṇā*. The English word 'love' is unfortunately grotesquely ambiguous. It can mean lust, in the sense of sexual craving, as when we speak of making love. It can mean a greedy liking: 'Oh, I love chocolate.' It can mean natural affection, as when we speak of a mother's love for her child, or brotherly love. Then there's romantic infatuation, which we can also call projected love, because it involves projecting onto the loved person qualities that he or she does not really possess, or not in the degree that we think they possess them. This is, in case you haven't tumbled to it, being in love. Finally, there is altruistic or sacrificial love. We don't have a word for this in English, though the Bible refers to it when it says, 'Greater love hath no man than this, that he lay down his life for his friend.'[299] It's important to distinguish the different meanings of the word love, otherwise there will be confusion in our thinking and probably confusion in our personal life as well. By love Rimpoche means *mettā*, or *maitrī* in Sanskrit, so when he says, 'Radiate love,' he means radiate *mettā*, or radiate *mettā* and *karuṇā*. This Pāli word *mettā* is cognate with *mitta* (*mitra* in Sanskrit), which means simply 'friend'. *Mettā* is the intense, non-sexual, altruistic, delighted affection that you feel for a friend, and it's love in this sense that Rimpoche is asking us to radiate.

Spiritual friendship is one of the cornerstones of our movement. Just a few months ago I was in the United States, and during my visit I had personal talks with about fifty people connected with the Movement there. I was naturally interested to know what had drawn them to the FWBO, especially as some of them had been connected with other Buddhist groups. There were several factors, but there was one thing that everybody mentioned, and two thirds of them put it at the top of their list. What had drawn them to the FWBO, they said, was its friendliness, its sense of sangha, spiritual community. It wasn't just that members of the FWBO happen to be friendly men and women. It was more that the FWBO actually believes in friendship, has faith in it, and values it. In some other Buddhist groups, I gathered, friendship is not exactly encouraged, or sometimes even discouraged in favour of faith in the guru, even, I'm afraid, blind faith.

So people in the FWBO make an effort to practise friendship, to be true friends to one another. But obviously our practice of friendship is not perfect. It's not easy to be a real friend. There are so many obstacles to friendship, perhaps now more than ever. In his talk on Going for Refuge and friendship, Subhuti enumerated certain obstacles to friendship: (1) passivity, (2) impatience, (3) a romantic view of friendship, (4) lack of commitment, (5) sexual relationships, (6) faction, (7) lack of forgiveness. And in his talk 'Have we Friendship in the Order?' Subhuti speaks of four areas to which we need to pay positive attention if there is to be depth in friendship: (1) immaturity, (2) lack of trust and competitiveness, (3) superficiality in our conception of friendship, and (4) sexual relationships.[300]

I would say that friendship is deep to the extent to which it incorporates the transcendental, or rather, deep to the extent that it is itself incorporated in the transcendental. It is deep to the extent that it is altruistic and egoless. I once spoke of communication as mutual awareness leading to mutual self-transcendence,[301] and deep friendship can be spoken of in similar terms. We can radiate love only to the extent that we live united. True friendship is the efflorescence of egolessness. To radiate means, according to the dictionary, 'to emit from a centre'. The centre is the middle point, and a point is defined as that which has position without magnitude. We can radiate love only from the centre of our being. We can radiate love only from egolessness, from *śūnyatā*, only from that point within ourselves which has position without magnitude.

'Cherish the doctrine, live united, radiate love' is the message that Rimpoche gave to his students, and that he still gives to each and every one of us. It's the message, moreover, that he gave not just in words but in deeds, through the medium of his own life. Rimpoche indeed cherished the doctrine, studying it intensively, especially during the earlier part of his life. He practised the doctrine, observing the ethics of a bodhisattva, cultivating the *pāramitās*, and living the life of a monk, and he propagated the doctrine, especially towards the end of his life. He taught the students of his own school, cooperated with visiting Buddhist scholars, especially those from the West, and gave advice and inspiration to visiting members of the FWBO. He once said that he regarded Sangharakshita's disciples as his own, and he could say that because he lived united with other real Buddhists. He was totally free from competitiveness and jealousy. On more than one occasion, as I saw myself during my time in Kalimpong, he really suffered at the hands of bigots, but he didn't bear a grudge. He was always willing to forgive, because he was not the victim of egotism. And finally, Rimpoche radiated love, *mettā* and *karuṇā*, friendliness. All those who came in contact with him, even for a short time, experienced this for themselves. This is why we remember Rimpoche today, and why we're celebrating the anniversary of his death. We're celebrating it because he was the embodiment of his own message, because he himself cherished the doctrine, lived united, and radiated love. In other words, we are celebrating the anniversary of Rimpoche's death because of the supreme quality of his life, and because his life is worth remembering, bearing in mind, reflecting upon, and deriving inspiration from. We're celebrating the anniversary of his death because we want to make his life a permanent part of the heritage of the FWBO.

REJOICING IN THE MERITS OF DHARDO RIMPOCHE

I rejoice in the merits
Of the Guru of Dhartsendo;
I rejoice in his life
Of mindfulness and compassion.
I rejoice in his confident turning
Of the Wheel of the Immaculate Dharma,
And in his faultless wielding
Of the Diamond Sceptre of Wisdom.
I rejoice in his proclamation
To his disciples both young and old,
To his disciples both near and far,
Of the threefold inspiring message
To cherish the Doctrine, live united, and radiate love.
I rejoice in his practice
Of the six perfections:
In his practice of unfailing Generosity;
In his practice of flawless Ethics and Manners;
In his practice of infinite Forbearance;

In his practice of inexhaustible Vigour;
In his practice of unshakeable Concentration;
In his practice of profound and far-reaching Wisdom.
Humbly and heartily,
Gratefully and reverentially,
With body, speech, and mind,
I rejoice in the merits
Of the Guru of Dhartsendo,
I rejoice in the merits
Of Dhardo Rimpoche.

THE FIVE PILLARS OF THE FWBO

Manchester Town Hall, 6 April 1991

It was more than twenty years ago that I paid my first visit to Greece, which for me meant ancient Greece, classical Greece, and among other places I visited Delphi, the fulfilment of a long-held wish. As I wandered round looking at the ruins of the great temple of Apollo, I couldn't help remembering that in ancient days – in the days of the glory that was Greece, when the temple stood four-square and beautiful – over the portal of the temple was an inscription that was famous throughout the whole of the classical world, and is not unknown even today: 'Know thyself'. The ancient Greeks had a certain understanding of these words, and we perhaps understand them in another way, but however we understand them, it's certainly not easy to know oneself. One could even go so far as to say that when we're young – when we're under 40 – we usually don't know ourselves at all. Usually we are quite blind, quite ignorant. Not only do we not know ourselves; perhaps it doesn't even occur to us that there is something to know that we don't know. Self-knowledge is not something we prize at that early stage of our life. It's only later on in life that we start knowing ourselves, partly as the natural result of our ordinary human maturity and partly as the result of our increased experience of life, and especially of other people with whom we come into contact in all sorts of ways. Very often that experience is painful, even very painful. We may even go so far as to say that very often it's only through painful experiences that we start to know ourselves. In any case, self-knowledge is something that we achieve to any depth comparatively late in life, and we tend to achieve it slowly and with difficulty.

This is true not only of the individual man and woman, but also of the collectivity. The ancient Greeks as a whole did not know themselves. The Athenian people did not know themselves, at least until after the Peloponnesian War. Medieval England did not know itself, and modern America perhaps does not know itself. One might even argue that the group as such never knows itself, or at most knows itself in the person of a few individuals who are more than just members of their group, individuals like – in the case of ancient Greece – Thucydides. But it is not only the group, the ethnic collectivity, that does not know itself. A spiritual movement does not know itself. The FWBO does not know itself. That is to say, it doesn't know itself until later on in its history. Today we celebrate the twenty-third anniversary of the FWBO, so we attained our collective majority two years ago. We could say that we are collectively – even if not always individually – grown up, so we should as a movement be a bit more mature. We should be beginning to know ourselves, to see ourselves.

Beginning to see ourselves, what do we see? How do we see the spiritual movement of which we are a part? Speaking personally, I see the FWBO in a number of different ways. I see it as a tree, or perhaps a sapling – a sapling that has sprung from a seed planted twenty-three years ago and is already bearing fruit, already providing shelter and nourishment for people in many parts of the world. I see the FWBO also as a bed of lotuses, a garden, a road, a raft. I see it as a magnificent temple, which began twenty-three years ago as a tiny improvised shrine and is still very much in process of construction, with here and there great building blocks that have not yet been incorporated into the overall structure. Some people, looking at the FWBO from a distance, don't see it as a temple at all, but as a fortress, or a factory, or a barracks. Some of them, though they seem to be looking in the right direction, don't see anything at all. But it's not easy to see the FWBO as a temple. It's not easy to see the FWBO as it really is, even when one is quite close to it. In fact it's not easy to see it even when one is standing right inside it. But standing inside this temple that is the FWBO, what does one see? One sees space, light, a multitude of great golden figures, enormous vistas, and an overarching dome like that of the sky itself. One sees multiple arches, and above all, round the central shrine of the temple, five mighty pillars that support the entire edifice. It's about these five pillars that I want to speak this afternoon.

But first, a warning. I'm afraid I have sometimes to complain that people take my words and images rather more literally than they were intended. So please don't take my five pillars too literally. Don't think that there are only five, no more and no less. There may be other pillars that I haven't mentioned, or even seen. Moreover, don't think of the pillars as being necessarily pillars of stone, hard, fixed, and rigid. The Bible speaks of pillars of cloud and pillars of fire, and we can also have pillars of living light, pillars of living radiance. So, having issued those words of warning, what are the five pillars of the FWBO? They are ideas, practices, institutions, experiment, and imagination.

IDEAS

By idea I don't mean just a concept, a mental object, but something like what we have in mind when we speak of a 'bright idea'. An idea of this kind can usually be expressed in just one or two words; it's simple and in a sense abstract. But though abstract, an idea is seen as being full of possibilities, as opening up new horizons. An idea excites people, it stirs them up. An idea is often very moving, and more often than not it moves people to action, to change things, to change themselves, even to change the world. People are even ready to die for the sake of an idea. Ideas therefore occupy an important place in human life. Sometimes ideas change history. In ancient Greece there was Plato's great idea of justice, which dominates his most famous dialogue, the *Republic*. It's not quite justice in the sense of the English word, but near enough. There's Plotinus' idea of emanation. There's the medieval idea of degree, or hierarchy, as we would say nowadays, echoes of which are to be heard in several well-known passages in Shakespeare.[302] There's the idea, connected with that, of the great chain of being.[303] Coming on to the eighteenth century, we find the idea of reason, which didn't previously exist in that eighteenth-century sense, and in connection with the idea of reason, we find the idea of enlightenment; enlightenment with a small 'e', not in the Buddhist sense of *bodhi*. Towards the end of the eighteenth century we find the three interconnected ideas of liberty, equality, and fraternity, ideas which for a while convulsed a good part of the world. And in the nineteenth century still more ideas emerged:

the idea of progress, the idea of evolution, the idea of science in the modern sense of the term. We've grown used to these ideas. Perhaps we no longer find them very interesting, and in the case of one or two of them perhaps we have become rather disillusioned about them, but these ideas were once new, exciting, even controversial. Nowadays we have such ideas as relativity, the unconscious, repression, and so on, and I need hardly tell you what part they play in our lives.

In the same way, there are ideas that occupy an important place in the history of Buddhism and are still important to us today. Take, for instance, the idea of conditionality, which, even when briefly stated, brought about such a tremendous spiritual upheaval in Śāriputra, who became one of the Buddha's two chief disciples, that he attained Stream Entry.[304] There's the Mahāyāna idea of the perfect mutual interpenetration of all the phenomena of existence. On an occasion like this there's no need to multiply examples. You'll be sufficiently familiar with these Buddhist ideas.

When Buddhism first came to the West towards the end of the nineteenth century, we didn't encounter it as any kind of organization, or in any living way. We didn't come into contact with its practices, its institutions, its festivals, or its celebrations. We came into contact first of all with its ideas, and some of these struck some people very forcibly. At that time, not much more than a hundred years ago, most people in the West believed that they had only one life on earth followed by an eternity of either bliss or torment. But Buddhism taught the idea of karma and rebirth, the idea of a whole series of lives, both here on earth and in other realms, lives governed by an impersonal moral law. We've got used to this idea, but when it was first introduced in the West, for some people it was a real eye-opener which placed their lives within an infinitely broader context. Another Buddhist idea that struck people very forcibly was the idea of tolerance, the idea that people of different religions are not natural enemies, that they don't have to fight and kill each other, but they can live together peacefully, agreeing to disagree. Many of us are so used to the Buddhist idea of tolerance that we can't imagine what an eye-opener it was to many people when they first came in contact with it. In those days difference of religion, difference of sect, difference of belief could divide families, estrange brother from brother, father from son, as illustrated by many of the works of fiction of the Victorian period.[305]

So ideas occupy an important place in human life. They occupy an important place in history, an important place in Buddhism, and naturally, therefore, an important place in the FWBO. The ideas that form one of the pillars of the FWBO are of several kinds. There are well-known traditional Buddhist ideas like conditionality. Then there are those ideas that struck people when Buddhism first came to the West. Perhaps I should also mention the idea of non-theistic religion. Previously people had believed that religion was necessarily theistic, and even now some people in the West who regard themselves as Buddhists have difficulty with the idea of non-theism and would like to think that in some way Buddhism believes in God. Finally, there are ideas that are more or less distinctive to the FWBO, emphases on hitherto neglected aspects of the Buddha's teaching, or restatements of the Buddha's teaching in more contemporary terms. Among emphases on neglected aspects of the Buddha's teaching we may mention the idea of positive conditionality, the idea of Going for Refuge, and the idea of the spiritual community. And among restatements of the Buddha's teaching in more contemporary terms, we may mention the idea of the higher evolution and the idea of male friendship. I say male friendship not because I wish to exclude women from the notion of friendship, but because friendship between men has been rather frowned upon in the West in modern times, and it therefore needs to be emphasized in a way that is not so necessary in the case of friendship between women.

Very often we don't realize the power of ideas, the effect that they can have on people, and very often this is because we've got used to them. We've lost our beginner's mind. It's important therefore that we keep our beginner's mind – important for our own sake and also for the sake of other people. Then we will continue to find ideas – perhaps the very ideas that originally attracted us to Buddhism – stimulating and exciting. We will feel inspired by them, and we will want to communicate them to others. Sometimes I think we don't communicate our ideas sufficiently to the outside world, to the people we meet. Only too often, I suspect, we are too preoccupied with our own mental and emotional states. I would suggest that there should be a greater emphasis on ideas, that we should talk more about conditionality, Going for Refuge, non-theism, male friendship, and all the stimulating and exciting ideas that form one of the pillars of the FWBO.

Secondly, practices are a pillar of the FWBO. By practices I mean spiritual practices, especially the different forms of meditation. Spiritual practices have been important in Buddhism from the very beginning, as illustrated by a well-known passage in the *Mahāparinibbāna Sutta*, the *sutta* from the Pāli canon that deals with the last days of the Buddha. The *sutta* tells us that the Buddha was in Vaiśālī. He was on his way to Kusinārā, where he would finally pass away, but he spent the rainy season in Vaiśālī, and Ānanda was with him. Towards the end of his stay, the Buddha asked Ānanda to call together all the monks in the locality. It seems that he knew he did not have much longer to live and he wanted to give the monks his final advice. We can imagine them coming from their little wattle and daub huts, from their dwelling places among the trees, from caves, all gathering in response to Ānanda's summons. Perhaps they knew that the Buddha's end was near, so they came all the more quickly, eagerly, even anxiously. And when they'd gathered around the Buddha, he said, 'Monks, the principles (*dharmas*) which I have discovered and taught should be well learned by you and practised, developed and cultivated so that this best life (*brahmacarya*) should be enduring and last long for the benefit and happiness of men and gods. And which are those principles? They are as follows.' And the Buddha proceeded to give a list, in fact a list of lists. It comprises: (1) the four foundations of mindfulness; (2) the four right exertions; (3) the four bases of psychic power; (4) the five spiritual faculties; (5) the five strengths; (6) the seven factors of Enlightenment; and (7) the Noble Eightfold Path – altogether thirty-seven different items, which later on in Buddhist history became collectively known as the thirty-seven *bodhipakṣya-dharmas*, 'principles that are the wings of Enlightenment', aids to the attainment of Enlightenment.[306]

What we notice about these principles is that they are all things to be done. They are all groups of mental exercises, and some are forms of meditation. On that solemn occasion the Buddha doesn't say anything about doctrine, not even conditionality. He speaks only of spiritual practices, which suggests that practices are very important indeed. We may recall here the first verse of the *Dhammapada*: *manopubbaṅgamā dhammā*, 'Mind is the first of things.' These practices are important because mind is important. They're important because it is important to change the mind from unskilful to skilful, from impure to pure, from unenlightened to Enlightened. And practices, both those mentioned by the Buddha on that occasion and others, are the means by which this change is brought about. They are the means by which the mind is transformed from the saṃsāric to the nirvāṇic mode – not the only means, but the central, most direct means. They are specific, concrete. You can't practise just meditation or just mindfulness in a general way, not if you're a beginner, someone who hasn't gained Stream Entry. You need specific methods, specific exercises, concrete things to do. Moreover, practices are something that you do regularly, even daily, not just when you happen to feel like it.

Some people say that spiritual practices are a form of mental or psychological conditioning. Well, they are. We need not be afraid of this word conditioning, because our minds are already conditioned. They're conditioned by our upbringing, by our education, by the work we do, by our environment, by our relations, acquaintances, and sexual partners. They're conditioned by the newspapers we read and the television programmes we watch. They're conditioned by the different groups to which we belong. Our minds are conditioned in so many ways, and for the most part in ways that are unskilful, impure, and saṃsāric. Spiritual practices are meant to undo that, to make our negatively conditioned mind into a positively conditioned mind. It's only a positively conditioned mind that can become an unconditioned mind, only a positively conditioned mind that is capable of gaining Enlightenment. Positive conditioning is important, so spiritual practices are important, and it's for this reason that in the FWBO we have many practices, virtually all of which are from the Buddhist tradition. In particular we have the mindfulness of breathing and the development of universal loving-kindness, the six element practice, various types of visualization, and the Going for Refuge and Prostration practice. There are also different sets of ethical precepts: the five precepts, the ten precepts, and so on. In traditional Buddhist societies *dāna*, or giving, is also a very important spiritual practice. In the FWBO, I feel, we don't as yet give sufficient attention to this practice, particularly perhaps in the case of those working and earning out there in the world.

Some of you might be surprised to hear that institutions are a pillar of the FWBO. In some quarters nowadays 'institution' is regarded almost as a dirty word, rather like the words 'discipline' and 'obedience'. When institutions are mentioned we tend to think of prisons and mental hospitals and *One Flew Over the Cuckoo's Nest*.[307] But according to the dictionary an institution is 'an organization or establishment founded for a specific purpose, such as a hospital or college'. Institution is thus a neutral word, like the word organization, and there's no need for us to be afraid of using it. The society in the midst of which we live is made up of institutions, and without them society could hardly exist – human beings, even, could hardly exist. Human beings want to achieve various specific purposes. They want to acquire knowledge, for example, or to be cured of disease. But they can't achieve that purpose by themselves, so they band together to found an organization or an institution. Most people belong to or make use of quite a few. Next time you feel tempted to be critical of them, you could make a list of all those to which you yourself belong. The length of the list might surprise you.

Institutions are principally of two kinds, the mundane and the spiritual, and some fulfil both purposes to some extent. Mundane institutions are not necessarily bad – some are, but others provide the necessary basis for spiritual institutions, or at least make it easier for spiritual institutions to function. Mundane institutions, one could say, belong to the lower evolution, while spiritual institutions belong to the higher evolution. Mundane institutions ideally enable one to develop as a healthy, happy group member, while spiritual institutions enable one to develop as an individual, not in isolation but in cooperation, even in spiritual community.

The institutions that are pillars of the FWBO are spiritual institutions, and at present there are mainly three: the public centre, the residential spiritual community, and the team-based right livelihood business (or co-op, as we used to say), the famous 'three Cs'. They're not mutually exclusive. One and the same person can belong to any two of them or even to all three, in varying degrees. The specific purpose of the public centre is to be a meeting point between the FWBO, in particular Order members, and the outside world. At the centre, members of the public can come in contact with the ideas of Buddhism, ideas that may change their lives, they can learn some of the practices of Buddhism, especially meditation, and they can start making friends with spiritually like-minded people. The specific purpose of the residential spiritual community is to provide a positive alternative to the family, whether nuclear or extended, a situation in which spiritually like-minded people can live together in a way that is expressive of Buddhist values, and can intensify their friendships and deepen their experience of the Dharma, especially their experience of Going for Refuge. And the specific purpose of the team-based right livelihood business is to enable people to support themselves in an ethical manner and to develop spiritually through working together, as well as to make a profit that can be given to the Movement as *dāna*.

We need these institutions. We need our centres, our communities, and what used to be called our co-ops, because we need other people, and other people need us. As anyone who has made a serious attempt knows, it is not easy to lead the spiritual life, that best life, that *brahmacarya*, of which the Buddha spoke. It's not easy to develop as an individual. It's not easy to be a true Buddhist. We need the help and cooperation of others who are trying to do the same thing. We need to meet with one another in our centres, we need to live with one another in our communities, and we need to work with one another in our team-based right livelihood businesses. In a sense we have no choice. It is not that we are free either to live in institutions or not. The only choice we have is whether to live more in mundane institutions or more in spiritual institutions, and if we want to develop as individuals we will choose to live more in spiritual institutions. We shall try in fact to live in them as much as we can. If we choose – whether consciously or by default – not to live in spiritual institutions, we shall unavoidably live in mundane institutions and be influenced and conditioned by them. So let us not listen to those for whom 'institution' is a dirty word. Let us live in centres, communities, and co-ops as much as we can. Let us rejoice in their merits, let us appreciate them, let us be proud of them, let us realize that spiritual institutions are one of the pillars of the FWBO.

EXPERIMENT

We live in a changing world, and the FWBO itself is changing and developing all the time – developing, we trust, in an organic manner. We are confronted by changing conditions all the time. We meet different kinds of people, and we come in contact with different cultures, especially when the FWBO spreads to a country where previously it had no presence, or to a different part of the same country, or a different social group. We may find that the existing way of doing things in the FWBO is not quite appropriate to the new conditions, so that we have to adapt and develop new approaches, new methods of presentation, new modes of communication. And in order to do this we shall have to experiment. Otherwise the FWBO may not succeed in establishing itself in a new environment and may not even survive in the old environment.

According to the dictionary, an experiment is 'a test or investigation, especially one planned to provide evidence for or against a hypothesis'. There are two points to note here. First, an experiment is planned, and has a definite purpose. It's not done at random. It's the result of serious thinking, even study. It's not a matter of doing something in a whimsical, irresponsible way just to see what will happen. Second, to conduct an experiment, we need a working hypothesis, which is, again having recourse to the dictionary, 'a suggested explanation for a group of facts or phenomena accepted as a basis for further verification'.

Let me give you one or two concrete examples. Suppose there's an FWBO centre somewhere in Britain, perhaps in a new geographical area, and suppose that as part of its regular activities this centre conducts pujas, but very few people come to them. Perhaps on some occasions nobody comes at all. So what do the Order members running the centre do? I'm assuming that they're very intelligent people. The first thing they do is study the situation carefully. Only too often we not only hypothesize but even speculate without bothering to ascertain the facts. So they ascertain the facts of the case, making allowances for fortuitous circumstances. People may not have come to the puja because it was raining, for example. Then, having ascertained the facts and made allowance for circumstances, the Order members concerned frame a hypothesis. In this case the hypothesis might be, 'People don't come because the pujas aren't colourful enough.' So they proceed to investigate their hypothesis, not theoretically – that's only too easy to do – but practically. They carry out a planned experiment. They organize a whole series of much more colourful pujas, and in this way they test their hypothesis. If more people attend and keep on attending, the hypothesis can be taken as verified, and more colourful pujas can become a feature of that centre's activities. If it makes no difference, or if even fewer people attend, the hypothesis is not verified, and the Order members concerned will have to frame another hypothesis and conduct another experiment. Alternatively, suppose there's a meditation centre and not many people come on retreat. The Order members concerned may hypothesize that this may be because there's not enough verbal instruction on the retreats they run, and they may then proceed to carry out an experiment.

So experiment as one of the pillars of the FWBO is a serious matter. It's not something to be conducted in a frivolous or irresponsible way. Also, experiments should be properly monitored. Week by week people should observe what is going on and records should be kept. Only then can real comparisons be made. Sometimes, I'm afraid, experiments of this sort are held at centres without any monitoring or record-keeping, but such experiments are obviously useless. One is left with vague personal impressions which don't help at all. Not only should all experiments be properly monitored, and records be kept, but the results of the experiments, negative or positive, whether the hypothesis is verified or not, should be communicated to the rest of the Movement for its information through suitable channels.

Experiments should be made by a number of experienced people working together. This will normally mean that they'll be made by a number of Order members. And they should be planned to test such hypotheses are in accordance with the spirit of the Movement. For instance, you shouldn't test the hypothesis, 'Would more people come to pujas if beer was served afterwards?' The hypotheses tested should also represent an organic development or application of the spirit of the Movement. There must be continuity between the old way of doing things and the new, not an abrupt break. Experiments should not be sprung on people, especially if they're accustomed to doing things in a particular way and they're not necessarily looking for a new approach. If you sit down expecting the Sevenfold Puja, it's disconcerting, maybe even annoying, if someone suddenly starts leading a quite different puja which he or she may have thought up overnight. And finally, and very importantly, one should not have recourse to experiment out of restlessness or simply a desire for change.

It's difficult to describe imagination in the way I've described the four other pillars. In fact, I was quite doubtful whether I should call this pillar imagination at all. I thought of calling it the pillar of vision, but then I thought it could be confused with vision in the sense of Perfect Vision or Insight, and that wasn't quite what I meant. I also thought of calling it the pillar of magic, or the pillar of mystery or the pillar of myth; but in the end I decided on imagination, though even this is not very satisfactory. I could give you the dictionary definition of imagination, or even read you an extract from Coleridge, but I think this would not help much, so instead I'm going to ask you to do something I should perhaps ask you to do more often. I'm going to ask you to use your imagination. Your own imagination should be able to tell you what imagination is, and whereabouts in the temple you will find this particular pillar of the FWBO. But let me give you a few hints. Look for imagination in the realm of myth, especially in the myth of the Order, the myth of the Movement, in archetypes and ideals, in poetry in the broadest sense of the term. More concretely, look for it in ritual and ceremony, in meditation, and in the scriptures, especially some of the great Mahāyāna *sūtras*. Look for it in the fine arts. Look for it in all these places, and in many others. If you do this, you will get at least a glimpse of imagination, and you'll be able to see that imagination is in truth one of the pillars of the FWBO.

These, then, are the five mighty pillars of our temple, which is still very much in the process of construction, but in which we live, or at least gather from time to time. So let us learn to recognize these five pillars for what they are. Let us familiarize ourselves with them. Let us know our temple. Let us know our movement. Let us know ourselves. Let us realize that ultimately it is our ideas, our practices, our institutions, our experiments, and our imagination that are the five pillars of the FWBO.

FIFTEEN POINTS FOR OLD – AND NEW – ORDER MEMBERS

WBO Day, Goldsmiths' College, 1993

I won't be giving you a lecture today. I think I was at my peak as regards giving lectures between twenty and thirty years ago, which is unfortunate for those of you who came along later, but some of those lectures are on tape for you to listen to if you want to. There will not be any spectacular verbal pyrotechnics on this occasion. I'm just going to present to you, in a plain and straightforward manner, from a list of more than forty points I jotted down recently, fifteen points which I have selected as being of relevance to most Order members. We already have our fifteen points for new – and old – Order members so this time I have reversed the title and I am going to call it 'Fifteen points for old – and new – Order members.'

1. REDUCE INPUT

My first point is relatively simple and straightforward. I don't know anything about computers, so this point is not intended to have anything to do with them, but it often strikes me that we are subject to enormous input through our senses and our mind. So much impinges on us every day, even every hour. First of all, people impinge on us, not just the people with whom we are in close contact, but those we pass in the street or see on the Tube or in other casual ways. On a Tube train, you can become aware that some of the people sitting in the carriage are in quite strange mental states – talking to themselves, or nodding their heads, or in a stupor, very tired after the day's work or even before the day's work begins. Because one can't help noticing people, they have an effect on one, contributing their input all the time.

Then there's the sound of traffic. My little flat at Sukhavati in Bethnal Green is relatively quiet, but even there I hear the traffic. Through the window of my study I can see planes coming and going every few minutes. I can hear police, ambulance, and fire engine sirens. I can hear glass being broken, and all sorts of goings on. In the distance I hear drilling and people shouting slogans. And when I go out, it all becomes much louder, especially in the heart of the city. Then there are the sounds of radios and televisions. There are also the things we read. If we are regular newspaper readers, they impinge on us all the time. Often we are not conscious of this, because it registers subliminally, but it affects us, probably more than we know.

So, reduce input. We may not be able to shut out all the input all the time, but we can be much more selective about what we choose to let in. We need to make an effort to be more selective about what we read, the television programmes we watch, and even the contact we have with our friends. We deliberately tune in to certain channels on the radio and television, and we should apply that principle to everything. We are a receiving station all the time, but we don't have to allow all these outside influences to play on us constantly without any control or restriction. Be more selective, and try to make sure that the influences that are impinging on you are positive.

We can reduce input drastically by going on solitary retreat. Don't take too many things with you. Don't take too many books, not even Dharma books, and don't stay in a place where you're likely to find a television set or even a radio. These things are very seductive. An Order member wrote to me some time ago and said, 'When I was on my solitary retreat I didn't watch too much television.' He seemed to think it not unusual or unacceptable to spend two or three hours a day watching it, and maybe for him it did represent a drastic reduction of input, but when we are on retreat we should reduce input much more than that. We should have no contact with people, or with the outside world at all, as far as possible.

We have a daily solitary retreat when we meditate. Almost the first thing we do is reduce input by closing our eyes. We try to meditate in a quiet place for the same reason. The things that impinge on us come mainly from the outside world, so first of all you reduce external input, and then you become more aware of internal input, the wandering thoughts, fancies, ideas, reflections, and worries, and you work on reducing those. Only when you've done all that do you really start meditating, and only then can you have contact with any deeper or higher levels within yourself. Writers and artists have to do the same sort of thing.

2. THINK CLEARLY

This is an old chestnut which I think will bear bringing to your notice yet again. Framed in more traditional terms, it is not so much 'Think clearly' as 'Cherish right view.' You notice I don't say 'Cherish Perfect Vision'. That would be premature, because there is no Perfect Vision without right view. Right view is the mundane form of Perfect Vision, and Perfect Vision is the transcendental counterpart of right view. Unless you have right view, you have very little chance of achieving Perfect Vision, which is why right view is so important. The Buddha had all sorts of things to say about right view. He didn't distinguish linguistically between right view and Perfect Vision, simply speaking in terms of *sammā-diṭṭhi* (Pāli; *samyag-dṛṣṭi* in Sanskrit), but it is clear from the context which he is talking about. Right view is important because wrong view leads downward. There is a Pāli term, *niraya*, which means 'downward', or 'downward path'. If you entertain wrong view, and especially if you cling to and insist upon it, you are very definitely on the downward path, so right view is of very great importance. No right view, no Perfect Vision. No Perfect Vision, no liberation, no Enlightenment, no real spiritual progress.

In order to cherish right view we have to learn to think, to reason. Sometimes I'm surprised how difficult people seem to find this. I'm not even speaking of thinking clearly. So often we are swayed by our negative emotions, but we are not aware of this, not aware that we are not really thinking. But to cherish right view we have to learn to think clearly, to reason correctly. Some time ago Subhuti led a series of weekends on the study and practice of logic. I believe that those who attended them found them very useful, and perhaps others who know a little about logic could restart them. There isn't much point in studying the Dharma if you can't think clearly, or even think at all. That, logically and psychologically, must come first. We have arts weekends and events, and even arts retreats, which is fine, but we must not neglect the other side of things.

Sometimes we use words very loosely and inaccurately. Our speech is often laden with jargon from various sources, and that does not conduce to clarity. So let us understand the meaning of the words we speak, and especially the words we write, and consult the dictionary if necessary. I think the most useful book in the world, leaving aside the scriptures, is the dictionary. If I was ever to be invited on *Desert Island Discs*, the book I would ask to take with me to my desert island would be a dictionary.[308] And it would not be just any old dictionary, but Dr Johnson's dictionary, which not only defines words beautifully and precisely, but also contains examples of how writers of the past have used words, providing an anthology of extracts which show how the words are used in literary or sometimes scientific contexts. If someone uses a word you don't understand, or if it's ambiguous, ask for clarification. Otherwise you may be discussing or arguing at cross purposes.

Nowadays, as I hardly need tell you, wrong views are pouring in upon us all the time. Open the newspapers and you will find wrong views. Read a recently published book, listen to a political speech or a talk on almost any topic, and you will encounter wrong views. We live in the midst of this society, so we can't help being affected by it, but we must be on the alert and realize that many of the views we encounter are quite inconsistent with the Dharma. We have to be able to think clearly, reason correctly, and understand the meaning of the words used. It is especially important that we don't mix up with the Dharma the ideas and ideologies with which we come into direct or indirect contact. It is all very well to try to speak the language of contemporary life, but we have to be careful that when we speak that language we don't allow ourselves to be misled and start to think in contemporary terms which are inconsistent not only with clarity of thought, but with right view. Be very wary of fashionable ideas and ideologies and isms, and stick to the Dharma. You can express the Dharma in relatively straightforward English up to a point, but be careful when you start using words and expressions and even borrowing philosophies and semi-philosophies from sources that are very different from or even inimical to the Dharma itself.

3. DISTINGUISH FACT FROM VALUE JUDGEMENT

This is a specific example of what I've just been talking about. I've found that it's something that people find very difficult to do. If we say, 'It's raining,' that's a factual statement, but if we say, 'The weather is bad,' that's a value judgement, though we don't always realize this. Rain may be bad from our point of view, if we want to go out for a walk, but the farmer may be delighted that it is raining. In India, after a long period of very hot weather, people are very pleased when the rain starts falling, because if the monsoon is delayed, it may mean starvation. At the first drop of rain they dance for joy, like the peacocks that are supposed to dance for joy when the first raincloud appears. So their value judgement would be different from ours. We often confuse these two types of statement, especially when talking about other people. We might say, 'Oh, they're not a very good person,' but that is not a statement of fact. If you wanted to put it in factual terms, you would have to say what they had done, and give your value judgement about it separately. Someone else might give a quite different value judgement.

Different value judgments occur in different religions. I've been thinking about blasphemy recently because of the Salman Rushdie case.[309] You can't really have a law of blasphemy because different people consider different things blasphemous. To an orthodox Christian, if you say that Jesus Christ is not God, that is blasphemy, and hundreds of years ago you could have been burned at the stake for saying it. But if you say that Jesus Christ *is* God, that is blasphemy to a Muslim, for whom only God is God. So those are two completely different value judgements about Jesus. To consider that he is the son of God is a value judgement, and to consider that he is *not* the son of God, but an ordinary man, is another value judgement. What for a Christian is blasphemy to deny, for a Muslim is blasphemy to assert. So before you say something about someone, ask yourself, 'What are the facts?' Sometimes people think they're disagreeing about facts when really they're disagreeing about value judgements. A lot of the confusion that arises in discussion between people, even in the pages of *Shabda* sometimes, springs from the fact that value judgements are not sufficiently distinguished from statements of fact.[310]

We are all Buddhists, we all go for Refuge to the Buddha, Dharma, and Sangha, and we all seek to follow the spiritual path. There are various models for following the spiritual path, and one of them is what has been called the developmental model. When we adopt this model, we think of following the spiritual path in terms of our individual development from a lower to a higher stage, and assess what we do, what we say, and even what we think, in terms of whether or not it conduces to our spiritual development. This is quite legitimate. But there is also an illegitimate use of the developmental model. I'll give you a few crude examples of the sort of thing I've heard: 'I think I ought to have a holiday this year. Maybe I'll go to Greece for a month. I think it would be good for my spiritual development.' 'I think I ought to start getting angry with people. I think it would be good for my spiritual development.' 'I think I ought to get into a sexual relationship. I think it would be good for my spiritual development.' You want to do something, but you justify it, at least to your Buddhist friends, by putting it in terms of your spiritual development. After all, people can't quarrel with your wanting to develop spiritually, so that's the way you express your intention. It would take a rather bold and insightful spiritual friend to challenge a statement like that.

People have tried this sort of thing on me in the past. I remember someone saying to me in India, 'Oh, I'm sure, Bhante, that someone as wise as you would not think so and so….' Wanting to appear wise, you may find it difficult not to think what that person wants you to think. It is very difficult to challenge the words used when the values they embody are held in common. The language of spiritual development is common to all of us, but it can be misused. So if someone tells you, or if you tell yourself, that something would be good for your spiritual development, challenge it. Just because the slogan of spiritual development has been invoked, it doesn't mean that it is beyond question. If someone tries to justify their action like this, respond with a challenge: 'Wait a minute, did you say a holiday in Greece? For three months? Why do you think that would conduce to your spiritual development? Is three months necessary? Do you need a rest, or do you need a solitary retreat? Or do you need to work harder?' Don't just accept the statement. There shouldn't be a full stop at the end of it, but a big question mark, and if your friend doesn't put that question mark there, put it in yourself, in their interests and in the interests of intellectual and spiritual honesty.

5. THINK MORE IN TERMS OF RENUNCIATION

Thinking in terms of giving things up will help to counterbalance any possible misuse of the developmental model. You could ask yourselves not 'What do I need for my spiritual development?' but 'What could I give up?' It is very unlikely that it will be bad for you to give up things you find difficult to give up. If you're not sure what to give up, ask your spiritual friends. Giving up using bad language might be an appropriate suggestion for some people, or giving up smoking. If someone is drinking more than just a very little alcohol – sherry in their trifle, for instance – you could suggest that they give it up. You could give money. We get lots of opportunities to do that because there are so many fundraising appeals. It is a very good and healthy thing to be asked to part with money, because that's one of the things that, quite frankly, we don't find it easy to part with, especially if we don't have much of it to begin with. If somebody doesn't have any money, obviously we should share with them whatever we have. We need to think much more in terms of renunciation. It is not only those who are *bhikkhus* or *anagārikas* who have to think in terms of giving things up. Every Buddhist needs to do it, regardless of their lifestyle.

If we think more in terms of renunciation, it will help to counteract the dreadful prevalence of consumerism that surrounds us on all sides. Advertisements are not interested in telling you what you can do without. They are very interested in telling you what you can't possibly do without. If you pick up a colour supplement or one of those enclosures that come through the post, you see pictures of all those household gadgets and holidays and clothes and accessories which you apparently must have. You can counteract this to some extent by thinking more in terms of renunciation. When you see an advertisement for a glossy new car, don't ask yourself, 'Would it be good for my spiritual development to buy this car?' Instead, say to yourself, 'Wouldn't it be good if I gave up even the thought of acquiring a car?'

We can't think exclusively in terms of spiritual development, taking that language literally; we also have to think in terms of renunciation, because there is no spiritual development without it. We can't always wait for things to drop away from us. Sometimes we have to actually give them up, even though it might be rather painful at first. And looking at it the other way round, there is no renunciation without spiritual development. I don't mean renunciation through feelings of irrational guilt, which you shouldn't be having anyway. We shouldn't think of development and renunciation as antithetical, much less still contradictory. If we renounce unskilful things, practices, words, and activities, we really will develop spiritually, it really will help us. I'm not saying think *only* in terms of renunciation, but think *more* in terms of renunciation, especially as a means of counteracting any possible misuse of the developmental model.

6. DON'T ACCEPT YOURSELF

To some people this may sound like blasphemy. They may say, 'Of course you must accept yourself. It's the first thing you must do.' But let us look a little more closely into the matter. First of all, what does 'accept' mean? I wanted to be quite sure of this, so I consulted my old friend Dr Johnson, on whom I find I can rely. In his dictionary he defines the verb 'to accept' as 'to receive with approbation, with approval'. But surely there is much in ourselves of which we don't approve, much of which perhaps we strongly disapprove. We shouldn't want to hang on to that personal characteristic, whatever it is. We should want to reject it. So we should modify the popular statement about accepting ourselves and say, 'Let us accept what is skilful in ourselves, but let us reject what is unskilful.' There is no spiritual development without such an attitude. It's a form of renunciation.

I know I'm being a bit provocative, but consider the truth to be found in the provocation. In our current culture and way of looking at things, we are becoming rather self-indulgent. There is widespread talk nowadays, especially in psychotherapeutic circles, about accepting yourself, and this term has become rather misused, rather like the developmental model. So conduct an experiment: don't accept yourself. Say to yourself, 'If I get angry sometimes, why should I accept that? I don't accept it. If I accept it, I'm not going to grow in that respect. If I'm mean, if I don't like to part with my money, why should I accept that? I want to grow spiritually.' One should not think in terms of accepting oneself totally. Such acceptance is suitable only for an infant, not for anybody who has reached any degree of maturity. So don't accept yourself.

Also, don't accept what is unskilful in your friends. Say, 'I'm not going to put up with that. You acted unskilfully, you told a lie, you let me down. I'm not going to let you off the hook.' Let there be no collusion. Sometimes there is mutual collusion: 'You let me get away with this and I'll let you get away with that.' Sometimes I get reports of chapter meetings where Order members have told their fellow chapter members they're thinking of doing something quite questionable, or at least something that ought to be looked at more closely, but other chapter members just say, 'That's fine, go ahead.' In some chapters a vigorous examination will take place concerning what that person proposes to do, but only too often there is collusion and the person is let off the hook. This can be a serious misuse of the whole concept of acceptance. Receive with approbation what is skilful in yourself and others and reject with disapprobation what is unskilful.

7. REJOICE IN ONE ANOTHER'S MERITS

This is also a bit of an old chestnut, but never mind. It really is important, especially as this is a gathering of Order members. Rejoice in each other's merits. If an Order member has done something good, positive, useful, noble, or heroic, rejoice in that. This applies especially to senior Order members; not that others are excluded by any means. Some of our senior Order members are quite remarkable people, and I often feel very proud of them. It would be invidious to mention any names, but I feel a lot of confidence in many of them, and feel I will be in a strong position to hand over responsibility when the time comes. We should rejoice in one another's merits, and especially in the merits of our older and more experienced Order members, who contribute so much to the Order and to the Movement.

Occasionally, I'm sorry to say, I become aware of a bit of sniping at senior and responsible Order members. They do sometimes make mistakes. Anybody may make mistakes. But sometimes the sniping seems to come from a spirit of competitiveness or at least from a lack of full appreciation. Don't let this get in the way. Sometimes prominent people lay themselves open to being sniped at just because they are prominent, but in many cases they are prominent because of the good they are doing, the leading part they are taking, the greatness of the contribution they are making. So let us make a definite attempt to rejoice in others' merits, and especially in the merits of those who are doing more than we are. Perhaps you're not objectively in a position to do much for the Dharma, but don't let that restrain you. Let us rejoice in the merits of those who are doing more than we are.

I'll mention one particular Order member because he's absent, and that's Lokamitra. I rejoice in Lokamitra's merits almost every day, whenever I think of him, because he has done so much for our movement in India. If it had not been for Lokamitra I don't think there would be well over a hundred Order members in India. There would not be a Karuna Trust, because the Karuna Trust would not have any channels into which to pour the wealth that it has gathered. Most of the things that Lokamitra has done, I could not have done myself. He has a particular combination of qualities that enables him to be very effective in that situation. So I rejoice in Lokamitra's merits.[311] I take him as a particularly conspicuous example, and also because he happens not to be present, but there are others in whose merits I rejoice in practically equal measure, who have also contributed so much to the Movement. I rejoice in the merits of each and every one of you. I don't think there is anybody who has not made a significant contribution, even if only within his or her local sangha, to the well-being of the Movement. So let us all rejoice in the merits of other Order members.

In order to rejoice in people's merits we have to know them, but even if we haven't met certain other Order members, we can read about them, for instance in *Shabda*. I was disappointed a few months ago to hear an Order member say, 'I never read *Shabda*.' We should all read *Shabda*. I can hold myself up as an example in this respect, if not in others. I read my *Shabda* as soon as I get it, and if it's late, I enquire for it, because I am eager to rejoice in your merits when I read about all the good, noble, and even heroic things you have been doing. Read your *Shabda*, so that you know what other Order members are doing and can rejoice in their merits in an intelligent way. Just saying, without knowing anything about them, 'Oh yes, I rejoice in the merits of all Order members' is not nearly enough. But if you rejoice in the merits that you really see and appreciate in other Order members, you will take pride in them, and you will become proud of the whole Order.

I sometimes think that we don't take enough pride in ourselves. We should rejoice in our own merits and be proud of our Order. After all, in the last twenty-five years, between us we really have created something that is worthwhile. It is quite staggering to think of the number of people who have come into contact with us, continued with us, or even just passed through the Movement. So let us take pride in the Order. That means sticking up for the Order too. If someone misrepresents or criticizes the Order, or seems not to have a clear idea of what it is all about, don't hesitate to correct them. Do it appropriately, but don't let them get away with it.

If we rejoice in one another's merits and if we are proud of the Order, we will also trust one another. I feel that there is not quite enough trust within the Order. Perhaps this is a hangover from our experience of the world. You would be a very foolish person if you trusted the world, and I certainly don't. I don't trust the media. I don't trust most of the authors I read, including those who write about religious, social, and political matters. I've got a well-developed faculty of distrust which has helped me to survive some very difficult situations. Some people tell me that I often look suspicious, and that's quite natural when dealing with the outside world, but it is not appropriate within the Movement, and least of all within the Order. So trust one another, don't suspect one another. Take it that one another's motives are pure until you have reason to think otherwise. And if that does happen, take it up in a positive manner with the person concerned. If you can't trust one another, you can't work together. Those of you who work in team-based right livelihood businesses will know that mutual trust is of the essence of the matter, both in spiritual and in practical terms.

8. DON'T ARGUE, DISCUSS

What's the difference between arguing and discussing? It's quite simple: when you get into an argument, what you are concerned with is to win, to defeat the other person, whereas the aim of discussion is to find out the truth of the matter cooperatively. You're not thinking in competitive terms. You're not trying to beat or confuse or confute the other person. You're just trying to get at the truth of the matter, or at least trying to understand it. If you're not careful, what starts off as a genuine discussion can become an argument. It's difficult sometimes to tell where the one passes over into the other, and you can find yourself deep in a real argument in a very unpleasant way, having had no intention to do that. Be alert, and when you enter into a discussion, especially one about a subject on which you and the other person or people concerned have strong feelings, be careful that it doesn't degenerate into an argument. Ego will always try to smuggle itself into discussion and when that happens, discussion will turn, unfortunately, into argument.

9. DO NOT KEEP TOO MANY OPTIONS OPEN TOO LONG

Our movement having expanded so much within the last twenty-five years, there are many options open to us, or at least to those who don't have responsibilities outside the Movement. The temptation is to keep hoping that something better will turn up. Maybe you're invited to join the team of a certain centre. You think that it wouldn't be a bad thing to do, but then you think, 'I don't want to live in an industrial town. I'll wait to see if I get an offer from a centre in an agreeable country town, or preferably right out in the country.' Perhaps you get such an invitation, and then you think, 'I'd prefer to live somewhere with a better climate. I need sunshine for the sake of my spiritual development.' So you go on keeping your options open, thinking that something better may turn up.

If you keep your options open, you don't have to commit yourself. Maybe you rather like sitting on the fence. Maybe you even think it's a noble thing to do. I'm sure there's an appropriate rationalization. Perhaps you've got a mistaken idea of freedom and independence: 'I don't want to bind myself by committing myself to this or that.' But freedom is found in commitment, not in refraining from commitment. I'm talking about specific commitments, not the commitment represented by one's Going for Refuge. Freedom is found in commitment because when you commit yourself, it's the act of your whole person, or of as much of your whole person as you are able to muster. If you keep your options open indefinitely, you stultify yourself. If you've just left a situation which was rather demanding, it's legitimate to keep your options open for a while. Just look around and see what the options are, and think about what you really want to do, what would genuinely be in the interests of your spiritual development, and in the interests of other people and of the Movement. Consult your spiritual friends. And then commit yourself. And don't commit yourself just for a short time.

The fact that we can move around so easily these days sometimes means that people get restless after a year or two and they want to move on, but you can't achieve anything substantial unless you commit yourself to it for a relatively long time – in the case of a commitment to working in a centre, a period of say four or five years.

10. KEEP YOUR PROMISES

I have become aware that sometimes people, even Order members, don't keep their promises. They undertake to do something, maybe to arrange the flowers on the shrine, but they don't do it. This is very regrettable. If you can't keep your promises, you're not an individual. Individuality implies continuity, implies that the 'you' of today is able to act upon the decisions and promises of the 'you' of yesterday. If you can't do that, if you're at the mercy of passing whims and fancies and change your mind and forget or default on your promises, there is no continuity in you, and to that extent there is no individuality. You also let other people down. So you should give very great importance to this: don't let other people down, but keep your promises.

That means not making promises lightly. Years ago, when I was in India, people used to ask me why I wouldn't promise to do something, and I would say, 'I'm not going to promise because I take my promises seriously.' If you take your promises seriously, you will not promise easily or lightly, but once you have promised, your word will be your bond, and people can absolutely rely upon you. It is very frustrating when those who are trying to organize something are told, 'Oh yes, I'll help you do this, I'll help you do that,' but then the promises are broken. It is also frustrating when people say, 'Well, I might be able to help you. Perhaps I will.' If you can only say that sort of thing, don't say anything at all. Say either yes or no. If someone is trying to organize something and he's got a couple of dozen people who can only say, 'Well, perhaps I can help you,' that's no use whatever, because to be able to plan things he has to know who he can rely upon and what he can rely on them for. We could even say that ordination itself represents a promise. You promise the Buddha, Dharma, and Sangha to observe the ten precepts which you take at the time of ordination. And the precepts themselves are promises: I promise not to harm other living beings, I promise not to take the not-given, and so on.

11. BE MORE CEREMONIOUS

I'm referring here not to religious ceremonies or rituals, but social ceremonies. To give an example, when you've got a new chairman, it would be a good idea to have a ceremony to mark that event as having a special significance. Invest it with a bit of glamour. If you do things ceremoniously, it underlines the significance of the event and introduces an aesthetic and even an archetypal element. It isn't just some official business arrangement. A chairman is a very important person, not just someone who presides at the centre's council meetings, but a focal point for the whole of that centre. He has a spiritual relationship with the centre, and with every person within the mandala his centre represents. The installation of a new chairman is a very important and even solemn occasion, so let it be underlined with a bit of ceremony. When people come back after they have been ordained, welcome them back ceremoniously. Not so long ago I heard that when a new Order member came back to his community, although they knew he was due to arrive, there was not a single person there to welcome him. That was quite unfortunate. I know that usually people are welcomed back when they've been ordained, but let it be done on an even grander scale, and more ceremonially.

And also connected with this, better manners. I know that lots of us think that manners are old-fashioned, middle-class things, but let us look at them in a more aesthetic way and try to do things elegantly and beautifully. Frankly, I'm sometimes embarrassed by the uncouth manners even of Order members. They seem to have no social savoir-faire. On this occasion I was introduced beautifully, but it is not always done like that. Sometimes someone stumbles up and says, 'Ha, ha, yeah, Bhante's going to give a little talk....What's he going to talk about?' It's really awful and I cringe. It's not quite so bad when it happens within the FWBO, where we can understand and forgive, but if people from the outside world witnessed it, what on earth would they think of us? It isn't a question of being formal in a stuffy way, but of doing things correctly and mindfully and gracefully, with a certain elegance, and also of speaking clearly and distinctly. Here I must congratulate Sinhadevi on her beautiful enunciation.[312] I appreciate things like that, and I think we should pay more attention to that sort of thing. It's a matter of our own self-respect, and it creates a pleasing impression on those who are listening to us. If you give a talk, why not listen to the tape, make a few notes, and ask your friends what they thought of it? Were there too many ums and ahs, or too many uncomfortable pauses, or did you slur your words or get your facts wrong? Manners are important. Here there is a particular *micchā-diṭṭhi* or wrong view that I should mention, the *micchā-diṭṭhi* of spontaneity, or pseudo-spontaneity. People say, 'You've got to be spontaneous. You've got to be yourself.' But if your self is an untidy, uncouth, unorganized self, why should you let it persist? Why should you inflict it on other people? Keep it to yourself. Do not accept that self. It is not worth accepting. Reject it and get a new one that will be better for everybody concerned.

Let's not have a clumsy, uncouth movement. It's very important when new people come to centres to have a proper way of welcoming them. We shouldn't just sidle up to people and say, 'Where are you from?' That's not the way to do it. It's even worse to ignore visitors while you have a chat with a friend. We must be very conscious of our manners, our customs, our behaviour, and the degree of ceremoniousness appropriate to the occasion. Our Indian friends are so good at this sort of thing. Sometimes they go over the top, but that's better than neglecting ceremoniousness. Lokamitra sometimes used to say to me at the end of a meeting, when I had received forty, fifty, or sixty garlands, 'Come on, Bhante, they can offer the garlands to your chair. You don't have to stay.' But I made a point of staying because there was so much devotion on the part of the people who were giving the garlands. Even though I was tired, even though I would have liked a cup of tea, and maybe I had been sitting on a very uncomfortable seat, or on the floor, for three hours, I would say, 'No, let them finish,' because I could see what it meant to them. Even if ceremoniousness goes over the top a bit, which it is unlikely to do in England, let us not mind.

12. MOVE TOWARDS COMPLETE *BRAHMACARYA*

I say 'complete' because everybody is already observing *brahmacarya* to some extent. It isn't a question of some people being totally celibate and others totally non-celibate. We are all moving, slowly or rapidly, now or later on, towards complete *brahmacarya*. But let us be more aware of that. Let us ask ourselves, 'Could I give up a bit more? Could I put my sexual relationship or relationships a bit more towards the periphery of my mandala?' Sexual relationships have a tendency to slip and slide and snuggle their way towards the centre of the mandala, but don't let them do that. Check up on them from time to time. That's all I'm suggesting. If you can do that, you are moving towards complete *brahmacarya*. I won't say any more about this because we recently had an excellent issue of *Golden Drum* on the topic.[313]

13. REMEMBER YOU ARE A CITIZEN

Perhaps this point surprises you. But you are not just a Buddhist, you are also a citizen of a particular country, and as a citizen you enjoy certain benefits. In England it's customary to grumble about the government, the country, the monarchy, the press, and almost anything you can think of, but we enjoy a lot of benefits, and we lead relatively peaceful lives. We are looked after by our government, at least to some extent. We are protected by the police, at least to some extent. We should be aware of that, and be grateful for it. There are people living in other parts of the world who don't enjoy the benefits we enjoy as citizens. We are very fortunate, and we should be grateful. It is not enough to pay our taxes and then forget what society does for us. We can't altogether cut ourselves off from the society of which we are a part. Yes, we want to create a Buddha-land within it, and we will have to undermine the existing society to some extent in order to do that. In the long run we would like to undermine it completely, but that is going to take a very long time, and in the meantime we can appreciate the benefits we receive from the positive features of the existing society and make our own contribution.

FWBO centres are in a position to have a positive influence on local life. For instance, those who have school-going children should take an active interest in the affairs of the school. It is very easy to join a parent-teacher association. Recently I heard that the local authority in which one of our big public centres is situated was looking for a Buddhist to fill a vacant place on the governing body of a school. I only heard about it afterwards, and was really disappointed that no one had been found to take up that position, even though there were Buddhist parents in that area. We could even think in terms of participating in local government. I'm not suggesting that we should get involved in party politics, but we should try to make a positive contribution as Buddhists through the medium of local government to the well-being of the locality in which our centre is situated. Sometimes questions of planning permission affect our centres. If a road was going to be built right next to your centre, that would be a concern. That's a selfish interest, but apart from that, we should do what we can for people living in the locality, whether they are coming along to the centre or not, whether they are Buddhists or not. Please remember that you have a responsibility to your fellow citizens, as well as a more spiritual responsibility to the Movement and your fellow Order members.

14. THINK OF OTHERS

This is connected to the previous point. Think especially of those who don't have the benefit of the Dharma. That means thinking of expanding into different areas. I would like to see Order members becoming more adventurous – taking part, for instance, in the Angulimala project.[314] I think there are only three or four people involved at the moment, and that is quite disgraceful. Those who are in a position, practically and psychologically, to do some prison visiting, please contact Angulimala and see how you can help. We can't afford to rest on our laurels. Think of all the people we could reach out to if we had more centres, not only in this country but elsewhere. I get a lot of letters from people who have found the FWBO, and they say, 'I'm so pleased and so grateful that I've made contact with the FWBO. It's made such a difference. It's changed my life.' There must be tens of thousands of people, even hundreds of thousands, who could write that letter if there were FWBO centres in their areas. In this country, and in places like Eastern Europe and South America, there are tremendous opportunities for communicating the Dharma and bringing real hope and inspiration to other people.

15. BE HEROIC

Years ago I gave a lecture called 'The Heroic Ideal in Buddhism', and perhaps I should have given hundreds of lectures on that theme.[315] Heroism above all is needed in the spiritual life. Spiritual life is not easy. To fight and struggle with oneself is not easy. To counteract the unskilful side of oneself is not easy. To make spiritual progress, to develop, to renounce, all these things are not easy by any means, so we need to be heroic, for our own sakes, and if we are to spread the Dharma. There are so many obstacles. Think of the Mahavihara in Pune. For just one signature, Lokamitra had to go to the same government office forty times. So we need to be heroic. If Lokamitra had not been such a hero he would never have been able to accomplish what he has.[316]

We need to be heroic nowadays because the world is becoming not just a difficult but a very dangerous place. After the end of the Cold War, many people thought that things were going to become easier, politically speaking, but it looks to me as if they are becoming worse, or have become worse, in many parts of the world. In this country we may not have such an easy time in the future as we had in the immediate past. Maybe there won't be disasters here, but I'm fairly sure there will be disasters in other parts of the world that are going to affect us. We shall have to be quite tough to survive and carry on with our Dharmic work. So far, in this country at least, we have had a pretty easy time. We have had no real difficulties compared with those faced by people in other countries, including India, where many of our Order members, Mitras, and Friends have a very difficult time. Heroic qualities are needed if the Movement is to survive and flourish.

As most of you will be aware, in a few months' time I will be 68. How many more years are left to me, I don't know. Nobody knows. For the last twenty-six years I have been deeply involved with the work of the FWBO and WBO. They have been my life. But that is not going to go on indefinitely. I may manage to hang on for another ten years, but I'm going to be passing on sooner or later, and that is going to make at least some difference. There will have to be a transition from being with me to being without me. I want to make that transition as easy as possible, so I have already started handing over some of my responsibilities to some of the more senior and experienced Order members, and in the next couple of years I want to see that process completed.

During the last few years, despite having handed over quite a few responsibilities, I seem to have more to do than ever before, which is in some ways disappointing, but in other ways reassuring, because the increased responsibilities are mainly due to the Movement expanding so much. But in the next few years, I want to hand over as much as I possibly can to the public preceptors and the presidents. It is with a view to doing that that we have recently set up what we are calling

FWBO Central, which means splitting the present Padmaloka FWBO in two, so that one half of Padmaloka is concerned with the men's ordination process and the other half is concerned with the Order Office, my own personal affairs, public relations, and so on. My idea is to hand over more and more of my responsibilities to this new body. I wouldn't like any one person to have to bear the responsibilities that I bear at the moment, so I'm hoping to be able to hand over my remaining responsibilities and any that may arise to this small body, mainly of preceptors and presidents, who will function through FWBO Central, so that as and when I do pass on, which we hope will not be too soon, there will be the proper machinery in place and a smooth transition.[317] Then, if you feel like it, you will be able to mourn my passing without having to worry about how the Movement is going to carry on without me.

Having succeeded in handing over my responsibilities, what am I going to do? Well, that's no problem at all. If I don't have anything to do, I won't mind in the least. But I expect I'll do more writing. There are quite a few books and pamphlets and papers I'd like to write. I'll go on seeing people individually. I may appear at functions and beam amiably on everybody. I may do a little travelling. I'd like to revisit India, and I'm going to America shortly. I'd very much like to revisit New Zealand and Australia, and I'd like to visit a few new places. I've always been fascinated by Mexico and Istanbul. I'd like to do some irrelevant things, just because I'd like to do them. But I have a strong sense of duty, and I will only be able to do this with a clear conscience after I have handed over my responsibilities properly. I'm communicating this just to keep you fully in the picture, and no doubt you will be informed, through *Shabda* and in other ways, of other developments as they take place.

That's all for the time being. Let me recapitulate, to help fix things in your minds a bit. I have brought to your attention a second set of fifteen points: (1) Reduce input, (2) Think clearly, (3) Distinguish fact from value judgement, (4) Don't misuse the developmental model, (5) Think more in terms of renunciation, (6) Don't accept yourself, (7) Rejoice in one anothers' merits, (8) Don't argue, discuss, (9) Don't keep too many options open too long, (10) Keep your promises, (11) Be more ceremonious, (12) Move towards complete *brahmacārya*, (13) Remember you are a citizen, (14) Think of others. In some ways they are all summed up in this last point: (15) Be heroic.

THE RAIN OF THE DHARMA

In 1994, Sangharakshita made a six-week tour of North America, an auspicious pradakṣiṇa, *as he called it, moving in a clockwise direction around the continent as one would circumambulate a stupa. The tour had three purposes, he said. First, he wanted to see with his own eyes all four of the* FWBO *groups then existing in North America: Aryaloka Buddhist Center in New Hampshire, the San Francisco Buddhist Center, and the groups in Seattle and Missoula. Secondly, he conferred the first two Western Buddhist Order ordinations on American soil, those of Saramati, from Missoula, and Karunadevi, from San Francisco. And his third purpose was to launch* The Drama of Cosmic Enlightenment, *his commentary on the parables, myths, and symbols of the* White Lotus Sūtra. *In San Francisco he spoke at the Zen Center and began his talk with warm words for the great teachers associated with it, including its founder Shunryū Suzuki Roshi; he also mentioned people who had been associated with the centre with whom he had a personal connection: Lama Govinda and Dr Edward Conze.*[318] *He also told the audience about his own teachers; that section of the talk is not included here because his teachers are more fully introduced in a talk elsewhere in this volume. In Seattle he spoke in a second-hand bookshop, a setting which, he confessed to his audience, was a kind of Pure Land as far as he was concerned, having always been a great reader. And in Missoula he spoke to a gathering chaired by the newly ordained Saramati, aka Professor Alan Sponberg. In all three places he visited, he gave a talk with the same name, 'The Rain of the Dharma', but substantially different, though overlapping content. The following text combines the three talks.*

I was born in a very ordinary part of South London in a very ordinary family, and grew up as a very ordinary boy. I was rather adventurous and mischievous. I remember my mother crying because I was so naughty. But when I was about 8, an abrupt stop was put to my activity when I was diagnosed, mistakenly as it subsequently transpired, as having some sort of valvular heart disease. The treatment in those far-off days was immobilization, so I was confined to bed and not allowed to move for two whole years. I wasn't even allowed to sit up by my own efforts, and I had to keep very, very quiet. My parents found it difficult to keep me amused, especially as I wasn't supposed to be *very* amused, because then I would get excited, and being excited was not good for my heart, but fortunately, my father discovered that I liked reading, so he took all his books and his father's books out of a cupboard, and later on a neighbour lent me the sixty-one parts of a children's encyclopaedia, and that kept me quiet for quite a while. Thus I acquired the habit of reading, and I still read a lot, perhaps more than is really good for me. By the time I was allowed out of bed, and had quite literally learned to walk again, I was established as an avid reader.

One day, when I was 14 and living in Torquay, I borrowed from the public library a couple of volumes called *Isis Unveiled*, by Madame H. P. Blavatsky. I'd never come across anything like it before. Madame Blavatsky is critical of dogmatic materialistic science and dogmatic, pseudo-spiritual religion, and she rather has it in for the Roman Catholic church, and especially the Jesuits. I had been going to church, though not taking it very seriously, but after reading those two volumes – and I think I read them twice – I realized that I wasn't a Christian. I continued reading all sorts of things – philosophy, religion, psychology, history, archaeology – and I happened upon two Buddhist texts, both translated from Chinese, which have played a very important part in the history of Far Eastern Buddhism: the *Sūtra of Wei Lang* (nowadays called the *Sūtra of Huineng*) and the *Diamond Sūtra*. When I read these two works, I at once felt, 'Yes. This is what I believe. This is what I've always believed. I am a Buddhist, and I always have been.'

So I was quite conscious that I was a Buddhist when I was 16, but for two years I was a Buddhist on my own, until in 1943 I came in contact with the London Buddhist Society, which had been founded in 1925, the year of my birth, by Christmas Humphreys. The first two articles I wrote for the society's magazine struck notes which have been characteristic of me ever since. The first article was called 'The Unity of Buddhism'.[319] Even then I felt that the Buddhist tradition has a unity, despite all the different groups, sects, schools, and traditions. And the second article, which wasn't published, perhaps because it was a bit technical, was on *pratītya samutpāda*, conditioned co-production, as Dr Conze translates it (the more traditional translation is 'dependent origination') which has been an important part of my thinking and teaching ever since those early days.

In those days the London Buddhist Society used to meet in rooms above a teashop in Great Russell Street, just a few doors along from the British Museum. That was the Buddhist movement in Great Britain in those days, just that little group of people. One Saturday afternoon, eight or ten of us were sitting and meditating. I don't know what meditation we practised – maybe we were just sitting quietly – and then in the distance we heard a tremendous explosion, and the windows of the room rattled. I'm glad to say that nobody moved. At least we'd learned enough of Buddhism not to be frightened, even by a bomb.

I was transferred with the army to India, Sri Lanka, and Singapore, and after the war I became a sort of wandering holy man, a freelance sadhu. I spent a couple of years quite literally with a begging-bowl in South India, and then I became ordained as a Buddhist monk. I settled in Kalimpong in the eastern Himalayas for fourteen years, and there I met some famous Tibetan lamas just as they were coming out of Tibet, some of whom became my personal teachers. I remember meeting Trungpa Rimpoche within weeks of his arrival from Tibet. He was much too young to be one of my teachers, only 19, and he didn't know a word of English and I knew only a few words of Tibetan, so we could only smile at each other, but we remained in contact for quite a long time afterwards. Altogether I had eight principal teachers, six of them Tibetan, one Chinese, and one Indian. Only one of them is still alive, and that is Chattrul Sangye Dorje, who had a great influence on Thomas Merton.[320] He's a very strange character. He's a practitioner of Dzogchen, and he doesn't normally give initiations or teachings. You just have to get along with him and understand him as best you can. If you ask him a question he doesn't give you a straight answer. He's a bit

Zen-like. All you get is some sort of Tibetan koan, or he does something apparently rather crazy. Some of my own students have visited him, and some went with offerings which were rudely refused, but another was given initiation on the spot. So Chattrul Sangye Dorje is quite unpredictable, but he's very highly respected by Dharma practitioners, especially by the Tibetans.[321] In India I also had extensive contact with the ex-Untouchable Buddhist community.

I returned to England in 1964 and for a couple of years the Hampstead Buddhist Vihara in London was my headquarters. I gave lots of lectures and taught meditation, but after a while I realized that I wasn't satisfied with the way things were going. The Buddhist Society was still carrying on, and there were other smaller groups, but I felt that the time had come for a new Buddhist movement, so in 1967 I started the Friends of the Western Buddhist Order, and a year later I started the Western Buddhist Order itself. We started our activities in a tiny basement underneath a shop that sold Japanese things run by one of our members. I've always thought it significant that we started in the heart of London, near Charing Cross Road and several well-known theatres. I used to jokingly compare us to the early Christians in the catacombs beneath the sinful city of Rome.

I started with meditation classes, significantly, and the teaching and practice of meditation has been very important in the FWBO ever since. We see it as the key to everything else. No meditation, one might say, no Buddhism. There are so many different kinds of meditation that it can be confusing to the beginner, but our meditation classes were quite simple. We taught, and we still teach, two methods. First of all, there's the mindfulness of breathing, *ānāpānasati*, as it's called in Pāli. I learned this in Singapore from a distinguished Sinhalese *bhikkhu* called Bhikkhu Soma, who had revived the practice in his own country and had written about it quite extensively, and I've practised it ever since.[322] Later on I introduced a second practice, which we also still teach, called the *mettā bhāvanā*, the development of universal loving-kindness. The Pāli and Sanskrit term *bhāvanā* is often used in Buddhist texts for what we call meditation. *Bhāvanā* comes from a root word meaning 'to be', and *bhāvanā* means to make become, to develop. Sometimes the Chinese equivalent of *bhāvanā* is translated as 'cultivation': you cultivate the mind, you develop the mind, make it bloom into higher states of consciousness and produce the thousand-petalled lotus. So the *mettā bhāvanā* is the development, the cultivation, of *mettā*, which is a feeling of friendliness, of love, towards all living beings, first of all towards oneself – this is very important – and then a near and dear friend, then a neutral person, then an enemy, then all four, then everybody, all beings throughout the world.

Mindfulness and *mettā* make a very good combination. Most people find mindfulness marginally easier than *mettā*, but we found that if you practise only mindfulness you become over-sensitized, and if you practise it too rigorously or wilfully, you can become a little emotionally alienated, so we balance it with the *mettā bhāvanā*. But if you just do the *mettā bhāvanā*, there's a danger that you may become a bit over-sentimental, so we balance it with mindfulness, which as it were calls you back to yourself, makes you a bit more real.

After a year or two, people weren't satisfied with coming along to a weekly class or lecture. They wanted a bigger dose of the Dharma. So we started organizing retreats. We would hire a house in the country, and a group of us would go on retreat, away from the world, immersing ourselves in the Dharma for a week or ten days, meditating, studying Dharma texts, perhaps practising yoga, practising t'ai chi ch'uan, and developing friendships with one another. People used to love these retreats. On many an occasion when I was about to leave I'd see a little cluster of people sadly, even tearfully, hanging around the gate, unwilling to accept that the retreat was at an end. Over time some of them started saying, 'It's so wonderful living with other Dharma practitioners. Couldn't we live together all the time?' Those who didn't have family commitments started forming residential spiritual communities, living together, sometimes with a common purse, meditating together every day, studying the Dharma together, and developing their friendships. Some of these early communities were very primitive. People squatted in derelict, unwanted properties (which was legal then). They were very happy, and that was a formative stage in the development of our movement. These days communities are comparatively lavish, but some people still think back to those good old days when they unrolled their sleeping bags on the floor and set up a little shrine and that was their community.

Then another development took place. The people who were living in communities still had to go out to work, and sometimes they had very uncongenial or unethical jobs, so some of them started thinking, 'It's wonderful living together, but wouldn't it be even more wonderful if we could work together too?' They started setting up little businesses, and this developed into a very important wing of our movement, our team-based right livelihood businesses. As well as providing ethical work and a context for Dharma practice and spiritual friendship, these businesses give financial support to our Buddhist movement. One of our principles from the very beginning has been that we don't ask the general public for support, but support ourselves financially. This might be an aspect of the FWBO which particularly appeals to North Americans, who are well-known for their rugged individuality and self-sufficiency. It's a very Zen principle, as I sometimes like to tell people. One of the Zen masters said, 'A day of no working is a day of no eating', and we've taken this principle to heart.

I mentioned that during my first two years back in England I saw the need for a new Buddhist movement. At that time there were a number of Buddhist societies up and down the country, all very small, and one of their features was that membership was open to all. Even people who had a mild interest in Buddhism, or perhaps no interest at all, but who for some reason wanted to join a Buddhist society, could do so by simply paying a subscription, and once you were a member, you could be elected as an office-bearer, become secretary or chairman, even president. This, I realized, was a great weakness, because it meant that sometimes a Buddhist society was run by people who were not deeply committed to Buddhism, and therefore the society could not be run effectively. I'd seen the same sort of thing in India to an even greater degree because the principal Buddhist organization there was dominated by people who were Hindu, and who in some cases were not sympathetic to Buddhism or saw Buddhism in a very distorted way. Seeing that we needed a different kind of organizational structure, I decided to start not another society, but an order. An order differs from a society inasmuch as it consists entirely of committed Buddhists. A Buddhist should be committed to the Three Jewels by definition, but by committed Buddhists I mean not just nominal Buddhists, not just born Buddhists, but people who really believe in the Dharma and try to practise it, people who take the Buddha as their ultimate teacher, his Dharma as the path that they follow to develop spiritually, and the Sangha, those who are more spiritually developed than themselves, as those to whom they look for guidance and inspiration – in other words, people who go for Refuge, in the traditional phrase, to the Buddha, the Dharma, and the Sangha. The Western Buddhist Order is thus a *Buddhist* order. One can't emphasize this sufficiently.

The Western Buddhist Order is Western in the sense that we try to practise the Dharma under the conditions of modern Western life. We're not living in the Middle Ages, or in Tibet or Thailand. We're living in the West in the midst of a technological society with all sorts of strains and problems, and trying to devise ways of practising the Dharma under those conditions, which have not prevailed in the world before. We're living in very unnatural times, and we have to find some way of practising the Dharma even under these conditions. I must emphasize that in the Western Buddhist Order we don't try to adapt Buddhist principles to Western culture. If anything, it's the other way around. We feel that it's Western culture that has to learn to adapt to Buddhist principles.

I sometimes say that our order is unified, and it's unified in two senses especially. First of all, it is neither monastic nor lay. It does not consist of monks and nuns, but neither does it consist of lay people. It consists simply of people who commit themselves to the Buddha, Dharma, and Sangha, regardless of whether they are following a monastic or a lay lifestyle. We have a little phrase which encapsulates our attitude: 'Commitment is primary, lifestyle is secondary.' Your lifestyle is only your particular expression of your commitment, of your Going for Refuge. You don't have to be a monk or a nun to practise the Dharma, and practise it fully. Some members of the Order have an ordinary job and family responsibilities, while others are living celibate lives and working full-time for the Dharma, but they are all equally members of the Order. We are all one on the basis of our commitment to the Three Jewels. And secondly, the Western Buddhist Order – and the Trailokya Bauddha Mahasangha in India – is a unified order in the sense that it is open to both men and women on equal terms. In some of the Eastern Buddhist traditions ordination is not open to women, but this is not the case with the Western Buddhist Order.

Ordination within the Western Buddhist Order is the point at which you consciously and deliberately decide that that is what you want to do, and your Going for Refuge to the Three Jewels is recognized by other members of the Order. You are a genuine, authentic, practising, committed Buddhist. The ordination ceremony has two parts. There's the private ordination, when the person to be ordained meets with his or her preceptor and repeats after him or her the Refuges and Precepts. Members of the Western Buddhist Order take ten precepts: to abstain from taking life, from taking what is not given, and from sexual misconduct, to abstain from speech which is false, harsh, unharmonious, or frivolous, and also to abstain from mental states dominated by greed, hatred, or ignorance and confusion. We take these precepts because we believe that it is not sufficient just to go for Refuge; that Going for Refuge must find ethical expression in your observance of, or your attempts to observe, the ten precepts. It's very important, according to Buddhist tradition, that there should be a firm ethical basis to your attempt to lead a spiritual life. Having taken the Refuges and Precepts from their preceptor, the person being ordained is given a mantra – I won't say anything about that because it is more private – and a new name, because by virtue of their ordination, they've achieved a new birth, a new life. They're a new person, and sometimes you see a profound change in someone after they've been ordained. The name is usually a traditional Buddhist name expressive of the character or the aspirations of the person being ordained. It reminds them all the time of who they are and what they're aspiring to. People are usually very interested to find out their new name, and other people are very interested too – but until the public ordination only the person being ordained and their preceptor know the secret. Wherever possible, when someone has received their private ordination they remain in total seclusion for twenty-four hours, reflecting on what has just occurred.

Then, a while after this period of seclusion, the length of time depending on how many people are receiving their private ordinations, there follows the public ordination, where the whole process is repeated, with variations, in the presence of as many other members of the sangha as possible. The person being ordained recites the Refuges and Precepts, and is given a white *kesa*, or a yellow *kesa* if they are leading a celibate life. *Kesa* is a Japanese term derived from the Sanskrit *kaṣāya*, which means simply robe, and the *kesa* is the external token of your ordination. Their new name is announced, and there are great rejoicings. The occasion represents the acceptance of that person as an Order member, a committed Buddhist, by the whole community.

Being ordained is not as simple as this short description might make it sound. Some Buddhist communities accept members very quickly and easily, but it usually takes at least four or five years of preparation to become a member of our Order, and it can take eight or ten. One of our members took twenty years, but she got there in the end. It depends to some extent on the amount of time that people have available to practise meditation, study the various texts that we prescribe, and go on the various retreats. At present the preparation concludes with a four-month retreat with other people who are going to be ordained, in total seclusion from the rest of the world. For men in Europe that usually takes place at our men's retreat centre in Spain, Guhyaloka; for the women there is a shorter retreat (shorter for practical reasons) at the women's retreat centre in Shropshire, England.[323] It's not easy to become a member of the Western Buddhist Order. We don't hurry or push people into it. It must come as a result of their own steady, gradual spiritual development.

So the FWBO is Buddhist in the full traditional sense, but it has certain special features of its own. As we have seen, it is a purely Buddhist movement. Secondly, the Western Buddhist Order is open to both men and women on equal terms. And thirdly, the FWBO is ecumenical. I myself have had teachers in the East of several different traditions – Theravāda, Nyingmapa, Gelugpa, and Chan or Zen – and we do not identify with any one form of Eastern Buddhist tradition, but draw inspiration, encouragement, and spiritual guidance from them all, because basically they're all one, inasmuch as they stem ultimately from the Buddha's Enlightenment.

In the early days of the FWBO in London I gave lectures on many of the Buddhist scriptures handed down by the different schools, and in 1970 I gave a series of eight lectures on the *Saddharma Puṇḍarīka*, or *White Lotus Sūtra*. These lectures have been transcribed and edited to produce the book that we're launching today.[324] The *White Lotus Sūtra* is one of the most important of all Buddhist canonical texts, and it has greatly influenced the development of Buddhism in the Far East. In China and Japan whole philosophical and spiritual traditions have been founded on its teachings. For hundreds of years before it was written down, the teaching would have been transmitted orally, like so many Buddhist scriptures. The *Saddharma Puṇḍarīka*, which is one of the most important of the great *Vaipulya* Mahāyāna *sūtras*, was evidently written down in two forms of Sanskrit some time around the first century BCE.

Chinese scholars have a lot to say about the meaning of the full title, the *Saddharma Puṇḍarīka Sūtra*, and I'll say a few words about it, because that will give us some clues to its teaching, and to Buddhism more generally. To take the last word first, *sūtra*, literally 'thread', means a discourse of the Buddha. When you give a talk, you string together a number of topics on a common thread, and that thread is the *sūtra* (Pāli *sutta*). So a *sūtra* is a Buddhist canonical text purporting to record the words of the historical Buddha Śākyamuni. I say 'purporting' because according to modern scholarship many of the *sūtras*, and especially many of the Mahāyāna *sūtras*, do not so much record the actual words of the Buddha as try to recast in contemporary form something of the spirit of the Buddha's teaching. The *suttas* of the Pāli canon are probably closest to the actual teaching of the Buddha so far as we can make out, to the letter of the teaching, one might say. Though they transmit quite a lot of the letter, the Mahāyāna *sūtras* are more concerned to transmit the spirit of the Buddha's teaching, and do not hesitate to amplify and expand it. The people who composed the *sūtras* must have been highly imaginative, because they clothed the Buddha's teaching in a very colourful and attractive literary form.

The *Saddharma Puṇḍarīka Sūtra* is a Mahāyāna *sūtra*, and rather a lengthy one, comprising a whole volume containing some twenty-eight chapters. *Saddharma* is of course related to the word *dharma*, a Sanskrit word derived from a verbal root meaning 'to support'. That which we term Dharma supports two things: life, existence in its broadest sense, and, more specifically, spiritual life, life which is dedicated to a spiritual path. Dharma therefore means, first of all, something like cosmic law, law governing the entire universe on all levels, and secondly, something like the law of the spiritual life, those laws which make spiritual life possible. Dharma is that which makes it possible for us to lead a spiritual life, to grow spiritually as human beings. The Buddha's teaching is called the Dharma because it reveals that cosmic spiritual law, and the Buddha is called the Enlightened one, or the awakened one, because he has awoken to the truth of that law, and having awoken to it, he reveals it to others. The Buddha himself emphasized that he did not create or invent the Dharma; he discovered it and then communicated it.

In the title *Saddharma Puṇḍarīka Sūtra*, to Dharma is added the prefix *sad*, which means something like true, real, actual, so when we speak of the *Saddharma* we distinguish the Buddha's teachings from the many misleading teachings which were current in his day and which he criticized. Adding the word *puṇḍarīka* at once takes us into a totally different world, a world of symbol, imagination, and myth. The *puṇḍarīka* is the white lotus. In India there are many different kinds and colours of lotus, and Sanskrit has names for each of them, but the *puṇḍarīka* is the king of lotuses. It is a symbol of perfect purity, representing the truth existing in the midst of falsehood, purity existing in the midst of impurity. Those who are familiar with the Pāli scriptures may recollect that immediately after the Buddha's Enlightenment he reflected that the truth, the Dharma, that he had discovered was so profound that he wondered whether it could be communicated to other human beings, whether they were ready to receive it, or whether they were so deep in the mud of the world, so to speak, that they wouldn't take any interest in it. He was inclined at first not to teach, but then, we are told, compassion, *karuṇā*, arose in his heart, and out of that feeling of compassion, which was inseparable from his wisdom, he decided that he would take the trouble to try to communicate the Dharma to unenlightened human beings. And then he had a sort of vision. He saw the whole of humanity stretching out before him like a lake of lotus plants, all at different stages of growth. Some were still sunk in the mud, others were emerging from the surface of the water, and some were standing clear and beginning to open their petals. So the Buddha saw that there were at least some human beings who were ready to receive his message, and he started teaching. No doubt he retained in his mind that vision of humanity like a bed of lotus flowers throughout the whole of his ministry, throughout the remaining forty-five years of his life.

The Tibetan tradition has the famous mantra, *oṃ maṇi padme hūṃ*, and *padme* is usually translated as 'in the lotus', so to paraphrase, when we chant the words *oṃ maṇi padme hūṃ* we're reminding ourselves that the *maṇi*, the potential for Enlightenment, is in the *padme*, the lotus of our own heart. The symbol of the lotus thus occupies a very important place in Buddhist spiritual life, symbolism, art, and literature, and the *Saddharma Puṇḍarīka Sūtra* blossoms forth like a lotus in the midst of the world, standing for something pure and perfect, the teaching of the Buddha.

Sometimes books about Buddhism give the impression that it is all ideas and concepts, and sometimes people say, 'Oh yes, Buddhism's a very admirable teaching, but I'm afraid it's too intellectual for me,' as though they think you've got to have a degree in Indology or Buddhist studies to be able to make anything of it, but although Buddhism certainly does speak the language of concepts – it has a great and profound philosophy, in fact many philosophies, and you can take your pick – it also speaks the language of parables and myths and symbols.

The *Saddharma Puṇḍarīka Sūtra* speaks both languages. Years ago in Bombay I had a friend who was a very interesting character. He was a Polish Jew, but he'd been a Jesuit, and then he'd become a follower of Krishnamurti and Ramana Maharshi. He was quite a bit older than me, and he used to treat me in a rather fatherly fashion, as sometimes older people will. Thinking that I was a young, inexperienced, unworldly Buddhist monk and needed a bit of advice from my more experienced seniors, he used to give me little lectures, and one day he said, 'There's a book that I think you should read, *Star Maker*, by Olaf Stapledon. You'll like it. It's just like a Mahāyāna *sūtra*.' And he further said, 'Mahāyāna *sūtras* are just like science fiction.' That's true, but I improved on it by saying that Mahāyāna *sūtras* are just like *transcendental* science fiction. In that respect Mahāyāna *sūtras* go beyond even such a good writer as Olaf Stapledon, who is one of the older science fiction writers and a bit out of fashion now, but still very much worth reading.[325] At least some Mahāyāna *sūtras* are full of parables and myths and symbols, and to that extent, yes, they do resemble science fiction. Perfection of Wisdom *sūtras* are rather different. They are rather conceptual, so you may want to put them aside for a while. But don't be frightened by the Mahāyāna *sūtras*. Just read them as you'd read a science fiction novel, and you'll get a lot from them, I'm sure. The parables, myths, and symbols of the *White Lotus Sūtra* have passed into the folklore of Far Eastern Buddhism, and my own book deals with some of them. I don't dwell much on the purely philosophical side of the *sūtra*'s teaching, because when I gave these talks originally in London, many people were under the impression that Buddhism was rather intellectual and I wanted to draw attention to this more beautiful, colourful, attractive side of the Buddha's teaching.

From a doctrinal point of view there are two principal themes reverberating through the *sūtra*. The first theme is that there are not in fact three *yānas*, but only one. Nowadays students of Buddhism usually understand by the three *yānas* the Hīnayāna, the Mahāyāna, and the Vajrayāna, but it is not these that are referred to here, but a quite different set of three: the *śrāvakayāna*, the *pratyekabuddhayāna*, and the *buddhayāna* or *bodhisattvayāna*. The word *śrāvaka* comes from a root meaning 'to hear', so a *śrāvaka* is one who hears, and the *śrāvakayāna* is the path or way of the hearers, of those who listen. By *śrāvakas* is understood the immediate disciples of the Buddha, those who listened to his teaching and as a result gained supreme Enlightenment for themselves, became, in traditional Buddhist terms, *arhants*, but according to tradition they did not teach, at least not in the way the Buddha taught, and the Enlightenment attained by the *śrāvaka* was somewhat inferior to the Enlightenment attained by the Buddha himself. Then we have the *pratyekabuddhayāna*. *Pratyeka* is usually explained in the commentarial sources in two ways, either as private and personal, or as relating to conditionality. *Pratyekabuddhas* are those who do not hear the Dharma from another, but discover it by their own efforts, and the Enlightenment they attain is the supreme Enlightenment of a Buddha, not the relatively inferior Enlightenment of the *arhant*, but after gaining that Enlightenment they do not teach.[326] And finally there's the *buddhayāna* or *bodhisattvayāna*. Bodhisattvas hear the teaching from a Buddha, achieve supreme Enlightenment by their own efforts, and then teach the Dharma.

So we have these three spiritual paths, these three goals. So far as we know from the Pāli scriptures, the historical Buddha did not teach that there were three *yānas* in this sense. He certainly did not use this nomenclature. So far as we can make out from the scriptures, he taught one *bodhi* for all. The *bodhi* that the Buddha himself had realized was the same as that realized by his disciples. Sometimes their *bodhi* was spoken of as *anubodhi*, a following *bodhi*, a *bodhi* that they realized following in his footsteps, but the two realizations were one and the same. But it seems that after the Buddha's passing away, his disciples, or the disciples of his disciples, started feeling that the Buddha was a man of such extraordinary spiritual attainment that his Enlightenment must have surpassed even that of his *arhant* disciples, great though they were, and they started distinguishing between a higher *bodhi* attained by the Buddha and a lower *bodhi* attained by his *arhant* disciples, *samyak sambodhi* and just *bodhi*. Then in between the *samyak sambuddha* and the *arhant* was interpolated the *pratyekabuddha*, so that you had three *yānas*, three ways, three spiritual ideals, and you could take your choice. According to some Buddhist schools, for instance the

Sarvāstivāda, you could choose either to be a bodhisattva and become a *samyak sambuddha*, or to be a *pratyekabuddha* and neither teach nor have a teacher yourself, or to follow the lower goal of the *arhant*, the *śrāvakayāna*. But the *White Lotus Sūtra* says that there's only one goal for all, that of the *samyak sambuddha*, and one path for all, *ekayāna*. So the *White Lotus Sūtra* represents a return to the spirit of the Buddha's original teaching. This is one of the two major themes of the *White Lotus Sūtra*, and one of the reasons why it has been of such great importance, especially in Far Eastern Buddhism.

The fact that all Buddhists follow the same spiritual path finds expression in the fact that all Buddhists go for Refuge to the Three Jewels: the Buddha, the Dharma, and the Sangha. As I mentioned earlier, I distinguish three levels of Going for Refuge: provisional, effective, and real. Real Going for Refuge is synonymous in traditional Buddhist terms with Stream Entry and also with what is known as the opening of the Dharma Eye.[327] It means that your faith in the Three Jewels has become absolutely unshakeable, like the Himalayas themselves, and your observance of the precepts is also firmly established. The traditional phrase is that no *śramaṇa*, no *brāhmaṇa*, not even Brahmā himself together with Māra the evil one, could shake your faith in the Buddha, the Dharma, and the Sangha.[328] Moreover, there is a distinct, unmistakable element of *vipaśyanā*, or in Pāli *vipassanā*, clear vision, which means a vision of the transcendental not as something distant, but here and now, actually realized, at least to some extent. *Vipaśyanā* represents a close approach to the Unconditioned itself, the *asamskṛta*, and according to tradition one approaches the Unconditioned when one goes for Refuge in that real sense by way of one of three transcendental *samādhis*.

These transcendental (*lokuttara*) *samādhi*s are so called because they're associated not with the world but with the transcendental dimension, with the *asamskṛta*, the Unconditioned, the uncompounded. One focuses on that. These three *samādhis* are sometimes described as three doors.[329] The first of these is the door of *śūnyatā*. You get *śūnyatā* into view, you get some glimpse of egolessness, selflessness, and that's a door through which you can approach the Unconditioned. Then there's the door of *animitta*. *Nimitta* literally means a sign, but it can also mean a word or a concept, and *animitta samādhi* is where you approach the transcendental by bypassing all words and all thoughts. This is a very distinctive experience, and when you have it, you realize that all words, all concepts, are totally inadequate, they don't mean anything at all. And then there is the *apraṇihita samādhi*, which literally means the directionless. This approach is by way of not going in any particular direction, because you've no particular desire to do so. You don't have any desire anyway, and you don't see any particular direction in which you could go. According to the earliest tradition, one can approach the Unconditioned by way of one or another of these three *samādhis*, and this is synonymous with what I've come to call the real Going for Refuge. So the Going for Refuge is very important indeed. In fact, it is the central and definitive act of the Buddhist life. It's what all Buddhists have in common. It is neglected in some Buddhist circles, but I was interested to find recently that there has been a revival of interest in its significance. Abbot Tenshin Anderson's talk 'Speaking of the Unspoken' is reported in the current *Shambhala Sun*, and this extract is of the greatest importance:

> For many years at the Zen Center I never really noticed that I had taken refuge in buddha, dharma, sangha. Now I've learned, again from Dogen's mouth and through Dogen's life. As he was dying, what was he doing? The last practice he did was to walk around a pillar upon which he had written 'buddha, dharma, sangha'. And he said, 'In the beginning, in the middle, and in the end, in your life, as you approach death, always, through all births and deaths, always take refuge in buddha, dharma, sangha.'
>
> This fundamental practice that all Buddhists do, many Zen students had never even heard about. It was said, but we didn't hear it because it wasn't emphasized strongly enough. In some way, our sitting practice is so essential that we may feel we can overlook some of these more basic practices.[330]

I find myself very much in agreement with those sentiments. But it's time we passed on to the second great doctrinal theme of the *White Lotus Sūtra*: the eternity of the Buddha, or literally the infinite life of the Buddha. Even in the more archaic Pāli texts, we find a distinction drawn between the *rūpakāya* and the *dharmakāya*.[331] The *rūpakāya* is the Buddha's physical body, his physical presence as we encounter it in history, and the *dharmakāya* is his inner spiritual, transcendental realization, we could even say his transcendental personality. *Kāya* literally means body, so *rūpakāya* is often translated as 'form body' and *dharmakāya* as 'Dharma body', but *kāya* really means something more like the Greek *hypostasis*, more like 'person' – person without personality.[332] You've got the Buddha as he appears to unenlightened people, in a physical, human form, and the Buddha as he is in the depths of his being, as he is in Reality, as he is at one with the absolute. But there aren't two Buddhas; there's only one Buddha, who is *rūpakāya* on one level and *dharmakāya* on another. This is basic Buddhist teaching, found in the Theravāda and also in the Mahāyāna, especially in the Madhyamaka, but the Yogācārins introduced a refinement, a third *kāya*, the *sambhogakāya*, literally 'body of glory', the archetypal Buddha.

Here we're concerned with the distinction between the *rūpakāya* and the *dharmakāya* as reflected in the *Saddharma Puṇḍarīka Sūtra*. All three *kāya*s are important, but the *White Lotus Sūtra* emphasizes the *dharmakāya*. It may be that by the time the *sūtra* was written down, the *dharmakāya*, the Buddha as he was in absolute reality, had come to be obscured by historical recollections of the *rūpakāya* Buddha, but the *White Lotus Sūtra* emphasizes very strongly that the Buddha is not to be identified with his material form, with his historical personality. He's not to be regarded as limited in the depths of his being by considerations of time and space. In reality the *dharmakāya*, the real Buddha, transcends time and space. He is infinite, eternal. That is the distinctive emphasis of the *White Lotus Sūtra*.

I would suggest, however, that many of us today need the opposite emphasis, an emphasis on the human, historical Buddha. When I lived in Kalimpong and came in contact with Tibetan Buddhists, I was surprised to find that many of them hadn't heard of Śākyamuni Buddha. Well, they might have heard the name, but it didn't mean anything to them. They knew all about Amitābha, Tārā, Avalokiteśvara, Mañjuśrī, and Padmasambhava, but they didn't know anything about Śākyamuni. In their case the *sambhogakāya* had overshadowed the *rūpakāya*. But we need to remember the *rūpakāya*, for the Buddha in his human historical existence can be a great source of inspiration to us. It's from him, as represented in the Pāli canon, that the whole tradition of Buddhism has come down to us in all its forms. If we read the Pāli scriptures, even in summary, we'll discover many stories in which the Buddha illustrates not just features of the Dharma but also aspects of his own personality in a very inspiring way. We can derive very great inspiration indeed from the life of the human historical Buddha, so perhaps we need to give more attention to him, following his life step by step from the Enlightenment to the final *parinirvāṇa*.

These are the two main themes, doctrinally speaking, of the *White Lotus Sūtra* – the theme of one *yāna* and the theme of the eternal Buddha – but the *sūtra* is not primarily a doctrinal work. Its approach is not intellectual, and it speaks mainly the language of parables, myths, and symbols. Nowadays many people are very interested in these, perhaps influenced by Carl Gustav Jung, who initiated a great movement in this direction. The term 'parable' may be familiar to you from the New Testament – the parable of the good shepherd, and so on – but the Buddhist scriptures have their parables too. Although sometimes people think that the Buddha just taught in an intellectual way, or just held up a flower, he also taught in beautiful parables. Those of the *White Lotus Sūtra* are especially brilliant and famous, and among them one of the most important is the parable of the rain cloud.

Although I was born and brought up in England, and I've now spent more than twenty years back there, I still feel more at home in India, and among the many features of Indian life that I recollect with great affection is the rainy season. For the rest of the year it's hot and dry, and everything withers, so people, and especially farmers, are very happy when they see those first dark rain clouds looming on the horizon. Although in rainy England the expression 'the rain of the Dharma' might have a rather depressing ring, for Indian Buddhists it has a very positive and special significance. The rainy season also has a spiritual significance, because in the Buddha's day the wandering monks used to stay in one spot during that period and devote themselves to intensive meditation, study, the recitation of *suttas*, and so on, and in the last eight or nine years of my life in India, I too spent the rainy season virtually in seclusion, scarcely stepping outside my vihara. Given all these associations, it isn't surprising that there should be a parable of the rain cloud in the *Saddharma Puṇḍarīka Sūtra*.

I'm going to read you the parable. It's a feature of the *White Lotus Sūtra* that it says everything twice, first in prose and then in verse, once for the prosaic people and once for the poetic people, perhaps. It is believed by some scholars that the verse portion is earlier, being in somewhat more archaic Sanskrit, heavily mixed with Prakritisms, while the prose portion conforms more closely to the rules of classical Sanskrit. I'll read the poetical version, in William Soothill's translation from Kumārajīva's Chinese version. Kumārajīva translated it from Sanskrit into Chinese at the beginning of the fifth century of the Common Era, and his translation, which is apparently a very beautiful piece of work from a literary point of view, was of great importance for practically the whole of Chinese, Korean, and Japanese Mahāyāna Buddhism. We have several English translations of it now. The Buddha says:

It is like unto a great cloud
Rising above the world,
Covering all things everywhere,
A gracious cloud full of moisture;
Lightning-flames flash and dazzle,
Voice of thunder vibrates afar,
Bringing joy and ease to all.
The sun's rays are veiled,
And the earth is cooled;
The cloud lowers and spreads
As if it might be caught and gathered;
Its rain everywhere equally
Descends on all sides,
Streaming and pouring unstinted,
Permeating the land.
On mountains, by rivers, in valleys,
In hidden recesses, there grow
The plants, trees, and herbs;
Trees, both great and small.
The shoots of the ripening grain,
Grape vine and sugar-cane.
Fertilized are these by the rain
And abundantly enriched;
The dry ground is soaked,
Herbs and trees flourish together
From the one water which
Issued from that cloud,
Plants, trees, thickets, forests,

According to need, receive moisture.
All the various trees,
Lofty, medium, low,
Each according to its size,
Grows and develops
Roots, stalks, branches, leaves,
Blossoms and fruits in their brilliant colours;
Wherever the one rain reaches,
All become fresh and glossy.
According as their bodies, forms
And natures are great or small,
So the enriching (rain),
Though it is one and the same,
Yet makes each of them flourish.
In like manner also the Buddha
Appears here in the World,
Like unto a great cloud
Universally covering all things;
And having appeared in the world,
He, for the sake of the living,
Discriminates and proclaims
The truth in regard to all laws.
The Great Holy World-honoured One,
Among the gods and men
And among the other beings,
Proclaims abroad this word:
'I am the Tathāgata,
The Most Honoured among men;
I appear in the world
Like unto this great cloud,
To pour enrichment on all
Parched living beings,
To free them from their misery
To attain the joy of peace,
Joy of the present world,
And joy of Nirvana.
Gods, men, and every one!
Hearken well with your mind.'[333]

So this is the famous parable of the rain cloud. Of course, the rain cloud is the Buddha showering down the rain of his teaching, the Dharma, and the plants are all living beings, the cosmic sangha, we could say. As the parable says, the rain falls on all alike – that is, the Buddha communicates the Dharma to all – and we find that the historical Buddha really did that. He was born into a well-to-do, even princely, family, but he communicated the Dharma to everyone he chanced to meet: wandering holy men, priests, brahmins, warriors, merchants, flower sellers, untouchables, scavengers, the learned, the unlearned, men, women, and children. So the rain of the Dharma falls on all alike, but the plants, the beings, on which it falls grow each in accordance with their own nature. We all learn and practise the Dharma, we all grow towards the same Enlightenment, but we develop spiritually each in our own way, even though it is one and the same Dharma that helps us to grow.

Even after Enlightenment, differences of temperament would seem to persist. We can think for instance of the Buddha's two chief disciples, Śāriputra and Maudgalyāyana. They both came from brahmin families, they went in search of a teacher together, together they became the Buddha's disciples, and they remained close friends for the rest of their lives, but although they were both Enlightened beings, temperamentally they were very different. Śāriputra was calm and quiet. He was a thinker, and gave philosophical discourses. Maudgalyāyana was a very strong character. He was credited with psychic powers, which apparently Śāriputra didn't have, and on one occasion when there was someone present in the assembly who shouldn't have been there, Maudgalyāyana apparently took him by the arm and forcibly removed him, something that Śāriputra probably wouldn't have done. So here we see these two chief disciples of the Buddha, close friends and equally Enlightened, but very different in character. If we consider the great Enlightened beings of the Tibetan tradition, we can think of Milarepa living in the midst of the snows wearing just a loincloth, meditating and singing his songs, not caring for book knowledge, and Tsongkhapa in his monastery, observing the Vinaya, writing all those books and commentaries, engaged in all those philosophical discussions. They had quite different temperaments, the yogi and the scholar-monk, the freelance and the traditionalist, but both were Enlightened beings. According to some commentaries even the Buddhas are distinguished by difference of temperament. According to one Pāli commentary there are three kinds of Buddha:

those in whom wisdom or *jñāna* predominates, those in whom *maitrī* or love predominates, and those in whom *karma* or activity predominates, and our Buddha, Śākyamuni, the commentary says, is a Buddha in whom *jñāna* predominates, which is why according to that commentator Buddhism is such an intellectual tradition.[334] We always have to take this factor of temperament into account, and not be misled by it.

We find this within our Western Buddhist Order. If you get five or ten Order members together, the first thing you'll notice is that they look very different. One looks quite staid and respectable. Maybe he's a professor or something like that. Another looks like a hippie, or at least an ex-hippie. You get men, you get women. You get highly intellectual people and very emotional people, people who are devoted to meditation and people who are devoted to study, people who are rather shy and people who are very extrovert. Within the Order, as we get to know each other better we get to recognize that these differences of temperament don't matter. They don't keep us apart. Deep down, by virtue of our commitment to the Three Jewels, we are one. I would say that I myself have presented a different sort of personality at different stages of my career. If you happened to watch that video of the early years of the FWBO recently made by one of our members, you probably wouldn't recognize me.[335] We all have these different facets of our personalities, and this is what makes us as human beings such fascinating creatures, and so interesting to get to know. But underneath all this diversity, especially if one is committed to the Three Jewels, there is unity. Enlightenment does not negate individuality. Enlightenment only negates ego, and the passions and biases based on ego.

For the growth of a plant, five things are needed. First of all there needs to be a seed, and then the seed needs soil, warmth, light, and rain. Similarly, if we are to grow spiritually, we need five things. The seed, especially according to the Mahāyāna, is the potentiality for Enlightenment that exists in each and every human being. According to Buddhist teaching, every human being, even those who appear beyond hope, is capable of spiritual development if he or she only makes the effort. Someone may appear very, very far from Enlightenment, from spiritual life, or perhaps even from ordinary human life, but deep down that potential is there. We think of somebody like Aṅgulimāla, who was a mass murderer, following a perverted tantric cult, but who eventually realized the error of his ways, became a disciple of the Buddha, and gained Enlightenment.[336] So there's hope for us all. However unethical we've been, however unspiritual, we can always change.

In the *White Lotus Sūtra* itself there's a chapter about Devadatta, a cousin of the Buddha who became a disciple, but unfortunately became very jealous of the Buddha, and wanted to start something of his own, and even tried to murder the Buddha. But in the *White Lotus Sūtra* the Buddha says that even Devadatta will one day gain supreme Enlightenment. So although Devadatta is the Judas-cum-Devil of Buddhism, he's not excluded from Enlightenment.[337] According to Christian tradition Judas is in hell and will remain there, and most Christians believe that Satan will stay in hell for ever too. Only one Christian thinker, Origen, ever dared to say that Satan would ultimately be saved.[338] But in the Buddhist tradition we believe that even Devadatta, who was so opposed to the Buddha and who on three separate occasions tried to kill him, will one day gain full Enlightenment. However low you sink, you can reverse direction, you can rise, you can change your life. That spiritual seed is there, that potential is there, however deeply it may be buried, and in many human beings it is buried very deeply indeed. This shows the supreme spiritual optimism of Buddhism, how it sees the gold of the potential for Enlightenment underneath the muck of the ordinary human psyche.

We could see the soil that is needed for the growth of the plant in two different ways. First of all, we could say that the soil isn't outside ourselves. *We* are the soil in which the plant of spiritual life will grow. The soil is the human body, speech, and mind. Any gardener knows that soils vary: some are stony, some are full of clay, some are full of gravel, and some contain a lot of rich decomposed organic matter. How this applies to human beings and the spiritual life I'll leave you to work out for yourself. Another way we could see the soil is that we need circumstances that are favourable to spiritual growth: leisure, health, and facilities of various kinds. We can still develop if circumstances are unfavourable, but it's much more difficult. In the West, we're very fortunate that usually these facilities lie ready to hand. Many of our Indian Buddhist friends aren't so lucky. For example, I heard of a young woman who became a Buddhist and wanted to take up meditation. She came from a family with eighteen members who all lived together in a hut with only one room, but she was determined to meditate, so every morning she got up very early and meditated sitting on a shelf on one side of the hut. And recently I heard about an old woman who wanted to go on one of our retreats. In India it usually costs a hundred rupees for a week's retreat: that's about two pounds sterling or five dollars. This old woman didn't have a hundred rupees, so she worked for a month as a farm labourer, digging up and carrying stones, saved up the money, and then came on a week's retreat. That's what people in India have to face if they want to practise the Dharma. We don't have those difficulties. We have access to books, free time, health, and leisure. But do we make the best use of those facilities?

Thirdly, for spiritual growth we need heat. In other words, we need spiritual friendship. In the Buddhist life friendship is very important, and in the FWBO we often speak of two kinds of spiritual friendship: vertical and horizontal. Vertical spiritual friendship is the friendship you have with those who are spiritually more developed than yourself, particularly with your spiritual teacher, while horizontal spiritual friendship is the friendship you have with your peers, with people who are on the same spiritual path as yourself and on roughly the same level. We need horizontal spiritual friendship, sangha, just as much as you need vertical spiritual friendship. In some Buddhist sanghas vertical spiritual friendship is greatly stressed, and horizontal spiritual friendship is rather neglected, and that can lead to problems. So in the FWBO we try to develop both the vertical spiritual friendship and the horizontal spiritual friendship, and we find that works very well. There's a beautiful saying in the Pāli canon, where Ānanda, the Buddha's close disciple, comes to him and says, 'Lord, I think that spiritual friendship is half of the holy life,' and the Buddha says, 'No, Ānanda, spiritual friendship is not half of the holy life. It's the whole of it.'[339] Spiritual friendship, both vertical and horizontal, is absolutely necessary for the spiritual life. Sometimes people following the spiritual path feel very lonely. Perhaps their family and their work associates don't understand or sympathize. We need the companionship and support of other members of the sangha. You can't have a cold spiritual life any more than you can have a dry spiritual life. Your spiritual life has to be warm, and that warmth comes from your own emotional positivity, generated to some extent through meditation experience, to some extent through your experience of the fine arts, but perhaps above all for most people from your experience of horizontal spiritual friendship.

Fourthly, for spiritual growth we need light, by which I mean intellectual clarity, clear thinking. In Buddhism we distinguish three kinds of *prajñā* or wisdom. First of all, there's the wisdom that comes from reading or hearing the scriptures: *śruta-mayī-prajñā*. Secondly, there's the wisdom that comes from reflecting upon them: *cinta-mayī-prajñā*. Very often people don't reflect on what they read, and perhaps sometimes what we read isn't worth reflecting on, but when we read the Buddhist scriptures, or any Buddhist book, if it's worth reading, it's worth turning it over in our minds so that we don't only remember the ideas in a superficial sense, but deeply absorb them, reflect on them, and try to work out their implications. Thirdly, there is *bhāvanā-mayī-prajñā*, the wisdom that comes through meditation. These three kinds of wisdom promote intellectual clarity, or a clarity which is even more than intellectual.[340]

Buddhism is certainly not an intellectually woolly teaching. If it's woolly, it isn't Buddhism. Some people think that being a Buddhist means being very intellectual, but others think that it means being nice and fuzzy and vague, that it means sacrificing the intellect. One may talk of going beyond the intellect, but T. S. Eliot once said, 'It's true that you have to go beyond the intellect, but first you've got to have an intellect.'[341] I recently attended a Buddhist conference and I'm afraid some of the discourses on Buddhism were very vague. For that sort of anti-intellectual, sub-intellectual, sentimental, vague Buddhism I coined a special term: candyfloss Buddhism, or, to translate into American English, cotton candy Buddhism. Cotton candy Buddhism is pink, sticky, sweet, and there's an awful lot of it, but it doesn't amount to very much. So we mustn't be dry-as-dust intellectual Buddhists, but we mustn't be cotton candy Buddhists either. We need intellectual clarity, even intellectual hardness. We must be able to think, we must be able to reason things out. The Buddha himself emphasized the importance of the rational as well as the mystical approach, and we have to be able to combine the two. One Buddhist scholar called the Theravāda, which is one of the main surviving forms of Buddhism, Buddhist rationalism tinged with mysticism, and Mahāyāna Buddhism mysticism tinged with rationalism, and this combination is very characteristic of Buddhism.[342] Buddhism has developed the reason very fully. Buddhist philosophy is vast and profound, and sometimes very technical. But there's also Buddhist mysticism, the Buddhism of higher spiritual states, transcendental experience, and we have these two, rational Buddhism – not rationalistic, but rational – and mystical Buddhism, blended beautifully together. We need intellectual clarity, clear thinking, as well as positive emotion to the nth degree.

And fifthly, for spiritual growth we need the rain of the Dharma, but that rain has to be pollution-free. Nowadays we have a great problem with pollution, and even rain is polluted; sometimes we even have acid rain. We need the rain of the Dharma, but it mustn't be acid rain, a Dharma which is mixed with non-Dharmic elements. Buddhist teachers in both the East and the West are becoming increasingly alive to this danger, as the following two quotations illustrate. The first is from Sulak Sivaraksa, a leading Thai Buddhist, who said in an interview 'In exile from Siam' which was published in the summer 1992 issue of the Buddhist magazine *Tricycle*:

> The Buddhists in China and Burma have suffered so much. The mistake they made was to compromise with the Confucians. The compromise was fatal for Buddhism in China. The Confucians say, 'Why don't you live for the next world and leave this world to us?' And most of East Asian Buddhism took part in that. The Japanese Buddhist clergy make a lot of money on funerals. But until the people die they leave their lives in the hands of the Confucians who run the country. And what 'Confucian' means here is that the big boss is the emperor. Everyone follows the big boss. And when you work you serve the big boss. You do not upset the status quo.

And the second quotation is from Roshi Philip Kapleau, who is a very well-known and highly respected American Zen roshi, in an interview published in the summer 1993 issue of *Tricycle*, in an article called 'Life with a capital L'. The editor of *Tricycle* introduces Kapleau Roshi's comments thus:

> Recently I was at a meeting in Santa Fe with a mix of Buddhists from all different traditions, and someone said that we get so caught up in identifying corruption – money, sex, power – that we've lost sight of the real corruption in Buddhism, which is the way the teachings are being altered to make them palatable to an American sangha.

And Kapleau Roshi, who is himself American, says:

> I fully agree. That is, if you mean making the practices easier or less disciplined. Then there are other corruptions as well, such as the appropriation of fundamental elements of Zen training by psychotherapists who give them a psychological twist. Or you find therapists teaching their patients meditation and equating it with spiritual liberation. Another threat to the integrity of Zen, and in many ways the most bizarre, is that of Zen teachers sanctioning Catholic priests and nuns as well as rabbis and ministers to teach Zen.

I'm very much in agreement with both these Buddhist teachers. We need the rain of the Dharma desperately, more today than ever before, but that rain needs to be pure, unmixed with Catholicism, or Vedānta, or secular ideologies. In traditional Buddhist terms, we need to go for Refuge. We need to do what the great Dōgen did. We need to inscribe the words 'Buddha, Dharma, Sangha' on a pillar, literally or metaphorically, and circumambulate that pillar constantly. Alternatively, in the words of the *White Lotus Sūtra*'s parable of the rain cloud, we need to stretch out our hands to the Buddha, the great rain cloud. We need to saturate every corner of our beings, saturate our whole lives, with the rain of the Dharma. We need to grow towards Enlightenment, towards Buddhahood, as each one of us has the potential to do.

THE DISAPPEARING BUDDHA

St James's Church, Piccadilly, 1994

Dr Broom and friends: I must begin by saying how glad I am to be here in St James with you all this evening. Dr Broom invited all those who have not been here before to put up their hand, and I should have put up my hand, as I haven't been inside this building before. Of course I've glimpsed it from the outside on my way to the Royal Academy, and once or twice I've strolled around the colourful stalls outside, but I didn't find my way inside, so I'm all the more glad to be here this evening. I'm glad to have been able to witness the little preliminaries, the rigmarole as they were called, and especially the lighting of the candles. I was asked to name a quality which could be associated with one of those three candles, and the quality I thought of was courage. I thought that probably everybody who comes here says something like peace or compassion or faith, so I'd be a bit different, but I also thought of courage for a definite reason. In the world of today, to uphold spiritual values we need a great deal of courage. Love isn't enough; we need courage to implement that love and act upon it. Truth *is* enough, but we also need courage to stand by the truth in the midst of a world that only too often seems to deny it.

I was glad to witness and take part in the ceremony also because I felt myself to be on familiar ground. In the context of Buddhist worship we often light candles and offer them to the Buddha, sometimes reciting a little verse that goes something like this: 'This light I offer to the Buddha, the Enlightened one who destroys the darkness of ignorance.' So the lighting of candles has that association for me. But light is a universal symbol, found in all spiritual traditions. During my days in India, I often saw the Hindu Diwali, the festival of lights. In some towns there was no electricity or gas, just oil lamps, and the whole of the town would be illuminated by rows and rows of these little lamps, in the windows, on the doorsteps, on the edges of the flat roofs, all symbolizing the triumph of light over darkness, the forces of good over the forces of evil. It was beautiful to see. Light in Buddhism represents spiritual knowledge, transcendental insight, the higher wisdom. The Buddha is represented as saying to his disciples, describing his attainment of Enlightenment, 'There arose in me knowledge, there arose in me wisdom, there arose in me light.'[343] It's not a coincidence that the Buddha is known in English as the En*light*ened One. And it's about the Buddha that I want to speak this evening.

At this point I have to confess that, glad as I am to be here this evening, it's a very long time since I was in a church, apart from sightseeing, and it's even longer since I spoke in a church. Looking up in my records, I discovered that the last time was on Sunday 15 July 1987, almost exactly seven years ago, when I delivered a sermon in the chapel of King's College, Cambridge. I don't remember what I said – I very often don't – but I remember that the congregation, which was about three hundred strong, consisted mainly of American tourists, and they had come not to hear me, but to hear the famous King's College choir.[344] But anyway, this evening I'm going to do more or less what I did on that occasion. Since I'm in Rome, if I can say that in an Anglican building, I'm going to do what Rome does – or at least what I think Rome may still do. I'm going to give a sermon on a text. It might not be quite what trendy C of E vicars do nowadays, and I must admit that for quite a few years I was rather prejudiced against the word sermon, and didn't like to hear the Buddha's discourses to his disciples referred to as sermons. But in recent years I've changed my mind, concluding that after all sermon is a good old English word. It comes to us via the old French from the Latin *sermo*, discourse, probably from *serere*, which means to join together, and some of our greatest English literature exists in the form of sermons. One thinks, for instance, of the sermons of John Donne and Jeremy Taylor, and even Cardinal Newman.[345]

My talk will be a sermon to the extent that it is based on a text, which I'm going to take from the Pāli *Mahāparinibbāna Sutta*. The

Buddhist scriptures are absolutely enormous. Christians are quite lucky to have just a one-volume Bible, though admittedly it's quite a thick volume, even when printed on India paper. Muslims are even luckier; they've got something much smaller. But there are several hundred volumes of Buddhist scriptures, so if you're a Buddhist who takes their studies seriously, you've got a problem. This evening we're going to consider a text from the Pāli canon. Pāli scriptures are divided into three great collections. First of all, there's the collection of discourses or sermons delivered by the Buddha. Secondly, there's the collection of rules for monks and nuns. There are not so many of these, only five or six volumes, which most monks and nuns find quite sufficient, and many of the rules are in any case no longer relevant in the modern world. And then there's a third collection whose name, Abhidharma, is rather difficult to translate, but we could say that it's the collection of the more analytical, more philosophical teachings.

The collection of discourses by the Buddha consists of four groups, the first of which is known as the group of long discourses, all those classified as long regardless of their subject matter. In the Pāli recension of the scriptures, there are thirty-four of these, some of them being about the same length as one of the Christian gospels. I'm going to take my text from discourse number sixteen, the *Mahāparinibbāna Sutta*, the discourse or sermon of the great decease – the decease being that of the Buddha. Out of reverence for the Buddha, Buddhists don't usually speak of his death, but of his *mahāparinibbāna*, which means something like final passing away, or great decease. Before the Buddha passed away at the age of about 80, he went on an extensive farewell tour. He went on foot, which for a man of his age was quite an undertaking, but he wanted to bid farewell to the groups of his disciples who were scattered all over north-eastern India, so he walked from village to village, town to town, and wherever he went he gave teachings. The *Mahāparinibbāna Sutta* tells the story of that final tour, describing the Buddha's meetings with various groups of disciples and the teachings he gave right up to the very end, when he passed away lying between two beautiful *sāl* trees.

In the passage I'm going to read, the Buddha is addressing Ānanda, who was one of his cousins and accompanied the Buddha day in and day out for about twenty years. On account of his closeness to the Buddha he is sometimes known as the St John of Buddhism, St John being the beloved disciple of Jesus. In this passage, the Buddha is addressing

Ānanda on what you might think is a rather strange subject: the eight great kinds of assemblies.

> Ānanda, these eight (kinds of) assemblies. What are they? They are the assembly of Khattiyas, the assembly of Brahmins, the assembly of householders, the assembly of ascetics, the assembly of devas of the realm of the Four Great Kings, the assembly of the Thirty-Three Gods, the assembly of māras, the assembly of Brahmās.
>
> I remember well, Ānanda, many hundreds of assemblies of Khattiyas that I have attended; and before I sat down with them, spoke to them or joined in their conversation, I adopted their appearance and speech, whatever it might be. And I instructed, inspired, fired and delighted them with a discourse on Dhamma. And as I spoke with them they did not know me and wondered: 'Who is it that speaks like this – a deva or a man?' And having thus instructed them, I disappeared, and still they did not know: 'He who has just disappeared – was he a deva or a man?'
>
> I remember well many hundreds of assemblies of Brahmins, of householders,... of Brahmās, and still they did not know: 'He who has just disappeared – was he a deva or a man?' Those, Ānanda, are the eight assemblies.[346]

Let's get into this gradually. Of the eight assemblies, the Khattiyas are mentioned first. The Khattiyas (Pāli, *Kṣatriyas* in Sanskrit) are the nobles, the warriors, the land-owning caste of ancient India. The Buddha himself was born into this caste, and so was Ānanda. But the Buddha did not attach any importance to hereditary caste, and no distinction of caste was observed within the sangha or spiritual community that he founded. On one occasion the Buddha said that just as the great rivers of India lose their separate identities on reaching the mighty ocean, so on becoming members of his sangha, people from the different castes lose their identities as members of those castes and all become simply spiritual sons and spiritual daughters of the Buddha, regardless of their social origin.[347]

The Brahmins were the hereditary priests of what wasn't exactly Hinduism then, but more like Vedism. They believed in the four Vedas not as literary documents – in fact they were transmitted orally – but as revealed truth, divine revelation. The Brahmins officiated at a variety of sacrifices, including animal sacrifices, based on Vedic texts, and they were very keen to maintain their socio-religious status. In later generations they liked to style themselves as gods on earth. The Buddha, it's not surprising to learn, clashed with them on a number of occasions, because he did not accept their hereditary pretensions. Quite a number of Brahmins actually became the Buddha's disciples. Śāriputra, for instance, usually regarded as the Buddha's chief disciple, was by birth a Brahmin. His official title was the *Dharmasenāpati*, which means commander-in-chief of the Dharma, and reminds us of his courage. You can't be the commander-in-chief even of an ordinary army without courage, unless you stay right behind the lines, and to be commander-in-chief of the Dharma, the spiritual truth, you need infinitely more courage than that. Then there's the assembly of householders, the *gṛhapatis*, the heads of families. In India in those days, as still today, families weren't nuclear but joined. You could have fifteen, twenty, up to a hundred people, all living under the same roof or collection of roofs as one family with a single head, the *gṛhapati* (Pāli *gahapati*). These householders were engaged in trade. And then we have the ascetics, the non-Vedic, even anti-Vedic, religious wanderers and teachers who were the alternative people of those days. The Pāli word for them is *samaṇa*, which means one who makes an effort – that is to say a spiritual effort, an effort in the direction of spiritual development. The Buddha's contemporaries, according to the Pāli scriptures, regarded him as a *samaṇa*, and to his disciples he was the *mahāsamaṇa*, the great *samaṇa*.[348]

Khattiyas, Brahmins, householders, and ascetics, who make up the first four of the eight assemblies, are all human beings, but the members of the next four assemblies are not human at all. They're supernatural, or rather supernormal beings, because according to Buddhism the supernatural is also natural in the sense that it's included in the realm of what Buddhists call conditioned existence, within the higher reaches of the *saṃsāra*. In this text the Buddha mentions only four kinds of supernormal beings, but if we look at the Pāli texts as a whole we'll find about thirty different kinds mentioned. This is much too complicated to go into this evening, fascinating though it might be, so I'm going to simplify things, group the members of the fifth and sixth assemblies together, and call them angels, to translate them into roughly corresponding Christian terms. In this way we have a double assembly of angels of two different kinds. But there are still two assemblies left.

Continuing to translate into roughly corresponding Christian terms, let's translate the assembly of *māras* and the assembly of the Gods of the Thirty-Three into the assembly of Satans and the assembly of archangels.

The Buddha, the text tells us, appears in all eight of these assemblies, and before doing so, he adopts their appearance and speech. Like St Paul, he becomes all things to all men, or rather all human beings.[349] But the Buddha becomes all things not only to all people but to all angels, all archangels, and even all Satans. A very important principle is involved here. If the mythological framework bothers you, forget about that and concentrate on the principle involved, which is that if you want to communicate with people – and don't forget that the Buddha entered these assemblies in order to communicate the Dharma – you must meet them halfway. You must adopt their appearance, look like them, and speak their language both literally and metaphorically. This principle applies at all levels from the highest to the lowest, from a Buddha's communication to our own communication with one another.

We can understand why it's necessary for us to speak other people's language, because if we didn't, whether literally or metaphorically, they wouldn't understand us. But why do we need to look like them in the interests of effective communication? In the case of the Buddha, if he had appeared as he was in reality, it would have been too much for them, whether they were gods or human beings. It would be like Zeus appearing to Semele in his full splendour. You may remember that in Greek mythology, when Zeus appeared as himself at Semele's rash request, she was burnt up by his overpowering splendour.[350] There's a parallel to that in the Christian tradition, because according to the Gospel, the three disciples of Jesus who witnessed his transfiguration were confused and frightened – they could not bear it, presumably because they'd had a glimpse of Jesus as he really was.[351]

But on our own level, why is it important for us to look like others, at least to some extent, when we want to communicate with them? Let me give you an example from my own experience. As you heard a little earlier on, I returned to England from India some thirty years ago, having spent twenty years in the East. For nearly all that time I lived as a Buddhist monk, and when I returned to England at the invitation of Buddhist friends in London to teach the Dharma, I came as a Buddhist monk. Not only was I a monk, I looked like one, complete with flowing yellow robe, which was a bit inconvenient for getting on and off buses, and shaven head, which wasn't adapted to the English winter. In the few years I spent teaching Buddhism while looking like a Buddhist monk, I had some success, but I encountered certain difficulties, one of which was that on account of my ascetic, spiritual, holy appearance, people started projecting onto me in the Jungian sense. Sometimes they projected positively, but sometimes they projected rather negatively. They felt me to be a rather threatening figure. That happened because I appeared different, because I was other, because I was strange.

Not long after I arrived back in England I was interviewed by various journalists, mainly from women's magazines, and I remember being asked, 'Are you allowed out of the monastery?' 'Are you allowed to speak to people?' as though I was some sort of Buddhist Trappist. I was also asked 'Who sent you?' I used to say 'Nobody sent me. I was invited, and I accepted the invitation.' They seemed to think that some pope-like figure in the mysterious East had sent me on a secret mission, and they were surprised, and sometimes a bit disappointed, when they learned I'd come under my own steam. So people projected onto me, whether positively or negatively, and because they did that they weren't able to experience me or communicate with me as I really was – not just in the ultimate metaphysical sense, but even in the more conventional sense – so communication between us could not go beyond a certain point, and I found there was a limit to what I could teach. Teaching isn't just laying down the law, spelling out the facts. It's a genuine communication, person to person, heart to heart, mind to mind, even soul to soul. I was happy in robes in India, where they were quite convenient, especially in hot weather. But in Britain I decided after a few years not to wear robes except on ceremonial occasions when a little colour was called for. I also allowed my hair to grow. In fact, I must confess I allowed it to grow somewhat longer than it is now, and this upset some people very much indeed. It was an eye-opener to me how much it shocked them. I was just the same, I was still myself, I'd only changed the externals, but externals mean a lot to people. I realized in the end that some people at least had become upset because I'd disturbed their projections onto me. But on the whole I found that I was able to communicate better, heart to heart and mind to mind, and I was therefore able to communicate more effectively. And at that point I founded the FWBO, but that's another story.

So perhaps we can get a glimpse of the rationale for appearing like other people. To give another example, I had a friend in Calcutta who was a great devotee of Sri Ramakrishna, the famous Bengali mystic of the nineteenth century. She told me that when she was a little girl, she was taken by her mother to see Ramakrishna's widow, whose name was Sarada Devi, and who was herself revered as a great spiritual teacher. In Bengali, as in other Indian languages, the word for goddess and lady is the same, *devi*, so when my friend's mother told her 'We're going to see Sarada Devi,' the little girl got very excited. The great day came, and along she went to see the *devi*, the goddess. But when her mother asked her, 'What did you think of the *devi*?' she said '*Devi*? There wasn't any *devi*, only an old widow woman.' She was accustomed to seeing images of Hindu gods and goddesses with six, eight, or ten or twelve arms, but here was this little old widow with just two. She was deeply disappointed. This is the kind of expectation that we can build up. When I had my yellow robes on, sometimes people saw six or eight or ten arms, and when there were no more yellow robes and definitely only two arms, they were very disappointed. But on the whole, appearing like other people enables us to communicate better. We are all different anyway, but we mustn't be too different, otherwise people will project onto us, and projection interferes with communication. Perhaps this is the reason bishops no longer go around with their mitre and crozier as they did in the Middle Ages. You'd be very surprised if you met a bishop in full regalia walking along Piccadilly, wouldn't you? And perhaps it's even the reason some clergyman no longer wear their dog collars.

But let's go back to our text. Having adopted their appearance and speech, the Buddha addresses the members of the various assemblies. The text speaks of him delivering a discourse on the Dharma. This word Dharma (Sanskrit; *Dhamma* in Pāli) has a number of meanings, but in this context it means something like truth or reality. It is, in a manner of speaking, the objective content of the Buddha's spiritual, transcendental experience. The text doesn't tell us what the Buddha says – it simply says he delivers a discourse on the Dharma – but it does tell us the effect of that discourse. Whether gods or human beings, the Buddha's hearers are 'instructed, inspired, fired and delighted'. This is very important. A religious discourse shouldn't just instruct us, shouldn't just communicate factual information even of a religious nature, useful though such information might be. It should inspire us with enthusiasm, fill us with overwhelming delight. One often listens to a discourse or sermon with feelings very far removed from overwhelming delight, but if it can't inspire and delight us, it won't affect us. It won't sink in, we won't remember it, it won't help us to change our lives. I don't give many talks these days, but I used to give hundreds in India. I used to go round many villages and towns, and sometimes I'd give a talk in a place where I'd given one fifteen years earlier, and people would still remember it. They didn't always remember the principles or the rules, but they'd remember the stories, because the stories had delighted them, fired them, even inspired them. This is a very important point.

So we see that the Buddha's hearers, each of the eight assemblies, are instructed, inspired, fired, and delighted. He even enters the assembly of the *māras* or Satans, and although they are wicked, even evil, supernormal beings, he adopts their appearance and speech – he doesn't shrink from that – and they too are instructed, inspired, fired, and delighted. Think what an achievement that is! Presumably they are permanently changed. Presumably they cease to be Satans and become angels. This is an example of the radical optimism of Buddhism, its conviction that even the weakest or most monstrously evil person can change. If we look at the Christian tradition, this is perhaps reminiscent of Origen's belief that even the Devil will eventually be saved – a belief which the church as a whole has not shared, unfortunately.[352]

After they have been instructed, inspired, fired, and delighted by the Buddha's discourse on the Dharma, the members of the different assemblies say, 'Who is it that speaks like this? A deva or a man?' The Buddha has come among them like one of themselves, but they know that he can't be. They've never been so deeply affected before. When we read a wonderful poem by a poet of whom we've never heard, we want to know who they are, and in the same way the Buddha's hearers ask, full of wonder, 'Who is it that speaks like this?' They know that whoever has spoken to them is not one of them, even though he appears like one of them, so they try to identify him, categorize him. This is what we usually do. We try to understand the unknown with the help of the known, the unfamiliar with the help of the familiar. Very often it works, but sometimes it doesn't.

The members of the assemblies operate with two principal categories. They ask, 'Is he a god or a man?' It seems not to occur to them that there could be a third category. This is very much the situation in the West today. The Buddha has appeared among us not in the flesh but on the pages of books and in images, some of them very inspiring and beautiful. We've become acquainted with his teachings, at least to some extent, and perhaps we've been impressed by them. So we ask, 'Who is the Buddha?' Sometimes, though, we don't wait for an answer, but try to answer the question ourselves. We seek to categorize the Buddha by applying to him terms with which we are already familiar, just as the Khattiyas, the Brahmins, and the others do in our text. Thus we see him either as a human teacher rather like Socrates or Confucius, or as a kind of oriental god. If we're a bit more sophisticated, we may think that the Buddha was a human teacher who was made into a god by his followers. Sometimes scholars even speak of the Buddha as a human teacher in the Theravāda and a deified figure in the Mahāyāna. You may remember those famous lines of Kipling from his poem 'Mandalay', which reflect the popular view of the Buddha as a god: 'Bloomin' idol made o' mud/Wot they called the Great Gawd Budd.'[353] This is how some of our ancestors not so long ago saw the Buddha, 'the Great Gawd Budd'. Hindus very often see the Buddha as the ninth incarnation of their own god, Vishnu. But Buddhists don't accept that the Buddha was either a human being in the ordinary sense or a god or God.

In the West the question is complicated by the fact that Buddhists are seen to worship the Buddha. Buddhists offer not only candles to the Buddha, but also incense, flowers, food, *tormas*, and even symbolical representations of the whole universe. To the Christian or ex-Christian Westerner this rather suggests that the Buddha is being treated as God, or even that he is God for Buddhists, because in the West worship is only offered to God. But in Buddhism worship is offered to anyone who is superior, especially spiritually superior. Eastern Buddhists will often speak of worshipping their parents or their teacher, even their primary school teacher. They use the same word, derived from the Pāli and Sanskrit *pūjā*. So the fact that Buddhists worship the Buddha does not mean that they regard him as God, or a god.

What then is the Buddha? Buddhists usually say that he is neither man nor god, but belongs to a third category. They say that he is one who has completely eliminated greed, hatred, and delusion, one who knows absolute reality from his personal experience, possesses supreme wisdom, and manifests infinite compassion. He has achieved all this by his own human efforts, but has gone so far beyond humanity as we know it that he can no longer be called a man, without nonetheless assuming the cosmic functions that we usually associate with the idea of God. In short, he is the Buddha.

The word Buddha is a title, not a proper name. It means one who is awake – awake to reality. But the Buddha is known by a number of other titles. In the Buddhist scriptures he's often referred to as the *Tathāgata*, and sometimes he uses that term to refer to himself in the third person. There's a lot of discussion about the meaning of *Tathāgata*, and more than one grammatical analysis, but I won't bother you with that. It literally means 'he who goes' and also 'he who comes'. The Buddha goes through wisdom from the mundane to the transcendental, and through compassion he comes back from the transcendental to the mundane, in order to teach the path to liberation. The Buddha is the embodiment of both wisdom and compassion. Buddhism is not a cold religion, as people sometimes think. It stresses compassion just as much as wisdom. *Tathāgata* has another meaning: 'one who acts as he speaks, and speaks as he acts'. This might seem a rather prosaic virtue, but if we reflect a minute, we will see that our own words and acts are very rarely in anything like harmony. There's almost always a discrepancy, whether slight or great, between what we profess and how we behave. But in the Buddha's case, speech and action are in perfect harmony at the highest conceivable level. The Buddha is an Enlightened being, and speaks and acts like one.

The Buddha is also known as *Lokavidu*, which means 'knower of the world'. This doesn't mean that he is worldly-wise, though he certainly wasn't lacking in worldly wisdom. It means that he knows mundane existence as it really is. He knows that existence is transitory, involves suffering, and possesses no inherent reality of its own. This knowledge is not merely theoretical, but a matter of real experience, and he therefore acts in accordance with it. We, by contrast, worldly-wise though we may be, do not know mundane existence as it really is. We like to think that the world is permanent, pleasurable, and possessed of an inherent reality, and thus we tend to become very attached to the world. We cling on to this or that aspect of it and in this way we create suffering for ourselves and very often suffering for others too.

The Buddha is sometimes called the *Jina*, which means the conqueror or the victor. He's known as the *Jina* not because he has conquered others but because he has conquered himself. In the *Dhammapada*, which is one of the shortest and most popular Buddhist texts, the Buddha says, 'Though one should conquer in battle thousands upon thousands of men, yet he who conquers himself is (truly) the greatest in battle.'[354] Another of the Buddha's titles is *Bhagavān*, which means one who is possessed of all positive auspicious qualities: compassion, wisdom, purity, generosity, and so on. The Buddha is usually spoken of or addressed as *Bhagavān* when he is regarded as an object of devotion.

And then there is the title *Mahāvīra*, which means great hero. Here the quality of courage comes in. The Buddha had the courage to face the forces of darkness and evil, both within his own mind and outside it. He was not a meek and mild character, but vigorous, bold, fearless, and resolute. I rather shocked some of my friends a few years ago when they asked me which historical character I thought most resembled the Buddha and I said at once, 'Julius Caesar'. Why? Because of his promptitude and courage. If Caesar saw that something was to be done – I'm not speaking now of whether it was right or wrong – he did it without hesitation, delay, shilly-shallying, wobbling, uncertainty, doubt, or scepticism. He was the embodiment of self-confidence, and so was the Buddha, on an infinitely higher spiritual plane. Don't take this too literally, but I would say that the Buddha was the Julius Caesar of the spiritual life. After all, the Buddha was born into a warrior family. He didn't have a bookish education, he didn't go to university. He couldn't even read or write. There's an incident in one of the Gospels where Jesus is represented as writing characters on the ground in the dust, but the Buddha isn't represented as being able even to do that.[355] In the India of his day there was no literacy – knowledge was transmitted by word of mouth – and that was how he learned the traditions of his community, listened to religious teachers, and gave his own teachings. He was educated in all sorts of martial arts, he was prompt, bold, and vigorous, and he directly sublimated those qualities into the spiritual path. Once he told his disciples, 'You're warriors because you fight for ethics (*sīla*), for meditation (*samādhi*), for wisdom (*paññā*), and for freedom (*vimutti*).[356] The Buddha was a great hero, a *Mahāvīra*.

The Buddha was also called *Lokajyeṣṭha*, which roughly means the elder brother of the world, and he was so called because he was born before us, not as a human being, but as a Buddha. This suggests that what the Buddha has attained, we too can attain. At present we are unenlightened, but we can become Enlightened, or at least make progress towards Enlightenment if we make the effort. If we practise ethics, meditation, and develop wisdom, we'll be liberated.

But it's time we got back to our text. The Khattiyas and others were delighted by the Buddha's discourse on the Dharma, but they didn't know who had spoken to them. The Buddha didn't identify himself. He just vanished. We may think that we're in a better position than the Khattiyas and the others. We may think we know who it was. After all, in this text the Buddha tells us, or at least he tells Ānanda. But do you really know who the Buddha is, even after hearing the text, even after listening to me for the last hour and ten minutes? I'm reminded of early Indian art depicting the Buddha gaining Enlightenment under the bodhi tree, teaching his disciples, subduing a mad elephant, and so on. The strange thing about these representations is that the Buddha himself is not shown. Trees, buildings, animals, and crowds of people are represented, but where you would have expected to find the Buddha, there's an empty space, around which everything is happening. Sometimes in the space there's a symbol: a bodhi tree, if the scene is that of the Buddha's Enlightenment; a stupa if the scene is that of his final passing away; a *dharmacakra*, a wheel of the Dharma, if the Buddha is teaching; and so on. But why the empty space? Why the symbol? Originally it was thought by Western art critics that the artists felt that they could not do justice to the figure of the Buddha, but later it was realized that this was not the real reason. They did not represent the Buddha because they wanted to convey the fact that he was a transcendental being, *lokuttara*, beyond the world, because he'd realized the transcendental sense of Nirvāṇa.

We can go further than that. In reality the Buddha, Nirvāṇa, and so on are not objects as opposed to perceiving subjects; in reality, they transcend the subject–object duality. But although they are not objects, we think and speak of them as though they were. We can hardly do otherwise, if we are to speak of them at all. So the Buddha appears to the Khattiyas and the others as one of themselves, as an objectively existing personal being, and he instructs, inspires, fires, and delights them, and then he disappears. The disappearance means that he is not really an object. He transcends the subject–object distinction. He is not included in the picture. It's no use asking who he is if that means trying to identify him as a particular kind of person. There's a famous verse from the *Diamond Sūtra*, one of the best known of the Mahāyāna Buddhist scriptures, in which the Buddha is represented as saying:

> Those who by my form did see me,
> And those who followed me by voice,
> Wrong the efforts they engaged in,
> Me those people will not see.
>
> From the Dharma should one see the Buddhas,
> From the Dharmabodies comes their guidance,
> Yet Dharma's true nature cannot be discerned,
> And no one can be conscious of it as an object.[357]

The Dharma is not an object, and neither is the Buddha, so one can't know who he is by asking what kind of object he is. So how can one know the Buddha? Perhaps a story from the Zen tradition may throw some light on the matter, and with this I'll conclude. The legendary founder of the Zen tradition was Bodhidharma, an Enlightened master who went from South India to China in the sixth century. When he'd been in China for a while, he met the emperor, who was a very pious Buddhist and had built temples and monasteries, distributed lots of money in alms, and so on. When he met Bodhidharma, the emperor, who was rather proud of all his good deeds, asked him how much merit he had accumulated as a result of performing them. But Bodhidharma said, 'No merit at all.' The emperor was deeply shocked, but when he'd recovered he asked another question: 'What then do you teach?' If you don't teach that good deeds should be performed and produce merit, what on earth do you teach? And Bodhidharma replied, 'Vast emptiness and nothing meritorious within.' Vast emptiness is a Buddhist term for ultimate reality beyond the subject–object duality and therefore beyond self, beyond the accumulation of merit and so on. The poor emperor became still more confused, but he managed to come out with one more question. 'Well, if you teach that there's just this vast emptiness, nothing meritorious within, who are you that is standing before me?' If everything is empty, if there's no subject–object distinction, who are you? Bodhidharma's reply was short and to the point. He said, 'I don't know.'[358] So the emperor was left wondering, just as the Khattiyas and the others were left wondering when the Buddha disappeared, and just as we perhaps are left wondering. But if we wonder long enough, and deeply enough, perhaps one day we shall get an answer to the question, 'Who is the Buddha?'

INTELLECT, EMOTION, AND WILL

Opening of the new Manchester Buddhist Centre, 1996

Order members, Mitras, and Friends: I need hardly say how happy I am to be here with you all on this occasion of the dedication of the shrine-room of the new Manchester Buddhist Centre, and the consecration of this beautiful new image. My association with the Manchester Buddhist Centre goes back quite a long way, probably nearly twenty years. My first visit was to a small terraced house which was the centre in those days, with a rather untidy kitchen and lots of hi-fi equipment. Later the centre moved to other premises with tidier kitchens, and today we find ourselves in the midst of a centre which is bigger and more beautiful than ever, in fact superlatively beautiful.

I have always enjoyed my visits to this city with its fine cultural facilities, especially its art gallery, where I like to pay my respects to the Pre-Raphaelite paintings, and I'm enjoying this visit to this new Manchester Centre. And now I'm supposed to be giving a talk or lecture. In the early days of the FWBO there used to be quite a lot of discussion as to whether I should give talks or lectures. People thought of a lecture as something formal, while a talk was more informal, and they used to think that a talk was much better than a lecture because informality was much better than formality. But regardless of whether they were lectures or talks, I did give quite a lot of them, and people still listen to recordings of them. Only a few days ago I received a letter from an unknown correspondent who seemed to be an orthodox Christian, and he'd just been listening to a talk I gave at the Hampstead Buddhist

Vihara thirty years ago on Buddhism and the Bishop of Woolwich.[359] He wrote raising various points and in particular he wanted to know how I could be so sure that there were no valid arguments for the existence of a personal creator God. So at least some of these talks have survived on tape, and some have been edited and published in book form. Perhaps it's a good thing that the thousands of talks I gave in India were never tape-recorded. The Spoken Word team would be growing grey over their labours; they're already busy enough.[360]

After all these years you may not be surprised to hear that I've rather gone off giving lectures. It's like so many things: you enjoy it a lot at first, but after a while the novelty begins to wear off. Someone asked me recently whether I have ever felt nervous before giving a lecture, but I never have, not even before my first lecture, which I gave when I was 21, in Singapore.[361] But I've become a little tired of giving lectures. It's a very valuable activity, and I'm glad to hear that the new Manchester Buddhist Centre will soon be the setting for a number of what I'm sure will be splendid lectures by *dharmacāris* and *dharmacāriṇīs* alike. I must admit – just between ourselves – that some Order members give better talks than I do these days. I was quite good in my prime, twenty-five or thirty years ago, but now I'm not so good at giving lectures, frankly. For example, I listened to the lecture that Subhuti gave at the opening of the Nottingham Buddhist Centre. I'm a bit of a connoisseur of lectures and I know a good one when I hear it, and Subhuti's lecture was very good indeed. In fact, it was a classic. I knew that I was going to be giving a talk today, but I couldn't help thinking that Subhuti's lecture is so appropriate to the opening of a new Buddhist centre that perhaps you could just play the tape and dispense with me. I didn't venture to suggest that because I thought perhaps the idea might not be very well received, even though I'm sure you think very highly of Subhuti's lectures.

Although I've gone off giving lectures, and may never give another, I'm quite happy to read a paper. You may think that's rather strange, because preparing a talk is relatively easy, whereas a paper can take weeks to write, but I prefer to prepare and read a paper because I feel that I can express myself more fully and accurately and pertinently and perhaps with less possibility of misunderstanding when I commit myself to writing. But I haven't had time to prepare a paper for this occasion, having been busy with preparations for my forthcoming tour, about which I shall have something to say later on.

So if I don't want to give a lecture and I haven't got a paper to read, what shall I do? My plan is just to share with you a little of my current thinking. I enjoy thinking and reflecting, and there are all sorts of things to think about and reflect upon: Dharmic things and non-Dharmic things, personal things, literary things, artistic things, current affairs, even the current political situation, friends and contacts in the Buddhist world, books that I am reading and have read, experiences that I had perhaps forty years ago. I spend quite a lot of time reflecting on all these things, especially those that have some bearing on the FWBO and on the Dharma.

Of course I've written quite a few books, as well as giving lectures and talks and seminars, so I have expressed thoughts, opinions, and conclusions on all sorts of subjects. Subhuti has recently tried to bring together my thoughts on leading topics of general Dharmic interest in a book.[362] But I haven't stopped thinking, and my thinking is still changing. I certainly don't consider my thinking to be complete, which means that I don't think that the FWBO is complete. Thirty years ago the FWBO was a tiny seed. It has now sprouted and put forth many shoots, and it's put down very deep roots, but its growth is by no means complete. In the last few years I have seen developments that I did not altogether foresee. I didn't have a detailed blueprint for the FWBO. There were just some leading ideas, a general sense of direction, a broad, general vision.

You won't be surprised to learn that some of my current thinking is in connection with Going for Refuge to the Three Jewels. Incidentally, someone made the point recently that some of us have got into the habit of speaking simply of Going for Refuge, or even 'my Going for Refuge', without mentioning what it is that we're Going for Refuge to. So don't just say, 'I'm not too sure about my Going for Refuge nowadays.' Talk about Going for Refuge to the Three Jewels. Make it explicit, make it concrete – then it'll become plainer and clearer.

But who is it that goes for Refuge? Well, *we* go for Refuge, especially if we're Order members. To take it a bit further, there's no collective Going for Refuge. The group as such does not go for Refuge, at least not effectively or really. It's the individual who goes for Refuge. But who is this individual that goes for Refuge? What are they like? I'm not concerned with anything deeply metaphysical. I'm not going to raise the question of the *anātman* doctrine, or relative and absolute truth, or anything of that sort. I'm speaking in quite everyday terms. It's the individual who goes for Refuge, so what's that individual like? What is that individual made up of? Very broadly speaking there's a *nāma* and a *rūpa*, a mind and a body, connected we know not how; that's a great mystery. But if we look at the mind, the individuality, the psyche, we can distinguish three distinct aspects. They're not altogether different, they're not demarcated in any hard and fast way, but we can distinguish them. There's an intellectual aspect, an emotional aspect, and a volitional aspect, the aspect of will. We think, we feel or emote, and we will. I want to try to relate these three aspects to our Going for Refuge to the Three Jewels. It would seem that they don't all come into play at once or equally, and this is because we're not integrated beings, but in many ways quite divided.

So what happens? Let's look at the way we come into contact with the Three Jewels. First of all we come to know about the Buddha. We hear about him, or read about him. We learn the historical facts. We know that he was born in the borderlands between the present-day Nepal and the present-day India, into a patrician, even princely family, and we know he went forth from the household life when he was 29 years of age. We know how he sat beneath the bodhi tree and gained Enlightenment, and how he taught his Dharma and gathered disciples. Here it's our 'intellect', for want of a better term, that comes into play. I wish we didn't have to use this term intellect, which has been grossly devalued in recent centuries, but we don't seem to have any other term to replace it, so I'll use it within quotation marks. We have this 'intellectual' knowledge about the Buddha.

But you can know the historical facts about the Buddha's life without being a Buddhist. There may be non-Buddhist scholars who know them much better than you do. But there's no feeling. That's the difference. When you know the historical facts about the Buddha, it's simply your 'intellect' that is coming into play, but if you dwell upon certain episodes in the life of the Buddha, you will start developing a feeling for him. Perhaps you come across that incident where the Buddha sees an old monk lying sick and neglected by the other monks. He calls upon Ānanda, his faithful attendant and disciple, to help him lift the sick monk onto a bed and wash him and care for him, and then he calls together the other monks and asks them why they are not looking after the sick man. He says, 'Monks, we have no father and no mother. We should care for one another.'[363] Or you might read the story of Kisāgotamī, the woman who had lost her only child, and come to know how tactfully and compassionately, but at the same time how profoundly and radically the Buddha dealt with her case, how he consoled her in the best possible way.[364] Then you're not just learning facts about the Buddha's life story, but beginning to have some feeling for his compassion, his wisdom, his unremitting energy as he preached the Dharma for so many years, and then the Buddha is no longer just an object of your knowledge, but also an object of your emotion. You can go on to contemplate his attributes systematically, to build up your feeling for him. You can do the Sevenfold Puja, which enhances your devotional feelings. Perhaps if you're an Order member, you do a visualization of Śākyamuni. When you visualize Śākyamuni or any other Buddha or bodhisattva, it isn't an emotionally neutral exercise. There must be some feeling for the person, the transcendental person.

As you develop more and more feeling for the Buddha you become drawn towards him, and you want to become more like him. This is when will comes into play. It isn't easy to become like the Buddha. You have to make an effort. So in this way 'intellect', emotion, and will each in turn comes into play and it's only when they are all present, when we know about the Buddha, we feel for the Buddha, and we have the will to become like the Buddha, that we are able effectively to go for Refuge.

I suspect that, like intellect, the term will has had rather a bad press in the FWBO. People think it's a very good thing to be into your feelings; you've got to be very vulnerable and sensitive these days, especially if you're a man. But will is not thought of so well, probably because will and willing are often confused with wilfulness, and wilful is one of the things that a good Order member or Mitra or Friend must not be. If someone isn't getting on very well with their meditation, or they're having difficulties in personal relationships, they're often told, 'My dear, I'm afraid you're being too wilful. Don't try so hard! Relax! Give yourself an easy time!' Sometimes it's necessary to relax, and real wilfulness certainly is a weakness, but strong and steady willing is quite a different thing. *Cetanā*, in the sense of will or conscious intention (the word is equated with karma), plays a crucial part in the Buddhist life.[365] It's no accident that I've always translated the term *bodhicitta* not as the thought of Enlightenment, but as the will to Enlightenment. No doubt 'will to Enlightenment' has disadvantages, but not nearly so many as 'thought of Enlightenment'. Furthermore, according to tradition, dhyānic states, states of superconsciousness, are states of willing, inasmuch as they represent a mental or psychical activity that has highly positive karmic consequences. So don't underestimate the importance of will in the spiritual life. It's not enough to know about the Buddha, to feel devotion for the Buddha, even to dedicate ourselves to the Buddha; we have also to will to be like the Buddha. There's no spiritual life without will. We might even define spiritual life as the constant willing of the Good, with a capital G, in all circumstances and under all conditions.

I've spoken about knowing, feeling, and willing in relation to the Buddha, but what about the Dharma and the Sangha? Well, the same principles hold good. There's such a thing as intellectual or academic study of the Dharma without any feeling for it, much less any will to embody it in one's own life. It's very important that we should be able to distinguish books about the Dharma which are merely informative from books written by people who have some feeling for the Dharma as well as knowledge about it. Years ago, people who were quite hostile to Buddhism used to write about it. They certainly had feelings about the Dharma but those feelings were very negative. We need to have an intellectual, even an academic knowledge of the Dharma, but we must also have a positive feeling for the Dharma. Then we will have real interest in and enthusiasm for Dharma study, and when the will comes into play, we will want to will the Dharma in our own lives, make it operative: practise the precepts, meditate, and so on.

Then what about the Sangha? This term is used rather loosely these days. I might get a letter from someone saying that the Brighton sangha is much bigger than it was five years ago, and sometimes you hear references to the women's sangha, or the Mitra sangha. These are extensions in the usage of the word, but I don't think that matters; they're not illegitimate, and they fulfil a certain purpose. But if we look at the meaning of sangha in the more traditional sense we see that there are really two: the sangha of *āryas*, and the sangha of non-*āryas*. The *āryas* are those who have gained the transcendental path, the path leading directly to Nirvāṇa, whether they are occupying the lower or the higher stages of that path: the Stream Entrants, the great bodhisattvas, and so on. And the non-*āryas* are all those who, though they may be effectively Going for Refuge, have not yet reached the transcendental path. Their Going for Refuge is not yet real. As with the Buddha and the Dharma, we can come to know the Sangha. We can learn about the lives of the members of the Āryasaṅgha – say Milarepa or Hakuin – and after coming to know about their lives, we can develop a feeling for them and aspire to be like them, develop the will to be like them. The same applies to the great bodhisattvas, in fact to all the figures on the Refuge Tree. We can get to know about them, read the stories of their lives, develop some feeling for them, and then, with the will coming into play, actively aspire to be like them. That's relatively straightforward.

But what about the sangha of non-*āryas*? For practical purposes, this consists of all those who are effectively Going for Refuge with whom we are in personal contact. Perhaps we could say that it includes also those whose Going for Refuge to the Three Jewels is provisional, all those who are actively involved in the same Buddhist centre as us. In other words, the sangha of non-*āryas* consists of all of you. When you come to the same centre, it's not enough just to know the names of other people and a bit about them. It's important to develop positive feelings for them, to feel happy that they're attending your centre. If I made fifteen points for people attending the new Manchester Buddhist Centre, one point (which would apply to all FWBO centres) would be: make newcomers feel welcome. People who have been involved with a centre for a few years don't always remember what it feels like to be a newcomer. To begin with you've had to pluck up your courage to come to this strange, exotic, apparently oriental-looking place. You go along on your own, you nervously enter, and there are a lot of people there, all talking vigorously to one another. No one takes any notice of you, no one seems to see you, and you can feel very isolated. I know this does occasionally happen. When regulars go along to the centre, perhaps you haven't seen your friends for a long time, or you've got an important item of council business to discuss, so you seize the chance to talk about that, and meanwhile the new person is standing there neglected. It's very important that you acknowledge that a new person has come in, and go out of your way to make them feel welcome and show them the ropes.

When you get to know people who have been coming along to the centre for quite a while, it's not enough just to know about them. You need to enter into a positive relationship of friendship with them, to develop care for them and a willingness to help them. I think there's been a breakthrough in FWBO centres in the last two or three years, and now people do rally round and help one another when help is needed. We all know in theory, and in many cases in practice, that *kalyāṇa mitratā* is one of the fundamental principles of the FWBO. It's something that we stress, and I suppose we have to admit that at least in the early days we talked about it so much because there was so little of it around. Things have changed, and though we go on talking about it, there is now quite a lot of it around, both vertical spiritual friendship with those who as far as we can see are more experienced, even more advanced, in the spiritual life than we are ourselves, and horizontal spiritual friendship with those who are on approximately the same level as us.

When I came back to Britain thirty-two years ago, people coming along to meditation classes or going on retreats seemed to think it wasn't quite the done thing to talk to the other people coming along. In fact, in some Buddhist circles it was definitely discouraged. You were supposed to go along, listen to the teacher, take something in and go away with it, if possible without speaking to anybody. People genuinely thought that this was the right and proper thing to do, that this was what Buddhists did. Indeed, they thought that you shouldn't even talk to other people about Buddhism or the fact that you were a Buddhist. The classic example was of a lady who came to see me one day and said, 'Bhante, I've been a Buddhist for seventeen years, but not even my best friends know!' She evidently felt that this concealment was a great achievement. But we want every FWBO centre to be a place where the theory and practice of *kalyāṇa mitratā* is thoroughly understood. It should be an oasis of friendliness in the midst of the desert of a world which unfortunately is often a rather unfriendly place.

But I need to sound a little note of warning. *Kalyāṇa mitratā* is an excellent thing, but there is a danger, a near enemy, and that is mere socializing. We have to remember that an FWBO centre is not a social centre and we shouldn't treat it as such. I'll give you a little example – not from the FWBO, so no centre needs to think that I'm getting at them. I was staying at a yoga centre as a guest for a few days, and at the same time a spiritual group was having a weekend retreat there. One day I was sitting in my room when two people who were on the retreat came and sat on a bench outside my window and started talking. They talked for two or three minutes about their meditation. One asked the other, 'How's it going?' and he said, 'Not so bad.' And then they started talking about cars, and they talked about cars for at least half an hour. That's the sort of thing I mean. Our context is spiritual, and let's keep it that way. Let's be glad to see our friends, enquire after their health and what they're doing, but let's make sure that the *kalyāṇa mitratā* we're here to experience doesn't slide insensibly into socializing and idle chatter. Remember the words of the dedication ceremony: 'Here may no idle word be spoken.'[366] That should be taken quite literally. It's something that we should remember and take very much to heart.

In the East they have the custom (which we also follow here) of leaving one's shoes outside the shrine-room. That's not just so that you don't carry any dirt in; it has a symbolic significance. Don't take your worldly affairs into the shrine-room, or even into the Buddhist centre. Leave them behind with your shoes. Perhaps you could make that a practice. Well, don't leave your shoes outside in the street because you might not find them there afterwards. Not everyone in Manchester is Buddhist. But when you leave your shoes outside the shrine-room door, think to yourself, 'Here I leave my shoes. Here I leave all thoughts about family and job. Here I leave my greed, hatred, and delusion, and go into the shrine-room with no other thought than the Dharma.' That could be quite a useful spiritual exercise. Only if we behave in this spirit will we be able to make real use of the centre.

Well, so much for my rather rambling current thinking on Going for Refuge to the Three Jewels. I have also had some thoughts specifically about the Dharma, or perhaps I should say about *prajñā*, *prajñā* being the 'subject' of which Dharma is the 'object'. I'm sure you all know there are three kinds of *prajñā*: *prajñā* based on hearing, *prajñā* based on reflection, and *prajñā* based on meditation.[367] These are usually treated, and indeed experienced, not only as successive, but as progressive. The *prajñā* that arises as a result of reflection is of a rather higher kind than that which arises in dependence upon simply hearing, and the *prajñā* that arises on the basis of meditation is a rather loftier kind than that which arises merely on the basis of reflection. But they can also be regarded as occupying the same level, and *prajñā* or insight can arise equally in dependence on all three.

Take the classic case of Śāriputra. Śāriputra and his friend Maudgalyāyana were originally the followers of a Brahmin teacher, but they became dissatisfied with his teaching and started looking for another teacher. Śāriputra, we are told, happened to encounter Aśvajit, one of the Buddha's first five disciples, was impressed by his appearance, and asked him whose disciple he was and what his master taught. Aśvajit told him that the Buddha taught 'the cause of those phenomena that arise from causes, as well as their cessation', that is, the teaching of conditioned co-production, *pratītya-samutpāda*, which is the whole of the Buddha's teaching on the philosophical side. On hearing those words, Śāriputra attained insight on the spot.[368] Many of the Buddha's other disciples had that experience too, both during the Buddha's own lifetime and afterwards.

We ourselves don't usually develop insight simply by hearing (or reading) the Dharma, though we mustn't overlook the fact that it's possible. We read all about the four noble truths, the Noble Eightfold Path, conditioned co-production, the seven *bodhyaṅgas*, *śūnyatā*, Nirvāṇa, but for some reason insight just doesn't arise. So what do we have to do? We have to reflect upon what we've read. It just hasn't sunk in deep enough. We can't have been sufficiently receptive, otherwise insight would have arisen. So we have to reflect, and if we reflect long and hard enough, insight, *prajñā*, may arise. Well, sometimes it does, but very often it doesn't. We reflect and reflect, but nothing seems to happen. So we have to meditate. Indeed, that's why we meditate. If *prajñā* had arisen when we heard or read or reflected, we wouldn't need to meditate, except for the sheer pleasure of it, because *dhyāna* experiences are very pleasurable and there's nothing wrong with skilful pleasure of that sort. It's the higher hedonism of Buddhism. Buddhism isn't puritanical or pleasure-denying. You can have as much pleasure as you like – enjoy yourself, revel in the *dhyānas*. In the Sixties people used to talk about being blissed out. But it's really because of our realization that insight hasn't arisen that we have to meditate, and if we meditate long and hard enough, eventually insight, *prajñā*, does arise. But we don't just meditate. Although we have found that study and reflection haven't led to the arising of insight, that doesn't mean that we give up those practices. We carry on studying, reading, and hearing the Dharma, and we also carry on reflecting on it, and with those two as a basis, we meditate. In that threefold way we usually manage to break through in the end. Very few people develop insight just on the basis of hearing or reading, though that does happen, or just on the basis of reflection, though that happens too. But even if you don't need meditation as a support for the development of *prajñā*, it's nonetheless a very pleasant experience.

I'll conclude by saying a few words about my forthcoming tour. I shall be visiting FWBO centres in the United States, Canada, Australia, and New Zealand, accompanied for the whole journey by Paramartha, and for part of it by Manjuvajra. I won't be engaging in any public activities – at least that's what I think at present. I'll just be meeting Order members, Mitras, and Friends informally, and doing a little sightseeing. As far as I know I shall be away for six or seven months, which will be the longest period I've been away from the UK since the FWBO was started. But although I'm going away from the UK, I won't be going away from the FWBO, but simply going from one part of it to another, which will remind me how wonderfully the FWBO has grown in the last twenty-eight years.

I sometimes ask myself how it has all happened. Sometimes it seems like a miracle. I remember that first FWBO centre, which was called the Triratna Buddhist Shrine and Meditation Centre, situated in that tiny basement in Monmouth Street in central London. It held at a tight squeeze about twenty-two people, and that's where we started, with one class a week to begin with, and then two. On one occasion just one person turned up for a class. I like to tell this story to encourage Order members who get discouraged when not many people turn up. And now we've got so many centres, so many communities. We've got right livelihood businesses, arts centres, publications. We've got a whole new Buddhist movement, and now this splendid new Manchester Buddhist Centre. I must congratulate all of those who were involved in its creation. It really is a magnificent achievement, and I rejoice in everybody's merits.

While I'm away, anything may happen. I'm well aware that I'm now nearly 71, so that even in the ordinary nature of things, never mind accidents, I may never come back to the UK. This may be my last public appearance. We must never forget that death may come to any of us at any time, and the older you get the more the odds are stacked against your continuing to exist. This applies not just to me, but to each and every one of you. So we should make the best possible use of our time to practise the Dharma. Sometimes we don't realize how lucky we are. I get letters from people telling me how they made contact with the FWBO, and sometimes it's by the merest fluke that they happened to see a leaflet or a poster, or read something in a book, or hear something from a friend. My own first real access to the Dharma apart from my own reading came during the war, when I started attending classes at the Buddhist Society, which was the only Buddhist organization in Britain then and had about a dozen regular members. But now, quite apart from the FWBO, which has dozens of centres in this country, so many other traditions are represented, and the Dharma is easily accessible to us. So let us make full use of the Dharma, let us take the Dharma seriously. We've more reason than ever to practise it because we are living in very difficult times. I'm not a prophet, I don't have a crystal ball, and I may not see the next millennium, but I suspect that the next few decades in the world are not going to be easy and that we shall need the Dharma more than ever. Here in Manchester not many weeks ago you had a painful reminder of that fact. I heard about the bombing on the radio and shortly afterwards I phoned the centre but there was no reply. I phoned the community and Mokshapriya was there, standing guard over the centre. The area had been evacuated but he'd decided to stay and keep an eye on things. The purpose of my call was to assure myself that no one connected with the centre had suffered any harm. He assured me that they hadn't, but told me that the centre had a few broken windows, which have since been repaired. I'm thankful that the damage was not worse and that work could continue.[369]

Despite what I've said, I hope that I will live to pay a few more visits to this Manchester Buddhist Centre, and meet you all again. Meanwhile, no doubt you'll be making good use of the centre, you'll be meditating here, studying the Dharma, enjoying spiritual friendship with one another, and working in so many different ways. I'm sure if I am able to come again I shall find the Manchester Buddhist Center bigger and more beautiful than ever. I congratulate all of you on what you've achieved so far. I hope that you may all put more and more into the centre and get more and more out of it. I hope and trust that the Manchester Buddhist Centre will continue to radiate the light of the Dharma more and more brightly. May that light touch and transform the lives of more and more people.

REFLECTIONS ON GOING FORTH

Order Convention, August 1997

Dharmacāris and *dharmacāriṇīs*: My original idea for this evening was to read a selection of my own poems on the topic of Going Forth, but on looking through my poems, I found there are very few that have even a tenuous connection with Going Forth. I then thought perhaps I could find some English poetry on going forth from this or that situation, but I didn't meet with any success. So the only option is to give a talk. I have to admit that I'm not much inclined to give talks these days. I think I was at my best as a speaker some twenty-five or thirty years ago and that therefore the FWBO has not heard me at my best as a speaker at all, because my best belonged to a period before the FWBO was started. I say this partly so that you won't expect too much. I am pleased to say that nowadays we have some very good speakers indeed within the Order, among both *dharmacāris* and *dharmacāriṇīs*. I hope – sometimes I almost pray – that as the years go by, *dharmacāris* and *dharmacāriṇīs* will be better speakers than I ever was. It's not enough for disciples to be as good as the teacher. They have to do better, at least in some respects – otherwise the Movement doesn't grow. If in every generation the disciples do a little less well, in a few hundred years you've got quite a degree of decline, so I expect each and every Order member to do better than I have ever done, in at least a few respects, and then we can be quite confident about the future of our Order.

Anyway, I had better start my talk! On 18 August 1947, I was in India, staying in the little hill station of Kasauli, in East Punjab. That morning, I got up as usual. I must have meditated – we were meditating nearly every morning then – and instead of putting on my usual clothes, I put on a saffron-coloured sarong and shirt. My friend and I had dyed our previously white sarongs and shirts the previous day with *gerua mati*, a red earth used for that purpose by sadhus and ascetics in India. In the previous two or three days we'd given away all our possessions and destroyed our identification papers. I had breakfast with a friend and then I went forth, taking with me only the robes I was wearing, a blanket, and a few books and notebooks, among which was the copy of the *Dhammapada* which I had with me for several years. So that was my Going Forth fifty years ago.

I was very young, one week short of my twenty-second birthday, and obviously the step I took that morning was a very important one for me. In Going Forth in that way, I was following, as I believed, in the footsteps of the Buddha. The Buddha, too, went forth from home to homelessness at an early age. There are some grounds for thinking that he was 19, but most accounts say 29. But at a relatively early age he left his family, his friends, and his circle of acquaintances, and gave up his civil identity. If he wasn't actually a prince, he was certainly the son of a leading citizen from a patrician high-caste family. He gave all that up. He renounced all worldly ambitions, and I suppose I was trying to do likewise. Though I was only 21, I had had some experience of worldly life. I had been in the army for three years and before that I had worked in local government for two years. Before that I had been in commerce for a year, and before that I had received what little schooling I did receive. But my experience of worldly life had not left me with any worldly ambition, so I was trying to do what the Buddha had done, to go forth from all that. I can't claim that on that day I realized the full significance of what I was doing, but it did mark a turning point in my life, and thereafter my life could not be the same.

So now, fifty years later, almost to the day, I want to place my youthful experience within a broader context and try to get a deeper understanding of the significance of Going Forth. Let us go back to the beginning, which for Buddhists is the Buddha's Enlightenment beneath the bodhi tree. In what that Enlightenment consisted is impossible to say. It's beyond conception, beyond thought. But one can say provisionally that it had three great aspects. First of all, there was the aspect of purity. The Buddha's mind was free from greed, from hatred, and from delusion. Even while we pronounce those words, it's very difficult, if not impossible, for us to frame an idea of what it's really like to be free from those three mental states. Every moment of our waking consciousness we're conscious of elements within our minds of greed, aversion or dislike, and delusion. Imagining all those states not being there and something very pure and positive in their place is very difficult for us, but nonetheless we have to make that effort. Another aspect of the Enlightenment experience is compassion. We sometimes feel pity for human beings and even animals who suffer or are persecuted, but it's not easy to feel even a glimmer of real compassion, because in that state there's no distinction between self and others. One feels for others as for oneself; one does not experience the usual subject–object, self–other dichotomy. It's very difficult for us to form an idea of a state of that kind, but the Buddha's mind when he gained Enlightenment was full of compassion in that sense. And thirdly, there's the aspect of wisdom, in which the Buddha saw things not from any limited perspective, not in any distorted fashion, but as they really are. Again, it's very difficult for us to form a concept of a state of that kind. So purity, compassion, and wisdom are the three great principal aspects, so far as we can imagine them, of the Buddha's Enlightenment.

This evening we're concerned just with the wisdom aspect, the fact that the Buddha saw things as they really are. What did he see when he looked at the world? In brief, he saw three things. He saw, first of all, that there is nothing in existence that is static, nothing that does not change. He saw that everything is in process. And secondly, he saw that this process is not random. Any phenomenon that arises does so in dependence on certain conditions, and it ceases to exist when those conditions cease to exist. And thirdly, he saw that things have no permanent, unchanging being or selfhood, that they are *śūnya*. He saw, moreover, that this principle of conditionality applies at all levels of existence: on the physical-inorganic level, on the physical-organic level, on the non-volitional mental or psychological level, on the ethical or karmic level, and on the dharmic or spiritual level. These are the five *niyamas*. Proceeding quickly, because this is familiar ground, these five *niyamas* can be divided into three groups. First of all, there are those that are governed only by the principle of action and reaction between pairs of opposites – that is to say, the physical-inorganic and organic *niyamas*. Secondly, there are those that are governed by the principle of action and reaction between pairs of opposites and also the principle of action and reaction between factors where the succeeding factor augments (instead of undoing) the effect of the preceding factor. Herein are included the ethical or karmic level and the lower reaches of the dharmic or spiritual level. And thirdly, we have those *niyamas* that are governed only by the principle of action and reaction where the reaction is augmented.[370] The second and third of these groups, corresponding between them to the fourth and fifth *niyamas*, are explained in detail in the twenty-four links of the complete *nidāna* chain. The *nidāna* chain is divided into two sections, each comprising twelve *nidānas*. The first is the mundane section, with its action process and its result process and its three points of transition from the one to the other. The second is the spiritual section, and this is divided into two subsections, consisting respectively of reversible and irreversible *nidānas*. The two are separated by Stream Entry. The mundane section of the chain makes up the round of existence, and the spiritual section makes up the spiral path.

All this will be familiar ground to you, but in case anyone has got lost, let's go back to Siddhārtha Gautama, before he became the Buddha. In the *Ariyapariyesenā Sutta* of the *Majjhima Nikāya* of the Pāli canon, the Buddha tells the monks how he came to go forth. First, he explains that there are two kinds of search – the noble search (*ariyapariyesenā*) and the ignoble search (*anariyapariyesenā*). The Buddha says:

> Bhikkhus, there are these two kinds of search: the noble search and the ignoble search. And what is the ignoble search? Here someone being himself subject to birth seeks what is also subject to birth; being himself subject to ageing, he seeks what is also subject to ageing; being himself subject to sickness, he seeks what is also subject to sickness; being himself subject to death, he seeks what is also subject to death; being himself subject to sorrow, he seeks what is also subject to sorrow; being himself subject to defilement, he seeks what is also subject to defilement.[371]

The Buddha then proceeds to give a detailed account of what may be said to be subject to birth, to ageing, to sickness, death, sorrow and defilement. After which, he proceeds:

And what is the noble search? He is someone being himself subject to birth, having understood the danger in what is subject to birth, seeks the unborn supreme security from bondage, Nibbāna; being himself subject to ageing, having understood the danger in what is subject to ageing, he seeks the unageing supreme security from bondage, Nibbāna; being himself subject to sickness, having understood the danger in what is subject to sickness, he seeks the unailing supreme security from bondage, Nibbāna; being himself subject to death, having understood the danger in what is subject to death, he seeks the deathless supreme security from bondage, Nibbāna; being himself subject to sorrow, having understood the danger in what is subject to sorrow, he seeks the sorrowless supreme security from bondage, Nibbāna; being himself subject to defilement, having understood that danger in what is subject to defilement, he seeks the undefiled supreme security from bondage, Nibbāna. This is the noble search.

Bhikkhus, before my enlightenment, while I was still only an unenlightened Bodhisatta, I too, being myself subject to birth, sought what was also subject to birth; being myself subject to ageing, sickness, death, sorrow, and defilement, I sought what was also subject to ageing, sickness, death, sorrow, and defilement. Then I considered thus: 'Why, being myself subject to birth, do I seek what is also subject to birth? Why, being myself subject to ageing, sickness, death, sorrow, and defilement, do I seek what is also subject to ageing, sickness, death, sorrow, and defilement? Suppose that, being myself subject to birth, having understood the danger in what is subject to birth, I seek the unborn supreme security from bondage, Nibbāna. Suppose that, being myself subject to ageing, sickness, death, sorrow, and defilement, having understood the danger in what is subject to ageing, sickness, death, sorrow, and defilement, I seek the unageing, unailing, deathless, sorrowless, and undefiled supreme security from bondage, Nibbāna.'

Later, while still young, a black-haired young man endowed with the blessing of youth, in the prime of life, though my mother and father wished otherwise and wept with tearful faces, I shaved off my hair and beard, put on the yellow robe, and went forth from the home life into homelessness.[372]

You notice, by the way, that the Buddha says nothing about leaving wife and child, as the later, more romantic accounts would have it.[373] But tonight I'm concerned with just one thing, in fact with just one word: *pariyesenā*. This word is made up of two parts, the prefix *pari*, meaning 'around', and the noun *esenā*, meaning 'desire, longing'. *Pariyesenā* therefore means a searching around, an investigation, an enquiry. The usual translation is simply 'quest'. The *ariyapariyesenā* is the noble quest and the *anariyapariyesenā* is the ignoble quest. I want to point out something which I think has not been noticed before. The same word, *pariyesenā*, is used to describe both. This point is of crucial importance both theoretically and practically. People who are new to Buddhism are fond of asking, 'Doesn't Buddhism contradict itself when it says that desire must be eliminated? How can desire be eliminated without the desire to eliminate it?' This question is supposed to completely floor the unfortunate Buddhist, but it is based on a misunderstanding. It's not a question of there being one kind of desire which is trying to commit hara-kiri. There are two kinds of desire with two radically different objects. There is the desire, *esenā*, for what is conditioned and there is the desire for Nirvāṇa. The first is represented by the *anariyapariyesenā*, the ignoble quest, and the second is represented by the *ariyapariyesenā*, the noble quest.

The fact that there are these two kinds of desire is reflected in another pair of terms: *kāmachanda* and *dhammachanda*. *Chanda* is a very strong term indeed. According to the Pali Text Society's *Pāli–English Dictionary*, it means impulse, excitement, intent, resolution, will, desire for, wish for, delight in. *Kāma* is sensuous experience and *dhamma* is the Buddha's teaching inasmuch that teaching reflects reality. There's also the term *taṇhā* (*tṛṣṇā* in Sanskrit) – literally thirst or drought but usually translated as craving, another very strong term. Unlike *esenā* and *chanda*, it has no positive counterpart and is almost always used in an entirely negative sense. (That is something Sagaramati discusses in the book which was launched earlier this evening.)[374] It's craving, *kāmachanda*, *taṇhā*, which, based on ignorance, keeps the wheel of life revolving. It's the energy that powers the wheel of life. But what is the energy that powers us onto the spiral path? What makes the transition from the round to the spiral? What powers us is the *ariyapariyesenā*. What powers us is *dhammachanda*.

So it's not enough to eliminate *taṇhā*, craving, desire for the conditioned. We also have to cultivate the positive *esenā*, the positive *chanda*. In fact, it's doubtful if we can simply eliminate *taṇhā*. It's more a question of gradually replacing desire for conditioned things with desire for Nirvāṇa. A desire for conditioned things, as we know only too well, is very, very powerful. It's the energy that powers the wheel of life as it turns again and again. It powers every aspect of ordinary unenlightened human existence: our personal life, our domestic life, our social and political life, our professional life, much of our cultural life, and even some of our so-called religious life. It's not easy to get away from craving, and we can get out of its grip only to the extent that our *dhammachanda* is stronger, which means that our *dhammachanda* has to be very strong indeed. It has to be a powerful emotion, an act of concentrated will, not just an idea faintly tinged with emotion. It's no accident that the ancient Greeks spoke of philosophy, which means the love of wisdom, but for us love is often a very weak term. It would be better if we spoke of a passion for wisdom, even a craze for wisdom.

Unfortunately, philosophy has become a purely intellectual exercise and, similarly, Buddhism has become in some quarters simply a subject for academic study. Only too often we set up an idea of the *ariyapariyesenā*, an idea of the spiral, and then we try to grasp it by means of an intellect powered by the energy of craving. The result is very often literalism. But this is not the way. The way is initially to learn simply to concentrate on the idea of the *ariyapariyesenā*, the spiral. We have to learn to appreciate it in the full sense of that word, to be moved by its beauty, to find it emotionally stirring. Then from deep within us there will arise the first glimmering of the *ariyapariyesenā* itself. This is presumably what happened to Siddhārtha. The fourth sight was a sadhu, a wanderer, and it was seeing him that prompted Siddhārtha's decision to go forth. The first three sights turned him away from conditioned existence, but it was the beauty of that fourth sight, the sadhu in his yellow robes, the wanderer, that moved him to go forth in the direction of Nirvāṇa, the Unconditioned, to go forth from home into homelessness.[375] His going forth, his *pabbajjā*, to use the traditional term, was the movement away from conditioned things and towards Nirvāṇa. It was a movement made possible by a shift in the emotional centre of his being, occasioned by his seeing the four sights, whether literally or metaphorically.

My own going forth, I have to admit, was occasioned by something less radical. The immediate occasion was my disillusionment with organized religion as I'd so far encountered it as represented by the Maha Bodhi Society of India and my old friend Pandit-ji, though no doubt deeper forces were also at work.[376] I certainly did feel that I was following in the footsteps of the Buddha, even though I was far from realizing the full significance of what I was doing. Perhaps I still don't realize its full significance now, fifty years later. But at least I am now able to place it within a broader context. In any case, there were important differences between the Buddha's Going Forth and my own. Apart from the obvious ones, there was the fact that I went forth as a Buddhist. Siddhārtha Gautama was not a Buddhist. Buddhism didn't exist then. Some Indian scholars are fond of saying that he was a Hindu, but that wasn't the case either. He was just Siddhārtha Gautama. I was a Buddhist before my Going Forth because I had gone for Refuge to the Buddha, the Dharma, and the Sangha. The Buddha to be had not gone for Refuge to anyone. He didn't follow in anyone's footsteps. He was a pioneer.

So what is the relation between going forth and Going for Refuge? There are different levels of Going for Refuge – the cultural, the provisional, the effective, and the real – and similarly there are levels of going forth. The cultural going forth is when someone in a Buddhist country becomes a monk without any sense of vocation, just because it's part of their culture. This is often accompanied by a strong sense of socio-religious status. Then there's provisional going forth, when you give up worldly life for a time just to see what it's like to be without all these things. This happens to some extent when you go on a long retreat. Effective going forth is when you are making a sustained, systematic effort to give up worldly attitudes, with the help of at least a degree of external renunciation. And real going forth is the equivalent to Stream Entry. When we compare going forth and Going for Refuge, we have to compare cultural with cultural, provisional with provisional, and so on. As Order members, we are basically concerned with effective and real Going for Refuge, so we are concerned with effective and real going forth. Both of these are expressions of the movement from the mundane to the transcendental, the going forth being more general, more philosophical (taking philosophical in the ancient Greek sense) and Going for Refuge being the more specific, more religious form of the same thing. We can go forth without Going for Refuge, but we can't go for Refuge without going forth. Perhaps you'd like to reflect on that.

There are many different ways in which we can go forth, and I want to spend the rest of this talk going into some of them. I'll deal with them under three headings: going forth in respect of one's body, going forth in respect of one's speech, and going forth in respect of one's mind. This tripartite division of the human person is reflected in the distribution of the ten precepts: three precepts for the purification of body, four for the purification of speech, and three for the purification of mind. The ten precepts themselves represent a going forth from the unskilful to the skilful, from the impure to the pure, and this particular going forth follows immediately from the act of Going for Refuge. This is well known to you, so I am not going to say anything about it. I want to speak about aspects of going forth that may not have occurred to you. But before going on to these, I'd like to say just one thing. I sometimes get the impression that not all Order members are as scrupulous about the observance of the ten precepts as they might be. The ten precepts are really very important. They're an expression of our Going for Refuge. They're the foundation of our spiritual progress, of meditative experience, and of real understanding of the Dharma. If our observance of the precepts is lax, our Going for Refuge will be weak, and our spiritual progress will be slow, uncertain, or even non-existent. So be very careful about your observance of the precepts, and about your ethical life in general. Encourage one another to observe the precepts and discuss your mutual observance of them at chapter meetings. If everyone does that, the ethical health of the Order will be assured.

GOING FORTH IN RESPECT OF THE BODY

One's physical body obviously occupies space, and one goes forth in respect of one's body when one moves physically from one place to another. The Buddha moved from Kapilavastu in the foothills of the Himalayas to the forests of Magadha, and I moved from Kasauli in the Punjab to South India, having already moved from England to the Indian subcontinent, from the West to the East. A change of place, a change of environment, is very important. The physical body is equipped with five senses and these five senses feed the mind, so change of place is never just change of place. It is also a change of experience. We're not just passive. We react to our experience, we respond to our environment. Sometimes aspects of ourselves which can't come into play in one environment come into play in another. We all know how different we feel when we go on retreat, especially when that retreat is in the countryside. Sometimes people say that they literally feel reborn after a few days. A new self comes into existence. I've often spoken about how in the very early days of the Movement I saw people change in two or three days, simply by being lifted out of their workaday urban environment and put down in the countryside on retreat, in a more congenial environment and with positive, inspiring things to do. This was one of the things that convinced me of the need to transform the world as well as the self, because without transforming the world to a degree it is very difficult to transform the self. In a more ideal world, it's easier for people to develop spiritually, so we need to work towards the creation of such a world.

Nowadays people often go abroad on holiday or on a business trip, but going forth only for a short while, sometimes taking your family with you, does not constitute a going forth, but going abroad can be an expression of your Going for Refuge when you go to live in another country solely in order to communicate the Dharma. This represents a very important step in one's spiritual development, especially if one devotes oneself to communicating the Dharma in the new country, and provided one does not succumb to worldly pleasures, forgetting one's original purpose. A number of Order members have taken this step. Some have moved from England to North America and to Germany. Others have moved from Australia and New Zealand to England. The courage and determination of such Order members is to be admired. It's a truly heroic step that they've taken, even though travel is so much easier now than it was in the Buddha's day, or even in my day. Nor must we forget those who come to the UK from other parts of the world in quest of ordination. That too is a going forth.[377]

A second way of going forth in respect to the body concerns its upkeep. The body's senses are constantly clamouring for satisfaction, so a good deal of our attention is centred on the body. Some of this attention is necessary and some of it is unnecessary. It's necessary to feed and clothe the body, and keep it clean and healthy, and this shouldn't be neglected, but a lot of the attention we give to the body is unnecessary, even harmful. Sometimes we eat simply out of neurotic craving. We give too much thought to what we wear and spend too much money on clothes. Then there's the question of cosmetics, and even cosmetic surgery, which is very expensive, and some people go in for tattoos.

Now I know that most Order members don't give unnecessary attention to the body. Very few of you, so far as I know, buy designer clothes. But that is the modern trend, and we have to be careful that we're not affected by it. Especially as the Movement becomes bigger and more prosperous, we may start thinking that we're entitled to a higher standard of living. So let us go forth in respect of the body in this way. Let us live as simply as possible. Let's give the body only what it really needs. Let's try consciously to reduce our expenditure on its upkeep. Let's concern ourselves with it objectively. All this applies more to Order members in the West, but even Order members in the East need to be careful. It's only too easy to be seduced by the attractions of the middle-class lifestyle and think that this is the lifestyle appropriate to an Order member.

I mentioned that going forth in relation to one's body is a going forth in space on the surface of the earth – a horizontal going forth, if you like – but the third aspect of going forth in respect to the body is more of a vertical going forth. (Perhaps the second one comes somewhere in between, but you can work that one out for yourself.) So what is vertical going forth with respect to the physical body? It's really very simple. You go forth vertically in respect to the body when you meditate – that is to say, when you really meditate, not just when you are trying to concentrate, but when you ascend into the *dhyānas*. For the time being you leave the body behind, or you have only a very peripheral awareness of it. No messages come to you from the senses, or if such messages do faintly come, you ignore them because you're absorbed in that higher state of consciousness. This vertical going forth helps us to realize that the physical body is not the be-all and end-all of our existence. It helps to remind us that we are not to identify ourselves exclusively with the physical body. It doesn't matter how you attain that higher state of consciousness. You can take the mindfulness of breathing practice as your point of departure, or the *mettā bhāvanā*, or you can contemplate your chosen Buddha or bodhisattva. What is important is that you should become absorbed in that higher state and be oblivious of everything else, at least for a short time each day. This will give you inspiration, renew your spiritual vision, and help you to live more in accordance with the Dharma.

We also have the opportunity to go forth vertically in respect to the body when we die. I've spoken of meditation as a kind of death and death as a kind of meditation. When we die, the gross physical body is no longer there, so we have the opportunity to go forth vertically to a higher state of existence, but we'll be able to do that at the time of death only if we have had some experience of such going forth during our lifetime. Otherwise, we shall be obliged to go forth horizontally, to be reborn in much the same circumstances as before.

GOING FORTH IN RESPECT OF SPEECH

Obviously one goes forth from wrong speech to right speech. Right speech is the most difficult to practise of all the precepts because we have innumerable opportunities to practise wrong speech. We have hundreds of opportunities every day to say what is not quite true, to speak a little roughly or harshly or unkindly, to talk idly, frivolously, or without any real meaning, even to slander and backbite and misrepresent. So we need to be very aware of our speech, especially on occasions like this when the Order is gathered together. On such occasions you meet lots of old friends and want to make up for lost time, and it's easy to find your tongue running away with you.

When one moves to another country, one often has to go forth from one's native language. You use your own language without thinking, but using the new language is much more difficult. You feel clumsy and unspontaneous. You can't say what you want to say. You can't understand people, and they can't understand you. You feel stupid, or like a small child. All this can feel very humiliating and frustrating. Perhaps you're a brilliant talker with wonderful power of expression in your own language, but your limited knowledge of the new language makes you seem stupid. This state of affairs doesn't last long, maybe not more than three or four years, but to begin with life can be quite difficult and painful, though at the same time very interesting. The courage and determination of those Order members who go and live abroad for the sake of the Dharma is to be very much admired, especially when it involves having to learn a new language, because there is a going forth in respect of both body and speech, so they are doubly heroic. I'd like all Order members – and Mitras even – to be prepared for this heroism. I would like every Order member to learn at least one foreign language, even if you have at present no intention of working for the Dharma abroad. It has been said that when you learn a new language, you acquire another soul, but you also lose something. You don't lose your old self, but it may be modified by the impact of the new one, so you lose a bit of your self. You cling a little less tightly to your old linguistic and national identity. In other words, you go forth in respect to speech.

We now come to an aspect of going forth in respect of speech which is even more radical. The fact is that we talk far too much. We need, from time to time, to go forth from speech altogether. We need to observe silence. This is not a very popular practice in the FWBO. I believe that sometimes people coming along to an FWBO centre from some other spiritual group are very impressed by our friendliness and our organizational skills, but they're not always impressed by our capacity for silence. But going forth from speech is very necessary. During the war we used to say that careless talk costs lives, and it also wastes energy. I am really surprised when young people complain of a lack of energy – when I say young, I mean anyone under 50 – but I think one of the reasons they lack it is that they talk too much. When you observe silence, you accumulate and refine energy. This brings me to one of my pet abominations, the business lunch, when people try to do two quite different things at the same time: to eat and to talk business. Both are important, but each needs your undivided attention. If anything, eating is the more important of the two. You need to eat slowly, mindfully, and quietly, otherwise you won't digest your food properly, and you won't enjoy your meal. So keep eating and business separate. Eat quietly together first, then talk. The same applies to the business breakfast, which is quite popular in some FWBO circles, and the *kalyāṇa mitra* lunch. By all means have a meal with your friend, but don't eat and talk at the same time. This applies very much to occasions such as conventions and Order weekends. In any case, speech is not the only form of human communication. Sometimes, indeed, we talk to avoid communication. We have to remember that silence also can be a form of communication. Silence enables you to tune in to your friend's wavelength, to be more receptive to them. So let's try to give a little more space to silence in our lives, especially when we meet with our friends. On some previous conventions, the noise at mealtimes was quite deafening, which is why we introduced silent breakfasts. Let's learn to value silence more and let's have more periods of silence on retreats and when we meet as an Order. It is said that Mozart was once asked what was the most important part of his music and he replied 'the pauses'. Pauses, silence, should be an integral part of our lives.

This brings me to a third aspect of going forth in respect of one's speech, one which you may find more acceptable and enjoyable than the last. It's going forth from speech into song. I'm not referring to singing in the shower, though I am not against that, but to something that has recently arisen within the FWBO which I am very glad to see: choral singing. This very positive development has taken place, I am glad to say, without any initiative on my part. I'm told that singing is very good for us physically, and it's also good for us emotionally, especially when we sing with others. I once said that an orchestra is a spiritual community, at least when it is playing, and the same is true of a choir. I'd like every centre to have its own choir and its own choirmaster, who should be a trained musician. In a way, the choirmaster is no less important than the Mitra convenor or the chapter convenor. Eventually there should be a national choirmaster, and choirmasters should meet together from time to time just as Mitra convenors do. On special occasions, local choirs should join forces. This has already happened a few times. But we should be careful what kind of music we sing together. It should be music that is noble and inspiring or peaceful and meditative, music that helps raise the level of consciousness of both the singers and the listeners. The words should be in keeping with the music, and they should be words we can sing with heartfelt conviction. Perhaps we could start producing our own choral music. We have composers and poets in the Movement; perhaps they should sometimes join forces. Above all, we should regard singing in choir as a spiritual practice, and approach it with awareness, emotional positivity, and a sense of responsibility.

GOING FORTH IN RESPECT OF THE MIND

This is the primary going forth in the sense that it's what gives life to one's going forth in respect to one's body and one's speech. There is much that could be said about this, but this evening I'm going to confine myself to two aspects. First of all, there is going forth from the *kāmaloka* to the *rūpaloka*. The *kāmaloka* is the world of the physical senses, the material world, and the mind that is concerned with sense experience. It's in this world that we live most of the time, and it's with the things of this world that we are usually most concerned – food, drink, clothing, sex, shelter, and so on. The *rūpaloka* is the world of archetypes: not just Jung's archetypes of the collective unconscious, but also the archetypes of the super-collective superconsciousness. We have access to the *rūpaloka* through dreams, through great works of art, literature, and music, and through images, myths, and symbols. The greatest works of art are those that speak to us of this world most directly and profoundly. We experience the *rūpaloka* by means of what Buddhism calls the divine eye, the *divya-cakṣus*, together with the divine ear, the *divya-śrotra*. In other words, we experience that higher realm, the *rūpaloka*, by means of the imagination – not imagination in the popular sense but in the sense in which Coleridge uses the term.[378] To avoid confusion, we can distinguish between imagination in the ordinary sense and the imaginal faculty, the faculty that gives us access to the *rūpaloka*, this higher archetypal realm. It's by means of the imaginal faculty that we experience the imaginal world, the world of *devas* and brahmās, angels and archangels, light, colour, and sound, the world that at its highest levels reflects the transcendental. We should go forth to this world, live more in this world. We should go forth to it in dreams and visions, through the fine arts, music and poetry in their highest and finest expressions, and above all, in meditation. In Sanskrit, *rūpa* can mean beauty, so the *rūpaloka* is the world of pure beauty. There's no doubt that we need beauty in our lives. Beauty nourishes and inspires us, and without it we tend to dry up, even to perish. So, let us go forth from the *kāmaloka* to the *rūpaloka*, and let us dwell there as much as we can.

The second aspect of going forth in respect of one's mind is a going forth from *manas* to *āryajñāna*. Intellectually, *manas* is the rational mind, and emotionally it is the ego-consciousness. It operates within the dualistic framework of subject and object, self and others. More often than not, it concerns what we experience through the five physical senses and the lower mind, the mind that is concerned with sense experience. *Manas* is also the faculty of abstract thought. It is capable of generalizing and drawing conclusions from the perceptions of the five senses and the lower mind. In a sense, *manas* is the scientific mind, though the greatest scientists seem also to possess a degree of imagination. Reason as such is not to be despised. *Manas* is not be despised, and from an evolutionary point of view, it has taken humanity a long time to develop it. But it does not represent the last word in human development. Beyond *manas*, there is *āryajñāna*. *Āryajñāna* means noble knowledge, and it is noble in the sense that it is transcendental. Being transcendental, it is non-dual. It is knowledge without a subject and without an object, knowledge in which there is nothing to know and nobody to know it. At the same time, it is not a state of unconsciousness like deep sleep – it is pure, blissful, radiant, non-dual awareness. Being non-dual, it can't be an object of knowledge, but for practical purposes we think of it as such. We think of it as something to which we go forth from *manas*. Obviously, this is not easy, and it's hardly possible for us to start out immediately without preparation, but we can make a good beginning by becoming more aware of the extent to which we are dominated by *manas*, by the rational mind, by our ego-consciousness. Indeed, dominated is too weak a word. We are usually identified with *manas*, identified with our ego-consciousness, and we have to become more aware of this; we have to stand back from our selves. Then perhaps we can start slowly turning round and facing in the direction of the *āryajñāna*, even start moving towards it. When that happens, we will have begun to go forth from *manas* to *āryajñāna*. We will have started transforming our effective Going for Refuge into real Going for Refuge.

So much, then, for my reflections on going forth. There is a going forth in respect of one's body, a going forth in respect of one's speech, and a going forth in respect of one's mind. We go forth in respect of the body when we go to live in another country, especially when we do so for the sake of the Dharma; when we live more simply, reducing our bodily needs; and when we meditate in the sense of experiencing the *dhyānas*. We go forth in respect of speech when we go forth from our own language through learning a new language, when we observe silence, and when we sing as members of a Dharma choir. And we go forth in respect of the mind when we go forth from the *kāmaloka* to the *rūpaloka* and from *manas* to *āryajñāna*. In going forth in these ways, we move from the *anariyapariyesenā* to the *ariyapariyesenā*, from the ignoble quest to the noble quest, from *kāmachanda* to *dhammachanda*, from the round of mundane existence to the spiral of spiritual development. In other words, we follow in the footsteps of the Buddha. And one day, it is to be hoped, we shall arrive, as the Buddha arrived, at the foot of the bodhi tree.

A LIFE FOR THE DHARMA

Birmingham Buddhist Centre, 26 January 1999

A few years ago I gave a lecture on great Buddhists of the twentieth century.[379] It was one of the longest talks I've ever given in England, something over two hours. In India I often used to give Dharma talks lasting that long, but here people don't usually have the stamina to listen to such a long talk, and they start fidgeting and looking out of the window. On that occasion I spoke about five great Buddhists. There was Anagārika Dharmapala of Sri Lanka, who restored the Buddhist holy places around the turn of the twentieth century and did a great deal toward the revival of Buddhism in the land of its birth. Then there was the intrepid Alexandra David-Néel, the first woman to make the journey to Lhasa. Thirdly, I spoke about Dr B. R. Ambedkar, the great leader of the ex-Untouchables, under whose leadership hundreds of thousands of his followers took refuge in the Buddha, the Dharma, and the Sangha. The fourth great Buddhist was Lama Govinda, who was of German birth and for many years concentrated on the subject of Tibetan mysticism, as he called it, on which subject he wrote an important book.[380] And fifthly, there was Dr Edward Conze, who devoted more than twenty years of his life to the translation of the Prajñāpāramitā corpus of Mahāyāna *sūtras*.

They were all truly great Buddhists. They were very different in character, background, education, nationality, and culture, but they possessed certain important qualities in common. They were all single-minded. Dharmapala was single-minded about the restoration of Bodh Gaya and other Buddhist holy places. Alexandra David-Néel was single-minded about getting to Lhasa, which she did in disguise. Dr Ambedkar was single-minded about emancipating his people from the socio-religious slavery of many centuries. Lama Govinda was single-minded about getting to Tibet, especially to western Tibet and the old temples and monasteries of Tsaparang. And Dr Edward Conze was single-minded in his devotion to the translation of those thirty-odd difficult and abstruse texts of Mahāyāna Buddhism, the Prajñāpāramitā *sūtras*. They were also all fearless. They were prepared to face and overcome opposition, even ostracism. Not surprisingly, all five of them were quite unconventional, and they were also self-motivated, autonomous, so they were true individuals. In short, all five were heroes, and in the case of Madame David-Néel a heroine, in the best sense of the term. I concluded my lecture by saying that we need to cherish our heroes and heroines, not put people up on a pedestal and then knock them off it for the sake of amusement. We need to admire our heroes and heroines, cherish their memory, and rejoice in their merits.

Great Buddhists are to be found not only in the twentieth century, but in all the centuries that have elapsed since the *parinirvāṇa* of the Buddha. They are found in Asian countries and are beginning to be found in Western countries too, speaking different languages and following different forms of Buddhism. But a difficulty arises. My five great Buddhists of the twentieth century all lived quite recently, and we know quite a lot about them. Some of them wrote autobiographies, and there are many documents about them. I had some kind of personal contact with each of them. But with regard to the great Buddhists of previous centuries it's very different. We often know very little about them, and sometimes the greater they were, the less we know about them. Think of Nāgārjuna, think of Asaṅga. How much do we really know about them? Perhaps we've seen thangkas, Tibetan painted scrolls, representing them. We see Nāgārjuna sitting on his raft floating on the ocean, and a mermaid-like figure, a *nāga* princess, coming up from the depths of the ocean and offering him the Perfection of Wisdom *sūtras*. In the case of Asaṅga we have thangkas representing the bodhisattva Maitreya looking down from the Tuṣita *devaloka* and sending down a ray of multicoloured light along which come teachings which Asaṅga records. These pictures are vivid and inspiring, but we don't have much in the way of concrete information about these great Buddhists of earlier days. We have their writings, for which we must be very grateful, and in a sense we can know Nāgārjuna, Asaṅga, Vasubandhu, Dharmakīrti, Śāntideva, and others through their writings. We can even feel that we know them very well, despite the deconstructionists. We can know what they thought, even how they felt. But there's very little solid biographical information.

Nāgārjuna and Asaṅga were both Indian, and India didn't go in for history or biography. So far as I recollect, in the whole of classical Sanskrit literature there is only one historical work, and that is the *Rājataraṃgiṇī*, the chronicle of the kings of Kashmir. The ancient Indians cultivated almost every other form of literature – drama, commentary, *sūtras* in the Brahminical sense, philosophical exposition, hymns – but not history or biography. Generally speaking, what we know about the great Buddhists of India comes from occasions when they or their disciples came in contact with people from other countries, especially China and Tibet. Traditionally the Chinese and the Tibetans are rather fond of biography and history. The Chinese cultivated those two genres quite intensively, and the Tibetans did likewise, under the influence of Buddhism.

This evening I want to speak about a great Indian Buddhist who went to Tibet in the eleventh century of the Common Era and came to play a crucially important part in the development of Tibetan Buddhism, and who is therefore deserving of our highest respect. I refer to Dīpaṃkara Śrījñāna, generally known as Atiśa, which means something like the great lord. Comparatively speaking we know quite a lot about Atiśa. We have the Tibetan translations of his writings. His original writings were in Sanskrit, and their colophons sometimes contain biographical information. We have several biographies written in Tibetan by disciples, and disciples of disciples, and records of some of Atiśa's personal teachings to his disciples – not formal treatises, but teachings in the form of what came to be called precepts, teachings suited to the character, temperament, and state of spiritual development of a particular disciple. It's possible to extract a straightforward biographical account from all this material, and naturally, Buddhists being Buddhists, there are also plenty of legends. What I shall try to do is give an outline of the generally agreed facts of Atiśa's career in India and Tibet, and dwell in particular on those episodes that have significance for us today – that is, for people who are trying to practise the Dharma in the industrialized, secularized, urbanized, competitive, consumerist, materialistic, violent society in which at the end of the twentieth century of the Common Era we find ourselves living, fortunately or unfortunately.

Atiśa was born in the year 982 CE, about fifteen hundred years after the Buddha, so he came at the end of a very long period of development of the Dharma in India. He was as far removed from the Buddha in time as Martin Luther was from Jesus, which gives us some idea of the historical perspective involved. Incidentally, it is rather unfortunate that we have to refer to dates in Buddhist history as occurring either CE or BCE. It used to be BC or AD, but there has been some improvement, and we now say CE, 'Common Era,' or BCE, 'before the Common Era'. Even this is rather unfortunate, though, because it suggests a break in the continuity of Buddhist history which is not really there. We're now living in the 2,545th year of the Buddhist era, at least according to the Southern reckoning.[381] So we should try not to allow the break suggested by CE and BCE to influence us when we survey the history of Buddhism.

Atiśa was born in Bengal in eastern India. We're not sure exactly where, but it may have been in a village near Dhaka, the capital of the present-day Bangladesh. All the accounts agree that he was born of noble parents, and his father may even have been the local chief, the local raja. Later accounts tend to represent Atiśa as having been the son of a great king. His biographers take as their model the legendary life of the Buddha, because if you can represent any great Buddhist as having been the son of a king and the heir to the throne, when he gives it all up it's even more impressive. But it seems that his father was really not much more than the local chief, no doubt an important man, but within a relatively small area. Atiśa received a good education, studied various arts and sciences, and according to some accounts he was married at an early age to five wives – that suggests he probably did come from the nobility – and had seven sons and two daughters, so presumably he wasn't lacking in worldly experience. Strangely, considering his later career, his religious life at this time was almost entirely Tantric. In a way, though, this is not surprising. Atiśa lived towards the end of the Buddhist period in India, and within 300 years of his death Buddhism had practically disappeared from the land of its birth, the last blow having been given by the destruction of the great monastic universities by the Muslim invaders. Even in Atiśa's day, Buddhism was more or less confined to north-eastern India.

Indian Buddhism passed through three great phases of historical development, each lasting five or six hundred years: a phase during which the Hīnayāna was dominant, a Mahāyāna phase, and a Vajrayāna or Tantric phase. By the time Atiśa was born, the Vajrayāna or Tantric Buddhism was predominant in that part of India where Buddhism still survived. Atiśa therefore grew up in a Tantric atmosphere. It is said that he received his first Tantric initiation from his father, and after that he associated with many famous Tantric yogins and teachers of the Mahāyāna. Some accounts say that among his teachers were some of those on the list of eighty-four *mahāsiddhas* or 'great perfect ones'.[382] So during these early years, when he was still living at home with his family, Atiśa was practising Tantric meditation, taking part in the *gaṇacakras* or Tantric feasts, and listening to the secret Tantric songs, which imparted esoteric instruction. According to at least one account he even went to the land of Uḍḍiyāna and practised the tantras in the company of the *ḍākinīs*, whatever that might mean. In this way he spent many years gaining a thorough knowledge of the Vajrayāna and its rituals and meditations.

But despite his thorough immersion in the Vajrayāna, and his vast acquaintance with Tantric disciplines and teachings, he was not satisfied. He felt he had not made any real spiritual progress. He had certainly not gained Enlightenment. In theory the Vajrayāna is not just the latest phase in the development of Indian Buddhism, but also the most advanced stage of the Buddhist spiritual path, at least according to the *triyāna* system. But here was Atiśa, who had practised the Vajrayāna systematically, thoroughly, and sincerely for fifteen or more years, with some of the greatest Tantric yogins as his teachers, still not satisfied with his spiritual progress. He felt there was something missing, something he hadn't achieved, something he hadn't experienced. Perhaps in a sense everything was lacking, everything was missing. So what had gone wrong? Well, to put it in a few words with which we are very familiar, he had been following the path of irregular steps. Before he could go forward he had to go back. He had to start following the path of regular steps.[383]

This is what happens to us not once but perhaps many times in the course of our spiritual life. We find that we've got stuck. We've been practising all these years and doing all the right things – maybe we've been good Buddhists of one sort or another for twenty years – but perhaps the time comes when we feel that we're not making progress, or even that we've never made any progress. If we reach that point, it's no use blaming conditions or our lifestyle: 'I'm so busy with my work and family, I'm so busy running classes at the Buddhist centre.' It's no use blaming your teacher: 'Oh, if only my teacher had given me more time, if only I could see him every day, sit at his feet every day, look into his eyes, I'm sure then I would make more progress.' Sometimes people start thinking that their teacher doesn't care for them much and they'd better start looking for another one. That's 'shopping around'. And it's no use blaming your fellow disciples for not helping and supporting you enough. In this sort of state, the best thing to do is retrace your steps, go back to fundamentals. There's a great deal of mental confusion around these days. You read it in the newspapers, you hear it on the radio, and I'm sure if you watched television, which I don't, you'd find lots and lots of it there. You find mental confusion in some of the books you read, and even in some of the Buddhists you meet. If we are mentally confused, as we usually are when we're not making spiritual progress, we have to go back to meditation. That may seem a dull, prosaic remedy, back to the old cushion, back to the old mindfulness of breathing, back to the old *mettā bhāvanā*, but that's what we have to do. If we are mentally confused, if we are not able to develop wisdom and make real spiritual progress, we have to go back to meditation, because, as the Buddha said, 'It is the concentrated mind that sees things as they really are.'[384]

If our meditation is unsatisfactory, if we don't have much time for it, or if we are troubled by all sorts of wandering thoughts and distractions – what happened yesterday, what has to be done tomorrow – we have to get back to *śīla*, to ethics. We have to practise the precepts more carefully and vigorously, because an ethical life is an integrated life, and the more integrated we are, the easier we shall find it to achieve mental concentration. It's no use leading an ethically unintegrated life and despite that trying to meditate. But what can we do if our practice of ethics is not very successful? Perhaps we find it difficult not to be cruel, and maybe we do sometimes take things we haven't been given. As for the third precept, the less said about that the better. And what about speech? This is the easiest precept of all to break, the precept according to which we should abstain not just from false speech but from harsh speech, divisive speech, and useless speech. Most of us have to admit that we break this precept many times a day. You're very unlikely to kill anybody or steal anything in the course of the day, and you're not very likely to commit adultery, but you're almost certain to infringe the speech precepts. And there's that fifth precept which is a matter of some controversy, whether it requires total abstention from drink and drugs or just not taking too much. And those are just the five precepts; there are also the ten precepts, the ten *kuśala-dharmas*.

If we find even the practice of ethics difficult, what shall we do? Is it possible to go back to something even more fundamental? Well, fortunately it is. If even the practice of ethics is difficult, we should practise *dāna* or giving. At the very least we can do that. Through giving we learn to empathize with other people, and imaginative identification with other living beings is the foundation of ethics. In this way we get back to the path of regular steps, and we start making progress again.

So this is what Atiśa did. He retraced his steps from the Vajrayāna to the Mahāyāna, and from the Mahāyāna to the Hīnayāna, and at the age of 29 he became a monk. He gave up all his Tantric rituals and paraphernalia and *gaṇacakras* and feasts, and he became a monk in the Mahāsāṃghika branch of the monastic order. It's not clear where he was ordained or under whom, but apparently he was ordained at one of the great monastic universities of north-eastern India, and thereafter he spent two years studying. He studied the Tripiṭaka in the sense of studying the Vinaya; the *Āgamas*, which are the Sanskrit counterparts of the Pāli *Nikāyas*; and the *Mahāvibhāṣā*, which is a commentary on the seventh and last book, the *Jñānaprasthāna*, of the Sarvāstivādin Abhidhamma Piṭaka. But these Hīnayāna works didn't satisfy him. He wanted to study the great classical Mahāyāna works too, but he couldn't find any teachers, and although he got hold of some important texts, others were no longer available, at least in that part of India. Atiśa realized that he would have to continue his studies abroad, and he decided to go to Indonesia, which was then a great centre of the Mahāyāna. There's the great stupa of Borobudur in Java, but Atiśa didn't go there. He went to the island of Sumatra, to the city of Srivijaya, which was then the capital of a great empire (the site is now occupied by the city of Palembang). He had to go by sea, and the voyage took thirteen months.

Let's pause to compare Atiśa's position with our own. We don't have to go abroad to study the Dharma; we can study it at home. There's no shortage of material; we can even study the Dharma in our own language. So many important texts have been translated into English, German, French, Spanish, and many other Western languages. As well as the texts, there are books about Buddhism, histories, expositions of its philosophy, and so on. Fifty years ago, when I was relatively new to Buddhism, if two or three books about Buddhism, including translations, came out in a single year, that was a great event, and if you were seriously interested in Buddhism, you knew each and every book that was published. But nowadays there are thousands of books on the different forms of Buddhism, different Buddhist practices, schools, art, architecture, and so on. Very often we don't know where to start. Just think of the scriptures in Pāli, Sanskrit, and Chinese that have been translated into English, and all the commentaries. Sometimes people wonder if we have to study all of it. Do we have to work our way through the whole of the Pāli Tipiṭaka? And there are those great Mahāyāna *sūtras*, hundreds of pages of them – do we have to study all of them? Dr Conze translated thirty-odd Prajñāpāramitā *sūtras* alone, which is just one group of Mahāyāna *sūtras*. Do we have to make our way through all of these?

Well, I'm going to say something about that in my next lecture here.[385] But whether we make our way through a few Buddhist texts or many, whether we study for many hours a week or just half an hour, we can study the Dharma at home, both metaphorically and literally. We can practise meditation here, we can go on retreat here, we can enjoy spiritual friendship here, and above all, there is nothing to stop us from Going for Refuge to the Buddha, the Dharma, and the Sangha here. In Western countries we have it very easy. Everything is available, everything is accessible. We don't always realize just how fortunate we are, so we don't always take full advantage of those opportunities. We even sometimes complain that we don't have even better advantages. So let us remember Atiśa and others like him in Buddhist history. Atiśa had to go abroad to study the Dharma, and that meant making a dangerous voyage lasting thirteen months. We can get to India in thirteen hours, go round all the holy places to pay our respects, and be back home within the week. So let us admire Atiśa's heroism, let us admire his devotion to the Dharma, and let us try to imbibe something of his spirit.

Atiśa spent twelve years in Sumatra, from the age of 32 to 44. He studied with the great teacher Dharmakīrti, not to be confused with the famous Indian logician of that name of a few centuries earlier.[386] The

Sumatran Dharmakīrti had studied in India in his younger days, it seems. So at the feet of Dharmakīrti, Atiśa became thoroughly acquainted with the great classical works of the Mahāyāna, especially with the writings of Nāgārjuna, Asaṅga, and Śāntideva, and we're told that he paid particular attention to the teachings connected with the arising of the *bodhicitta*, the aspiration to achieve supreme Enlightenment not just for one's own benefit, but for the sake of all living beings. Atiśa's interest in those teachings was certainly not just theoretical. He really took them to heart. Atiśa was a Mahāyāna Buddhist in the broadest sense, and the *bodhicitta* is the heart of the Mahāyāna. It is the arising of the *bodhicitta*, the will to universal Enlightenment, that makes a bodhisattva a bodhisattva. So Atiśa was inspired by the bodhisattva ideal, and he tried to develop the *bodhicitta* within himself. How successful he was in doing this we shall see.

Probably those twelve years of intensive study in Sumatra passed very quickly. At any rate, at the age of 44 Atiśa returned to India, and not long after his departure from Sumatra, the island was conquered by a South Indian Hindu king, and Buddhism started to decline there. Still later, Sumatra and the neighbouring island of Java and the other smaller islands were conquered by the forces of Islam, and Indonesia became part of the Muslim religious empire. Atiśa spent the next fifteen years in north-eastern India, particularly at the great monastic university of Vikramaśilā.[387] During that time he seems to have been very busy. He wrote a number of books in Sanskrit, some of which were subsequently translated into Tibetan with the help of Atiśa himself, he taught many disciples, he engaged in vigorous debate with various non-Buddhist teachers, and he even found time to meditate, as well as discharging administrative responsibilities within the monastery.

During this period, two important events occurred. The first was that war broke out between a Hindu king of western India and the ruler of Magadha, Magadha being the kingdom within which Atiśa lived, and which was ruled by some of the later Pala kings. The Hindu king was the aggressor and at first he was very successful, and the Pala king's troops were defeated, but eventually the tide of battle turned, the Hindu king was defeated, and he and his troops were at the mercy of the victors. Atiśa took the king and the defeated warriors under his protection, and did not allow them to be harmed, because he had great influence with the Pala king, who may have been his disciple. Not only that; Atiśa played an active role in the negotiation of a peace treaty between the Hindu king and the Pala ruler of Magadha. So this was a very important event in Atiśa's life.

The second, even more important event was that Atiśa received an invitation to visit Tibet. This, indeed, was the crucial event in his life. In order to understand how he came to receive this invitation, we will have to go a little into the history of Tibet. Buddhism was introduced there in the seventh century of the Common Era, along with a good deal of Indian culture. Before that time Tibet didn't have a written literature, or even an alphabet. In the eighth century, Buddhism was given a further impetus in Tibet, mainly due to the work of Śāntarakṣita and the great guru Padmasambhava. In the ninth century the king of Tibet called a great Buddhist council and arrangements were made for the systematic translation of Buddhist scriptures into the Tibetan language, using the newly devised Tibetan alphabet, which was based on a contemporary Indian alphabet.[388] So far, so good. Buddhism seems to have been well established in Tibet by that time.

But then a terrible setback occurred. It seems there was a certain amount of opposition to the establishment of Buddhism, and the pious Buddhist king was assassinated, to be succeeded by a very anti-Buddhist king who destroyed monasteries and forced monks to return to lay life. During that king's reign Buddhism was practically wiped out. But those who live by the sword will die by the sword, and the king was assassinated in his turn – by a monk, I'm sorry to say. The Tibetans maintain that the monk was activated by pure bodhisattva compassion, wanting to prevent the king from performing any more evil deeds and to save Buddhism in Tibet. That may have been the case, but it is not a course of action that Buddhism generally recommends. Further disasters followed. Tibet disintegrated politically, and the whole country was overrun by freelance Tantric teachers from India. They weren't all Buddhists. There were all sorts of strange Hindu sects, and some of them went so far as to teach that the practice of the tantra consisted in the enjoyment of two things: wine and, predictably, sex. Some of these Tantrics even practised ritual human sacrifice and cannibalism. So one can see that they were quite extreme, and had strayed a very long way from the Buddha's teachings and from the Vajrayāna.

Meanwhile, a descendant of the last king of old Tibet had migrated to western Tibet and there set up a separate kingdom. He and his descendants were devout Buddhists, and they did their best to revive true Buddhism, at least in that part of Tibet. One of those descendants was Jñānaprabha, and this brings us to the eleventh century of the Common Era, the century of Atiśa. Jñānaprabha seems to have heard of Atiśa; at any rate he sent a delegation to Vikramaśilā to invite him to visit Tibet, the delegation being led by the king's own nephew. They found it difficult enough to get to Vikramaśilā, but when they got there they must have found it rather frustrating because they had difficulty meeting Atiśa. In fact, it seems that it took them two years to meet him. Sometimes people complain if they can't meet a monk or holy man within the next week, but these unfortunate people had to wait a couple of years, it seems, and even then they had to meet Atiśa secretly, because they didn't want the authorities of Vikramaśilā to know that their greatest scholar had been invited elsewhere.

But eventually they managed to find a way of meeting Atiśa personally, and they extended the invitation. In those days, if you invited a monk to visit your place or give lectures you had to give him a generous offering, and the delegation presented Atiśa with a large quantity of gold. We're told that Atiśa was deeply moved by the invitation. These people had come all the way from the Land of Snows, taking months to get there. Some members of the delegation had died along the way. But at last the survivors of the party had reached Vikramaśilā, and here they were, inviting him to visit Tibet. Atiśa was also greatly moved by their gift: not by the gold itself, but by the story of how it had come to be collected. It seems that Jñānaprabha had been fighting a war-like tribe on the borders of western Tibet, and he was captured. His captors can't have been very sympathetic to Buddhism, because they gave him a terrible choice. They said they were prepared to release him, but only on condition that he renounced his refuge in the Three Jewels. For Jñānaprabha, a devout Buddhist, that was an impossible condition, and he refused. So his captors set another condition: if your subjects can give us gold equivalent to your weight, we will release you. Word was conveyed to Jñānaprabha's nephew, who spent a number of years collecting gold from all over western Tibet. But even after all those years he still hadn't collected quite enough. He had collected enough to ransom the king's body but not enough to ransom his head. By the time Jñānaprabha heard this, he was quite old, so he sent a message to his nephew telling him not to bother to collect any more gold. His subjects had been sufficiently hard-pressed to raise all the gold collected so far. He said, 'Let me die in captivity. I am old and my time is nearly finished anyway. Use the gold to invite Atiśa to Tibet. In this way, though a captive, I will be of some service to the Dharma before I die.' This was the gold that was presented to Atiśa, who was deeply moved by Jñānaprabha's deep devotion to the Dharma and spirit of self-sacrifice. So Atiśa felt he had to take the invitation to visit Tibet seriously. These Tibetans seemed very sincere people, really committed to the Dharma and desirous of truer Buddhist teaching.

It seems that Atiśa didn't ask the other monks whether they thought he should go. He didn't even think about the matter in the ordinary sense. We're told that he consulted the bodhisattva Tārā. It seems that Atiśa had been devoted to Tārā since his childhood, and regarded her as his *yidam*, his *iṣṭa devatā*, his tutelary divinity. So, at this turning point in his life, he consulted her. We don't quite know how he established communication. There's more than one version of this important episode. But it seems he had a vision of Tārā and she spoke to him, or perhaps words were impressed upon his heart. And Tārā said, 'Accept the invitation, go to Tibet.' But she also said, 'If you go to Tibet your life will be shortened by twenty years.' So Atiśa accepted the invitation. After all, he took the bodhisattva ideal seriously. He couldn't leave at once – he had to hand over his responsibilities and get the permission of the head of the monastery – but eventually he left Vikramaśilā for western Tibet in 1040 CE. He was then 58 years of age.

Before we accompany him on his journey, I want to look at a few points. First of all, there's this question of his consulting Tārā. What does it mean to consult her, or any other bodhisattva? Who or what is Tārā? Tārā, like the other archetypal bodhisattvas, is a particular manifestation of the *dharmakāya* in an ideal human form, in this case a female form, so when we are in contact with Tārā, we are in contact with the *dharmakāya*, with the transcendental. This contact may take the form of a vision, as it did for Atiśa, or another form, but whatever form it takes, that contact affects us deeply. It may even transform us. After all, contact of that kind amounts to an insight experience, and that experience may throw light on our existing condition, and show us what we have to do next. But we have to be careful. It is easy to mistake our whims and fancies, our subjective imaginings, for the voice of Tārā. In Atiśa's case there was no such danger, and he could go ahead and do what Tārā advised him to do. But in our case there is a danger, so even if we have heard the voice of Tārā, we would be well advised to consult our spiritual friends and ask for their advice too. In the broadest sense, consulting Tārā, or any archetypal bodhisattva, means acting in accordance with our awareness of what is highest and best in us, and also beyond us. That is what Atiśa did. He decided to go to Tibet, even though going there would shorten his life by twenty years. Like Jñānaprabha, he was prepared to sacrifice his life, or a substantial portion of his life, for the sake of the Dharma. And that is the great test: are we willing to die for the Dharma, are we willing to die for the Three Jewels?

In this country we have no difficulty practising the Dharma if we want to. Here Buddhists are not persecuted or discriminated against. But if they were, how many of us, I wonder, would pass that test? It's a question we have to ask ourselves. One thing I do know is that you will be able to die for the Dharma if you have lived for the Dharma. Fortunately for us there are still people, even towards the end of this twentieth century, who live for the Dharma. Just a few days ago I was reminiscing to a few friends about two Indian Order members who lived for the Dharma: Shakyananda and Sanghasena. They lived for the Dharma, and they died for the Dharma. They were both old men when I ordained them quite a few years ago, and they both suffered from various ailments, especially Shakyananda. But that didn't stop them. Year after year they went from village to village and town to town, giving talks on Buddhism, encouraging people to practise the Dharma. Sanghasena was a small, quiet man, who operated in the northern part of Maharashtra, so he was known as the lion of the north, and Shakyananda, who was a very fat, jolly man – I used to call him the Buddhist Falstaff, except that he didn't have any of Falstaff's weaknesses – operated in the southern part of Maharashtra, so he was known as the lion of the south. Between them in a few years, perhaps six or seven, they must have covered a thousand villages and towns, bringing the Dharma to each and every one of them, and they both died in harness. One might say they both sacrificed their lives for the sake of the Dharma, except that they worked so hard and so happily. They didn't get burned out or anything like that. They loved their work, they were joyful despite their ailments, and they communicated that joy in the Dharma to thousands of people. If they hadn't worked so hard, they might have lived a few more years. They weren't great scholars, in fact they weren't scholars at all, but they were living embodiments of compassion and energy, and in my opinion worthy successors in spirit of Jñānaprabha and Atiśa, and examples to us all. I would like them to be remembered, which is why I'm mentioning them at this point.

But it's time we returned to Atiśa and his journey. It took him two years to reach the Nari region of western Tibet, partly because on the way he spent a whole year in Nepal. We know the route he followed, and we know that he made the first half of his journey on the back of an elephant – presumably supplied by the king – and the second half on horseback. He was accompanied by about thirty people, including monks and translators, and we know quite a lot about his journey, but I'm not going to say much about it, because I want to get him to Tibet as quickly as possible. I'll just outline the route he followed, in case anybody feels like following in his footsteps, which wouldn't be difficult to do. From Vikramaśilā he went to Bodh Gaya, where he made offerings and paid his respects to the *vajrāsana*, the site of the Buddha's Enlightenment. Then he went up into Nepal, into the Kathmandu Valley, to the Swayambhunath *caitya* or stupa, which is still there, on the outskirts of the present-day Kathmandu. From there he proceeded in a westerly direction and eventually he arrived in Palpa in western Nepal. As I mention in my memoirs, in 1950 I spent some time in Palpa. In Atiśa's time it was the capital of Nepal, but when I visited it, it wasn't much more than an overgrown village.[389] There Atiśa stayed for quite a while, writing books and building and endowing a large monastery with the king's help. From Palpa the party made its way to Lake Manasarovar, whose magical beauty is wonderfully described in Lama Govinda's *Way of the White Clouds*.[390] Atiśa was now in Tibet, and from the famous lake he travelled to Thon, and from Thon to the Ngari area of western Tibet. He was given a splendid reception by the local rulers and accommodated in the Tholing Monastery, and this was his headquarters for the next three years, years which were of crucial importance for the success of his mission. During that time he met Rinchen Zangpo, the greatest Tibetan scholar of the day; he composed his most important and influential work; and he met the man who became his chief Tibetan disciple.

Before dealing with these major events I want to mention a minor one, by way of light relief. When Atiśa reached the Tibetan border, he was received by a delegation of local rulers who made him welcome, offering him a drink in a beautiful porcelain cup with dragons on it. Atiśa asked, 'What's this delicious drink?' and one of the translators told him it was called *chai* – tea. Of course it was Tibetan tea, prepared with salt and butter, but Atiśa seems to have taken to it, and according to Tibetan sources he even composed a poem in praise of tea. But let us go back to the main story, and his meeting with Rinchen Zangpo.

Rinchen Zangpo was a great scholar. He'd studied the Dharma in India, in fact he'd made three trips there. He had translated many Sanskrit texts into Tibetan, mainly Perfection of Wisdom or Prajñāpāramitā texts, and many, many tantras. He's still referred to as 'the great translator'. He had also founded many temples and monasteries, not only in western Tibet but also in what is now Ladakh and other parts of north-western India. At the time of Atiśa's arrival in Ngari, Rinchen Zangpo was 85 years old, even older than Atiśa. He was a distinguished person, and a member of the religious establishment, and at first, perhaps not surprisingly, he treated Atiśa with a certain amount of reserve. Until Atiśa's arrival he'd been the leading Buddhist monk in the area. But thanks to Atiśa's diplomatic and genuinely Buddhist behaviour, Rinchen Zangpo was won over. He invited Atiśa to come and stay with him for a while at his monastery, and Atiśa went, maybe with some of his disciples. He found that this monastery was large and beautiful, with many images of Buddhas and bodhisattvas arranged in different chapels. On his arrival, Atiśa went round all these chapels, escorted by Rinchen Zangpo, and paused for a few minutes in front of each image, whether of Tārā, Avalokiteśvara, Śākyamuni, Sitātapatrā, or Mañjughoṣa. There must have been hundreds of them, and before each he stopped and recited a Sanskrit verse in praise of that Buddha or bodhisattva. Rinchen Zangpo, who hadn't heard these verses before, thought they were beautiful, and wondered where Atiśa had learned them, so when they had finished their tour, he said, 'Excuse me, but what *ślokas* were you chanting? Where did you learn them? When were they composed?' Atiśa said, 'Well, I composed them on the spot.' This shows not only his great devotion, but his great skill in the spontaneous production of poetry in Sanskrit *śloka* form. So, Rinchen Zangpo began to have a great respect for Atiśa.

The next incident is not easy to explain; there are different accounts and interpretations of what happened. It seems that Rinchen Zangpo used to get up very early in the morning and practise Tantric meditation: *sādhanas* of different Buddhas and bodhisattvas, various mandalas, and so on. One morning Atiśa asked him how he practised, and Rinchen Zangpo replied that he practised all those different *sādhanas* one after the other, as though one had to be added to the others in order to produce the total effect. He was under the impression, so far as we can understand, that they were essentially different from one another. But Atiśa disagreed, and explained that all the different *sādhanas* should be practised together, and that one practised them together by practising any one of them deeply, for in principle all *sādhanas* were the same. There was no question of finishing with Tārā and then going on to Mañjughoṣa, as though there was something in the Mañjughoṣa *sādhana* that was not in the Tārā *sādhana*. He explained that what you encounter in the depth of your practice of a particular *sādhana*, you also encounter in the depth of the practice of any other *sādhana*. So in a sense you need to practise only one *sādhana*. You don't have to collect *sādhanas*, as though it is only the totality of all the *sādhanas* considered separately that will help you to achieve what you want to achieve through the Tantric path. Rinchen Zangpo was greatly impressed by this explanation and he felt more respect than ever for Atiśa, and thereafter he helped him with his translation work. When Atiśa left Ngari, Rinchen Zangpo shut himself up in his room and devoted himself entirely to the practice of meditation as explained by Atiśa. He did this for ten years, and it is said that eventually he attained Enlightenment. By that time he was nearly a hundred, which shows that one is never too old to learn.

Before leaving the Ngari area, Atiśa composed his most important and influential work, the *Bodhipathapradīpa* or *Lamp for the Path to Enlightenment*, and also his commentary on that work.[391] The original text consists of sixty-eight verses divided into two parts, the first dealing with the Mahāyāna and the second with the Mantrayāna or Vajrayāna. The first part is much longer than the second, which suggests that Atiśa was concerned not to emphasize the Vajrayāna. We must remember that at that time Tibet was overrun by freelance Tantric teachers from India, some of whom had given the Tantra a very bad name. Atiśa was concerned to emphasize ethical and spiritual values, and the Mahāyāna – the bodhisattva ideal, the development of the *bodhicitta*, the practice of the *pāramitās* and so on – and he tended to play down the Tantra, though he couldn't ignore it completely. After all, he'd practised it himself in his youth, and at that time it was believed that the tantras were *Buddhavacana*, the word of the Buddha, in other words that they had been taught by the Buddha himself, though not necessarily in his human form. So Atiśa was in rather a quandary. He couldn't accept the tantras wholeheartedly, but he couldn't reject them, so it seems he simply played them down. Today we know that the tantras were not literally taught by the Buddha Śākyamuni, the historical Buddha. We know that they came into existence many hundreds of years later, and that some of them contain many non-Buddhist features or elements, so we're free to reject whatever in them is not in accordance with the fundamental principles of Buddhism.

Some Tibetan commentators maintain that Atiśa played down the tantras as a result of the influence of Dromtön, his chief Tibetan disciple. As a Tibetan, Dromtön was no doubt well aware of the damage that had been done to the Dharma in Tibet as a result of wrong Tantric teaching. This brings us to Dromtön himself. In a way it's remarkable that although Dromtön was Atiśa's chief disciple, and although he subsequently became the founder of the Kadam school based on Atiśa's teaching, he never became a monk, but remained a layman. But he was very highly respected, and a man of deep spiritual realization. He seems to have met Atiśa just as he was about to leave or perhaps had just left Ngari to go back to India, having spent three years in Tibet. Dromtön persuaded Atiśa to visit central Tibet. In any case, the road back to India was blocked at the time as there was a war going on. Atiśa therefore spent ten years in central Tibet, in the Lhasa area, and visited Samye, the oldest monastery in Tibet, which had been founded in the eighth century by Śāntarakṣita and Padmasambhava. In this ancient monastery Atiśa found copies of Sanskrit Buddhist texts that were no longer available in India – further evidence of the extent to which Buddhism had already declined in the land of its birth. Wherever he went, Atiśa gave teachings, composed books, and translated texts from Sanskrit into Tibetan with the help of his interpreters. In his personal teaching he placed particular emphasis on Going for Refuge to the Three Jewels, and he is often known as the Refuge Lama because he placed such emphasis on that supremely important act of the Buddhist life. He also encouraged the practice of the ten precepts and the development of the *bodhicitta*, including the development of *mettā* and *karuṇā* as the basis of the development of the *bodhicitta*. In addition to these practices he encouraged the worship of four holy persons: Śākyamuni the Buddha, Avalokiteśvara, Tārā, and Acala. Acala means 'Immovable One', and he's an aspect of Vairocana, the Buddha of the centre of the mandala, in wrathful bodhisattva form. He's very popular in Japanese Buddhism, where he is known as Fudō, and he is represented as a wrathful, muscular, almost angry figure, carrying a noose or lasso and a sword and attended by two small acolytes.

Atiśa spent his last days in Nyetang, south of Lhasa, and died there in 1054, aged 73. It's said that his tomb can still be seen there, or at least it could until recently. Before his passing away Atiśa appointed Dromtön as his successor. From existing sources we get a definite impression of Atiśa's character. Although he was a great scholar and a man of great spiritual attainment, it's clear that he was very modest and unpretentious. He had a charismatic personality, as we say nowadays, but I get the impression that the charisma was of a mild and gentle persuasive kind. It seems from all accounts that he was exceptionally kind and compassionate. He had a great love of animals. He was courteous, mild, gentle in speech and in behaviour. But above all he was characterized by a tremendous spirit of self-sacrifice. He did indeed give his life for the Dharma.

Dromtön lived for nine years after Atiśa's death. He too was an extraordinary person. He kept Atiśa's disciples together, he preserved his teachings, and he founded Reting Monastery near Lhasa to act as a spiritual centre for the movement of spiritual regeneration inaugurated by Atiśa. There he began what became known as the Kadam school of Tibetan Buddhism, which was firmly based on Atiśa's teaching and example. It was called the Kadam school because it was based on the word – *ka* in Tibetan, *vacana* in Sanskrit – of the Buddha; that is, it was based on the teachings of the Buddha as contained in the scriptures. Like Atiśa, the Kadam school accepted all the scriptures, both Hīnayāna and Mahāyāna, and drew inspiration and guidance from them all. The attitude of the Kadam school was thus ecumenical or non-sectarian. It paid particular attention to six non-canonical works, six *śāstras* as they are called. There were two by Asaṅga, the *Yogācārabhūmi* and the *Mahāyāna Sūtrālaṃkāra Kārikā*; and two by Śāntideva, the *Śikṣā-samuccaya* and the *Bodhicaryāvatāra*; and the other two works to which the school gave particular attention were the *Jātakas*, which recount the stories of the Buddha's previous lives, and the *Udānavarga*, an anthology roughly corresponding to the Pāli *Dhammapada*. Naturally the Kadam school also studied Atiśa's own writings, especially the *Bodhipathapradīpa*. Three centuries later the Kadam school became the basis for Tsongkhapa's Gelug school, which is also known as the New Kadampa school, and became the dominant school of Tibetan Buddhism, to which the Dalai Lamas belong. There's no time to go into all that this evening. But we've seen something of the state of Buddhism in India and Tibet in the tenth and eleventh centuries, and something of the life and work of a very great Buddhist of that period. We've appreciated how fortunate we are today to have such easy access to the Dharma in all its forms, and how important it is that we should follow the path of regular steps, and make full use of our spiritual opportunities. So let us rejoice in the merits of Atiśa, let us be thankful for the example he has given us, and let us try to imbibe a little of his spirit of self-sacrifice. Let us too try to give, in our own measure, a life for the Dharma.

COMMUNICATING THE DHARMA

International Chairmen's Event, Padmaloka 1999

It's quite a long time since I was last in Norfolk, this beautiful county, and I don't like to think how long it is since I was last at Padmaloka, but today I've been walking around and refreshing my memory of this auspicious place. I'm very happy to see all the improvements that have been made and are in the process of being made. At lunch, looking around at everybody present, it occurred to me that not so many years ago there were not as many Order members in existence as we now have chairmen and chairwomen. At the very first Order convention, there were twenty-seven of us assembled in the front room at Aryatara.[392] Well, you certainly couldn't get the Order into the front room at Aryatara now. We have grown, we have developed, and we have been communicating the Dharma. I must admit that when the organizers of this event wrote to me inviting me to speak to you on this theme, I was a bit surprised. I thought, 'Well, surely they know by this time. Haven't they been doing it all these years? And haven't I, in any case, said quite a lot in one way or another about communicating the Dharma?' I'm not sure I have anything new to say, so perhaps my talk will be more of a reminder than imparting any new information.

I assumed that I was being invited to speak on the subject of communicating the Dharma verbally, although the Dharma can be communicated in all sorts of other ways, for example through visual images – Buddha and bodhisattva figures represented in thangkas and embodied in sculptures, and also the wheel of life. You also communicate the

Dharma, and you certainly reinforce your written or spoken word, through your living personal example. Years ago someone who had been on one of the London Buddhist Centre's winter retreats told me that what had impressed them most was not the talks, wonderful though they were, nor the meditation, inspiring though they'd found it, but the harmonious manner in which the members of the team had worked together to run the retreat. The team was communicating the Dharma just by running the retreat in such a harmonious way, living and working just like those famous Anuruddhas whose lives we sometimes study.[393] So the Dharma is not communicated only through words, but that is what I am going to take this topic to mean this evening. I'm not going to give a lecture, just another of my sets of fifteen points.

1. KNOW YOUR SUBJECT

This may seem obvious, and it is, but what does knowing your subject mean? It certainly doesn't mean swotting it up at the last minute for the purpose of the talk you are going to be giving. When people ask me how long it takes me to prepare a talk, I sometimes say it takes a lifetime. I'm reminded of a little anecdote from the biography of the painter James Whistler. He was asked in a famous court case, in which he sued John Ruskin and was awarded £1,000 in damages, how long it had taken him to paint a certain picture, for which he was asking 200 guineas – a lot of money in those days. He said, 'It took me two days.' So the opposing counsel said, 'You mean you're asking 200 guineas for the work of two days?' 'No,' he said, 'I'm asking it for the experience of a lifetime.'[394] The experience of a lifetime had gone into painting that picture even though it took him only two days to paint it. In much the same way, some of the talks I've given have grown out of reflections that I've been considering for many years. It's not that I suddenly think of talking about this or that. It's the culmination of a long process of reflection, and when my reflections come to a certain point and an opportunity offers itself, I give a talk. Choose a subject that you have been reflecting on for some time, so that when you come to give the talk it is just the culmination of that process.

But it is not enough just to know your subject. You also need to love it, or even be in love with it, and want to talk about it out of the abundance of that love. You know that when you are in love you want to talk about it with someone, at least with your best friend. You want to tell them what you feel, how wonderful he or she is, because you are just bursting with those emotions. Well, you should feel the same way about the Dharma. You should be enamoured of the subject, as well as knowing about it. Of course, when you are in love you don't necessarily know the other person, so the analogy is not quite complete, but you see what I'm getting at. It is not enough to know something about the subject of your talk; you must have enthusiasm for it and be able to communicate that. So know your subject, love your subject.

2. PREPARE

This second point may seem to contradict the first one, but it does so only superficially. Even though you know and love your subject, don't be overconfident. Prepare well, look up references, make notes, and don't rely on last-minute inspiration. Otherwise, you may find yourself at a loss for words and simply go rambling on, and it will be obvious to everybody that you haven't prepared, which will be very sad and disappointing. However well you know the subject, sit down beforehand, give yourself sufficient time, and make notes. Even write the talk out if you think it necessary, but do prepare. Give the audience, and the subject, that degree of respect.

3. DON'T CONCEAL YOUR IGNORANCE

Don't pretend that you know what you don't know, don't try to bluff. Audiences aren't stupid, even though sometimes they might look it. Some members of the audience will be able to see through your bluff and they won't be impressed. If there are things you don't know, make it clear that you are a bit tentative about this or that, or haven't fully gone into something else. With regard to the talk as a whole, you should be sufficiently knowledgeable. Often people try to bluff for the same reason that they rely, unwisely, on last-minute inspiration: because they haven't prepared very well, or even at all. Don't try to pull the wool over the eyes of your audience.

4. KNOW YOUR AUDIENCE

If you are giving a talk at the Buddhist centre, you will usually know your audience, and you will adjust your talk accordingly, but if you are invited to give a talk to some other Buddhist group or to a class in a school or college, or a women's institute or something of that sort, try to find out something about them in advance. Find out whether they have had a Buddhist speaker before, what is likely to be their level of knowledge about Buddhism, what their misunderstandings are likely to be. Do a little research, especially when you are trying to communicate the Dharma to a group of people outside the FWBO, and prepare your talk accordingly. This is quite important because otherwise you might prepare a talk that is beyond the understanding of the people that you are addressing, or it may fall below their level of understanding, and in both cases that will be disappointing.

It is sometimes a good idea to stand for a minute or two before you start speaking and just look at your audience. Who's there? What are they like? Old or young? Smart? Quiet-looking or otherwise? Are they attentive, or do they look a bit bored already? At least some of them will be aware of you looking at them, and that will establish a rapport between you. What sometimes happens is that a speaker is a bit nervous and they come up to the lectern and just start speaking, not even looking at the audience. That is not how to communicate the Dharma or anything else. You should be very aware of the people to whom you are speaking throughout the talk. One of the disadvantages of reading your talk, and I've suffered from this myself, is that it is difficult to keep one eye on the audience and another eye on your notes, but if you are reading your talk, at least lift up your head and look at your audience from time to time. Many years ago in India I had the experience of hearing a very distinguished Buddhist giving a talk to a very distinguished gathering. He held his text low down in front of him and mumbled his lecture, never once looking at the audience. What he had to say was quite important, but most people didn't even hear it.

Keep as much eye contact with the audience as possible, and be prepared to vary your talk a little if you see signs of restlessness, because clearly you've got to get their attention again. Within the FWBO people are usually quite polite, but if it's a public lecture, people may just get up and walk out. People used to walk out of my lectures in London years ago, usually when I had something not very appreciative to say about Christianity. If you notice someone walking out, you may realize the reason, and you may need to adjust your talk accordingly. If you just need to get the attention of a restless audience, very often, people being what they are, you can get it with a story or a joke. It is not always easy to produce the right anecdote or the appropriate joke when you need it, but have a stock of them up your sleeve for use in emergencies.

You may think that it is not easy to keep in touch with a big audience, but I can assure you it is, if you go the right way about it. If there are thousands of them, you can't maintain eye contact with all of them, but when there's a very large gathering there's usually some empathy between the audience members which can help with maintaining contact between you and the people to whom you are speaking.

5. BE GENUINE

Don't put on an act. Some people are born actors but that's not really the way to communicate the Dharma. Recently I was in Germany and visited some of Lama Govinda's disciples, especially Advayavajra, who is the leader of the main Arya Maitreya Mandala group.[395] They were talking about the different Western teachers who had been functioning in Germany, and they mentioned one who came onto the stage to give his talk while he was still shaving. It wasn't clear whether he wanted to convey that he was such a busy and popular man that he didn't even have time to shave before coming onto the stage, or whether it was a gimmick. One must be wary about putting on an act, though it sometimes attracts people's attention. Sometimes speakers do it in less obtrusive ways. Sometimes out of shyness or embarrassment, they are not able to be themselves. I don't mean that you should 'be yourself' in the current sense, which usually means not being yourself at all, but putting on some kind of act of 'being yourself', being pseudo-spontaneous and natural and all the rest of it. Just be yourself in the authentic sense. Don't try to put on some kind of act to impress people. You shouldn't need to make an effort to be yourself. Just be yourself and it should be easy. Of course, on another level, one might ask what is this 'self'? It's a good question, and I ask it because I've brought a bit of work with me, a book that I have undertaken to review for the *Times Higher Education Supplement*. It's an interdisciplinary study of the self, about twenty papers by distinguished people from neurologists to theologians. I've got to read it and think of something to say about it in 1,500 words.[396] So yes, the self is perhaps not a simple subject after all. When I say, 'Be yourself,' you might say, 'What self?' – but that's another question altogether.

6. COMMUNICATE THE DHARMA

This may seem very obvious, but I'll say it anyway. The aim is to communicate the Dharma, not yourself or your pet ideas and theories. You should not be concerned with communicating the Dharma in 'your' way. Sometimes people think, 'Well, I've got my own way of communicating the Dharma.' There's a slogan the advertisers use: 'Let's do it your way.' But that's not the Dharmic attitude. You shouldn't think in terms of trying to put yourself across as a communicator of the Dharma. You yourself will come across, for better or for worse you will make an impression, but the less impression you make, and the greater the impression the Dharma makes, the better. You should be transparent, a medium for the Dharma. Your mind should be on the Dharma, your heart should be with the Dharma, not on yourself or your special, individual way of communicating it.

7. AVOID FASHIONABLE TERMINOLOGY

Avoid slang. Don't try to be 'with it'. Don't be like one of those vicars who try to put the gospel across by jumping around with the young people to show that they are still young at heart. Apparently it just doesn't work, because it isn't credible. Don't try to spice your communication of the Dharma with fashionable terminology, or any kind of wrong speech. I probably shouldn't have to say this, but don't use harsh or indecent language in your communication of the Dharma. Don't try to show how up to date or streetwise you are. Just think in terms of communicating the Dharma in a way that will be accessible to the people in front of you.

8. DRESS APPROPRIATELY

This may seem quite a minor point, but you have to think about the situation you're going to be in. Is it a Rotary Club? Is it a school? Is it another Buddhist group? Dress appropriately for the occasion, and however you dress, whether formally or informally, don't be sloppy. Even if you are going to address a convention of bikers, at least be neat and tidy. You don't have to be like them to communicate with them. If you look sloppy and careless, that communicates an impression of unmindfulness, that you don't care about yourself or the impression you make, and that will subtly affect your communication of the Dharma. Give some attention to your personal appearance. You don't have to tart yourself up, but be presentable.

9. WATCH YOUR GESTURES

I'm afraid that both live and on video I've seen Order members with their arms flailing around. I've seen people twiddling with buttons, fiddling with pencils, and even fiddling with their kesa. It looks dreadful, especially if you are talking about mindfulness and you yourself are plainly an embodiment of the very opposite. It doesn't go down well, it doesn't convince people, it's not in keeping. Use appropriate gestures, but do it with intention, don't let it just happen, so that you just don't know what your arms or your legs or your head are doing while you are speaking. It creates a very negative impression, especially if you speak to other Buddhist groups where mindfulness is emphasized. I did hear that at least one Buddhist group had the impression that members of the Western Buddhist Order were very unmindful. I suspect that someone had been to speak to their group and had been quite unmindful with regard to their gestures or general demeanour. Try not to laugh at your own jokes, at least not immoderately. And watch your posture. Don't try to be over-casual, that's just putting on an act. Don't walk around while you're talking. Be aware of the tone of your voice. Sometimes your subject matter might make it appropriate to raise your voice or lower it to a whisper. But above all, watch your gestures; it's a form of mindfulness of the body.

10. DON'T TALK DOWN TO PEOPLE

If you talk down to your audience it means you haven't found out enough about them, and you're not aware of them. Even if you are talking to children, be very careful not to talk down to them. Years ago I spent a lot of time among the newly converted disciples of Dr Ambedkar, and some of my fellow monks definitely used to talk down to them in the sense that they would only talk about the five precepts, thinking that their audience weren't very well educated so they needed something simple. But especially if I'd given two or three lectures in a particular place, I made a point of going into points of Buddhist philosophy. I used to talk about the Buddhist conception of Nirvāṇa, what we mean by *anattā*, even *pratītya-samutpāda*, to people who were virtually illiterate, because I realized that intelligence has very little to do with formal education. If you put things in the right way, if you are clear in your own mind about these topics and you communicate clearly, less educated people can understand at least something of what you are saying. Never talk down to your audience, whatever their age, and whatever their standard of education. Of course, be careful that you don't say things that go above their heads. You can say a few things, perhaps, that are beyond their understanding, as a reminder that you don't, and they don't, understand everything about Buddhism. But the bulk of what you say must be serious and intelligible to them and deal with fundamentals, and above all, not be condescending in any way.

11. DON'T BE APOLOGETIC

If you are going to talk about the Noble Eightfold Path don't start by saying, 'I don't know much about the Noble Eightfold Path; I haven't studied it very much.' People might wonder why you are talking about it in that case. I sometimes wonder why people feel it necessary to be apologetic. It's a sort of false humility, perhaps. Don't brag about your knowledge, but don't be apologetic either. Have confidence. You've studied the Dharma, you've reflected upon this subject, so you don't need to be apologetic. At the same time your presentation can be modest – modestly confident or confidently modest.

12. BE AWARE OF THE OCCASION

Perhaps this applies most to talks given within the context of the FWBO. If you've been asked to speak at a Wesak celebration, say something about Wesak, something about the Buddha's Enlightenment and its significance. Don't go off on some interesting spiel on an unrelated topic.

Similarly, if you are invited to speak at somebody's funeral, say something about that person, something about impermanence, something about death. You might think this is obvious, but I heard not so long ago that someone gave a talk at a centre and after the talk, whoever was giving the vote of thanks proceeded to speak about something that had no connection whatever with the topic of the talk. Consider the occasion and speak appropriately, in a tone and with emotions appropriate to the occasion. In the case of Wesak, obviously you can speak in a joyful way, while if it's Parinirvana Day, a more solemn tone is appropriate. If you are giving a little talk on the occasion of the name-giving of somebody's baby, be joyful and celebratory, because this new little being has come into the world and may grow up to be a good human being, perhaps even a Buddhist, even an Order member. And similarly, if it's someone's birthday party, you don't want to be the skeleton at the feast, however appropriate skeletons may be on other occasions. I am sometimes surprised by the extent to which people are not mindful of the occasion and therefore don't speak appropriately.

13. BE SYSTEMATIC

Have a structure. Give your talk a definite beginning, middle, and end. It need not have an obvious structure, but its shape must be clear in your own mind. There must at least be an introductory bit, a substantial bit in the middle, and a winding up at the end. A well-written story gives a sense of satisfaction because it's whole, it has a beginning, a middle, and an end. There are stories which are very cleverly written and don't follow that formula, but you need to be a genius to be able to pull that off. In the same way, it's possible to give a talk that doesn't have a definite structure and at the same time is very satisfactory, but you need to be very experienced and something of a genius to be able to do that, so I wouldn't recommend it. If your talk doesn't have a structure, even though you may be quite knowledgeable about the subject, you may ramble a lot because you have lost the thread.

14. DON'T BE AFRAID OF REPEATING YOURSELF

The old saying is that when you give a speech, you should first of all tell the audience what you are going to tell them, then you tell them, then you tell them what you've told them. The point is that people don't take everything in the first time. I talked a while ago about being aware of your audience. With experience you can see when someone's thoughts are wandering; it's evident from their posture, their expression, and sometimes even the movement of their eyes. They're going to miss part of your talk, or even great chunks of it, while they're wool-gathering. They may miss more than they take in. So don't be afraid to repeat yourself. You don't have to repeat everything, but perhaps at the end there should be a little summary of the points that you want people to take away with them. If it's a long and complex talk containing a lot of material, the chances are that what people will take away with them will either be a story or the last few things you said. If you give them a little warning that you are near the end of your talk, they will start perking up and listening, knowing that it's going to come to an end soon. Then you can reiterate your main points. Sometimes you need to do that, so don't be afraid of repeating yourself.

That is, don't be afraid of repeating yourself intentionally. Sometimes people repeat themselves like the needle on an old-fashioned gramophone, saying the same few words over and over again because they can't think of what to say next. I remember some painful experiences of this sort in India, especially with the politicians. They usually didn't know anything about the Dharma, but they would insist on chairing my talks. Once in Agra I'd given a talk and the person chairing had to say something, so he said, 'What we really need to do is to publish little books on Buddhism, little pamphlets ... little pamphlets, publish little pamphlets on Buddhism ... little pamphlets, we need to publish little pamphlets on Buddhism.' He just couldn't get further than this, and then he had to sit down. So repeat yourself, but do it intentionally, and let the repetitions have a definite place in the structure of your talk.

15. SPEAK CLEARLY

Project your voice. If you are inexperienced, station a friend at the back of the hall and ask him to signal if he can't hear you properly. Enunciate clearly, don't mumble, speak in such a way that the people can understand every word you say. You may have to iron out your pronunciation a bit, or even your accent, but you should be prepared to do that in the interest of communicating the Dharma effectively.

You shouldn't be too concerned about preserving your individual way of speaking. Concentrate on communicating the Dharma. That's why you're speaking. It may even be necessary to take elocution lessons. It is also important to pronounce words correctly. You might not want to use too many Pāli or Sanskrit words, depending on the nature of your audience, but if you do use them, take the trouble to find out the correct pronunciation, as well as the correct pronunciation of words in your own language. And don't drawl, or speak in an affected manner, or anything of that sort.

LOOKING AHEAD A LITTLE WAY

Combined Order Convention, Wymondham College, 1999

Dharmacāris and *dharmacāriṇīs*: I've been here at Wymondham College on the Order convention with the *dharmacāriṇīs* for the last ten days, and I must say it has been an exceptionally positive experience. I believe I've had lunch or dinner with some 156 *dharmacāriṇīs*, which is one of the advantages of being the founder of a spiritual movement. I've seen a couple of dozen of them individually too. Apart from that I didn't do very much with them, apart from reading some poems, but as I was getting on with my own work, I was aware of them meditating and studying and doing their prostration practice and their *kalyāṇa mitra yoga*, and I was very conscious of the positive, serene, and happy atmosphere that was generated. I think that the *dharmacāris* are very fortunate to have been able to come into that atmosphere.

So for the last ten days I've been living in quite another world. I haven't seen a newspaper, and I haven't listened to the radio, so that outside world has seemed rather remote, even a little dream-like. But I do have some recollection of things that were going on before I came here and no doubt are still going on. I have been very aware of certain issues that are in people's minds, here in Britain and in other parts of the world. And one of the things I've been conscious of is that people are preparing to celebrate the millennium, the two thousandth anniversary of the alleged birth of Jesus Christ. (I say alleged because even those who believe he existed seem now to accept that he was born at least four years before the conventionally accepted date.)

Although we're aware of all this going on, I think it's important that we as Buddhists don't allow ourselves to be carried away by the hype. This millennium is not our millennium. I'm not saying that you shouldn't go to see that famous dome on which so much energy, time, skill, and money has been expended, and in any case the exhibitions within the dome will be by no means entirely Christian. Some Christians have in fact complained vociferously that Christianity has not been allocated sufficient space. It seems they're being squeezed into some little corner of a multifaith exhibition and they're not very happy about that. One can understand it – it is after all their millennium.[397] We Buddhists celebrated a half millennium of our own more than forty years ago, May 1956 to May 1957: 2,500 years of Buddhism. I was in India at that time and took part in the celebrations, and even helped to organize some of them. It was a very colourful and emotional year for all Buddhists.[398]

Christians see the birth of Jesus Christ as a turning point in history, and conventionally history is divided into what happened BC and AD, though non-Christian historians have suggested that if there is to be any such distinction then it should be expressed as 'Common Era' and 'Before Common Era'. Moreover, scholars have suggested that if there is a turning point in history it's to be found not in one particular year but in a whole period, in the years centring around 500 BCE, the period from about 800 to 200 years BCE which has been termed the Axial Age. According to the German philosopher Karl Jaspers, in those years the spiritual foundations of humanity were laid, simultaneously and independently, in China, India, Persia, Palestine, and Greece. It was the age of the great Individuals, with a capital I: the age of Confucius and Isaiah, Socrates and Plato, the Upanishadic sages and the Greek tragic poets. And most importantly for Buddhists, it was the age of the Buddha.[399]

Buddhists certainly see the appearance of the Buddha on the stage of history as a turning point, but not in the same way that Christians see the appearance of Christ. For Christians, Christ is absolutely unique. He is the incarnate *logos*, the incarnate son of God, and his sacrificial death on the cross is the central event in the history of the whole world. That history, according to Christian tradition, began with the Creation and will end with the Last Judgement, when the trumpet will sound in the heavens and the entire human race will be summoned before the throne of God to be judged by Christ. For Buddhists, however, the

Buddha is not absolutely unique. He is *relatively* unique, if one can use such an expression, in the sense that he is unique within a certain world period. According to Buddhist tradition there have been other Buddhas before him and there will be other Buddhas after him in future world periods. A Buddha is one who rediscovers the path to Enlightenment after it has been lost to humanity.

Christianity and Buddhism thus have two different visions of history. The Christian vision is linear. It begins with Creation and the Fall of Man, reaches its climax in the life and death of Christ, and ends with the Last Judgement. Before the Creation and after the Last Judgement there is only eternity. This linear vision has dominated Western thought since the rise of Christianity, and in modern times it finds expression in Marxism, which has been described, from a certain point of view, as a secularized version of the Christian linear vision of history. This underlies modern notions of the indefinite progress of the human race, but certain happenings in the twentieth century have rather undermined that idea. We are less confident now than we were a hundred years ago that the history of humanity is a history of uninterrupted progress on all fronts. We realize now that there can be a falling back to an earlier, more primitive, less civilized state of development. For Islam too, history is a single story, with a definite beginning and a definite end. Its climax is not the life of Jesus Christ, even though Muslims do have the greatest respect for Jesus, short of recognizing him as the incarnate son of God. For Muslims the climax of the historical process is the life of Mohammed and the revelation of the Koran, 600 years after the appearance of Christ, and Mohammed's departure from Mecca to Medina in 622 CE. Of course, both the Christian and the Muslim visions of history have roots in Judaism. One may therefore speak of the linear vision of history as the Semitic vision. It is the vision common to all three Abrahamic faiths, Judaism, Christianity, and Islam, as well as to Marxism and much of modern thought.

Buddhism, by contrast, sees history as proceeding not in a straight or single line, but in a series of cycles. Within each of these cycles there is a process of growth, maturity, and decay, and this cyclical process Buddhism sees as applying not only to human history but to the whole world, in fact to the whole universe, to the whole of phenomenal existence, or to what Buddhists traditionally call *saṃsāra*. It has a vision of phenomenal existence as being like a great ocean without beginning and without end, without boundaries. Upon this infinite ocean, millions upon millions of waves are constantly rising and falling, and these waves are universes or worlds. And upon these waves that are universes, there are millions upon millions of smaller waves. These waves are civilizations, or empires or religions or nations or individuals, and these too are constantly rising and falling, undergoing the process of growth, maturity, and decay.

Christianity and Islam both see themselves as continuing triumphantly to the end of time, to the Last Judgement. Judaism sees itself as continuing until the coming of the Messiah. Buddhism, however, sees itself as subject to the same cyclical process as everything else. Buddhism too, as an organized religion, is born, develops, matures, declines, and dies. Many Buddhist texts purport to predict this decline,[400] and indeed in many parts of the Buddhist world it has come to pass. It happened centuries ago in central Asia, India, and Indonesia, which once had thriving Buddhist cultures and civilizations. In all these areas Buddhism has passed through the complete cycle. In more recent times Buddhism has seriously declined in China and Tibet, and elsewhere in the East to an extent. In the Buddhist East as a whole, Buddhism has been in decline for at least a thousand years, which is a sobering thought. Individual Buddhists, and even small groups of Buddhists, may have pursued the path even to Enlightenment here and there, but there have been fewer and fewer such individuals and groups, and Buddhism has had for centuries less and less influence on the surrounding civilization and culture.

But the cyclical process is complex. There are waves upon waves, cycles within cycles, and upon the back of a larger wave that is falling there may be a smaller wave that is rising. Within an overall cycle of decay, there may be a cycle of growth. Within declining Buddhism we see arising movements of revival and reform, usually associated with the life and work of an outstanding individual. In Tibet we had the outstanding achievement of Atiśa, the founder of the Kadampa tradition. In Japan there was Hakuin, the revitalizer of Rinzai Zen. In more recent times in China there was the remarkable figure of the abbot Taixu, who did so much for the revival of Buddhism in that country after the collapse of the Manchu dynasty that he is known to Chinese Buddhists as Bodhisattva Taixu.

During the twentieth century, Buddhism has been on the whole in decline. We all know what has happened in China and in Tibet, where it has been openly attacked by the forces of militant Marxism. Elsewhere in the East it has been undermined by industrialization and urbanization, and weakened by the inroads of Christianity and Islam, to such an extent that some of the Buddhist leaders in some of the traditionally Buddhist countries have become seriously alarmed. Thus, the wave of Buddhism in the world on the whole has been falling. But there are smaller waves, some of them very small indeed, that are rising, and I believe two of those waves are of particular significance. One of them has arisen in India, where Buddhism had been virtually dead for nearly a thousand years, and the other has arisen in the West, where Buddhism was unknown until very recently. The FWBO is part of that wave. It is also part of the wave that has arisen in India, where it is known as the TBMSG. One could say also that these two waves are made up of a multitude of smaller waves, and the FWBO/TBMSG is itself made up of hundreds, even thousands of waves: the different chapters, city centres, country retreat centres, communities, team-based right livelihood businesses, choirs, and so on. There are even the individual Order members, Mitras, and Friends, all of whom are, I trust, undergoing on the whole a process of growth and upward development, making some progress up the spiral path. That progress will be made by their consciousness, their *citta* for want of a better term, even if their physical body is in a process of decline. If that is the case, and it will be the case sooner or later for all of us, our attitude should be that of the poet William Butler Yeats, who says:

> An aged man is but a paltry thing,
> A tattered coat upon a stick, unless
> Soul clap its hands and sing, and louder sing
> For every tatter in its mortal dress.[401]

As Buddhists, as men and women who have gone for Refuge to the Three Jewels, we have every reason to clap our hands and sing, both literally and metaphorically, whatever the state of our mortal dress. But to return to the image of the wave, there are big waves, small waves, and very small waves, but they are all composed of water, and in the same way all the different sects and schools and traditions and forms of Buddhism are composed of the Dharma. They are all expressions, under different conditions and circumstances, of the Buddha's teaching. Some of them are comprehensive in scope, some are more limited, and some are one-sided in one way or another, but all are part of the great wave that we call Buddhism. All have the taste of liberation.

I often speak of six distinctive emphases that are characteristic of our own particular wave.[402] Of these, the most important is our emphasis on the centrality to the Buddhist life of the act of Going for Refuge to the Three Jewels. It is the most important both practically and theoretically. Everything else flows from it, directly or indirectly. To the extent that you go for Refuge, to that extent you are a Buddhist. Going for Refuge is found in all forms of Buddhism, or at least they all refer to it, but unfortunately it is often spoken of, at least in English, as *taking* Refuge. This used to be the standard way of putting it, and some people still do say it, but the Pāli word used in the scriptures is definitely *gacchāmi*, 'I go'. 'Taking' Refuge has the wrong connotation, a connotation of appropriation and possession, even of grasping. Let us be careful never to speak of taking Refuge. But though Going for Refuge is found in all forms of Buddhism, it rarely has a central place in them. That place is usually taken by something else – monastic ordination, for example, or a particular kind of meditation, or some other spiritual practice. In our own tradition, however, Going for Refuge is central. We seek to place the Three Jewels at the heart of our lives and orient all our activities towards them, directly or indirectly.

All this is well known to you, so there's no need for me to enlarge upon it, but I'd like to remind you of the four levels of Going for Refuge. There's first of all, the ethnic or cultural Going for Refuge; secondly, there's provisional Going for Refuge; thirdly, there's effective Going for Refuge; and fourthly, there's real Going for Refuge. An understanding of these four is absolutely fundamental. Ordination represents a recognition by our spiritual friends that we are effectively Going for Refuge, but ordination is not enough. We must not rest on our laurels. We are not effectively Going for Refuge unless we are making a serious effort to achieve real Going for Refuge, to gain Stream Entry or achieve the arising of the *bodhicitta*. We must ask ourselves if we are really making that effort, really keeping alive the flame of that aspiration, because if we're not going forward, inevitably we shall slip back, perhaps into a merely provisional or even a purely formal Going for Refuge. A convention is obviously a good time to think about such things, a good time to make an extra effort to make our Going for

Refuge real. It is not simply a time for socializing or catching up with the news, though that has a place to a limited extent, especially if you haven't seen someone for a long time.

Ordination is the ritual recognition that a man or woman is effectively Going for Refuge to the Three Jewels, and that he or she intends to continue to do so. The final word with regard to someone's readiness for ordination rests with the public preceptor, the senior Order member who conducts the ordination ceremony. Originally that responsibility rested solely with me. I conducted all the public ordinations and the private ones too. A few years ago, however, I started handing on that responsibility to a number of senior Order members and at present there are seven of them. In order of seniority within the Order they are: Dhammadinna, ordained in August 1973; Subhuti, ordained in November 1973; Sona, ordained in 1974; Srimala, ordained in 1975; Padmavajra, ordained in 1976; Sanghadevi, ordained in 1977; and Suvajra, ordained in 1978. They've all been ordained for more than twenty years, which is quite a big slice of anybody's life. These seven people are responsible between them for the men's and women's ordination processes. Together with the presidents of some centres they make up the Preceptors' College and Council of the Western Buddhist Order/ Trailokya Bauddha Mahasangha.[403]

The responsibility I have handed on to the public preceptors is a very weighty one. I know just how weighty it is, because I bore it alone for more than twenty years. It is they who are responsible, in the end, for admitting new members of the Order, which means that it is they who determine, to an extent, the character of the Order, even the future of the Order. All Order members have an important part to play, but the part played by the public preceptors is special. I would like to take this opportunity of declaring that I have complete confidence in them, both individually and collectively. I am sure that they will fulfil the responsibility that I have entrusted to them with complete fidelity and integrity. But they will be able to fulfil it properly only with the support and cooperation of each and every one of you, and I therefore call upon you to give them that support and cooperation sincerely and wholeheartedly. I haven't quite handed on all my responsibilities. I'm still, it seems, head of the Order. But I want to hand that on too. I'm now nearly 74, and by the time I'm 75 I want to have handed on the headship of the Order. How or to whom I shall hand it on I have not yet decided, but I hope to make an announcement regarding the matter in a year's time, around my seventy-fifth birthday – if I live that long.

In the meantime, I trust you will all carry on deepening your Going for Refuge. So now at last I'm looking ahead a little way. The fact that I'm doing so means that I believe that the Order, that the Movement, has a future. You won't necessarily have an easy time. You may well encounter a good deal of opposition. Buddhism itself may encounter a good deal of opposition. In the Buddhist world as a whole, Buddhism has been on the decline for nearly a thousand years. Only in the West and in India, broadly speaking, is it part of a rising wave. But if that wave is to keep on rising, it will have to struggle and work very hard. *You* will have to struggle, and work very hard. In India you will have to struggle against the all-pervading influence of Hinduism, and the relentless pressure to Hinduize Buddhists, to put you back into the caste system. In the West you will have to struggle against pseudo-liberalism, against some aspects of New Age ideology, against the attempts to mix Buddhism with Christianity, and against materialism and consumerism, and very often you will have to stand alone. You will have to risk unpopularity, perhaps even persecution. People want others to like them, they want to be in with the crowd, and that tempts them to compromise their principles, their ideals, even their Buddhist ideals. You will probably have to face that temptation. Perhaps you are sometimes having to face it even now. But if the Movement is to have a future, you will have to resist temptations of that kind. You will have to be true individuals, not afraid to be in the minority as Buddhists, not afraid to stand alone. You will have to have the courage of your convictions, the courage of your experience and your insight.

So far I've spoken of opposition coming from outside, but there is another kind of opposition to be faced, an even greater danger that may come from within. That danger is, in a word, disharmony. It's not enough for the Order to be unified. It has to be united in its common commitment to the Three Jewels. Human beings being what they are, there will always be differences of opinion and personality clashes, but these should be resolved as soon as they arise. Resolving them should be an absolute priority. That doesn't necessarily mean that we should just go on talking about them. That sometimes merely prolongs the conflict. Sometimes it is best simply to intensify our practice of the Dharma and leave the problem to look after itself. As Order members you are making an effort to rise from effective Going for Refuge to real Going for Refuge, and that is the real solution to the problem. If a sufficient number of Order members achieve real Going for Refuge, or make a genuine effort to achieve it, there will be harmony in the Order. If Order members are in harmony, if *you* are in harmony, the Order will be strong, and able to resist both the dangers from without and the dangers from within.

More than that, if the Order is spiritually united, if it is in harmony, then a truly wonderful thing will happen. The Order will become the locus for the manifestation of the *bodhicitta*. As you all know, we sometimes liken the Order to the eleven-headed and thousand-armed Avalokiteśvara. This is not just a manner of speaking, a figure of speech. We should take it very seriously, even literally. Let us go back for a moment to the four levels of Going for Refuge. Order members go for Refuge effectively, that is, they're making a wholehearted effort to achieve real Going for Refuge, to achieve Stream Entry. When that happens, a radical transformation in the nature of the Going for Refuge takes place. The Going for Refuge ceases to be 'my' Going for Refuge. 'I' cease Going for Refuge. Something else takes over, at least to an extent. In Mahāyāna terms this something else is the real *bodhicitta*.

There are four levels of the arising of the *bodhicitta*, corresponding to the four levels of Going for Refuge. In the first place, there's an ethnic or cultural arising. This is not really an arising at all. It just consists in the formal acceptance of the bodhisattva ideal as part of one's Mahāyāna Buddhist cultural heritage. Secondly, there's a provisional arising of the *bodhicitta*. This occurs when you try to act in accordance with the bodhisattva ideal, to act altruistically, even if only very intermittently. And thirdly, there's the effective arising. Here you are wholeheartedly committed to acting in accordance with the bodhisattva ideal and you make a serious effort to practise the six *pāramitās*, but there's still the possibility of backsliding, and you may even give up the *bodhicitta* altogether. Fourthly, there's the real arising of the *bodhicitta*. Here you have achieved at least a degree of real wisdom and you are therefore practising this and the other *pāramitās* as *pāramitās*. Your practice of them is a transcendental practice and there is no possibility of falling back.

I have spoken in the past of the arising of the *bodhicitta* as the altruistic dimension of Going for Refuge. Strictly speaking, this applies only to the first three levels of the arising. In the case of the real arising, the distinction between self and others has begun to be seriously eroded. The real *bodhicitta* is therefore neither individualistic nor altruistic, so there is no question of the arising of the real *bodhicitta* being 'my' arising. 'I' do not develop the real *bodhicitta*, 'I' am not a bodhisattva, any more than it is 'I' who really go for Refuge, or 'I' who gain Stream Entry. In both cases, what we can only describe as a non-egoistic stream of spiritual energy, and perhaps even consciousness, has begun to take over. Early Buddhism does not have much to say about this. Perhaps the Buddha himself did not have much to say about it; perhaps he was content simply to demonstrate it in his life. But the Mahāyāna *sūtras* have a great deal to say about it, especially in their teaching about the bodhisattva ideal.

I won't say anything more about this now. I have talked about it elsewhere, for instance in my 1969 lectures on the bodhisattva ideal, which will soon be appearing in book form.[404] Now I want to focus on what happens when a number of people achieve this non-egoistic Going for Refuge, this non-egoistic arising of the *bodhicitta*, when this stream of non-egoistic spiritual energy starts manifesting through a number of people simultaneously. Those people will be literally hands or arms, or even faces, of Avalokiteśvara. There will be no question of any conflict between them. They will function in perfect harmony. They will be something for which we have no expression in English. It will be a true sangha, an Āryasaṅgha. Our Order has a future only to the extent that it is such a sangha, or contains such a sangha as its nucleus. It is therefore imperative that each and every one of you should seek to transform your effective Going for Refuge into a real Going for Refuge, should seek to attain Stream Entry or the arising of the real *bodhicitta*. It is up to you. The future of the Order, of the Movement, is in your hands.

I need hardly say how much the world needs the Dharma, needs such an Order and such a movement as ours. I have done what I can. I have started the Order, started the Movement. Next year I will be handing on the headship of the Order. I will then have no formal responsibilities. This does not mean that I shall be going out of circulation. I will still be more than happy to see people, and no doubt I will be putting in an appearance at centres from time to time, as the mood takes me. Of course, I will be doing some writing. Whether I will be at the next convention I can't say. In any case I am very happy indeed to be at this one. I'm happy to have had the opportunity of sharing with you some of my thoughts, happy to have had the opportunity of looking ahead a little way.

LIVING AND WORKING TOGETHER

European Buddhist Union conference, Berlin, 24 October 1999

Friends: I am very glad to be here in Berlin once again and to be speaking under the auspices of the European Buddhist Union on the subject of 'living and working together'. The title was selected for me by our organizers, and even though it isn't a subject on which I would have chosen to speak, I have decided to take it as a challenge. On this occasion we are clearly concerned not just with Buddhist theory, but also with Buddhist practice, and sometimes it's good for our Buddhist practice to do things that we haven't chosen to do. But how should one interpret 'living and working together'? Of course, one can live and work with animals, and living and working with machines is becoming increasingly common, but I take it that the organizers have in mind living and working with people. People play a very important part in our lives and we can't get on without them. Even solitary hermits like Milarepa were at least brought up by other people. Other people are in fact indispensable to us, whether for good or evil. The French existentialist thinker Jean Paul Sartre said, 'Hell is other people,' but we could also say that heaven is other people – sometimes – and even that purgatory is other people. People affect us in all sorts of ways, directly and indirectly, and most deeply and most crucially through our personal relationships with them.

Most of us are involved in relationships of different kinds, with different people, at different levels, in different situations. From one point of view, our whole life could be seen as a network of personal relationships of varying degrees of importance and intensity. In a very important *sutta*, the *Sigālaka Sutta*, which is found in the *Dīgha Nikāya*, the 'long discourses', the Buddha deals with what were in the India of his day the six basic relationships of human life. To begin with, he talks about how parents should treat their children, and how children should behave towards their parents, and secondly, he discusses the relation between teachers and pupils – teachers meaning secular teachers, schoolteachers. Thirdly, the Buddha talks about the duties of the husband towards the wife and of the wife towards the husband, and here too he goes into some detail. Fourthly, he goes into the question of the relation between friends and companions: how they should behave towards each other, and how they should help each other in the various vicissitudes of life. Fifthly, he deals with the relationship between the master or employer and his servants or employees, laying down some very interesting principles which are still valid today, 2,500 years later. And sixthly and lastly, the Buddha deals with the relation between spiritual teachers and their disciples.[405] Almost everything that the Buddha has to say about these six relationships of human life is relevant today. I won't go into any more detail now – we don't have time – but the *Sigālaka Sutta* is well worth studying. On the present occasion I would just like to make two general points about the *sutta* before going on to deal with something more fundamental.

The first point is that nowhere in this *sutta* does the Buddha say anything about rights. He doesn't say anything about the rights of children, or the rights of the husband or wife, or the rights of workers or employers. He speaks throughout about duties and responsibilities. Nowadays in the West the discourse of rights has been carried to absurd lengths. This is especially the case in the United States, but it's beginning to happen in Britain too. What happens is that people endow themselves and others with all sorts of imaginary or unreal rights and then start fighting for the legal recognition of those rights. There is even talk in some quarters of a right to happiness. A couple of months ago in the United States two teenagers took their parents to court and sued them for not having given them a happy childhood. This is the sort of pass to which we have come. But in Buddhism the emphasis is not on rights, but on duties, and of course if everybody does their duty, everybody will have their rights. If parents do their duty as far as children are concerned, children won't need rights, and it's the same with regard to the other relationships. There is no word for rights in Pāli and Sanskrit, as though the emphasis on duties and responsibilities was so strong that no concept of rights was necessary.

This brings me to my second general point, which is that according to Buddhism duties are mutual and reciprocal. The husband has a duty to his wife, but the wife also has a duty to her husband. The employer has a duty to employees, but employees also have a duty towards their employer. There is no one-sidedness, but mutuality and reciprocity. The Buddha's teaching about mutual human relationships has had an enormous influence on traditional Buddhist societies, especially in the mainly Theravādin countries of South-east Asia, helping to shape those societies in a very positive manner, but this teaching is not applicable only to Buddhists and Buddhist societies. It is a universal teaching, which can be equally well practised by Christians, Hindus, Jews, and all people; it is relevant to human social life everywhere in the world.

Despite this, the teaching has its limitations. It is universal, but only on the ethical level. It does not contain all the Buddha's teachings. There are many, many other teachings in other parts of the Pāli canon, as well as in the Sanskrit Buddhist literature, which go far beyond just ethics, *śīla*, as it's called in Buddhism. There are teachings about *samādhi*, concentration and meditation, and about *prajñā*, *vipaśyanā*, the higher spiritual wisdom and insight. So let's go into those higher, or deeper, levels. It is clear that relationships are between people, but who or what are people? We speak of *other* people. In other words, other people are other. One could even say, being a little philosophical, that they represent *the* other, the not-I. Of course, trees and mountains are not-I. Tables and chairs are other. But people represent the other, they *are* other, in a rather special sense, and our relationships with other people are normally more important and more intense than our relationships with things. Usually our relationships with things are intense only when we start treating them as people, or quasi-people. I know there are people who say that their cat or their dog is their best friend, but that's a little exceptional. Usually our most important and most intense relationships are with other people, and that's perhaps because in our relationships with other people we experience ourselves, we are conscious of ourselves. Even when we only think of other people, whether positively or negatively, we can have a very strong experience of them and ourselves in relation to them. We can say that every human relationship is bipolar – that is, it has two poles between which it operates, a self pole and an other pole, an I pole and a you pole. Here we begin to come to the crux of the whole matter, and in a way to the crux of Buddhism.

Our experience as human beings is dualistic. In it there's a subject and an object, a self and an other, and usually we take both, and the duality between them, to be absolutely and irreducibly real. But according to Buddhist teaching the duality is only relatively real, and there is a higher level where the subject–object duality is transcended, a level where self and other are not experienced as we usually experience them. This is the level of *prajñā* or wisdom. It's also the level of *karuṇā* or compassion in the sense of *mahākaruṇā*. In a word, it is the level of Enlightenment or awakening, of *bodhi*. As Buddhists it's our ultimate aim to reach that higher level and become Enlightened. That is why we go for Refuge to the Buddha, the Dharma, and the Sangha, and we seek to reach that goal by following the Noble Eightfold Path, by practising the six or the ten *pāramitās*, and so on. But where do we do all of this? We do it inevitably and inescapably here in this world, in the context of our relationships with other people. We do it even *through* our relationships with other people, or at least some of them. We do it, in a word, *together* with other people.

Usually we get together with other people to fulfil some need of our own, whether healthy or neurotic, to achieve some objective we can't achieve on our own, and usually a certain amount of compromise is necessary: 'You scratch my back and I'll scratch yours.' We fulfil our need and we allow the other person to fulfil theirs. We get on together more or less well, but often our needs clash with those of other people, or there is a profound disagreement as to how to achieve a common objective. Everybody in the world wants peace, for example, but how to achieve it? There are so many different views. When that happens, whether on a larger or a smaller scale, there's conflict, there may even be war, and togetherness based on the satisfaction of common needs breaks down, at least for a time.

But there is another kind of togetherness, another way of being with other people. That is when our common objective is spiritual, nothing other than Enlightenment, a realization that transcends the subject–object dichotomy. In this way we arrive at a highly paradoxical situation, in which egos come together with the objective of achieving egolessness. Perhaps it's difficult for us to imagine that, but such a situation is described in *sutta* 31 of the *Majjhima Nikāya*, the collection of middle-length discourses of the Buddha.

Apparently the Buddha was on his travels when he came to a sort of park or woodland area where three of his monk-disciples were living quietly together, so he thought he would go and see how they were getting on. Even in the Buddha's day monks didn't always get on well together, and sometimes there were serious quarrels. One of the three monks, Anuruddha, saw the Buddha coming and went forward to greet him respectfully. The Buddha said, 'I hope, Anuruddha, that you are all living in concord. I hope you are living with mutual appreciation. I hope you are living without disputing. I hope you are living blending like milk and water. I hope you are living viewing each other with kindly eyes.' And Anuruddha said, 'Yes, we are indeed living in that way.' The Buddha wanted to know how the three were living together in greater detail, and Anuruddha said, 'I think it is a great gain for me that I am living with such companions in the spiritual life. I act towards them with thoughts of *mettā*, both openly and privately, thinking that I should set aside what I want to do and do what they want to do. We are different in body, we are three, but we have only one mind.' And each of the other monks told the Buddha exactly the same thing.

The Buddha wanted to know even more practical details, so he asked further questions, and they replied. Being monks, they went begging into the nearest village for their food. They didn't all come back together, because they would beg separately and one might have further to go than the others, so Anuruddha explained, 'Whoever gets back first makes the seats ready, sets out the water for drinking, and separate water for washing, and puts the refuse bucket in its place.' This sort of thing is still relevant in communities even today. Anuruddha went on to explain that whichever monk came back last put away the seats, and the water for drinking, and the water for washing. He put away the refuse bucket after washing it, and he swept out the eating place. Whichever of the three happened to notice that the pots of drinking water, water for washing, or water in the latrine were low or empty attended to them. They didn't have to talk about these things, but did them by mutual agreement, observing silence, but once every five days they got together to talk about the Dharma.[406]

This gives a very beautiful picture of how at least some of the monk disciples lived together in the Buddha's day. There are several key phrases here. They live together 'like milk and water blended'. When you mix milk and water, you can't tell which is which, unless you subject the liquid to chemical analysis. The three monks were like that. In a sense you couldn't tell one from the other: they had three bodies, but only one mind. This gives us an ideal, at a very high level and within a monastic context, for living and working together. You might say that the monks were living together, but they weren't working, but actually they *were* working. They spent much of their time in meditation, and meditation is hard work. If you don't believe me, try it! In Pāli the term for a meditation subject is *kammaṭṭhāna*, which means the place of work. The meditation subject, whether it's your breath or something you visualize, is a place where you work, and you have to work very hard.

So here we have these three monks living and working together. They're different in body, but they're of one mind, and their living and working together helps them to transcend their separate selfish interests. They cooperate for a higher purpose. You might think that was all very well if you were living in the forest as a monk in the Buddha's day, but that it isn't possible to live like that today, but you would be wrong. In the Friends of the Western Buddhist Order we have developed a way of living and working together which we call team-based right livelihood businesses. Right livelihood is the fifth step of the Buddha's Noble Eightfold Path, so it's an integral part of Buddhist theory and Buddhist practice. These right livelihood businesses are team-based in the sense that people work together in them as Buddhists, as people who have gone for Refuge to the Buddha, the Dharma, and the Sangha, whose ultimate common objective is the attainment of Enlightenment.

In Britain we have at present thirty-one such businesses, some large and some quite small, between them employing – or rather supporting, because we don't give wages in the ordinary sense – 232 full-time workers and 48 part-time workers. Among the businesses we have an import-export business, vegetarian restaurants, wholefood shops, gift shops, and a publishing house,[407] and all these businesses have four objectives.

Their first objective is to provide the people working in them with the means of material support. The emphasis is on what people need, not on what they might want. People don't work in team-based right livelihood businesses for the money. They get support according to their needs, so a man or woman without dependants will get less than someone with dependants, whether children or aged parents. The amount of support you get is not related to the degree of your responsibility within the organization; a manager or director who is single may get much less financial support than an ordinary worker who has dependants. So things are done very differently from how they're usually done out in the world. Everyone working in these businesses is encouraged to lead as simple a life as possible. That is one of the reasons why idealistic young people want to work there; they want to give more to society than they take from it. If one tries to live simply, cutting down on one's needs and certainly cutting down on one's wants, then craving will be diminished, and I need hardly say how important this emphasis in the spiritual life is nowadays. In an organization like a team-based right livelihood business there's no place for consumerism.

The second objective of team-based right livelihood businesses is to provide ethical work. They aim to conduct their business in a way that does not exploit or take unfair advantage of anybody, that does no harm to the workers or to any other living beings, whether human or animal. The biggest of our businesses imports handicrafts from some of the developing countries, and we make sure that those handicrafts are produced under ethical conditions. We won't buy where underage children are employed or where people work under sweatshop conditions. Also, we make sure that the work does not involve undue physical or mental strain. It would be a bit paradoxical if as a Buddhist you were working in a Buddhist team-based right livelihood business and you ended up at the end of the day feeling stressed and unable to meditate. People in team-based right livelihoods work very hard indeed, but they enjoy their work and they don't get stressed – well, maybe for an hour or two, but not more than that. They get six weeks of paid holiday every year, and they can use that period for ordinary holidays, or for retreats, or for spending time with their families.

Thirdly, the team-based right livelihood situation provides a context for the development of spiritual friendship. The Buddha once said that spiritual friendship is the whole of the spiritual life.[408] Some people who work in these businesses not only work together, but also live together in residential spiritual communities, so they meditate together and study the Dharma together, and this helps to create a very intense situation which is highly conducive to spiritual development and is not in principle unlike that of the three monks in the Pāli *sutta*.

The fourth of the objectives of the team-based right livelihood businesses is to make a profit, and some of them make a lot of money. A small amount is put back into the business to finance development, but most of the profit is given away as *dāna. Dāna* or generosity is one of the most important of Buddhist spiritual practices, helping to counteract one's craving and attachment. Over the years our team-based right livelihood businesses have given millions of pounds to support the Dharma activities of the FWBO.

So here we have an example of people living and working together as Buddhists. There are other ways of doing that, but this is one about which I happen to know something. We may say that living and working together is a spiritual practice in itself, helping us to overcome our self-centredness and ultimately to transcend the subject–object duality and attain Enlightenment. I hope that as we enter the twenty-first century (even though of course it's not our Buddhist twenty-first century) there will be more and more team-based right livelihood businesses, not just in the FWBO, but within the sanghas of the various other Buddhist traditions. This will surely be one way of consolidating the influence of the Dharma in the West.

SEEING THINGS AS THEY REALLY ARE

Berlin Buddhist Centre, 25 October 1999

I'm glad to be here again, about a year and a half since my last visit, and once again to be surrounded by members of our German sangha, because I can see there are people here not just from Berlin but from Essen and other places.

Buddhism celebrated its 2,500th anniversary more than forty years ago. As I was in India at that time, I was closely associated with the celebrations in Delhi, Sarnath, and other places. So Buddhism is a very old religion. One could also say that it's a very young religion, but that's from another point of view. In the last 2,500 years Buddhism has spread to many countries and many cultures. It spread from India into Sri Lanka and other South-east Asian countries, into China and Japan, into Indonesia, and into Tibet, and it created many different ways of practising the Buddhist spiritual path. There are hundreds of methods of Buddhist meditation, for instance. Buddhism produced an enormous literature in scores of languages, and gave rise to a number of religious sects. So in the course of its long history, Buddhism has become little by little a very rich and complex thing, and now it has come to the West in all its richness and complexity. Well, in fact it isn't Buddhism itself that has come to the West, but a number of its Eastern forms. We have representatives of Theravāda Buddhism, Zen Buddhism, Tibetan Buddhism, and Japanese Pure Land Buddhism, and each of these traditions exists, even in the West, in different forms. For example, we have Sinhalese Theravāda, Burmese Theravāda, and

Thai-style Theravāda, each with its own unique flavour, and we have a number of Zen traditions, especially in the United States, and a number of forms of Tibetan Buddhism: the Gelugpa tradition, Sakyapa tradition, Kagyupa tradition, and so on. One of my Tibetan teachers told me that there were fourteen forms of Kagyupa Buddhism. Indeed, there are so many forms of Buddhism that it's difficult to see Buddhism. As we say in English, we can't see the wood for the trees.

All this has happened in comparatively recent times. Nearly sixty years ago, when I became a Buddhist, or rather when I realized that I was a Buddhist, there were so few books on Buddhism available in English that one could read them all in the course of a few weeks. I bought a few of them, and the rest I borrowed from the library of the Buddhist Society in London. But now, it's probably not an exaggeration to say that several hundred new books on Buddhism are published every year in English alone. It's quite difficult to keep up with all this literature, and I gave up trying about twenty years ago. At the same time, some of the new books being published, both translations and original works, are very important. Sometimes it's hard to see the wood of Buddhism for the trees – that is, all the books.

But this confusion, this complexity, is only apparent. If we get down to rock bottom, Buddhism is a very simple thing. In fact, it is possible to reduce Buddhism to just two teachings, so that if you really get hold of these two teachings, you will have got hold of Buddhism. It's like finding in the midst of the forest one big tree which is quite clearly the king of the forest. The first of these two teachings is that it is possible for human beings to change. It's possible for a human being to change radically, to change from an unenlightened human being to an Enlightened human being, and to make that change by virtue of their own human efforts. And the second teaching is that really radical change takes place in a human being when they get rid of their delusions, when they begin to see things as they really are, as the traditional term has it. 'As they really are' translates *yathābhūta*, which is also sometimes translated as 'according to reality' or 'according to the truth'.

Quite a lot of people are under the impression that they already see things as they really are. People usually think that they are realists, practical people who know what's what. They think they know all the facts and understand what life is all about. But according to Buddhism, such people don't see things as they really are – in fact, just the opposite.

People almost always have a distorted view of reality, seeing things the wrong way round, or even upside down. When I was a child we used to see distorting mirrors in fairgrounds. You would stand in front of the mirror and your head would look enormous and your body would look tiny, or you might even see yourself upside down. Well, according to Buddhism, that's how we usually see things. We're the victims of what Buddhism calls the four *viparyāsas*, the four upside down views. The first of these is seeing what is impermanent as permanent, the second is seeing what is painful as pleasurable, the third is seeing what is not possessed of permanent, unchanging selfhood as being possessed of such selfhood, and the fourth is seeing what is not beautiful as beautiful. I will say something about each of these in turn.

So first of all, seeing what is impermanent as permanent. We may say that we know very well that the house we live in isn't going to last for ever, that one day it's going to crumble or be pulled down. We may say that we know that our human relationships are impermanent. People go away, or die; friendships and relationships come to an end. We may think we know all this. But do we really know it? Suppose you were to go home this evening and find that while you were out at the Buddhist lecture your house had burned down. Would you say, 'Oh well, I knew it was impermanent. That's what Bhante said in his lecture'? Or suppose someone very near and dear to us dies suddenly, as sometimes happens. We don't just shrug our shoulders and say, 'Oh well, I knew they'd die one day.' We feel the loss very deeply, sometimes so deeply that we are seriously affected for weeks or months. There are some losses that some people never seem to get over. So what does this mean? It means in brief that there are two ways of knowing. There's knowing superficially, just mentally or theoretically, and there's knowing with our whole being, knowing in our very bones. Usually we don't know in that sort of way. We don't see with that sort of clarity and intensity, with the result that in effect we do see the impermanent as permanent, so that we tend to cling onto it, become attached to it, and in the long run that usually means suffering. I'm not suggesting that we should not feel, and even feel deeply, the loss of someone close to us. I'm certainly not suggesting that the good Buddhist should be devoid of feeling. But there are two kinds of feeling, selfish feeling and unselfish feeling, and it is unselfish feeling, what we call in Buddhism *mettā* and *karuṇā*, loving-kindness and compassion, that should be cultivated. If we do this, when we lose someone near and dear to us, we will feel the loss not so much for our sake, but for theirs.

The second *viparyāsa* is seeing what is painful as pleasurable. This doesn't mean that there's no such thing as pleasure or happiness in the world. There certainly is, and we all experience it sometimes. But we also find that it doesn't last. It's not ultimately satisfying. We all want happiness. We go in search of it, consciously or unconsciously, and there's nothing wrong with that. It's perfectly natural. But according to Buddhism we search for happiness in the wrong place. We don't look for it in the spiritual life, in Enlightenment, in the Unconditioned. We look for it in conditioned things, so sooner or later we're going to be disappointed, and we're going to suffer. We suffer ultimately because as human beings we have deep down in us the potential for Enlightenment, and we cannot be truly and fully happy until we have realized that potential or we are well on the way to realizing it. In Goethe's famous drama *Faust*, the character Faust makes a bet with Mephistopheles, the devil, saying, 'If you can give me a really satisfying experience, even for one moment, then I'm yours for ever.' Mephistopheles does his best and gives Faust many experiences, but Faust is never completely satisfied, and in the end Mephistopheles loses the bet and Faust escapes; in fact, in the last scene he goes to heaven, despite all his mistakes. The world cannot give Faust a perfectly satisfying experience, and Mephistopheles can give only worldly things, so in the end he loses the bet.[409] You could say that we are all Faust, and we are all Mephistopheles. They're both in us. Sometimes they agree, and sometimes they disagree. No doubt they were both in Goethe as well. We have all sorts of experiences and enjoyments, but in the end they leave us dissatisfied, and we begin to realize that satisfaction is to be found elsewhere – in what in Buddhism for want of a better term we call Enlightenment. This realization is what sets us following the spiritual path.

The third of the *viparyāsas* is seeing that which is not possessed of permanent, unchanging selfhood as being possessed of such selfhood. At this point we start entering rather deep philosophical waters. The most prominent feature of our experience as human beings is that it is dualistic, that there's a perceiving subject and a perceived object, an I and a you, or an I and an it. Buddhism holds in all its schools that this duality is not ultimately real – not totally unreal, but only relatively real – and that this level of dualistic experience is transcended in the experience of Enlightenment. Language is a bit contradictory here, but Enlightenment is an experience in which paradoxically there is neither subject nor object. It's a state we can only describe as pure, blissful, non-dual awareness. Buddhism does not speak of Enlightenment in terms of a higher self. In Enlightenment there's no self at all. But for us in our ordinary everyday experience there is very much a self, our own psychophysical being, and we identify with that self. In effect for us our self is the centre of the universe. *We* are the centre of the universe, and that's why we act selfishly or without consideration for other people, thinking only of our own interests. For us the self possesses the ultimacy that really belongs only to the Unconditioned or Enlightenment.

The fourth *viparyāsa* is seeing what is not beautiful as beautiful. Here the Pāli word for beautiful is *subha*, which can also be translated as pure. The literal meaning is shining, attractive. So what do we mean by seeing the not-beautiful as beautiful? I'll try to make this clear by referring to an episode in the Pāli scriptures. What I've been saying so far about the *viparyāsas* might have seemed a bit abstract, but with this fourth *viparyāsa* perhaps I can be a bit more concrete. According to the Pāli scriptures the Buddha had a cousin called Nanda, a handsome young man who was inspired by the Dharma and decided to become a monk, so he shaved his head, wore the yellow robe, and went begging for alms in the nearest village every day. Everything went on all right for a few weeks, but then he started telling the other monks that he was thinking of going back to being a layman. News of this reached the ears of the Buddha, as that sort of thing usually did, so he sent for Nanda and said, 'Come on, tell me. Why do you want to give up being a monk?' So Nanda said, 'Well, I just don't feel happy. I feel very depressed, very dissatisfied.' The Buddha asked him why, and in the end Nanda came clean. He said, 'Well, as I left my house to become a monk, there was a girl looking out of the window.' Her name, according to the Pāli text, was Janapadakalyāṇī. *Janapada* means a country or a district, and *kalyāṇī* means a beautiful or auspicious woman, so the name means 'the most beautiful woman in the country'. Some translators render it 'beauty queen'. This young woman saw Nanda going off to become a monk, and she said, 'See you later!' And Nanda said to the Buddha, 'I can't forget what she said. I can still hear her saying in that beautiful voice, "See you later!" I just can't stop thinking about her.'

So what did the Buddha do? He didn't waste time giving a sermon. He had supernormal powers, and when it was necessary he made use of them, so he just seized Nanda by the arm and took him up into a higher heavenly world. According to Indian belief, and even the Pāli scriptures, above our world there are lots of heavenly worlds, and the Buddha took Nanda up into the Indra *devaloka*, the heavenly world of Indra, the king of the gods. Indra is always attended by five hundred beautiful nymphs, incomparably more beautiful than human women. The Buddha, using his skilful means, said to Nanda, 'What do you think of these nymphs?' Taken aback, Nanda said, 'They're so beautiful, much more beautiful than that girl I left behind. In comparison she looks just like a monkey with its tail, nose, and ears cut off.'[410] That wasn't very polite, of course, and let's hope that the girl never heard about it. But what does this story mean? It means there are degrees of beauty. As we develop spiritually, and especially as we meditate, we're able to appreciate the higher degrees of beauty more and more, whether we see it in human beings, in great works of art and literature, or in nature. In the Buddhist tradition there are methods for enhancing our appreciation of this subtler, more refined beauty; for example the *kasiṇa* exercises, in which one concentrates on a disc of pure colour.[411]

Nowadays in the Western world some people regard beauty as a rather old-fashioned thing, and even some artists don't think in terms of beauty. In England we have an annual art competition called the Turner Prize, named after one of our greatest English artists, famous especially for his beautiful landscapes, the way in which he depicted the sea, storms, clouds, and sky. This year one of the shortlisted works for the prize was a bed in which the artist had been sleeping for a few weeks. The sheets were dirty, there were old socks on the bed, and so on. I wouldn't be surprised if it won the prize.[412] People seem to have lost their sense of beauty, which is rather sad.

We have to admit that from a philosophical point of view the concept of beauty is rather problematic. Is beauty objective, inherent in the object, or is it subjective, in the eye of the beholder? Schopenhauer has some interesting things to say about this. He says that we see something as beautiful when we see it without desire, without craving, when we do not relate it to our own personal needs.[413] Seeing the beautiful as beautiful means seeing it without reference to our own desires, not confusing the beautiful with what is merely desirable. Perhaps we could say that only the Buddha really sees the true beauty of the world, because only the Buddha is totally free from craving and selfish desire.

So these are the four *viparyāsas*, the four upside down views: seeing the impermanent as permanent, seeing the painful as pleasurable, seeing what is devoid of permanent, unchanging selfhood as being possessed of such selfhood, and seeing what is not supremely beautiful as beautiful. This is the way we usually see things, but we have to reverse the process. We have to learn to see the impermanent as impermanent, we have to see the pleasurable as not being in the long run either permanent or ultimately satisfying, we have to learn to see the self as being only a relative and not an absolute reality, and we have to learn that what we see as beautiful is only relatively beautiful, that there's a higher beauty that has nothing to do with selfish desire. To begin with, we shall understand this only conceptually. This is what we call mundane right view, and it is the first step of the Buddha's Noble Eightfold Path. There are seven other steps, and if we practise them, mundane right view will eventually be transformed into transcendental right view, which is an aspect of Enlightenment. So right view is of crucial importance. It is an integral part of our Going for Refuge. When we go for Refuge to the Dharma, in particular, we move away from wrong views and towards right views.

Wrong views are not merely wrong in some theoretical, abstract manner. The *viparyāsas* can have disastrous consequences, for us and for other people. There are two other wrong views that the Buddha often mentions. First of all, there is the wrong view that actions do not have consequences, have no ethical significance, that good actions are not productive of happiness or bad ones of suffering. This is of course the opposite of the teaching of karma. And then there is the wrong view that there are not, and nor have there ever been, Enlightened beings in the world. This wrong view denies that it is possible for human beings to gain Enlightenment, maintaining that what we call Enlightenment is no more than a pipe dream, that there is no higher reality.[414]

Wrong views don't just have a disastrous effect on our spiritual life. They can also have a disastrous effect on our ordinary worldly life, particularly when they take the form of political ideologies. In the twentieth century we have seen the rise of two disastrous ideologies, Marxist communism and fascism, which have brought immense suffering to hundreds of millions of people. Marxist communism is inflicting such suffering even now in its Chinese form, especially on the unfortunate people of Tibet. It's therefore important that we should think clearly, that we should think for ourselves and not allow ourselves to be swept off our feet by mass movements. It's important that we should not be taken in by slogans or soundbites, or allow ourselves to be over-influenced by the mass media or the advertising industry. Just think how many advertisements we encounter in the course of the day, all trying to get us to spend money, encouraging us to be more and more greedy. We shouldn't allow ourselves to be taken in by these things. We shouldn't even allow ourselves to be taken in by Buddhism, or by what purports to be Buddhism. The Buddha is recorded as saying, 'Test my words as the gold is tested in the fire by the goldsmith.'[415] So let us test all views in the fire of our own reason and experience. If we do that radically and thoroughly, wrong views will be reduced to ashes, and right views will come out bright and shining. So let us try to turn the four *viparyāsas* the other way round. Let us try to see things as they really are.

THE TRUE MIRACLE

Berlin, 27 October 1999

Nowadays in all the principal cities of Europe we find many different Buddhist groups, following different Buddhist traditions, and that's quite remarkable, because not much more than a hundred years ago Buddhism was hardly known at all in the West, except by travellers to the East and scholars who had specialized in oriental languages. Whatever ideas were in circulation about Buddhism were sometimes very strange. Some people had the impression that Buddhism is pessimistic and nihilistic, that Buddhism teaches that life is simply bad, and the best thing that one can do is never to be reborn again, but to be absorbed into some sort of nothingness. Some ideas about the Buddha himself were even stranger. Some well-reputed scholars seriously maintained that the Buddha was a sort of sun god, and I remember reading one article which said that he was identical with the Nordic god Woden. Towards the end of the nineteenth century, other strange ideas about the Buddha circulated. Some people thought that he was a sort of religious reformer, like Martin Luther, maintaining that just as Luther was critical of the corrupt Roman Catholic church, the Buddha was critical of the corrupt Hinduism of his day and wanted to reform it. I have also met people who believe that the Buddha was an early Indian rationalist, something like Bertrand Russell.

But in the Buddhist scriptures we find a very different sort of Buddha: a Buddha who works miracles. Some people aren't very happy with those parts of the Buddhist scriptures where the Buddha gives exhibitions of supernormal powers, but they are there. One miracle was particularly famous: the *yamaka prātihārya*, (Sanskrit, Pāli *pāṭihāriya*) which was not just a miracle (*prātihārya*), but a double (*yamaka*) miracle.[416] According to these accounts, the Buddha ascended into the air and walked up and down. We've heard of someone walking on the water, but here was the Buddha walking in the air. I wouldn't like to say which was the greater miracle. And the Buddha didn't just walk in the air. From one side of his body flames came shooting out, and from the other side of his body water flowed. This is the *yamaka prātihārya*. In modern times some people have tried to explain it along Jungian lines. Fire is masculine, water is feminine, and emitting both at the same time could be understood as a union of opposites, while the Buddha walking up and down up in the air represents that higher level on which all opposites are unified, so it could be regarded as a symbol of the integration of the self at a higher level.

Let's leave aside those explanations, though, because in the Pāli scriptures one certainly doesn't find just miracles, but also a lot of very important teachings about ethics, meditation, the higher wisdom, social matters, human relationships, right livelihood, and so on, and one saying of the Buddha is especially relevant. One day he put the question, 'What is the greatest miracle?' No doubt his disciples were expecting him to mention the *yamaka prātihārya*, or perhaps a miracle even greater than that, but the Buddha said that the greatest miracle, far greater than any *yamaka prātihārya*, is when a human being changes from a dark way of life to a bright way of life, gives up an unethical way of life and starts living an ethical and spiritual life.[417] So the same person who is performing the *yamaka prātihārya* and other miracles is saying that the greatest miracle is that kind of change which takes place in the human being. In other places in the scriptures the Buddha even says, 'I look down upon what people usually regard as a miracle. The real miracle is that change of heart in the human being.' The *yamaka prātihārya*, the great miracle, can be understood metaphorically, but what the Buddha says about the greatest miracle of all has to be taken quite literally. The true miracle is when we transform our own life.

The Buddha himself performed this true miracle in the earlier part of his life. When the Buddha was relatively old, he sometimes used to reminisce to his disciples about his experiences before he became fully Enlightened, and in the Pāli *sutta* called the *Ariyapariyesanā*, the 'Noble Search', he thinks back to the time when he was quite young, maybe 18 or so, and remembers, 'Being myself subject to conditions, limited, contingent, I went in search of those things which were also conditioned, also limited, also contingent. Being myself subject to birth, old age, disease, and death, I went in search of those things which were also subject to birth, old age, disease, and death. Then a thought occurred to me: suppose instead of going in search of that which is subject to birth, old age, disease, and death, I was to go in search of that which transcends birth, old age, disease, and death?' So he decided to leave home, and he became a sort of wandering ascetic. He cut off his hair and beard, wore the clothes of a beggar, and went in search of teachers.[418] He made contact with various teachers and was satisfied with their teachings for a while, but he felt they didn't go far enough, so he left them and practised self-mortification by himself. In those days many people in India believed that if you mortified the flesh your spirit became purer and you could see the truth more easily. Later the Buddha rejected that attitude, and taught a middle way between self-indulgence and self-mortification.

In another *sutta* of the Pāli canon, the Buddha describes how at one time before his Enlightenment he was living by himself in the jungle and trying to meditate, but he kept experiencing a terrible fear. It didn't seem to have any particular cause. It just came, and it seemed as though it was going to completely overwhelm him. What should he do? In the end he decided he wouldn't do anything. If the fear arose when he was sitting, he would carry on sitting until it passed away. If it arose when he was walking up and down, he would carry on walking up and down. And if it came when he was lying down, he would carry on lying down. He wouldn't run away from the fear. He would face it. He'd let it come and let it go, and in the end it went for good.[419] I mention this incident because even nowadays people who practise meditation from time to time experience this sort of fear, and it's reassuring to know that the Buddha himself before his Enlightenment had the same sort of experience.

The Buddha was on his own for about six years, seeking Enlightenment, and at the end of that period he found himself on the bank of a river, sitting underneath a tree, and he felt ready just to meditate. In that way he found what he was looking for. He experienced that higher transcendental state which we call supreme Enlightenment or *sambodhi*.[420] In the course of that attainment he passed through various experiences, but I won't go into that this evening. Let's just think of the Buddha sitting beneath the bodhi tree, as it was afterwards called, enjoying the bliss of his newly attained Enlightenment. Until then he had been a bodhisattva, someone who is in search of *bodhi*, Enlightenment, awakening, but after his Enlightenment he was called the Buddha, the one who has achieved *bodhi*. Buddha is therefore not a name, but a title. But what is a Buddha? To say that he is one who has attained *bodhi* doesn't help us much. In the West, even among Western Buddhists, there has been quite a bit of confusion as to what a Buddha is, because even though we are Buddhists, we are still very much under the influence of traditional Western categories of thought. In the West traditionally on the one hand there is God and on the other hand there is the human being. God is the creator, human beings are what or who has been created, and there is a big gulf between the two. A human being cannot become God.

When we come into contact with something new, we try to fit it into the old categories, so the question arose among Western students of Buddhism, to which of these two categories did the Buddha belong? Was he a god or an ordinary human being? Perhaps the general view was that the Buddha was a human being, but that after his death he'd been made into a god by his followers. Some scholars said that according to the Theravāda school, the Buddha was a man, but the Mahāyānists later on turned him into a god. Some people also pointed to the fact that in the Buddhist countries of the Far East the Buddha is worshipped. If you go into a temple, you see big, beautiful Buddha images and people lighting candles, offering flowers, lighting incense sticks, and prostrating themselves on the floor, worshipping the Buddha. With our Western Christian background, we tend to think that if you're worshipping something, you must be regarding it as God, but that's not the Buddhist view, or the Hindu view either. In Buddhism you are said to worship anything you look up to. Buddhist literature speaks of worshipping the Buddha and the bodhisattvas, but also of worshipping your teachers and your parents, and your elders generally, so there's not the distinction between worship and respect which we usually find in the West.

For Buddhism, the categories are unenlightened human being and Enlightened human being. God doesn't come into the picture at all. Buddhism is a non-theistic religion. Some people are puzzled by this, because in the West we've become accustomed to identifying religion with theism, with a personal creator God who created the universe, but in Buddhism there's no such concept, and people in Buddhist countries have difficulty understanding it. I was told by some of my Thai Buddhist friends that when Christian missionaries first arrived in Thailand they wanted to translate the Bible into the Thai language, but they were shocked to find that in Thai there was no word for God, so they had to create a new word: 'the Buddha who created the universe'. To Thai Buddhists this was nonsense, because the idea of the Buddha and the idea of creating the universe were quite antithetical.

The Buddha represents a third category, neither man nor God, but Enlightened human being, free from greed, hatred, and delusion, full of wisdom and compassion, living not for his own sake but for the sake of all human beings, and showing them how they too can become Enlightened. We could regard him as representing a higher evolutionary development, as being the forerunner of a new, higher species of human being. This kind of evolution is different from biological evolution, which I sometimes call the lower evolution, in that the lower evolution is a collective thing, but the Buddha's attainment of Enlightenment is an individual achievement, the result of his own individual human effort. Nowadays quite a lot of people believe that we're living at the dawn of a new age, usually called the Age of Aquarius, when they say we'll all be lifted up to a higher level of happiness almost without any effort of our own. But in Buddhism there's no room for believing in an age of this sort, or this kind of collective development. In Buddhism spiritual development is very much an individual affair, even though individuals can help one another in their spiritual development. For most people, indeed, such help is absolutely necessary, and that's why we have sangha. Sangha in the highest sense is one of the Three Jewels, the others being the Buddha and the Dharma, and it is to the Buddha, Dharma, and Sangha that we commit ourselves. Sangha is very important. We can't get far by our own efforts. We need the help and inspiration of other people. But nonetheless, we ourselves have to make the effort. The Buddha says in the *Dhammapada* that the Buddhas only show the way.[421]

Why don't we make that effort? If we're Buddhists, or think of ourselves as Buddhists, why don't we make more effort than we do? I'm afraid the truth is that usually it's because we don't really want to. There's an English saying, 'You can lead a horse to water, but you can't make it drink' – a very ordinary saying, but it contains a deep truth. Usually we're quite satisfied with things the way they are, and with ourselves as we are. We know we're not perfect, but we're not so bad – not so bad as some people, anyway – so we're reasonably satisfied with ourselves. We haven't committed any major crimes. We haven't got *too* many faults.

Even if we get a bit dissatisfied with ourselves as we are and try to make an effort, it isn't easy. We're faced by all sorts of difficulties and obstacles. Some of these obstacles are external. If you're trying to change, if you're trying to become more ethical, to lead a spiritual life, the world doesn't usually help or cooperate. In fact, the world may think you're a decidedly odd sort of person, though maybe not so much now as in the past. When I came back to the West in 1964, people in Britain had hardly heard of meditation, but now most people have at least heard of it, and if you mention that you're meditating, they probably won't think you're crazy. But nonetheless many people still have a deep resistance to anything of a spiritual nature, and if we try really hard to lead a different, better kind of life, the world won't necessarily give us an easy time.

The internal obstacles are even more serious and dangerous. In traditional Buddhist terms the biggest obstacle to our search for Enlightenment is simply craving, in Sanskrit *tṛṣṇā*, a very strong word which literally means thirst – the kind of thirst you would feel if you were in the midst of a desert without water. It's craving that motivates us most of the time. Buddhism recognizes various forms of it, including the craving for experience, enjoyment, through the senses or the lower mind, and the craving to go on existing in this world, or another world rather like this one. Sooner or later our craving gives rise to suffering, because inevitably it gets frustrated in one way or another. We certainly don't always get what we want.

Buddhism traditionally speaks of three main kinds of suffering. The first is simply called 'the suffering which is suffering', the kind you feel when someone sticks a pin in you or speaks harshly to you. Then there's the suffering of change. You experience something which is very pleasant, you like it very much, you become attached to it, but then it changes and no longer gives you the satisfaction that it used to, and this is a source of suffering. And the third kind of suffering is the suffering which is conditioned existence itself. Philosophically this is the most important of these three kinds of suffering, and it reflects the fact that nothing that is conditioned, worldly, impermanent, can give us full and lasting satisfaction. The human heart needs something more. You may have everything from a worldly point of view, but you're not satisfied. There's something missing.

In the course of my life as a Buddhist and as a teacher I've come across thousands of people in that sort of situation. They may be leading a happy life. They may have a good wife or husband. They may have children. Their domestic life may be happy. Their professional life may be successful. They may go on holiday to Spain or Greece, may get a new car every two years, have a colour television, go to discos on Friday nights, but nonetheless they feel that something is missing. According to the *Ariyapariyesanā Sutta*, this is how the Buddha himself felt, when he was living in his father's house. According to the later legendary accounts, he had untold luxury and enjoyment. I won't go into the details. You might start envying the Buddha in those days! He had everything, but in a sense he had nothing, and that's why he went forth from home. Many of us are in the same sort of position. We may not actually go forth, though if you're young you might go and wander for a few months, but even if we don't literally leave home, we start looking for something. Maybe we start reading books about spiritual teachings, or we go to lectures. Sooner or later, in one way or another, we come across something – a specific teaching, or an account of somebody's life, or something else – that moves us deeply, something to which we feel a response.

Some people come into contact first of all with the Buddha. I know people whose lives have been completely changed after seeing an image of the peaceful, compassionate Buddha, through which they intuited the sense of a higher experience, an experience which they themselves would like to achieve. Other people respond more strongly to the Dharma teachings, drawn perhaps by the more philosophical teachings. This was the case with me. I came across the Perfection of Wisdom *sūtras* when I was about sixteen, and I felt such a strong attraction to them that after reading them I thought, 'This is what I believe, this is what I accept. I'm a Buddhist' – even though for two years after that I was not in contact with any other Buddhist. And some people are attracted by the idea of sangha. It really inspires them to see people working together happily for the sake of a spiritual ideal. Just a few days ago here in Berlin we had the Congress of the European Buddhist Union, and this was an experience of sangha for many of the people present. They were able to meet with friends from so many different Buddhist traditions, all of them united in their Going for Refuge to the Buddha, Dharma, and Sangha, and collaborating to make that Congress a success. I came across another example of this years ago in relation to the big open retreats we used to hold (and still do). These retreats used to be very popular with people who had no previous experience of Buddhism or of the FWBO, and after the retreats they would come and tell me something which I found very interesting. They told me that they liked the meditations and enjoyed the lectures, and the food was good, but the thing that impressed them most was the harmonious way in which the Order members who were running the retreat worked together. They said they'd never seen people working together in that way before. In other words, they saw the sangha in operation. The sangha was what some people were looking for, and that was what moved them to become involved with the Buddhist tradition.

When we experience this sort of response, whether it's to a teaching, or someone's life story, or a group of people, a distinctive positive emotion arises within us. In Sanskrit it is called *śraddhā*. It's usually translated into English as faith or belief, but that's not a very good translation. It's certainly not believing to be true something which can't be proved. *Śraddhā* is the emotion you feel when you come into contact with something that you recognize to be spiritually higher, and to which your heart, in fact your whole being, goes out. Etymologically the word *śraddhā* means 'placing the heart on'. As Buddhists we place the heart on the Buddha, the Dharma, and the Sangha. We have this tremendous emotional response to them, and it's that which motivates us in our spiritual life. In Buddhist teaching we have the phrase 'In dependence upon suffering arises *śraddhā*'. Before, we were dissatisfied, perhaps suffering from a sort of existential anguish, so we started looking for something else, and when we found something to which we responded, *śraddhā* arose.

When we come in contact with something higher, something in response to which we experience *śraddhā*, we experience a deep sense of contentment, and because we feel happier, we behave better. Because we're leading more ethical lives, we become calmer, more concentrated, more mindful, more integrated, especially if we take up the practice of meditation. We also become more compassionate, patient, and tolerant.

In this way a process of transformation begins to take place. Our craving is transformed into *śraddhā*, and *śraddhā* is transformed into a whole series of positive spiritual emotions. But it's not easy to do this, and I hope I haven't given the impression that it is. Craving is very powerful. In one way or another it dominates our lives, and it therefore puts up a tremendous fight, because it doesn't want to be transformed. Spiritual life can be a struggle for quite a while. But because it's a struggle, it's also a heroic life. One could even say that a real Buddhist has to be a hero. There will no doubt be ups and downs in your spiritual life. Sometimes craving will win. Sometimes you will win – that is, *śraddhā* will win. Sometimes the struggle may be so difficult that you feel like giving it up altogether, especially if you feel that you've been struggling for many years but you seem to be just the same as before. Naturally we like to see results. If you find that after practising meditation for fifteen or twenty years you still leave things on the bus, you're bound to think you're not making much progress.

To encourage people, I like to tell the story I once heard in India of the twentieth blow that eventually splits the rock. Spiritual life is like that. For a long time it may seem that you're not making any progress, but deep down a change is taking place. So don't lose hope. One day you will give that twentieth blow, and then something will really happen. You may not gain Enlightenment on the spot, but at least there'll be a big breakthrough. From what I've observed, working with people over so many years, this is very much the pattern. You go on for a few weeks, or a few months, or even a few years, practising steadily, and nothing much happens, but one day for no apparent reason you break through to a new level of spiritual experience. For a while you carry on steadily on that new level, and then there's another breakthrough. Sometimes it comes very unexpectedly, when you're on a meditation retreat, or washing the dishes, or walking along the street. But if you keep up the steady practice of the precepts and meditation it will come.

There are many setbacks, but you mustn't mind that. Once you've set your feet on the spiritual path, the fact that you've done that and you know you've done it will mean that despite all your difficulties, you'll feel deep down a very deep happiness, because you're doing the best thing you can possibly do with your human life. You're actualizing your deepest or highest potential. Buddhism used to be presented in purely negative terms, as though it consisted simply in getting rid of craving, and giving things up, but this is very one-sided. Buddhism also consists in the development of positive emotional states like *śraddhā*, happiness, joy, and contentment.

But even these positive qualities are not enough. It's not enough for the process of the transformation of craving to be going on steadily. It has to be made irreversible. You have to reach what is called in Buddhism the point of no return, that point in your spiritual development where you've gathered such momentum that you cannot fall back. This is traditionally called the point of Stream Entry, the point at which you enter the stream which will one day carry you to Enlightenment. When you reach the point of no return, you perform a miracle: not the attainment of Buddhahood itself, but a miracle nonetheless. But for this miracle to take place, another very important factor has to come into play. *Śraddhā* is not enough. Happiness and joy are not enough. Concentration is not enough. We have to develop *prajñā*, wisdom; we have to be able to see things as they really are, which was the subject of my talk a couple of evenings ago.[422]

So we've seen that Buddhism is a non-theistic religion. We've seen that the Buddha is neither God nor a human being, but an Enlightened human being, which is a wholly distinct category with which until now we haven't been familiar in the West. The Buddha shows how others may become Enlightened like him, but he only shows the way. We have to make the effort ourselves. We won't be carried to Enlightenment by some collective zeitgeist. We have to transform craving, by which we are usually dominated, into *śraddhā* and all the other positive emotions. As I hope I've made clear, this certainly isn't easy. We usually experience many setbacks. But to make that effort, to engage in that struggle, is the most worthwhile thing that we can possibly do with our lives, and if we engage in it even to a limited extent, we will have performed a true miracle. We will have performed on our own selves the miracle of change. We will have made the transition from the path of darkness to the path of light.

THE 2000S

THE CELEBRATION OF SANGHARAKSHITA'S SEVENTY-FIFTH BIRTHDAY

Aston University, Birmingham, 26 August 2000

Order members, Mitras, and Friends: The first thing I want to do is to thank those who have organized this celebration so beautifully, efficiently, and punctually. I also want to thank all of you for attending, and all those who have given me cards and all sorts of gifts and offerings, which I've received not just from those gathered here but from people in many different parts of the world. I'm deeply grateful and appreciative.

I'm not going to say much this evening. For once I find myself rather lost for words – a rather unusual experience for me, in view of all the millions of words that have been recorded. The first thing to say is that it seems quite incredible that I am now 75. The time seems to have gone so quickly. It's as though the last seventy-five years have been a dream. It does seem very strange that I should have had seventy-five years of life, and it also seems incredible that our Buddhist movement has been in existence for more than thirty years. In the early days, when we had been in existence for two years, we used to be amazed by that, and now it is thirty-two years, in fact a little more. It also seems quite incredible that today I am publicly handing on the last of my formal responsibilities.

For quite a few years I was president of all the FWBO centres. I handed on that responsibility ten years ago. I also used to conduct all the ordinations, both private and public, and I handed that responsibility on a few years ago as well. But tonight I am handing on the headship of the Order. I know there has been quite a bit of speculation about who is going to be that favoured person. I also know that some people have been rather dreading being landed with that responsibility. I have been thinking about this for quite a while. In fact, only yesterday someone handed me a confidential file in which I found a letter I dictated over twelve years ago, just before I had my prostate operation, with my last instructions about the Order, just in case I didn't survive the operation.[423] On reading it I was a bit surprised to find that I had it more or less worked out even then.

One of the things I decided quite early on was that I wasn't going to hand on the responsibility for being the head of the Order to any one person, however talented, gifted, and capable. I felt it would be almost unkind to hand that weighty responsibility to one person. So to whom, or to what, is it going to be handed on? I won't keep you in suspense any longer: I am handing on the responsibility to the College of Public Preceptors. The College has at present eight members, though it may grow. I will read out their names in order of seniority within the Order. First of all there is Dhammadinna, ordained in August 1973. Then there is Subhuti, also ordained in 1973, in November. Next comes Sona, ordained in 1974, and Srimala, ordained in 1975, followed by Padmavajra, ordained in June 1976. Next comes Surata, ordained in August 1976, and Sanghadevi, ordained in 1977, and eighth and lastly, there's Suvajra, ordained in 1978. Together with the presidents of certain centres, these Order members make up the Preceptors' College and Council of the WBO/TBM. At present there are nine such presidents who are not also public preceptors. In order of seniority in the Order, they are Nagabodhi, ordained in January 1974, Devamitra, ordained in January 1974, Vessantara, ordained in August 1974, Kamalashila, ordained in November 1974, Dhammarati, ordained in 1976, Kulananda, ordained in May 1977, Kovida, ordained in 1978, Cittapala, ordained in 1982, and Moksananda, ordained in 1985.

The College of Public Preceptors will have a chairman who will also be the chairman of the combined College and Council. I am using the word 'chairman' provisionally, because this and other nomenclature may be changed in due course. The chairman will be elected from among the public preceptors by the whole College and Council. He or she will serve for a term of five years and will be re-electable. The first chairman is, however, being designated by me: Dharmachari Subhuti. New members of the College of Public Preceptors will be appointed by the existing members of that college. Presidents are elected by the council of the centre concerned, and may be invited to join the council at the discretion of the College of Public Preceptors. Other matters of internal organization will be settled by the College, or by the College and council, as appropriate. Perhaps I should also mention that three public preceptors are also presidents: these are Subhuti, Sona, and Sanghadevi. And there are also two members of the council who are neither public preceptors nor presidents: Lokamitra and Ratnaguna. Thus we have two separate but closely related bodies, the College of Public Preceptors and the council of public preceptors and presidents, and it is to the College that I am handing on the headship of the Order.

That is the structure I have set up in order to ensure the continuance, consolidation, and expansion of the WBO and FWBO after my death, whenever that may be. Two questions remain to be answered. What will be the function of the College of Public Preceptors, and what will I be doing now that I have handed on the last of my responsibilities? With regard to the first of these questions, it is the public preceptors who have the ultimate responsibility for accepting people into the Order, and they are already exercising that responsibility. I have decided not to define their function any further than that, except to say that they will be doing whatever I have been doing over the years. If you like, the College is the collective reincarnation of me, and they will be functioning in the same spirit. For the last five years most of the public preceptors and presidents have been living in Birmingham, either at Madhyamaloka or at the Park Hill community, and the others have visited from time to time. In this way they've got to know one another even better than they already did, and they've also had regular contact with me, so they know my mind. The public preceptors and the presidents have been working harmoniously together, which gives me great satisfaction and augurs well for the future health of the whole movement.

So what will I be doing, now that I've handed on the last of my responsibilities? Well, I certainly won't be disappearing from the scene, at least not for the present. I'm not going to retire to the Bahamas or the south of France. I won't even be going on holiday. In fact, I will be doing many of the things I've been doing for the last few years: writing memoirs, reading page proofs, going for walks, visiting second-hand bookshops, appearing at centres for book launches, poetry readings, and so on, meditating, listening to music, perhaps writing a few more poems. I shall also be seeing people. In this connection I want to clear up what seems to be a misunderstanding. From time to time a little rumour goes round that says that I am not seeing people any more, or even that I don't want to see people. That is certainly not the case. I have always seen people, and I want to go on seeing people, both in groups and individually. It is not always possible to see me immediately, but if you want to see me, don't hesitate to write and ask, and if I can fit you in, I will gladly do so.

That's really all I have to say. As I said at the beginning, it seems incredible that I am now 75. I can't say that I feel it, but my birth certificate says quite clearly that I am. Fortunately my health is good, except that my blood pressure is rather high, so I may be around for a few more years. I don't know. Death may come to any of us at any time. So let us make the most of one another while we have the opportunity. Let *kalyāṇa mitratā* flourish amongst us more and more.

FIELDS OF CREATIVITY

London Buddhist Centre, 2001

In the course of the year since I last visited the London Buddhist Centre, quite a lot has happened, in the world, in the FWBO, and in my own life. One of the important things that has happened for me personally is that I have at last finished writing my latest volume of memoirs, or rather I've finished dictating them, because the last ten chapters have had to be dictated, for reasons of which most of you are aware.[424] So they're finished, and they are to be published next year. The title of this new volume is *Moving Against the Stream*, and it covers the period from August 1964, when I returned to England after an absence of twenty years, up to April 1967, when the FWBO was founded.[425]

Someone asked me recently whether any particular themes have emerged from the memoirs. At first I thought not. I've been working on the book off and on for about five years, and it was difficult to get an overview of it. But when I thought about it, one theme I did see emerging was my reconnection with Western culture after twenty years in the East. Even while I was in India I was keeping up my contact to some extent with English literature, history, and so on, and I was writing poetry, but I didn't have any opportunities to see any Western visual art or hear any classical music. But once I got back to England I started re-engaging with Western culture, especially in the course of the tour of Italy and Greece which I made in 1966 in the company of a friend. This was a very rich experience, and I have written about it at some length in *Moving Against the Stream*.[426] Not only was I re-engaging with Western culture,

I was also having to present the Dharma in terms accessible to a Western audience. In India I had been accustomed to addressing Indians brought up in their very distinctive and rich and ancient culture. Some people were Westernized, Western-educated, and versed in Western culture, but many of them had very little higher culture at their disposal at all. I was addressing a very different sort of audience in the West, and I started presenting the Dharma in somewhat different terms. The fundamental principles were the same wherever I was teaching, but I was re-engaging in different ways with Western culture, and that was to be of importance for the future of the FWBO. There are a few other threads in this volume. For example, at the time of my arrival back in England, there were only two Buddhist organizations in Britain, and they'd been at loggerheads for about a year and weren't on speaking terms, so one of the threads is an account of how I tried to bring them together. Another important thread is the development of one of the most important friendships of my life, and that story I have told in some detail.[427]

Those of you who have read my memoirs will recollect that the previous volume ends in 1957, at the end of the Buddha Jayanti year. The new volume begins in 1964. What about the intervening period? It's unlikely that I shall be able to fill in those missing years myself, but all is not lost, because the gap has been filled to some extent by my old friend Khantipālo in his new book *Noble Friendship*.[428] Khantipālo arrived in India from England in 1959 and came to see me in 1960. He had been ordained as a *śrāmaṇera* or novice monk in London about a year earlier by a Sri Lankan *bhikkhu* who was another old friend of mine, and on his arrival in Bodh Gaya, where he was going to stay at the Thai monastery for a while, he heard that there was an English monk, Sangharakshita by name, in Kalimpong, so he and my Thai *bhikkhu* friend Vivekananda came to see me.[429] Khantipālo spent three years in India, and one year was spent with me in two lengthy instalments, plus that first short meeting. I remember him very well. He is ten years younger than me, and quite a bit taller, rather angular and awkward in his movements, with a high forehead and a regular dome of a head. But I soon found that he was very sincere, very willing to learn. In the book he says somewhere that as a young man he was very conceited. That's for him to say, but I certainly didn't notice any trace of conceit during the time he was with me. He was very humble, receptive, helpful, and cooperative. And yes, we did develop something of a friendship.

On one occasion he spent about six months with me uninterruptedly, partly during the rainy season, and we paid weekly visits to one of my teachers, Yogi Chen, who lived as a hermit on the outskirts of the Kalimpong bazaar and spent most of his time meditating. He allowed himself half an hour a day in which to write, and produced quite a lot of books that way. He didn't usually receive visitors, but I was allowed to see him whenever I wished, so I was already visiting him once a week on Saturdays. I took Khantipālo to meet him because Yogi Chen was a great meditator and very deeply versed in the Dharma, and I thought it was good that Khantipālo should become acquainted with him. At that time Khantipālo was called Sujiva, the well or happily living one, which I felt was quite appropriate. He became Khantipālo when he became a fully ordained monk or *bhikkhu*. We had many discussions with Yogi Chen, and eventually he offered to give a series of lectures just for the two of us on the subject of meditation: Hīnayāna, Mahāyāna, Vajrayāna, Chan, the whole field of Buddhist meditation, in which he was deeply versed. So week by week we went along. Yogi Chen prepared his talks very carefully, and for one hour we listened and Khantipālo made extensive notes, and when we got back to the vihara, he typed them out and showed them to me. I made suggestions and corrections, we checked them with Yogi Chen, and in this way a book was produced, eventually published as *Buddhist Meditation, Systematic and Practical*.[430]

In his book Khantipālo gives an engaging picture of our life at the Triyana Vardhana Vihara. When it was read to me recently, I was a bit shocked to realize how simply we were living. Khantipālo doesn't exactly complain about the food, but he clearly found it very simple, sparse even, and of course we didn't usually eat after twelve o'clock. It isn't surprising that when I returned to England after twenty years I weighed only eight and a half stone. I took Khantipālo on tour with me among the Indian people who had recently converted to Buddhism under the guidance of Dr Ambedkar, and he assisted me greatly during one of my extensive tours, in the course of which I visited scores of towns and villages, and gave many, many lectures.[431] In Pune we held a month-long training course for some fifty newly converted Buddhists, held in the evenings because everybody had a full-time job. That was a historic occasion, quite a milestone, and at least one person who was present later became a member of our Order. So Khantipālo and

I had a very good, even a quite deep contact. He also writes about his impressions of India, and about the time he spent in Nepal, where he met people that I had met many years earlier. The book is very readable, and I hope that quite a few of you will find time to read it.

Now that I've finished writing my memoirs I have much more time for reflection and meditation. Just a couple of weeks ago I was in Birmingham, at Madhyamaloka, sitting on the patio in the sunshine, and for some reason thoughts about creativity started coming into my mind.[432] One of the thoughts that occurred to me was that nowadays we use the term 'creative' rather loosely. It's been rather debased, rather vulgarized. Some time ago I heard of something called 'creative accounting', which used to be called falsification! All sorts of things have become creative. If you take a piece of paper and scribble on it a bit, you're being creative, apparently. You could even win a prize. The terms creative and creativity have become rather overworked and clichéd, and have lost much of their significance. So what is creativity really? Let's linger on the topic briefly, though I don't want to spend too long considering it in the abstract, because I want to get on to something more concrete. Creativity, we could say, means bringing something new into existence, but it isn't just that, because not everything that is new is creative. People nowadays set great store by being original, but you can't be original by trying to be original. That is an artificial originality, not the real thing. You can only produce something original if *you* are original. That doesn't mean being eccentric. It means being yourself, being in touch with yourself, knowing who and what you are, having or developing insights, vision, imagination. If you can be yourself in that way, you will produce something original, something that partakes of the nature of creativity.

So much for the more abstract aspect of the topic. Now let's go into the crux of the matter: the different fields of creativity, the different ways in which we are creative. The first field is the obvious one of the arts: music, poetry, literature in general, film, the visual arts, painting, sculpture. These are all at their best manifestations of creativity. They are original in the sense that they are the products, the expressions, of someone's original, actually experienced vision, imagination, even insight.

The second field of creativity is perhaps less obvious: meditation. Some of you may think of meditation as a hard slog, but when you're meditating, you're actually being creative. What are you creating when you meditate? You're creating skilful (*kuśala*) mental events. Previously there was probably a mixture of thoughts passing through your mind – unskilful thoughts, wandering thoughts, disturbed thoughts, unconcentrated thoughts – but when you meditate, you bring into existence a succession of skilful, wholesome, *kuśala* mental events. The deeper you go in meditation the more meditative you become, and the more continuous is the stream of positive mental events you produce. So meditation is a highly creative activity. You are bringing into existence and hopefully sustaining something positive, wholesome, and skilful, and with practice you can do this uninterruptedly, or at least with only intermittent breaks. You don't just do it when you're sitting on your meditation cushion. Ideally you do it, with the help of awareness, whatever you're doing. Meditation is thus one of the most creative activities in which we can possibly engage. We could also more specifically refer to some of the Mahāyāna and Vajrāyāna meditation practices in which we use our imagination. We're being creative when we visualize the Pure Land, or when we visualize the figure of Avalokiteśvara, or Mañjughoṣa, or Padmasambhava, or Tārā. That is a more specialized form of meditation as creativity – *sādhana*, as we call it – and it has tremendous emotional and spiritual value for those who engage in it.

The third area within which creativity manifests itself is friendship. When two people meet and become friends, and especially when they become spiritual friends, they have an influence on each other and create something between them: a relationship, an experience, a mental state which we call friendship. The English word friendship is rather weak, and even the word *mettā*, even *kalyāṇa mitratā*, is a rather weak expression for the kind of experience that is brought into existence when two friends get together and when communication between them is deep and honest and sincere and intense. A lot can happen within the context of a friendship. As you interact with your friend with openness and honesty, rough edges get smoothed, corners get rounded off, and you learn to do for the sake of your friend what you would hardly perhaps even do for yourself. In this way friendship becomes what I've called a mutual transcendence of egoism.[433] Śāntideva sheds light on this in his *Bodhicaryāvatāra*.[434] If you get a number of people in a relationship of mutual friendship, something very precious can be produced.

In his *Ethics*, Aristotle says that friendship is possible only between the virtuous, by which he doesn't mean the goody-goody; he wasn't interested in that sort of virtue. Virtue really means something like excellence, so Aristotle means that in order to be truly friends, you must have some principle, some ideal, on which the friendship is based. In the context of Buddhism, *kalyāṇa mitratā* is based on the fact that both people are living and working for the Dharma, and they are therefore helping each other to engage more deeply with the Dharma to which both of them are committed. In this way there comes about that mutual transcendence of self, and the friendship becomes a manifestation of creativity. Something new is brought into existence. If you have a real friendship with someone, you get from it something you don't get from your relationship with your parents, or your employer, or your children, or your sexual partner. You get something completely different, completely new, unique. Unfortunately, nowadays very few people in the world seem to have any experience of this.

The fourth field within which creativity manifests itself may surprise or even shock you. It's institutions. Groans all round! The word institution has rather a bad press, even within the FWBO. But institutions are very important. Without them there's no civilization, no culture. Everything that is alive is organized, and disorganization means death. If you look at a plant, so long as it has life, it has structure, it has organization, and when it dies, it withers and disintegrates. It's the same, obviously, with the human being. So long as we are alive, we are a structure of bones and blood, flesh and phlegm, bile, and all the other things mentioned in the ten stages of the decomposition of a corpse, and when we die, the body becomes disorganized, reverting to the elements of which it consists and from which it was originally drawn.[435] That which is alive is organized, and if you're not organized, you're not alive.

Organization within the context of civilization and culture is a very important manifestation of creativity. It usually takes a lot of people to bring an institution into existence, and it takes a long time for them to do it, a long time for the institution to develop within itself sufficient life, energy, and vitality to be able to survive under changing circumstances. In the world there are all sorts of organizations and institutions, and among them of course is the FWBO. We need not hesitate to refer to the FWBO as an institution, even though the word has unpleasant connotations for some people. If someone can think of a better word, I'd be glad to hear it. The FWBO as an institution has been built up, created, over the years. So many people have put their creativity into it. The London Buddhist Centre, which we originally called Sukhavati, is an institution. Twenty-odd years ago, some thirty people worked on this semi-derelict old fire station and transformed it over a period of some two and a half years into our present London Buddhist Centre, from which so many people have benefited. This was not just the bringing into existence of an institution in the ordinary, rather negative sense of the term, but a great creative achievement, the creation of something valuable, important, and beautiful.[436] We have many other institutions – centres, team-based right livelihood businesses, chapters, communities – into which we put our creative energy.

So these are these four areas in which creativity manifests: the arts, meditation, friendship, especially spiritual friendship, and institutions, especially those which we ourselves are in the process of building up.

In the course of my reflections over the last few weeks, I've been wondering how I would characterize my life, if I was asked to be quite objective and to look back at my life as though it was somebody else's. It occurs to me that, to be quite honest, I'm not a religious-minded person in the conventional sense. I don't think I've ever been pious, and I wouldn't like to be described as religious. It seems to have all the wrong connotations. So how would I describe myself? I think I'd like to describe myself as a creative person, someone whose life has been an expression of creativity, even if only in a small way. After all, I've written quite a bit of poetry, and quite a few volumes of memoirs. I'm well aware that in some quarters my poetry is considered rather old-fashioned and non-experimental, but never mind, I've expressed myself through that medium, so I think I can justly say I've been creative in that way, whatever the objective value of that creation may be. And I've had the good fortune to come into contact with very good spiritual teachers and spiritual friends, people like Yogi Chen. I've had the opportunity of taking up meditation and having meditative experience, including experience of the *sādhanas* I mentioned, so in this respect also my life has been an expression of creativity. And I've been very fortunate in my friendships. I consider it one of the great blessings of my life that I have had so many good friends, both in India and in the West. Some have been friends for decades now, and some, sadly, have departed this life. Dr Johnson famously said that it's important to keep one's friendships in constant repair.[437] It's important to keep in contact with one's friends, and I have tried to do that. I have a number of good old friends, and I'm glad to say that even in my old age I seem to be making new friends as well. And when we come to institutions, I think I can say I've played a significant part in the creation of the FWBO. Now I've been able to hand on many responsibilities to the College of Preceptors and to the Council, and they are continuing that work of creativity, as are all those who are in one way or another involved in our movement. We are all engaged in one great creative endeavour, manifesting itself in many cases in the creation of our institutions.

I consider myself very fortunate to have been able to lead a life of creativity, and I can say that a creative life is a happy life. If you're being creative, whatever the difficulties, you are happy. If you're painting a picture or writing a poem, you may be experiencing all sorts of technical difficulties and you may even be tempted to give up, but deep down you're very happy. Creativity, in the broad sense I've tried to describe, is a very positive experience. While you are creating, you are happy, and if you're not creating in any way, or only in a very limited way, then the likelihood is that you're not very happy.

In an early talk, *Mind – Reactive and Creative*, I described the creative mind as the mind that is independent, spontaneous, aware, and the reactive mind as the mind that doesn't originate anything, but just re-acts, the dependent, repetitive, mechanical mind.[438] It occurred to me recently that I could add another epithet to that list. The reactive mind is not just *non*-creative. It can be *anti*-creative, destructive.

That reminds me of something I've been listening to recently, Ted Hughes' translation and reading of that great Anglo-Saxon epic *Beowulf*. It's well worth reading, and it's illustrative of the destructive aspect of the reactive mind. The poem was written down in the tenth century – there's only one surviving manuscript – but it seems that it was composed, perhaps orally, some time around the eighth century, and relates to happenings which probably occurred in the fifth or sixth century, though scholars differ on all these points. The story, or at least the first half of it, is set in what is now Denmark, and it begins with a description of the descent of the king of the Danes. The king was very famous, and attracted many young men into his service. He was a just ruler, he accumulated great riches, and one day he decided to build a magnificent hall. Apparently he sent for architects and artists from all over the world – this can't be historically accurate, but it is what the poem says. This great hall was built, and the poem describes it as a wonder of the world, adorned inside and outside with gold that glittered from afar. It's referred to as a mead hall, the hall in which the warriors gather to drink mead, rejoice, and celebrate. The first time the hall was used, when the king and queen were there, and all the king's men, the court minstrel started singing a song of the creation of the sun and the moon, the earth, and all living things. When I read this poem for the first time many years ago and came to this passage, it struck me as being of great archetypal significance. It's almost as though this great hall, adorned with gold, represents the civilization and culture of the whole of humanity, the values that we've created over the centuries since the dawn of history.

So there was great feasting and rejoicing in the hall, and everyone was happy – all except one. The monster Grendel was not happy about all that rejoicing. I don't know what the name Grendel means, but it has a harsh sound, as of the grinding of teeth: Grrrendel. Grendel is described as being descended from Cain, who according to the Old Testament murdered his brother Abel. So one night Grendel crept up, broke down the door of the hall, slaughtered thirty of the men sleeping there, and took them away to devour them. Night after night he came and pillaged the hall, so that it became deserted, and the song of the minstrel was heard there no more. One other significant detail is that the hall was also the throne room of the king, and we're told in a rather mysterious way that Grendel was 'kept from the throne'. That, I'm sure, has deep significance which I may go into at some other time.

Word of Grendel's destruction of the hall spread far and wide, even to distant countries, and to cut a long story short, the hero Beowulf, who comes from the land of the Geats, which seems to be not far away, perhaps in southern Sweden, comes to the great hall, and he and his men sleep there. Grendel comes and kills one man, but when he comes to Beowulf, Beowulf has in his hand the strength of thirty men, so he seizes Grendel's arm and wrenches the arm right off, and Grendel dies. So once again there is feasting and music and singing in the great hall. But that's not the end of the story, because Grendel has a mother. We're not told her name. She's just referred to as Grendel's mother, and she lives where Grendel also used to live, at the bottom of a deep dark pool in the middle of a sinister forest up in the mountains. Very upset at her son's death, she comes to the hall and snatches the king's close friend and favourite advisor and gets away before Beowulf can catch her. The next morning Beowulf and the king follow her track and discover this lake overshadowed by rocks and trees deep in the forest, and Beowulf plunges down into the depths, where he kills Grendel's mother. I think there is some significance in this. Grendel comes to the hall and he is defeated there, but in order to defeat Grendel's mother, Beowulf has to track her and go down into those depths. It's as though she represents a force even more primordial than Grendel himself. This is only half the story. In the other half, which takes place fifty years later, Beowulf fights and kills a dragon, and is killed himself at the same time. But here I'm using the story as an illustration of the fact that the reactive mind can be destructive. Grendel symbolizes, or embodies, that aspect of the reactive mind which is not only not creative, but opposed to creativity.

We can see this destructive force operating within all the fields of creativity I've mentioned. In the arts we can see it in the carpings of small-minded critics who can't appreciate true greatness. Recently I've been listening to the music of Richard Strauss. One of his compositions is called *The Life of a Hero*, and in the opening movement you get the hero scene, while in the second movement you get all sorts of sharp little quavering sounds which according to the programme notes represent the critics who criticized the composer's music. Of course, being criticized doesn't mean that you're a genius, but even a genius may be criticized, and in the field of the arts you get this sort of niggling criticism. But where the destructive force operates most is perhaps within the psyche of the artist himself or herself. Some artists start off very well. They're inspired. Perhaps they are geniuses. But then, wanting success, they start giving the public what they want, producing what will sell, perhaps because they've got domestic responsibilities, or because they want to build a magnificent house and entertain in style. Such compromise is the working of the reactive mind in its destructive aspect within the psyche of the artist. The Pre-Raphaelite painter John Everett Millais, for example, produced some wonderful work in his early days, but towards the end of his life, though he did paint some fine pictures, he seemed to compromise more and more, because the public wanted pretty pictures like *Bubbles*.[439] Writers compromise too. George Gissing's fine novel *New Grub Street* tells the story of a novelist who sets out with great ideals but gradually starts writing things that the public want to read, to bring in a lot of money. The real-life Grub Street was a London street where in the days of Samuel Johnson hack writers lived and sold their pen to the highest bidder.[440]

And then we come to meditation. Here, the anti-creative force manifests itself when meditation becomes just a matter of technique, when you think that if you get the right technique and practise it regularly, even forcibly, you're sure to obtain results. You can start seeing meditation as an end in itself, almost a magical solution to your problems if you can just go on doing it, however repetitively and mechanically, although the practice has lost whatever life it originally had. So it's very important that we refresh our meditation practice from time to time.

And then there's the question of how that destructive impulse manifests in the sphere of friendship, and human relations generally. Aristotle said that friendship is possible only between those who are free. He didn't think there could be friendship between a free man and a slave, because slaves are not their own masters, and in order to be friends you both have to be independent.[441] The destructive element comes in when one of the friends is dependent on the other in an unhealthy way, so that they are no longer emotionally and spiritually free. Sometimes one friend dominates or controls the other, or even takes over the life of the other in the interests of so-called friendship, but this is not true friendship. One could say that the same destructive element enters in when the individual is taken over by or made to submit to the group. They may be swallowed up by the group, or perhaps they even want to be swallowed up by the group.

The destructive aspect of the reactive mind can also manifest in the field of institutions. To take an obvious example, it manifests when a universal religion becomes an ethnic religion, and this is a danger facing all universal religions. There's always a gravitational pull by virtue of which they're in danger of becoming ethnic religions.[442] We have to be on our guard against that all the time.

The destructive, anti-creative aspect of the reactive mind can operate in all the four fields I have mentioned. But there's another way in which this reactive mind can be characterized. It's more than destructive; it's devouring. I have recently been reflecting on William Blake, an excellent example of a truly great artist and poet, and one of the most creative people in the history of English art and literature. In *The Marriage of Heaven and Hell*, Blake distinguishes between what he calls the prolific and the devouring.[443] The prolific is that which is enormously and constantly productive. Many of the greatest artists and writers were prolific, producing not just one or two masterpieces, but dozens. One thinks of the great Greek dramatists, Sophocles, Euripides, and others, who according to tradition each produced a hundred or more plays, only a fraction of which survive, unfortunately. In the Renaissance, painters like Titian, Tintoretto, El Greco, Rembrandt, Rubens, and Michelangelo were hugely prolific. Think how prolific Shakespeare was, and Goethe, and Dickens, and the great Russian novelists. And in the East, the Sufi poet Jalal al-Din Rumi was constantly creating, sometimes in a state of ecstasy, dictating verse after verse after verse, and in modern times the great Bengali poet Rabindranath Tagore was endlessly creative, producing not only an enormous amount of lyric poetry, but short stories, novels, and plays. In his old age he started painting and produced about two thousand paintings, and he composed and set to music two thousand songs which are still sung all over India. So many of the greatest artists and poets have been very, very creative.

Meditation can be prolific too. They say that one good turn deserves another, but one good, skilful thought produces another, so the more you meditate, the more you are likely to meditate. Meditation is prolific in another way too, because if you are a meditator, if you are creative in that particular way, you can teach meditation. When I started the FWBO, I didn't keep my experience of meditation to myself, but began teaching meditation to others, and over the years thousands of people have learned to meditate. Not only within the FWBO, but wherever meditation is taught, there is that creation and recreation of a very positive state of mind. Back in the Sixties we had something called Transcendental Meditation. I don't think there was anything very transcendental about it, but it popularized the practice of meditation, and we can be very grateful to the Maharishi Mahesh Yogi for that. Meditation is inherently prolific because once you have a meditative experience, just as when you have a positive experience of any kind, you want to share it with other people.

Friendship is prolific too. If you make a new friend, you normally like to introduce them to your old friends, so in that way a network of friends grows up. Sometimes we speak of the FWBO itself as being fundamentally a network of friendship. Network, one might say, is another word for organization. I'm reminded of the simile in one of the Mahāyāna *sūtras* of a flame being lit from another.[444] The first flame doesn't lose anything by propagating itself, and the flame of friendship passes from one person to another, and then another, until there are all these flames burning brightly together within what we might describe as the mandala of friendship.

So that's the prolific. As I mentioned, Blake says in *The Marriage of Heaven and Hell* that there are two kinds of person, the prolific and the devouring. What corresponds to devouring in the reactive, anti-creative mind is a very important word in Buddhism, which occurs in the chain of the *nidānas* depicted in the outermost circle of the wheel of life: *tṛṣṇa*, craving. Craving is the urge to devour something, whether it's another person, or an idea, or a thing.

In the *nidāna* chain, you have first of all the cause process of the past life: *avidyā*, ignorance, and the *saṃskāras*, the factors conducing to rebirth, and then in this life you have first of all the effect process of the present life. First there's *vijñāna*, the seed of consciousness that comes into being in the womb of the mother. Then you have *nāma-rūpa*, the psychophysical organism that comes into existence in dependence upon that *vijñāna*, that initial consciousness. In dependence upon that you have the six sense organs, including mind. Then you have contact with an external object, physical or mental, and then *vedanā*, feeling, whether pleasant, painful, or neutral. That's the end of the result process, but not the end of the chain, because what usually happens is that in dependence upon feeling, especially pleasurable feeling, there arises thirst, craving. You want to devour that pleasant experience, person, idea, or possession. And in dependence upon *tṛṣṇā*, craving, there arises *upādāna*, clinging. I need not trace the process any further. The crucial point I want to make is that at the point at which the result process of the present passes over into the cause process of the present, what we have to do is maintain our awareness. When we experience *vedanā*, whether pleasant, painful, or neutral, we have to be careful not to allow the reactive mind to come into operation. We must be creative. We must respond. And especially when we experience *duḥkha*, when we experience suffering, we should try to develop *śraddhā* or faith.

When we are enjoying ourselves we don't usually stop and ask, 'Why am I enjoying myself? Why should I be so happy?' That sort of state is not conducive to the asking of philosophical questions. But when we experience suffering, whether it's physical suffering or loss of some kind, we may start thinking that there must be something more than this life of alternate suffering and pleasure, and perhaps we start lifting our mind to something higher, for want of a better term, to higher values, to something more truly satisfying. In Buddhist terms, our aspiration eventually comes to rest on the Three Jewels, the Buddha, the Dharma, and the Sangha, and faith, in the sense of the placing of our heart on the Three Jewels, arises. In this way we take the first step out of the round and up the spiral which leads eventually to Enlightenment. In dependence upon faith there arises a feeling of joyous contentment, a deep, heartfelt satisfaction. In dependence upon that there may arise an ecstatic state, an intense bubbling joy. In dependence upon that there arises an even more lofty experience, which consists in the calming down of the previous experience without any lessening of its intensity. In this way we come to *sukha*, a truly blissful experience. We then become concentrated, experiencing *samādhi*, and when we're concentrated, we're able to see things as they really are, and that really does constitute a tremendous turning point in the spiritual life. From then onwards the attainment of Enlightenment is certain.

We may seem to have come a long way from Bhikkhu Khantipālo and his book *Noble Friendship*, but we haven't really. Those of you who have heard me speak before will know that after these long detours I come back to the original point. Khantipālo was a remarkable person. After his three years in India, he spent about twelve years in Thailand as a fully ordained monk. He then moved to Australia, set up a meditation centre near Sydney, and a few years ago he decided he didn't want to be a *bhikkhu* any more and broadened out his spiritual approach, and he is now involved in the creation of the Bodhicitta Centre, a Buddhist centre in north-eastern Australia.[445] So Khantipālo's life has been a life of creativity, just as mine has been, and he has lived a happy, fulfilling life. He's written a number of books, so his creativity has expressed itself in literary terms. He is a person with considerable experience of meditation; he's been creative in that way too. And he has made many friends. His book is called *Noble Friendship*, and it is about his friendship with me, and with my old friend Buddharakshita, who was his teacher for a while,[446] and with Vivekananda, the Thai *bhikkhu* who was one of my closest friends at that time. He's also been creative in the sphere of institutions. I'm very pleased to see the appearance of this book of his. Reading it, or having it read to me, I was touched to find how deeply Khantipālo was affected by the time he spent with me, and the way he remembered me with so much affection and appreciation, especially as since those days we haven't had much communication until the last few years. I was quite moved by some parts of this book, and I hope you will be too.

LOOKING BACK – AND FORWARD

Birmingham Buddhist Centre, April 2007

About five years ago I had the unpleasant experience of partially losing my eyesight. Throughout my life I've been a great reader, so to lose my eyesight even partially was quite an affliction, but there are always compensations even for afflictions like that, and one of these was that I started listening to the radio more. Listening to the radio over the years, I have noticed that every now and then an anniversary is celebrated. The two hundredth anniversary of the battle of Trafalgar was celebrated with a few programmes. More recently there have been programmes around the fiftieth anniversary of the signing of the Treaty of Rome, and at present we're in the midst of all sorts of programmes about the Falklands War of twenty-five years ago. Looking to events of a Buddhist nature which have been celebrated in recent months, last October there was the fiftieth anniversary of Dr Ambedkar's conversion to Buddhism, which was followed by the conversion of hundreds of thousands of people in India and elsewhere.

It seems that anniversaries have both a collective importance and an individual importance. They form part of our history, they remind us of what has happened, and they help create continuity, a story, a collective or personal identity. And so it is that today we are celebrating the fortieth anniversary of the founding of the FWBO. I must say that I was a little disappointed when I learned that there wasn't going to be the usual big national celebration here in the UK. I understand that plans are afoot to have a big celebration of our forty-first anniversary next year, and I suppose we shall have to be content with that. I'm assured that it will be something rather different and very attractive and many people are expected to attend.[447] But even though there isn't a national celebration of FWBO Day this year, we are celebrating it here in Birmingham and I am very glad to see that people from a number of other centres have come to take part.

Naturally my thoughts fly back to those early days forty years ago. Sometimes it seems a long time ago, sometimes not long at all. I was 41 then, still a comparatively young man. We started very small, just a handful of people, and we didn't have a centre of our own. Our first classes were held in a basement below a shop in Monmouth Street in central London. The basement was about twelve feet square, and with a bit of juggling we could get twenty chairs in, because in those days people did not sit on the floor to meditate. When we had our inaugural dedication we allowed a few people to stand, so we squeezed in twenty-four people, and recited a dedication ceremony that I'd composed the evening before.[448] Thus we dedicated our Triratna shrine and meditation room, and that was how and where the FWBO began.

We started with meditation classes, which is significant in itself, meditation being such an integral part of the Buddhist spiritual life. We very soon had two or three meditation classes a week; there was quite a demand for them. There was quite a big turnover but our classes were usually full, with eight or ten or twelve people, though one evening when I came along to take the class I found that only one person had come. That's the sort of thing that happens, as all of you who take classes at FWBO centres know only too well, and we have to practise patience and optimism and not lose heart. I certainly didn't lose heart on that occasion because there were other encouraging signs.

The first meditation I taught was the mindfulness of breathing, and after a while I started teaching the *mettā bhāvanā* as well. Both these practices, especially the mindfulness of breathing, had been very important in my own spiritual life for quite a few years, and they continue to be taught in all our FWBO centres, laying a firm foundation for our practice of meditation, and the spiritual life generally. From the mindfulness of breathing we can go to mindfulness of the body and its movements, mindfulness of our feelings, our emotions, mindfulness of every thought that passes through our mind, every imagining, every dream, and we can go on to mindfulness of the Dharma, mindfulness of the teaching of the Buddha, even eventually mindfulness of reality itself. The mindfulness of breathing can take us a very long way, and we shouldn't doubt that. Similarly, from practising the *mettā bhāvanā* we can go on to practise the other *brahma vihāras*: the *karuṇā bhāvanā*, the *muditā bhāvanā*, and the *upekṣā bhāvanā*. The *upekṣā bhāvanā* is the *bhāvanā* of complete tranquillity, within which it is difficult to make any distinction between how we feel towards others and how we feel towards ourselves, and that can lead us right into the heart of the Dharma, into *śūnyatā*. So these two practices, seemingly so simple and straightforward, are the twin pillars of our practice of meditation. We may take on other practices in the course of our spiritual life, and they may be very helpful, but at rock bottom we need these two practices.

After a while of coming along to classes, there were people who wanted a more extended practice of meditation. They wanted to go deeper. If you're just sitting for a couple of hours, you can't always go very deep, especially if you're coming straight from work, as many people did. So we started holding week-long retreats in the countryside. We went to a place called Quartermaine in West Sussex, and another bigger place called Keffolds, and we had what has come to be a standard FWBO retreat consisting of talks, meditation, periods of silence, walks and talks together, pujas, study, and so on. I have very pleasant memories of those far-off days. I can remember the day when I introduced communication exercises. I noticed that people didn't always find it very easy to communicate with one another, so I wondered what to do. A bit more mindfulness, even a bit more *mettā bhāvanā*, might not be enough. Then I bethought myself of these exercises I had learned in India many years before from an Englishwoman who had devised them on the basis of advice she'd received from various teachers. I introduced these exercises and they had an almost miraculous effect. People really opened up with one another. After that the communication exercises came to be a regular part of the FWBO repertoire, and I believe they're sometimes still used on retreat if the leader feels that people aren't opening up with one another sufficiently.[449]

At the end of a week's retreat, people would loiter at the gate waiting for their transport home, looking very sad. They'd been increasingly happy throughout the week, and they were very sorry that the retreat had ended. In the course of the retreats, I noticed such a remarkable change in people. They would arrive looking rather tired, perhaps a bit fed up, but as the days progressed, they became happier, more positive, more communicative, and one could see with one's own eyes that the Dharma – even a little of it – really did work. This showed me very clearly that conditions are important. If you wish to practise the Dharma, it's a duty to yourself, almost, to do your best to create the conditions and the lifestyle that enable you to practise.

This takes me back to a time in my own life when a change in conditions made a very big difference to me, and had a lasting effect. Today, as well as celebrating the fortieth anniversary of the FWBO, we're also celebrating the sixtieth anniversary of my Going Forth. In my memoirs I describe how I went forth from a place called Kasauli with a friend, having given away my worldly possessions and wearing yellow robes, shaven-headed, and all that.[450] I spent a couple of years wandering here and there, staying in different places. I have sometimes asked myself why I did it and what I learned. It was sixty years ago, and it's not easy to say exactly what my motivation was, except that I wanted to lead a thoroughly Buddhist life, as close to the life of the Buddha as I could. But one of my motivations was that I wanted to go forth from civic and national identity. I was in India as an Englishman, a foreigner, and I threw away my identification papers so that I could be anonymous, at least in my own mind. One of the things I learned was that you might not identify yourself in your own mind with any particular group or social class or nationality, but other people will want to identify you, and you sometimes have to fight quite hard to retain your non-identity. But that was my ideal: not to consider myself in my heart of hearts as being English as opposed to some other nationality. I understood that to be an essential part of the attitude of the spiritual life of the monk. Subsequently I discovered that most monks in the East were intensely nationalistic, which rather disappointed me. But I still uphold the ideal that we should try to see ourselves as Buddhists, as citizens of the world, and not identify ourselves too closely with any particular nationality or culture or conditioning of that kind.

As I wandered, I came to know a lot about India at a grass roots level. I knew what village life was like, and small-town life, and the open road, and that gave me a great love of India and the Indian people which deepened as the years went by. In those days I described myself as a freelance wandering ascetic, freelance meaning that I didn't belong to any Buddhist group or society or organization or order. Not having any means of livelihood, I was dependent on other people, at one stage begging my food, especially after I was ordained as a *śrāmaṇera* and had a begging-bowl. Sometimes there was no shelter and we slept in the open, but I don't think we ever went hungry. That experience was important, because it showed me in a very concrete way how dependent we are on other people. Today I had lunch. I expect most of you did too. So how was it that I had lunch? I didn't prepare it myself. It was prepared by Sanghadeva. How was it that he was able to prepare it? Well, the vegetables come from a man who delivers them once a week. He gets them from the wholesaler, I think, and the wholesaler perhaps gets them from the farmer, or perhaps there are more intermediate stages. We are very dependent on other people – not only dependent but interdependent, as I was sharply reminded every day during my wandering period. Much of the time we slept in a different place every night, just once or twice settling down for a while, so I developed a sense of detachment from place. Even after coming back to England I lived happily in a number of different places, wandering having taught me to be independent of place and quite happy to move to a new one. Even now, if I go to stay somewhere for a few days, I feel at home wherever I happen to be. That is part of the legacy of those wandering days all those years ago.

Back in England, I started giving lectures in hired halls, and they were very well attended. Many people came to the meditation classes, and after a while people started living together in communities. Our first community came into existence during that period, at Sarum House, as it was then called, in Purley. (It was later given the name Aryatara.) I believe there's still a community of some kind there, so there's an element of continuity. So in the course of those five years quite a lot happened. We got off the mark quite quickly. There was a lot of enthusiasm, a lot of interest. There weren't many of us but we were all very closely connected and saw each other very frequently, meeting in classes and lectures, at the poetry group that we started, or in tea shops and cafés. Ananda was a great lover of tea shops. He used to work on his poetry and his novel – the first of many – sitting in a tea shop or coffee bar, and I sometimes used to meet him and we'd walk along the Embankment by the River Thames discussing the Dharma and poetry and Zen, and the form of the novel, and all that sort of thing.[451] I have many happy memories of that period.

We were helped by the spirit of the times. In the late Sixties and early Seventies there was an atmosphere of experimentation and all sorts of areas of life were changing. We had the Beatles and all sorts of other groups, and along with the Beatles there was the Maharishi, a colourful character whose high-pitched cackle I remember hearing on the radio. There was guru Maharaj, the boy guru whom people flocked to see, though he's quite forgotten now. Zen was in the air, and something else was in the air too – not in the FWBO, but if one joined a queue to watch a certain type of film, there'd be a pall of smoke hanging over the whole queue. Those were the days of psychedelic drugs and experimenting with oriental music and new forms of literature. Jack Kerouac's novels were popular and so were the works of Erich Fromm. There was definitely a spirit that was supportive of any new spiritual venture rather than antagonistic to it. Not everybody was affected by this zeitgeist, but some people were, and we were able to take advantage of this.

I've sometimes thought that if I'd returned to this country ten years earlier it would have been very difficult to found the FWBO, and if I'd arrived ten years later, I would have missed the bus. It seems that 1964 was just the right time to arrive, and after a spell at the Hampstead Vihara, I started the FWBO in 1967. Some cultural and social conditions supported us. At that time there was a widespread movement of squatting – that is, occupying an empty house – especially in London. The government attempted to stop it with the Criminal Law Act of 1977, but for a time some of our friends didn't have to pay rent, and that helped. Also, it was very easy for young people to get work then. They didn't mind giving up work for a few months because they knew that as soon as they needed money, they could get a job. It isn't quite like that now, so people are more economically conscious. So we had the advantage of riding on the crest of that wave.

Things have changed since then, though it's difficult to say exactly how. The economic imperative seems stronger, and the forces of materialism, consumerism, and individualism are rampant, and all that tends to move against any attempt, collective or individual, to lead the spiritual life. We are up against it, as I know from some of the people who come to see me. It isn't easy to try to lead a spiritual life nowadays. Of course, it's never been easy; indeed, it's intrinsically difficult. At the time of his conversion, Dr Ambedkar said, 'Make no mistake, Buddhism is a very difficult religion to practise.' And some of my Tibetan friends used to quote a proverb: 'If it isn't difficult, it isn't religion.' That's very uncompromising indeed. So the present time isn't the only time in history when it's been difficult to lead a spiritual life. Even just trying to be objective and see things as they are on the everyday level has always been difficult.

I'm reminded of Sir Francis Bacon's doctrine of the idols. Bacon was one of the first great modern philosophers, roughly a contemporary of Shakespeare, and he wrote a number of important philosophical works which I suspect are not much read nowadays. In a work called *Novum Organum* he tried to overthrow the logic of Aristotle and replace it by something more empirically grounded, propounding a doctrine of what he called the idols, those things in the human mind that prevent us from seeing things truly.[452] He was thinking in terms of what we would call scientific truth, or what was then called natural philosophy, but what he said has a wider applicability.

The four idols he identified were the idols of the tribe, the idols of the cave, the idols of the market place, and the idols of the theatre. By tribe he meant the whole human race, *Homo sapiens*, and by the idols of the tribe he meant the mental limitations which we share in as much as we are all human beings, and which get in the way of our seeing the truth. One of the biggest idols he identified is our love of comfort. We prefer comfort to truth and tend to believe what pleases and appeals to us, and this leads to what he called superstition. One could bring in here belief in a personal God. People usually believe in God not because they've been intellectually convinced but because they want to feel safe, comfortable, protected, even loved. Idols of this sort are common to all human beings. We're all subject to the temptation to believe something because it feels comfortable to believe it. And then there are the idols of the cave. These are the personal limitations of individual human beings, their personal conditioning due to which they see things in a particular way, have certain prejudices, preferences, and so on. The market place is where people meet, where they exchange views and ideas, so the idols of the market place are the limitations that arise due to the nature of language, the difficulties of using language properly, reasoning properly and being clear in our thinking and in our definitions. By the idols of the theatre, Bacon doesn't mean theatre in the usual sense; he uses the word in a rather strange way. According to him, the idols of the theatre are simply, as we would say, wrong views, systematized into erroneous systems of belief or thought. Bacon propounded this doctrine of four idols many years ago, but I think they're still applicable, and form a useful framework for us to look at ourselves and our conditioning.[453] An Order member who is especially interested in philosophy might like to lead study on these four idols. It would be quite an interesting and stimulating exercise.

If we are trying to lead a spiritual life, we are up against it both individually and collectively. There are all sorts of ideologies by which we may be ensnared. Individualism is one of the most prevalent and lethal ones, but there are also consumerism, commercialism, and materialism in general. Our Buddhist thinking can be affected by the other ideologies that are around. We find people trying to bring together Buddhism and Christianity, or the Dharma and some form of therapy. When I was teaching at Yale in the United States, someone came to see me who was very enthusiastic about behaviourist psychology and convinced that it was more or less the same thing as Buddhism, and he found it very difficult to accept my view that the two are really rather different.[454] So there is the possibility that the purity of the Dharma may be adulterated by ideological elements that have no connection with it. I'm sure you can think of examples that you've encountered, or even had to wrestle with from time to time.

I recently came across an interesting book by Dzongsar Khyentse Rimpoche, who is a modern incarnate lama, believed to be an incarnation or *tulku* of one of my own teachers, Jamyang Khyentse Rimpoche. Dzongsar Khyentse Rimpoche is well acquainted with English and has quite a good knowledge of Western culture, and you may have heard of him as the director of a film called *The Cup*.[455] He's recently published a book called *What Makes You Not a Buddhist?* – quite an interesting question. He's had extensive experience of teaching the Dharma, especially Tibetan Buddhism, in various parts of the Western world, and he must have come across some rather strange Buddhists, what one might call hybrid Buddhists: half Buddhist and half something else. As a result, he has written this book, in which he says that what makes you not a Buddhist is that you don't wholeheartedly accept and entrust yourself to the four seals, the four *Dharma mudrās*.

So what are the four *Dharma mudrās*? They are a well-known traditional list.[456] The Rimpoche has produced his own version, some of which may sound familiar, some perhaps not:

All compounded things are impermanent.
All emotions are pain.
All things have no inherent existence.
Nirvana is beyond concepts.[457]

The word *mudrā* has many meanings, but the one that's relevant here is 'seal'. If a document has somebody's personal or official seal attached to it, you know that the document is genuine. Nowadays we use not seals but signatures. The *Dharma mudrās* guarantee that this is the Buddha's teaching. If a teaching bears these four seals it's authentic. If it doesn't bear them, or if it contradicts them or disagrees with them, it can't be Buddhist. This should give us a great deal of food for thought. More often than not we tend to ask the question 'What is it that makes one a Buddhist?', but Rimpoche has turned it around to ask 'What is it that makes one *not* a Buddhist?'

You're not a Buddhist if you don't accept that all compounded things are impermanent. And that means *all*. If you make any little exceptions, you're not a Buddhist. Your belief does not bear the Dharma seal. 'All emotions are pain' is a more difficult one, perhaps. Emotions like hatred, fear, jealousy, anxiety, and uncertainty are obviously painful, but some people would say that emotions like love are not painful. However, if they are not immediately painful, sooner or later they will become painful if what is occasioning the emotion is lost for any reason. In any case, no positive emotion can give you complete and final happiness. And then, all things have no inherent existence. There's no permanent unchanging soul or self. That is one of the basic doctrines of the Dharma. And the fourth *Dharma mudrā* is that Nirvāṇa is beyond concepts. It's very easy to talk slickly about Nirvāṇa, or Enlightenment, or *bodhi*, but do we really understand what it is? It's much better if we think of it as a mystery, something beyond our conception. We could also think of the Buddha not as that well-known historical figure Siddhārtha Gautama, someone about whom we know quite a lot, but as a very mysterious, distant personality, if we can even use the word 'personality' of him at all, someone almost luminous. We know quite a lot about the circumstances of the Buddha's life, what he did, his effect on his contemporaries, especially his disciples, but do we really know what he was like? Do we really have any understanding of what his experience of Enlightenment was? We have to recognize that Nirvāṇa is beyond conception.

So Dzongsar Rimpoche has performed a very useful service, and given us all something to think about. We have to ask ourselves, do we really accept, do we really believe, do we really have faith in these four *Dharma mudrās*? If we don't, we have to accept that we're not Buddhists after all, or at least much less Buddhist than we thought. I hope that Rimpoche's book will be found in FWBO bookstores, and that at least some of you will read it and study it. I think it's very appropriate that on this day when we're celebrating the fortieth anniversary of the FWBO we should go back to fundamentals, asking ourselves not just what makes us Buddhists, but also what makes us *not* Buddhists. The four *Dharma mudrās* are common to the whole Buddhist world, and in theory all Buddhists accept them. We just have to be certain that that is really the case so far as we personally are concerned.

ON TĀRĀ

Taraloka Retreat Centre, May 2007

I am very glad to be here at Taraloka once again, and to see the new extension and all sorts of other improvements and additions, and I'm especially pleased that in the grounds there is now a cabin shrine dedicated to Tārā, and that I can be here for its dedication, in view of the connection I have with this bodhisattva. Many years ago in Kalimpong I received a Tārā initiation from one of my teachers, Chattrul Sangye Dorje. I'd heard about him from a Sikkimese Buddhist friend, who told me that there was a very great Tibetan lama visiting Kalimpong and that I should certainly meet him. My friend said, 'He has a reputation for being a bit eccentric. No one knows exactly what he's going to do or say next. But he will probably be quite pleased to see you, and he might even give you a teaching if he's in the mood.' I didn't know Tibetan, so I needed an interpreter, so this friend came along with me, and I met the Rimpoche. He didn't look very prepossessing. In fact, he looked a bit grim, roughly dressed, and with a rough look, as though he was the sort of person you wouldn't care to meet on a dark night, but he also exuded an atmosphere of kindness and compassion, despite his rather grim expression. We got talking, and I believe we talked for about four hours, discussing all sorts of things, including meditation. In the end I asked him rather tentatively if he would give me a meditation, and if he would tell me what he thought my *yidam* was. To my surprise, he said that he would be very pleased to do so. He reflected for a few moments – I think he closed his eyes – and then he said, 'Your *yidam* is Dolma Jang-gu.' (That's the Tibetan name for Green Tārā.) Saying that Green Tārā had been the *yidam* of many pandits of Tibet and India, and he was sure that doing her *sādhana* would be of great benefit to me as well, he proceeded to explain to me exactly how she was to be visualized. A few days later he came to see me, and in the meantime I'd written down what he told me about the practice, so I took the opportunity of checking it with him. That was how I received my own introduction to Green Tārā nearly fifty years ago. I have done the practice off and on ever since then, and I've been very happy to hand it on to other Order members, some of whom have handed it on to others in their turn.

Green Tārā is sometimes called Śyāma Tārā. *Śyāma* is a Sanskrit word which literally means 'dark', and it refers to a very dark green. To me it seems that this beautiful rich green is very appropriate for Green Tārā, because it represents something dark and mysterious, like the deep green of the sea, or the midst of the forest. Another name for her is Khadiravaṇī Tārā, which means 'she of the *khadira* grove', a *khadira* being an acacia tree. Perhaps it would be a good idea if here at Taraloka you were to plant an acacia grove, a *khadiravaṇī*. You might not all live to see them as fully-grown trees, but many of you would, and I think it would give you a further sense that this really is Tārā's place.

Green Tārā represents compassionate action, and I've always associated Chattrul Sangye Dorje with that quality. His compassion doesn't just remain in his heart or his mind, but gets embodied in action. I've recently been hearing that he's been emphasizing the practice of releasing animals and birds from captivity, and the importance of being vegetarian. He said recently in an interview that he only became a vegetarian himself when he was 46, because he was born and brought up in Tibet, where it isn't easy to be vegetarian, but now he's in India, it's easy to be vegetarian, and he thinks that Buddhists in India and in the West should all take up that practice. This is very much in accordance with my own thinking. It seems to me that if one claims to be a Buddhist, and to be practising the five precepts, one obvious application of the first precept is to be a vegetarian. Recently I heard that a certain lama went to stay with Chattrul Sangye Dorje and placed a photograph of his own teacher on Chattrul Sangye Dorje's shrine. When Chattrul Sangye Dorje saw it, he said, 'Take it away. I don't want a meat-eater's photo on my shrine.' He's that sort of lama. He's not always polite. His intention is to teach the Dharma, and if you really want to teach the Dharma and you don't want to dilute it, sometimes you have to be a bit rough, or even a bit rude.

The most recent news I have of Chattrul Sangye Dorje is that about a month ago he went off on his wanderings again, at the age of 95. It's always been his custom to wander off to some holy place or shrine, or up into a range of mountains, and it seems that he's still doing that sort of thing even at his advanced age. I don't know exactly where he is – maybe nobody knows – but no doubt in due course we'll hear about his whereabouts.[458] So that's Chattrul Sangye Dorje, from whom I received the Green Tārā initiation. I subsequently received other Green Tārā initiations from two other teachers, Jamyang Khyentse Rimpoche and Dudjom Rimpoche, and I feel very fortunate to have received this initiation from these three great teachers.

I saw compassionate action manifested in the life and work of Chattrul Sangye Dorje and my other teachers, but what is it? It's very important to understand that true compassion is not just ordinary kindness. It's very much more than that. It is an emotion, if we can call it that, which springs from an absence of egotism. It's very important to make a distinction between pity and compassion; one gets a sense of this distinction in an interesting novel by Stefan Zweig called *Beware of Pity* which was popular in our sangha at one time.[459] Pity is weak, but compassion is strong. Pity springs from the ego, but compassion springs from a realization of non-ego. True compassion is inseparable from wisdom. The compassionate action that Green Tārā represents is compassion in this sense. If we want to engage in compassionate action, we have to work on transcending the ego-sense, at least to some extent. In the course of our FWBO practice, and especially when preparing for ordination, we do the six element practice, which is one of the most direct ways of attacking the ego-sense.[460] It's important to remember that compassionate action is action which springs from wisdom, action in which there isn't any trace of self-interest or egotism. Green Tārā makes the gesture that says, 'Don't be afraid.' Fear, of course, comes from ego, and ego is always anxious to protect itself. Ego itself is afraid, ego itself is fear, so where there is ego, there is fear, and where there is no ego, there is no fear. So Tārā represents not just true compassion, and the action that springs from it, but also fearless action, fearless because there is no ego behind the action.

Tārā assumes a number of different forms. There is a traditional mandala of twenty-one Tārās, and among them perhaps the best known, apart from Green Tārā, is White Tārā, who stands for long life, and also for merit and for *jñāna* or wisdom. White Tārā has seven eyes: two in the usual place, an eye in the middle of her forehead, eyes in the palms of her hands, and eyes in the soles of her feet. In other words, she looks out from every part of her body. She is the embodiment of awareness. Awareness expresses itself, looks out through, those eyes. So as well as embodying compassion, she also embodies absolute mindfulness, absolute awareness.

I received the White Tārā initiation from Dhardo Rimpoche, shortly before my return to the West, as a sort of parting gift. I was especially pleased to receive this initiation from him because I knew him very well. I'd known him by that time for twelve years, and we'd spent a lot of time together. We'd travelled together, studied together, and engaged in all sorts of Buddhist activities together, and he was a very good friend. He had many wonderful bodhisattva-like qualities, and he was a particularly mindful and aware person, so it seemed appropriate that I should receive from him the initiation of White Tārā, the embodiment of awareness.

So these are my associations with Tārā. I'm happy to be here on this occasion, and happy that I shall be leading this little procession in the direction of the shrine-room. I hope it won't be raining too hard, but whether it's raining or not, we'll get there, and we'll follow the little programme that has been outlined, and dedicate the shrine to Tārā.

FORTY YEARS ON: THE SIX DISTINCTIVE EMPHASES OF THE FWBO

Manchester Buddhist Centre, 7 April 2008, with additions from talks on the same theme given in Berlin, Padmaloka, and elsewhere between the late 1990s and 2010.

The weekend before last, at Wymondham College, we celebrated the fortieth anniversary of the Western Buddhist Order, and on the Saturday evening I had dinner with eight very senior Order members. They'd all been ordained for thirty or more years, and it was a very interesting experience after the meal was over just sitting together and reminiscing, one person saying, 'Do you remember this?' and somebody else saying, 'Well, do you remember *that*?' There followed some stories of the early days which gave us a great deal of amusement. People were reminiscing about the first time they set eyes on this person or that, the first time they saw me, and I told the story of the first time I ever saw Vajradaka, who was one of the eight present. It was on the occasion of a jumble sale in Camden Town – in those days we raised money by having a jumble sale every now and then, and we were quite pleased when we managed to raise two or three hundred pounds. I remember arriving for the jumble sale, and behind one of the stalls there was a very tall young man. He was only about 18, and he was wearing a beautiful white silk suit. He had long black hair and flashing black eyes which were turning in all directions. Someone else said that he remembered that Vajradaka had golden boots. I didn't remember his boots, but I certainly remembered that white silk suit, and the long black hair, and the flashing eyes. Even after more than thirty years I can still see them in my mind's eye.

As we recalled the things that happened in those early days, people were remarking on the number of activities we already had. There were so many retreats, so many meditation sessions. There were communication exercises, classes, and public lectures. Of course a lot of the events were led by me. I used to give all the lectures, lead all the classes, and someone used to say that I also made the tea and cut the sandwiches. I don't quite remember doing that, but it's not impossible. Quite a number of people were living in squats in those days. It was perfectly legal then, before that particular loophole was closed, so they used to live very cheaply, just get part-time work from time to time, and spend the rest of the time engaged in FWBO activities. As we reminisced, several people were saying that they remember it not only as a very busy time, but also a very joyful time. One or two even felt that the time when we were creating the FWBO and the WBO together was the happiest time of their whole life.

So that's the situation that the Order and the FWBO grew out of. Then we were only a few dozen, maybe fifty at the most. Now there are more than 1,500 Order members, and there must be double or even treble that number of Mitras worldwide, so we've expanded, and in many cases our experience of the Dharma, our communication with one another, and our understanding and sympathy have deepened over the years. It was out of our happy association with one another all those decades ago, that the Western Buddhist Order and the Friends of the Western Buddhist Order gradually emerged. But what was it that held us all together? What was it that united us? What were the common principles which we shared and on the basis of which we cooperated, especially in the case of those who were Order members? This is what I want to talk about this evening. I want to say a few words about what I call the distinctive emphases of the FWBO, emphases that differentiate us from other Buddhist movements of the past and present.

Of course we are very much a Buddhist movement and share with the rest of the Buddhist world the general characteristics of all schools and traditions, especially with regards to teachings. Like the rest of the Buddhist world we study and try to practise the four noble truths and the Noble Eightfold Path, conditioned co-production (*pratītya-samutpāda),* the six or the ten *pāramitās*, and the four *saṃgrahavastus*. We share a preoccupation with *śīla,* with ethics. We share various meditation practices: in all our centres we teach the mindfulness of breathing and the *mettā bhāvanā*. Other practices that we have in common with all other Buddhists are ritual, worship, chanting, pilgrimage, and study, symbols like the Buddha image, the wheel of life, and the mandala, and teachings about wisdom – *prajñā, śūnyatā, anātman*. So we have a great deal in common with the rest of the Buddhist world. At the same time we have our own distinctive features or characteristics.

1. THE CENTRALITY OF GOING FOR REFUGE

Our first distinctive feature is our emphasis on the centrality of Going for Refuge to the Buddha, the Dharma, and the Sangha. Many years ago I realized that the thing that all Buddhists have in common is that they all go for Refuge to the Buddha, the Dharma, and the Sangha, and thinking back to those early days of the Order, this was obviously the factor that united us. We came from many different backgrounds. There were different lifestyles among us; many were single, but some were married. But overriding all those differences there was the fact that we were all Going for Refuge. In many parts of the world Buddhists are divided into those who are monks and those who are lay people and who in many cases are expected simply to serve and look after the monks, but over the years I became convinced that this sort of division, especially when it was carried to extremes, was quite disastrous, both for the monks and for the lay people. It lost sight of what was fundamental, it lost sight of what people had in common: the Going for Refuge to the Buddha, the Dharma, and the Sangha. In quite a few Buddhist traditions the Going for Refuge has been marginalized. It isn't altogether absent, but it is there in a very attenuated form. There are many Buddhists who recite the words 'To the Buddha for Refuge I go', whether in Pāli, Tibetan, or another language, but that's all that their Going for Refuge amounts to. But the Going for Refuge is – or should be – quite central for Buddhists. To the extent that we go for Refuge, to that extent we are Buddhists.

The Pāli scriptures tell many stories of people going to see the Buddha. All sorts of people went to see him – a prince, a businessman, a young man-about-town, a distraught mother who had just lost her baby, and many more – and the Buddha gave to each person a Dharma teaching that was appropriate to their situation. They would be deeply affected by what he said to them, as though their whole life had been turned upside down, and quite spontaneously they would say, 'I go for Refuge to the Buddha, I go for Refuge to the Dharma, I go for Refuge to the Sangha.' This is what Going for Refuge to the Three

Jewels is. Someone is confronted by the Dharma, which they haven't heard before, it has a tremendous effect on them, and they respond. That response is Going for Refuge, and it is this that we see as being of central importance.

One of the reasons I saw this so clearly was that when I was in the East I was often made to feel that if you wanted to be a real Buddhist, you had to become a monk. This put monasticism at the centre, and I felt that this was entirely wrong. It is Going for Refuge that should be at the very centre of the Buddhist life. In later years I formulated the slogan 'Commitment (that is, commitment to Going for Refuge) is primary and lifestyle is secondary', or even 'Commitment is primary, ethical behaviour is secondary, and lifestyle is tertiary.'

Over the years I came to see that there are different levels of Going for Refuge, and I eventually concluded that four different levels can be distinguished. The first is what I call cultural Going for Refuge. This is common in the Buddhist countries of the Far East. Someone is born into a Buddhist family and they go along to the temple and learn to recite *Buddhaṃ saraṇaṃ gacchāmi*, but they don't think about it: it's just part of the culture. In a sense cultural Going for Refuge is not really Going for Refuge at all. Then there is what I call provisional Going for Refuge. Someone has some idea about going for Refuge and maybe they want to do it, but they are not quite sure about it; they want to try it out first. This happens quite a bit in the West. Thirdly, there is effective Going for Refuge, which for all practical purposes is the key. Effective Going for Refuge takes place when you sincerely wish to go for Refuge to the Buddha, Dharma, and Sangha with your whole heart. You recognize Enlightenment as the true goal of human life, you see the Dharma as the path to the realization of that goal, and you look up to fellow travellers on that path who are more advanced than you are. It is this effective Going for Refuge that is synonymous with ordination within our Order. In other words, when other Order members are satisfied that someone is effectively Going for Refuge, then he or she is ordained.

There is a fourth level of Going for Refuge, the real Going for Refuge. The difference between effective and real Going for Refuge is that if you are effectively Going for Refuge, you can fall back. Of course, you may recover yourself and get onto the path again, so that your Going for Refuge again becomes effective; even to go for Refuge effectively is difficult, and sometimes people do slip back. But once you reach the level of real Going for Refuge, your Going for Refuge has become so deep, so genuine, has transformed your whole being to such an extent, that you can't possibly fall back.

So Going for Refuge – especially effective Going for Refuge and real Going for Refuge – is of central importance to us. There are many other Buddhists who go for Refuge very sincerely, but Going for Refuge may not have in their spiritual life the central place that it has in the spiritual lives of the people in our community.

2. A UNIFIED ORDER

The second of our distinctive emphases is that we have a unified order, in the sense that it is open to men and women on equal terms. Members of the Order, whether men or women, have equal responsibilities, equal position, equal duties. There is no difference made between them on the basis of gender. That's rather unusual. In some parts of the Buddhist world ordination of nuns has died out completely, and in other parts the nuns are definitely subordinated to the *bhikkhus*, and there is no question of them being given equal status. So when we say that members of the Western Buddhist Order, whether men or women, have equal responsibility, equal duties, observe the same precepts, live the same kind of life as Order members within their respective lifestyles, this is not only revolutionary, it's really quite radical. Within the FWBO I think we're so accustomed to seeing *dharmacāriṇīs* functioning in just the same way as *dharmacāris*, giving talks, leading classes, giving ordinations, it's so much part of the world in which we live that we don't realize how radical it is, historically speaking. It's sometimes very difficult for Buddhists outside the FWBO to see and to recognize the radical nature of what we are doing.

At the same time, we are not a *unisex* Buddhist order. It's not like a unisex hairdressing salon. When you become a member of the Order, you don't have to cease to be a man. You don't have to try to tone down your masculine attributes and attitudes, as long they are in harmony with the Dharma and with ethical principles. You don't have to develop your feminine side or anything of that sort. And the same applies to women: they need not feel obliged to develop their masculine side in the rather one-sided manner some people say we should.

There is nothing wrong with being a man. I'm afraid it's necessary to say that these days because in the course of the last thirty years, ever since I've been back in Britain, I have heard so much propaganda to the effect that it is not a very good thing to be a man. According to the propaganda, men are rather inferior creatures. They have all these nasty habits. They are very aggressive, responsible for all the wars that have ever been started, and all the bloodshed. They are cruel, narrow-minded, not sympathetic or empathetic like women, not very touchy-feely. They have got to develop their feminine side or perish. But don't let anybody, whether within or outside our movement, make you feel ashamed of being a man, or being a woman. We need well-rounded characters, whether men or women, who are not ashamed of being men and women and can happily collaborate when the occasion requires.

Perhaps I need hardly mention that in addition to being open to both men and women on equal terms, the Order is open to all people regardless of colour, sexual orientation, or national and cultural background. We come from many different backgrounds and there are different lifestyles among us, but overriding all those differences is our common Going for Refuge to the Buddha, the Dharma, and the Sangha. This is what unites us. So this is our second distinctive emphasis.

3. A NON-SECTARIAN APPROACH: INSPIRATION FROM ALL BUDDHIST SCRIPTURES

The FWBO does not identify itself exclusively with any one Eastern Buddhist tradition. We don't say that we are Theravādin or Mahāyāna, that we follow Tibetan Buddhism or that we are a Vajrayāna tradition. We are simply Buddhists. We are a Buddhist movement, a Buddhist tradition, even a Buddhist lineage, and we feel free to draw upon the enormous wealth of the entire Buddhist tradition. The Buddhist scriptures are very extensive, so we have to choose which to study – a choice which will be in accordance with our spiritual needs. We also feel free to derive inspiration from great works of Western literature, but our primary sources of inspiration are from within the Buddhist tradition, especially the scriptures. People in our sangha love and appreciate the *Dhammapada*, the *Udāna*, and the *Sutta-Nipāta* from the Pāli canon, and texts like the *Laṅkāvatāra* and the *White Lotus Sūtra* from the Mahāyāna tradition. Among later works, the *Bodhicaryāvatāra* of Śāntideva is a great favourite, and the songs of *Milarepa* are also very popular. We derive inspiration, guidance, and faith from them all. There is a vast treasury from which we can take whichever ideas, principles, and practices help us to develop as Buddhists within the context of the society and culture within which we live. Not everybody is inspired by the same texts, but this is our principle: to feel free to draw inspiration and guidance from the whole vast heritage of Buddhist scriptures.

4. THE IMPORTANCE OF SPIRITUAL FRIENDSHIP

Our fourth distinctive emphasis is the great importance that we attach to spiritual friendship, which is the bedrock of the sangha. I know that this is one of our features that many people find especially attractive. I get many letters and visitors, and people often tell me the story of how they came in contact with our movement, sometimes after experiencing other forms of Buddhism. From what people tell me, I would say that the two things that draw most people to us and which they continue to value most are our clear presentation of the Dharma and the experience of sangha. That people appreciate this emphasis on spiritual friendship so much suggests that very often that element is lacking in the outside world. You may have friends, or at least acquaintances, but you may not have people whom you know so well that you can open your heart to them, and have a full and deep communication about everything that concerns you, whether material, practical, emotional, or spiritual.

Years ago I was very struck by the passage in the Pāli scriptures in which Ānanda comes to the Buddha and says, 'Lord, I've been reflecting, and I truly believe that friendship is half the spiritual life.' And the Buddha replies, 'No, Ānanda. Spiritual friendship is not half the spiritual life. Spiritual friendship is the *whole* of the spiritual life.'[461] The first time I read that and really understood it, my hair almost stood on end. It seemed an extraordinary statement, but there it was in the Pāli scriptures. No Buddhist tradition that I'm aware of, in the course of the last 2,500 years, has ever taken that extraordinary utterance of the Buddha seriously. It's that teaching that we try to explore. What did the Buddha mean? In what way is spiritual friendship the whole of the spiritual life? The short answer is that in the course of spiritual friendship the ego gets gradually worn away. You rub up against one another, challenge one another, encourage one another. You try to get beyond your petty needs and desires, your selfishness, your egotism. This is one of the benefits of living in a residential community too.

You can't always have things your own way. When you live on your own, you don't have to consider anybody else, and that can encourage individualism, but spiritual friendship is the enemy of individualism, the enemy of egotism. This is why in the FWBO spiritual friendship is very highly valued, and so is the sangha in the broadest sense, spiritual association with others who have the same Buddhist ideals as oneself.

5. RIGHT LIVELIHOOD

Team-based right livelihood is another distinctive emphasis. In all forms of Buddhism right livelihood is mentioned, and it is one of the steps of the Buddha's Noble Eightfold Path, but the traditional explanation is much too simple for modern times. It is a purely negative explanation: not to manufacture or deal in weapons of war, not to deal in poisons, and not to deal in living beings, which can be understood as including animals as well as human beings.[462] But much more than that is needed. The world in which we live is one in which ethical considerations are often not allowed to get in the way of making money. One of the conclusions I arrived at very early on in the history of our movement was that we ought to try to make inroads into the economic life of society by starting up a form of economic activity based on ethical principles. It isn't enough just for the individual Buddhist to have an ethical occupation, although that is important. I am happy to say that over the years team-based right livelihood businesses have become a very important part of the total structure of our movement and provide a very positive situation for those who work in them. Of course, if you work out there 'in the world', try to follow an occupation which doesn't oblige you to violate your Buddhist ethical principles, but if at all possible, go a step further and join a team-based right livelihood business.

A team-based right livelihood business should have four essential features. First of all, the business must be run on ethical lines. It must not cut corners ethically in order to make more money, or do or encourage anything of an unethical nature. Secondly, the business should give those working within it sufficient support – not wages or salary but support – to meet reasonable living requirements. As a Buddhist one should try to live as simply as possible, using as few of the earth's resources as possible within reasonable limits, not spending too much on clothes or amusements or unnecessary travel or anything frivolous. Leading a simple life is easier if one is living in a residential community. Thirdly, a team-based right livelihood business should provide a framework for spiritual practice and especially for the development of friendships. Very often in the workplace personal relationships are not of the best, and people are not generally thinking in terms of helping one another to grow spiritually or even psychologically, but within the team-based right livelihood business, cooperation and friendship should be such that people are helped to grow as Buddhists and deepen their Going for Refuge. And fourthly, team-based right livelihood businesses should make a profit. There is no virtue in not making a profit, and it is important to do so in order to give financial support to other, non-profit-making activities of the Movement. One of the reasons why in the early days I was keen that we should have team-based right livelihood businesses was my concern that this Western Buddhist movement of ours should not be dependent on donations from wealthy Buddhists in the East. I felt that this would be very demoralizing. We should stand on our own feet, be self-supporting. I used to quote that old Zen saying, 'A day of no working is a day of no eating.'

From what I have seen, the team-based right livelihood situation is highly positive – not for everybody, but for many, many people. Apart from a vihara-type situation, which will attract only a few people, I think that team-based right livelihood is about the most positive situation that one could have. A situation in which the members not only work together but also live together in communities, and share puja, meditation, and study, is very intensive, almost monastic. People who have come through team-based right livelihood have a definite character. They are usually quite positive, they've got lots of energy and idealism, and they seem to be healthier than people in other situations. I know that at the moment team-based right livelihood is going out of fashion within our movement. I am rather sorry to see that, and hope that sooner or later there will be a revival. In any case, it's very important that however we choose to earn our living, we look at the ethical implications of what we are doing. But if we can work together as Buddhists, supporting ourselves and our families, if we have them, by means of team-based right livelihood, with all that that implies in the way of possibilities of developing spiritual friendship and creating *dāna* for the Movement, that is so much the better.

6. THE SPIRITUAL VALUE OF THE ARTS

Our sixth distinctive emphasis is that we attach spiritual value to the arts. I've always seen the practice and appreciation of art as something that has an important place in the spiritual life. Beauty should have an important place in the spiritual life because the appreciation of beauty, whether in the form of art or natural beauty, is an essential part of human life. Poetry, literature, and great music have the capacity to develop our sensitivities, refine our emotional life, and open the way to the experience of meditative states, which is very helpful from the point of view of the spiritual life. Speaking from my own experience, even before I came into contact with the Dharma, which I did when I was 16, I was inspired and uplifted by the poetry I read – Shelley, Shakespeare, Milton, Wordsworth – and by the great art I saw. An experience of the arts can play a very important part in our lives. I am not saying that everybody needs to be widely read or knowledgeable about the arts, but a poem or a picture can be a source of great inspiration. We all know how inspiring we find certain Buddha and bodhisattva images, thangkas, and icons, and we shouldn't underestimate the importance of these aids.

In Western literature we often come across insights which are very close to those of Buddhism. Recently I got a recording of selections from William Wordsworth's poetry, including his 'Lines Written a Few Miles above Tintern Abbey'. I've read this poem a number of times before, but listening to it this time, read by a very good reader, it came as a bit of a revelation. It really did seem that in a section of this poem Wordsworth had given expression to a state of meditative calm which opened into what we may describe as vistas of insight. There was no Buddhist language of course, nor even any abstract philosophical language, but I couldn't help feeling that in this poem Wordsworth showed that he had had an experience very close to what Buddhists experience when they become absorbed in meditation, when they dwell in higher states of consciousness and try to look into the heart of things.[463]

To give another example, when I lived in Kalimpong, students used to come to me for help with their English studies, and one day I was going through a poem by Shelley, 'The Cloud', with two or three of them. As I explained the deeper significance of the poem, line by line and verse by verse, I got quite concentrated, quite immersed in it, and it suddenly dawned on me that I was not just explaining the meaning of the poem; I was explaining the Dharma.[464] This was a great eye-opener for me. We can find in the best of our own literature insights that come very close to those of the Dharma, so we shouldn't hesitate to make connections with what is best in our own cultural tradition. From the arts, from poetry, from music, from drama, from dance, we can derive something that adds to and supports our spiritual life. In all Buddhist countries art, literature, and poetry has been produced, much of it inspired by Buddhism, so it is only natural that within our own movement we not only appreciate the arts, but also create them. We're very fortunate to have some very creative people indeed.

THE GROWTH AND PROSPERITY OF THE SANGHA

FWBO International Retreat, Taraloka, 25 May 2008

Thank you, Parami, for those kind words of introduction. I suppose I'd better begin by apologizing for bringing the rain, but I'm sure the farmers won't mind, and I'm sure we're all quite happy sitting here dry and comfortable and listening to the sound of the rain on the roof of the tent.

People sometimes ask me what I've been doing, and nowadays it's not difficult to answer that question, because there are certain things that I can no longer do. I can't any longer see to read or write, which used to occupy a lot of my time, so I have more time for other things. I see people most days – Order members, Mitras, and other friends – and I talk with them, explore the Dharma with them, and sometimes study with them. I also have quite a lot of time for quiet reflection and contemplation and looking back over the happenings of the last so many years.

I must admit that I also listen to the radio sometimes, especially to the news, and a few weeks ago there was quite a lot on the radio in connection with the Olympics. I'm not very interested in the Olympics – I've never been much of a sportsman, as those of you who've read my memoirs will have gathered – but I couldn't help hearing about the forthcoming Olympics in Beijing, and about the Olympic torch which is being passed from one band of people to another, from one country to another, even at one point going to the top of Mount Everest, on the way to China. The handing on of the torch from one group of people to another in so many countries put me in mind of something that I've encountered in the Buddhist scriptures, where the Buddha speaks of handing on the lamp of the Dharma to his disciples.[465] Also, in Chinese Buddhism there is a quite important text called the *Transmission of the Lamp of the Dharma*, which is a history of the way the Dharma came to China, as it came to so many countries in the East, being passed from master to disciple down through the ages.[466]

The difference between the transmission of the Olympic torch and the transmission of the light of the Dharma from one generation to another is that the Olympics are competitive. People are not only doing their best, but trying to outshine their competitors and win that coveted medal. But for the followers of the Buddha, to whom the light of the Dharma is transmitted and who pass it on in their turn, there is no question of competition, or even cooperation. It's about collaboration, spiritual friendship. We often speak of our own movement as constituting a network of spiritual friendships, a network which includes people from all sorts of cultural backgrounds, racial backgrounds, class backgrounds, even former religious backgrounds. This is one of the characteristics of the FWBO, and we attach a great deal of importance to it.

This reminds me of something that the Buddha said to his disciples at a time when it seems he was concerned about the preservation of the spiritual movement he had started. On this occasion he had been questioned about a political matter. In the India of the Buddha's day there were various kingdoms and tribes, and some of these were expanding so aggressively that they were in the process of swallowing up some of the small republican tribes. It would seem that a representative of one of these tribes came to ask the Buddha about the conditions under which his tribe could survive and prosper. The Buddha gave him some very good advice of a more or less ethical-cum-political nature, and he then proceeded to give parallel advice to his followers. He was speaking to monks, but the principles he outlined were applicable to all his followers. He was concerned for the future of the movement he had founded, which after all existed in the midst of the world, a world which was not much more favourable to the continuity of a spiritual movement than the world is today.[467]

The first thing the Buddha said was that his disciples should meet regularly and in large numbers. I'm very glad to see that on this occasion that advice is being followed quite literally. One could even say that we've been gathering repeatedly, because there have been other gatherings of our sangha in the course of the year, but here we are on the forty-first anniversary of the founding of the FWBO, gathering together in large numbers. I hope that this tradition will be maintained. I know that some people don't like large gatherings, but when we gather together united by a common devotion to the Dharma, it's not the same as when people gather for some more secular purpose like watching a football match or a film. When we meditate together, when we do puja together, when we listen to talks about the Dharma together, a completely different atmosphere is generated, and a quite different level of consciousness is sometimes reached.

There was another incident in the Buddha's life when one of his disciples suggested to the king of the region that they should go to visit the Buddha. It was the night of the full moon, and the king was led to a clearing in the middle of the forest, where the Buddha was sitting with his disciples, all in perfect silence. Such was the atmosphere generated, such was the deep peace that the king felt, just seeing the Buddha and his disciples all sitting there, that he exclaimed, 'I wish that my son could enjoy such peace as this.' The king himself had committed certain wicked actions and couldn't hope to experience much peace in his lifetime, but although he was a wicked man, he was very fond of his son and wanted him to enjoy peace of mind, and he could think of no greater blessing than the peace of mind experienced by the Buddha's disciples as they sat there in the moonlight.[468] Likewise, when we gather together, whether we're sitting in silence or communicating with one another, whether we're chanting or meditating, since we're united in the Dharma, something collective is generated, even quite a different level of consciousness, and I know that many of you have experienced this on a number of occasions.

The Buddha's second point was that he wanted his disciples to gather together in harmony and disperse in harmony. Harmony is a wonderful word. We often use it in connection with music, speaking of instruments agreeing, blending, and producing a beautiful and inspiring sound. Harmony among people, harmony within the sangha, is a very precious and valuable and beautiful thing. Sometimes I'm asked if I ever feel disappointed by anything, and I have to admit that there is one thing that does sometimes disappoint or disturb me, or even pain me, and that is when I hear of disharmony within the sangha, whether it's within the Order, within a chapter, at a particular Buddhist centre, or within the

Buddhist community generally. It's incumbent on those of us who belong to the sangha to do everything that we can to promote harmony, not just the harmony of external agreement, but the harmony that comes when we have a deep feeling for one another, an appreciation for one another, and a realization that we are all treading the same spiritual path. We will not always agree, but it should be possible to maintain harmony even when there is disagreement about this or that issue.

This brings me to the question of tolerance. There's a lot of talk about tolerance these days, especially in interfaith circles. The day before yesterday I was in London, at Lambeth Palace, attending a meeting of religious leaders with the Dalai Lama, and in that context there was a lot of talk about love, compassion, and tolerance, but I have found over the years that the idea of tolerance is often misunderstood.[469] To be tolerant does not mean that you have to agree with what others say. Differences of opinion, differences of belief, are inevitable, but the fact that one differs in belief, doctrine, or practice from someone else does not mean that one should have a negative attitude towards them, or that one should not regard them with what the Buddha called the eye of friendship.[470] We don't have to accept that all teachings are the same in order to be tolerant. That's a false conclusion. We have to recognize that there are significant differences between the religions of the world. When the Dalai Lama spoke on that occasion, he made a clear distinction between theistic and non-theistic religions, and I was very glad to hear him do so at a gathering where there were followers of both. To be tolerant does not mean maintaining that everyone basically believes the same thing or worships the same God. There can be differences of opinion and harmony at the same time, and that should certainly be the case within the Buddhist community. We may have our little differences, practical and theoretical, differences of doctrine, differences of method, but that should not mar the overall harmony. There may be a little discordant note here and there, but sometimes a discordant note can contribute to the overall harmony.

The third point that the Buddha made was also very important, though it may sound rather strange to modern ears. He said that within the sangha there should be no change to any accepted practice or formulation. For instance, the laws which governed the sangha should be kept unchanged. In modern times people are very fond of changing things. People are crazy for something new, so the idea that you can't change anything will strike them rather strangely, and they may not like it. But we have to try to understand what the Buddha meant. He certainly didn't mean that the *bhikkhus* could not change anything at all. In fact, on another occasion he said that they could abolish the minor rules if they thought fit, though after his death they decided not to abolish them.[471] The point that the Buddha was making was that there has to be continuity. There can be developments within Buddhism, within the sangha, and within the FWBO, but they have to be in harmony and continuity with whatever has gone before.

This gathering itself is an example of that. We're celebrating the founding of the FWBO, and this time it's a week-long celebration, not just one day. I can't remember when we started celebrating FWBO Day, but it was quite a long time ago, and for a while we celebrated it just on one day, usually the day before we celebrated WBO Day. Over the years the nature of the celebration changed, and last year for some reason no official celebration was organized at all. I was not very happy about that, so I decided I'd give a talk on FWBO Day at the Birmingham centre. We had a very good turnout. I gave a talk, Dharmamati led a rather lengthy puja, and that was our FWBO Day celebration. Nobody organized it, and it wasn't announced much beforehand, but people came from all quarters of the British Isles, it seems. Coaches were turning up outside, and the Birmingham Buddhist Centre was absolutely packed.[472] But this year I'm very glad to see that so many people have gathered for a whole week of meditation and talks and puja, so that the anniversary of the founding of the FWBO is being celebrated, but in a way that it hasn't been celebrated before. There has been a change, but there has been continuity. I think this illustrates what the Buddha was getting at when he told his disciples they should not change anything. He didn't mean that literally nothing at all should be changed, and in the course of Buddhist history a number of things have been changed, sometimes for the better, sometimes for the worse. The principle to remember is that the change should be in accordance with what has gone before. It should be the continuation of the tradition in another form, not something completely new.

The Buddha's fourth point is perhaps not on the face of it very popular nowadays. He said that elders – elders in the spiritual sense – must be respected. Within the FWBO there are now people who have been practising meditation, and studying and practising the Dharma, for a very long time, some of them for as many as thirty or even forty years, so a lot of experience has been built up. We need to recognize that there are some people with more and deeper experience, perhaps with a clearer vision of the Dharma, than we have ourselves. I have noticed that it's not necessarily those who are well known within the Movement and frequently appear in public who have the deepest spiritual experience or the most consistent spiritual practice. I see quite a few people – Order members and Mitras – and I'm sometimes quite impressed by the level of maturity and the depth of experience of people who may not be well known within the Movement, but who have been practising the Dharma for a very long time. It doesn't always show in any obvious way, but I think if one meets someone who has been practising for a long time, one should take it for granted that they are an elder and that respect is due to them. This is not very much in accordance with the modern outlook, but there are so many ways in which the Dharma is quite opposed to aspects of modern thinking and belief.

Fifthly, the Buddha made the point – and I'm paraphrasing here – that there should be no backsliding. It's very easy to be carried away by one's first enthusiasm for the Dharma and for meditation, and perhaps for a while, maybe for some years, all goes well. But then doubts may creep in, or external influences play their part, or one takes on other responsibilities, and the practice of the Dharma is relegated more and more to the circumference of one's personal mandala, and one gradually drifts away. The Buddha said that this falling away from one's original inspiration is something to be greatly guarded against. If too many people within the sangha fall away, the whole sangha will decay and eventually perhaps disappear. So this is one of the most important points that the Buddha made to his early disciples. Safeguard your original vision, keep up your contact with your spiritual friends, if you're an Order member keep up your membership of a chapter, and make sure that you never fall away from the spiritual path. If a sufficient number of members of the sangha safeguard their vision, then the future prosperity of the Movement will be assured.

Sixthly, the Buddha said that within the spiritual community there should be a place for a minority of people who are devoted to more intensive spiritual practice. We all know that some people practise more intensively than others. The Buddha was insistent that if the health of the whole sangha is to be maintained, there must be at least some people within that community who are devoted wholeheartedly, with body, speech, and mind, whether to the practice of meditation, or the study of the Dharma, or the practice of the Dharma in some other way. If there isn't that smaller body of more intensely committed people, the health of the whole movement will suffer. So we need to make a space, make opportunities, for those who want to devote themselves to long periods of solitary meditation, or Dharma study, or work for the Dharma in any other way. We need that small core of people who do their best to live out the Dharma in every aspect of their lives in a very intense way.

The last thing I want to mention strikes a very positive note. The Buddha said that the members of his sangha should welcome new members. We might think that that was a rather obvious thing to say, but sometimes groups, even spiritual groups, can tend to become a little exclusive, and not as welcoming to new people as they could be. When new people come along, whether to a centre or a retreat, make them feel welcome. We mustn't forget that if someone comes along for the first time to a Buddhist centre or group, or goes on retreat, it's all very new and strange, and they may not feel quite comfortable at first, so it's our responsibility to make them feel at home and extend genuine friendship towards them. We should welcome those who want to join the sangha, treat them as brothers and sisters, and make them as happy and comfortable as we can. The Buddha added that at the same time we should be mindful and we should direct *mettā* towards the whole of the existing membership of the sangha. So in giving this advice to his followers, almost the last words the Buddha speaks are about *mettā* and mindfulness. He strikes this double note: that we should extend our *mettā* towards all our fellow members of the sangha, and we should practise mindfulness. These are the two great pillars of Buddhist life and practice.

I'm sure that in the course of the last week you've all had many opportunities of demonstrating *mettā* towards other people who are here and many opportunities of practising mindfulness. I'm very glad that I could have this opportunity of coming here today, even though I did bring the rain, and the opportunity to remind you of some of the things that the Buddha said with regard to the welfare of the spiritual community he founded, words of advice that are as relevant today as they were 2,500 years ago when the Buddha first uttered them.

RECOLLECTIONS OF MY EARLY LIFE, AND SOME REFLECTIONS ON REBIRTH

Sheffield Buddhist Centre, July 2008

This evening I was having dinner with the Sheffield Evolution shop team and they were telling me rather proudly that they are one of the five remaining Evolution shop teams in the FWBO staffed entirely by members of the sangha. Team-based right livelihood has always been very close to my heart and I am glad to know that it is flourishing here in Sheffield, along with other FWBO activities.

In the course of the conversation over dinner the subject of South London came up. When I look back, I think how extraordinary it is that someone whose life has been devoted to the Dharma, someone who ended up founding a Buddhist order, should first have seen the light of day in South London of all places. I was brought up in a very ordinary working-class family. My father was a French polisher who was sometimes out of work and my mother was an ordinary housewife. It seems very strange that someone like me should emerge from those surroundings.

My life, the whole force of my being, had a definite direction from the very beginning. When I was about 8 or 9 and confined to bed because of illness I first learned about the Buddha, Siddhārtha Gautama, and the founders of other religions, from the pages of an encyclopaedia. Mohammed didn't appeal to me particularly and I don't think even Zarathustra did, but the Buddha certainly appealed to me, and the images of the Buddha in my encyclopaedia stuck in my mind. A few years later I was in Brighton with my family on holiday and happened to see in the window of a bric-a-brac shop a small brass image of the Buddha. I think it must have been a tiny replica of the famous Kamakura Buddha of Japan. I went into the shop and bought it with my pocket money. I must have been 12 or 13. I bought at the same time a few sticks of incense which I later came to know as Indian incense, very black and very sweet, and when we got home I used to put this little Buddha image on a table and burn one of my precious incense sticks. I did this without understanding the significance of what I was doing. My parents must have seen me doing it but they were used to me having strange interests and ideas, and nothing was said.

During the next few years I immersed myself in literature and philosophy. I attended church for a while but it didn't make much impression on me, and when I was about 14 or 15 I realized that I was definitely not a Christian. What was I? I didn't know, not yet. But a time came when, in the course of my reading, I came across books on Buddhism and, more important still, actual Buddhist texts, or rather translations of Buddhist texts. In particular I came across translations of the *Diamond Sūtra* and the *Sūtra of Wei Lang* – the *Platform Sūtra* as it is usually called – and when I read these, especially the *Diamond Sūtra*, I at once felt, 'This is what I really believe. This is what I have always believed.'

I had not as yet met any other Buddhists. I was all on my own. I don't think I talked about my interest in Buddhism with anybody I knew. But eventually I came to hear of the London Buddhist Society, and I started corresponding with the editor of their magazine and going along to their classes. This must have been in 1943. I made friends there, and started to meditate after a fashion. I can't remember what sort of meditation we did, but the Buddhist Society had published a book called *Concentration and Meditation* which I must have read.[473] Mr Humphreys, the founder of the Buddhist Society, used to recommend that we started off by learning to concentrate on a matchbox, which some of us duly did. It was the midst of the war, and on one occasion I was at the Buddhist Society's premises above a tea shop in Great Russell Street when a bomb fell. We were sitting on our chairs meditating – no one sat on cushions in those days – or at least our eyes were closed and we were inwardly concentrated, perhaps on a matchbox, perhaps on something else, when suddenly there was the noise of a tremendous explosion. A bomb had fallen so close by that the windows rattled, but we didn't move – so we weren't doing badly for beginners.

Then I was conscripted into the army, though in view of my medical history I had not expected that they would take me. I didn't like the army at all and ignored it as much as I could, while continuing to pursue my own interests, and reading books on Buddhism whenever I had the opportunity. Many of my friends in the unit were dismayed when we heard that we were going to be sent to India, which seemed to them like going to the ends of the earth, so far away from their families. Of course I wasn't pleased to be separated from my family either, but I was very pleased with the idea of going to India, the land of the Buddha. As I found out, though, in those days there were hardly any Buddhists in India, so I carried on with my study of Buddhism through reading books. For about a year I was in Singapore, still in the army, and there I made friends with a number of Chinese Buddhists, so I got to know something about Chinese Buddhism at that time.

After I had been in the army for four years the war ended and, as you will know if you have read my memoirs, I took up a wandering life in India.[474] I wasn't just a tourist. I did it properly. I shaved my head, shaved off my beard, and donned the saffron robes of the wandering monk. With a Bengali companion I spent a couple of years wandering around India, sometimes staying in ashrams, sometimes in caves, and devoting myself to meditation and to the study of the Dharma. Most of the people with whom I came into contact were Hindus, and I spent time with some famous Hindu teachers, but I was always quite clear that it was to the Dharma that I wanted to devote my life.

A turning point came when I was staying in a cave on the Arunachala mountain and had a vision of the red Buddha, Amitābha. It was a rather unusual vision, or at least so I thought at the time, because this red Buddha was seated on a red lotus which was floating on the waters of the ocean. In his right hand the Buddha was holding a red lotus and behind him, to one side, the sun was setting, and the light of the setting sun was glittering on the waves.[475] I had never seen a picture like this, and for many years I thought that it was not quite traditional, but not many years ago someone sent me a picture postcard from Nepal. The picture was part of a thangka, and there was the red Buddha holding up a red lotus, just as in my vision. Somebody else told me that when they visited Kalimpong and went to see the temple built by

Dudjom Rimpoche they saw the same Buddha in one of the paintings on the walls.[476] So it seems that my vision wasn't as untraditional as I originally thought.

It was a very vivid experience, and I took it to mean that it was time I got myself properly ordained and joined the monastic sangha. I was ordained as a *śrāmaṇera* at Kusinara and subsequently as a *bhikkhu* at Sarnath. I was very fully on track, so to speak. Then I spent some time with Bhikkhu Kashyap studying Pāli. He took me up to Kalimpong and left me there, exhorting me to stay there and work for the good of Buddhism, which I proceeded to do by starting, among other things, the Young Men's Buddhist Association, which could be regarded as a sort of trial run for the FWBO. In the years that followed I continued to study, meditate, and practise the Dharma, and was fortunate enough to receive instruction and initiation from some very distinguished Tibetan lamas, as well as from a Chinese hermit yogi, Mr Chen. So fourteen productive years passed in Kalimpong. I did quite a lot of writing, including *A Survey of Buddhism*, and also got involved with the movement of mass conversion in the plains of India which had been started by Dr Ambedkar. So my life found a very definite force.

In 1964 I came back to England after an absence of twenty years, and three years later I started the FWBO and WBO. The rest is, as they say, history, and a history of which all of you are now part. As I look back now as an old man of nearly 83 I can't help thinking that there must have been some reason why I followed that particular course without any deviation. Even the army couldn't stop me studying Buddhism, and I wasn't captured by one of those famous Hindu teachers. I stuck to the Dharma. The Dharma was my path. It was the Dharma that I wanted to immerse myself in, to experience, to communicate. This was always clear to me. Sometimes I wonder where this tremendous urge came from, this urge which has played such a dominant part in my life for more than sixty years. Thinking of the ordinary working-class surroundings I was born into, what could account for my interest? I can only presume that some powerful *saṃskāra* carried over from a previous existence impelled me to follow a path I had followed before and reconnect with teachings and practices and experiences with which I had been connected in previous lives.

This has always been one of the considerations which has led me to accept the idea of rebirth. I use the word consideration deliberately, because it isn't a proof. Many people might say that I am quite mistaken and that my interest in Buddhism and devotion to the Dharma could be explained by some sort of gene in my makeup, but to me it really does seem as though I have been following a path in this life which I have trodden in previous lives.

I am now going to talk a bit about dreams. I wasn't expecting to talk about dreams, but I think I will. According to some Buddhist texts Siddhārtha had a number of significant dreams before his Enlightenment. In fact, I wrote a poem about one of them.[477] Dreams obviously make up an important part of our lives. In India there is a traditional division of the human psyche into four parts: the waking state, the state of deep, dreamless sleep, the dream state, and the state that covers all the higher meditative experiences. Dreams make up part of our experience, part of our personality almost. Many dreams are just shadows of things that have happened to us in the course of the day, but there are dreams of a quite different kind too, archetypal dreams that have a higher or deeper significance. I have had these archetypal dreams from time to time in the course of my life.

I remember in particular one such dream which repeated itself in various forms again and again over a number of years. The first time I dreamed it, which was in India before I came back to Britain, I dreamed there was a mountain in South India, at the foot of which was an ashram. This ashram was open to the public, and there were people coming and going, but behind the ashram was a secret stair cut out of the rock, and this led up to another ashram, which was much higher up and much smaller, and which people usually didn't know anything about. The stair opened onto a wide platform, and in the dream I climbed up and found myself on that platform looking out over a broad landscape with several factories dotted here and there. At the top of the stairs there was an elderly man in a white robe and behind him there was a showcase of the kind you see in Tibetan temples, with lots of Buddha images behind the glass. This was the archetypal dream. The public ashram was at the foot of the mountain and the secret ashram was above it, at the top of the stairs, distant or hidden or unknown, or sometimes even in ruins. In some of my dreams people had forgotten about its existence. I used to reflect on this dream and ask myself what it could designate. I won't tell you the results of my reflections. They vary from time to time. Perhaps you would like to reflect on that dream yourself and ask yourself whether you have had anything like it.

Now I want to fast-forward to five or six years ago, to the time when I had a whole year of chronic insomnia for which we have never discovered the cause. It was quite extreme, quite severe, amounting in fact to sleep deprivation. It was a very painful experience. Since I was able to sleep so little, my energy drained away, and I thought I might die. I felt utterly exhausted, and friends were very concerned. I was well looked after during that period and also very much helped by acupuncture. But it was a painful period, and all I could do was remain aware, practise patience, and try not to get frustrated.

However, there were compensations. In fact, there was a silver lining to that very dark cloud, or even a golden lining, because during that period I had some wonderful archetypal dreams which seemed to me to be of great significance. It felt like a real gift, a real reward, a very positive, even a genuinely spiritual experience. These dreams took many forms. In some of them all sorts of beautiful, brilliant jewels appeared. I have always been fond of precious and semi-precious stones for their beauty and their colours, and in my dreams I saw the most magnifcent stones, arranged in wonderful patterns and shapes. I also used to have dreams of wonderful scenery, very often mountain scenery such as perhaps doesn't exist on earth, very often at the edge of the sea. Sometimes I would be high up in the air looking down on the sea and the mountains, and sometimes I would be in subterranean chasms which contained all sorts of fissures. I had many, many such dreams, all of which I found very inspiring, and they helped to sustain me during that year of chronic insomnia.

You may wonder why I am going on about these dreams, but I will come to something that you may find more interesting. I also occasionally used to have vivid dreams of my teachers, and I still do. During the week before I handed on my responsibilities as head of the Order to a small group of senior Order members, each night I dreamed of several of my teachers and in the course of the week I must have dreamed of each of them a number of times. These dreams were very, very powerful, and of a sort of visionary brotherhood. I took them to mean that in handing on responsibility for the Order I was doing the right thing, and that what I was doing had the blessing of my teachers. It was of great importance to me, and perhaps of importance to the Movement as well, especially to the Order.

To connect this up with the question of rebirth, I have also had dreams relatively recently which seemed like recollections of experiences in another life. Of course I can't prove that they were, but some of these dreams have been of great intensity – not the kind of intensity of some of my archetypal dreams, but quite a different kind, as though they were recollections of things that had happened to me in previous lives. As far as I can make out, thinking it over afterwards, I was living in the eighth or ninth century in this country at a time when England was divided into seven or eight independent kingdoms which were sometimes at war. I was the prior of a little priory, believe it or not, and I had under me twenty-four monks. One day a representative of the king of the kingdom where I was living came and said, 'The king is at war with a neighbouring king. We need soldiers. You have got to send twelve of your monks to fight as soldiers for the king.' So, sadly, I had to acquiesce. A little later on (I don't know exactly how much later) the dream continued and I was in the presence of the king with other counsellors and advisers. The king was seated on his throne and we were all standing and addressing him in turn. Just after waking I could remember what I said to the king when it was my turn, but it didn't last and now I can't remember it, but I said something with regard to the political situation.

These dreams were of a special kind, different from ordinary dreams and even archetypal dreams, and I could only conclude that they were probably reminiscences of another life. So this is another of the considerations that leads me to accept the fact of rebirth. I think it is quite likely that some of the things that people experience in the dream state are recollections of events or experiences in previous existences. There are other considerations too. There was an English Buddhist, an *anagārika* called Francis Story who died in 1972, having spent much of his life in Sri Lanka. He was especially interested in rebirth and wanted to see if it could be empirically verified. He did a great deal of research, mainly in Burma, where he also spent quite a lot of time. He investigated a number of cases where young children spoke about having lived with some other family before, in some other place, and after investigating a number of these cases he came to the conclusion that in some of them, the only possible explanation was that the children were remembering their existence in a previous life, usually also in Burma, not very far away from where they had reincarnated, so to speak, in this current life.[478] So this is another consideration, and perhaps it has a little more weight than the others I have mentioned, which might appear to be of a rather subjective nature.

But we can go a step further. I have known at least two people who claimed to remember their previous existence: Lama Govinda and Dhardo Rimpoche. Dhardo Rimpoche of course was a *tulku*, an incarnate lama. I don't know whether other *tulkus* have any recollection of their previous existences. When I lived in Kalimpong and could have asked those I knew, I wasn't especially interested in the question of rebirth, or rather I wasn't interested in trying to establish it as a fact. I took it for granted, as did all the Buddhists around me. But I remember discussing it with Dhardo Rimpoche, and he told me that at one time he had been able to remember his previous life, but the recollection faded when he was about 7. He seemed to think that that was what often happened. Before the age of 7 one might well be able to recollect previous existences, but the present life crowded in upon one and those old memories were overlaid and eventually forgotten. Apparently his mother remembered how when he was very young, no more than 7 or 8, a female devotee had invited him for a meal, but had the impression that the young Rimpoche was not very willing to go. She expressed that feeling, and the young Rimpoche said, 'Why should I be unwilling to go to your house for a meal? I have done so many times before.' His mother took that to mean that he was referring to his previous existence, when he had indeed visited this woman's house a number of times. Dhardo Rimpoche confirmed that this is what he believed had happened. At the time I spoke to him he didn't have any direct memory of that previous existence, but he remembered that he had remembered.

Then there is the case of Lama Govinda. In his book *The Way of the White Clouds* he discusses the question of rebirth at some length and reports on some cases that he came across in Burma.[479] One day I happened to mention to him that his writings reminded me very much of those of the early German Romantics, which I read when I was in my teens. He smiled and said that he believed that he had been Novalis – one of those Romantic writers – in a previous existence. He had had a strange experience of reading something by Novalis and finding it very familiar, and then it came back to him that he himself had written it. All these considerations persuaded me that rebirth, or reincarnation, or metempsychosis, is a fact, not just a beautiful romantic idea.

There is something else to be borne in mind. In the Buddhist scriptures we are clearly told that the Buddha recollected his previous existences and was able to see the births and deaths and rebirths of other beings.[480] These days, people are not easily convinced if one invokes authority, even the authority of the Buddha. Some people doubt whether the Buddha himself really believed in rebirth. Sometimes they say that he simply adopted the teaching because it was current in his time. But the Pāli scriptures make it clear that not everybody in India at the Buddha's time believed in rebirth. Some of them were nihilists, materialists, and the Buddha sometimes had to convince them. So one can't argue that the Buddha believed in or taught rebirth simply because it was the common ideology of the time in India.[481]

Of course, I am aware that for many Western Buddhists and even for some people in the FWBO belief in rebirth is problematic. Over the years many people have asked me whether it is possible to be a Buddhist and not believe in rebirth. My standard answer is, 'Yes, you can be a Buddhist and not believe in rebirth. But as a Buddhist you accept full Enlightenment as the goal of the Buddha's teachings, so if you don't believe in rebirth, if you don't believe that you will have another chance later on, you will have to go all out for Enlightenment in this very life. You will have to sacrifice everything, give up everything. That is the only thing you can do which is consistent with your belief in the Buddha as the Enlightened One and your lack of belief in rebirth.' Usually that suggestion doesn't go down very well! In fact, some people are genuinely in a dilemma. They believe in the teachings of the Buddha up to a point and really do want to progress spiritually, but they don't believe in rebirth.

Buddhists in the East do believe in rebirth, which means they also believe that if they don't make it to the highest spiritual level in this life they can carry on with the journey in a future life. The danger is, and it's a real danger in many Buddhist countries, that people put off the real practice of the Dharma to a future life. It's a sort of get-out. If they find it too difficult in this life, all right, they will do it in another life under more favourable circumstances. Many people in Theravāda countries don't care much about the practice of the Dharma in this life; they are just aiming to be reborn when a Buddha is alive, so that then they can hear the Dharma directly from him, which will make it much easier to gain Enlightenment. That's a bit of a cop-out. Nonetheless, if, as a Western Buddhist, you don't believe in rebirth, you may feel a tremendous pressure to do it all now, in this life. No doubt you could, if you were sufficiently determined, but the idea that this is your only chance can give rise to a great deal of tension and anxiety which is rather counterproductive. The best thing is to follow a middle way. Let's do our best to progress spiritually as best we can in this life of ours, but let's not put ourselves under too much strain, believing that we have got to do it now or never, or die unfulfilled. Perhaps it's best to have the possibility of rebirth at the back of your mind, but not attach so much importance to the idea of future possibilities of treading the path to Enlightenment that you neglect to do so in this life, as some Eastern Buddhists do.

So, these are some of the thoughts that have been stirring in my mind recently. I think that we in the FWBO, and the WBO especially, perhaps have to ask ourselves whether we accept the idea of rebirth or not. We need to be quite clear about this, or at least try to be clear about it, because it isn't an easy thing to be clear about. We owe it to ourselves, and even to the Dharma, to ask ourselves what we really think, what we really believe. That will have its effect on our actual practice of the Dharma. So I will leave you with that little exhortation.

MINGLING SOULS

The launch of Dear Dinoo: Letters to a Friend, *Birmingham Buddhist Centre, 10 December 2011*

Most of you know, I think, that for the last fourteen years of my time in India I spent most of my time in a place called Kalimpong in the eastern Himalayas, but most years I would spend the winter months down in the plains. I used to spend time in Calcutta, Nagpur, Poona, and sometimes even Delhi, but in the early 1950s I spent more time in Bombay than any other city, partly because I had developed friendships with quite a few people there. In those days Bombay was a rather pleasant city – I gather it's changed a lot since then – and it was very cosmopolitan. There were Hindus and Muslims, Sikhs and Bahá'ís, Europeans of many nationalities, and Parsis. For some reason or other I developed friendships with quite a few people who belonged to the Parsi community, as my friend Dinoo did.

The word Parsi is a corruption of *Farsi*, a Persian word from which we derive our own word Persia. The Parsis are a community of people who left Persia, or Iran, about a thousand years ago, at a time when the Arab Muslims were invading and trying to convert everybody to Islam. The Parsis are Zoroastrians, followers of the prophet Zoroaster. Scholars are still discussing when Zoroaster lived – in fact there seems to have been a succession of Zoroasters – but it seems that even the last of them lived some time before the Buddha. Zoroastrianism is thus a very ancient religion, with its own prophet, its own scriptures, and its own symbols. The Parsis are fire worshippers. In Bombay there is still a Parsi fire temple into which non-Parsis are not admitted. The Bombay landscape is also marked by the towers of silence, where the Parsis practise what the Tibetans call wind or air burial. At the very top of these towers there is a kind of grille, and there dead bodies are exposed. The vultures come and devour the flesh, and the bones fall down into a pit below. One of my Parsi friends, Dr Mehta, told me that he had once gone with the attendants who carried the bodies up to the top of the tower and had seen what happened, but that's not a sight that many people would be prepared to see, unless they were good Buddhists doing a corpse meditation. The Parsis are a very Westernized, very cultured people, usually English-educated, and with a keen interest in religion and philosophy. It's quite a small community. They're scattered over western India, and the largest number is to be found in the city of Bombay, but I doubt whether they amount to more than a couple of hundred thousand.[482] They are a survival from a very remote past.

So this was the cultural background of my friend Dinoo. I remember very well how I happened to meet her, at a lecture I gave called 'Inspiration – Whence?' I was concerned to make the point that inspiration came not just from religion or mysticism, but could also come from the arts, from poetry, literature, drama, and so on.[483] I think this appealed to Dinoo because she was herself a meditator, she read widely, and she was an artist. She had visionary experiences, and in her meditations she sometimes used to see a face which she believed to be that of Maitreya Buddha. She executed a number of paintings of this face just as she saw it, one of which she gave me. It was circular and depicted a very European face, very white, with pink cheeks and blue eyes and masses of golden hair, and a beatific smile which did give one the impression of something out of this world. I took the painting back to Kalimpong, but the climate there, though agreeable in many ways, is not kind to books or paintings, and I'm afraid the painting collected mould and eventually disintegrated.

Dinoo was very excited by my talk, and she was keen to see more of me, and that I should meet her friends, including Dr Mehta.[484] She invited me to tea on the spot, and a day or two later I found myself in her sitting room among her books, looking out over the Arabian Sea. She had a ground-floor flat in Marine Drive, a rather prestigious address in those days. Over the following years I had tea with Dinoo whenever I happened to be in Bombay. She was a bit deaf in one ear, so she used to draw a stool up quite close to me, turn her good ear towards me, and listen very intently, almost like a little bird. We had varied conversations, covering the Dharma, Buddhism, literature, the arts, mutual friends, and so on, and in between meetings we corresponded. She was a very good correspondent, and some of her letters were quite a bit longer than mine.

The years rolled by, and in 1964 I came back to England. I was still in correspondence with Dinoo, and during one of my visits to Bombay thereafter I met her for the last time. When I was in India I had many good friends who were older than myself, which was in some ways a good thing – I was quite young then – but since they were much older than me, they passed away before me, and I've often felt their loss. Dinoo passed away about twenty years ago, and before she died she sent me all the letters I had written to her. I can't remember how that came about. Perhaps I mentioned that they would be useful to me if I came to write my memoirs or perhaps it was a spontaneous gesture on her part. When I looked through them, I was interested to see how many words she'd underlined. Dinoo was a great underliner. All her books were heavily underlined, and more than half of the text of some of my letters was underlined, sometimes twice.

I have kept these twenty-nine letters by me, and in the last couple of years, in preparation for my move into the country, whenever and wherever that may be, I've been putting archival material together with the help of Paramartha, so these letters were in my mind, and I dallied with the thought of bringing them out in book form.[485] But who was to help me do that? At that point somebody turned up who was available and willing, and that of course was Kalyanaprabha. So we set to work, or rather Kalyanaprabha did. I didn't have much to do except answer her questions. Before long she had put the letters together and had written dozens of notes and the introduction and the appendix, and there it was, potentially a book. I contacted Windhorse Publications – I thought I'd better offer it to them first – but they didn't want to bring it out. I think they had quite a lot on their plate at that time. So then I thought, 'Well, why shouldn't I bring it out myself?' I'd heard a bit about self-publication. Kalyanaprabha investigated, and to cut a long story short, with additional help from Shantavira and Dharmashura, we were able to bring out *Dear Dinoo: Letters to a Friend* and launch it this evening. I'm very pleased that we've been able to do that. I'm very grateful to Kalyanaprabha for all her work, and to Shantavira and Dharmashura for their assistance.

It has set me thinking a bit about letters in general. Letters are very important. The opening line of a verse letter by John Donne is, 'Sir, more than kisses, letters mingle souls'.[486] When you receive a letter, you experience something of another person's soul – if it's a proper letter, not just a hastily scribbled note or an even more hastily despatched email. There are so many kinds of letters. When I went back in history to discover when letter-writing started, I found myself back in ancient Babylonia, the land between the two rivers, the Tigris and the Euphrates, which we now call Iraq. Towards the end of the nineteenth century European archaeologists conducted excavations there, and they found thousands of baked clay tablets on which there was a strange kind of writing, now called cuneiform, in the language of the people who lived there as long ago as 3,000 years before the Common Era. It took scholars some time to decipher this script and the language on which it was based. Some of the tablets were inscribed with poetry, including the celebrated *Epic of Gilgamesh*, which is one of the earliest literary masterpieces of the world. But they also found an enormous number of letters – rather disappointingly, mostly business letters, for the ancient Babylonians were at the centre of a great empire with all sorts of trading relations. I thought it rather strange and not very inspiring that the oldest form of the letter, so far as we can tell, is the business letter.

Business letters have continued to be written right down to the present day. Nowadays they are often between us and our bank, but it's all been simplified. A couple of hundred years ago, if you wanted to pay someone some money, you would sit down and write, with a quill pen, a letter asking the man at the bank to pay a certain sum of money to that person. But now you just write a cheque – a cheque being an abbreviated business letter, a tradition that goes all the way back to the Babylonians. Not only do we write letters to the bank; the bank, in the form of the Bank of England, writes letters to us. Any bank note is inscribed 'Pay to bearer' and signed by the cashier of the Bank of England. That means that if you had a ten pound note, you could go to the cashier of the Bank of England and he would give you – well, what? After he'd got over his surprise he'd probably just give you another ten pound note. But some years ago, if you'd gone to the Bank of England, or to any bank, because in those days there were numerous banks issuing currency notes, and presented a ten pound note, they would have given you ten gold sovereigns. That wouldn't happen now because in Britain we've stopped using the gold standard.[487] In fact, we don't see gold sovereigns any more at all.

On the radio I've heard all sorts of things about the economic situation, and I recently heard about something called quantitative easing. I hadn't heard that expression before, but I heard that another term for it is 'printing money', which makes it easier to understand. The Bank of England prints money and distributes it in some way. Perhaps it throws banknotes into the street and people pick them up, or so one might imagine. But actually, as I learned, the Bank of England may not print money at all. You may not believe this, but apparently someone at the Bank of England gets up one day and says, 'Let there be seventy billion pounds,' and at once seventy billion pounds come into existence, just as in the Book of Genesis, God said, 'Let there be light,' and there was light. But although all that money comes into existence, do we see it? Do we hear it? It exists on paper somewhere perhaps, or perhaps just electronically. I'm afraid economics is a bit beyond me!

I've gone off the track a bit, but this is all in connection with those Babylonian business letters. It all goes back to Babylon, as so many things seem to. Another form of letter is the newsletter. During the Victorian period, if someone was travelling abroad, they would write a long letter about what they were doing, send it home, and it would be passed around the extended family. Nowadays newsletters are produced by groups, organizations, and individuals, and we get them on the radio too. I remember in particular Alistair Cooke's famous *Letter from America*, which he wrote and broadcast for more than half a century. The first of them was broadcast just after the war and the last of them went out not many years ago.[488]

There's also the didactic letter, a letter of instruction, and this can be philosophical, religious, or devoted to almost any subject. I was very impressed by the *Letters on Aesthetics* written by Friedrich Schiller, the great German poet and dramatist and disciple of Kant, to a prince who was his patron. Schiller starts with a short, simple letter on aesthetics, but as the correspondence continues, he gets deeper and deeper into the subject, until the letters are long and profound.[489] And there's the religious didactic letter, for example the letters of St Paul. They're usually called epistles, which sounds a bit grand, but some modern translations simply call them letters, and that's what they are. After his dramatic 'Road to Damascus' conversion, Paul travelled around Asia Minor and eventually went to Rome. He founded little groups of followers of the risen Jesus, and he'd write letters to them from time to time, admonishing and instructing them and telling them what to believe and what not to believe. These letters have been extremely influential on Christianity, which, theologically speaking, is based less on Jesus's sayings than on the densely theological argumentative epistles of St Paul. Some people think that we'd have been much better off if the emphasis had been on the sayings of Jesus.

Some years ago I read a beautifully written and serious novel about the life of Jesus, *The Brook Kerith*, by George Moore, the great Irish novelist. According to his story, Jesus did not die on the cross, but was surreptitiously taken down from it by Joseph of Arimathea, who features in the Gospels. George Moore gives a beautiful description, with apparently quite a bit of psychological and medical understanding, of how Joseph of Arimathea gradually nurses the wounded, stricken Jesus back to life. It's clear that the crucifixion has been a terribly traumatic experience, and it takes Jesus a very long time to get over it, and even to walk again. But eventually he does walk again, and then he has to decide what to do with his life. As he thinks things over, he realizes that he has made a terrible mistake. He realizes that he isn't the Messiah, and he misled people by claiming to be. He is not exactly just an ordinary man, but he is certainly not the Messiah. So he decides to go back to what he was doing before he started preaching – being a shepherd. He minds his flock for maybe twenty years or so, and then one day there comes to the town where he is staying a small, bald-headed man bringing the message that Jesus has risen from the dead. The now middle-aged shepherd and the enthusiastic convert Paul meet, and Jesus says, 'I didn't die on the cross. I'm still alive.' But Paul says, 'No, you rose from the dead. I know because it's been revealed to me.' So Paul goes on his way, visiting different cities, founding his groups of believers in the risen Jesus, and writing his epistles, and that's how we come to have the sort of Christianity that we have had for the last 2,000 years.[490]

So the letter is a very varied literary form, one of the most flexible literary forms that we have, along with the novel and the play. Next on my list of types of letter is what I would call the imaginary letter – for instance, letters composed to create a novel whose story is told through an exchange of letters. This is sometimes called the epistolary novel, and there are several famous examples. There's Goethe's novel, *The Sorrows of Young Werther*.[491] In English literature the classic example is Samuel Richardson's *Clarissa*. Richardson is known for his psychological insight, and in that way he's a very modern novelist, though he lived in the eighteenth century and was a contemporary of Dr Johnson. Famously, Dr Johnson once said about Richardson's novels, 'If you were to read Richardson for the story, you'd go and hang yourself.'[492] There's also an epistolary novel by Walter Scott called *Redgauntlet*.[493]

In some ways the most important kind of letter is the personal letter. In *The Paston Letters* we have a famous collection of letters written in the fifteenth century by members of the Paston family which throw a great deal of light on the life of the times. And there are even more personal letters, for instance Henry the Eighth's love letters to Anne Boleyn, which are in the Vatican library. Some of them have been published, so you can see exactly what the love-sick Henry wrote to Anne some two or three years before he cut off her head.

The eighteenth century was the century of letter-writing, when educated people were very conscious of the need to write a good letter. One famous collection of letters from this period is that written by Lord Chesterfield to his illegitimate son, Stanhope. Lord Chesterfield was keen to bring this young man on in the world, and concerned that he should know how to behave. The collection was published after Lord Chesterfield and Stanhope were both dead, having been sold to the publisher by Stanhope's widow. It was widely read, though Dr Johnson didn't think very highly of it, commenting that the letters teach 'the morals of a whore, and the manners of a dancing master', which I think was a little unjust.[494] Dr Johnson wrote letters too; he isn't particularly known for them, but they have been published in three volumes. One letter of his that became famous was written to that same Lord Chesterfield. When Johnson started working on his great dictionary he tried unsuccessfully to get an interview with Lord Chesterfield, but when the dictionary had been completed, Chesterfield apparently let it be known that he wouldn't mind if Johnson dedicated it to him. This upset Johnson, and he wrote the 'Letter to Chesterfield'. I wish I knew it by heart so I could repeat it for you, but it's one of the greatest put-downs in literary history, and well worth reading if you want to know how to do that sort of thing in style.[495]

To go a little further on in history, some of the most interesting personal letters are those written by the Romantic poets. We've got wonderful letters by Lord Byron, for instance. They're racy, personal, a bit slangy, and they cover a wide field, so you really get to know what sort of person Byron was. We've got a whole volume of very fine letters by Keats, mostly written to his brother and his sister-in-law. In a particularly famous one he talks about human life as a vale of soul-making. It was a Christian moralizing view that this life is a vale of tears, but Keats takes up that phrase and turns it.[496] The soul is not something that you're given, something that doesn't change. You can change and develop, and of course that's a very important idea which we have in the Dharma. We don't speak in terms of soul, though I don't see why we shouldn't in a poetic sense, but we do speak in terms of developing and transforming our whole being, our consciousness, and Keats had that sort of idea too. And then we've got some wonderful letters by Coleridge, six whole volumes of them. Coleridge really poured himself into his letters – his thoughts, his feelings, his fears, his literary criticisms, his philosophical ideas, his theological speculations, and pages and pages of self-analysis. It's a very rich collection. If you want to know Coleridge in any depth, read those letters, as well as the poems and Richard Holmes' two volumes of biography.[497]

Great writers carried on writing letters all through the nineteenth century, and coming closer to our own day we've got wonderful letters by D. H. Lawrence and Philip Larkin. When a selection of Larkin's letters was published just a few years ago, they created a bit of a scandal, because they expressed rather bluntly what some people considered rather right-wing views.[498]

Of course, we write personal letters ourselves occasionally. I've always felt that the writing of letters, like any other form of literary activity, is very important, and I'm still writing them, though I have to dictate them nowadays. I try to say in them what I really think and feel, which isn't always easy considering some of the people I have to write to. I write to some people who are older than me and some who are younger, and of course some of my correspondents, like my old friend Dinoo, have passed away, and that gives rise to reflections.

People who visit me often ask me two questions: what is it like to be old, and whether I think much about death. With regard to the first question I usually say that one of the things I've come to realize, especially after reading something written by one of Jung's disciples, is that old age is not just a preparation for death. Old age is a stage of life in its own right, to be enjoyed and benefited from. It gives you something quite distinctive that youth and middle age don't give, something that has a definite value of its own.[499]

I don't think about death much more than I have been thinking about it all these years, though I'm aware of it, and of course I'm reminded of it when friends pass on and I can no longer write to them or see them. I hope I'm ready for it. I think rather more about rebirth, because after death, according to the Dharma, there comes another life, a new beginning. I sometimes wonder where I will be reborn. There are all sorts of possibilities. I could be reborn in Africa or China or Russia. I could be reborn to a pair of Order members here in Birmingham, who knows? I do sometimes wonder how I would cope if I found myself reborn in surroundings which would be unfamiliar in comparison with those I experience now, but I don't think about it too much. I just hope that wherever I am reborn, whether on this earth or in some other world – possibly a heavenly world? – I will continue to have contact with the Dharma, so that I can study and practise it, and that I will still have spiritual friends, still have a sangha just like this one in Birmingham that I've had the pleasure of addressing this evening.

SOURCES

The talks in this volume have not been published before (with a couple of exceptions), but you could consult sources in the form of the original recordings. Recordings and transcripts were made over many years by many people – many thanks to everyone who has helped – and some talks were specially transcribed for this volume. We have done our best to correct mishearings, and endnotes provide references wherever possible. If you want to listen to any of them, at the time of writing (2021) almost all the talks can be found online at www.freebuddhistaudio.com, but a few of the later ones exist just as videos made by the Clear Vision Trust and (at present) to be found on Vimeo.

NOTES AND REFERENCES

THE 1960S

1 Sangharakshita has more to say about this in his memoir *Moving Against the Stream*, in chapter 29, 'Buddhism and the Bishop of Woolwich'; see *Complete Works*, vol. 23, pp. 210–15.

2 The Second Vatican Council took place between 1962 and 1965 and addressed various matters to do with the Roman Catholic church's relationship with the modern world.

3 Paul Tillich (1886–1965) was an influential theologian who emigrated from Germany to America in 1933. He is particularly associated with the idea of God as the ground of being.

Dietrich Bonhoeffer (1906–45) was a German theologian who was imprisoned and executed by the Nazis; of his many works, the *Letters and Papers from Prison* are particularly well known.

4 John Colenso (1814–83) was originally from Cornwall, and became the first Bishop of Natal. The questions about the Bible put to him by his African students made him question the literal accuracy of the Pentateuch of the Old Testament. His views, and his advocacy for native Africans, made him a controversial figure.

5 Śaṅkara, also called Śaṅkarācārya, was an Indian philosopher and theologian of the eighth century CE, and a renowned exponent of the Advaita Vedānta school of philosophy.

6 John A. T. Robinson, *The New Reformation?*, SCM Press, London 1965, p. 41.

7 The death of Socrates is described at the end of Plato's

Phaedo. Socrates died for others in the sense of holding to his principles. See Plato, *The Last Days of Socrates*, Christopher Rowe (trans.), Penguin, Harmondsworth 2010.

The first Vietnamese monk to self-immolate in protest at the persecution of Buddhists by the Vietnamese government was Thích Quảng Đức, who set himself on fire in 1963. Sangharakshita writes about the events in Vietnam in *Precious Teachers*, *Complete Works*, vol. 22, pp. 516–17.

Edith Cavell (1865–1915) was an English nurse and hospital matron who worked in Belgium during the First World War. She tended soldiers from both sides, and helped Allied soldiers to escape, for which she was executed by firing squad. She is remembered for her words: 'Patriotism is not enough; I must have no hatred or bitterness towards anyone.' Sangharakshita writes of her in *A Moseley Miscellany*, Ibis Books, Ledbury 2015, p. 119 (*Complete Works*, vol. 26).

8 Her name is Samding Dorje Phagmo, and she is the third highest-ranking person in the Tibetan hierarchy after the Dalai Lama and the Panchen Lama. Traditionally she is the abbess of Samding Monastery, and said to be an emanation of Vajravārāhī, a wrathful form of Vajrayoginī. The current incarnation, the twelfth of that line, lives in Lhasa (2021).

9 The story of how Milarepa built, tore down, and rebuilt a tower, again and again, at his guru Marpa's instruction is told in part 2, chapter 2, 'Ordeals' of the autobiography of Milarepa as told to Rechungpa. There are various translations; see, for example, Lobsang P. Lhalungpa, *The Life of Milarepa*, E. P. Dutton, New York 1977, pp. 49–56.

10 The disciple was Lama Ngokpa. Ibid., p. 69.

11 A version of the traditional guru yoga practice is described in chapter 4, 'The Cosmic Refuge Tree and the Archetypal Guru', in *Creative Symbols of Tantric Buddhism*, *Complete Works*, vol. 13, pp. 216–20. As developed and practised in the Triratna Buddhist Order, it has become known as the *kalyāṇa mitra yoga*; for more information on the practice, see *The Purpose and Practice of Buddhist Meditation*, *Complete Works*, vol. 5, pp. 558–65, and p. 753, note 538.

12 For more details of the practice, see *Creative Symbols of Tantric Buddhism* in *Complete Works*, vol. 13, pp. 260–6.

13 Among many canonical references to the five *indriyas*, the *Saṃyutta Nikāya* (v.193 ff.) describes them in various ways in a section on the faculties; see Bhikkhu Bodhi (trans.), *The*

Connected Discourses of the Buddha, Wisdom Publications, Boston 2000, pp. 1668ff.; see also F. L. Woodward (trans.), *The Book of the Kindred Sayings*, part 5, Pali Text Society, London 1979, pp. 169ff. See also *Complete Works*, vol. 1, pp. 279–94.

14 *Saṃyutta Nikāya* v.115 (*Mahāvagga* 46.53): Bhikkhu Bodhi, ibid., p. 1607; or F. L. Woodward, ibid. p. 98.

15 For more on the first three fetters, see Sangharakshita, *The Taste of Freedom*, ch. 1 (*Complete Works*, vol. 11) in which these three fetters are described as habit, vagueness, and superficiality.

16 Maitreya is revered by the Theravādins as the future Buddha. He is said to live in the Tuṣita Heaven awaiting the time for his birth as the Buddha-to-be. He is mentioned (in the Pāli form Metteyya) in the *Cakkavatti-Sīhanāda Sutta*, *Dīgha Nikāya* 26 (iii.36): T. W. and C. A. F. Rhys Davids (trans.), *Dialogues of the Buddha*, part 3, Pali Text Society, London 1971, pp. 73–4; or M. Walshe (trans.), *The Long Discourses of the Buddha*, Wisdom Publications, Boston 1995, pp. 402–3.

17 In William Blake's *The Marriage of Heaven and Hell*, published in the author's own illustrated edition in 1793, the voice of the Devil says, 'Energy is eternal delight', contrary to the error that 'God will torment Man in Eternity for following his Energies'.

18 René Guénon, *The Reign of Quantity and the Signs of the Times*, trans. Lord Northbourne, Sophia Perennis, New York 2001. This text is considered the magnum opus among Guénon's texts of civilizational criticism.

19 *Dhammapada* 100, trans. Sangharakshita.

20 See, for example, the *Brahmajāla Sutta*, *Dīgha Nikāya* 1 (i.8): M. Walshe (trans.), *The Long Discourses of the Buddha*, Wisdom Publications, Boston 1995, pp. 70–1; or T. W. Rhys Davids (trans.), *Dialogues of the Buddha*, part 1, Pali Text Society, London 1973, pp. 13–14. Also the *Saccasaṃyutta, Saṃyutta Nikāya* v.419–20: Bhikkhu Bodhi (trans.), *The Connected Discourses of the Buddha*, Wisdom Publications, Boston 2000, p. 1843; or F. L. Woodward (trans.), *The Book of the Kindred Sayings*, part 5, Pali Text Society, London 1979, pp. 355–6. These *suttas* list twenty-eight forms of *tiracchāna-kathā*, low talk, literally 'beastly talk'. The commentaries add another four: talk about sensuous enjoyment, self-mortification, eternity, and self-annihilation, bringing the number to thirty-two. (Information from Nyanatiloka, *Buddhist*

Dictionary, Buddhist Publication Society, Kandy 1988, p. 211.)

21 In Christian theology, the tripartite view holds that humankind is a composite of three distinct components: body, spirit, and soul. See, for example, 1 Corinthians 2:12–3:4.

22 James Boswell, *The Life of Samuel Johnson*, Jones & Co, London 1827, p. 361.

23 Wesak is a Burmese corruption of the name of the month *Vaiśākha*. Many Buddhists today prefer to call the festival Buddha Day, Buddha Jayanti, or *Vaiśākha Pūrṇimā*.

24 Sangharakshita came into contact with the German-born lama in 1950 through the magazine he founded soon after arriving in Kalimpong.

> Lama Govinda … hailed the appearance of *Stepping-Stones* with great enthusiasm, sending me letters of advice and encouragement after every issue, and promising support and cooperation

(*Facing Mount Kanchenjunga*, *Complete Works*, vol. 21, p. 87). Articles for publication followed; and then a visit to Kalimpong from the lama and his Parsi wife, Li Gotami. Sangharakshita found in Lama Govinda 'a kindred spirit' (ibid., chapter 13). They remained in contact for the rest of Lama Govinda's life. His final letter to Sangharakshita, from America where he spent the last years, was written just four days before he died in January 1985.

25 Sangharakshita learned these communication exercises in the early 1960s from Muriel Payne, an English educationalist working in India who had found that teachers, generally speaking, taught very badly and came to the conclusion that this was because they were not able to communicate, either with their pupils or with each other. She therefore devised a series of communication exercises. Sangharakshita gathered a couple of dozen friends and arranged for Miss Payne to conduct a series of workshops, at which she taught these exercises, which Sangharakshita was convinced brought one to a level of communication way beyond that which normally exists between people. 'During those exercises I experienced communication as I had never done before, especially when I did the exercises with her.' Each person says, turn by turn, a banal phrase such as, 'Do birds fly?' In Sangharakshita's experience, 'Through a verbal exchange that does not have any objective meaning you experience the other person as though there is, one might almost say, a merging of

your two beings – it is very like that experience of the angels merging that Raphael describes in *Paradise Lost*.' Some years later, when leading FWBO retreats, Sangharakshita introduced these exercises and they proved very successful. (Condensed from a conversation with Mahamati and Subhuti in 2009.)

26 Voltaire was an eighteenth-century French writer, philosopher, wit, and critic of Christianity. This saying comes from his 1736 work *The important examination of the Holy Scriptures*, attributed to Lord Bolingbroke, but written by Voltaire. It is sometimes also attributed to the American writer Mark Twain.

27 Alfred North Whitehead, *Religion in the Making*, Cambridge University Press, Cambridge 2011, p. 6.

28 T. S. Eliot, *Choruses from 'The Rock'*, part 3 (1934).

29 Julian Huxley (1887–1975) was a British evolutionary theorist who popularized science through books and articles, and presentations on radio and television. He was a founding member of the World Wildlife Fund and first director-general of UNESCO (United Nations Educational, Scientific and Cultural Organization). 'Personalia' is chapter 4 of Julian Huxley, *Religion without Revelation*, Max Parrish, London 1959, pp. 65–96.

30 These talks were published as *The Essence of Zen*; see *Complete Works*, vol. 13, pp. 319–64.

31 Sangharakshita writes about his friendship with Clare Cameron in *The Rainbow Road from Tooting Broadway to Kalimpong* in *Complete Works*, vol. 20, pp. 87, 100 and 103. See also the section on Clare Cameron in *Dear Dinoo: Letters to a Friend*, in *Complete Works*, vol. 21, pp. 338 and 479.

32 These articles were published in *Early Writings 1944–1954*; see *Complete Works*, vol. 7.

33 S. Radhakrishnan, *A History of Indian Philosophy*, Cambridge University Press, 1922, vol. i, pp. 130–1. See also Yamakami Sogen, *Systems of Buddhistic Thought*, Calcutta University, 1912, ch. 7.

34 See note 13.

35 Aristotle, *Politics*, book 1 section 1253a:

> He who is unable to live in society or who has no need because he is sufficient for himself, must be either a beast or a god: his is no part of a state.

36 Sangharakshita describes his travels with Buddharakshita in *The Rainbow Road from Tooting Broadway to Kalimpong*; see *Complete Works*, vol. 20, pp. 158–443. For an account of Buddharakshita in his vihara, see Khantipālo, *Noble*

Friendship, Windhorse Publications, Birmingham 2002, pp. 69–80.

37 This is the famous first line of a prose work by the poet John Donne, in *Devotions upon Emergent Occasions*, published in 1624. The passage begins, 'No man is an island, entire of itself' and ends, 'Any man's death diminishes me, because I am involved in mankind. And therefore never send to know for whom the bells tolls; it tolls for thee.'

38 Robert Spence Hardy (1803–1868) was an English Wesleyan missionary to India and Ceylon who wrote several books on Buddhism and Christianity.

39 Robert Caesar Childers' Pāli–English dictionary was first published in 1872–5. A facsimile copy was published in 2007 by the Oriental Book Centre, Delhi.

40 The Pali Text Society was founded in 1881 'to foster and promote the study of Pāli texts'. It still keeps in print the texts T. W. Rhys Davids himself translated, and the *Pāli–English Dictionary* he produced with William Stede, as well as the rest of the Pāli canon.

41 For example, Max Müller produced *Buddhist Mahayana Texts*, now back in print, and originally published in the Sacred Books of the East series, which was edited by Müller himself, comprised fifty volumes, including sacred texts of Hinduism, Buddhism, Daoism, Confucianism, Zoroastrianism, Jainism, and Islam, and was published by the Oxford University Press between 1879 and 1910. Müller wrote three of the volumes, and collaborated on three others.

42 Samuel Beal, *A Catena of Buddhist Scriptures from the Chinese*, Trübner, London 1871.

43 Right Reverend P. Bigandet, *The Life or Legend of Gaudama, the Buddha of the Burmese*, Kegan Paul, Trench, Trübner & Co., London 1911.

44 In 1906 the short-lived 'Buddhist Society of England' (later the Buddhist League) was founded by R. J. Jackson, who had come to Buddhism after reading Arnold's *The Light of Asia* and attending a lecture in Cambridge, and Colonel J. R. Pain, an ex-soldier who served in Burma, and presided over by T. W. Rhys Davids, the famous scholar of Pāli and founder of the Pali Text Society. Pain and Jackson, together with Dr E. R. Rost, a member of the Indian Medical Service, opened a Buddhist bookshop at 14 Bury Street, Bloomsbury, near the British Museum, in 1907. Lectures were given in the back of the shop and the three self-confessed Buddhists spoke in the parks from a portable platform painted bright orange and bearing the slogan 'The word of the

Glorious Buddha is Sure and Everlasting'. Information from Christmas Humphreys, *A Buddhist Students' Manual*, The Buddhist Society, London 1956, p. 30.

45 Francis Payne discovered Buddhism through the bookshop in Bury Street. Christmas Humphreys reports,

> The shop, with its bright yellow front, attracted the attention of Mr Francis Payne as he came out of the British Museum. He entered and demanded of J. R. Pain, whom he found in charge, 'Why are you bringing this superstition to England?' Said Pain, 'Don't be in such a hurry – read the books.' 'He showed me *Lotus Blossoms* by Bhikkhu Silacara', wrote Payne years later, 'and I had to conclude that Bhikkhu Silacara must be inspired, for he knows how to convert.' Soon after, Francis Payne was himself giving lectures on the Dhamma, and later played a valuable part in the development of Buddhism in England.

Ibid., pp. 30–1, 46–7, 50.

46 Christmas Humphreys (1901–1983) was an English barrister, and later a judge, whose theosophical interests led him to Buddhism. His first contact with it was through Coomaraswamy's *Buddha and the Gospel of Buddhism*, which he found in a London bookshop when he was seventeen.

> Having discovered that I could with ease sit in the correct cross-legged position for meditation, and that I seemed to 'remember' the principles of the Dhamma almost as fast as I read them, I lightly regarded Buddhism as an old friend once more encountered.

Ibid., p. 52. He wrote many books, widely read at a time when there was little information about Buddhism available in English.

47 Daisetsu Teitaro Suzuki (1870–1966) was a Japanese scholar whose series of three books *Essays in Zen Buddhism*, published between 1927 and 1934, made Zen known in the West for the first time.

48 The English Sangha Trust was founded by the English monk Bhikkhu Kapilavaddho (William Purfurst), who had been ordained in Thailand but soon gave up the robe to marry and become a pub landlord. See *Moving Against the Stream*, *Complete Works*, vol. 23, pp. 46–7.

49 John Wycliffe (c.1320–1384) translated the Bible into English for the first time, believing that everyone should have direct access to Christian teachings rather than only through the priesthood, whose wealth and power he questioned.

His followers were known as 'Lollards' (a derogatory name) and their movement can be seen as a precursor to the Reformation, which is why Wycliffe is sometimes called its morning star.

50 In 1810 seven Bishops voted against the Bill to abolish capital punishment for stealing from shops property to the value of five shillings. On that occasion not a single Bishop voted in favour of the abrogation of the monstrous and barbarous punishment of death for a comparatively small offence.

Speech in the House of Commons in 1899 by Mr H. Lewis, as reported by *Hansard*, the official parliamentary record.

51 E. M. W. Tillyard, *The Elizabethan World Picture*, first published in 1942.

52 Francis Bacon (1561–1626) was a philosopher and statesman who served as Lord Chancellor of England under James I. He died in Highgate after contracting pneumonia; he had been carrying out an experiment with snow.

53 Bishop George Berkeley (1685–1753) was an English philosopher, an empiricist who, in his *Principles and Three Dialogues*, defends two metaphysical theses: idealism (the claim that everything that exists either is a mind or depends on a mind for its existence), and immaterialism (the claim that matter does not exist). His contention that all physical objects are composed of ideas is encapsulated in his motto *esse est percipi* (to be is to be perceived).

54 Joseph Butler (1692–1752) was an influential theologian and philosopher and a Christian apologist. He was bishop of Bristol from 1738 to 1750.

55 The Cambridge Platonists were a group of English seventeenth-century thinkers associated with the University of Cambridge. The most important philosophers among them were Henry More (1614–87) and Ralph Cudworth (1617–88).

56 'Lobsang Rampa' was Cyril Henry Hoskins (1910–1981), who believed himself to be 'hosting' the spirit of a Tibetan lama, Tuesday Lobsang Rampa (born on a Tuesday). His *The Third Eye: the Autobiography of a Tibetan Lama* was published in England in 1956. The title refers to an operation which he claimed opened his third eye. He was unmasked by the British press in 1958, but went on to write many other books including *Living with the Lama: 25 Years with Lobsang Rampa*, dictated to Rampa by his cat, Mrs Fifi Greywhiskers.

57 Reginald Horace Blyth (1898–1964) was born in England, imprisoned as a conscientious objector during

the First World War, and moved to Korea, then Japan, as a professor of English. He was interned by the Japanese in 1941 and finished work on *Zen in English Literature and Oriental Classics* while still in the internment camp; it was first published in 1942 by the Hokuseido Press, Tokyo.

58 Arthur Schopenhauer mentions this idea in the preface to *The World as Will and Representation* (1818).

> I surmise that the influence of Sanskrit literature will penetrate no less deeply than did the revival of Greek literature in the fifteenth century.

Arthur Schopenhauer, trans. E. F. T. Payne, *The World as Will and Representation*, vol. i, Dover Publications, New York 1969, p. xv.

59 Lal Bahadur Shastri (1904–66) was India's second Prime Minister. His sudden death was the subject of a 2019 film, *The Tashkent Files*.

60 For a little about Bhikkhu Mangalo, see *Moving Against the Stream*, *Complete Works*, vol. 23, pp. 24–6.

61 The reference is to Alfred North Whitehead (1861–1947), a prominent English mathematician and philosopher who co-authored the highly influential *Principia Mathematica* with Bertrand Russell. 'Religion is what the individual does with his own solitariness' is repeated several times in Whitehead's *Religion in the Making*, which originated in a series of four lectures delivered in King's Chapel, Boston, during February 1926. See Alfred North Whitehead, *Religion in the Making*, Cambridge University Press, Cambridge 2011, pp. 6, 37, 48.

62 Julian Huxley (1887–1975) was an English biologist and the first director-general of UNESCO (see also note 29). This passage is from his introduction to Pierre Teilhard de Chardin's book, *The Phenomenon of Man*, Harper Torchbooks, New York 1964, p. 13.

63 *The Winter's Tale*, Act IV, Scene iv, lines 112–4.

64 This phrase 'leaping sideways' (*ōchō*) is from Pure Land Buddhism, although evidently not used quite in this way; it means

> turning away from and thus abandoning the usual procedure of trudging along the path in a straightforward fashion, ascending step by step. Instead, by facing the Buddha directly and gaining his intercession, one 'leaps' to a stage close to that of the Buddha's own attainment. For Shan-tao, the originator of this phrase, this sideways leap meant experiencing *bodhicitta*, which he equated with *darśana-mārga*.

Mark L. Blum, 'Pure Land Buddhism as an Alternative Mārga', in *Critical Readings on Pure Land Buddhism in Japan*, vol. 1, ed. Galen Amstutz, Brill, Leiden 2020, pp. 44–5.

65 John Middleton Murry (1889–1957) was an English writer on social issues, politics, religion, and literary criticism. For what he called metabiology, see his book, *God: being an introduction to the science of metabiology*, Jonathan Cape, London 1929.

66 Chapter 3, 'The ground of our being', in John A. T. Robinson, *Honest to God*, SCM Press, London 1963, pp. 45–63.

67 For example, at *Aṅguttara Nikāya* i.174 we find

> Those who fall back on God's creative activity as the essential truth have no desire (to do) what should be done and (to avoid doing) what should not be done, nor do they make an effort in this respect. Since they do not apprehand as true and valid anything that should be done or should not be done, they are muddle-minded, they do not guard themselves, and even the personal designation 'ascetic' could not be legitimately applied to them.

Bhikkhu Bodhi (trans.), *The Numerical Discourses of the Buddha*, Wisdom Publications, Boston 2012, p. 267; see also F. L. Woodward (trans.), *The Book of the Gradual Sayings*, vol. i, Pali Text Society, Oxford 2000, p. 158.

68 *Dhammapada* 165.

69 *Dīgha Nikāya* 11 (i.222) in M. Walshe (trans.), *The Long Discourses of the Buddha*, Wisdom Publications, Boston 1995, pp. 178–9; or T. W. Rhys Davids (trans.), *Dialogues of the Buddha*, part 1, Pali Text Society, London 1973, p. 282.

70 See, for example, *Itivuttaka* 100: 'Bhikkhus, I am ... an unsurpassed physician and surgeon.' John Ireland (trans.), *The Udāna and the Itivuttaka*, Buddhist Publication Society, Kandy 1997, p. 226.

71 See, for example, *Visuddhimagga* 512; Bhikkhu Ñāṇamoli (trans.), *The Path of Purification*, Buddhist Publication Society, Kandy 1991, p. 520; or Pe Maung Tin (trans.), *The Path of Purity*, Pali Text Society, London 1975, p. 608. In *Foundations of Buddhism, Oxford University Press*, Oxford 1998, p. 63, pp. 282–3 (note 8), Rupert Gethin refers to research which concludes that there is no evidence that the Buddha borrowed the schema of the four noble truths from Indian medical tradition, and that it is more likely to have been the other way round.

72 The *viññāṇa-sota* is referred to in the Pāli canon, for example in the *Sampasādanīya Sutta*, *Dīgha Nikāya* 28 (iii.105),

in which it is said that the practitioner 'comes to know the unbroken stream of human consciousness as established both in this world and in the next'. See M. Walshe (trans.), *The Long Discourses of the Buddha*, Wisdom Publications, Boston 1995, p. 420; or T. W. and C. A. F. Rhys Davids (trans.), *Dialogues of the Buddha*, part 3, Pali Text Society, London 1971, p. 100. For an explanation of the *ālaya-vijñāna*, see *Complete Works*, vol. 2, pp. 279–82, and also pp. 174–8 in this volume.

73 John Locke (1832–1704) was an English philosopher according to whom, as expressed for example in *Essay Concerning Human Understanding*, at birth the human mind is a 'blank slate'.

74 See *Complete Works*, vol. 3, p. 199. For one of many canonical references see *Dīgha Nikāya* ii.308: M. Walshe (trans.), *The Long Discourses of the Buddha*, Wisdom Publications, Boston 1995, p. 346; or T. W. Rhys Davids (trans.), *Dialogues of the Buddha*, part 2, Pali Text Society, London 1971, p. 340.

75 Erich Fromm coined the term biophilia in his book *The Heart of Man* (1964).

76 See, for example, the *Brahmajāla Sutta*, *Dīgha Nikāya* 1 (i.13–17 and i.34–6); M. Walshe (trans.), *The Long Discourses of the Buddha*, Wisdom Publications, Boston 1995, pp. 73–5 and 83–6; or T. W. Rhys Davids (trans.), *Dialogues of the Buddha*, part 1, Pali Text Society, London 1973, pp. 27–30 and 46–9.

77 *Udāna* 6.4. For Sangharakshita's commentary, see *Complete Works*, vol. 10, pp. 594–9.

78 Jaideva Singh, *An Introduction to Madhyamaka Philosophy*, Bharatiya Vidya Prakashan, Varanasi 1968, p. 36:

> The approach to truth adopted in Hīnayāna was one of mystically-tinged rationalism, that adopted by Mahāyāna was one of super-rationalism and profound mysticism.

79 'This Mahāyāna doctrine was essentially a sophistic nihilism', L. A. Waddell, *The Buddhism of Tibet, or Lamaism, with its Mystic Cults*, W. H. Allen and Co., London 1895, p. 11. Waddell refers to 'fiendesses' throughout the book.

80 D. L. Snellgrove, *The Hevajra Tantra*, Oxford University Press, London 1959.

81 Edward Conze, *Further Buddhist Studies*, Bruno Cassirer, Oxford 1975, pp. 180–2.

82 George Grimm, *The Doctrine of the Buddha: the Religion of Reason and Meditation*, Akademie-Verlag, Berlin 1958. In the preface to this edition, Max Hoppe writes that the lengthening of the title

(originally published as *The Doctrine of the Buddha: the Religion of Reason*) was in accordance with one of George Grimm's last wishes.

83 This visit is briefly described in *The Rainbow Road from Tooting Broadway to Kalimpong*, *Complete Works*, vol. 20, p. 122.

84 These were published as *The Buddha's Noble Eightfold Path*; see *Complete Works*, vol. 1, especially on pp. 479–82.

85 An edited version of the talk referred to appears in *Ritual and Devotion in Buddhism*, Windhorse Publications, Birmingham 1995, pp. 25–36 (*Complete Works*, vol. 11).

86 The beginning of the Vinaya Piṭaka's *Mahāvagga* ('great chapter') tells the story of the Buddha's life from the moment of his Enlightenment, and includes his first teachings, his encounter with Kassapa of Uruvelā, the 'Fire Sermon', and his meeting with King Bimbisāra. See I. B. Horner (trans.), *The Book of the Discipline*, part 4, Pali Text Society, Oxford 1996, pp. 1–52. There are many more stories of meetings and encounters with the Buddha in the *Mahāvagga* and elsewhere in the Vinaya Piṭaka; for example, part 7 of the *Cullavagga* includes the story of the Buddha and Devadatta; see I. B. Horner (trans.), *The Book of the Discipline*, part 5, Pali Text Society, London 1975, pp. 259–85.

87 J. J. Jones (trans.), *Mahāvastu*, Luzac, London 1949 (vol. i), 1952 (vol. ii), 1956 (vol. iii).

The *Lalitavistara Sūtra* is published as Gwendolyn Bays (trans.), *The Voice of the Buddha*, Dharma Publishing, Berkeley 1983.

The *Abhiniṣkramaṇa Sūtra* is published as Samuel Beal (trans.), *The Romantic Legend of Śākya Buddha*, Motilal Banarsidass, Delhi 1985 (first published 1875).

Kosho Yamamoto (trans.), *Mahāyāna Mahāparinirvāṇa Sūtra*, Karinbunko, Japan 1974.

Aśvaghoṣa, *The Buddhacarita*, trans. E. H. Johnston, Motilal Banarsidass, Delhi 1984.

88 See, for example, the *Mahāparinibbāna Sutta*, *Dīgha Nikāya* 16 (ii.155): M. Walshe (trans.), *The Long Discourses of the Buddha*, Wisdom Publications, Boston 1995, p. 270; or T. W. Rhys Davids (trans.), *Dialogues of the Buddha*, part 2, Pali Text Society, London 1971, p. 173. Also the *Uposatha Sutta, Udāna* 5.5: John D. Ireland (trans.), *The Udāna and the Itivuttaka*, Buddhist Publication Society, Kandy 2007, p. 70.

89 The *Ninety-five Theses* or *Disputation on the Power and Efficacy of Indulgences* is a list of propositions written

in 1517 by Martin Luther, professor of moral theology at the University of Wittenberg, Germany. They advance Luther's arguments against what he saw as the abuse of the practice of clergy selling plenary indulgences, which were certificates believed to reduce the time spent in purgatory for sins committed by the purchasers or their loved ones.

90 Edward Parrinder, *The Christian Debate: Light from the East*, Gollancz, London 1964.

91 Billy Graham (1918–2018) was an evangelical preacher who held mass rallies.

92 See Edward Conze, *Buddhism: Its Essence and Development*, Windhorse Publications, Birmingham 2001, p. 39.

93 A famous example of a discourse addressed to a layman is the *Sigālaka Sutta*, in which the Buddha comes across a young man called Sigālaka standing in the river worshipping the six directions, and explains that true worship of the six directions consists of carrying out one's duties in regard to six kinds of relationship. See the *Sigālaka Sutta* (also known as the *Sigālovāda Sutta*), *Dīgha Nikāya* 31 (iii.180–93): M. Walshe (trans.), *The Long Discourses of the Buddha*, Wisdom Publications, Boston 1995, pp. 461–9; or T. W. and C. A. F. Rhys Davids (trans.), *Dialogues of the Buddha*, part 3, Pali Text Society, London 1971, pp. 173–84. For Sangharakshita's commentary on the text, see *What is the Sangha?* part 3, 'The Network of Human Relationships', in *Complete Works*, vol. 3, pp. 521ff.

94 This was the English Sangha Trust's meditation centre in Biddulph, Staffordshire.

95 This was G. P. (Gunapala Piyasena) Malalasekera, who was influenced by Anagarika Dhammapala and was founder president of the World Fellowship of Buddhists. He was Sri Lanka's High Commissioner to the UK from 1963 to 1967.

96 Bill Revill's enthusiasm for these talks is described in *Moving Against the Stream*, in chapter 29, 'Buddhism and the Bishop of Woolwich'; see *Complete Works*, vol. 23, pp. 211–2. Sangharakshita's destination when he was 'away for a few weeks' was Greece; the journey is described in *Crossing the Stream*; see *Complete Works*, vol. 23, pp. 246–320.

97 In the first verse of Rudyard Kipling's poem 'The English Flag'.

98 The four sights are not mentioned in the Pāli canon as concrete encounters of the historical Buddha. They are presented as 'the thought occurred to me ...': see *Sukhamāla Sutta*, *Aṅguttara*

Nikāya i.144, in Bhikkhu Bodhi (trans.), *The Numerical Discourses of the Buddha*, Wisdom Publications, Boston 2012, pp. 239–42; or F. L. Woodward (trans.), *The Book of the Gradual Sayings*, vol. i, Pali Text Society, Oxford 2000, p. 128; also section 13 of the *Ariyapariyesanā Sutta*, *Majjhima Nikāya* 26 (i.163): Bhikkhu Ñāṇamoli and Bhikkhu Bodhi (trans.), *The Middle Length Discourses of the Buddha*, Wisdom Publications, Boston 1995, p. 256; or I. B. Horner (trans.), *The Collection of the Middle Length Sayings*, vol. i, Pali Text Society, London 1976, p. 207. In early Pāli sources the legendary account of the four sights is only described in connection with the Buddha Vipassī; see the *Mahāpadāna Sutta*, *Dīgha Nikāya* 14 (ii.22–8): M. Walshe (trans.), *The Long Discourses of the Buddha*, Wisdom Publications, Boston 1995, pp. 207–10; or T. W. Rhys Davids (trans.), *Dialogues of the Buddha*, part 2, Pali Text Society, London 1971, pp. 18–22. In later texts, for example the *Nidānakathā*, *Buddhavaṃsa*, and *Lalitavistara*, the story is applied to the Buddha. The *Mahāvastu* gives a particularly graphic account of the four sights; see J. J. Jones (trans.), *Mahāvastu*, vol. ii, Pali Text Society, London 1987, pp. 145–53. See also Aśvaghoṣa, *Buddhacarita*, book 3, verses 26–62.

99 Let blood dry up, let flesh wither away, but I shall not stir from this spot till Enlightenment be attained.

These dramatic words are from the *Lalitavistara Sūtra*; see Gwendolyn Bays (trans.), *The Voice of the Buddha*, vol. ii, Dharma Publishing, Berkeley 1983, p. 439. See also Aśvaghoṣa, *Buddhacarita*, E. H. Johnston (trans.), Motilal Banarsidass, Delhi 1984, p. 186; and the *Appaṭivāṇa Sutta*, *Aṅguttara Nikāya* i.50; see Bhikkhu Bodhi (trans.), *Numerical Discourses of the Buddha*, Wisdom Publications, Boston 2012, p. 142; or F. L. Woodward (trans.), *The Book of the Gradual Sayings*, vol. i, Pali Text Society, Oxford 2000, p. 45.

100 *Dhammapada* 165.

101 O Bhikṣus, my words should be accepted by the wise, not out of regard for me, but after due investigation – just as gold is accepted as true only after heating, cutting, and rubbing.

Ganganatha Jha (trans.), *The Tattvasaṅgraha of Shāntarakṣita*, Motilal Banarsidass, Delhi 1986, vol. ii, p. 1558, text 3588.

102 This story is passed down in, for example, the *Atthasālinī*, Buddhaghosa's commentary on the first book of the

Abhidhamma. See Pe Maung Tin (trans.), *The Expositor*, vol. i, Pali Text Society, London 1921, pp. 18–20.

103 S. Radhakrishnan, *Indian Philosophy*, vol. i, George Allen & Unwin, London 1940, p. 613.

104 See, for example, Nārada Mahā Thera, *A Manual of Abhidhamma* (being the *Abhidhammattha Saṅgaha* of Bhadanta Anuruddhācariya), Buddhist Missionary Society, Kuala Lumpur 1979. See also Sangharakshita, *Know Your Mind* (*Complete Works* vol. 17), an analysis of mental states based on the Yogācarā version, as presented by a Tibetan commentator.

105 See the *Abhidhammattha-saṅgaha* of Ācariya Anuruddha, chapter 1, section 10, in Bhikkhu Bodhi (ed.), *A Comprehensive Manual of Abhidhamma*, Buddhist Publication Society Pariyatta Editions, Onalaska WA 1999, p. 45:

> Smile-producing consciousness (*hasituppādacitta*): This is a *citta* peculiar to Arahants, including Buddhas and Paccekabuddhas who are also types of Arahants. Its function is to cause Arahants to smile about sense-sphere phenomena.

106 'The Structure of Consciousness' in Lama Anagarika Govinda, *The Psychological Attitude of Early Buddhist Philosophy*, Rider and Co., London 1961, pp. 89–97. There is a diagram of the pyramid on p. 89.

107 For Sangharakshita's analysis of the Abhidharma's teachings on mind and mental functions, see *Know Your Mind* in *Complete Works*, vol. 17.

108 This incident is known as 'Brahmā's request'. See p. 188.

109 This is the truth that 'this being, that becomes'; in Pāli *imasmiṃ sati, idaṃ hoti; imassuppādā, idaṃ uppajjati; imasmiṃ asati, idaṃ na hoti; imassa nirodhā, idaṃ nirujjhati*. See, for example, the *Cūḷasakuludāyi Sutta*, *Majjhima Nikāya* 79 (ii.32); I. B. Horner (trans.), *The Collection of the Middle Length Sayings*, vol. ii, Pali Text Society, Oxford 1994, p. 229; or Bhikkhu Ñāṇamoli and Bhikkhu Bodhi (trans.), *The Middle Length Discourses of the Buddha*, Wisdom Publications, Boston 1995, p. 655. Also *Nidānasaṃyutta*, *Saṃyutta Nikāya* ii.28, in C. A. F. Rhys Davids (trans.), *The Book of the Kindred Sayings*, part 2, Pali Text Society, Oxford 1997, p. 23; or Bhikkhu Bodhi (trans.), *The Connected Discourses of the Buddha*, Wisdom Publications, Boston 2000, p. 552.

110 For a detailed account, see Sangharakshita, *What is the Dharma?*, chapters 2 and 7

('The Dynamics of Being' and 'The Spiral Path') in *Complete Works*, vol. 3, pp. 187–204 and pp. 258–79.

111 *Udāna* 1.10. For Sangharakshita's commentary, see *Complete Works* vol. 10, pp. 458–68.

112 Alan Watts, *This is It and Other Essays on Zen and Spiritual Experience*, John Murray, London 1961.

113 Buddhaghosa lists these five kinds of *prīti* (Pāli *pīti*) at *Visuddhimagga* 143–4; see Bhikkhu Ñaṇamoli (trans.), *The Path of Purification*, Buddhist Publication Society, Kandy 1991, pp. 140–2; or Pe Maung Tin (trans.), *The Path of Purity*, Pali Text Society, London 1975, pp. 166–7.

114 One use of this image is to be found in a story told about the Vedānta master of the early twentieth century, Swami Vivekananda. His biographer reports:

> Witnessing the religious ecstasy of several devotees, Narendra one day said to the Master that he too wanted to experience it. 'My child,' he was told, 'when a huge elephant enters a small pond, a great commotion is set up, but when it plunges into the Ganga, the river shows very little agitation. These devotees are like small ponds; a little experience makes their feelings flow over the brim. But you are a huge river.'

Another version of this simile is found in the *Himavanta Sutta*, *Saṃyutta Nikāya* v.63:

> Monks, the *nāgas* depend on the king of snowy mountains to increase their substance, and account for their power. Increased and empowered they descend into small pools, then into large pools; then they descend into small rivers, and then into large rivers; and finally they descend into the great gathered waters of the ocean. Thus their body becomes great and full. Just like that, monks, the monk depending on virtue, supported by virtue, seriously takes up the practice of, and produces, the seven factors of awakening and attains the greatness and fullness of them.

Here, the mythic *nāgas* are the ones making the progress. In Pāli, *nāga* frequently means elephant, but it can also mean any large or particularly impressive animal. The image of overflowing water to describe the transition from one positive mental state to another is given in the *Upanisa Sutta*, *Saṃyutta Nikāya* ii.32; see Bhikkhu Bodhi (trans.), *The Connected Discourses of the Buddha*, Wisdom Publications, Boston 2000, p. 556; or C. A. F. Rhys Davids (trans.), *The Book of the Kindred Sayings*, part 2, Pali

Text Society, Oxford 1997, p. 27.

115 *Cūḷadukkhakhandha Sutta*, *Majjhima Nikāya* 14 (i.94): see Bhikkhu Ñāṇamoli and Bhikkhu Bodhi (trans.), *The Middle Length Discourses of the Buddha*, Wisdom Publications, Boston 1995, pp. 188–9; or I. B. Horner (trans.), *The Collection of the Middle Length Sayings*, vol. i, Pali Text Society, London 1976, pp. 123–4.

116 This is the sixth of the eight qualities of the great ocean described by the Buddha in the *Uposatha Sutta*, *Udāna* 5.5. For Sangharakshita's commentary, see *Complete Works*, vol. 10, pp. 557–72. See also *The Taste of Freedom* in *Complete Works*, vol. 11.

117 The three *āsravas* (Pāli *āsavas*) are listed in many places in the Pāli canon; for example, see the *Mahāsaccaka Sutta*, *Majjhima Nikāya* 36 (i.249). See Bhikkhu Ñāṇamoli and Bhikkhu Bodhi (trans.), *The Middle Length Discourses of the Buddha*, Wisdom Publications, Boston 1995, p. 342; or I. B. Horner (trans.), *The Collection of the Middle Length Sayings*, vol. i, Pali Text Society, London 1976, p. 303. A few sources list a fourth *āsava*, *diṭṭhāsava*, the mental poison of wrong views; for example, the *Mahāparinibbāna Sutta*, *Dīgha Nikāya* 16 (ii.81). See M. Walshe (trans.), *The Long Discourses of the Buddha*, Wisdom Publications, Boston 1995, p. 234; or T. W. Rhys Davids (trans.), *Dialogues of the Buddha*, part 2, Pali Text Society, London 1971, pp. 327–37.

118 *Laṅkāvatāra Sūtra* 108, 42, 80, and 168 respectively. See D. T. Suzuki (trans), *The Laṅkāvatāra Sūtra*, Motilal Banarsidass, Delhi 1990, pp. 93, 38, 71, and 145.

119 John Blofeld, *The Zen Teaching of Huang Po on the Transmission of Mind*, Rider & Co., London 1958, pp. 29–30.

120 See note 53.

121 See Daisetz Teitero Suzuki, *Studies in the Laṅkāvatāra Sūtra*, Routledge & Kegan Paul, London 1972, pp. 104, 340, 397–8.

122 For more about the 'turning about', the *parāvṛtti*, see Sangharakshita, *The Meaning of Conversion in Buddhism*, chapter 4 (*Complete Works*, vol. 2, chapter 5, pp. 275–85).

123 This was Ramana Maharshi (1879–1950), who went to live at the Arunachala Hill at Tiruvannamalai in South India following a spiritual experience when he was 16 years old. He remained there for the rest of his life and an ashram grew up around him. He was widely regarded as a holy or enlightened teacher, and was associated with the Hindu Advaita Vedānta tradition. He spent years meditating in the

Virupaksha Cave where, much later, Sangharakshita meditated and saw a vision of the Buddha Amitābha.

124 A famous quotation from the Smaragdine Tablet, an ancient alchemical document ascribed to Hermes Tresmegistus, states the 'Hermetic correspondence' between higher and lower levels of reality:

> That which is above is like that which is below and that which is below is like that which is above, to accomplish the miracles of one thing.

125 The *Jātakas* and *Avadānas*, the 'Birth Stories and Glorious Deeds', are stories and celebrations of the previous lives of the Buddha. See *The Eternal Legacy* in *Complete Works*, vol. 14, pp. 61–71.

The *Mahāvastu* has been translated by J. J. Jones and was published by the Pali Text Society.

The *Lalitavistara Sūtra* is published as Gwendolyn Bays (trans.), *The Voice of the Buddha*, Dharma Publishing, Berkeley 1983.

The *Abhiniṣkramaṇa Sūtra* is published as Samuel Beal (trans.), *The Romantic Legend of Śākya Buddha*, Motilal Banarsidass, Delhi 1985 (first published 1875).

The Light of Asia is available in many editions, including one published by Windhorse Publications.

The *Nidānakathā* has been published as T. W. Rhys Davids, *Buddhist Birth Stories.*

Asvaghosa's *Buddhacarita*, trans. E. H. Johnston, is published by Motilal Banarsidass, Delhi 1984.

126 J. J. Jones (trans.), *Mahāvastu*, vol. iii, Luzac, London 1956, p. 156.

127 See Eugene Watson Burlingame (ed.), *Buddhist Legends*, part 3, Luzac, London 1969, pp. 45–7.

128 The Kanheri Caves are a group of caves and rock-cut monuments cut into a massive basalt outcrop in the forests of the Sanjay Gandhi National Park, on the former island of Salsette in the western outskirts of Mumbai, India. They contain Buddhist sculptures and relief carvings, paintings, and inscriptions, dating from the first to the tenth centuries CE.

129 'The union of opposites must play a decisive role in the alchemical process,' C. G. Jung, *Psychology and Alchemy*, Routledge & Kegan Paul, London 1953, p. 456.

130 See the *Dhammapada* commentary, published as Eugene Watson Burlingame (ed.), *Buddhist Legends*, Luzac, London 1969, part 3, pp. 53–4. See also W. H. D. Rouse (trans.), *The Jātaka*, vol. iv, Allen & Unwin, London 1981, no. 483, p. 168.

131 Genesis 28:10–19.

132 See, for example, Aśvaghoṣa, *Buddhacarita*, E. H. Johnston (trans.), Motilal Banarsidass, Delhi 1984, book 12, verses 67–8, pp. 200–1.

133 *The Three Jewels* was indeed published, the first edition by Rider in 1967. It now appears in *Complete Works*, vol. 2, and the section referred to here is to be found in chapter 4, 'The Legends', pp. 31–8.

134 Hieronymus Bosch (1450–1516) was a Dutch painter whose most famous work is a triptych called *The Garden of Earthly Delights*, which depicts all kinds of strange figures, especially in the hellscape in the right-hand panel.

135 See 'The Defeat of Māra' in the *Lalitavistara Sūtra*: Gwendolyn Bays (trans.), *The Voice of the Buddha*, vol. ii, Dharma Publishing, Berkeley 1983, pp. 463–8.

136 For more about this, see 'The Buddha's Victory' in the collection of that name, *Complete Works*, vol. 11.

137 The story of the Buddha, Māra, and the earth goddess seems first to have been introduced to the accounts of the Buddha's journey to Enlightenment in the Mahāyāna tradition's *Lalitavistara Sūtra*. For a translation, see Gwendolyn Bays (trans.), *The Voice of the Buddha*, vol. ii, Dharma Publishing, Berkeley 1983, pp. 481–2.

138 Mother Erda appears in *Das Rheingold*, the first of the four operas of Richard Wagner's Ring cycle, first staged in 1876.

'Hertha' is a long poem written in 1869 by the Victorian poet Algernon Swinburne, who described it as 'a dramatic monologue narrated by the Teutonic goddess of fertility Hertha – Mother Earth'.

139 The Buddha's vision of humanity like a bed of lotuses is described at *Saṃyutta Nikāya* i.138; see Bhikkhu Bodhi (trans.), *The Connected Discourses of the Buddha*, Wisdom Publications, Boston 2000, p. 233; or C. A. F. Rhys Davids (trans.), *The Book of the Kindred Sayings*, part 1, Pali Text Society, London 1979, p. 174; also *Vinaya Piṭaka* i.6; see I. B. Horner (trans.), *The Book of the Discipline*, Part 4, Pali Text Society, Oxford 1996, p. 9.

140 *Udāna* 2.1.

141 Rabindranath Tagore, *Gitanjali* (Song Offerings), no. 95.

142 Sangharakshita subsequently gave at least two talks on Padmasambhava; see pp. 285 and 317.

143 A new edition of the *Rinchen Terdzö* was published, with additions, at the instigation of Dilgo Khyentse Rimpoche in the late 1970s. It was published again, with revisions, in seventy-three volumes in 2018, by the Shechen Monastery, Kathmandu; copies are available from the monastery.

144 This teacher was evidently Yogi Chen, who says:

> Among Tibetans there is a well-known saying, 'When the iron bird flies everywhere, then my Dharma will go to the West.' This I heard from my esteemed Guru, Ganga Rimpoche, who quoted it as being the words of the Guru Rimpoche Padmasambhava.

C. M. Chen, *Buddhist Meditation: Systematic and Practical*, p. 3. The prophecy is said to be one of the *Lungten Gyatsa* ('one hundred prophecies'), a Nyingma collection of *terma* prophecies. 'Iron bird' is almost certainly a reference to the Tibetan year of the iron bird (which occurs every sixty years), and most translations specify 'the land of the red-faced people' rather than 'the West'; Tibetans historically consider this to refer to them.

145 W. Y. Evans-Wentz (ed.), *The Tibetan Book of the Dead*, trans. Lama Kazi Dawa-Samdup, Oxford University Press, London 1957, p. vi.

146 T. S. Eliot, 'Burnt Norton', part 1, in *Four Quartets*.

147 See Lama Anagarika Govinda, *Foundations of Tibetan Mysticism*, Century Hutchinson, London 1987, p. 123.

148 W. Y. Evans Wentz (ed.), *The Tibetan Book of the Dead*, trans. Lama Kazi Dawa-Samdup, Oxford University Press, Oxford 1957, pp. 202–5.

149 Edward Conze, 'The Hevajra Tantra: a critical study', *Bulletin of the School of Oriental and African Studies*, vol. 23, 3 (1960).

150 *Dhammacakkappavattana Sutta*, *Saṃyutta Nikāya* 56.11 (v.421): see Bhikkhu Bodhi (trans.), *The Connected Discourses of the Buddha*, Wisdom Publications, Boston 2000, pp. 1843–6; or F. L. Woodward (trans.), *Book of the Kindred Sayings*, part 5, Pali Text Society, London 1979, pp. 356–60.

151 There doesn't seem to be a passage in the *Gaṇḍavyūha Sūtra* that specifically makes this comparison, but the Huayan school of Buddhism picked up the general idea from the *sūtra*, and from the *Avataṃsaka Sūtra* as a whole, and made it a key part of its approach to the Dharma. See D. T. Suzuki, *On Indian Mahāyāna Buddhism*, Harper and Row, New York, Evanston and London 1968, pp. 156–7; and D. T. Suzuki, *Essays in Zen Buddhism*, third series, Rider and Company, London 1958, pp. 87–9.

152 Vinaya Piṭaka ii.173 (*Cullavagga* 7.10): see I. B. Horner (trans.), *The Book of the Discipline*, part 5, Pali Text Society, London 1975, pp. 271–2.

153 Uriah Heep is a character in Charles Dickens' novel *David*

Copperfield. While constantly claiming to be 'umble, Heep in fact has ambitions to become rich and powerful by entirely deceitful and unscrupulous means.

154 Jung discusses this in *Mandalas and Symbolism* (*Collected Works* 9.i) and also in *Commentary on the Secret of the Golden Flower*. For the latter see, for example, C. G. Jung, *Psyche and Symbol*, Anchor Books, New York 1958, p. 319.

155 Samuel Taylor Coleridge wrote to an unknown correspondent on 10 March 1804, of Sir Thomas Browne's 1658 work *The Garden of Cyrus* (whose subtitle is *The Quincuncial Lozenge, or Network Plantations of the Ancients, naturally, artificially, mystically considered*):

> You have quincunxes in heaven above, quincunxes in earth below, and quincunxes in the water beneath the earth; quincunxes in deity, quincunxes in the mind of man, quincunxes in bones, in the optic nerves, in the roots of trees, in leaves, in petals, in every thing.

156 In Hindu creation mythology, our world was born through a 'golden lotus', the opening from the womb of the universe. Buddhist cosmology tends to favour other creation stories, but in the Chinese Buddhist tradition we find the golden lotus:

> The overspreading ocean then produced a thousand-leafed lotus, golden-coloured and resplendent.

Samuel Beal, *A Catena of Buddhist Scriptures*, Trubner & Co., London 1871, p. 16.

157 Karl Jaspers, *The Nature of Psychotherapy: a critical appraisal*, Manchester University Press, 1965, p. 1.

158 Erich Fromm distinguishes between what he calls humanistic religion and what he calls authoritarian religion. This is the theme of his 1950 work *Psychoanalysis and Religion*.

159 Augustine of Hippo (354–430 CE) was one of the foremost church fathers of Christianity. In his major work, *The City of God* (*De Civitatis Dei*), book 16, chapter 32, he considers Abraham's willingness to sacrifice his son Isaac at God's command: 'Of course Abraham could never believe that God delighted in human sacrifices; yet when the divine commandment thundered, it was to be obeyed, not disputed.' Henry Edward Manning (1808–1892) was a well-known cleric in the Church of England, but in 1851 he converted to Catholicism and later became Archbishop of Westminster.

160 See note 71.

161 W. Liebenthal (trans.), *The Sūtra of the Lord of Healing (Bhaiṣajyaguru Vaiḍūryaprabhā Tathāgata)*, Peiping 1936.

162 This conversation takes place in chapter 5 of the *Vimalakīrti-nirdeśa*. Vimalakīrti's statement, and Sangharakshita's commentary on it, is to be found in *The Inconceivable Emancipation*, *Complete Works*, vol. 16, pp. 522–3.

163 Buddhaghosa, *Visuddhimagga* 573: 'The ordinary man is like a madman' (*ummattako viya hi puthujjano*); see Bhikkhu Ñāṇamoli, *The Path of Purification*, Buddhist Publication Society, Kandy 1991, p. 591.

164 Vladimir Solovyov, *The Meaning of Love*, trans. Thomas R. Beyer Jr., Lindisfarne Press, Great Barrington 1985, chapter 4, part 2:

> Just as what excites the fetishist, the hair or the feet, are only parts of the woman's body, so this same body, in its whole structure, is only a part of the woman's being. Nevertheless the countless lovers of the woman's body, in and for itself, are not termed fetishists, do not acknowledge themselves to be insane and do not submit to treatment of any kind. In what however does the difference lie here? Can it be that the hand or the foot represents a lesser superficiality than the whole body?

165 This verse is attributed to Bodhidharma. See D. T. Suzuki, *Essays in Zen Buddhism (First Series)*, Rider & Company, London 1949, p. 20 and p. 176. For further commentary on the verse, see *The Essence of Zen* in *Complete Works*, vol. 13, pp. 335–64.

166 *Hansard* is the verbatim record of UK parliamentary proceedings.

The 'Little Red Book' is *Quotations from Chairman Mao Zedong*, which was published by the Chinese leader in 1964.

167 The narrative of Xuanzang's journey is available as Li Rongxi (trans.), *The Records of the Western Regions Visited During the Great Tang Dynasty*, Numata Center for Buddhist Translation and Research, Berkeley 1996.

168 Psalms 146:3.

169 This is declared in hymn 10.90 of the *Rig Veda*, dedicated to the *Puruṣa*, the Cosmic Being. The verse about the creation of the Varṇas (verse 12) is believed by some scholars to be an insertion. For more about the verse, see *Ambedkar and Buddhism*, *Complete Works*, vol. 9, pp. 77–8.

170 For example, this is the theme of *Dhammapada* chapter 26, 'The Brāhmaṇa'.

171 See, for example, *Majjhima Nikāya* i.392–3; Bhikkhu Ñāṇamoli and Bhikkhu Bodhi (trans.), *The Middle Length Discourses of the Buddha*, Wisdom Publications, Boston 1995, p. 498; or I. B. Horner (trans.), *The Collection of the Middle Length Sayings*, vol. ii, Pali Text Society, Oxford 1994, p. 60. Also *Majjhima Nikāya* i.176; Bhikkhu Ñāṇamoli and Bhikkhu Bodhi (trans.), *The Middle Length Discourses of the Buddha*, Wisdom Publications, Boston 1995, p. 270; or I. B. Horner (trans.), *The Collection of the Middle Length Sayings*, vol. i, Pali Text Society, London 1976, p. 221.

172 This is called anthimeria, from the Greek word *anti-meros*, which means 'one part for another'. It is a rhetorical device that uses a word in a new grammatical shape, often as a noun or verb, and thus replaces one part of speech with another; for example, 'The thunder would not peace at my bidding', Shakespeare, *King Lear*, Act IV, Scene vi.

173 The historian was Minhaj-i-Siraj, and his book was called *Tabaqat-i-Nasiri*.

174 This was Akbar the Great, the third Mughal emperor, who reigned from 1556 to 1605.

175 Matthew 19:29; John 2:4.

176 Søren Kierkegaard, *The Present Moment*, no. v.4.

THE 1970S

177 This is the second lecture in that series, which was given in 1970. The first lecture of the series, 'How Consciousness Evolves', appears in edited form in chapter 9 of *What is the Sangha?*, *Complete Works*, vol. 3, pp. 475–85, and some other lectures from the series, 'Individuality, True and False', 'The Individual and the Spiritual Community', The Problem of Human Relationships', and 'Is a Guru Necessary?' also appear in that volume; see 'Sources, vol. 3, pp. 697–8. 'Meditation versus Psychotherapy' appears in *The Purpose and Practice of Buddhist Meditation*, see Complete Works, vol. 5, pp. 653–65.

178 See *A Survey of Buddhism*, chapter 1, section 17, in *Complete Works*, vol. 1, pp. 149–68.

179 The series was published as *The Buddha's Noble Eightfold Path*; see *Complete Works*, vol. 1, pp. 567–78.

180 No recording of this talk seems to exist.

181 This story is about Tenno, a disciple of Nanin. He had become a teacher when Nanin asked him this question, after which he went back to being a pupil. The story is told in Paul Reps, *Zen Flesh,*

Zen Bones, Penguin Books, Harmondsworth, 1971, p. 43.

182 This talk appears in edited form in *What is the Sangha?*, *Complete Works*, vol. 3, pp. 521–9.

183 Wilhelm Reich (1897–1957) was a radical and controversial psychiatrist (of the next generation after Sigmund Freud). One of his best known ideas was 'character armour' – the idea that emotional trauma was stored in the musculature of the body, forming a kind of armour against further attack; the armour could be released through massage, he believed.

184 Mr Micawber is a character in Charles Dickens' novel *David Copperfield* and 'Something will turn up' is his catchphrase.

185 Freud wrote about his theories of psychosexual development in the 1905 work *Three Essays on the Theory of Sexuality*.

186 Karen Horney was a German psychoanalyst who later worked in the United States. She disagreed with some of Freud's theories. She outlined these character types in her 1945 work *Our Inner Conflicts*.

187 Wilhelm Reich described these character types in his 1933 work *Character Analysis*.

188 This saying has been variously attributed – for example to Herbert Spencer, to Charles Darwin, and also to the biologist Thomas Henry Huxley, who is reported to have referred in conversation with Spencer to 'a beautiful theory, killed by a nasty, ugly little fact'.

189 Carl Jung's book *Psychological Types* was first published in 1921.

190 Erich Fromm (1900–1980) identifies these five character orientations in his book *Man for Himself: An Inquiry into the Psychology of Ethics* (1947).

191 *Bhagavad Gītā* 4.13.

192 At *Visuddhimagga* 102–110, Buddhaghosa identifies six 'kinds of temperament'. As well as 'greedy' and 'hating'; the other four are 'deluded', 'faithful', 'intelligent', and 'speculative'. See Bhikkhu Ñāṇamoli (trans.), *The Path of Purification*, Buddhist Publication Society, Kandy 2010 (fourth edition), pp. 102–111; or *The Path of Purity*, trans. Pe Maung Tin, Pali Text Society, London 1975, pp. 118–28.

193 At *Visuddhimagga* 97 Buddhaghosa says that loving-kindness and mindfulness of death are generally useful meditation subjects whereas all others are 'special meditation subjects'. Bhikkhu Ñāṇamoli (trans.), *The Path of Purification*, Buddhist Publication Society, Kandy 1991, p. 97.

194 William Sheldon (1898–1977) was an American psychologist who constructed a classification system that associated physiology and psychology,

which he outlined in *The Varieties of Human Physique* (1940) and other works.

195 See note 13.

196 W. Y. Evans-Wentz (ed.), *Tibetan Book of the Great Liberation*, Oxford University Press, London and Oxford 1970, pp. 102–92.

197 Lama Govinda, *Foundations of Tibetan Mysticism*, Rider, London 1973, pp. 190–5.

198 W. Y. Evans-Wentz (ed.), *Tibetan Book of the Great Liberation*, Oxford University Press, London and Oxford 1968, pp.106–9.

199 Ibid., pp. 145–7. See also Yeshe Tsogyal, *The Life and Liberation of Padmasambhava*, Dharma Publishing, Emeryville 1978, pp. 253–60.

200 Ganganatha Jha (trans.), *The Tattvasaṅgraha of Shāntarakṣita*, Motilal Banarsidass, Delhi 1986.

201 Samye monastery has been destroyed and rebuilt a number of times in its history. At the time of writing (2021) it is an active monastery again.

202 George N. Roerich, *The Blue Annals*, Motilal Banarsidass, Delhi 1979, p. 42.

203 This Latin phrase, which means 'The Devil is God turned upside down', is an ancient Kabbalistic aphorism. H. P. Blavatsky discusses it in *The Secret Doctrine*, vol. 1, Theosophical University Press, Pasadena 1888, pp. 411–23.

204 Evans-Wentz (ed.), *Tibetan Yoga and Secret Doctrines*, Oxford University Press, Oxford 1967, pp. 172–209.

205 This was Kachu Rimpoche. Sangharakshita describes his connection with this mysterious lama in *Precious Teachers*, Windhorse Publications, Birmingham 2007, chapter 8 (*Complete Works*, vol. 22, pp. 466–77). The story of the banner of victory on the vihara roof is also told in Sangharakshita, *In the Realm of the Lotus*, Windhorse Publications, Birmingham 1995, p. 27 (*Complete Works*, vol. 26).

206 See note 143.

207 See note 144.

208 See *The Rainbow Road from Tooting Broadway to Kalimpong*, *Complete Works*, vol. 20, pp. 409–10.

209 Ibid., pp. 425–6.

210 The Pāli text called the *Udāna* records a sequence of verses said to have been uttered by the Buddha in this way; for the text, and Sangharakshita's commentary on it, see *Complete Works*, vol. 10, pp. 419ff.

211 SOCRATES: Surely you're following, Theaetetus; it's my impression at any rate that you're not inexperienced in things of this sort.

THEAETETUS: Yes indeed, by the gods, Socrates, I wonder exceedingly as to why (what) in the world

> these things are, and sometimes in looking at them I truly get dizzy.
>
> SOCRATES: The reason is, my dear, that, apparently, Theodorus' guess about your nature is not a bad one, for this experience is very much a philosopher's, that of wondering. For nothing else is the beginning (principle) of philosophy than this.

Plato, *Theaetetus*, trans. Seth Bernardette, University of Chicago Press, Chicago 1986, 155c–d.

212 To take one of very many examples, see the *Tevijja Sutta*, *Dīgha Nikāya* 13, Maurice Walshe, *The Long Discourses of the Buddha*, Wisdom, Boston 1995, p. 195:

> At this the young Brahmins Vāseṭṭha and Bhāradvāja said to the Lord: 'Excellent, Reverend Gotama, excellent! It is as if someone were to set up what had been knocked down, or to point out the way to one who had got lost, or to bring an oil-lamp into a dark place, so that those with eyes could see what was there. Just so the Reverend Gotama has expounded the Dhamma in various ways. We take refuge in the Reverend Gotama, in the Dhamma, and in the Sangha. May the Reverend Gotama accept us as lay-followers having taken refuge from this day forth as long as life shall last!'

See also T. W. Rhys Davids (trans.), *Dialogues of the Buddha*, part 1, Pali Text Society, London 1973, p. 332.

213 See Dwight Goddard (ed.), *A Buddhist Bible*, Beacon Press, Boston 1970, p. 112.

214 See *Sāmaññaphala Sutta*, *Dīgha Nikāya* 2 (i.47–50): M. Walshe (trans.), *The Long Discourses of the Buddha*, Wisdom Publications, Boston 1995, pp. 91–3; or T. W. Rhys Davids (trans.), *Dialogues of the Buddha*, part 1, Pali Text Society, London 1973, pp. 65–8.

215 See Kenneth W. Morgan (ed.), *The Path of the Buddha*, Ronald Press, New York 1956, p. 347.

216 Sukhavati was the name given to the building that was to become a residential community and the London Buddhist Centre. The building project to turn this derelict old fire station into a Buddhist centre began in 1976 and the centre was opened in 1978.

The FWBO *Newsletter*, no. 33 (Winter 1977) reports from Norwich:

> Four members of Sukhavati community came to do some building work for the Rainbow vegetarian restaurant recently opened by one of the Norwich mitras. The strong, positive

presence left a considerable impression on more than just those involved with the Centre.

217 As he suggests in this talk, this seems to have been the first time that Sangharakshita spoke about levels of Going for Refuge. Here he posits six levels; in later presentations he identified four. See for example p. 596 or p. 666 below.

218 See, for example, the *Vasala Sutta* of the *Sutta-Nipāta*, in which the Buddha says:

> One does not become an outcast by birth, one does not become a brahmin by birth. It is by deed that one becomes an outcast, it is by deed that one becomes a brahmin.

Sutta-Nipāta 1.7, verse 21; for this translation see H. Saddhatissa, *The Sutta-Nipāta*, Curzon Press, Richmond 1994, p. 14.

219 At the time of writing (2021) the guidelines for becoming a Mitra in the context of the Triratna Buddhist Community are as follows: you become a Mitra when you (1) consider you are a Buddhist, (2) want to live in accordance with the five ethical precepts, and (3) believe that the Triratna Buddhist Community is the appropriate spiritual community for you.

220 William Blake's conception of the 'emanation' is complex. A brief idea of it is given by Northrop Frye in his study of Blake's work, *Fearful Symmetry*:

> Abstract ideas are called spectres by Blake and Spectre with a capital letter is the Selfhood. The corresponding term is 'Emanation,' which means the total form of all the things a man loves and creates. In the fallen states the Emanation is conceived as outside, and hence it becomes the source of a continuously tantalizing and elusive torment. In imaginative states it is united with and emanates from the man, hence its name.

Northrop Frye, *Fearful Symmetry*, Princeton University Press, Princeton 1969, p. 73. Communication through emanations is described in Plate 88 of *Jerusalem* (which Blake produced between 1804 and 1820).

221 Sukhavati was the name given to the building that was to become a residential community and the London Buddhist Centre.

222 See above, p. 285.

223 Yeshe Tsogyal, *The Life and Liberation of Padmasambhava*, Dharma Publishing, Emeryville 1978, pp. 50–1.

224 Ibid., p. 142.

225 Ibid., p. 182.

226 Ibid., pp. 30–5.

227 In William Blake's complex mythology, Urizen embodies conventional reason. He is usually depicted as a bearded old man, for example in Blake's painting 'The Ancient of Days'. He appears in several of Blake's mythological works, including the one named after him, *The Book of Urizen*, one of Blake's prophetic books, which was first published, with illustrative plates, in 1794. The work is a kind of parody of the Book of Genesis.

228 The eighteen kinds of *termas* are enumerated at Yeshe Tsogyal, *The Life and Liberation of Padmasambhava*, Dharma Publishing, Emeryville 1978, pp. 330–3.

229 The talks (given in 1976) were edited and published as *Transforming Self and World*, a commentary on the *Sūtra of Golden Light*; see *Complete Works*, vol. 16, pp. 227ff.

THE 1980S

230 The story is told in the *Dhammapada* commentary, as the occasion on which the Buddha spoke *Dhammapada* verses 197–9. See Eugene Watson Burlingame (trans.), *Buddhist Legends, Translated from the Original Pali Text of the Dhammapada Commentary*, Harvard University Press 1921, part 3, xv.1, pp. 70–2.

231 Edith Cavell (1865–1915) was an English nurse and hospital matron who worked in Belgium during the First World War. She tended soldiers from both sides, and helped Allied soldiers to escape, for which she was executed by firing squad. She is remembered for her words: 'Patriotism is not enough. I must have no hatred or bitterness towards anyone.' Sangharakshita writes of her in *A Moseley Miscellany*, Ibis Books, Ledbury 2015, p. 119 (*Complete Works*, vol. 26).

232 'Tis dangerous when the baser nature comes
Between the pass and fell incensèd points
Of mighty opposites.

Hamlet, Act V, Scene ii.

233 A reference to George Orwell's dystopian novel *Nineteen Eighty-Four*, first published in 1949.

234 These are all fictional Utopias, to use the title of the first. Sir Thomas More's *Utopia*, a satire about a fictional island of that name, was first published in 1516.

Bacon's *New Atlantis* depicts the creation of a utopian land where 'generosity and enlightenment, dignity and splendour, piety and public spirit' are the commonly held qualities of the inhabitants of the mythical Bensalem. Though unfinished, it was published in 1626.

The City of the Sun is a philosophical work by the Italian philosopher Tommaso Campanella, written in 1602, shortly after his imprisonment for heresy and sedition. A Latin version was written in 1613–14 and published in Frankfurt in 1623.

In *News From Nowhere* (1890), William Morris imagines a utopian future in which money, 'wage slavery', and marriage have been abolished.

235 'The Lotos-Eaters' was published by the English poet Alfred Lord Tennyson in a poetry collection published in 1832.

236 This was King Viḍūḍabha. The story is told in the *Dhammapada* commentary, and concludes with the Buddha's exhortation which became *Dhammapada* 49. See Eugene Watson Burlingame (trans.), *Buddhist Legends, Translated from the Original Pali Text of the Dhammapada Commentary*, Harvard University Press 1921, part 2, iv.3, pp. 44–5.

237 See note 98.

238 *Dhammapada* 197–201, trans. Sangharakshita.

239 See *Complete Works*, vol. 14, pp. 285–304.

240 The volume was eventually written and published as *Moving Against the Stream*; see *Complete Works*, vol. 23.

241 This scene is described in a chapter called 'Meditations in Monmouth-Street' in Charles Dickens' 1836 work *Sketches by Boz*, a collection of fifty-six pen portraits of London scenes and people. Curiously, Dickens also commented on those who inhabited the basements of Monmouth Street:

> The inhabitants of Monmouth-street are a distinct class; a peaceable and retiring race, who immure themselves for the most part in deep cellars,... and their habitations are distinguished by that disregard of outward appearance and neglect of personal comfort, so common among people who are constantly immersed in profound speculations, and deeply engaged in sedentary pursuits.

242 The lectures in the series 'Aspects of Buddhist psychology' appear in this volume; see pp. 138–234.

243 The lectures were eventually published as *The Buddha's Noble Eightfold Path*; see *Complete Works*, vol. 1, pp. 469ff.

244 See note 25.

245 Vinaya Piṭaka ii.258–9 (*Cullavagga* 10.5). See I. B. Horner (trans.), *The Book of the Discipline*, part 5, London 1975, p. 359. See also *Aṅguttara Nikāya* iv.280, in Bhikkhu Bodhi (trans.), *The Numerical Discourses of the Buddha*, Wisdom Publications, Boston 2012, p. 1193; or E. M. Hare (trans.), *The Book of the Gradual Sayings*, vol. iv, Pali Text Society, Oxford 1995, pp. 186–7.

246 In fact this didn't happen until the spring of 2010, when the name of the Order was changed to the Triratna Buddhist Order, and the FWBO/TBMSG became the Triratna Buddhist Community.

247 The talk now appears in *Complete Works*, vol. 2, pp. 287–306.

248 This was the International Buddhist Cultural Conference; see *Facing Mount Kanchenjunga*, *Complete Works*, vol. 21, pp. 393–4.

249 *Golden Drum* ran for 39 quarterly issues, the last issue appearing in November 1995. It was replaced by *Dharma Life*, which was published from 1996 to 2005.

250 R. E. Emmerick (trans.), *The Sūtra of Golden Light*, Luzac, London 1970, p. 12.

251
> The door of the Truth is covered by a golden disc. Open it, O Nourisher! Remove it so that I who have been worshipping the Truth may behold It.

Īśopaniṣad 15.

252 In the *Sāmaññaphala Sutta*, *Dīgha Nikāya* 2 (i.52–60), King Ajātasattu describes the views of various spiritual teachers he's met, including Purāṇa Kassapa, an eternalist, and Ajita Kesakambalin, an annihilationist. See M. Walshe (trans.), *The Long Discourses of the Buddha*, Wisdom Publications, Boston 1995, pp. 93–9; or T. W. Rhys Davids (trans.), *Dialogues of the Buddha*, part 1, Pali Text Society, London 1973, pp. 69–76.

253 *Collins Concise English Dictionary*.

254 The story of how the Buddha told Mahāprajāpatī Gautamī the criteria by which the Dharma can be known is to be found at Vinaya Piṭaka ii.258–9 (*Cullavagga* 10.5): see I. B. Horner (trans.), *The Book of the Discipline*, part 5, Pali Text Society, London 1975, p. 359; and *Aṅguttara Nikāya* iv.280–1, in E. M. Hare (trans.), *The Book of the Gradual Sayings*, vol. iv, Pali Text Society, Oxford 1995, pp. 186–7; and Bhikkhu Bodhi (trans.), *The Numerical Discourses of the Buddha*, Wisdom Publications, Boston 2012, p. 1193.

255 Alfred Tennyson's poem 'The Palace of Art' was first published in 1832, and a new edition with many revisions appeared in 1842. In *The Religion of Art* (see *Complete Works*, vol. 26, pp. 149–50), Sangharakshita discusses the poem, in which, as he says,

> Tennyson has described with his usual abundance of vivid pictorial detail the fate of 'A Glorious Devil, large in heart and brain, That did love beauty only' and who had therefore planned to devote his life to the solitary enjoyment of whatever

masterpieces of painting, music, and poetry had been produced by man.

256 The inspiration came from *The Sūtra of Golden Light*, on which Sangharakshita gave an influential series of lectures in 1976, later published as *Transforming Self and World*; see *Complete Works*, vol. 16, pp. 225ff.

257 Sangharakshita recalled those walks in his 1997 poem 'Letter to Ananda'; see *Complete Works*, vol. 25, pp. 420–1.

258 *The History of My Going for Refuge* is included in *Complete Works*, vol. 2, pp. 397ff.

259 This very volume fulfils part of that wish, though it has taken more than thirty years to produce it. But after Sangharakshita made this statement, the Spoken Word Project produced a number of books based on lectures and seminars, and all of those books appear in the *Complete Works*. Not all of the seminars are in the *Complete Works*, but all exist in transcript form, to be found on the website freebuddhistaudio, and there are plans to produce edited versions of all of them.

260 Guhyaloka, or the 'secret realm', is a valley in the Sierra Aitana mountains of southern Spain, where ordination retreats for men have been held annually since 1987. At the top of the valley is the retreat centre; a house for the resident community is at the bottom, while midway between the two is a bungalow where Sangharakshita used to stay when he visited the valley.

261 The charity Aid for India was founded by members of the Western Buddhist Order in 1980 and in 1987 was renamed the Karuna Trust, which continues to fund social projects of many kinds in India and beyond.

262 In 1988 about 18% of Order members were women; in 2021 the figure is 40%.

263 In the Triratna Buddhist Order, a man or woman who becomes an *anagārika* observes the same ten precepts as all other Order members, the only difference being that the third precept is observed in the form of abstention from unchastity (*abrahmacariya*); that is, they are committed to celibacy. For more about this, see *Forty-Three Years Ago*, in *Complete Works*, vol. 2, pp. 608–9. We currently have (2021) 72 anagārikas, 54 women and 18 men.

264 *The Ten Pillars of Buddhism* appears in *Complete Works*, vol. 2, pp. 307ff.

265 Thich Nhat Hanh, *The Miracle of Mindfulness*, first published in 1975. Thich Nhat Hanh died in January 2022.

266 The bodhisattva's *saṃvara-śīla* or sixty-four precepts are included in the appendix to *Complete Works*, vol. 2, pp. 657–9.

267 See note 246.

268

> Society must have either the sanction of law or the sanction of morality to hold it together. Without either, society is sure to go to pieces. In all societies, law plays a very small part. It is intended to keep the minority within the range of social discipline. The majority is left and has to be left to sustain its social life by the postulates and sanction of morality. Religion in the sense of morality must therefore remain the governing principle in every society.

From 'Buddha and the Future of His Religion', an article by Dr Ambedkar first published in the *Maha Bodhi*, April/May 1950. For this passage in the article and Sangharakshita's commentary on it, see *Complete Works*, vol. 10, pp. 63ff.

269 See this volume, pp. 338ff.

270 This refers to the Buddha's advice to the Vajjians:

> As long as the monks hold regular and frequent assemblies, they may be expected to prosper and not decline.

Mahāparinibbāna Sutta, *Dīgha Nikāya* 16 (ii.76–7): see Maurice Walshe (trans.), *The Long Discourses of the Buddha*, Wisdom Publications, Boston 1995, p. 233; or T. W. Rhys Davids (trans.), *Dialogues of the Buddha*, part 2, Pali Text Society, London 1971, p. 82.

271 'Fierce friendship' was much talked about at a certain period of the FWBO's history. An article in *FWBO Newsletter* 47 (Autumn 1980) explained the role of criticism in friendship, declaring robustly that 'the offering of criticism by a spiritual friend, unlike dispraise, really is an act of friendship, for it shows a living concern for the person being criticized, a refusal to be indifferent to their shortcomings. What could be more loving than that?' This kind of approach could obviously be used insensitively, as Sangharakshita points out here.

272 'Harry the Ticker' appears briefly in Sangharakshita's memoir *The Rainbow Road from Tooting Broadway to Kalimpong*; see *Complete Works*, vol. 20, pp. 95–6.

273 John Keble (1792–1866) was an English clergyman and poet who in 1827 published *The Christian Year*, which became one of the most popular collections of verse of the nineteenth century. From one of its poems, 'Hues of the Rich Unfolding Morn', were derived the words of the hymn 'New every morning is the love'.

274 *Saṃyutta Nikāya* ii.29 (12.22). See C. A. F. Rhys Davids (trans.), *The Book of*

the Kindred Sayings, part 2, Pali Text Society, Oxford 1997, p. 24; also Bhikkhu Bodhi (trans.), *The Connected Discourses of the Buddha*, Wisdom Publications, Boston 2000, p. 553.

THE 1990S

275
> World history travels from east to west; for Europe is the absolute end of history, just as Asia is the beginning.

Georg Wilhelm Friedrich Hegel, *Lectures on the Philosophy of History*, Cambridge University Press, Cambridge 1975, p. 197.

276 *The Rainbow Road from Tooting Broadway to Kalimpong*, *Complete Works*, vol. 20, p. 448.

277 Vinaya Piṭaka i.47 (*Mahāvagga* 1.25): see I. B. Horner (trans.), *The Book of the Discipline*, part 4, Pali Text Society, Oxford 1996, p. 61.

278 The research institute was called the Magadh Institute of Post-Graduate Studies and Research in Pali and Allied Languages and Buddhist Learning, founded at Nalanda in 1951. It later came to be known as Nava Nalanda Mahavihara and was granted university status in 2006.

279 The first volume appeared in 1956 on the occasion of the Buddha Jayanti, and the rest followed over five years, guided to completion with enormous effort by Bhikkhu Kashyap. At one point he sold his house to pay the salaries of workers when payments had been delayed.

280 Professor Narain taught at Princeton University for a while, and among his students was Alan Sponberg, an American scholar who was himself to become a professor and in 1993 was ordained as a member of the Western Buddhist Order, Saramati, who helped to establish the Rocky Mountain Buddhist Center in Missoula, Montana. Professor Narain died in 2013.

281 Kenneth W. Morgan, *The Path of the Buddha*, Ronald Press Company, New York 1956.

282 *A Survey of Buddhism* was first published in 1957 and appeared in vol. 1 of the *Complete Works*. As stated here, it has just a few brief references to Tibetan Buddhism.

283 Dhardo Rimpoche explained his vision for what came to be known as the Indo-Tibetan Buddhist Cultural Institute (ITBCI) in Kalimpong when Sangharakshita first met him in 1954:

> The school would teach Tibetan and Buddhism in the morning, Dhardo Rimpoche explained, and modern subjects in the afternoon. There were many refugee children in Kalimpong, and he was anxious that they should grow up with

> a knowledge of their own religion and culture. At the same time, he realized that they had to be equipped to meet the demands of life in the modern world.

Sangharakshita, *Precious Teachers*, *Complete Works*, vol. 22, p. 422.

284 The charity Aid for India was founded by members of the Western Buddhist Order in 1980 and in 1987 was renamed the Karuna Trust. The charity continues to support many projects in India, including Dhardo Rimpoche's school, until it closed in December 2021.

285 Suvajra, *The Wheel and the Diamond: The Life of Dhardo Tulku*, Windhorse Publications, Glasgow 1991.

286 René de Nebesky-Wojkowitz's *Oracles and Demons of Tibet: The Cult and Iconography of the Tibetan Protective Deities* has been reprinted by various publishers since its original publication in 1956.

287 Chattrul Sangye Dorje died in 2015 at the age of 102.

288 Thomas Merton (1915–1968) was an American Trappist monk whose interest in meditation and other faiths brought him into contact with the Dalai Lama, D. T. Suzuki, Thich Nhat Hanh, and others. He met Chattrul Sangye Dorje in 1968, and recorded his impressions of the Rimpoche in his journal; see Thomas Merton, *The Asian Journal of Thomas Merton*, New Directions, New York 1975, pp. 143–4.

289 The Rimé movement was started in Tibet by Jamyang Khyentse Wangpo (1820–92) and Jamgön Kongtrül (1813–99). Ringu Tulku explains:

> *Ris* or *Phyog-ris* in Tibetan means 'one-sided, 'partisan' or 'sectarian'. *Med* means 'no'. *Ris-med* (Wylie), or *Rimé*, therefore means 'no sides', 'non-partisan' or 'non-sectarian'. It does not mean 'non-conformist' or 'non-committal'; nor does it mean forming a new School or system that is different from the existing ones. A person who believes the Rimé way almost certainly follows one lineage as his or her main practice. He or she would not dissociate from the School in which he or she was raised. Kongtrül was raised in the Nyingma and Kagyu traditions; Khyentse was reared in a strong Sakyapa tradition. They never failed to acknowledge their affiliation to their own Schools.

Ringu Tulku, *The Ri-me Philosophy of Jamgön Kongtrul the Great: A Study of the Buddhist Lineages of Tibet*, Shambhala Publications, Boston and London 2006, chapter 1.

290 The disciple's Dharma name was Jivaka. Sangharakshita tells this story in various places, and chapter 48, 'The Man in the Pit', of *Moving Against the Stream* introduces Jivaka and also describes this vision; see *Complete Works*, vol. 23, pp. 387–91.

291 Following the death of Dudjom Rimpoche, Dilgo Khyentse Rimpoche became head of the Nyingma school in 1987. He died in Bhutan in 1991.

292 Dudjom Rimpoche died in 1987. His book *The Nyingma School of Tibetan Buddhism: Its Fundamentals and History* was published in an English translation by Wisdom Publications, Boston, in 2005.

293 Jambhala, a bodhisattva in the 'family' of Ratnasambhava, is represented as a stout, deep-yellow figure, holding in his left hand a mongoose with jewels pouring from its mouth.

The red *ḍākinī* Kurukullā, sometimes considered to be a form of the bodhisattva Tārā, carries a bow and flowery arrows, a hook, and a noose, to shoot her 'victims' and pull them in (out of compassion, of course).

For a description of the rite of fascination (and the other three Tantric rites: purification, destruction, and prospering), see *Creative Symbols of Tantric Buddhism*, *Complete Works*, vol. 13, pp. 277–80.

294 A *phowa* is a Vajrayāna Buddhist meditation practice. It may be described as transference of consciousness with one's yidam. See *Precious Teachers*, *Complete Works*, vol. 22, pp. 554–5.

295 See *Moving Against the Stream*, *Complete Works*, vol. 23, p. 376 et seq.

296 *Aṅguttara Nikāya* i.259, in Bhikkhu Bodhi (trans.), *Numerical Discourses of the Buddha*, Wisdom Publications, Boston 2012, p. 342; or F. L. Woodward (trans.), *The Book of the Gradual Sayings* vol. i, Pali Text Society, Oxford 2000, p. 239. Bhikkhu Bodhi's translation is: 'To laugh excessively, showing one's teeth, is childishness.'

297 A number of works by Dilgo Khyentse Rimpoche have now been published, and in 2011 Shambhala Publications produced a *Collected Works* in three volumes.

298 The school closed in December 2021.

299 John 15:13.

300 Subhuti's talks on spiritual friendship were published as a booklet by Padmaloka Books and Subhuti later published a book on the subject, *Buddhism and Friendship*, Windhorse Publications, Cambridge 2004.

301 See p. 37 above.

302 For an analysis of Shakespeare's references to the medieval idea of hierarchy, see E. M. W. Tillyard, *The Elizabethan World Picture: A*

study of the idea of order in the age of Shakespeare, Donne and Milton, Vintage Books, New York 1959.

303 Ibid., 'The Chain of Being', chapter 4.

304 Śāriputra, who was looking for a teacher, came upon the Buddha's disciple Aśvajit, who told him that the Buddha's teaching could be summed up in the truth of universal conditionality. The story is told at Vinaya Piṭaka i.39 (*Mahāvagga* 1.23): see I. B. Horner (trans.), *The Book of the Discipline*, part 4, Pali Text Society, Oxford 1996, pp. 52–4. See also *What is the Dharma?*, *Complete Works*, vol. 3, p. 93.

305 It is the Russian novels of the nineteenth century in which this is a strong theme; see, for example, Ivan Turgenev's 1862 novel *Fathers and Sons* and Fyodor Dostoevsky's *The Brothers Karamazov* (1880).

306 The thirty-seven *bodhipakṣya-dharmas* are enumerated in the *Parinibbāna Sutta* at *Dīgha Nikāya* ii.120 (and many other places in the Pāli canon): see M. Walshe (trans.), *The Long Discourses of the Buddha*, Wisdom, Boston 1995, p. 253; or T. W. and C. A. F. Rhys Davids (trans.), *Dialogues of the Buddha*, part 2, Pali Text Society, London 1971, p. 128.

307 *One Flew Over the Cuckoo's Nest* by Ken Kesey is a 1972 novel (later made into a film) about a mental hospital tyrannized by the cruel Nurse Ratched.

308 *Desert Island Discs* is a BBC radio programme in which 'castaways' are exiled on an imaginary desert island and are asked to name the eight pieces of music they would want to have with them. They are also 'given' a copy of the Bible (or a substitute for those of other faiths) and the complete works of Shakespeare, and invited to take another book of their own choosing.

309 This case surrounded the publication in the UK in 1988 of Salman Rushdie's novel *The Satanic Verses*, to which many Muslims took grave exception – to the extent that the Ayatollah in Iran issued a fatwa against Rushdie.

310 *Shabda*, the Order's private newsletter, is circulated monthly. It began in 1974 at a time when Order members gathered together once a month in London to report in about their lives. These reports formed the basis of the newsletter. As the Order expanded and it was no longer possible to gather together regularly in one place, reports were sent by letter (replaced these days by email).

311 Lokamitra (b. 1947) was ordained by Sangharakshita in 1974. In 1977 he travelled to India to visit the Buddhist holy places, Kalimpong (where Sangharakshita had lived for many years), and Pune, where

he studied yoga with B. K. S. Iyengar. On his way to Pune he arrived in Nagpur on the very day that Dr Ambedkar's followers were celebrating the twenty-first anniversary of the mass conversion to Buddhism. He was so moved by what he saw that he decided to stay and work in India with Dr Ambedkar's Buddhist followers to create an Indian wing of the Order and movement that Sangharakshita had inaugurated and to date he has worked there for over forty years.

312 Sinhadevi, who evidently introduced this talk, is an Irish *dharmacāriṇī* with a beautiful lilting voice.

313 In fact two consecutive issues of *Golden Drum* discussed the topic: *Golden Drum* nos. 6 and 7, August–October 1987 and November–January 1987–8.

314 Angulimala, the Buddhist Prison Chaplaincy, was founded in the 1980s by British-born Ajahn Khemadhammo (b. 1944), who trained and worked as an actor, went on to receive *bhikkhu* ordination in the Theravāda tradition in Thailand, and for thirty-five years has run Angulimala. The historical Aṅgulimāla was a notorious murderer who was famously converted to Buddhism after an encounter with the Buddha. *Aṅgulimāla Sutta*, *Majjhima Nikāya* 86 (ii.98–105): see Bhikkhu Ñāṇamoli and Bhikkhu Bodhi (trans.), *The Middle Length Discourses of the Buddha*, Wisdom Publications, Boston 1995, pp. 710–17; or I. B. Horner (trans.), *The Collection of the Middle Length Sayings*, vol. ii, Pali Text Society, Oxford 1994, pp. 284–92.

315 The lecture 'The Heroic Ideal in Buddhism' was delivered in 1969. An edited version appears in chapter 4 of *Who is the Buddha?*; see *Complete Works*, vol. 3, pp. 44–56.

316 The Mahavihara in Dapodi, Pune, was opened in 1991; the story of the obstacles faced by Lokamitra are briefly described in *Complete Works*, vol. 10 (pp. 366–71), in the section called 'Keeping the Mahavihara beautiful'.

317 At the time of writing (2021) these responsibilities are held by the College of Public Preceptors, which has forty-four members.

318 San Francisco Zen Center was established in 1962 by Shunryū Suzuki Roshi (1904–1971), well-known as the author of *Zen Mind, Beginner's Mind*, and his American students.

Lama Govinda moved to San Francisco in the late 1970s, and the Zen Center sangha took care of him until his death in 1985.

Dr Edward Conze taught at the University of California, Berkeley, in 1971–2, and at

Suzuki Roshi's suggestion a number of Zen Center students attended Conze's lectures and seminars.

319 The article was published in *Early Writings 1944–1954*, Ibis Publications, Ledbury 2014, pp. 33–8 (*Complete Works*, vol. 7, pp. 31–6).

320 See note 288.

321 Chattrul Sangye Dorje died at the very end of 2015.

322 See *The Rainbow Road from Tooting Broadway to Kalimpong*, *Complete Works*, vol. 20, pp. 144–5.

323 The first women's retreat centre, Taraloka, was founded in 1985, followed by the ordination training retreat centre for women, Tiratanaloka, which was founded in 1994. At the time this talk was given (1990) women's ordination retreats were being held at Taraloka. With the founding in 2007 of Akashavana, an ordination retreat centre for women located in the remote mountains of Aragón in northern Spain, annual three-month ordination retreats for women were established. For those unable to attend a long retreat, two-week retreats are held both at Akashavana and locally.

324 This was *The Drama of Cosmic Enlightenment: Parables, Myths, and Symbols of the White Lotus Sūtra*; see *Complete Works*, vol. 16, pp. 1ff.

325 Olaf Stapledon (1886–1950) was a British philosopher and author. *Star Maker* (1937) is regarded as one of the finest works of science fiction of the twentieth century. It includes descriptions of a multiplicity of universes.

326 There is much more to be said about the mysterious *pratyekabuddha*. A good account is to be found in Reginald Ray, *Buddhist Saints in India*, Oxford University Press, Oxford and New York 1994, chapter 7.

327 The Dharma Eye is one of the 'five eyes' of the Buddhist tradition; for a description see Sangharakshita, *Complete Works*, vol. 9, pp. 251–2. The first of the Buddha's disciples whose 'Eye of Truth' was opened was Kondañña, one of the five ascetics to whom the Buddha first taught the Dharma. See *Saccasaṃyutta*, *Saṃyutta Nikāya* v.423; Bhikkhu Bodhi (trans.), *The Connected Discourses of the Buddha*, Wisdom Publications, Boston 2000, p. 1846; or F. L. Woodward (trans.), *The Book of the Kindred Sayings*, part 5, Pāli Text Society, London 1979, p. 359.

328 See, for example, the *Aggañña Sutta*, *Dīgha Nikāya* 27 (iii.84): M. Walshe (trans.), *The Long Discourses of the Buddha*, Wisdom, Boston 1995, p. 409; or T. W. and C. A. F. Rhys Davids (trans.), *Dialogues of the Buddha*,

part 3, Pali Text Society, London 1971, p. 79.

329 These are the entrances to liberation, the three *vimokṣa-mukhas*, or doors to emancipation (also known as the three *samādhis*). For more about them, see chapter 14, 'The Goal', in *The Three Jewels*, *Complete Works*, vol. 2, pp. 121–2. See also 'Perfect Samadhi', *The Buddha's Noble Eightfold Path*, *Complete Works*, vol. 1, pp. 586–7,

330 Abbot Tenshin Anderson, 'Speaking the Unspoken', Talk One, *Shambhala Sun* (June 1993), p. 31; also included in Reb Anderson, *Warm Smiles from Cold Mountains: Dharma Talks on Zen Meditation*, Shambhala Publications, Boulder 2016, chapter 8.

331 The Early Hīnayānists, for instance,

> conceived Buddha's *rūpakāya* as that of a human being, and his *dharmakāya* as the collection of his *dhammas*, i.e. doctrines and disciplinary rules collectively.'

Nalinaksha Dutt, *Aspects of Mahāyāna Buddhism and its Relation to Hīnayāna*, Luzac and Company, London 1930, p. 97.

332 It was the Stoics who first used *hypostasis* as a philosophical term, to refer to objective or concrete reality, stating that, for example, objects in nature such as rain and hail have *hypostasis*, i.e. reality, in contrast to a rainbow, which exists 'according to semblance'. The term was adopted by later philosophers and theologians, including the Neoplatonist Plotinus, who in the *Enneads* set out his doctrine of the three *hypostases* or first principles (these being the mind, the soul, and the One), and the early Christian theologians, who used the term in various ways, including to refer to the Trinity, and as a kind of synonym for *persona*.

333 W. E. Soothill (trans.), *The Lotus of the Wonderful Law*, Curzon Press, London 1987, pp. 125–7.

334 We haven't managed to trace this in the Pāli commentaries, but the commentary on the *Sutta-Nipāta* includes a passage about how long it takes 'for the aspiration of buddhas to be achieved', in which the Buddha explains that it takes different numbers of incalculable aeons depending on whether wisdom, faith, or energy is predominant. See Bhikkhu Bodhi (trans.): *The Suttanipāta, together with its commentaries*, Wisdom Publications, Somerville 2017, p. 402.

335 This was probably 'An Opening of the Heart', released

by Suryaprabha's Lights in the Sky in 1993.

336 The story of Aṅgulimāla's encounter with the Buddha is told in the *Aṅgulimāla Sutta*, *Majjhima Nikāya* 86; see Bhikkhu Ñāṇamoli and Bhikkhu Bodhi (trans.), *The Middle Length Discourses of the Buddha*, pp. 710–7; or I. B. Horner (trans.), *The Collection of the Middle Length Sayings*, vol. ii, Pali Text Society, Oxford 1994, pp. 284–92.

337 In chapter 12 of the *White Lotus Sūtra*, 'Devadatta', the Buddha says that in a former life, 'through the good friendship of Devadatta I was enabled to become perfect in the six *pāramitās*' and foretells that Devadatta will become a Buddha called Devarāja, 'King of the Gods'. See, for example, Bunnō Katō et al. (trans.), *The Threefold Lotus Sūtra*, Weatherhill, New York & Tokyo 1978, p. 209. The story of Devadatta according to the Pāli canon is told at Vinaya Piṭaka ii.188 (*Cullavagga* 7.3): see I. B. Horner (trans.), *The Book of the Discipline*, part 5, Pali Text Society, London 1975, p. 264.

338 The theologian Origen (c.185–c.253) was born in Alexandria and was inspired by Plato. A passage in his *De Principiis* (*First Principles*) has been interpreted as meaning that even Satan will be saved. On the other hand, in a letter to his friends in Alexandria, Origen is said to have exclaimed that only a lunatic would prophesy the salvation of the devil. In fact, the Greek bishop Gregory of Nyssa (c.335–c.395) evidently also averred that Satan would be saved, for example in his treatises *On the Soul and Resurrection* and *The Catechetical Oration*.

339 *Maggasaṃyutta*, *Saṃyutta Nikāya* v.2: see Bhikkhu Bodhi (trans.), *The Connected Discourses of the Buddha*, Wisdom Publications, Boston 2000, pp. 1524–5; also F. L. Woodward (trans.), *The Book of the Kindred Sayings*, part 5, Pali Text Society, London 1979, p. 2.

340 The three levels of wisdom are enumerated in, for example, the *Saṅgīti Sutta*, *Dīgha Nikāya* 33 (iii.219): see M. Walshe (trans.), *The Long Discourses of the Buddha*, Wisdom Publications, Boston 1995, p. 486; or T. W. Rhys Davids (trans.), *Dialogues of the Buddha*, part 3, Pali Text Society, London 1971, p. 212.

341 In his essay 'Tradition and the Individual Talent' Eliot doesn't say quite this, but does say,

> Only those who have personality and emotions know what it means to want to escape from these things.

T. S. Eliot, *The Sacred Wood: Essays on Poetry and Criticism*, Alfred A. Knopf, New York 1921.

342 Jaideva Singh, *An Introduction to Madhyamaka Philosophy*, Bharatiya Vidya Prakashan, Varanasi 1968, p. 36:

> The approach to truth adopted in Hīnayāna was one of mystically-tinged rationalism, that adopted by Mahāyāna was one of super-rationalism and profound mysticism.

343 See the *Dhammacakkappavattana Sutta*, *Saṃyutta Nikāya* v.421; Bhikkhu Bodhi (trans.), *The Connected Discourses of the Buddha*, Wisdom Publications, Boston 2000, pp. 1844–5; or F. L. Woodward (trans.), *The Book of the Kindred Sayings*, part 5, Pali Text Society, London 1979, p. 357; also I. B. Horner (trans.), *The Book of the Discipline*, part 4, Pali Text Society, Oxford 1996, p. 15–16.

344 This talk or sermon, 'The Priceless Jewel', was delivered at King's College, Cambridge, on Sunday 15 July 1987; it appears in *Complete Works*, vol. 16, pp. 211–23.

345 John Donne (1572–1631) was an ardent love poet in his younger years, but later, as Dean of St Paul's Cathedral, the writer of the *Holy Sonnets*. His published sermons include the one with the famous passage beginning 'No man is an island entire of itself'.

Jeremy Taylor (1613–1667) was on the Royalist side in the English Civil War. Many of his most admired sermons were published with the title Golden Grove, that being the name of the Montgomeryshire home of Lord Carbery where he found refuge during the period of the Commonwealth.

John Henry Newman (1801–1890) was a theologian, philosopher, and poet, ordained first within the Church of England and then the Roman Catholic church. Among his published sermons is the collection called *Parochial and Plain Sermons*, published in 1834.

346 *Dīgha Nikāya* ii.109–10 in Maurice Walshe (trans.), *The Long Discourses of the Buddha*, Wisdom Publications, Boston 1995, pp. 248–9. See also T. W. Rhys Davids (trans.), *Dialogues of the Buddha*, part 2, Pali Text Society, London 1971, p. 117.

347 *Udāna* 5.5. For Sangharakshita's commentary, see *Complete Works*, vol. 10, pp. 557–72.

348 For example, the Buddha is addressed as *samaṇa* at *Dīgha Nikāya* i.4. and i.87, and at Vinaya Piṭaka i.8 and i.350.

349 1 Corinthians 9:22.

350 In Greek mythology, Semele's liaison with Zeus enraged Zeus's wife, Hera, who, disguised as an old nurse, coaxed Semele into asking Zeus to visit her in the same splendour in which he would appear before Hera. Zeus had already promised to grant

Semele her every wish and was thus forced to grant a wish that would kill her: the splendour of his firebolts, as god of thunder, destroyed Semele.

351 Matthew 17:1–8.

352 See note 338.

353 The English writer Rudyard Kipling wrote and published his poem 'Mandalay' in 1890. The poem is set in colonial Burma, and the protagonist is a working-class soldier, back in grey restrictive London, recalling the time he felt free and had a Burmese lover, now unattainably far away.

354 *Dhammapada* 103, trans. Sangharakshita.

355 John 8:6.

356 Dr Ambedkar quotes this saying of the Buddha in *The Buddha and his Dhamma* (Siddharth Publications, Bombay 1991, p. 327) and Christmas Humphreys also quotes it in *Zen Buddhism* (Unwin Paperbacks, London 1984, p. 27), but in neither case is a source given, and so far it has not been traced, although Christmas Humphreys avers that it is of the canon of the 'Southern School' of Buddhism.

357 *Diamond Sūtra* section 26, trans. Edward Conze (*Buddhist Wisdom Books: The Diamond Sūtra and the Heart Sūtra*, George Allen & Unwin, London 1975). For Sangharakshita's commentary, see *Wisdom Beyond Words*, *Complete Works*, vol. 14, pp. 499–500.

358 This story is told in Case 1 of the Zen classic *The Blue Cliff Record*. See, for example, K. Sekida (trans.), *Two Zen Classics*, Weatherhill, New York 1996, p. 147.

359 Reproduced above, pp. 2ff.

360 Collections of Sangharakshita's lectures and edited seminars were published from the earliest days of the FWBO, but in the early 1990s a new initiative called the Spoken Word Project began to edit books published by Windhorse Publications, the first titles being *The Drama of Cosmic Enlightenment* and *Wisdom Beyond Words*, and many Spoken Word titles appear in these *Complete Works*. And the present editor, who was also a member of the Spoken Word team, is indeed going grey over her labours.

361 See *The Rainbow Road from Tooting Broadway to Kalimpong*, *Complete Works*, vol. 20, p. 149.

362 Subhuti, *Sangharakshita: A New Voice in the Buddhist Tradition*, Windhorse Publications, Birmingham 1994.

363 The story is told at Vinaya Piṭaka i.301–3 (*Mahāvagga* 8.26): see I. B. Horner (trans.), *The Book of the Discipline*, part 4, Pali Text Society, Oxford 1996, pp. 431–4. See also Sangharakshita, *The Buddha's Victory*, chapter

4, 'A Case of Dysentery', *Complete Works*, vol. 11.

364 For the story of Kisāgotamī, see C. A. F. Rhys Davids and K. R. Norman (trans.), *Poems of Early Buddhist Nuns (Therīgāthā)*, Pali Text Society, Oxford 1997, pp. 88–91. See also *Complete Works*, vol. 3, pp. 357–8 or vol. 4, pp. 11–13.

365 For more about *cetanā*, see Sangharakshita, *Know Your Mind*, Windhorse, Birmingham 1998, pp. 89–94 (*Complete Works*, vol. 17). For a canonical reference to *cetanā* as a synonym for karma, see *Aṅguttara Nikāya* iii.415; see Bhikkhu Bodhi (trans.), *The Numerical Discourses of the Buddha*, Wisdom Publications 2012, p. 963; or E. M. Hare (trans.), *The Book of the Gradual Sayings*, vol. iii, Pali Text Society, Oxford 1995, p. 294.

366 Sangharakshita composed the dedication ceremony to dedicate the FWBO's first ever shrine-room in April 1967; see *Moving Against the Stream*, *Complete Works*, vol. 23, p. 429. The dedication ceremony continues to be used to dedicate Triratna shrine-rooms and retreats. It can be found in *Puja: The Triratna Book of Buddhist Devotional Texts*, seventh edition, Windhorse Publications, Cambridge 2008, pp. 36–7.

367 See p. 515 above. Also Sangharakshita discusses the three levels of wisdom further in, for example, *What is the Dharma?* in *Complete Works*, vol. 3, pp. 302–3. They are enumerated in, for example, the *Saṅgīti Sutta*, *Dīgha Nikāya* 33 (iii.219): see M. Walshe (trans.), *The Long Discourses of the Buddha*, Wisdom Publications, Boston 1995, p. 486; or T. W. Rhys Davids (trans.), *Dialogues of the Buddha*, part 3, Pali Text Society, London 1971, p. 212.

368 The story of Śāriputra and Aśvajit is told at Vinaya Piṭaka i.39 (*Mahāvagga* 1.23): see I. B. Horner (trans.), *The Book of the Discipline*, part 4, Pali Text Society, Oxford 1996, pp. 52–4. See also note 109 above.

369 On 15 June 1996 the Provisional Irish Republican Army detonated a lorry bomb in central Manchester, about 400 metres from the Manchester Buddhist Centre. It caused significant damage to the city's infrastructure and economy, but the area had been evacuated and there were no fatalities.

370 From Sangharakshita, *What is the Dharma?*, chapter 10 (*Complete Works*, vol. 3, pp. 316–17):

> The Buddha identified five orders of conditionality, five *niyamas*, as Buddhaghosa subsequently called them: physical inorganic; physical organic (i.e. biological); psychological; karmic; and

transcendental. Unless one has the insight of a Buddha, one cannot be sure which *niyamas* have brought about what particular effect. The example usually given is that of a fever. If one gets a fever, it may be a chill caused by a sudden change in temperature; or one may have caught a viral infection; or perhaps one has succumbed to illness as a result of some kind of mental strain; or it may have been caused by an unskilful action committed in the past; or it may even be the effect on one's system of transcendental insight. Thus the same end result may have been brought about by something physical, something biological, something psychological, something karmic, or something transcendental – or a combination of two or more of these.

The five orders of conditionality or *niyamas* are enumerated by Buddhaghosa in his commentary on the *Dhammasaṅgaṇī*, the first book of the Abhidhamma Piṭaka, vol. ii. Pe Maung Tin (trans.), *The Expositor*, ch. 10, ed. C. A. F. Rhys Davids, Pali Text Society, London 1921. Another of Sangharakshita's sources is C. A. F. Rhys Davids, *Buddhism: A Study of the Buddhist Norm*, Williams and Norgate, London 1912, pp. 118–9.

371 *Majjhima Nikāya* 26 (i.161–2) in Bhikkhu Ñāṇamoli and Bhikkhu Bodhi (trans.), *The Middle Length Discourses of the Buddha*, Wisdom Publications, Boston 1995, p. 254.

372 Ibid. (i.162–3), pp. 255–6.

373 For example, a stirring account of Siddhārtha's leaving the palace is given in the *Mahāvastu*; see J. J. Jones (trans.), *Mahāvastu*, vol. ii, Pali Text Society, London 1987, pp. 155–6.

374 Robert G. Morrison, *Nietzsche and Buddhism: A Study in Nihilism and Ironic Affinities*, Oxford University Press, New York 1997.

375 See pp. 132ff. above for a more detailed description of the four sights.

376 See *The Rainbow Road from Tooting Broadway to Kalimpong*, *Complete Works*, vol. 20, pp. 223–5.

377 It's still the case that people sometimes come to the UK in order to train for ordination, but increasingly there are ordination training courses in different countries around the world.

378 The English poet Samuel Taylor Coleridge made a distinction between imagination and fancy, explaining in chapter four of his 1817 work *Biographia Literaria* that they are not different words for the same thing or lower and higher

degrees of the same power, but two very different faculties, imagination being creative, but fancy being a mechanical process that receives the images that come to it and reassembles them in a different order.

379 See *Complete Works*, vol. 6.

380 Lama Anagarika Govinda, *Foundations of Tibetan Mysticism*, Century Hutchinson, London 1987.

381 The Buddhist countries of south-east Asia use a lunisolar system to determine their calendar, i.e. dates are based on the phase of the moon as well as the time of the solar year. They are based on an older Hindu system, but differ from the Indian system in that they don't rely on apparent reckoning based on the sun as observed from earth, but use a version of the Metonic cycle, which is based on the fact that every nineteen years or so, the phases of the moon recur on the same days of the year.

382 Keith Dowman, introduction to *Masters of Mahāmudrā*, State University of New York, New York 1984, p. 2.

383 The distinction between the two is explained in the talk 'The Path of Regular Steps and the Path of Irregular Steps', in *The Taste of Freedom*, Windhorse Publications, Birmingham 1997, pp. 27–48 (*Complete Works*, vol. 11).

384 For example, the *Dasuttara Sutta*, *Dīgha Nikāya* 34 (iii.288): see M. Walshe (trans.), *The Long Discourses of the Buddha*, Wisdom Publications, Boston 1995, p. 519; or T. W. Rhys Davids, *Dialogues of the Buddha*, part 3, Pali Text Society, London 1971, p. 262.

385 This was the lecture 'Standing on Holy Ground', which appears in *Complete Works*, vol. 25, pp. 3–21.

386 The earlier Dharmakīrti was a scholar of Nālandā University in the sixth or seventh century CE; he could be said to be an example of a 'Buddhist nominalist'. Atiśa's Sumatran teacher was also known as Lama Serlingpa. In Song 132 of Atiśa's Tibetan biography, written around 1355, he says:

> Then we went to Lama's residence, the Silver Parasol Palace, and took our seats.... After we had settled there, the Lama in order to introduce to me the characteristics of dependent origination began his teachings from the *Abhisamayālaṃkāra* in five sessions. Staying in the Silver Parasol Palace, I continued with my practices of listening, concentration, and meditation. Lama Serlingpa guided me throughout this process of practice.

387 Vikramaśilā was founded by the Pala king Dharmapala in the late eighth or early ninth century, and was destroyed at the end of the twelfth

century, along with the other major centres of Buddhism in India. We know about Vikramaśilā mainly through Tibetan sources, especially the writings of the monk historian Tāranātha. In its day it was one of the largest Buddhist universities, with more than a hundred teachers and about a thousand students. It produced eminent scholars who were often invited by foreign countries to spread Buddhist learning, culture, and religion. Atiśa was the most distinguished of its scholars.

388 This was the Religious Council of the Fire Dragon Year held by King rTse-lde – see George N. Roerich, *The Blue Annals*, Motilal Banarsidass, Delhi 1979, p. 70.

389 Its full name is Palpa-Tansen, and it's called Tansen in the memoir *The Rainbow Road from Tooting Broadway to Kalimpong*; see *Complete Works*, vol. 20, pp. 424–41.

390 Lama Anagarika Govinda, *The Way of the White Clouds*, Rider, London 1984, pp. 210–1.

391 See Geshe Sonam Rinchen, *Atisha's Lamp for the Path to Enlightenment*, Snow Lion Publications, Ithaca 1997.

392 The first Order convention took place at Aryatara in 1974. According to the transcript of the recordings made, the programme included four plenary sessions on 'The Spiritual Development of the Individual Order Member', 'Communication within the Order', 'The Order and the World', and 'The Functioning of the Order'.

393 This is a reference to the Buddha's visit to Anuruddha, Nandiya, and Kimbila, who say they are getting along 'as milk and water blend'; see *Cūḷagosinga Sutta*, *Majjhima Nikāya* 31 (i.207): Bhikkhu Ñāṇamoli and Bhikkhu Bodhi (trans.), *The Middle Length Discourses of the Buddha*, Wisdom Publications, Boston 1995, pp. 301–6; or I. B. Horner (trans.), *The Collection of the Middle Length Sayings*, vol. i, Pali Text Society, London 1976, pp. 257–62.

394 Petra ten-Doesschate Chu, *Nineteenth-Century European Art*, Pearson, London 2006, p. 349.

395 Lama Govinda founded the Arya Maitreya Mandala in 1933, initially in India, but in the 1950s branches were opened in other countries. Advayavajra took over from Lama Govinda as head of the Arya Maitreya Mandala in 1982. He died in 2007.

396 The review, titled 'Searching for me, Me*, or I?', appears in *A Moseley Miscellany*, Ibis Publications, Ledbury 2015, pp. 260–3 (see *Complete Works*, vol. 26).

397 This was the Millennium Dome, which was constructed in South-East London as a multicultural celebration of the

millennium in the year 2000. It was a politically controversial project and failed to attract the numbers of visitors hoped for, but was recreated as the O2 Arena, a huge concert venue.

398 See *In the Sign of the Golden Wheel*, *Complete Works*, vol. 22, pp. 304–28.

399 See Karl Jaspers, *The Origin and Goal of History*, Routledge and Kegan Paul, London 1953.

400 The question of the disappearance of the Dharma is a recurring preoccupation in the Buddhist tradition, but the decline is not always seen as inevitable. See, for example, the *Cakkavatti-Sīhanāda Sutta*, *Dīgha Nikāya* 26 in M. Walshe (trans.), *The Long Discourses of the Buddha*, Wisdom Publications, Boston 1995, pp. 395–405; or T. W. Rhys Davids (trans.), *Dialogues of the Buddha*, part 3, Pali Text Society, London 1971, pp. 59–74. This *sutta* tells the story of a wheel-turning king (i.e. a king who rules according to the Dharma) who, when the 'sacred Wheel-Treasure' disappears, continues to govern according to his own ideas, as a result of which selfishness, lying, and greed increase in the kingdom, and there is a terrible decline, to the dreadful point at which there is a 'sword-interval' during which people mistake one another for wild beasts and fight among themselves. But even then, there are some beings who think, 'Let us not kill or be killed by anyone!' – and they hide and live on roots and fruits of the forest until the fighting stops. And then the thought occurs to those beings, 'It is only because we became addicted to evil ways that we suffered this loss of our kindred, so let us now do good! What good things can we do? Let us abstain from the taking of life – that will be a good practice.' And so, in time, wholesome practices increase, and in the end another Buddha, Metteyya (Sanskrit Maitreya) arises. The story is interesting for the way it seems to show that some vestige of skilfulness can remain in some people even when the Dharma has, or appears to have, disappeared. In the Mahāyāna tradition, the *Lotus Sūtra* in particular includes precautions, in its characteristically mythical terms, to guard against the disappearance of the Dharma in what are predicted to be dark times ahead. In chapter 13, 'Exhortation to Hold Firm', thousands of bodhisattvas promise to protect and preach the *Sūtra* 'in the evil age to come', when 'living beings will decrease in good qualities, while they will increase in utter arrogance....' Bunnō Katō et al, (trans.), *The Threefold Lotus Sutra*, Kosei Publishing, Tokyo 1995, pp. 215–20.

401 This is the second stanza of W. B. Yeats' poem 'Sailing to Byzantium', written in 1926.

402 See pp. 663ff. for a full account.

403 Over the years these responsibilities have been handed on to others in turn, but still within the College of Public Preceptors, which at the time of writing (2021) has forty-four members.

404 The lectures were first published by Windhorse Publications as *The Bodhisattva Ideal* in 2000; see *Complete Works*, vol. 4, pp. 1–213.

405 *Sigālaka Sutta*, *Dīgha Nikāya* 31; see M. Walshe (trans.), *The Long Discourses of the Buddha*, Wisdom Publications, Boston 1995, pp. 461–9; or T. W. Rhys Davids (trans.), *Dialogues of the Buddha*, part 3, Pali Text Society, London 1971, pp. 173–84.

406 See also *Cūḷagosinga Sutta*, *Majjhima Nikāya* 31 (i.207): see Bhikkhu Ñāṇamoli and Bhikkhu Bodhi (trans.), *The Middle Length Discourses of the Buddha*, Wisdom Publications, Boston 1995, pp. 301–6; or I. B. Horner (trans.), *The Collection of the Middle Length Sayings*, vol. i, Pali Text Society, London 1976, pp. 257–62. See also MN 128.

407 Triratna right livelihood businesses have appeared and disappeared over the years, and at the time of writing (2021), some of the businesses mentioned here are no more – the publishing house being a notable and obvious exception! At present, right livelihood businesses around Triratna include Evolution Arts in Brighton, Lama's Pyjamas and an arts centre in East London, Dana Cafe in Sheffield, New View Residential Property Services in Cambridge, as well as outreach in the form of Breathworks, Wildmind, freebuddhistaudio, and the running of websites, urban Buddhist centres, retreat centres, and administrating and servicing the Order and Community.

408 See note 339.

409 The pact that Faust makes with Mephistopheles is that the devil can take his soul only

> When, to the Moment then,
> I say
> 'Ah, stay a while! You are so
> lovely!'

J. W. Goethe, *Faust I*, scene iv. But Faust's restlessness never ceases and the devil has no chance to seize his soul. However, in the final act of *Faust II*, Faust experiences a moment of bliss when he dedicates himself to helping the lives of others.

410 See Eugene Watson Burlingame (trans.), *Buddhist Legends* (*Dhammapada Commentary*), part 1, Pali Text Society, Luzac, London 1969, pp. 218–23; and *Udāna* 3.2. For Sangharakshita's commentary

on the latter, see *Complete Works*, vol. 10, pp. 504–7.

411 For more about the *kasiṇa* practice see *The Purpose and Practice of Buddhist Meditation*, *Complete Works*, vol. 5, pp. 566–71. There are ten *kasiṇas* described in Buddhaghosa's *Visuddhimagga* 118–175; see Bhikkhu Ñāṇamoli, *The Path of Purification*, Buddhist Publication Society, Kandy 1991, pp. 118–70.

412 The Turner Prize was inaugurated in 1984, and named after the artist J. M. W. Turner (1775–1851). The shortlisted work referred to was 'My Bed' by Tracey Emin, which was entered for the prize in 1999, didn't win, but was sold at auction for £2,546,500.

413

> At the moment at which, freed from the will, we give ourselves up to pure will-less knowing, we pass into a world from which everything is absent that influenced our will and moved us so violently through it. This freeing of knowledge lifts us as wholly and entirely away from all that, as do sleep and dreams; happiness and unhappiness have disappeared; we are no longer individual; the individual is forgotten; we are only pure subject of knowledge; we are only that *one* eye of the world which looks out from all knowing creatures, but which can become perfectly free from the service of will in man alone. Thus all difference of individuality so entirely disappears, that it is all the same whether the perceiving eye belongs to a mighty king or to a wretched beggar; for neither joy nor complaining can pass that boundary with us.

Arthur Schopenhauer, *The World as Will and Representation*, trans. R. B. Haldane and J. Kemp, third book, section 38.

414 See, for example, the *Mahācattārīsaka Sutta*, *Majjhima Nikaya* 117 (iii.72); Bhikkhu Nanamoli and Bhikkhu Bodhi (trans.), *The Middle Length Discourses of the Buddha*, Wisdom Publications, Boston 1995, p. 934; or I. B. Horner (trans.), *The Collection of the Middle Length Sayings*, vol. iii, Pali Text Society, Oxford 1993, p. 114.

415 See note 101.

416 For an account of the 'twin miracle', see notes 126 and 127.

417 The Pāli canon example that comes closest to this is to be found in the *Kevaddha Sutta*, *Dīgha Nikāya* 11 (i.211–4); M. Walshe (trans.), *The Long Discourses of the Buddha*, Wisdom Publications, Boston 1995, pp. 175–6; or T. W. Rhys

Davids (trans.), *Dialogues of the Buddha*, part 1, Pali Text Society, London 1973, pp. 276–9. But this is really about the 'miracle of instruction' rather than the miracle of human change itself. Sangharakshita's source might be a work he often consulted: Paul Carus, *The Gospel of Buddha* (Studio Editions, London 1995, p. 172), where the Buddha is quoted as saying,

> Is it not a wonderful thing, mysterious and miraculous to the worldling, that a man who commits wrong can become a saint, that he who attains to enlightenment will find the path of truth and abandon the evil ways of selfishness?

Unfortunately, Carus doesn't give a clear source for this section of his compilation, but it is perhaps from the Chinese Buddhist tradition.

418 *Ariyapariyesanā Sutta, Majjhima Nikāya* 26 (i.163) in Bhikkhu Ñāṇamoli and Bhikkhu Bodhi (trans.), *The Middle Length Discourses of the Buddha*, Wisdom Publications, Boston 1995, p. 256; or I. B. Horner (trans.), *The Collection of the Middle Length Sayings*, vol. i, Pali Text Society, London 1976, p. 207.

419 *Bhayabherava Sutta, Majjhima Nikāya* 4 (i.22): see Bhikkhu Ñāṇamoli and Bhikkhu Bodhi (trans.), *The Collection of the Middle Length Discourses of the Buddha*, Wisdom Publications, Boston 1995, p. 102–7; or I. B. Horner (trans.), *Middle Length Sayings*, vol. i, Pali Text Society, London 1976, pp. 21–30.

420 *Ariyapariyesanā Sutta, Majjhima Nikāya* 26 (i.167–8): Bhikkhu Ñāṇamoli and Bhikkhu Bodhi (trans.), *The Middle Length Discourses of the Buddha*, Wisdom Publications, Boston 1995, p. 259–60; or I. B. Horner (trans.), *The Collection of the Middle Length Sayings*, vol. i, Pali Text Society, London 1976, p. 211.

421 *Dhammapada* 276.

422 See pp. 610–17.

THE 2000S

423 Sangharakshita described the circumstances of his illness and his decision to write down his wishes in a letter to the Order, included in *Through Buddhist Eyes*, Windhorse Publications, Birmingham 2000, pp. 106–30 (*Complete Works*, vol. 24, pp. 329–54).

424 Sangharakshita started to suffer from the eye condition called macular degeneration at this time, and was thereafter unable read or write.

425 See *Moving Against the Stream*, *Complete Works*, vol. 23.

426 Ibid., pp. 234–315.

427 The attempt to bring the two organizations together is described in chapter 7,

'Healing the Breach', ibid., pp. 42–50.

The friendship was with Terry Delamare, first introduced in ibid., pp. 95–105.

428 Khantipālo, *Noble Friendship: Travels of a Buddhist Monk*, Windhorse Publications, Birmingham 2002.

429 Bhikkhu Vivekananda, 'a short Thai of indeterminate age' who had once been a kick boxer, is introduced in *Precious Teachers*, *Complete Works*, vol. 22, p. 525.

430 C. M. Chen, *Buddhist Meditation, Systematic and Practical*, published by Dr Yutang Lin, El Cerrito 1989.

431 These tours are described in *Dr Ambedkar and the Revival of Buddhism II*, *Complete Works*, vol. 10, which also includes notes of some of the talks.

432 Sangharakshita lived in the annexe of the large community called Madhyamaloka in Moseley, Birmingham, from 1994 until 2013, when he moved to Adhisthana in Herefordshire.

433 This could be a reference to the talk 'The Buddha's Philosophy of Right Speech', in this volume, pp. 31–7:

> You think about somebody else's needs so much so that you tend to forget about yourself, and the other person is so preoccupied with your needs that they tend to forget about their own self. Thus you get a situation of mutual helpfulness leading to mutual self-transcendence, a reciprocity of helpfulness within a context of increasing selflessness.

434 Śāntideva, *Bodhicaryāvatāra*, ch. 8, verses 112 ff. See also *The Endlessly Fascinating Cry*, *Complete Works*, vol. 4, pp. 631–4.

435 The corpse meditation is described in Sangharakshita, *Creative Symbols of Tantric Buddhism*, *Complete Works*, vol. 13, pp. 225–7. Sangharakshita also describes various forms of this meditation in chapter 11, 'The Threefold Path: Meditation', in *What is the Dharma?*, *Complete Works*, vol. 3, pp. 344–6. For traditional descriptions see, for example, the *Mahāsatipaṭṭhāna Sutta*, *Dīgha Nikāya* 22 (ii.295–7): M. Walshe (trans.), *The Long Discourses of the Buddha*, Wisdom Publications, Boston 1995, p. 338–9; or T. W. Rhys Davids (trans.), *Dialogues of the Buddha*, part 2, Pali Text Society, London 1971, p. 332.

436 The building project to turn the old fire station into a Buddhist centre began in 1976 and the centre was opened in 1978.

437
> If a man does not make new acquaintances as he

> advances through life, he will soon find himself left alone. A man, Sir, should keep his friendship in constant repair.

According to his biographer, James Boswell, the remark was made by Dr Johnson in 1755 to the painter, Sir Joshua Reynolds. See 1755: aetat 46 in James Boswell, *Life of Johnson*, first published in 1791.

438 The lecture 'Mind – Reactive and Creative' appears in *Buddha Mind*, in *Complete Works*, vol. 11.

439 The painter John Everett Millais (1829–96) was one of the founder members of the Pre-Raphaelite Brotherhood. His later works were enormously successful, making him one of the wealthiest artists of his day, but some former admirers, including William Morris, saw this as a sell-out. Millais notoriously allowed his painting *Bubbles* to be used for a sentimental soap advertisement.

440 George Gissing (1857–1903) published *New Grub Street* in 1891.

441 Aristotle, *Nichomachean Ethics*, Book 8, section 11 (trans. W. D. Ross):

> But neither is there friendship towards a horse or an ox, nor to a slave qua slave. For there is nothing common to the two parties; the slave is a living tool and the tool a lifeless slave. Qua slave then, one cannot be friends with him. But qua man one can; for there seems to be some justice between any man and any other who can share in a system of law or be a party to an agreement; therefore there can also be friendship with him in so far as he is a man. Therefore while in tyrannies friendship and justice hardly exist, in democracies they exist more fully; for where the citizens are equal they have much in common.

442 See the talk 'Religion: Ethnic and Universal', in this volume, pp. 235ff.

443 The second plate of William Blake's *The Marriage of Heaven and Hell*, composed between 1790 and 1793, includes the text:

> The Giants who formed this world into its sensual existence and now seem to live in it in chains, are in truth the causes of its life & the sources of all activity, but the chains are the cunning of weak and tame minds which have power to resist energy, according to the proverb, the weak in courage is strong in cunning. Thus one portion of being is the Prolific, the other the Devouring: to the devourer it seems as if the producer was in his chains, but it is not so, he only takes

portions of existence and fancies that the whole.

444 The Buddha said: 'Observe those who bestow knowledge of the Way, for to help them is a great joy and many blessings can thus be obtained.' A Sramana asked: 'Is there any limit to such blessings?' The Buddha replied, 'They are like the fire of a torch from which hundreds and thousands of people light their own torches. Thus the darkness is swallowed up. Such is the nature of those blessings.'

Section 11 of the *Sūtra of Forty-two Sections*, trans. John Blofeld (Chu Ch'an), Buddhist Society, London 1977, p. 13.

> Just as millions of lamps can be lit from one lamp, without the one lamp being exhausted or diminished by all the lamps taking their flame from it, in the same way from the one lamp of the aspiration for omniscience the lamps of aspiration for omniscience of all buddhas of past, future, and present are lit, yet the one lamp of aspiration for omniscience is not exhausted, and shines undiminished by the lights of the lamps of aspiration to omniscience proceeding from it.

Thomas Cleary (trans.), *The Flower Ornament Scripture*, Shambhala Publications, Boston and London 1993, p. 1483.

445 In 1973 Khantipālo established Wat Buddha Dhamma in New South Wales, and in 1991 he established the Bodhicitta Buddhist Centre in Queensland. In 2010 he was re-ordained as a novice in the Vietnamese Mahāyāna tradition under the name Minh An, 'Peace with Wisdom'. After a lifetime of service to Buddhism he finally succumbed to ill health and moved to a medical care facility in Melbourne, where he died in 2021.

446 Sangharakshita's Bengali Brahmin friend Robin Banerjee (1922–2013), who, as a wandering ascetic with Sangharakshita, took the name Satyapriya, was ordained as Buddharakshita; though he always used the Pāli form, Buddharakkhita. He is a significant figure in the memoir *The Rainbow Road from Tooting Broadway to Kalimpong*, *Complete Works*, vol. 20, chapters 16–47. He went on to found the Bangalore Maha Bodhi Society, and helped establish schools and hospitals. He published many books on Buddhism under the name Acharya Buddharakkhita, including a translation of the *Dhammapada* (published by the Buddhist Publication Society, Kandy, in 1998).

447 The celebration took the form of a week-long international retreat at Taraloka; for the talk Sangharakshita gave on that occasion, 'The Growth and Prosperity of the Sangha', see pp. 674ff.

448 See *Moving Against the Stream*, *Complete Works*, vol. 23, p. 429. The dedication ceremony composed for that occasion continues to be used to dedicate Triratna shrine-rooms, retreats, and even projects to the Three Jewels. It can be found in *Puja: The Triratna Book of Buddhist Devotional Texts*, seventh edition, Windhorse Publications, Cambridge 2008, pp. 36–7.

449 See note 25.

450 *The Rainbow Road from Tooting Broadway to Kalimpong*, *Complete Works*, vol. 20, pp. 224–6.

451 Ananda (Stephen Parr, b. 1944) was one of the first twelve Order members ordained by Sangharakshita on 7 April 1968. Today (2021) he is the longest-ordained member of the Triratna Buddhist Order. Ananda has devoted his life to poetry, and to writing as a spiritual practice. Through the 'Wolf at the Door' retreats he developed with his friend Manjusvara, he inspired people from all around the world in this transformative practice.

452 Sir Francis Bacon (1561–1626), a philosopher and poet, held high office at the courts of Elizabeth I and James I. His *Novum Organum* was published in Latin in 1620. The title means 'New Organum', the old *Organum* being a work on logic by Aristotle. Francis Bacon's description of the four idols comes at the end of part 1.

453 For an article by Sangharakshita on the idols of the market place, see *Golden Drum* no. 33, May–July 1994, p. 28 (*Complete Works*, vol. 11).

454 Sangharakshita taught Buddhism as a visiting lecturer in philosophy at Berkeley College, Yale, in 1970. He described the experience in *1970 – A Retrospective* see *Complete Works*, vol. 23, pp. 453–62.

455 *The Cup* is a Tibetan-language film released in 1999 about two young football-crazed novice monks in a remote Himalayan monastery in India who desperately try to obtain a television so that they can watch the 1998 World Cup final.

456 The list of the four *Dharma mudrās* is particularly to be found in Tibetan Buddhism, and is based on the marks of conditioned existence or *lakṣaṇas* taught in early Buddhism. Usually three *lakṣaṇas* are listed – unsatisfactoriness, impermanence, and insubstantiality (no-self) – but as Sangharakshita notes in

chapter 11 of *The Three Jewels* (*Complete Works*, vol. 2, pp. 81–2), sometimes a fourth *lakṣaṇa*, 'Nirvāṇa alone is peace', is added to the original set of three. It is this list of four that appears as the four *Dharma mudrās*.

457 Dzongsar Jamyang Khyentse, *What Makes You Not a Buddhist?*, Shambhala Publications, Boston 2007, p. 3.

458 Chattrul Sangye Dorje died in 2015 at the age of 102.

459 Stefan Zweig was an Austrian writer; *Beware of Pity* was published in 1939.

460 For details of the six element practice, see *The Purpose and Practice of Buddhist Meditation*, *Complete Works*, vol. 5, pp. 478–97. For a canonical reference see, for example, the *Mahāhatthipadopama Sutta*, *Majjhima Nikāya* 28 (i.184–91): Bhikkhu Ñāṇamoli and Bhikkhu Bodhi (trans.), *The Middle Length Discourses of the Buddha*, Wisdom Publications, Boston 1995, pp. 278–85; or I. B. Horner (trans.), *The Collection of the Middle Length Sayings*, vol. i, Pali Text Society, London 1976, pp. 230–8.

461 See note 339.

462 For this list of kinds of wrong livelihood, see, for example, *Aṅguttara Nikāya* iii.208; Bhikkhu Bodhi (trans.), *The Numerical Discourses of the Buddha*, Wisdom Publications, Boston 2012, p. 790; or E. M. Hare (trans.), *The Book of the Gradual Sayings*, vol. iii, Pali Text Society, Oxford 1995, p. 153.

463 William Wordsworth, 'Lines Composed a Few Miles above Tintern Abbey' (first published in *Lyrical Ballads*, 1798), lines 48–50:

> … with an eye made quiet
> by the power
> Of harmony, and the deep
> power of joy,
> We see into the life of things.

464 Shelley's 'The Cloud', a metaphor for the unending cycle of nature, was published in 1820. See also *Facing Mount Kanchenjunga*, *Complete Works*, vol. 21, pp. 78–9.

465 See, for example, *Mahāparinibbāna Sutta*, *Dīgha Nikāya* 16 (ii.100–102); T. W. and C. A. F. Rhys Davids (trans.), *Dialogues of the Buddha*, part 2, Pali Text Society, London 1971, p. 108; or M. Walshe (trans.), *The Long Discourses of the Buddha*, Wisdom Publications, Boston 1995, p. 245.

466 *The Jingde Record of the Transmission of the Lamp* is a thirty-volume work consisting of putative biographies of the Chan (or Zen) patriarchs and other prominent Buddhist monks. It is available in English as *Records of the Transmission of the Lamp*, trans. Randolph S. Whitfield, in eight volumes.

467 The tribe was that of the Vajjians, who found themselves under attack by King Ajātasattu, and their emissary was Vassakāra. See the *Mahāparinibbāna Sutta*, *Dīgha Nikāya* 16 (ii.72–8): M. Walshe (trans.), *The Long Discourses of the Buddha*, Wisdom Publications, Boston 1995, pp. 231–3; or T. W. Rhys Davids (trans.), *Dialogues of the Buddha*, part 2, Pali Text Society, London 1971, pp. 78–83.

468 The king was King Ajātasattu, and the disciple was the king's physician, Jīvaka. See the *Sāmaññaphala Sutta*, *Dīgha Nikāya* 2 (i.47–50): M. Walshe (trans.), *The Long Discourses of the Buddha*, Wisdom Publications, Boston 1995, pp. 91–3; or T. W. Rhys Davids (trans.), *Dialogues of the Buddha*, part 1, Pali Text Society, London 1973, pp. 65–8.

469 This meeting, instigated by the then Archbishop of Canterbury, Rowan Williams, took place on 23 May 2008. Speaking about the meeting, the archbishop said,

> The religious leaders who had gathered to welcome His Holiness the Dalai Lama listened with great appreciation to what he had to say about the priority of compassion in all our religious traditions.

470 For example, the Buddha said to Anuruddha and his friends, 'I hope you are living viewing each other with kindly eyes.' See pp. 606–7, and note 393.

471 The Buddha said this at the very end of his life, as recorded in the *Mahāparinibbāna Sutta*, *Dīgha Nikāya* 16 (ii.154): see M. Walshe (trans.), *The Long Discourses of the Buddha*, Wisdom Publications, Boston 1995, p. 270; or T. W. Rhys Davids (trans.), *Dialogues of the Buddha*, part 2, Pali Text Society, London 1971, p. 171. However, no one asked the Buddha which he considered the minor rules to be – no doubt it wasn't the right time to ask such a question – so after his death all the rules were retained. According to Nāgasena, the Buddha was testing the *bhikkhus'* resolve to adhere to all his instructions after his *parinirvāṇa*. See T. W. Rhys Davids (trans.), *The Questions of King Milinda*, Motilal Banarsidass, Delhi 1992, vol. i, pp. 202–4 for a detailed discussion of this issue.

472 This was the talk 'Looking Back – and Forward', which appears in this volume, pp. 649ff.

473 *Concentration and Meditation: A Manual of Mind Development*, under the authorship of Christmas Humphreys, was eventually published by Stuart & Watkins of London in 1968, but existed informally before that, as

Christmas Humphreys explains in the preface of a new edition published by Element Books in 1987:

> My name appears as author, and in fact I drafted the material, section by section, for consideration at weekly meetings of the small society then known as the Buddhist Lodge. All present at each meeting had their say and many a point was carefully debated. I am therefore grateful to those unknown persons who helped to produce the book which finally appeared.

474 The story of those wandering years is told in *The Rainbow Road from Tooting Broadway to Kalimpong*, *Complete Works*, vol. 20.

475 Ibid., p. 345.

476 This was the Zangdokpalri Monastery, established in Kalimpong by Dudjom Rimpoche in 1946 and consecrated by the Dalai Lama in 1976.

477 'Siddhārtha's Dream', in *Complete Works*, vol. 25, p. 295, referencing *Mahāvastu* ii.137; see J. J. Jones (trans.), *Mahāvastu*, vol. ii, Luzac, London 1952, pp. 131–2.

478 See Francis Story, *The Case for Rebirth*, Buddhist Publication Society, Kandy 1959; and Francis Story, *Rebirth as Doctrine and Experience*, Buddhist Publication Society, Kandy 1975.

479 Lama Anagarika Govinda, *The Way of the White Clouds*, Rider, London 1984, pp. 120–5.

480 The Buddha's recollection of his previous lives is described as one of the experiences that culminated in his Enlightenment; for one of several examples, see the *Bhayabherava Sutta*, *Majjhima Nikāya* 4 (i.22): Bhikkhu Ñāṇamoli and Bhikkhu Bodhi (trans.), *The Middle Length Discourses of the Buddha*, Wisdom Publications, Boston 1995, p. 105; or I. B. Horner (trans.), *Middle Length Sayings*, vol. i, Pali Text Society, London 1976, p. 28.

481 For example, the *Sāmaññaphala Sutta* reports that when King Ajātasattu asked the different sages of the day what the fruits of the homeless life are, a teacher called Ajita Keskambalī told him that there is no such thing as karma, and that after death, the body reverts to the elements and that's that. See *Dīgha Nikāya* 2 (i.55): M. Walshe (trans.), *The Long Discourses of the Buddha*, Wisdom Publications, Boston 1995, pp. 95–6; or T. W. Rhys Davids (trans.), *Dialogues of the Buddha*, part 1, Pali Text Society, London 1973, pp. 73–4.

482 According to the 2011 census there were in fact fewer than 60,000 Parsis in India that year.

483 An outline of this talk is given in the memoir *In the Sign of the Golden Wheel*; see *Complete Works*, vol. 22, p. 269.

484 Sangharakshita describes his acquaintance with Dr Dinshah Mehta in ibid., pp. 282–6 and 295–9. Also in *The Monk and The Prophet*, *Complete Works*, vol. 21, pp. 599–619.

485 The move into the country eventually took place in 2013, when Sangharakshita moved to the property he named Adhisthana in rural Herefordshire, which was his home for the last six years of his life.

The letters are now published in *Complete Works*, vol. 21, pp. 455ff.

486 John Donne (1572–1631) was an English poet and theologian. Quoted here is the first line of his verse letter, 'To Sir Henry Wotton'. Henry Wotton (1568–1639), poet and diplomat, was a friend of Donne from his student days, and remained a close friend throughout Donne's life. Sangharakshita quotes these lines in his own verse letter, 'Letter to Ananda', *Complete Works*, vol. 25, pp. 420–1.

487 The gold standard is a monetary system in which a country's currency or paper money has a value directly linked to gold. The gold standard is not currently used by any government; Britain stopped using it in 1931.

488 Alistair Cooke was a British-born broadcaster who lived in America and recorded a fifteen-minute radio programme every week on an issue that was current in the US. The series ran from 1946 to 2004, making it the longest-running speech radio programme with the same presenter.

489 Friedrich Schiller's *Letters on the Aesthetic Education of Man*, often referred to as *Aesthetic Letters*, is perhaps his best-known theoretical work. Published in his journal *Horen* in 1795 and written in the form of letters to his new patron, the Prince of Schleswig-Holstein-Augustenburg, they are dauntingly ambitious, encompassing a diagnosis of the French Revolution; a critique of the Enlightenment; a transcendental account of beauty; an analysis of human psychology; an assessment of art's psychological and political importance; and an image of a new, ideal form of government designed to allow humans to reach their full potential (*Stanford Encyclopedia of Philosophy*).

490 George Moore's novel *The Brook Kerith: A Syrian Story* was first published in 1916. It divided opinion; a court case was brought accusing the author of blasphemy, but the magistrate ruled that the book

was based on the assumption that Christ was merely a man and not a divine person, an assumption that the author had a perfect right to make.

491 Johann Wolfgang von Goethe wrote *The Sorrows of Young Werther*, a loosely autobiographical novel, in six weeks in the spring of 1774, when he was 24.

492 *Clarissa, or the History of a Young Lady*, by Samuel Richardson, was first published in 1748. Dr Johnson's words are recorded by James Boswell:

> Why, Sir, if you were to read Richardson for the story, your impatience would be so much fretted that you would hang yourself. But you must read him for the sentiment, and consider the story as only giving occasion for the sentiment.

James Boswell, *The Life of Samuel Johnson*, vol. 3, Henry G. Bohn, London 1846, p. 208.

493 Sir Walter Scott (1771–1832) was a Scottish historical novelist. *Redgauntlet*, published in 1824, is about the Jacobite rebellion of the previous century, the Jacobites being those who supported the restoration of the Stuarts to the British throne.

494 James Boswell, *The Life of Samuel Johnson*, ed. David Womersley, Penguin 2008, p. 144.

495 The letter was sent in February 1755. A typical extract reads:

> Is not a patron, my lord, one who looks with unconcern on a man struggling for life in the water, and when he has reached ground, encumbers him with help? The notice which you have been pleased to take of my labours, had it been early, had been kind: but it has been delayed till I am indifferent and cannot enjoy it; till I am solitary and cannot impart it; till I am known and do not want it.

Lord Chesterfield was apparently not offended by the letter, but impressed by its literary style.

496 On Wednesday 21 April 1819 John Keats wrote to his brother George:

> The common cognomen of this world among the misguided and superstitious is 'a vale of tears' from which we are to be redeemed by a certain arbitrary interposition of God and taken to Heaven. What a little circumscribed straightened [sic] notion! Call the world if you please 'The vale of Soul-making'.

497 Samuel Taylor Coleridge (1772–1834) was one of the great English Romantic poets, also literary critic, philosopher, and lecturer. A new edition of his *Collected*

Letters was published in one volume (of 3,494 pages) by the Oxford University Press in 2000.

Richard Holmes' two volumes of Coleridge's biography are *Early Visions* (1989) and *Darker Reflections* (1998).

498 Anthony Thwaite (ed.), *Selected Letters of Philip Larkin*, Faber and Faber, London 1993.

499 The book referred to is James Hillman's *The Force of Character and the Lasting Life*, Random House, New York 1999.

INDEX

Abhidhammattha-saṅgaha 146, 715n
Abhidharma (Pāli Abhidhamma)
Piṭaka 142–3, 520, 567
commentaries 714n, 744n
Sangharakshita and 430, 431, 715n; *see also Know Your Mind*
tradition 140–9, 150, 151, 163, 166, 169, 179, 210, 366
Abhidharmakośa 143
Abhiniṣkramaṇa Sūtra 109, 182, 712n
Abhisamayālaṃkāra 745n
abhiṣeka (or *wonkur*) 20; *see also* Tantric initiation
the Absolute 167, 294; *see also* the Unconditioned, reality
knowledge of 297; *see also dharmadhātu*, wisdom of the
Acala (Fudō) 578
acceptance 392–3, 480–1
Adam 109, 186
Adhisthana 751n, 758n
adhiṣṭhāna (Tibetan *chin lap*) 14; *see also* blessings
Advaita Vedānta 7, 701n, 717n; *see also* Vedānta
Aggañña Sutta 738n
Aid For India 401, 435, 731n, 734n; *see also* Karuna Trust
AIDS 408
Ajātasattu (Sanskrit Ajātaśatru), King 308–9, 342, 676, 726n, 730n, 756n, 757n
Ākāśadhāteśvarī 222
Akashavana 738n
Akbar the Great 245, 723n
Akṣobhya 203–4, 213–14, 222
ālaya 175–6
relative and absolute 176–7, 218
ālaya-vijñāna 99, 174–6, 711n
alchemy 181, 184–5, 718n
alienated awareness 204–5, 258–69
mindfulness and 496
alienation, from nature 217
alms 133, 237, 429, 531
altruism 457, 458, 600
going for Refuge and, *see* going for Refuge…, altruistic dimension
Ambedkar, B. R. 401, 561, 562, 649, 654–5, 732n, 742n
Sangharakshita work with followers of 319–20, 364, 495, 526, 587, 636, 684, 736–7n, 751n
and social ethics 406, 732n
Ambedkar and Buddhism 722n
America xvii, 450, 462, 492, 497, 554
Amitābha 65, 204, 215–16, 222, 288, 449, 450, 507
Sangharakshita initiations 449, 450
Sangharakshita's vision of 683, 718n
Amoghasiddhi 204, 216–17, 222
anagārikas 373, 402, 479, 731n; *see also brahmacarya*
Ānanda 307–8, 466, 514, 520–1, 530, 536, 669
Ananda (Stephen Parr) 367, 372, 396, 404, 653, 731n, 754n, 758n

Ananda Metteyya (Allan Bennett) 71
anariyapariyesanā 269, 548, 550, 560
anattā (Sanskrit *anātman*) doctrine 62, 267, 296, 428–9, 587, 657, 665
and *attā* (self) 428
Anderson, R. 506, 739n
angels 97, 185, 354, 522–3, 526, 559; *see also* supernormal beings
anger 28, 31, 151, 265, 267; *see also* aversion, hatred
Aṅgulimāla 512, 737n, 740n
Angulimala, The Buddhist Prison Chaplaincy 489, 737n
Aṅgulimāla Sutta 737n, 740n
Aṅguttara Nikāya 280, 450, 710n, 713n, 714n, 729n, 730n, 735n, 743n, 755n
Ani-la 440–1
anima and animus 190–3
animals 33, 46, 88–9, 90, 356
five emblem 217
animitta samādhi 505–6; *see also* *samādhis*, three
annihilation, self- 703n
annihilationism 99, 387, 730n; *see also* nihilism
anti-nuclear activities 345–50
anubodhi 504
Anuruddhas 581, 606–7, 746n, 756n
anuyogayāna 297–8
Apollo 52, 461
Appaṭivāṇa Sutta 714n
apraṇihita samādhi 506; *see also* *samādhis*, three
archetypal
dreams 199, 685–7
experience, world of, *see rūpaloka*
images 199, 211
symbolism xiv, 110, 179–93, 642–3
in the life of the Buddha 181–93, 366
archetypes 118, 181, 190–3, 203–4, 211, 319, 472
of the collective unconscious 323, 333–4, 559
Jung, C. G.
four principal 190–1
use of term 181
arhants (Sanskrit *arahants*) 27, 107–8, 229, 504–5
smile of 146, 715n
Aristotle 68, 406, 638–9, 644, 655, 705n, 752n, 754n
ariyapariyesanā 548–51, 560
Ariyapariyesanā Sutta 548, 619–20, 624, 714n, 750n
Arnold, E. 71, 182, 706n, 718n
art, Buddhist 24, 29, 80, 139, 184, 186, 188–9, 191, 673
thangkas 562, 580, 672, 683
arts 24, 117, 182, 259–60, 393, 514, 559, 637, 643; *see also* culture, painting, poetry
and experience of *rūpaloka* 370
FWBO and the 405–6, 476, 543, 672–3, 748n; *see also* 'Wolf at the Door'
and higher evolution 87
and imagination 472
and religion, ethnic and universal 244
Arunachala mountain or Hill 683, 717n
arūpaloka 147, 370; *see also* spiritual world
Aryaloka Buddhist Center 375, 426, 492
āryas 229
and Āryasaṅgha 538–9, 600
four noble paths of the (*ārya-mārgas*) 27–8, 107–8
Aryatara 580, 653, 746n
Asaṅga 28, 169, 562–3, 569, 578
ascetics (*samaṇas*) 521, 522, 546, 652–3
five 738n
āsravas (Pāli *āsavas*) 164, 717n
assemblies 732n
eight great kinds of 521–3, 525–6
Aśvaghoṣa 109, 182, 712n, 714n, 718n, 719n
Aśvajit 542, 736n, 743n
Atiśa (Dīpaṃkara Śrījñāna) 298, 563–5, 567–79, 594, 745n, 746n
ati-yoga 296, 298, 299
attachment 27; *see also* clinging
Atthasālinī 714n
Augustine, Saint, of Hippo 228, 721n
authoritarianism 42, 228, 246
authority 50, 232–3, 243, 417, 689
Avadānas 182, 718n
Avalokiteśvara 213, 287, 292, 429, 507, 575, 578, 638
as an embodiment or symbol of the Order 405, 414–15, 472, 599–600; *see also* Order, myth of the
initiation of Sangharakshita 438
mantras 96, 502
Avataṃsaka Sūtra 111, 720n; *see also* *The Flower Ornament Scripture*
aversion 154, 157, 291, 356, 547; *see also* anger, hatred

awareness 100, 139, 158–9, 222, 259–60, 269, 558, 638, 646; *see also* mindfulness
Abhidharma and 148–9
alienated and integrated 204–5, 258–69
or consciousness, transcendental 88–9, 258, 263, 282
discriminating, *see vijñāna*
four dimensions of 259–63
and Māra 192; *see also* shadow
mirror-like 158
non-dual, pure or perfect 158, 176–7, 259, 560, 614
three levels of 263–4
White Tārā as embodiment of 662
Axial Age 339, 592

Bacon, F. 77, 355, 655–6, 708n, 728n, 754n
Bāhiya 157–8
Banerjee, R, *see* Buddharakshita
banner of victory 298, 441, 725n
bardos (Sanskrit *antarā-bhavas*) 197–8
Bardo Thödol, see Tibetan Book of the Dead
Beal, S. 70, 706n, 712n, 721n
beautiful (Pāli *subha*), seeing what is not beautiful as 612, 614–16
beauty 219, 308, 551, 615, 672, 730n, 758n
degrees of 615–16
Ratnasambhava and 214
world of, *see rūpaloka*
becoming (*bhāva*) 156, 387
begging-bowl 133, 157, 192, 429, 494, 653
beginner's mind 422–3, 465, 737n
being, great chain of 463, 736n
Benares (Vārāṇasī) xv, 240, 245
Benares Hindu University 429, 430
Beowulf 641–3
Berkeley, G. (Bishop) 77–8, 172, 708n
Berlin 602, 610, 618, 663
Berlin Buddhist Centre 610
Bhagavad Gītā 277–8, 724n
Bhagavān 529; *see also* Buddha
Bhaiṣajyaguru Vaiḍūryaprabhā Tathāgata 722n
Bhaiṣajyarāja 228, 722n
Bhaja Retreat Centre 375, 378
bhāvanā 495
bhāvanā-mayī-prajñā 515; *see also* wisdom, three levels of
Bhayabherava Sutta 620, 750n, 757n
bhikkhunīs (Sanskrit *bhikṣuṇīs*) *see* nuns
bhikkhus (Sanskrit *bhikṣus*) 13, 14, 429, 667; *see also* monks
anagārikas compared to 373
formalistic approach 428
Khantipālo as 636, 647
leading Refuges and Precepts 304–5
ordination of Sangharakshita 303, 684
Bhutan 64, 235, 433, 447, 735n
Bigandet, P. 70, 706n
Bihar 228, 238, 427, 430
Birmingham 630, 632, 637, 650, 699, 751n
Buddhist Centre 561, 649, 678, 691
Blake, W. 29, 331–2, 369, 393, 644–6, 703n, 727n, 728n, 752n
emanation as *ḍākinī* 314, 727n
blasphemy 477, 736n, 758n
Blavatsky, H. P. 70, 493, 725n
blessings (*adhiṣṭhāna*) 14, 17, 303, 364, 438, 640, 686, 753n
bliss (*sukha*) 21, 151, 154, 161–2, 335, 621, 647, 748n
Blofeld, J. 717n, 753n
The Blue Annals 293, 725n, 746n
The Blue Cliff Record 531, 742n
Blyth, R. H. 78, 708n
Bodh Gaya 133, 290, 359, 427, 432, 452, 561, 574, 635
bodhi 173, 504, 605; *see also* Enlightenment
Bodhicaryāvatāra 578, 638, 668, 751n
bodhicitta 214, 537–8, 569, 576–7, 596, 600; *see also* will, to Enlightenment
development of (*mūla yoga*) 19–20
four levels of 599–600
in Pure Land (Shin) Buddhism 86, 709n
real, WBO and manifestation of 405, 599–600
Bodhicitta Buddhist Centre 647, 753n
Bodhidharma 168, 173, 290, 531, 722n
bodhipakṣya-dharmas 466, 736n
Bodhipathapradīpa 576, 579, 746n
bodhisattva
Buddha as 621; *see also* Buddha, previous lives, *Jātakas*
of Compassion 292, 297, 415; *see also* Avalokiteśvara
of generosity (Jambhala) 448, 450, 735n
ideal 16, 123–4, 388, 405, 599–600
Atiśa and 569, 572, 576
lama as 15–17

bodhisattva (*cont.*)
of learning and culture (*Sarasvatī*) 453
ordination 17, 371, 373, 435, 452
of Power 297; *see also* Vajrapāṇi
precepts (*saṃvaraśīla*) 17, 296, 405, 731n
Śāntarakṣita as 293
vow 17, 19–20, 167, 371, 373
of Wisdom 229, 297, 453; *see also* Mañjughoṣa, Mañjuśrī
The Bodhisattva Ideal 600, 748n
bodhisattvas 9, 229, 231, 296–7, 308, 375, 504, 505, 538–9, 569
as Āryasaṅgha 539
consulting 572–3
ethics of 458; *see also* bodhisattva precepts
incarnate 17, 143
lay people as 124
and the mandala 20, 204, 211
meditating on 313; *see also sādhana*, visualization practice, *yidams*
as a non-egoistic stream of spiritual energy 600
peaceful and wrathful 578; *see also* deities, peaceful and wrathful
protecting the Dharma 747n; *see also* Dharma, protectors
renunciation of Nirvāṇa 9, 15–16, 147, 551
white 213
worship of 116, 167, 429, 575, 621
bodhisattvayāna (or *buddhayāna*) 296, 504
bodhi tree 111, 133, 164, 185, 186, 187–8, 189, 213, 560
bodhyaṅgas (Pāli *bojjhaṅgas*), seven 197, 466, 542, 716n
bodies
of the Buddha, *see* Buddha, bodies of
subtle 202, 205
body
awareness 260, 265, 268
going forth in respect of 553–6, 558–60
mindfulness of the 586, 650
precepts and 553
body, speech, and mind 33, 460, 513
and effective Going for Refuge 312, 374, 680
and going forth 553–60
and karma 155
transmutation of 20
Boin, E. 365
Bombay (Mumbai) 691, 692, 693, 718n
Bonhoeffer, D. 5, 8, 9, 701n
Bosch, H. 187, 719n
Boswell, J. 704n, 752n, 759n
Brahmā, and Brahmās 97–8, 189–91, 239, 323, 505, 559; *see also* gods
assembly of 521
brahmacarya 466, 469
'complete' 487–8; *see also anagārikas*, celibacy
Brahmajāla Sutta 703n, 711n
Brahmā Sahāmpati 188–9
Brahmā's request 110, 188–9
brahma vihāras 24, 651; *see also mettā bhāvanā*
Brahmins 50, 223, 240, 245–6, 278, 521
Buddha's criticism of 311, 522, 727n
Buddha's teaching on (true) 31, 311, 727n
Buddha teaching of 141, 240, 511, 521–2
hostility to Buddhism 62, 239, 242–3, 248
Browne, T. 218, 721n
Buddha 89, 90, 134, 140–1, 151–3, 159, 321–2, 501, 527, 530–1, 592–3, 621–2, 657; *see also* Gautama, Śākyamuni, Siddhārtha, *Tathāgata*
adopting appearance of others 523, 526
blue, *see* Akṣobhya
bodies (*kāyas*) of 205–6, 335, 506–7, 739n; *see also dharmakāya*, *trikāya*
as conqueror (Jina) 53, 370, 528–9
Day 704n; *see also* Wesak
death of, *see parinirvāṇa*
decision to teach 152, 502; *see also* Brahmā's request
disappearing 521, 530–1
effect of seeing or hearing 306–8, 624
first sermon 212; *see also* Dharma, teaching of, first
of the future, *see* Maitreya
golden or yellow, *see* Ratnasambhava
as great physician 98, 710n; *see also* Bhaiṣajyarāja; Buddhas, seven medicine
as the great *samaṇa* (*mahāsamaṇa*) 522, 741n
green, *see* Amoghasiddhi
Jayanti 433, 592, 610, 635, 704n, 733n; *see also* Buddha Day, Buddhism, 2500th anniversary of
life of 109–10, 131–4, 358–9, 536, 620–1, 652, 706n, 712n

archetypal symbolism in 181–93, 366; mythical incidents, 110, 618–19; *see also* Brahmā's request, earth goddess, Māra, Mucalinda, twin miracles
in English, *see The Light of Asia*
four sights 131–3, 358–9, 551, 713n, 714n
going forth 546, 548–50, 551–2, 553, 620, 744n
infinite 506–7, 508; *see also dharmakāya*
last days 466; *see also Mahāparinibbāna Sutta*
other titles for 528–30
previous lives, recollection of 689, 740n, 757n; *see also Jātakas*
Refuge, esoteric 17, 312, 313
second 196, 318–19; *see also* Padmasambhava
supernormal powers of 110, 615, 618–19; *see also* miracles
in Tibetan Buddhism 180–1, 507
white, *see* Vairocana
word of the (*Buddhavacana*) 64, 142, 196, 454, 501, 577, 578
to be 'tested like gold in fire' 136, 617, 714n
Buddhacarita 109, 182, 712n, 714n, 718n, 719n
Buddhaghosa 143, 161, 182, 229, 278–80, 710n, 714n, 716n, 722n, 724n, 743–4n, 749n
Buddhahood 58, 164, 199, 212, 231, 234
seeking externally 171
and symbolism of whiteness 213
Buddha-nature 193
Buddharakshita (or Buddharakkhita, formerly Robin Banerjee, Satyapriya) 68, 647, 705n, 753n
Buddhas
of different temperaments 511–12
female (consorts) 203, 204, 221–2, 297
five, mandala of 177, 180–1, 204, 211, 212–17, 219, 221–2, 297
as lamps 753n
seven Medicine 228
Buddhavacana 577; *see also* Buddha, word of
Buddhavaṃsa 714n
buddhayāna 504; *see also bodhisattvayāna*
Buddhism 7–8, 26, 43, 50, 57, 63–4, 93, 98, 106–8, 120–1, 130–1, 136, 139, 246–7, 515, 611, 617
2,500th anniversary of 433, 592, 610; *see also* Buddha Jayanti
accused of nihilism 103, 618
attitude to archetypes 191
basic 15, 93, 611
British 71, 305
'candyfloss' 515
cultural trappings/patterns 78, 119–20
and culture 78–9, 80–1, 310
'difficult to practise' 654–5
Eastern 120, 493, 503, 505, 610
effect on Hinduism 241–2, 249
and environmentalism 409–10
ethnic 252–3; *see also* going for Refuge, cultural
history 15, 115–16, 166–7, 210, 290, 564, 565, 568, 610, 678
decline 594–5, 598, 747n; and disappearance from India, 166–7, 236–43, 286, 564, 577, 594, 745–6n, 747n
in Tibet 290–2
how to approach 58, 60–7
importance of ideas in 465
as the middle way 387–8
mixing with other religions 369, 598, 656
as non-theistic religion 7, 11, 55–7, 62–3, 94, 99, 101, 113, 225, 228, 465, 621–2
one-sided approaches to 103–4
and philosophy 17, 91, 103–4, 106, 117, 139, 145, 169–70, 503, 515, 551, 587
positive and negative approaches to 626–7
preaching in the West 119–20; *see also* Dharma, FWBO propagating
and psychology xiv, 138–40, 150, 155, 179, 194, 291, 656
and psychotherapy 227–34
radical optimism of 513, 526
rational and rationalistic presentation of 104–6, 180–1, 209, 211, 219, 293, 295, 322, 502–3, 512, 515–16
reformation of 115–17
schools of 64, 93, 595–6, 610–11; *see also* individual schools
and science 56, 104–5, 117
seeing with new eyes 39–41
and theosophy 70–1, 72

Buddhism (*cont.*)
in Tibet 290–3; *see also* Tibetan Buddhism
and tolerance 75, 136, 137, 464
unity of 60, 494
and Going for Refuge 596
view of history 592–4; *see also* cosmology
in the West 69–74, 103, 119, 294–5, 368, 369, 383–4, 393, 464, 494, 618, 656
Western 108, 373
Buddhism in England xiii, 59–60
The Buddhist 73
Buddhist, 'movement' and 'society' differentiated 374
Buddhist League 706n
Buddhist Meditation, Systematic and Practical 636, 751n
The Buddhist Review 71
Buddhist scriptures 31–2, 63–5, 241, 321, 500, 508, 520; *see also sūtras*, canonical literature, Pāli canon, Tripiṭaka, and individual Nikāyas, *suttas* etc.
biographies of the Buddha 109–10, 181–2, 618–19
early translations into English 31–2, 70
inspiration from 382, 668–9
study of, in FWBO 368–9, 418, 454, 456, 500, 515, 608, 668–9; *see also* Dharma, study
Tibetan 63–4, 196–7, 286, 300, 570
The Buddhist Society (London) 44, 59–60, 68, 72–3, 91, 102, 137, 364–5, 377, 494, 495, 544, 611, 682, 707n
summer school 23, 24, 59, 68, 73
Buddhist Society of England (1906) 71, 706n
Burma 47, 63, 70–1, 123–5, 142, 428, 516, 687, 688, 742n
Butler, J. 77, 708n
Byron, Lord 698

Cakkavatti-Sīhanāda Sutta 703n, 747n
Calcutta 364, 368, 449, 691
Cameron, C. 59, 705n
Campanella, T. 355, 728n
canonical literature 108, 109, 210; *see also* Buddhist scriptures
Carus, P. 750n
caste system 50, 131, 223, 239, 242, 245, 278, 304, 427, 521, 598
Catena of Buddhist Scriptures 70, 706n, 721n
Cavell, E. 9, 343, 702n, 728n
Caxton Hall 91, 304
celibacy 373, 402, 498, 499, 731n; *see also brahmacarya*
Centre House, Kensington 366–7, 368
centres (of FWBO) 377–8, 385, 455, 468–9, 470–1, 486, 488–9, 595, 650, 664, 676, 680; *see also* Aryaloka, Berlin, London, Manchester, Missoula, Norwich, Nottingham, retreat centres, San Francisco, Seattle, Sheffield
first 365–7, 495, 543; *see also* Monmouth Street, Pundarika, Sakura
presidents of 490–1, 597, 630–2
and Sangha 539–41
ceremonies 167, 240, 438, 441, 472, 518
FWBO 439, 486
dedication 365–6, 541, 650, 743n, 754n
ordination 302–3; *see also* ordination, into WBO, private and public
ceremoniousness 486–7
cetanā 537, 743n
Ceylon 15, 47, 63, 70, 73, 105–6, 123, 142, 143, 278, 706n; *see also* Sri Lanka
Chan 64, 78, 79, 117, 170, 173, 309, 422, 500, 636, 755n; *see also* Zen
Yogi Chen and 443–4
chanting 24, 160, 241, 438, 453, 575, 664, 676
character types 271, 273, 279–80, 724n; *see also* psychological types, temperaments
extroversion and introversion 25, 65, 125, 273–5, 281–2, 512
Chattrul Sangye Dorje 436–7, 443, 494–5, 659–61, 734n, 738n, 755n
Chaucer 76
Chen, C. M, *see* Yogi Chen
'Cherish the doctrine. Live united. Radiate love.' 453; *see also* Dhardo Rimpoche, message of
Chesterfield, Lord 697, 759n
Childers, R. C. 70, 706n
China 116–17, 434–5, 516, 592, 594–5, 675
Christ 8–9, 43, 51, 94, 98, 131, 186, 191, 249, 591–3, 758–9n

Christianity 4–5, 7, 10–11, 42–4, 55, 57, 76, 94, 105, 112–14, 118, 167, 249–52, 265, 295, 739n
and archetypes, myth and symbol 106–7, 191–2
and belief 47–8
and Buddhism 61–2, 94, 595, 598, 656, 706n
criticism of other faiths 136–7
in England 75–8
and ethics 406–7
and hell 513
Kierkegaard criticism of 251–2, 723n
and the millennium 591–2
and paganism 253–4
Sangharakshita and 3–4, 50, 51, 129, 493, 682
St Paul and 33, 696, 704n
view of history 592–4
Cicero 406
cintāmaṇi 214
cinta-mayī-prajñā 515; *see also* wisdom, through reflection
citizenship 342, 353, 488–9, 652
citta 144–8, 151, 175, 595, 715n
citta-mātra 170–3; *see also* One Mind, Yogācāra school
Cittapala 631
cittas, three planes of 151; *see also* existence, conditioned, levels of
civil disobedience 346
clinging (*upādāna*) 156, 187, 646; *see also* attachment
Colenso, J. 6–7, 701n
Coleridge, S. T. 218, 472, 559, 698, 721n, 744–5n, 759–60n
College of Psychic Science xiv, 12
College of Public Preceptors, Triratna 737n, 748n; *see also* Preceptors' College and Council of WBO/TBM
commitment
and freedom 484–5
'is primary, lifestyle is secondary' 389, 498, 666; *see also* lifestyle, and commitment
to the Three Jewels 370, 371, 374, 389, 396, 497–8, 512; *see also* going for Refuge to the Three Jewels, effective
communication 209, 415, 523–4, 525; *see also* speech
argument and discussion compared 483–4
courteous, *see* manners
ḍākinī and 314–15
exercises 38, 367, 651, 664, 704n
FWBO experimentation with 470
and knowing your audience 583–4
and mutual self-transcendence 37, 458, 638, 751n
problem of 152–3, 209, 349–52
communities
Anuruddhas as example, *see* Anuruddhas
FWBO, residential 336, 375, 407, 419, 421, 455, 469, 486, 496, 595, 608, 632, 653–4, 664, 669–70, 671
compassion 43, 139, 547, 661, 756n; *see also karuṇā*
in action 660–1
Bodhisattva of 292, 297, 415; *see also* Avalokiteśvara
of the Buddha 189, 502, 528, 537
and egotism 661
and pity 9, 547, 661
and wisdom 9, 30, 222, 229, 502, 528, 661
union (*yogayāna*) 297
and world peace 339, 343–4, 349, 353
computers 473
concentration 25, 100, 148, 162–3; *see also* meditation, *samādhi*
forty methods of (*kammaṭṭhānas*) 280, 607, 724n
conditionality 21–2, 152–5, 296, 464, 465, 715n; *see also* conditioned co-production, dependent origination
cyclic, seen in history and Buddhism 593–5
cyclic and spiral 21–2, 153–4, 197–8; *see also nidānas*
levels of (five *niyamas*) 547–8, 743–4n
positive 465; *see also nidānas*, twelve positive, spiral path
conditioned, and unconditioned (*saṃskṛta* and *asaṃskṛta dharmas*) 144–5
conditioned co-production (*pratītya samutpāda*) 14, 153, 318, 322, 494, 542, 664; *see also* conditionality
conditioned existence, *see* existence, conditioned
conditioning 262, 467, 652
confession 160
confidence 216–17
Confucianism 7, 42, 53–4, 94, 117, 135, 228, 247, 250, 309, 706n
and Buddhism 516

Confucius 53, 247, 527, 592
consciousness 144, 217; *see also vijñāna*
at death 201–2
four kinds of 262
levels or states of 26, 46, 204, 558, 676; *see also* existence, conditioned, levels of; reality, levels of; realms; states; worlds
collective 322–3
deeper 22, 30, 322–3, 475; *see also* the unconscious
and evolution 88
higher 12–13, 82, 107, 169–70, 191, 220–1, 391, 404, 495, 555, 672; *see also dhyānas*
and integration 217–18, 220–1
progressive, *see nidānas*, twelve positive
and wheel of life 154, 156
pyramid of 147, 715n
sense, *see vijñānas*, five
and soul 698
store, *see ālaya-vijñāna*
transference of (*phowa*) 449, 735n
turning about in (*parāvṛtti*) 174, 176–8, 513, 717n
unification of 147; *see also* integration
consumerism 479, 598, 608, 654, 656
contact (*sparśa*) 155–6, 646
conversion 54, 71, 227, 243, 248, 654
Buddhism and
going forth 307–8
mass 304, 319, 561, 649, 684, 737n
the *parāvṛtti* 174, 717n
Hinduism and 245
Conze, E. 72–3, 103–4, 123, 168, 170, 210, 211, 492, 494, 561–2, 568, 711n, 713n, 720n, 737–8n, 742n
Cooke, A. 695, 758n
Coomaraswamy, A. 707n
corpse meditation 280, 639, 692, 751n
cosmic
Going for Refuge 315
law 501
lotus 220, 721n
tree, *see* world tree
cosmology
Buddhist 20, 141, 155, 203, 250, 292, 721n; *see also* Buddhism, view of history
world periods 318, 319
Indian 320
courage 5, 6, 7, 518, 522, 529, 554, 556, 598
craving 43, 98–100, 187, 207, 359, 362, 554, 608, 609, 646; *see also* desire, greed, *kāmachanda*, *tṛṣṇā*
Abhidharma and 146
and alienated awareness 267
aversion and wrong views 154, 291; *see also* greed, hatred and delusion; poisons, three
and feeling, gap or point between 156–7, 158, 165, 198
and recollection of death 195
and *śraddhā* 626
three kinds of 99
Creative Symbols of Tantric Buddhism 702n, 735n, 751n
creativity 32, 234, 359, 380, 634, 637–41, 643–7
cremation grounds 220–1, 289, 294, 324
Cūḷadukkhakhandha Sutta 162, 717n
Cūḷagosinga Sutta 581, 746n, 748n
Cūḷasakuludāyi Sutta 715n
culture xiv, 78, 243–4, 321, 348, 392, 394, 746n; *see also* arts
as channel for energies 380, 381
and institutions 639
and religion 45, 244, 246, 247
Western 62, 81, 392–4, 395, 498, 656
Sangharakshita and 634–5
The Cup 656, 754n

ḍākas 294, 314
ḍākinīs 191, 287, 289, 314, 334, 565, 702n
as esoteric Sangha Refuge 312, 314–15
five great 222; *see also* Buddhas, female
our own integrated 314–15
Padmasambhava and 294, 324–5, 331, 335–6
principle represented in staff 335
red, *see* Kurukullā
Dalai Lama 12, 16, 17, 65, 432, 435, 437, 579, 677, 702n, 734n, 756n, 757n
dāna 17, 124–5, 178, 467, 469, 567, 609, 671; *see also* generosity
Dante 76
Dao De Jing 59, 247
Daoism (Taoism) 7, 42, 53–4, 94, 117, 135, 216, 228, 247, 250, 706n
Darjeeling 285, 436, 438, 449
darkness
forces of 529

and light 215, 220, 278, 307, 354–6, 518–19, 627, 753n
Darwin, C. 84, 153, 724n
Dasuttara Sutta 745n
David-Néel, A. 561–2
Dawa-Samdup, Kazi 197, 720n
Dear Dinoo: Letters to a Friend 691, 693, 705n
death 194–208, 356–62, 387, 396, 543, 548–9, 620, 633, 639, 699
bardo of the moment of (*chikhai bardo*) 198, 200–2, 206, 207
demon of 356
and going forth 555–6
Hindu ceremonies 240
Kisāgotamī and 537, 743n
mindfulness or recollection of 195, 280, 724n
and Vajrasattva mantra 438–9
defilements 548–9
deities, *see also* gods, supernormal beings
knowledge-holding 204
nāga or serpent 323
peaceful and wrathful 203–5, 207, 221, 578, 702n
protector or guardian, *see* Dharma, protectors
tutelary (*iṣṭa devatās*) 572; *see also yidams*
Delamare, T. 450, 751n
Delhi 364, 610, 691
delight 160, 187, 261, 276, 332, 455, 526, 530, 550, 703n; *see also* joy
deluded types (*mohacaritas*) 278–80, 724n
delusion 131, 146, 151, 154, 356, 527, 611; *see also* ignorance; poisons, three
demon dagger (*phurba*) 285
demons 186–7; *see also* supernormal beings
of death and Impermanence 356
and gods 291–2, 318, 323–4, 331, 332, 335
transforming or subduing 323–36; *see also under* integration
in the West 323, 333–4, 335
dependent origination 151, 153, 494, 745n; *see also* conditionality
Desert Island Discs 476, 736n
desire (*rāga*) 28; *see also* craving, sensuous experience
and alienated awareness 267
and beauty 615
for Nirvāṇa (*dhammachanda*) 550–1, 560
two kinds of 550
deva, or *yidam*, as esoteric Dharma Refuge 191, 312, 313
Devadatta 513, 712n, 740n
devalokas 143, 169, 559; *see also* heavens; realms, higher
Indra 615
Tāvatiṃsa 143
Tuṣita 28, 143, 169, 562, 703n
Devamitra 631
devas 521, *see* also, gods, supernormal beings
world of, *see devalokas*
devils 725n, 730n, 740n; *see also* Satan, supernormal beings
in Blake 29, 703n
Mephistopheles 613, 748n
salvation of 526, 740n
devotion 14, 19, 23–4, 160, 167, 222, 314, 487, 529, 538, 712n
Atiśa and 568, 575
devotional practices 24, 160, 283; *see also* puja
Dhammacakkappavattana Sutta 212, 720n, 741n
dhammachanda 550–1, 560
Dhammadinna 597, 631
Dhammapada 31–2, 33, 36–7, 97, 135, 339, 357, 362, 368, 466, 529, 546, 579, 622, 668, 703n, 710n, 714n, 723n, 728n, 729n, 742n, 750n, 753n
commentary 185, 339, 357, 615, 718n, 728n, 729n, 748n
Dhammapala, Anagarika 713n
Dhammarati 385, 631
Dhammasaṅgaṇī 744n
Dhardo Rimpoche 96, 364, 431–6, 440–1, 447–9, 452, 662
biography by Suvajra 435, 734n
death anniversary 452, 459
message or motto of 453–9
previous life 688
rejoicing in the merits of 459–60
school, *see* Indo-Tibetan Buddhist Cultural Institute School
Dharma 61, 63, 134, 139, 141–2, 159–60, 322, 369, 454, 501
'come and see' (*ehipassiko*) 136
communicating the 580–90
FWBO propagating and publicizing 380–1, 407–8, 455–6, 469–70, 489, 490, 554, 583

Dharma, communicating the (*cont.*)
through stories 507–8, 526, 539, 589, 665, 712n, 718n, 719n, 740n, 743n, 747n
criterion given to Mahāprajāpatī Gautamī 393–4, 730n
decline and disappearance of 747n; *see also* Buddhism, history, decline
as doctrine 466
cherishing 454–6
effect of hearing 306–7, 624, 652, 665–6
engaging intellect, emotion and will with 538
esoteric teachings 196; *see also termas*
meaning of word (*dharma* (Pāli *dhamma*))
in Buddhism 140, 143–4, 212, 466, 501, 525; *see also dharmas*
in Hinduism 50
not mixing with other ideologies 404, 455, 476, 516–17, 585, 598, 656
protectors, or guardians of 191–2, 221, 292, 294, 295, 297, 331, 734n, 747n
as a raft 61–2, 454, 462
as rain 508–11, 516
Refuge, esoteric (*deva* or *yidam*) 191, 312, 313
seals (*mudrās*), four 656–8, 754–5n
study 368–9, 382, 396, 418, 496, 538, 567–8, 664, 680; *see also* Buddhist scriptures, study of
teaching of, first 152–3, 212
transmission of 231–2, 675
willingness to die for 572, 573
dharmacakra 203, 212, 530
dharmacakrapravartana mudrā 212
dharmacāris and *dharmacāriṇīs* 312, 373, 374, 398, 545, 591, 667–8; *see also* Order members
dharmadhātu, wisdom of the 177, 203, 212–13
Dharma Eye 505, 738n
dharmakāya 201, 298, 335, 454, 506–7, 572, 739n; *see also* Buddha, bodies of; reality
White Lotus Sūtra and 507
Dharmakīrti (Lama Serlingpa) 568–9
Dharmakīrti (scholar of Nālandā) 563, 569, 745n
Dharma Life magazine 730n
Dharmamati 678
Dharmapala, Anagārika 561
dharmas (Pāli *dhammas*) 143–5, 147, 149, 163
and *dharmakāya* 739n
ten *kuśala-* 567; *see also* precepts, ten
thirty-seven *bodhipakṣya-* 466, 736n
Dharmashura 693
dhātus, eighteen 291, 293
Dhyāna Bardo, *see* meditation, *bardo* of
dhyāna mudrā 215
dhyānas 542, 555; *see also* consciousness, levels of, higher
and the Buddha's *parinirvāṇa* 357
four 147, 357
and insight 542
diamonds 285, 459; *see also vajras*
Diamond Sūtra 59, 233, 368, 493, 531, 682, 742n
Sangharakshita's commentary 742n
diamond throne (*vajrāsana*) 186–7, 220
Dickens, C. 217, 271, 365, 645, 720–1n, 724n, 729n
dictionaries 135, 150, 151, 181, 392, 458, 468, 470, 476
Buddhist 703–4n
Dr Johnson's 476, 480, 697
Pāli-English 70, 368, 550, 706n
Dīgha Nikāya 97–8, 309, 387, 412, 466, 521, 603, 619, 675, 703n, 710n, 711n, 712n, 713n, 714n, 717n, 726n, 730n, 732n, 736n, 738n, 740n, 741n, 743n, 745n, 747n, 748n, 749n, 751n, 755n, 756n, 757n
Dilgo Khyentse Rimpoche 442, 446–51, 719n, 735n
Dīpaṅkara 327
directionless *samādhi* 506; *see also samādhis*, three
disciples 19, 143, 377, 603, 675
Ani-la as 440–1
of Atiśa 563, 569, 575, 577, 578
of the Buddha 141–3, 216, 231–2, 237, 464, 504, 511–13, 520, 522, 529, 542, 657, 675, 676, 678–9, 756n; *see also śrāvakas*
and case of dysentry 536–7, 742–3n
and *guru yoga* 19
Marpa and 18, 702n
need to meet in large numbers 412, 732n
Sangharakshita's 438–9, 495, 545, 660, 735n; *see also* Order members
Dhardo Rimpoche and 459
story of Tenno, Nanin and umbrella 260–1, 723n

discriminating
awarenesses, *see vijñāna*
wisdom 176, 215, 297
discrimination, racial 408–9
dispassion (*vairāgya*) 164
distraction 381, 421–3
and reducing input 473–5
divine eye, *see* eyes, divine
Dōgen 506, 517
Donne, J. 68, 519, 694, 706n, 736n, 741n, 758n
The Door of Liberation 368
doubt (*vicikitsā*) 27–8
The Drama of Cosmic Enlightenment 492, 738n, 742n
dreams 172, 175, 182, 192, 206, 218, 559, 650, 749n
archetypal 199, 685–7
bardo of 199–200, 206
Dromtön 577–8
dualism, *see* subject-object dualism
Dubash, D. 691–3, 698; *see also Dear Dinoo: Letters to a Friend*
Dudjom Rimpoche 442–3, 450, 661, 684, 735n, 757n
dukkha (Sanskrit *duḥkha*) *see* suffering
duties 125, 189, 406, 491, 603–4, 652, 713n; *see also* responsibility
Dzogchen 299, 494
Dzongsar Khyentse Rimpoche 656, 658, 755n

earth 214
goddess (Vasuṃdharā) 110, 187–8, 190–2, 213, 719n
and heaven, ladder between 12, 185–6
mother 188, 719n
earth-touching gesture (*bhūmisparśa*) 188, 213
eclecticism 52, 54
ecology 409; *see also* environment
ecumenism
FWBO and, *see* FWBO, ecumenism
in Tibetan Buddhism 437, 578, 734n
effort 46–7, 56–7, 97, 134–5, 522, 537, 596, 599, 622–3
in meditation 162–3, 178, 537
right 27, 135
ego 99–100, 173, 484, 512, 559–60, 605, 661, 669
no unchanging, *see* self, no-
ego-centric intellect, integration of 217–18
egolessness 458, 505, 605
egotism 13–14, 456, 459, 669–70
and compassion 661
Egyptian Book of the Dead 197
elements
eighteen (*dhātus*) 291, 293
five 217
four 220–1
Jungian interpretation 619
six, meditation practice 467, 661, 755n
elephants 102–3, 161, 203, 716n
Eliot, T. S. 45, 201, 515, 705n, 720n, 740n
emanations 314, 333, 438, 463, 702n, 727n
emancipation 167; *see also* liberation, freedom
emotions 657
negative 83, 187, 261, 266, 391, 475
positive 261, 314, 378, 394, 516, 627, 657
ḍākinī as spiritual 314–15
repression of, *see* repression
empiricism 75
energies, *see also* forces
direction of 380–2, 402
emotional 161–3, 391
misguided or scattered 335–6
unification of 161, 162–3; *see also* integration
energy 25, 29, 65, 148, 296
effect of silence on 557
'is eternal delight' 703n
mind as 99
non-egoistic stream of spiritual 14, 336, 600
or power, Bodhisattva of 297, 415; *see also* Vajrapāṇi
psychic 190
English Sangha Association 73, 137, 364–5
English Sangha Trust 73, 125, 137, 364–5, 449, 707n, 713n
Enlightened mind, as wish-fulfilling jewel (*cintāmaṇi*) 214
Enlightenment 47, 61, 62, 100, 135, 152, 158, 164, 177, 322, 546–7, 613–14
and altruism 373; *see also bodhicitta*, bodhisattva vow
aspects of 214–17, 222, 308
of the Buddha Śākyamuni 133–4, 189, 504–5, 620–1, 712n, 714n
anniversary of, *see* Buddha Jayanti, Wesak
and the dream state 199

Enlightenment (*cont.*)
glimpses of 25–6
importance of conditioning the mind for 467
and individuation 192
levels of 13, 504
as mandala 218–19, 221
potential for 43, 502, 511–13, 517, 529–30, 613; *see also* spiritual potential as seeds
private or solitary, *see pratyekabuddhas*
seat of, *see vajrāsana*
seven limbs or factors of (*bodhyaṅgas*) 197, 466, 542, 716n
with a small 'e' 463
thirty-seven wings of, *see bodhipakṣya-dharmas*
in this lifetime 689, 690
as ultimate Going for Refuge 315
as union or integration of opposites (*yuganaddha*) 184–5
will to 19, 296, 537–8; *see also bodhicitta*
as wisdom of the *dharmadhātu* 212–13
wrong views about 616
environment xvii, 409–10, 670
epistemology 106, 139, 145, 171
equality, wisdom of 177, 204, 214
equanimity, *see upekṣā*
esoteric Refuges, *see* Three Refuges, esoteric
The Essence of Zen 56, 705n, 722n
eternalism 730n; *see also* views, wrong
ethical or karmic level of conditionality 547–8
ethics 17, 116, 139, 146, 167, 188, 291, 296, 459, 529, 566, 625, 664; *see also* morality, precepts
and commitment and lifestyle 666
and economic activity 670; *see also* right livelihood
and Going for Refuge 499
Manu and 320–1
and meditation and wisdom 604
middle way and 387
in secular language 117
in society 406
European Buddhist Union Congress 602, 624–5
Evans-Wentz, W. Y. 72, 197, 286, 298, 720n, 725n
evolution xii, 46, 82–5, 379–80, 464
and biology 84, 88–9
as cosmic going for Refuge 315–16
Daoism and 247
diagram 88–90
and ethnic and universal religion 244
higher 46–7, 49, 58, 63, 65, 85, 88–9, 107, 159, 244, 251, 258–9, 269, 622
and effective going for Refuge 316
and lower evolution 87–90, 250, 253
and psychological types 270, 278, 280–4
religion as 282
as restatement of the Buddha's teaching 465
and institutions 468
theory of 85, 153
exertions, four right 466
existence
conditioned or phenomenal 144, 217, 356; *see also saṃsāra*
detachment from 164, 551
levels or planes of 21, 84–5, 147, 151, 168–70, 184, 547, 556; *see also* consciousness, levels of
poison of desire for (*bhavāsrava*) 99, 164
six worlds of 204; *see also* wheel of life
suffering of 623–4
three or four marks of 754–5n
structure of 12–13; *see also* evolution, higher, and lower
Unconditioned 163; *see also* the Unconditioned
experiment, *see* FWBO, five pillars of, experiment
ex-Untouchables 303–4, 319, 495, 561; *see also* 'untouchables'
eyes
Dharma 505, 738n
divine (*divya-cakṣus*) 189, 559
five 738n
of friendship (or kindly) 677, 756n
'perceiving' 749n

faculties
imaginal 559, 745n
individual and spiritual development 281
spiritual, *see* spiritual, faculties, five 65
of transcendental awareness 88
faith 25, 65, 148, 283, 505; *see also śraddhā*
fascination, rite of 308, 448, 735n
Faust 613, 748n
fear 620, 661

fearlessness 216, 661
feeling 144, 217; *see also vedanā*
and craving, gap or point between 156–7, 158, 165, 198
in Jungian sense 273–5, 281
feelings
awareness of 261–2, 265–6
repressed, *see* repression
subjective and objective truth 350–1
fetters 27–8, 703
fire 220–1
fire and water 184–5, 619
The Flower Ornament Scripture 646, 753n; *see also Avataṃsaka Sūtra*
forbearance (*kṣānti*) 459; *see also* patience, tolerance
force
mind as a 99
of Sangharakshita's life 681, 684
supra-personal, *see* energy, non-egoistic stream of spiritual
forces, *see also ḍākinīs*, demons, energies, shadow, supernormal beings
anti-creative 641, 644, 646; *see also* mind, reactive
or energies, primordial or supra-rational 294, 323–5, 332, 335, 529, 552, 643
of inspiration 294
of the unconscious or psyche 189–90, 293, 323–4
form
material, *see rūpa*
world of (*rūpaloka*) 147, 170
formless world (*arūpaloka*) 147, 170, 370
Forty-Three Years Ago 731n
Four Great Kings 521
four noble truths 14, 98, 121, 228, 296, 318, 322, 542, 664, 710n
four sights, Buddha and 131–3, 358–9, 551, 713–14n
freedom (*vimukti*) 164, 529; *see also* emancipation, liberation
and commitment 484–5
fear of 232–3
taste of xi, 164, 596, 717n
Freud, S. xiv, 93–5, 99, 117, 153, 366, 724n
theory of psychological types 272, 281
friendship 457–8, 469, 474, 539–40, 638–9, 640–1, 645–6, 752n; *see also* spiritual friendship
Cicero's dialogue on 406
and collusion 481
Dr Johnson on 640, 751–2n
fierce 416–17, 732n
as a flame being lit from another 645–6, 753n
male 465
obstacles to 458, 644
Sangharakshita and 68, 320–1, 333, 364, 416, 438, 635, 640–1, 662, 682, 683, 691–3, 704n
Fromm, E. xiv, 72, 93, 99, 227–8, 366, 654, 711n, 721n
theory of psychological types 275–7, 724n
FWBO (Friends of the Western Buddhist Order) xii, 373–7, 381, 386–7, 462–3, 595, 664
anniversaries (FWBO) Day xiv, xvi, xviii, 363–4, 365, 374, 385, 395, 462, 649–50, 676, 678
centres, *see* centres, FWBO
ceremonies, *see* ceremonies
characteristics shared with rest of Buddhist world 664–5
choirs 558, 595
co-ops 336, 375, 404, 468, 469; *see also* team-based right livelihood businesses
Dhardo Rimpoche and 432, 435, 453, 458–9
early years 653–4, 663–4
video of 512, 739n
ecumenism or non-sectarian approach 437, 454, 500, 668–9; *see also* inspiration, from whole Buddhist tradition
emphasis on Going for Refuge, *see* going for Refuge..., centrality of
five pillars of xvii, 463–72
experiment 463, 469–72
ideas 463–5, 468–9, 472
imagination 463–4, 472
institutions 463, 468–9, 472, 639–40, 641
practices 463, 466–7, 469, 472
founding of xiii, 364–8, 495, 524, 634, 650, 654, 743n
'Friends' with a capital F 374, 376, 381, 383, 595
future of 421, 490, 545, 597–8, 600, 632, 635, 677–9
in India, *see* Trailokya Bauddha Mahasangha Sahayak Gana, Aid for India, Karuna Trust

FWBO (*cont.*)
infrastructure (inc FWBO Central) 398, 490–1; *see also* FWBO, 'three Cs'
Mitras, *see* Mitras
in North America 492
as nucleus of a new society 385, 395
and ordination, *see* ordination, Western Buddhist Order
publications 375, 379, 398, 726n, 732n, 742n; *see also Golden Drum*
transcription of lectures and seminars xi, 366, 398, 455, 500, 534, 700, 731n, 742n
relationship with WBO 321, 368, 370, 378, 388, 415, 497, 600
residential communities, *see* communities, FWBO residential
respect for elders in 678–9
retreat centres, *see* retreat centres
Sangharakshita and 384, 386, 390, 401, 462–3, 490, 535, 543, 600, 632–3, 641, 653–4, 664, 670, 674, 684; *see also* FWBO, founding; ordination; Sangharakshita, handing on responsibilities
six distinctive emphases of xvi, 596, 663–73
and spiritual friendship, *see* spiritual friendship, FWBO and
and study, *see* Dharma, study
'three Cs' 336, 375, 407, 419, 468, 543, 640
women and 375–6, 667; *see also* Order members, women

Gainsborough, T. 76–7
Gampopa 368
Gaṇḍavyūha Sūtra 111, 216, 720n
Gautama 139, 240–1, 322, 338, 387; *see also* Buddha
Gelug school or Gelugpa tradition 14, 64, 196, 210, 298–9, 432, 500, 611
Dhardo Rimpoche and 432
and Kadam school 579
generosity 133, 160, 188, 296, 459, 479, 609; *see also dāna*
mudrā of 214
genius 152, 241, 588, 643
gestures 586, 661; *see also mudrās*
Gissing, G. 643, 752n
'The Glory of the Literary World' 363, 729n
God 5–7, 113–14, 120, 233, 710n, 725n, 759n; *see also* Brahmā
as archetype 191
in Blake 703n
in Buddhism 7, 8, 96–7, 134–5
Christian view of 228, 477, 592, 621, 701n, 710n, 721n
death of 44, 94
as father figure 94–7
in Hinduism 134
and interfaith circles 677
personal, creator 5, 7, 10, 42–3, 55, 94, 135, 276, 534, 621–2, 655
Shakespeare and 76
sun as symbol of 181
in Vedānta 7, 268
goddess, earth, *see* earth goddess
gods 204, 248, 291–4, 356; *see also* Brahmā, and Brahmās; deities; *devas*; supernormal beings
and demons 291–2, 318, 323–4, 331, 332, 335
and leisure time 355
turned into devils 295
world or realm of 203; *see also devalokas*, heavens
Goethe, J. W. von 369, 613, 645, 697, 748n, 759n
Going for Refuge and Prostration Practice (*mūla yoga*) 19, 467, 591
Going for Refuge to the Three Jewels xv–xvi, 17, 63, 69, 160, 246, 305, 369, 371, 454–5, 535–41
altruistic dimension or aspect 373, 405, 599–600; *see also* ordination, bodhisattva
Atiśa's emphasis on 577
centrality of 305–6, 371–2, 399, 506, 596, 665–7
cosmic 315
cultural 310–11, 596, 666
distinguished from 'taking Refuge' 596
Dōgen and 506, 517
effective 312–16, 371–2, 537, 539, 560, 596, 599–600, 666–7
and ordination into WBO 398–9, 596–7, 666
and FWBO institutions 469
levels of xvi, 310–16, 371–2, 505, 552, 596, 599, 666, 727n
in the Pāli scriptures 665, 726n
provisional 311–12, 539, 596, 666
real 315, 371, 372, 505–6, 552, 560, 596–7, 599–600, 666–7; *see also* Stream Entry
and Refuges and Precepts, *see* Refuges and Precepts

relation to going forth 552
Sangharakshita's 301–5, 552
significance of 305–6, 310
and *śrāvakayāna* 296
ten precepts as expression of 403, 553
ultimate 315; *see also* Enlightenment
going forth 307, 546–60, 624
of the Buddha 546, 548–50, 551–2, 553, 620, 744n
levels of 552
relation to Going for Refuge 552
in respect of body, speech and mind 552–60
Sangharakshita's 546, 551–2, 683
Golden Drum 383, 488, 730n, 754n
golden drum, in *Sūtra of Golden Light* 384
Govinda, Lama 36–7, 147, 206, 492, 561–2, 688, 704n, 715n, 725n, 737n
and Arya Maitreya Mandala 584, 746n
Foundations of Tibetan Mysticism 287, 720n, 725n, 745n
The Way of the White Clouds 574, 688, 746n, 757n
Graham, Billy 119, 713n
gravitational pull 163, 253, 644
Greece 79, 406, 461, 462, 463, 592, 634, 713n
greed (*lobha*) 28, 356, 617; *see also* craving
hatred, and delusion 393, 499, 541, 622; *see also* poisons, three
hatred and delusion, freedom from 546–7
greedy types (*lobhacaritas*) 278–80, 724n
Green Tārā 222, 436, 438, 660–2
Grimm, G. 104, 711–12n
group
and conditioning 467
and individual 394, 462, 644
and Going for Refuge 535–6
and religion 243–5, 247–51, 253
positive 311, 320–1
and spiritual community 456, 468
Guénon, R. 32, 703n
Guhyaloka 398, 401, 411, 418, 419, 420–1, 422, 500, 731n
guilt 160, 406, 480
Guru, Padmasambhava as the 286, 300, 319
Guru of Dhartsendo 459–60; *see also* Dhardo Rimpoche
Guru principle 332, 334
Guru Rimpoche 196; *see also* Padmasambhava
gurus 323, 723n; *see also* spiritual teachers
as esoteric Buddha Refuge 17, 312, 313
and spiritual friendship 458
in *sūtra* and *terma* traditions 299
Tantric (Vajrācārya) 17–20, 191, 286, 299–300
and the three *yānas* 15–20
guru yoga practice 19, 702n; *see also* *kalyāṇa mitra yoga*

Hakuin 368, 539, 594
Hampstead Buddhist Vihara xi–xiii, 2, 21, 31, 39, 49, 58, 67–8, 73, 82, 112, 128, 130, 137, 365–6, 372, 495, 533–4, 654
happiness 21, 28, 154, 162, 362, 466, 603, 613, 622, 626–7, 657, 749n
and creativity 641
and upside-down views (*viparyāsas*) 613, 616
'happy, healthy human beings' 321, 468
Hardy, R. Spence 69–70, 706n
harmony 37, 598–600, 676–8
Harry the Ticker 416, 732n
hate types (*dosacaritas*) 278–80, 724n
hatred 146, 187, 391; *see also* anger, aversion
Heart Sūtra 31, 103, 368
Sangharakshita's commentary 742n
heaven
Christian conception of 191
and earth 19
and cremation grounds 220–1
ladder between 12, 185–6
literal 276
heavens
in Buddhism 97–8, 169, 229, 356; *see also devalokas*, realms
of the Thirty-Three 185
hedonism, higher 542
Hegel, G. W. F. 277, 426, 733n
hell 29, 356, 513
torment, or suffering, state of 155, 204, 356
Heraclitus 422
Hermetic correspondence 181, 718n
heroism 489–90, 556, 562, 626, 737n
Hevajra Tantra 104, 210–11, 223, 711n, 720n

hierarchy
ecclesiastical 13, 17, 702n
medieval idea of 463, 735–6n
spiritual 12–15, 19
Himavanta Sutta 716n
Hīnayāna 15, 64, 116, 167, 210, 565, 711n, 739n, 741n
Atiśa and 567
lama in 15, 20
meditation, Yogi Chen and 636
Hinduism 12, 42, 50, 52, 54, 94, 134, 239–40, 244–8, 521, 706n
and Buddhism 62, 240–3, 249, 527, 598
and language 241, 250
Kashyapji and 427–8
theory of psychological types 277–8, 283
and Vedism 521
The History of my Going for Refuge xvi, 396–7, 731n
Hogarth, W. 76
Holmes, R. 698, 760n
Holy Grail 192
Honest to God 2, 4–5, 7–8, 114, 130, 135, 710n
Horney, K. 93, 272–3, 724n
householder, bodhisattva 228
householders 240, 521, 522; *see also* laity, lay men or lay people
household life
going forth from 288, 307–8, 536
Mahāyāna view 167
Huángbò (Huang Po) 170–1, 717n
Huayan school 64, 720n
Hughes, T. 641
Huineng 233; *see also Sūtra of Huineng*
humanism 8–9, 42, 62, 93, 98, 129, 227–8, 345, 721n
humours, four 229, 271–2
Humphreys, C. 16, 72, 91, 304–5, 444, 494, 682, 707n, 742n, 756–7n
The Hundred Thousand Songs of Milarepa 368
Huxley, A. 201
Huxley, J. 55, 56, 84, 705n, 709n, 724n
Huxley, T. H. 724n

the 'id' 99–100
ideal, worlds or utopias 355, 728n
idealism 708n
absolute and subjective 171–2
ideas, *see* FWBO, five pillars of, ideas
idols, four 655–6, 754n
ignorance (*avidyā*) 43, 154–6, 550, 582, 646; *see also* delusion
Māra as 187
poison of spiritual (*avidyāsrava*) 164
the Illuminator, *see* Vairocana
images
archetypal 199, 211; *see also* archetypes
eidetic 172
language of 209
Muslim attitude to 242
imaginal faculty 559, 745n
imagination 175, 182, 209, 295, 404, 502, 559, 637, 638
and ceremonies 472
distinguished from fancy 744–5n
and ethics 567
FWBO and, *see* FWBO, five pillars of, imagination
impermanence 163, 187, 207, 357–8, 588, 624, 657, 754n
demon of 356
seen as permanent 612, 616
imperturbability 164
the Imperturbable, *see* Akṣobhya
The Inconceivable Emancipation 722n
India
conditions for Dharma practice 513–14, 598
FWBO activities 482, 490, 731n; *see also* Aid for India, Karuna Trust, TBMSG
mass conversions to Buddhism 304, 319, 561, 649, 684, 737n
Sangharakshita in, *see under* Sangharakshita
Western Buddhist Order in, *see* Trailokya Bauddha Mahasangha
individual 90, 348, 536
developing as an 468–9
and group, *see* group, and individual
higher evolution of the 258, 269–70, 284, 622
and spiritual community 307, 395, 468, 723n
theories about 281–2
Bhagavad Gītā 277–8
Buddhaghosa 278–81
Freud 272
Fromm 276–7
Jung, *see* individuation process
true 244, 247, 250, 253, 255, 386, 562, 598, 723n
and universal religion 243–4
individualism 456, 654, 656, 670
individuality 99, 144, 216, 244, 246, 485, 497, 512, 536, 723n

individuals, non- 351–2
individuation process 190–2, 199, 218;
see also integration
Indonesia 567, 569, 594, 610
Sumatra 289, 567, 568–9
Indo-Tibetan Buddhist Cultural Institute (ITBCI) school 433, 435, 452–3, 458, 733n, 734n
Indra 427, 615
Indrabhūti 288–9
the Infinite Light, *see* Amitābha
initiations
of Padmasambhava by a *ḍākinī* 287
Sangharakshita's, *see under* Sangharakshita
Tantric, *see* Tantric initiations
Yogi Chen and 444, 448
insight 29, 163, 296–8, 315, 372, 472; *see also* Going for Refuge, real; Perfect Vision
alienated awareness mistaken for 267
and *dhyāna* 542
flashes of (*vipassanā*) 25, 414; *see also* vision, path of
having the courage of one's 598
and problem of communication 152
and three levels of wisdom 541
through contact with *dharmakāya* through a bodhisattva 572–3
through hearing the Dharma 541–2
through *kalyāṇa mitratā* 382; *see also* self-transcendence, mutual
through reflection 542; *see also* wisdom, through reflection
transcendental 404, 519, 744n
in Western literature 672
insights
of the bodhisattva 296
cosmic, of Daoism 247
and creativity 637
inspiration
from the arts and literature 369, 406, 668, 672, 692
from Buddhist scriptures 382, 668–9
forces of 294; *see also ḍākinīs*
loss of 419, 421, 679
from meditation 169, 298–9, 441, 555; *see also* visions
of others 378, 497–8; *see also kalyāṇa mitratā*
from Śākyamuni Buddha 507–8
from *termas* 332–3
from whole Buddhist tradition 368–9, 500, 578; *see also* FWBO, ecumenism
inspired utterance, *see udāna*
institutions 468–9, 644
and creativity 639–40, 647–8
integrated awareness 258–69
integration 23–4, 26, 29–30, 147, 190–3, 217–18, 536, 625; *see also* energies, unification of; individuation process; spiritual wholeness
and ethics 566
the mandala as symbol of 209, 218–23
of non-rational and supra-rational forces 294, 335; *see also ḍākinī*, our own integrated; demons, transforming
psychological xv
or union, of opposites 29, 184–6, 216, 359, 619
sexual symbolism 222–3; *see also yab-yum*
intellectual
aspect of mind 536–8
clarity 515–16
interconnectedness 129, 154, 171, 409; *see also* interpenetration
interpenetration, mutual 464
'In the seen, only the seen' 158, 716n
intuition 59, 166, 182–3
in Jungian sense 273–4, 275, 281–2
Islam 42, 53–4, 55, 135, 243, 249–50, 569, 593, 594, 595, 691, 706n
iṣṭa devatās 572; *see also yidams*
Italy 634
ITBCI school, *see* Indo-Tibetan Buddhist Cultural Institute school
Itivuttaka 710n

Jackson, R. J. 71, 706n
Jainism 7, 53–4, 135, 428, 706n
Jambhala 448, 450, 735n
Jamgön Kongtrül 734n
Jamyang Khyentse Rimpoche 437–9, 441, 442, 443, 446, 656, 661
and Kachu Rimpoche 440, 442
and Yogi Chen 443
Jamyang Khyentse Wangpo 734n
Jaspers, K. 225–7, 592, 721n, 747n
Jātakas 182, 578, 718n
jealousy 157, 187, 205, 208, 456
jewel (*maṇi*), in the lotus 502
Jewel Ornament of Liberation 368
Jewel-Producing One, *see* Ratnasambhava
jewels, three, *see* Three Jewels

Jina 53, 370, 528–9; *see also* Buddha
Jivaka 438–9, 735n
Jñānaprabha 571–4
jñānas, five, *see* wisdoms, five
Jogis 439
John, Saint 520
  Gospel According to 249, 457, 529, 723n, 735n, 742n
Johnson, S. 34, 77, 397, 476, 476, 480, 640, 697, 704n, 752n, 759n
joy (*prāmodya*) 21, 160, 378, 509, 510, 573, 627, 753n, 755n; *see also* delight
joy, sympathetic, *see muditā*
Judaism 42, 53, 54, 134, 135, 248, 250, 593, 594
Jung, C. G. xiv, 72, 93, 117–18, 172, 366, 508, 699, 760n
  and alchemy 184–5, 718n
  and archetypes, *see* archetypes
  collective unconscious 176
  and dreams 199
  and individuation process, *see* individuation process
  and mandalas 218, 721n
  and psychological types 271, 273–5, 281–2, 283, 724n; *see also* extroversion, introversion
  and the *Tibetan Book of the Dead* 197

Kachu Rimpoche 298, 440–3, 725n
  and Jamyang Khyentse Rimpoche 440, 442
Kadam school or Kadampa tradition 577, 578–9, 594
Kagyu school or Kagyupa tradition 14, 64, 298, 440, 611, 734n
Kalimpong 2, 34, 91, 96, 136, 180, 196, 235–6, 299, 385, 434, 447, 494, 635–6, 704n
  Sangharakshita's arrival in 430, 684
  Sangharakshita's teachers in 431, 432, 436–7, 441, 442, 443–4, 446–7, 449, 452, 459, 659, 684
  Sangharakshita's vihara in, *see* Triyana Vardhana Vihara
kalyāṇa mitras 202–3, 421, 557; *see also* spiritual friends
kalyāṇa mitratā 381–2, 386, 540–1, 633, 638–9; *see also* spiritual friendship
kalyāṇa mitra yoga 591, 702n; *see also guru yoga*
Kalyanaprabha 693
kāmachanda 550, 560; *see also* craving
Kamalashila 378–9, 631
kāmaloka 147, 370, 558–60
kammaṭṭhānas, forty 280, 607, 724n
Kangyur 64
Kanheri Caves 184, 718n
Kant, I. 45, 695
Kapilavastu 183, 338, 553
Kapleau, P. 516–17
karma 155–6, 250, 442, 464, 512, 616
  and *bardo* experiences 205
  and *cetanā* or will 537–8, 743n
  and *cittas* 146–7
  formations, *see saṃskāras*
  law of 146
  wrong views about 616, 757n
Karmalingpa, Rinchen 197
karuṇā 24, 381, 457, 459, 577, 605, 612; *see also* compassion
karuṇā bhāvanā 651
Karunadevi 492
Karuna Trust 482, 731n, 734n; *see also* Aid For India
Kasauli 545, 553, 652
Kashyap, Jagdish (Kashyapji) 427–31, 448, 684, 733n
kāyas, three, *see* Buddha, bodies of
Keats, J. 32, 78, 418, 698, 759n
Keffolds 426, 651
Kerouac, J. 654
Kevaddha 97–8
Kevaddha Sutta 749–50n
Khantipālo 635–7, 647–8, 705n, 751n, 753n
Kierkegaard, S. 251–2, 723n
kindness 404; *see also mettā*
Kingsway Hall xiv, 366
Kipling, R. 130, 527, 713n, 742n
Kisāgotamī 537, 743n
kliṣṭa-mano-vijñāna 174–5
knowledge
  of destruction of *āsravas* (*āsravakṣayajñāna*) 164
  'intellectual,' about the Buddha 536
  noble (*āryajñāna*) 559–60
  and vision... (*yathābhūta-jñānadarśana*) 163–4
knowledges, five, *see* wisdoms, five
Know Your Mind 715n, 743n
koans 230, 495
Koliyans 338, 340, 343, 349–50, 357
Koran 54, 233, 593
Kovida 631
Krishnamurti, followers of 320, 503
kriyāyogayāna 296–7

kṣānti, *see* forbearance, patience, tolerance
Kshatriyas (Pāli Khattiyas) 50, 131, 239, 278, 521, 522
Kulananda 631
Kumārajīva 509
kuṇḍalinī (*caṇḍālī*) 190
Kurukullā 448, 450, 735n
Kusinara 302, 357, 434, 466, 684

ladder 12, 185–6
 Jacob's 185
laity 80, 81, 123–4, 389; *see also* householders, laymen or lay people
 and monks xii, 123–7, 388–9, 429, 665
lakṣaṇas 754–5n
Lalitavistara Sūtra 109, 182, 187, 712n, 714n, 718n, 719n
Lama, Panchen 12, 16–17, 702n
Lama Dance 438
lamas 12–20, 202, 437, 440, 443, 660
 Gelug 299
 incarnate (*tulkus*) 12, 16, 431–2, 436, 438, 440, 442, 444, 447, 448, 656, 688
 Nyingma 298–9
 women as 16, 702n
language 117–18
 Buddhist use of Hindu 241, 250
 of concepts 179–80, 211, 503
 English 241
 and ethnic and universal religion 250
 Going Forth from 556–7
 of images, myth and parables 102–3, 105–11, 179–80, 209, 211, 503, 508
 learning a foreign 556–7
 limitations of 655
 literal and metaphorical 523
 monastic 123
 and propagating the Dharma 456, 476, 585
 secular 117
 of spiritual development, misuse of 478
Laṅkāvatāra Sūtra 168, 170, 173–4, 176, 210, 668, 717n
Larkin, P. 698, 760n
law-giver, *see Manu*
Lawrence, D. H. 698
laymen or lay people 14, 126, 389, 577, 713n; *see also* householders, laity
 as bodhisattvas 124
 as 'a third order' 127
legends 131–2, 141, 173, 192, 287–90, 318, 385, 563, 719n; *see also* myth
 banished by Abhidharma 142
 scholars and 110, 169, 287
letters 693–8
Lhalungpa, Lobsang 433, 702n
liberation 157, 197, 198, 202, 203, 204, 206, 528; *see also* emancipation, freedom
 three doors to 739n; *see also samādhis*, three transcendental
liberty, equality, and fraternity 463
life, *bardo* of 198, 199, 206
The Life and Liberation of Padmasambhava 319, 323–4, 332–3, 336, 725n, 727n, 728n
lifestyle 652, 665
 and commitment 388–9, 395, 498, 566
 monastic and lay 167, 498
 regular 381
 and renunciation 479
 simple 125, 555, 636, 670–1
light 172, 175, 181, 188, 515
 in the *bardo* 201–4
 Buddha of, *see* Vairocana
 Buddha of infinite, *see* Amitābha
 of the Buddha Śākyamuni 307–8, 519
 and darkness 215, 220, 278, 307, 354–6, 518–19, 627, 753n
 flame of friendship and inspiration passed like 646, 753n
 Prince of 331
 of vision 335
The Light of Asia 71, 182, 718n
links
 twelve, *see nidānas*, twelve cyclic
 twenty-four, *see nidānas*, twenty-four links
literalism 463
livelihood
 right, *see* right livelihood, team-based right livelihood businesses
 wrong 670, 755n
Lobsang Rampa (C. H. Hoskins) 78, 708n
Locanā 222
Locke, J. 99, 711n
logic 219, 242, 326, 430, 475–6, 655, 754n; *see also* reason
 language of 107–8
Lokajyeṣṭha 529
Lokamitra 482, 487, 490, 632, 736n, 737n
Lokavidu 528; *see also* Buddha

London Buddhist Centre xv, 317, 335, 385, 634, 640, 726n, 727n
building project 640, 726n, 751n
retreats 581
Lotus Born, *see* Padmasambhava
lotuses 184, 215, 218, 231, 288, 317, 502
Buddha's vision of lake of 189, 502, 719n
circle of enclosing mandala 220
FWBO as bed of 462
white (*puṇḍarīka*) 502
love 36, 160, 161, 215, 262, 276, 348, 657; *see also mettā*
and alienated awareness 264
as the Buddha loved 343–4
and courage 518
Dhardo Rimpoche and 453, 457
motto 'radiate love' 457–8, 459
for the Dharma 581–2
for humanity and the world 343, 349, 353
of life and death 99, 195
mode, and power mode 415–16
the principle of 354
loving-kindness, *see also mettā, mettā bhāvanā*, development of universal 467
Luther, M. 114, 564, 618, 713n

Madhyamaka school 28–9, 168, 507
Madhyamaloka 632, 637, 751n
madness of worldlings (*pṛthagjanas*) 229, 722n
Magadha 342, 553, 569–70
Maha Bodhi Society 73, 432, 552, 753n
Mahāhatthipadopama Sutta 755n
mahākaruṇā 605; *see also karuṇā*
Mahākāśyapa 231–2
Mahamati 705n
Mahāpadāna Sutta 714n
mahāparinibbāna 520; *see also parinirvāṇa*
Mahāparinibbāna Sutta 412, 466, 519, 520, 678, 712n, 717n, 732n, 736n, 755n, 756n
Mahāparinirvāṇa Sūtra 109
Mahāprajāpatī Gautamī 393, 730n
Mahāsaccaka Sutta 717n
Mahāsāṃghikas 567
Mahāsatipaṭṭhāna Sutta 751n
mahāsiddhas, eighty-four 565
Mahāvastu 109, 181–2, 183, 712n, 714n, 718n, 744n, 757n
Mahavihara, Dapodi, Pune 490, 737n
Mahāvīra, and Jainism 53
Mahāvīra, title of the Buddha 529; *see also* Buddha
Mahāyāna 15–17, 64, 100, 116, 167, 219, 515, 565, 711n, 741n, 747n
Atiśa and 565, 567, 569, 576
and the bodhisattva ideal, *see* bodhisattva, ideal
lama in 20
and the language of myth 110–11, 142, 166
meditation, Yogi Chen and 636
and the Perfection of Wisdom, *see* perfection of wisdom
schools, *see* Madhyamaka, Yogācāra, Zen
Vasubandhu and 143
Mahāyāna Sūtrālaṃkāra Kārikā 578
Mahāyāna *sūtras* 63, 110–11, 168, 182, 211, 228, 231, 368, 369, 382, 500–1, 503, 531; *see also* Perfection of Wisdom *sūtras*, and individual *sūtras*
and bodhisattva ideal 600
and imagination 472, 501
like transcendental science fiction 503
translation into English 70, 706n
vaipulya 210, 500
mahāyogayāna 297
Maitreya (Pāli Metteyya) 28, 181, 562, 692, 703n, 747n
Maitreya, (or Maitreyanātha) 168–9
Five Books of 169
Majjhima Nikāya 162, 368, 548, 606, 620, 714n, 715n, 717n, 723n, 737n, 740n, 744n, 746n, 748n, 749n, 750n, 755n, 757n
Malalasekera, G. P. 126, 713n
Malaysia 367
Māmakī 222
manas 174–7, 218, 320, 559–60; *see also* mind
Manchester Buddhist Centre 533–4, 539, 543, 544, 663, 743n
mandala 172, 211–23, 665
of the five Buddhas 177, 180–1, 204, 211, 212–17, 219, 221–2, 297
of friendship 646
Jung and 218, 721n
offering practice (*mūla yoga*) 20
Order and centres as 400, 486
personal 372, 488, 679
as quincunx 218, 721n
Mandāravā 289
Mangalo, Bhikkhu 80, 709n

Mañjughoṣa 415, 575–6, 638
initiation of Sangharakshita 438
Mañjuśrī 229, 453, 507
Manjusvara 754n
Manjuvajra 426, 543
manners 403–4, 459, 486–7
Manning, H. E. 228, 721n
mano-vijñāna 174–5, 177
mantras 287, 297, 576
Avalokiteśvara 96, 502
ordination and 499
Vajrasattva 20, 438–9
Mantrayāna 576; *see also* Vajrayāna
Manu 319–21, 334
Māra 110, 164, 186–8, 190–1, 192, 213, 327, 505, 719n
language of 456
māras, assembly of 521, 523, 526
Marcus Aurelius 134, 406
Marpa 18–19
marriage 14, 243, 244; *see also* weddings
in alchemy 185
The Marriage of Heaven and Hell 29, 644–5, 646, 703n, 752n
Marxism 242, 277, 593, 595, 616
Mātaraṃgara 329–31
materialism 455, 598, 654, 656, 689
matter, and spirit (*prakṛti*) and (*puruṣa*) 278
Matthew, Saint, Gospel According to 249, 523, 723n, 742n
Maudgalyāyana 357, 511
meditation 262, 466–7, 529, 566, 610, 637–8, 644, 645; *see also samādhi*
and alienated awareness 267–8
archetypal world and 192, 559; *see also rūpaloka*
bardo of (*Dhyāna Bardo*) 198, 200, 206, 207
and beginner's mind, *see* beginner's mind
at the Buddhist Society 682–3
classes 138, 366–7, 396, 653, 664
at Sakura 365, 650
in cremation grounds 289, 324
as a daily solitary retreat 474–5
and death 201
on death 195
decomposition of a corpse 280, 639, 692, 751n
and devotion 24
and dream state 199
effort in 162–3, 178, 537
esoteric (Vajrayāna) 116, 167, 288, 296–8; *see also kuṇḍalinī*, *tummo*, *phowa*
and ethics 566
and fear 620
four foundation yogas, *see mūla yogas*
FWBO teaching 467, 469, 495–6, 650–1
and going forth 555
and higher planes 147, 151, 168–9, 370; *see also devalokas*, *dhyānas*
and imagination 472, 638
inspiration from 169, 298–9, 441, 555; *see also* visions
kasiṇa exercises 615, 749n
mettā bhāvanā, *see mettā bhāvanā*
mindfulness, *see* mindfulness of breathing
and motivation 382
and ordination into WBO 500
pāramitā 188, 296
recollection practices, *see* recollection
retreats 162–3, 377, 626
right or perfect (*samyag-samādhi*) 27
sādhana practice, *see sādhana* practice
six element practice 467, 661, 755n
subjects, forty (*kammaṭṭhānas*) 280, 607, 724n
and temperament 280–1
as third level of wisdom (*bhāvanā-mayī-prajñā*) 515, 541
'Transcendental Meditation' 645
usefulness of Abhidharma in 149
and visualization, *see* visualization
as work 607
Yogācāra and 168, 172, 175
Yogi Chen and 444, 636, 751n
and Zen 230
Mehta, D. 692, 758n
mental states, or events 144–9, 715n; *see also citta*
friendship as 638–9
preoccupation with own 465
skilful, unskilful and neutral (*kuśala*, *akuśala* and *avyākata*) 146, 148–9, 151, 267, 291, 315, 356, 359, 638, 716n
Merton, T. 437, 494, 734n
metaphysics 7, 46, 57, 93, 98, 106, 171, 215, 291, 293, 366
Berkeley and 708n
Enlightenment and 186
and literalism 276
Mahāyāna and 64, 116, 167–8
middle way in 387

metaphysics (*cont.*)
and no-self 268
One Mind and 173, 176
plane, level or dimension of 9, 59, 171, 184, 234
mettā (Sanskrit *maitrī*) 24–5, 392, 457, 512, 638, 724n; *see also* love
Anuruddha and 606
and communicating the Dharma 381
and compassion (*karuṇā*) 381, 457, 459, 577, 612–13
directing to whole sangha 680
and the environment 409
and mindfulness, balancing 24, 496
mettā (Sanskrit *maitrī*) *bhāvanā* 25, 280, 348, 382, 422–3, 467, 495–6, 555, 650–1, 664
and world peace 348
Michelangelo 392, 393, 645
middle way 168, 359, 620, 690
FWBO ways of practising the 387–95
vajrāsana and the 188
The Middle Way magazine 59, 73
Milarepa 18–19, 72, 182, 368, 433, 511, 539, 668, 702n
Millais, J. E. 643, 752n
millennium 591–2, 746–7n
Milton, J. 392, 418, 672, 705n, 736n
mind 138, 139–40, 466–7; *see also* *citta*, *manas*
absolute or universal 86
archetypes as phenomena of 204–5, 207
creative 641; *see also* creativity
devouring and prolific 644–6, 752n
direct pointing to 231, 233
freedom of (*ceto-vimukti*) 164
functions (*caitta* or *caitasika*) 144–6
going forth in respect of 558–60
intellectual aspect of 536–8
mandala as picture of 219
'One Mind' 170–1, 173, 176, 177–8, 201–2, 230, 294, 298; *see also* Yogācāra school
precepts 553
as a process not a thing 99
reactive and anti-creative 154–5, 157–8, 641, 643–4, 646
reducing input 473–5
as sixth sense 155, 174–5
three aspects of 536, 537–8; *see also* emotions, intellect, will
mind consciousness, *see also* *mano-vijñāna*
afflicted (*manas*) *see* *kliṣṭa-mano-vijñāna*
mindfulness 25, 65, 90, 100, 148, 246, 251, 261, 283, 403; *see also* awareness
and alienation 266–7, 496
of the body 586, 650
of breathing 555
Confucianism and 247
Dhardo Rimpoche and 433–4, 459
in dream states 199–200
and eating 557
four foundations of 466, 650–1
lack of 382
and *mettā*
balancing 24, 496
Buddha's last words on 680
or recollection, of death 195, 280, 724n
when giving Dharma talks 585–6, 588
mindfulness of breathing (*ānāpānasati*) 25, 280, 382, 422, 423, 467, 495–6, 566, 650–1, 664
Mind Only doctrine (*citta-mātra*) 170–3; *see also* One Mind
'Mind – Reactive and Creative' xi, 641, 752n
Minhaj-i-Siraj 243, 723n
The Miracle of Mindfulness 403, 731n
miracles 403, 543, 618–19, 718n
true or greatest 619, 627, 750n
twin, of the Buddha 183–5, 619, 718n, 749n; *see also* Buddha, supernormal powers
missionaries 3, 46, 94, 119, 136–7, 252, 622, 706n
Buddhist 119
Missoula 492
(Rocky Mountain) Buddhist Center 733n
mitra, meaning of word 457
Mitra convenors 558
Mitras 312, 372, 374–5, 376, 381–3, 389–90, 595, 664, 679
guidelines for becoming 312, 727n
Order members and 416–17
Mohammed 53–4, 134, 140, 249, 593, 681
Moksananda 631
Mokshapriya 544
monastic code, *see* Vinaya
monasticism 123, 237–8, 240, 242, 299, 395, 666
Hīnayāna and 167

money 18, 334, 407, 479–80, 514, 531, 554, 617, 654, 694–5, 729n
team-based right livelihood businesses and 607–8, 609, 670
monk, and umbrella story 260–1, 723n
monks, *see also bhikkhus*
English Buddhist 80
and laity xii, 123–7, 388–9, 429, 665
Vietnamese, self-immolation of 9, 702n
wandering (*parivrājakas*) 237
Monmouth Street 365, 367, 375, 386, 543, 650, 729n; *see also* Sakura
moon 292, 296, 642, 745n
Buddha and monks meeting at full 676
and Buddhist celebrations 119–20, 237
Moore, G. 696, 758n
morality 406, 732n; *see also* ethics, precepts
moral rules, as a fetter (*śīlavrata-parāmarśa*) 27–8
More, T. 77, 355, 728n
Morris, W. 355, 729n, 752n
A Moseley Miscellany 702n, 728n, 746n
Mother Erda 188, 719n
motivation xvii, 379, 381–2, 652
'the Movement' 374–5; *see also* FWBO, Triratna Buddhist Community
Moving Against the Stream 634, 701n, 707n, 713n, 735n
Mozart, W. A. 557–8
Mucalinda 110, 189–91
muditā 24
muditā bhāvanā 651
mudrās 212; *see also* gestures
earth-touching (*bhūmisparśa*) 188, 213
of fearlessness (*abhaya*) 216
four Dharma 297, 656–8, 754–5n
mandala offering 20
of meditation (*dhyāna*) 215, 288
of supreme giving (*varada*) 214
wheel-turning (*dharmacakrapravartana*) 212
mūla yogas 19–20, 441
Müller, M. 70, 706n
Mumbai, *see* Bombay
Murry, J. Middleton 87, 710n
music 106, 393, 558, 637, 645, 672, 673, 676, 731n, 736n
and experiencing the *rūpaloka* 559
learning to listen to 260
lectures compared to xii, 83
and *prīti* 161
Sangharakshita and 632, 643
Muslims 53, 242, 245, 477, 564, 569, 736n
mystical experiences 151, 153, 202, 394
mysticism 78, 103, 515, 692, 711n, 741n
myth 106–11, 179–83, 211, 220, 254, 287, 325, 368, 418, 503, 559
language of, *see* language, of images, myth and parables
of the Order 472; *see also under* Avalokiteśvara
mythological framework, and principle 523

Nagabodhi 379, 631
Nāgārjuna 29, 168, 182, 562–3, 569
nāgas 189–90, 318, 323, 330, 716n
king of the, *see* Mucalinda
princess 562
Nagpur 364, 691, 737n
nairātmya 457; *see also* self, no-
Nālandā 219, 238, 242–3, 290, 317, 318, 430, 733n, 745n
crest 317, 335, 336
Nalanda Pāli Institute 430, 733n
nāma-rūpa 155–6, 536, 646
Nanda 614–15
Narain, Professor 430–1, 733n
nationalism 310, 342–3, 353
nature 46, 84, 260
alienation from 217
Daoism and 247
worship 53
Nebesky-Wojkowitz, R. de 435, 734n
Neoplatonism 12, 739n
Nepal 95, 239, 290, 303, 338, 436, 536, 574, 637
New Kadampa school 579; *see also* Gelug school
Newman, J. H. (Cardinal) 519, 741n
The New Reformation? 6, 8, 114–15, 118, 120, 128, 701n
Nichiren school 64
Nidānakathā 182, 714n, 718n
nidānas, see also conditionality
twelve cyclic 155–7, 197–8, 291, 293, 296, 356, 646
twelve positive 158–65, 197; *see also* spiral path
twenty-four links 322, 548
Nietzsche and Buddhism 550, 744n

nihilism 689, 744n; *see also* annihilationism
Buddhism accused of 103, 618
nirmāṇakāya 335; *see also* Buddha, bodies of; *rūpakāya*
Nirvāṇa (Pāli *Nibbāna*) 89, 121–2, 167, 370, 530, 549, 657; *see also* Enlightenment, the Unconditioned
and God 56
gravitational pull of 163
as only unconditioned *dharma* 144, 163
renunciation of by bodhisattvas 9, 15–16, 147, 551
niyamas, five 547–8, 743–4n
Noble Eightfold Path 26–7, 33, 98, 107–8, 135, 228, 322, 466, 542, 605, 607, 616, 664, 670
Sangharakshita's lectures on 259, 366–7, 712n, 723n, 729n, 739n
noble quest or search, *see ariyapariyesenā*
non-duality 9, 30; *see also* subject-object dualism; *śūnyatā*
non-returner 27–8, 107–8, 229
non-violence xvii, 346, 349, 353–5, 357, 361, 409
no return, point of 88, 253, 372, 627; *see also* Stream Entry
'normative' 112, 150–1
Norwich Buddhist Centre 309, 726n
no-self, *see* self, no-
Novalis 688
nuclear disarmament 345
nuclear war or holocaust 338–41, 343–7, 349–57, 359, 361–2, 401, 408
opportunity represented by 360–1
nuclear weapons 104, 340, 341, 347–8, 353–4, 356, 361
abolition of 341, 344–8, 353–4, 360
nuns (*bhikkhunīs* (Sanskrit *bhikṣuṇīs*)) 231, 373, 376, 388, 389, 440, 667, 743n
The Nyingma School of Tibetan Buddhism: Its Fundamentals and History 443, 450, 735n
Nyingma school or Nyingmapa tradition 14, 64, 196, 210, 288, 295, 298–300, 318–19, 440, 443, 450, 500, 720n, 734n, 735n
Sangharakshita's teachers and 432, 436–7, 440, 442, 443, 735n
nymphs, Nanda and the 615
oṃ maṇi padme hūṃ 96, 502
once-returner 27–8, 107, 229
One Mind 170–1, 173, 176, 177–8, 201–2, 230, 294, 298; *see also* Yogācāra school
opposites, *see also* subject–object dualism
in Jungian psychological types 274
reaction between 21–2, 153–4, 198, 344, 547–8, 718n, 728n
union, integration or transcending of 29, 184–6, 216, 359, 619, 718n
vertically arranged 22
Order, *see also* Western Buddhist Order, Triratna Buddhist Order
in India 482, 636; *see also* Trailokya Bauddha Mahasangha
Order members 374–5, 378, 389–90, 400, 512, 535, 552, 580, 595, 664, 733n, 754n; *see also dharmacāris* and *dharmacāriṇīs*, Western Buddhist Order
and contact with Sangharakshita 411–12
and Dhardo Rimpoche 432, 435, 458–9
fifteen points for 411–23, 473–91
and FWBO centres 415, 470–1, 484, 485, 534
and Mitras 416–17
moving abroad to communicate the Dharma 554, 556
and *sādhana* practice, *see sādhana* practice
senior 398, 481, 597, 663, 686
two who lived for the Dharma 573–4
women 376, 402, 731n; *see also dharmacāriṇīs*; ordination, into WBO, of women
ordination 485
bhikkhu (Sanskrit *bhikṣu*) or monastic xv, 13, 15, 371, 426, 447, 596, 737n
bodhisattva 17, 371, 373, 435, 452
of first Tibetans 292
into WBO 399, 498–500, 554, 597, 661; *see also* Going for Refuge to the Three Jewels, effective
in America 492
ceremony 376, 498–9, 597
first 367–8, 371, 754n
four grades of 371
and giving of new name 499
in India, *see* Trailokya Bauddha Mahasangha (TBM), ordinations into

only one 371, 373
and post-ordination process 419–21
private 367, 498–9
public 367–8, 371, 499, 597
retreats 376, 378, 398, 411, 418, 419–20, 500, 731n, 738n
Sangharakshita handing on responsibility for 376, 378–9, 381, 398–401, 410, 597, 630, 748n
significance of 371
training process 375–6, 419–21, 491, 499–500, 554, 597, 738n, 744n
of women 375–6, 498, 667, 738n
of Khantipālo 635, 636, 753n
of Sangharakshita xv, 68, 302–3, 426, 435, 452, 494, 684
Origen 513, 526, 740n
Orwell, G. 352, 728n

pacifism 357
Padmaloka 301, 364, 382, 398, 401, 418, 419, 421, 491, 580, 663
Padmasambhava xv, 19, 180, 195–6, 285–300, 317–36, 507, 570, 577, 638, 719n, 720n, 725n, 727n, 728n
Day 317–18, 323, 336
emanations of, *see* Tertöns
emblems of 285–6, 334–5
hidden teachings, *see termas*
'iron birds' prophecy 196, 300, 720n
Sangharakshita and 441, 719n
Padmavajra 597, 631
paganism 253, 254, 255
pain, *see also* suffering
mistaken for pleasure 613, 616
Pain, J. R. 71, 706n, 707n
painting 24, 76–7, 393–4, 581, 637, 641
Palestine 248, 592
Pāli 31
Pāli canon 63, 108, 109, 142, 211, 369, 428–9, 501, 507–8, 520, 619; *see also* Tipiṭaka
Pali Text Society and 70, 706n
Palpa-Tansen 574, 746n
Panchen Lama 12, 16–17, 702n
Pāṇḍaravāsinī 222
Pandit-ji 552
parables 108, 110, 287, 368, 503
blind men and the elephant 102–3, 711n
language of, *see* language, of images, myth and parables
of the rain cloud 508–11, 517
Paramartha 543, 693
Parami 674
pāramitās 188, 458, 576, 599, 605, 664, 740n; *see also* perfections, six
parāvṛtti 174, 176–8, 513
as conversion 174, 717n
parents 390–2, 395, 427
parinibbāna, mahā 520
Parinibbāna Sutta, see Mahāparinibbāna Sutta
parinirvāṇa 302, 322, 357, 756n; *see also mahāparinibbāna*
Parinirvana Day 588
Parrinder, E. 115, 713n
Parsis 691–2, 704n, 757n
path
downward (*niraya*) 475; *see also* views, wrong
eightfold, *see* Noble Eightfold Path
finding one's own 136
middle 27; *see also* middle way
of regular and irregular steps 565–7, 579, 745n
transcendental 27, 315, 538–9
of vision (*darśana-mārga*) 26–7, 29, 107–8, 322, 334, 709n
Path of Purification, see Visuddhimagga
paths, four noble (*ārya-mārgas*) 27–8, 107–8
patience (*kṣānti*) 17, 188, 296, 625, 650, 686; *see also* forbearance, tolerance
patriotism 342–3, 702n
Paul, Saint 523, 695–6
Corinthians 523, 704n, 741n
Payne, F. 71–2, 707n
Payne, M. 704n
peace
and abolition of nuclear weapons 341
world 342, 344, 349, 353–5, 362
perception, *see also samjñā*
inner (*pratyātmagocara*) 173
perceptual situation, eighteen elements (*dhātus*) of 291, 293
perfection of wisdom 28–9
Perfection of Wisdom (Prajñāpāramitā) *sūtras* 31, 72–3, 103–4, 108, 168, 210–11, 503, 561–2, 568, 575, 624; *see also Diamond Sūtra*
perfections, six 17, 213, 296, 459; *see also pāramitās*
Perfect Vision (*samyag-dṛṣṭi* (Pāli *sammā-diṭṭhi*)) 26–7, 472; *see also* insight
and right view 475–6, 616

Persia 53–4, 592
Peter of Greece, Prince 435–6
philosophy 45, 51, 77
'begins with a sense of wonder' 306, 726n
Buddhism and 17, 91, 103–4, 106, 117, 139, 145, 169–70, 503, 515, 551, 587
Graeco-Roman 405–6
and idealism 171
Sāṃkhya 277–8
phowa practice 449, 735n
pilgrimage 430, 568, 664
Platform Sūtra, see Sūtra of Huineng
Plato 32, 45, 51, 77, 283, 306, 369, 406, 463, 592, 701–2n, 726n, 740n
Platonists, Cambridge 77, 708n
pleasure 21, 153–4, 272, 542, 554
pain mistaken for 613, 616
Plotinus 45, 406, 463, 739n
poetry 45, 51, 78, 106, 179, 181–2, 224, 306, 307, 396, 418, 472, 559, 637, 641, 645, 653, 692, 694, 729n, 730–1n, 754n
Atiśa and 575
banished by Abhidharma 142, 166
Sangharakshita and 130, 398, 401, 545, 591, 632, 634, 640, 672–3
in *Shabda* 414
in the *White Lotus Sūtra* 508–9
poisons
five 100, 217
mental, *see āsravas*
three 335; *see also* craving, aversion and delusion; greed, hatred and delusion
Poona, *see* Pune
power
mode, and love mode 415–16
spiritual 20
powers, or strengths, five 466
prajñā, see wisdom
Prajnaloka 447
Prajñāpāramitā, *sūtras, see* Perfection of Wisdom *sūtras*
prajñās, five 222; *see also* Buddhas, female (consorts)
prakṛti 278
praśrabdhi 161
pratītya-samutpāda, see conditioned co-production
pratyekabuddhas (Pāli *paccekabuddhas*) 504–5, 715n, 738n
pratyekabuddhayāna 296, 504
preceptors 15, 17, 292, 302
private 499; *see also* ordination, private
public 490, 597, 631–2; *see also* ordination, public
Preceptors' College and Council of WBO/TBM 491, 597, 631–2, 641, 737n, 748n
precepts 455, 456, 626; *see also* ethics, morality
Atiśa's teachings as 563
bodhisattva (*saṃvaraśīla*) 17, 296, 405, 731n
five 33, 74, 467, 566–7, 587, 660
principles involved 124–5
and Stream Entry 505
ten
Atiśa and 577
śrāmaṇera 296, 302, 303, 731n
upāsaka 291
of WBO 402–3, 467, 485, 499, 553, 567, 667; *anagārikas* and, 373, 731n; and body, speech and mind, 553
Precious Teachers 702n, 725n, 735n, 751n
pride 331
honest or positive 277, 343, 386, 482–3
prison visiting 489, 737n
prīti (Pāli *pīti*) *see* rapture
progress
idea of 464, 593, 594
spritual, *see* spiritual, progress
projection 36, 190–3, 223, 234, 457, 524–5
Prometheus 108
pṛthagjanas, see worldlings
psyche
non-rational or primordial forces of, *see* forces, of the unconscious
traditional Indian divison into four states 685
psychic heat (*tummo*) 297
psychic power 317, 511
four bases of 466
psychoanalysis 92–101, 233–4, 272
psychological
conditioning 262, 283, 467
types 270–84; *see also* character types, temperaments
wholeness xv, 43, 46–9, 57, 63; *see also* integration
psychology xiv, 92, 117–18, 138, 147, 171, 174, 272, 366
analytical, of the Abhidharma xiv, 140, 145, 147, 149

and archetypes 190–2
and Buddhism xiv, 138–40, 150, 155, 179, 194, 291, 656
and higher evolution 87, 280
middle way in 387
of ritual 108
of spiritual development 150–65
and symbols 203–5
psychotherapy 138, 224–8, 230, 231, 232, 233, 234, 723n
pūjā 527; *see also* worship
pujas 24, 295, 311, 312, 336, 368, 413, 434, 455, 456, 651, 671, 676, 678
and experimentation 470–1
Pujas, Sevenfold 160, 367, 405, 471, 537
Puja: The Triratna Book of Buddhist Devotional Texts 743n, 754n
Pundarika xv, 285, 318
Pune (formerly Poona) 242, 364, 490, 636, 691, 736n, 737n
Pure Land school 204, 610, 638, 709–10n; *see also* Shin school
purification 20, 53, 240, 553, 735n
purity 546–7
puruṣa 278, 722n
Pythagoras 406

Quakers 3, 8
Quartermaine 367, 651
quest (*pariyesenā*) 550
ignoble, *see anariyapariyesenā*
noble, *see ariyapariyesenā*
The Questions of King Milinda 756n

racial prejudice xvii, 408–9
Radhakrishnan, S. 62, 143, 705n, 715n
The Rainbow Road from Tooting Broadway to Kalimpong 705n, 712n, 732n, 746n, 753n, 757n
Rajgir 430
Rākṣasas, Land of 290, 318
Ramakrishna, Sri 52, 96, 525
Ramana Maharshi 177–8, 503, 717n
rapture (*prīti*) 21, 154, 160–1, 362, 716n
rationalism 103, 105, 293, 515, 711n
Ratnaguna 632
Ratnaprabha 379
Ratnasambhava 204, 214, 222, 735n
Ray, R. 738n
realism, pluralistic 143
reality 8–9, 212–13, 234; *see also dharmakāya*
absolute or ultimate 9, 25, 48, 49, 86, 88–9, 387, 454, 507, 527, 531
in Christianity 42–3
wisdom of 203
alienation from 204–5
awareness of 89, 259, 262–3
bardo of (*chönyi bardo*) 198, 200, 202–5, 207
clear light of 201–2; *see also dharmakāya*
and hypostasis 507, 739n
levels or planes of 12–13, 169; *see also* consciousness, levels of
deeper 176, 199, 203, 323
and Hermetic correspondence 181, 718n
Madhyamaka view 168
and the mandala 211
and no thought 200
and perception 172
psychotherapy and 227
'seeing according to' 611–17
Yogācāra view 171–2
realization, inner (*pratyātmagocara*) 173, 182, 717n
realms
god, *see devalokas*
hell, *see* hell, torment, or suffering, state of
higher 143, 559; *see also* consciousness, levels of; *arūpaloka*; *devalokas*; *rūpaloka*; heavens
or worlds, six, of wheel of life 155, 203–4, 356
reason 475, 476, 559; *see also* logic
Blake's Urizen as conventional 331–2, 728n
idea of 463
rebirth xvii, 21, 43, 155–6, 176, 197–8, 250, 291, 315, 359, 387, 464, 556, 646, 689–90, 757n; *see also* reincarnation
bardo of 198, 200, 205, 207
the Buddha and 689; *see also* Buddha, previous lives
Confucianism and 516
extreme views about 387, 730n
recollection of previous lives 432, 688–9, 757n
Sangharakshita reflections on 684–5, 687–90, 699
spiritual 174, 202, 220, 227, 249, 317
and young hero 190, 193
of *tulkus*, *see* lamas, incarnate
receptivity 14, 19, 180

recollection 175
of the loathsomeness of food 280
of previous lives 432, 688, 757n
of the ten stages of the decomposition of a corpse 280
reflection (*cinta-mayī-prajñā*) 515, 535, 541–2, 581
reflection, Sangharakshita's practice of, *see* Sangharakshita, and reflection
Reformation 75, 77, 114, 116, 708n
reformation, new 114–27, 701n
Refuge
fourth 17
going for, *see* Going for Refuge to the Three Jewels
'taking' 19, 454, 506, 596, 726n
Refuge Lama, *see* Atiśa
Refuges, *see also* Three Jewels
esoteric 17, 312–15
Refuges and Precepts 301–5
and ordination 15, 302–3, 499
recitation of xv, 40, 301–3, 304–6, 310, 311, 312, 665, 666
Refuge Tree 19, 539
Reich, W. 265, 273, 724n
reincarnation 445; *see also* rebirth
rejoicing in merits 481–3
of Dhardo Rimpoche 459–60
relationships 602–5, 713n
transcendence of subject-object duality in 458, 605–7, 638–9, 704n, 751n
religion 41, 48, 61, 90, 129–30, 282, 721n
choosing 50–2
comparative 3, 51, 70, 94, 248
conventional 44–5, 48, 69, 155
and culture 45, 244, 246, 247
ethnic and universal 42, 54–5, 235–55
and higher evolution 87, 282
humanistic and authoritarian 227–8
irreligious use of 47
as morality, and society, Dr Ambedkar on 406, 732n
necessity of 44–5, 49
non-theistic 7, 10–11, 42, 55–7, 113, 135, 228, 677; *see also* Buddhism, as non-theistic religion
and psychotherapy 226–7
and solitude 82, 709n
teaching of in schools 51–2
and tolerance 136–7, 464; *see also* missionaries
universal, *see* religion, ethnic and universal
Voltaire's critique of 41, 705n
The Religion of Art 730n
religious observances, as fetter (*śīlavrata-parāmarśa*) 27–8
Renaissance 79, 645
renunciation 335, 369–70, 389–90, 395, 479–80, 552
repression 190–1, 192, 217–18, 223, 233–4, 265–6, 268–9, 293, 295, 464
responsibility 377–83, 400, 410, 489; *see also* duties
and rights 603–4
restlessness 471
retreat centres 375, 378, 471, 500, 595, 748n; *see also* Adhisthana, Akashavana, Guhyaloka, Padmaloka, Taraloka, Tiratanaloka, Vajraloka
retreats 125, 364, 554
FWBO 377–8, 581, 680, 743n
first 367, 426, 476, 496, 554, 625, 651, 705n
international 674, 678, 754n
and silence 557
single-sex 377, 402
'Wolf at the Door' 754n
long 552, 680
meditation 162–3, 626
ordination, *see* ordination, into WBO, retreats
rainy season 125, 236–7, 466
solitary 367–8, 381, 414, 418–19, 455, 474, 478, 680
reverence 13, 14
Revill, W. 128, 713n
Rhys Davids, C. A. F. 744n
Rhys Davids, T. W. 70, 706n, 744n
Richardson, S. 697, 759n
right livelihood 27, 135, 407, 455, 607, 619, 670
FWBO businesses, *see* team-based right livelihood businesses
rights and duties, or responsibilities 603–4
right speech, *see* speech, right
right view (*samyag-dṛṣṭi* (Pāli *sammā-diṭṭhi*)) 475–6, 616; *see also* Perfect Vision
Rig Veda 70, 722n
Rinchen Karmalingpa 197
Rinchen Terdzö 196, 299–300, 719n
Rinchen Zangpo 574–6
ritual 57, 78, 106, 108, 182, 449, 472, 664; *see also* ceremonies, pujas
ordination as 597; *see also* ordination ceremonies

in Tibetan Buddhism (Tantric) 64, 116, 167, 296–7, 565, 567, 570
Ritual and Devotion in Buddhism 712n
robes xii, xiii, 78, 126, 127, 279, 429, 436, 523–5; *see also* Western Buddhist Order, kesas
Rocky Mountain Buddhist Center 733n
Rohiṇī incident 339–41, 349–50
significance of 344, 349, 361
Root Verses of the Six Bardos 206–8; *see also The Tibetan Book of the Dead*
Rost, E. R. 706n
Rudra, *see* Tarpa Nagpo
Rumi, Jalal al-Din 645
rūpa 144, 145, 217, 536, 559
rūpakāya 506–7, 739n; *see also* Buddha, bodies of; *nirmāṇakāya*
rūpaloka 147, 170, 205, 370, 558–60
Rushdie, S. 477, 736n
Ruskin, J. 581

Sacred Books of the East 706n
Saddharma Laṅkāvatāra Sūtra, see Laṅkāvatāra Sūtra
Saddharma Puṇḍarīka Sūtra, see White Lotus Sūtra
sādhana practice 417–18, 555, 576, 638, 640, 660; *see also* visualization practice
sadhus 133, 546, 551
Sagaramati (Robert Morrison) 550, 744n
Sakura 364–7, 396; *see also* Monmouth Street
Śākyamuni 318–19, 327, 507, 512, 575, 578; *see also* Buddha
visualization 537
Śākyans 338, 340, 341, 343, 349–50, 352, 357, 361, 362
Sakya school or Sakyapa tradition 64, 298, 437, 611, 734n
samādhi 17, 148, 207, 604, 647; *see also* concentration, meditation
Perfect 739n
samādhis, three (transcendental) 505–6, 739n
Sāmaññaphala Sutta 309, 387, 726n, 730n, 756n, 757n
sambhogakāya 335, 507; *see also* Buddha, bodies of
Saṃdhinirmocana Sūtra 168
Samding Dorje Phagmo 16, 702n
sameness, wisdom or knowledge of 214–15, 297
saṃgrahavastus, four 664
samjñā 144, 171–2, 175, 217, 559
Sāṃkhya philosophy 277–8
Sampasādanīya Sutta 710n
saṃsāra 16, 21–2, 158, 394, 454, 522, 593–4; *see also* existence, conditioned or phenomenal
gravitational pull of 163, 253, 644
saṃskāras 22, 144–5, 155–6, 646, 684; *see also* idols, four
samyak sambodhi 151, 504; *see also* Enlightenment
samyak sambuddha 504–5
Samye monastery 292, 294–5, 317–18, 577, 725n
Saṃyutta Nikāya 25, 189, 212, 423, 514, 519, 702n, 716n, 719n, 720n, 732n, 741n
Maggasaṃyutta 740n
Mahāvagga 703n
Nidānasaṃyutta 715n
Saccasaṃyutta 703n, 738n
San Francisco Buddhist Center 492
San Francisco Zen Center 492, 506, 737–8n
Sangha 63, 134, 160, 538–41, 622; *see also* spiritual community
āryas, and non-*āryas* 229, 538–9, 600
caring for the sick 536–7
and caste 521
effect of experiencing 308–10, 421, 457, 624–5, 669
founding of 294–5
and Going for Refuge 69
importance of gathering in assemblies, large numbers 675–6, 732n
need for continuity alongside development 677–8
as Refuge 371
Refuge, esoteric 313–15
true, *see* Āryasaṅgha
unity of 412, 456–7, 675–6, 732n
four means of *saṃgrahavastus* 664
Sanghadevi 597, 631, 632
Sangharakshita 684, 758n
and Buddhism 59, 301–5, 377, 552, 611, 624, 669, 681–5
disciples 438–9, 495, 545, 660, 735n; *see also* Order members
Dhardo Rimpoche and 458–9
dreams 685–7
early life 493, 546, 681–3
experience in the army 416, 732n
experience of Going for Refuge 301–5, 552

Sangharakshita (*cont.*)
and friendship 68, 320–1, 333, 364, 416, 438, 635, 640–1, 662, 682, 683, 691–3, 704n
and the FWBO/Triratna, *see* FWBO, Sangharakshita and
Going Forth 545–6, 553, 652–3
handing on responsibilities 367, 376–9, 381, 383–4, 397–401, 410, 481, 490–1, 597–8, 600, 630–2, 641, 686, 748n
in India 302–4, 377, 387, 407, 426, 494–5, 508, 519, 534, 552, 561, 589, 610, 634, 651, 683–4, 691, 693, 704n; *see also* Kalimpong; Sangharakshita, Going Forth
decision to leave 364
dreams and visions in 683, 685
with ex-Untouchables 235, 319–20, 364, 495, 526, 587, 636, 684, 736–7n, 751n
return visits 364, 449
initiations 440, 443, 449, 684
Amitābha and *phowa* practice 449, 450, 735n
four, with Jamyang Khyentse Rimpoche 438
Green Tārā 436, 438, 659–60, 661
Jambhala and Kurukullā 448–9, 450
Mañjughoṣa 438
Padmasambhava 441
White Tārā 435, 662
insomnia 686
and lectures and talks xvi–xvii, 83, 363, 366–7, 446, 473, 526, 533–4, 545, 561, 583–4
'Legends' about 385
literary work 379, 397–8, 407, 491, 494, 632, 634, 693, 698, 704n
loss of sight 634, 649, 674, 750n
ordination of xv, 68, 302–3, 426, 435, 452, 494, 684
personality self-assessment xvii–xviii, 512, 640–1
and poetry 398, 545, 591, 632, 634, 640, 672–3
referred to as 'Bhante' 423, 487
and reflection 535, 581, 637, 640, 674, 685
reflections on rebirth 684–5, 687–90, 699
and robes 523–4, 525, 546, 652, 683
sādhanas 640; *see also under* Sangharakshita, initiations
seminars 367, 398, 535, 731n, 742n
teachers 364, 426–60, 492, 494–5, 500, 661, 683, 686; *see also* individual teachers
visions of
Amitābha 683, 718n
Vajrasattva mantra and 'the man in the pit' 438–9, 683–4, 735n
at Yale 656, 754n
Sangharakshita: A New Voice in the Buddhist Tradition 535, 742n
Saṅgīti Sutta 740n, 743n
Śaṅkara (Śaṅkarācārya) 7, 51, 701n
Śāntarakṣita 136, 290–4, 317–18, 570, 577, 714n, 725n
Śāntideva 563, 569, 578, 638, 668, 751n
Sarada Devi 525
Saramati (Alan Sponberg) 431, 492, 733n
Sarasvatī 453
Śāriputra 143, 357, 464, 511, 522, 541–2, 736n, 743n
Sarnath 212, 431, 610, 684
Sartre, J. P. 602
Sarvāstivāda 63, 167, 200, 289, 505
Abhidharma Piṭaka 142–6, 148
śāstras 454, 456, 578
Satan 186, 191, 523; *see also* devils
salvation of 513, 526, 740n
Satyapriya, *see* Buddharakshita
Schiller, F. 695, 758n
Schopenhauer, A. 45, 79, 615, 709n, 749n
science 84, 464
and Buddhism 56, 104–5, 117
and evolution 87
scientific approach, limitations of 110
Scott, W. 697, 759n
Seattle 492
seeds
planted by Sangharakshita 401
Yogācāra, of spiritual potential 176–8, 512–13
self 149, 616
being one's 584–5
empirical 173, 175–6, 178
higher 191, 220–1, 614
new 191, 193, 219, 554; *see also* spiritual rebirth
no- (*anattā* doctrine) 62, 267, 296, 428–9, 587, 657, 665
and other 547, 559, 600, 604–5; *see also* subject-object dualism
three levels of non-experience of 265–6
self-acceptance 480–1, 487

self-analysis 281, 698
self-awareness or knowledge 46–7, 69, 100, 258, 260–1, 281, 284, 461–2
self-centredness 160, 333, 405, 609
self-consciousness 46, 88, 90, 263, 282
self-help 135–6
selfhood
and Blake's Spectre 727n
no permanent, unchanging 547, 612–13, 616
self-indulgence 387, 480, 620
self-transcendence 9, 86
mutual, and communication 37, 458, 638, 751n
self-view, fixed (*satkāya-dṛṣṭi*) 27–8
Semele 523, 741–2n
Seneca 406
sensation
in Buddhist sense, *see vedanā*
in Jungian sense 273–4, 275, 281
sense-discriminating awarenesses, five (*vijñānas*) 174–6
sense organs (*ṣaḍāyatanas*) 155–6
senses, sense organs and consciousnesses, *see dhātus*, eighteen
sensuous experience (*kāma*) 99, 550, 559; *see also* desire
or desire
poison of (*kāmāsrava*) 164
world of (*kāmaloka*) 147, 170, 370
sermons 519–20
serpents, *see nāgas*
sex 160, 193, 254, 265, 283, 559, 570
abstention from, *see anagārikas*, celibacy
tantra and 298, 436
sexual
development, Freud and 272, 724n
relationships 458, 478, 487–8
symbolism 221–2
Shabda 413–14, 477, 482, 491, 736n
shadow 190, 192–3, 223; *see also* forces, of the unconscious
Shakespeare, W. 76, 78, 84, 241, 344, 392, 418, 463, 645, 672, 709n, 723n, 728n, 735n, 736n
Shantavira 693
Shastri, L. B. 79, 709n
Sheffield Buddhist Centre 681
Sheldon, W. 281, 724n
Shelley, P. B. 78, 418, 672, 755n
Sherab Ngawang 447
Shingon sect 212
Shin school 64, 65, 86; *see also* Pure Land school
Shinto 53–4, 94, 248, 250
shrine-rooms 309, 533, 541, 743n, 754n
shrines 303, 334, 365, 366, 462, 485, 660, 661, 662
Shudras 50, 239, 278
sickness 132, 228–9, 548–9
Siddhārtha 131–3, 186–8, 548, 551, 552, 681, 744n; *see also* Buddha
Sigālaka Sutta (or *Sigālovāda Sutta*) 603, 713n, 748n
signless *samādhi* 505–6; *see also samādhis*, three
Sikhism 54, 428
Sikkim 440, 442
Maharaja of 196, 440, 442
Śikṣāsamuccaya 578
śīla, *see* ethics, morality
silence 37, 157, 231–2, 557–8, 560, 651, 676
Singapore 377, 494, 495, 534, 683
Singh, J. 515, 741n
singing, choral 558
single-sex activities 283, 377, 402
Sinhadevi 486, 737n
Sitātapatrā 575
Sivaraksa, S. 516
six distinctive emphases of FWBO xvi, 596, 663–73
six element practice 467, 661, 755n
skandhas, five 144–5, 217
skilful means (*upāyakauśalyas*) 217, 615
skilfulness and unskilfulness 481, 553; *see also* ethics
skull cups 285, 334–5
sky 294
Smaragdine Tablet 181, 718n
Snellgrove, D. 104, 711n
society, and morality 406, 732n
Socrates 9, 134, 527, 592, 701–2n, 725–6n
solitary retreats 367–8, 381, 414, 418–19, 455, 474, 478, 680
solitude 82
Solovyov, V. 230, 722n
Soma, Bhikkhu 495
Sona 597, 631, 632
Songtsen Gampo 290
Soothill, W. 509, 739n
soul 33, 44, 226, 230, 387, 439, 524, 557, 698, 739n, 748n, 760n
soul-making, vale of 698, 759n
space, sphere of infinite 222
speech 279, 476

speech (*cont.*)
affectionate, kindly and loving 35–6, 416
going forth in respect of 552–60
harmonious 37
inspired (*udāna*) 306
perfect or right 32–8
precepts 33–7, 403, 541, 553, 566–7
right 27, 31, 33–5, 37, 135–6, 556
and speaking clearly 589–90
useless 33, 703n
Spencer, H. 274, 724n
spiral path 21–2, 154, 159–60, 165, 198, 548, 550–1, 560, 595, 647, 716n; *see also* conditionality, cyclic and spiral; *nidānas*, twelve positive
spirit, and matter (*puruṣa* and *prakṛti*) 278
spiritual 150–1
community 69, 81, 335, 370–1, 400, 465, 558; *see also* Sangha, spiritual group
conflict in 456
and group 321, 456, 468
and individual, *see* individual, and spiritual community
and institutions 468–9
leaving the 315
some people practising more intensively 679–80
development
misusing model of 478–80
and ordination into WBO 500
psychology of 150–65
and renunciation, *see* renunciation
Sangharakshita's teachers, levels of 443
self-centred 404–5
in team-based right livelihood businesses 608–9
energy 14, 336, 600
evolution, *see* evolution
faculties, five (*indriyas*) 25, 65, 283, 466, 702n
friends 370, 382, 478, 484, 573, 679; *see also kalyāṇa mitras*
friendship 381–2, 386, 396, 399, 423, 426, 455, 457–8, 496–7, 608; *see also* friendship, *kalyāṇa mitratā*
FWBO and 457–8, 514, 540, 608, 645–6, 669–70, 671, 675
horizontal 514, 540
Subhuti's talks and book 458, 735n
vertical 382, 514, 540
'the whole of the spiritual life' 514, 669
friendship and Ḍākinī Refuge 314
group 68–9, 680; *see also* spiritual community
hierarchy, *see* hierarchy, spiritual
life 67–8, 89–90, 135, 149, 219, 336, 538
central problem of 22–3
as complete turning about, *see parāvṛtti*
and heroism 489–90
as marriage of heaven and hell 29
obstacles and difficulties 623, 654–6
peaks of 25–6
self- and other-regarding attitudes 373
potential, as seeds 176–8, 512–13
power 20
practice 280, 283, 382, 384, 423, 466–7, 558, 609, 671, 754n
in FWBO, *see* FWBO, five pillars of, practices
progress 14–16, 25, 135, 146, 160, 190, 223, 475, 489, 553, 595
lack of 565–6; and 'twentieth blow,' 177–8, 626
quest, *see ariyapariyesenā*, quest
rebirth, *see* rebirth, spiritual
research station 128
teachers 14–15, 17, 18, 20, 160, 191, 193, 202, 371, 514, 525, 603, 730n; *see also gurus*, *kalyāṇa mitras*
transmutation, alchemy as 184–5
wholeness 43, 46–9, 57, 63; *see also* integration
world (*arūpaloka*) 21, 147, 154, 212, 370
Spoken Word Project 534, 731n, 742n
Sponberg, A. (Saramati) 431, 492, 733n
śraddhā 159–60, 625–7; *see also* faith
and suffering 625, 646–7
śrāmaṇera
ordination of Prajnaloka by Sangharakshita 447
ordination of Sangharakshita 302–3, 653, 684
śrāmaṇeras 14, 68, 436, 635
śrāvakas 296, 504; *see also* disciples, of the Buddha
śrāvakayāna 296, 504–5
Śrāvastī 157, 183
Sri Lanka 377, 388, 428–9, 494, 610, 713n; *see also* Ceylon
Srimala 597, 631
śruta-mayī-prajñā 515; *see also* wisdom, three levels of

Stapledon, O. 503, 738n
states, *see also* consciousness, levels of
dhyānic 538; *see also dhyānas*
four, of psyche in Indian tradition 685
higher spiritual 515–16
intermediate 198–200, 202, 206–7; *see also bardos*
Stoics 739n
Stonehenge 254–5
Story, F. 687, 757n
Stream Entry 27, 107–8, 229, 370, 464, 538, 542, 548; *see also* no return, point of
and real going forth and Going for Refuge 315, 372, 552, 599–600
within reach 378, 423
stupas 292, 436, 492, 530, 567, 574
subha, *see* beautiful
Subhuti 378, 379, 419, 421, 475, 597, 631, 632, 705n
talks and books 458, 534, 535, 735n, 742n
subject-object dualism 173–4, 177, 530–1, 547, 604–5, 609, 613–14; *see also* opposites, self and other
going beyond 215–16, 559–60, 613–14; *see also* non-duality
suffering (*dukkha* (Sanskrit *duḥkha*)) 43, 98–9, 121, 159, 228; *see also* pain
and *śraddhā*' 625, 646–7; *see also* spiral path
states of, *see* hell, torment, or suffering, state of
three main kinds of 623–4
and twelve positive *nidānas* 158–9
upside-down views (*viparyāsas*) and 613, 616–17
Sufism 12
Sukhamāla Sutta 713n
Sukhavati 309, 317–18, 474, 640, 726n, 727n
Sukhāvatī-vyūha Sūtra 111
Sullivan, H. S. xiv, 93, 366
Sumatra 289, 567, 568–9
sun 181, 212–13, 215, 222, 292, 384
śūnyatā 9, 296, 387, 457, 458, 542, 651, 665; *see also* void
first two kinds of 163
and One Mind 173
samādhi or door of 505
and wisdom of equality 177
śūnyatāvāda 17
supernormal beings 522, 526; *see also* angels, Brahmās, deities, demons, *devas*, gods, *māras*
Śūraṅgama Sūtra 307
Surata 631
A Survey of Buddhism 259, 433, 684, 723n, 733n
Suryaprabha 739–40n
Sūtra of Forty-two Sections 646, 753n
Sūtra of Golden Light 336, 368, 384, 730n
Sangharakshita's commentary on 728n, 731n
Sūtra of Huineng (or Wei Lang) 59–60, 368, 493, 682
sūtras (Pāli *suttas*) 454, 501; *see also* individual *sūtras/suttas*
Mahāyāna, *see* Mahāyāna *sūtras*
vaipulya 210, 500
sūtra tradition 299
Sutta-Nipāta 368, 668, 727n, 739n
Sutta Piṭaka 142
Suvajra 378, 379, 435, 597, 631, 734n
Suzuki, D. T. 72, 73, 707n, 717n, 720n, 722n, 734n
Suzuki, Shunryū 492, 737n, 738n
Swinburne, A. 188, 719n
symbolism, archetypal, *see* archetypal symbolism
symbols 108, 159, 181; *see also* myths
of integration, *see* mandalas
of, *saṃsāra*, *see* wheel of life
psycho-spiritual 203–5
representing the Buddha 530
of spiritual rebirth, *see* lotuses
of the transcendental, *see vajras*
of transformation or transmutation, *see* cremation grounds, fire

Tagore, R. 195, 645, 719n
Taixu, abbot or Bodhisattva 594
taṇhā (Sanskrit *tṛṣṇā*) 99, 156, 158, 550–1, 623, 646; *see also* craving
Tantra 288, 297–8, 326, 436; *see also* Tantric Buddhism, Vajrayāna
corruption of 570, 576, 577
tantras 209–11, 218–19, 222–3, 575, 577
Tantra Yogācāra 291
Tantric Buddhism 19–20, 191, 432, 702n; *see also* Tantra, Tibetan Buddhism, Vajrayāna
Atiśa and 564, 565, 576–7
Padmasambhava and 295–6
Tantric initiations (Sanskrit *abhiṣekas*, Tibetan *wongkurs*) 17, 18–19, 20, 206, 288, 565

Tantric initiations, of Sangharakshita, *see* Sangharakshita, initiations
Tantric rites, (or functions) 448, 735n
Tārā 375, 507, 576, 578, 638, 661–2
Atiśa and 572–3, 575
cabin at Taraloka 659, 662
different forms of 662
Green 222, 436, 438, 660–2
Sangharakshita and 436, 438, 659–60, 661
Khadiravaṇī 660
and Kurukullā 735n
White 213, 222, 435, 662
Sangharakshita and 435, 662
Taraloka Retreat Centre for women xvi, xviii, 375, 500, 659, 660, 674, 738n, 754n
Tarpa Nagpo (Black Salvation) 325, 331, 333–4
The Taste of Freedom xi, 703n, 717n, 745n
Tathāgata 216, 510, 528; *see also* Buddha
The Tattvasaṃgraha of Shāntarakṣita 136, 291, 293, 617, 714n, 725n
Taylor, J. 519, 741n
TBM, *see* Trailokya Bauddha Mahasangha
TBMSG, *see* Trailokya Bauddha Mahasangha Sahayak Gana
team-based right livelihood businesses 385, 395, 396, 407, 455, 468, 469, 483, 496–7, 543, 595, 607–9, 640, 670–1, 681, 726n, 748n; *see also* FWBO, co-ops
four objectives of 607–9, 670–1
single-sex 402
telepathy 110, 441
television 23, 417, 421, 474, 566
temperaments 271, 280, 511–12, 563, 724n, 739n; *see also* character types, psychological types
temple, FWBO as 462–3
Tengyur 64, 437
Tennyson, A. 355, 394, 729n, 730–1n
Ten Pillars of Buddhism 402–3, 731n
termas 196–7, 296, 299–300, 332–3, 720n, 728n
Tertöns 299, 319, 332–4
Tevijja Sutta 726n
Thailand 63–4, 142
thangkas 453, 562, 580, 672, 683
theology, four kinds of 122–3
Theosophical Society 70–2, 81
theosophy 707n
Theravāda 63, 93, 99, 116, 167, 200, 278, 388, 500, 515, 527, 610–11
independent Abhidharma tradition of 142–6
Thibaw, King 124
Thich Nhat Hanh 403, 731n, 734n
thinking
clear 475–6, 515–16, 617
in Jungian sense 273–4, 281
thoughts, awareness of 261–2, 266
The Three Jewels 186, 719n, 739n, 755n
Three Jewels 63, 159–60, 506; *see also* Buddha, Dharma and Sangha
commitment to 370, 371–2, 374, 388–90, 395, 412, 497–8, 512, 598; *see also* going for Refuge, effective
going for Refuge to, *see* going for Refuge
as unifying factor 456
Three Refuges, *see also* Three Jewels
esoteric forms 17, 312–15
Through Buddhist Eyes 750n
thunderbolts 213, 220, 285; *see also* *vajras*
Tibet 12, 15, 293, 400, 435
invasion by China 434–5
Tibetan Book of the Dead (*Bardo Thödol*) xiv, 72, 195–208, 212, 300, 366, 720n
Tibetan Book of the Great Liberation 286, 725n
Tibetan Buddhism 12, 14–15, 29, 63–4, 93, 228, 242, 296, 433, 610, 656; *see also* Tantric Buddhism, Vajrayāna
Atiśa and 563, 571–2, 574–9
and dancing 437–8
Dhardo Rimpoche and 432, 435
establishment of 290–3
literature 72, 368, 437–8
Padmasambhava and 196, 286–300, 317–18
and reincarnation 442
Rimé tradition 437, 734n
ritual (Tantric) in 64, 116, 167, 296–7, 565, 567, 570
and Śākyamuni Buddha 180–1, 507
schools of 210, 298, 440, 570, 579, 611; *see also* individual schools
Tibetan wheel of life, *see* wheel of life
Tibetan Yoga and Secret Doctrines 72, 298, 725n
Tillich, P. 5, 701n

Tillyard, E. M. W. 76, 708n, 735n
Tipiṭaka 64, 428, 430, 568; *see also* Pāli canon, Tripiṭaka
Tiratanaloka 738n
tolerance (*kṣānti*) 75, 136–7, 464, 677; *see also* forbearance, patience
Tolkien, J. R. R. 332
Tolstoy, L. 392
Trailokya Bauddha Mahasangha (TBM) 370, 482, 498, 597, 737n; *see also* Triratna Buddhist Order, Western Buddhist Order
  ordinations into 312, 376, 378–9
  Preceptors' College and Council of the WBO and 597, 631–2, 748n
Trailokya Bauddha Mahasangha Sahayak Gana (TBMSG) 595, 730n
tranquillity 24, 314, 651; *see also* *upekṣā*
transcendence 9, 322
  of subject-object duality in relationships 458, 605–7, 638–9, 704n, 751n
transcendental
  awareness or consciousness 88–9, 258, 263, 282
  path 27, 315, 538–9
  plane or dimension, the 59, 147, 151, 163, 184, 234, 505
  primitivism 247
  samādhis 505–6, 739n
  the
    represented by *vajra* 186, 220
    in the world 333
transformation
  Padmasambhava as principle of 334–5
  path of (*bhāvanā-mārga*) 26–7, 29, 107, 322, 334
  of self and world 335–6, 394–5, 554
Transforming Self and World 728n, 731n
Transmission of the Lamp of the Dharma 675, 755n
transmutation 185, 220–1
  alchemy as spiritual 184–5
tree
  bodhi, *see* bodhi tree
  FWBO as a 462
  world 185–6
Tricycle 516
tridents 285, 288, 335
Tri-Kāya (*trikāya*) 206; *see also* Buddha, bodies of
Tripiṭaka 63, 142, 210–11, 443, 567; *see also* Tipiṭaka
Triratna
  Buddhist Community 727n, 730n; *see also* FWBO
  Buddhist Order, *see also* Western Buddhist Order (WBO)
    College of Public Preceptors, *see* Preceptors' College
    in India, *see* Trailokya Bauddha Mahasangha
    name change 370, 730n
  Buddhist Shrine and Meditation Centre 366, 543, 650; *see also* Sakura
Trisong Detsen 286, 290
triyāna, *see yānas*, three
Triyana Vardana Vihara 128, 385, 437, 441, 636
tṛṣṇā (Pāli *taṇhā*) 99, 156, 158, 550–1, 623, 646; *see also* craving
Trungpa, C. 494
truth 56, 102–3, 136, 480
  absolute 29, 59
  and beauty 308
  objective 350–2, 361
  relative 7, 29
  two kinds of 182–3
truthful speech, *see* speech
truths, psychological and spiritual 109, 110
Tsongkhapa 298–9, 511, 579
Tucci, G. 196
tulkus, *see* lamas, incarnate
tummo 297
Turner, J. M. W. 76–7, 392, 749n
Turner Prize 615, 749n
turning about (*parāvṛtti*) (in the deepest seat of consciousness) 174, 176–8, 513

ubhayacariyāyogayāna 297
Udāna 102, 158, 164, 189, 306, 368, 521, 578, 615, 668, 711n, 712n, 716n, 717n, 719n, 725n, 741n, 748n
udāna, meaning 306, 725n
Udāna Sangharakshita's commentary 711n, 725n
Udānavarga 578–9
Uḍḍiyāna 288–90, 329, 565
the Unconditioned (*asamskṛta*) 163, 359, 361, 505–6; *see also* Nirvāṇa
the unconscious (mind) 22–3, 99, 106–8, 110, 162, 179–81, 190–1, 194, 325, 464
  collective 176, 293, 323, 331, 333–4, 336, 559

the unconscious (mind) (*cont.*)
Māra and 187; *see also* forces, or energies, primordial or supra-rational
tension with conscious mind 217–18
unconscious mental activity (*viññāṇa-sota*) 99, 710–11n
Unitarians 2–3, 8
'untouchables' 50, 223, 278, 511; *see also* ex-Untouchables
Upanishads 79, 384, 592, 730n
upāsakas and *upāsikās* 14, 312, 371
'*mahā-*' 373
upekṣā 24, 148; *see also* tranquillity
upekṣā bhāvanā 651
Uposatha Sutta 164, 712n, 717n

vaipulya sūtras 210, 500
Vairocana 203, 212–13, 219, 222, 297, 578
Vairocanarakṣita 292
Vaiśālī 228, 466
Vaishyas 50, 239, 278
vajra (Tibetan *dorje*) 186, 213, 220, 286, 288, 334, 335
double 216
Vajracchedikā Sūtra, *see Diamond Sūtra*
Vajradaka 663
Vajraloka Retreat Centre 375
Vajrapāṇi 415
initiation of Sangharakshita 438
vajrāsana 186–7, 220, 574
Vajrasattva, mantra
and death 438–9
and 'the man in the pit' 439, 735n
recitation practice (*mūla yoga*) 20
Vajravārāhī 702n
Vajrayāna 15, 17, 64, 116, 142, 166, 167, 210, 312–13, 565; *see also* Tantric Buddhism, Tibetan Buddhism
Yogi Chen and 443, 444, 448–9, 636
Vajrayoginī 702n
Vangisa 372
Vārāṇasī, *see* Benares
Vasala Sutta 727n
Vasubandhu 78, 143, 563
vedanā 144, 155–8, 646; *see also* feeling
Vedānta 94, 268, 517; *see also* Advaita Vedānta
Vedas 52, 246, 427–8, 521–2
vegetarianism 660
Vessantara 631
victory, banner of 298, 441, 725n
views
right, *see* right view
wrong (*micchā-diṭṭhis*) 164, 291, 454, 475–6, 487, 616–17
and Bacon's 'idols of the theatre' 655–6
or extreme 387, 730n
as a fourth *āsava* (Sanskrit *āsrava*) 717n
topsy-turvy or upside down, *see viparyāsas*, four
wrong, and value judgements 182, 266, 477
vigour (*vīrya*) 17, 188, 283, 460
vijñāna 144, 155–6, 221, 646
vijñānas
eight 174–6, 221
and five *jñānas* 176–7
five 174–6
Vikramaśilā 569, 571, 572, 574, 745–6n
Vimalakīrti-nirdeśa 228–9, 368, 722n
Sangharakshita's commentary on 722n
vimokṣa-mukhas, *see samādhis*, three transcendental
Vinaya 429, 511
Buddha's view of changes to 678, 756n
Vinaya Piṭaka 142, 210, 520, 567, 719n, 741n
Cullavagga 712n, 720n, 729n, 730n, 740n
Mahāvagga 109, 712n, 733n, 736n, 742n, 743n
viparyāsas, four 612, 616–17
vipassanā (Sanskrit *vipaśyanā*) 25, 393, 505, 604; *see also* insight
and real going for Refuge 505
Virgin Mary 106, 191
Virupaksha Cave 683, 718n
vīrya, *see* vigour
vision
clear, of transcendental, *see vipassanā*
and creativity 637
importance of retaining 404, 679, 735n
path of (*darśana-mārga*) 26–7, 29, 107–8, 322, 334, 709n
pillar of 472
right or perfect (*samyag-dṛṣṭi* (Pāli *sammā-diṭṭhi*)) *see* right view, Perfect Vision
Yogācāra philosophy as formulation of 169

visions 203, 205, 559, 572, 692; *see also* meditation, inspiration from
Atiśa's, of Tārā 572
Buddha's, of lotus lake 502
of Kachu Rimpoche 298, 441, 725n
Sangharakshita's, *see under* Sangharakshita
Yogi Chen's 444
visualization 19–20, 207, 537
practice 297, 423, 467, 555, 607, 638, 660; *see also sādhana* practice
Visuddhimagga 143, 161, 229, 278–80, 710n, 716n, 722n, 724n, 749n
Vivekananda, Bhikkhu 635, 647, 751n
Vivekananda, Vedānta master 52, 716n
void 171, 335; *see also śūnyatā*
wrong view of Nirvāṇa as 218
volition, *see saṃskāras*
Voltaire 41, 705n
vow, bodhisattva 17, 19–20, 167, 371, 373
vultures 286, 334, 692

Waddell, L. A. 103, 711n
Wagner, R. 188, 719n
Wangyal, Geshe 368
war 338–9, 342, 670, 682
in Magadha 569–70
nuclear 341, 347, 408
water 183–5, 189–90, 220–1, 502, 683
and fire 184–5, 619
as metaphor for One Mind 173
or rain of the Dharma, *see* parables, of the raincloud
Watts, A. 159, 716n
WBO, *see* Triratna Buddhist Order, Western Buddhist Order
weddings 305, 320, 321; *see also* marriage
Wesak (*Vaiśākha Pūrṇimā*) 34, 134, 302, 304–5, 374, 587–8, 704n
Wesley, J. 4
Western Buddhist movement 293, 671; *see also* FWBO
Western Buddhist Order (WBO) 370, 374, 388, 495, 497–500, 664; *see also* Triratna Buddhist Order
anniversaries xvi, 396, 663
Avalokiteśvara as embodiment or myth of 405, 414–15, 472, 599–600
and celibacy 730n, 754n; *see also anagārikas*
chapters 376, 381–2, 401, 412–13, 414, 415, 420, 423, 481, 553, 595, 676, 679
conventions 301, 545, 557, 580, 591, 596, 601, 746n
founding of 368, 737n; *see also* FWBO, founding; ordinations, into WBO, first
future of 545, 597, 600; *see also* FWBO, future of
growth of 400–1
headship of 597–8, 630–1
importance of harmony in 37, 598–600, 676–8
in India
start of 737n; *see also* Trailokya Bauddha Mahasangha (TBMSG)
support for social projects, *see* Aid for India, Karuna Trust
kesas 416, 499, 586
members, *see dharmacāris* and *dharmacāriṇīs*; Order members
name change 370, 405, 730n
newsletter, private, *see Shabda*
Order Office 491
Order weekends 413, 557
ordination into, *see* ordination
Preceptors' College and Council of the 597, 631–2, 748n
relationship with FWBO 321, 368, 370, 378, 388, 415, 497, 600
resigning from 315, 372
'society', not a 497–8
two wings of 402
a 'unified order' 498, 667–8
unity of, preserving and realizing 402, 412, 414–15, 512, 598–9, 665, 732n
women and 498, 500, 512; *see also* order members, women; ordination, of women
What is the Dharma? 736n, 743n, 751n
What is the Sangha? 723n
wheel, of conditioned existence, *see saṃsāra*
wheel of life 27, 154–5, 157–8, 197, 199, 203, 219, 291, 315, 356, 361, 550–1, 580, 646, 665
wheel of the law (*dharmacakra*) 203, 212, 459, 530
wheel-turning king 747n
wheel-turning *mudrā* (*dharmacakra-pravartana mudrā*) 212
Whistler, J. 581
Whitehead, A. N. 41–2, 705n, 709n
White Lotus Sūtra (*Saddharma Puṇḍarīka Sūtra*) 111, 210–11, 368, 501–3, 505–8, 513, 517, 668, 740n, 747n

White Lotus Sūtra (*cont.*)
Sangharakshita's commentary on 492, 500, 738n
White Tārā 213, 222, 435, 662
Who is the Buddha? 82, 737n
will
to Enlightenment 19, 296, 537–8; *see also bodhicitta*
and willing 537–8, 749n; *see also cetanā*
wisdom (*prajñā*) 25, 65, 139, 149, 283, 296, 529, 541, 547
all-performing 177, 204, 217, 297
Bodhisattva of 229, 297, 415, 453; *see also* Mañjughoṣa, Mañjuśrī
and compassion 9, 30, 222, 229, 502, 528, 661
of the *dharmadhātu* 177, 203, 212–13
discriminating or distinguishing 177, 204, 215, 297
energy or passion for 551; *see also dhammachanda*
of equality 177, 204, 214–15
freedom of (*prajñā-vimukti*) 164
Madhyamaka emphasis on 168
mirror-like 177, 204, 214, 297
perfect 25
perfection of, *see* perfection of wisdom
and real going for Refuge 315
and 'seeing things as they really are' 611–17, 627, 647
three kinds or levels of 515, 541–2, 740n, 743n
through hearing the scriptures (*śruta-mayī-prajñā*) 515, 542
through meditation (*bhāvanā-mayī-prajñā*) 515, 541, 542, 740n, 743n
through reflection (*cinta-mayī-prajñā*) 515, 535, 541–2, 581
through relationships 604–5
Wisdom Beyond Words 742n
wisdoms, five (*jñānas*) 100, 176–8, 204, 212–13, 297
distinguished from five *prajñās* 221–2
wise old man 191, 193
wish-fulfilling gem (*cintāmaṇi*) 214
withdrawal (*nirveda*) 164, 215
'Wolf at the Door' 754n
women
and FWBO/Triratna, *see* FWBO, women and
as lamas 16, 702n
in Western/Triratna Buddhist Order, *see* Order members, women; ordination, in WBO, of women
wongkur (or *abhiṣeka*) 20; *see also* Tantric initiation
Woolwich, Bishop of 4–10, 45, 94, 112–13, 118, 130, 534
Wordsworth, W. 78, 672, 755n
work 602–4, 654, 671, *see* also, right livelihood
meditation as 607
worldlings (*pṛthagjanas* (Pāli *puthujjanas*) 229, 722n, 750n
worlds, *see also* consciousness, levels of
of the gods 355; *see also devalokas*
higher 220–1, 288, 384
human 43, 204
of hungry ghosts (*pretaloka*) 204
ideal, or utopias 355, 728n
material 21, 147, 154, 212, 558
self-centred 333
of sensuous desire (*kāmaloka*) 147, 370, 558–60
six, *see* realms, or worlds, six
spiritual 21, 147, 154, 212; *see also arūpaloka*
of Tārā 375
three, or triple (Trailokya) 170, 370; *see also* existence, conditioned, levels or planes of
conquerors of (*trailokya vijayins*) 370
of the titans 204
or utopias, ideal 355, 728n
world tree 185–6
worship 14, 24, 116, 527, 578, 621, 664
true 713n
Wycliffe, J. 75, 707–8n
Wymondham College 591, 663

Xuanzang 238, 290, 722n

yab-yum 297; *see also* integration, or union, of opposites, sexual symbolism
Yale 656, 754n
yāna, one 508
yānas
nine 296–8
three (*triyāna*) 15, 116, 167, 210, 224, 296, 312, 504, 565
in the *White Lotus Sūtra* 503–4
Yeats, W. B. 595, 748n

Yeshe Tsogyal 286, 725n, 727n, 728n; *see also The Life and Liberation of Padmasambhava*
yidams 572, 659–60, 735n; *see also iṣṭa devatā*
(or *deva*) as esoteric Dharma Refuge 191, 312, 313
Yogācāra, Tantra 291
Yogācarā, version of Abhidharma 715n
Yogācārabhūmi 578
Yogācāra school xiv, 28–9, 99, 143, 166, 168–74, 175–9, 230, 366, 507
Mind Only doctrine (*citta-mātra*) 170–3; *see also* One Mind
sūtras 168
yogas, foundation, *see mūla yogas*
yogayāna 297
Yogi Chen 196, 443–5, 449, 636, 640, 684, 720n, 751n
Young Men's Buddhist Association (Kalimpong) 385, 684
Zangdokpalri Monastery 683–4, 757n
Zen 4, 8, 25, 72, 75, 78, 173–4, 216, 224–5, 230–2, 610, 611, 654, 707n, 709n, 716n; *see also* Chan
four fundamental principles of in verse 231–4, 722n
and going for Refuge 506
and psychotherapy 232–4
Rinzai 368, 594
Sangharakshita's talks on 56, 705n
story of Bodhidharma and emperor 531
teachings, appropriation of 517
texts 170, 368, 369, 742n
and work 497, 671
Yogi Chen and 443
Zeus 523, 741n
Zoroastrianism 52–4, 248, 250, 691, 706n
Zweig, S. 661, 755n

A GUIDE TO THE COMPLETE WORKS OF SANGHARAKSHITA

Gathered together in these twenty-seven volumes are talks and stories, commentaries on the Buddhist scriptures, poems, memoirs, reviews, and other writings. The genres are many, and the subject matter covered is wide, but it all has – its whole purpose is to convey – that taste of freedom which the Buddha declared to be the hallmark of his Dharma. Another traditional description of the Buddha's Dharma is that it is *ehipassiko*, 'come and see'. Sangharakshita calls to us, his readers, to come and see how the Dharma can fundamentally change the way we see things, change the way we live for the better, and change the society we belong to, wherever in the world we live.

Sangharakshita's very first published piece, *The Unity of Buddhism* (found in volume 7 of this collection), appeared in 1944 when he was eighteen years old, and it introduced themes that continued to resound throughout his work: the basis of Buddhist ethics, the compassion of the bodhisattva, and the transcendental unity of Buddhism. Over the course of the following seven decades not only did numerous other works flow from his pen; he gave hundreds of talks (some now lost). In gathering all we could find of this vast output, we have sought to arrange it in a way that brings a sense of coherence, communicating something essential about Sangharakshita, his life and teaching. Recalling the three 'baskets' among which an early tradition divided the Buddha's teachings, we have divided Sangharakshita's creative output into six 'baskets' or groups: foundation texts; works originating in India; teachings originally given in the West; commentaries on the Buddhist scriptures; personal writings; and poetry, aphorisms, and works on the arts. The 27th volume, a concordance, brings together all the terms and themes of the whole collection. If you want to find a particular story or teaching, look at a traditional term from different points of view or in different contexts, or track down one of the thousands of canonical references to be found in these volumes, the concordance will be your guide.

1. FOUNDATION

What is the foundation of a Buddhist life? How do we understand and then follow the Buddha's path of Ethics, Meditation, and Wisdom? What is really meant by 'Going for Refuge to the Three Jewels', described by Sangharakshita as the essential act of a Buddhist life? And what is the Bodhisattva ideal, which he has called 'one of the sublimest ideals mankind has ever seen'? In the 'Foundation' group you will find teachings on all these themes. It includes the author's *magnum opus, A Survey of Buddhism*, a collection of teachings on *The Purpose and Practice of Buddhist Meditation*, and the anthology, *The Essential Sangharakshita*, an eminently helpful distillation of the entire corpus.

2. INDIA

From 1950 to 1964 Sangharakshita, based in Kalimpong in the eastern Himalayas, poured his energy into trying to revive Buddhism in the land of its birth and to revitalize and bring reform to the existing Asian Buddhist world. The articles and book reviews from this period are gathered in volumes 7 and 8, as well as his biographical sketch of the great Sinhalese Dharmaduta, Anagārika Dharmapala. In 1954 Sangharakshita took on the editing of the *Maha Bodhi*, a journal for which he wrote a monthly editorial, and which, under his editorship, published the work of many of the leading Buddhist writers of the time. It was also during these years in India that a vital connection was forged with Dr B. R. Ambedkar, renowned Indian statesman and leader of the Buddhist mass conversion of 1956. Sangharakshita became closely involved with the new Buddhists and, after Dr Ambedkar's untimely death, visited them regularly on extensive teaching tours.

From 1979, when an Indian wing of the Triratna Buddhist Community was founded (then known as TBMSG), Sangharakshita returned several times to undertake further teaching tours. The talks from these tours are collected in volumes 9 and 10 along with a unique work on Ambedkar and his life which draws out the significance of his conversion to Buddhism.

3. THE WEST

Sangharakshita founded the Triratna Buddhist Community (then called the Friends of the Western Buddhist Order) on 6 April 1967. On 7 April the following year he performed the first ordinations of men and women within the Triratna Buddhist Order (then the Western Buddhist Order). At that time Buddhism was not widely known in the West and for the following two decades or so he taught intensively, finding new ways to communicate the ancient truths of Buddhism, drawing on the whole Buddhist tradition to do so, as well as making connections with what was best in existing Western culture. Sometimes his sword flashed as he critiqued ideas and views inimical to the Dharma. It is these teachings and writings that are gathered together in this third group.

4. COMMENTARY

Throughout Sangharakshita's works are threaded references to the Buddhist canon of literature – Pāli, Mahāyāna, and Vajrayāna – from which he drew his inspiration. In the early days of the new movement he often taught by means of seminars in which, prompted by the questions of his students, he sought to pass on the inspiration and wisdom of the Buddhist tradition. Each seminar was based around a different text, the seminars were recorded and transcribed, and in due course many of the transcriptions were edited and turned into books, all carefully checked by Sangharakshita. The commentaries compiled in this way constitute the fourth group. In some ways this is the heart of the collection. Sangharakshita often told the story of how it was that, reading two *sūtras* at the age of sixteen or seventeen, he realized that he was a Buddhist, and he has never tired of showing others how they too could see and realize the value of the '*sūtra*-treasure'.

5. MEMOIRS

Who is Sangharakshita? What sort of life did he live? Whom did he meet? What did he feel? Why did he found a new Buddhist movement? In these volumes of memoirs and letters Sangharakshita shares with his readers much about himself and his life as he himself has experienced it, giving us a sense of its breadth and depth, humour and pathos.

6. POETRY, APHORISMS, AND THE ARTS

Sangharakshita describes reading *Paradise Lost* at the age of twelve as one of the greatest poetic experiences of his life. His realization of the value of the higher arts to spiritual development is one of his distinctive contributions to our understanding of what Buddhist life is, and he has expressed it in a number of essays and articles. Throughout his life he has written poetry which he says can be regarded as a kind of spiritual autobiography. It is here, perhaps, that we come closest to the heart of Sangharakshita. He has also written a few short stories and composed some startling aphorisms. Through book reviews he has engaged with the experiences, ideas, and opinions of modern writers. All these are collected in this sixth group.

In the preface to *A Survey of Buddhism* (volume 1 in this collection), Sangharakshita wrote of his approach to the Buddha's teachings:

> Why did the Buddha (or Nāgārjuna, or Buddhaghosa) teach this particular doctrine? What bearing does it have on the spiritual life? How does it help the individual Buddhist actually to follow the spiritual path?... I found myself asking such questions again and again, for only in this way, I found, could I make sense – spiritual sense – of Buddhism.

Although this collection contains so many words, they are all intent, directly or indirectly, on these same questions. And all these words are not in the end about their writer, but about his great subject, the Buddha and his teaching, and about you, the reader, for whose benefit they are solely intended. These pages are full of the reverence that Sangharakshita has always felt, which is expressed in an early poem, 'Taking Refuge in the Buddha', whose refrain is 'My place is at thy feet'. He has devoted his life to communicating the Buddha's Dharma in its depth and in its breadth, to men and women from all backgrounds and walks of life, from all countries, of all races, of all ages. These collected works are the fruit of that devotion.

We are very pleased to be able to include some previously unpublished work in this collection, but most of what appears in these volumes has been published before. We have made very few changes, though we have added extra notes where we thought they would be useful. We have had the pleasure of researching the notes in the Sangharakshita Library at 'Adhisthana', Triratna's centre in Herefordshire, UK, which houses his own collection of books. It has been of great value to be able to search among the very copies of the *suttas*, *sūtras* and commentaries that have provided the basis of his teachings over the last seventy years.

The publication of these volumes owes much to the work of transcribers, editors, indexers, designers, and publishers over many years – those who brought out the original editions of many of the works included here, and those who have contributed in all sorts of ways to this *Complete Works* project, including all those who contributed to funds given in celebration of Sangharakshita's ninetieth birthday in August 2015, and to a further outpouring of generosity after Sangharakshita's death in October 2018. All these donors have made the publication of this series possible, and we are very grateful. Many thanks to everyone who has helped; may the merit gained in our acting thus go to the alleviation of the suffering of all beings.

Vidyadevi and Kalyanaprabha
Editors

THE COMPLETE WORKS OF SANGHARAKSHITA

I FOUNDATION

VOLUME 1 A SURVEY OF BUDDHISM / THE BUDDHA'S NOBLE EIGHTFOLD PATH
A Survey of Buddhism
The Buddha's Noble Eightfold Path

2 THE THREE JEWELS I
The Three Jewels
The Meaning of Conversion in Buddhism
Going for Refuge
The Ten Pillars of Buddhism
The History of My Going for Refuge
My Relation to the Order
Extending the Hand of Fellowship
Forty-Three Years Ago
Was the Buddha a Bhikkhu?

3 THE THREE JEWELS II
Who is the Buddha?
What is the Dharma?
What is the Sangha?

4 THE BODHISATTVA IDEAL
The Bodhisattva Ideal
The Endlessly Fascinating Cry (seminar)
The Bodhisattva Principle

5 THE PURPOSE AND PRACTICE OF BUDDHIST MEDITATION
The Purpose and Practice of Buddhist Meditation

6 THE ESSENTIAL SANGHARAKSHITA
The Essential Sangharakshita

II INDIA

7 CROSSING THE STREAM: INDIA WRITINGS I
Early Writings 1944–1954
Crossing the Stream
Buddhism in the Modern World: Cultural and Political Implications
The Meaning of Orthodoxy in Buddhism
Buddhism in India Today
Ordination and Initiation in the Three Yānas
A Bird's Eye View of Indian Buddhism

VOLUME 8 BEATING THE DHARMA DRUM: INDIA WRITINGS II
Anagarika Dharmapala and Other 'Maha Bodhi' Writings
Dharmapala: The Spiritual Dimension
Beating the Drum: 'Maha Bodhi' Editorials
Alternative Traditions

9 DR AMBEDKAR AND THE REVIVAL OF BUDDHISM I
Ambedkar and Buddhism
Lecture Tour in India, December 1981–March 1982

10 DR AMBEDKAR AND THE REVIVAL OF BUDDHISM II
Remembering Ambedkar
Buddha and the Future of His Religion
The Mass Conversion and the Years After, 1956–61
Lectures in India and England 1979, 1982–92
Wisdom before Words: The Udāna

III THE WEST

11 A NEW BUDDHIST MOVEMENT I
Ritual and Devotion in Buddhism
The Buddha's Victory
The Taste of Freedom
Buddha Mind
Human Enlightenment
New Currents in Western Buddhism
Buddhism for Today – and Tomorrow
Buddhism and the West
Aspects of Buddhist Morality
Dialogue between Buddhism and Christianity
Buddhism and Blasphemy
Articles and Interviews

12 A NEW BUDDHIST MOVEMENT II
Buddhism and the Bishop of Woolwich
Buddhism, World Peace, and Nuclear War
Previously Unpublished Talks

13 EASTERN AND WESTERN TRADITIONS
Tibetan Buddhism
Creative Symbols of Tantric Buddhism
The Essence of Zen
The FWBO and 'Protestant Buddhism'
From Genesis to the Diamond Sūtra

IV COMMENTARY

VOLUME 14 THE ETERNAL LEGACY / WISDOM BEYOND WORDS
The Eternal Legacy
The Glory of the Literary World
Wisdom Beyond Words

15 PĀLI CANON TEACHINGS AND TRANSLATIONS
Dhammapada (translation)
Karaṇīyamettā Sutta (translation)
Living with Kindness
Living with Awareness
Maṅgala Sutta (translation)
Auspicious Signs (seminar)
Salutation to the Three Jewels (translation)
The Threefold Refuge (seminar)
Further Pāli Sutta Commentaries

16 MAHĀYĀNA MYTHS AND STORIES
The Drama of Cosmic Enlightenment
The Priceless Jewel (talk)
Transforming Self and World
The Inconceivable Emancipation

17 WISDOM TEACHINGS OF THE MAHĀYĀNA
Know Your Mind
Living Ethically
Living Wisely
The Way to Wisdom (seminar)

18 MILAREPA AND THE ART OF DISCIPLESHIP I
The Yogi's Joy
The Shepherd's Search for Mind
Rechungpa's Journey to Enlightenment

19 MILAREPA AND THE ART OF DISCIPLESHIP II
Rechungpa's Journey to Enlightenment, continued

V MEMOIRS

20 THE RAINBOW ROAD FROM TOOTING BROADWAY TO KALIMPONG
The Rainbow Road from Tooting Broadway to Kalimpong

VOLUME 21 FACING MOUNT KANCHENJUNGA

Facing Mount Kanchenjunga
Dear Dinoo: Letters to a Friend

22 IN THE SIGN OF THE GOLDEN WHEEL

In the Sign of the Golden Wheel
Precious Teachers
With Allen Ginsberg in Kalimpong (essay)

23 MOVING AGAINST THE STREAM

Moving Against the Stream
1970 – A Retrospect

24 THROUGH BUDDHIST EYES

Travel Letters
Through Buddhist Eyes

VI POETRY AND THE ARTS

25 POEMS AND SHORT STORIES

Complete Poems 1941–1994
Other Poems
Short Stories

26 APHORISMS, THE ARTS, AND LATE WRITINGS

Sayings, Poems, Reflections
Peace is a Fire
A Stream of Stars
The Religion of Art
In the Realm of the Lotus
The Journey to Il Convento
St Jerome Revisited
A Note on The Burial of Count Orgaz
Criticism East and West
Buddhism and William Blake
Urthona Interviews
Madhyamaloka Reflections
Adhisthana Writings

27 CONCORDANCE AND APPENDICES

WINDHORSE PUBLICATIONS

Windhorse Publications is a Buddhist charitable company based in the UK. We produce books of high quality that are accessible and relevant to all those interested in Buddhism, at whatever level of interest and commitment. We are the main publisher of Sangharakshita, the founder of the Triratna Buddhist Order and Community. Our books draw on the whole range of the Buddhist tradition, including translations of traditional texts, commentaries, books that make links with contemporary culture and ways of life, biographies of Buddhists, and works on meditation.

To subscribe to the *Complete Works of Sangharakshita,* please go to: windhorsepublications.com/sangharakshita-complete-works/

THE TRIRATNA BUDDHIST COMMUNITY

Windhorse Publications is a part of the Triratna Buddhist Community, an international movement with centres in Europe, India, North and South America and Australasia. At these centres, members of the Triratna Buddhist Order offer classes in meditation and Buddhism. Activities of the Triratna Community also include retreat centres, residential spiritual communities, ethical Right Livelihood businesses, and the Karuna Trust, a UK fundraising charity that supports social welfare projects in the slums and villages of India.

Through these and other activities, Triratna is developing a unique approach to Buddhism, not simply as a philosophy and a set of techniques, but as a creatively directed way of life for all people living in the conditions of the modern world.

For more information please visit thebuddhistcentre.com